Business Management and Organizational Behaiour

Business Management and Organizational Behaviour

Karam Pal
Associate Professor
Haryana School of Business
Guru Jambheshwar University of Science and Technology
Hisar

TECHSAR™
NEW DELHI

Published and Printed by
Techsar Pvt. Ltd.
4435-36/7, Ansari Road, Daryaganj
New Delhi-110 002 (India)
E-mail: tech_info@techsarworld.com
Website: www.techsarworld.com

ISBN 978-93-80578-99-6

Reprint 2024

Foreword

This present book on **Business Management and Organizational Behaviour** is a meticulous addition in the literary-locale on the subject matter. The book, which has been divided into two parts, contains twenty-nine chapters in total. It provides a comprehensive coverage on the subject matter of business management fundamentals and organizational behaviour in a coherent and systematic manner. The book is an upshot of an incredibly absolute scholarly exercise. It is unique in countless requirements. Firstly, it has been written in a very practical tongue and diverse concepts have been logically explained. Anyone, who will read this text with a minimum of insightful background, can follow its compassion without a set twist. Secondly, by presenting an executive approach to business management and organizational behaviour and demonstrating the application of behavioural science within the workplace, the author has emphasized the role of management as a core integrating activity. Thirdly, in one docile volume the authors have condensed the spirit of the subject matter without going off beam from any imperative linkage and facet.

A reflective feature of self-instructional mode inside each chapter would encourage the students to decisively evaluate the key ideas and practices of business management and organizational behaviour. A glossary of key terms at the end of the book would enable the students to locate the relevant information quickly. The book is logically structured and clearly written, thus enabling easy access to the subject without compromising the academic reliability. The theories and concepts discussed in this textbook are clearly applied through appealing and relevant figures. This textbook offers a balanced view of management theories with stimulating, but practical illustrations for a whole range of readers particularly focusing on the students of MBA, MCom, BBA and BCom.

In fact, **Dr. Karam Pal** has thoroughly convinced me to realize that he has sincerely attempted his rich experiences of teaching and research for writing this book on **Business Management and Organizational Behaviour** that shows his preferred inclination in intellectual creation activities. He has provided in the book just what is considered necessary in the civic of Business Management and Organizational Behaviour.

I value that this book is a significant accrual to the accessible citations on the theme and as a result, it will serve as a legitimate textbook on the subject matter. I hope that those who will send this book may sense a easy approach to learn the subject with the finer passion. In my opinion the book will be appreciated by all individuals, may be the students, teachers, or professionals, who have a curiosity in the field of business process and organizational behaviour.

PROF. M. S. TURAN
Director, Distance Education
Guru Jambheshwar University of Science and Technology, Hisar–125001 (Haryana)

Preface

One can think of management functionally: as the action in measuring a quantity on a regular basis and adjusting an initial plan and the actions taken to reach one's intended goal. This applies even in situations where planning does not take place. Situational management may precede and subsume purposive management.

Modern management as a discipline began as an derivative of economics in the 19th century. Classical economists such as Adam Smith and John Stuart Mill provided a theoretical background to resource allocation, production, and pricing issues. About the same time, innovators like Eli Whitney, James Watt, and Matthew Boulton developed technical production elements such as standardization, quality control procedures, cost accounting, interchangeability of parts, and work planning. By the middle of the 19th century, Robert Owen, H. Poor, and M. Laughlin and others introduced the human element with theories of worker training, motivation, organizational structure and span of control. By the late 19th century, marginal economists Alfred Marshall and Leon Walrus and others introduced a new layer of complexity to the theoretical underpinnings of management. The first tertiary-level course in management was offered in 1881 by J. Wharton. By 1900, we find managers trying to place their theories on a thoroughly scientific basis. Examples include H. Towne's *Science of management*, Frederick Winslow Taylor's *Scientific management*, Frank Bunker Gilbreth's *Science of motion study*, and Henry L. Gantt's charts. J. Duncan wrote the first college management textbook in 1911.

The first comprehensive theories of management appeared around 1920. People like H. Fayol and A. Church described the various branches of management and their interrelationships. In the early 20th century, people like O. Tead, W. Scott and J. Mooney applied the principles of psychology to management, while other writers, such as Elton Mayo, M. Follett, C. Barnard, Max Weber, Rensis Likert, and Chris Argyris approached it from a sociological perspective. Peter Ferdinand Drucker called one of the earliest books on Management as a science *Concept of a Corporation.* It is the result of Alfred Sloan (head of General Motors) commissioning a study on the organization. Drucker went on to write 32 books, mostly along the same vein of study. H. Dodge, R. Fisher, and T. Fry introduced statistical techniques into management. In the 1940s, Patrick Blackett combined these statistical theories with microeconomic theory and gave birth to the science of operations research. Operations research, sometimes known as "management science", attempts to take a scientific approach to solving management problems, particularly in the areas of logistics and operations.

Some of the more recent developments include the theory of constraints, reengineering, and various information technology driven theories such as agile software development. The theory of constraints approach describes management decision-making as a continuous cycle of three basic questions—what to change? To what to change to? How to make the change happen? Towards the end of the 20th century, management was seen as consisting of a number of separate branches, including: Human resource management; Operations or production management; Strategic management; Marketing management; Financial management; and Information Technology management. In the 21st century, we find it increasingly difficult to subdivide management into categories in this way. More and more processes simultaneously involve several categories. Instead, we tend to think in terms of the various processes, tasks, and objects that can be managed. Different functional areas of management are: Change management; Communications management; Constraint Management; Cost management; Customer; Earned; Enterprise management; Facility; Integration management; Knowledge management; Marketing management; Micromanagement; Pain management; Perception management; Procurement management; Programme management; Project management; Process management; Product management; Quality management; Resource management; Risk management; Skills management; Spend management; Supply chain management; Systems management; Time management; and Stress management. This diverse conceptualization process in the field, leaves magnificent scope for youngsters to endow with the comprehensive of the theories, principles and practices in relevant areas for the diversity of stakeholders in the field.

The present book on **Business Management and Organizational Behaviour**, which is an improvement over 'Management Process and Organizational Behaviour' is an attempt to come up to the expectations of those readers particularly students who are wandering for inventive and reminiscent single textbook on the subject matters. For last more than a decade or so, the Business Management and Organizational Behaviour is being taught as a combined course in management programmes but there is an urgent need of such textbook that can help the students and teachers for both the areas. The book has been divided into two parts. First part contains the fundamentals of Business Management and has been divided into eighteen chapters. The second part is devoted to Organizational Behaviour and consists of eleven chapters. The basic concepts with suitable illustrations have been elucidated all the way through twenty-nine wide-ranging chapters in this textbook. All the chapters have been designed into a stable manner and the details provided in this text are in self-instructional manner. It is expected that the readers would find this book quite valuable and receptive. I would welcome suggestions, if any, from all places for the continuous improvements in this textbook.

KARAM PAL

Acknowledgements

At the very outset, I would like to put on record my special gratefulness to **Prof. M. S. Turan**, who has been a source of motivation to me all the way through this book-writing project. He has been very kind to have happily agreed to write a foreword for this textbook. He is basically an intellectual of high standing and most notably he is a teacher by compassion and temperament. In fact, his input in terms of observations, support, and intellectual inspiration has indeed imbibed the value to this book. I have no words to fittingly articulate my earnest gratitude but I simply salute him.

I would like to acknowledge the scholastic lend a hand by Dr. M.L. Ranga, our Honble Vice-chancellor, and Prof. R.S. Jaglan, our worthy Registrar, Prof. L.N. Dahiya, Prof. R. Vinayek, Prof. S.S. Chahal, Prof. Daleep Singh, and Prof. Ajay Rajan from M.D. University, Rohtak; Prof. S.L. Gupta, Prof. B.S. Bodlu and Prof. M.K. Jain from Kurukshetra University, Kurukshetra; Prof. Bal Krishan from H.P. University, Shimla; Prof. L.K. Bansal from Punjab University, Chandigarh; Prof. Sultan Singh from C.D.L. University, Sirsa; Prof. A.S. Chawla and Prof. Prem Kumar from Punjabi University Patiala; and Prof. H.L. Verma, Prof. Harbhajan Bansal, Prof. S.C. Kundu, and Prof. B.K. Punia from this University. I am also indebted to all my other colleagues in the department for their affirmative offers from time to time. It is plainly their love and affection that stimulated me to be attentive in academics dome.

I am also beholden to all our nearers and dearers especially who made considerable academic involvement in this at hand work. I sense gratefulness to the officers and officials of the university libraries in this part of the country who provided all cooperation in the effecting of this bookwork. I am especially gratified to I.K. International Publishing House Pvt. Ltd. for their untiring efforts in the systematic and ethological publication process.

I have parallel zeal to express our heartfelt appreciation to countless others who have contributed to this piece of knowledge both explicitly and categorically. Although academic help sought from the existing literature has been duly acknowledged at appropriate places but, at rest, I would like to show my gross gratitude to all of them. Hence, I thank one and all.

KARAM PAL

Contents

PART A

Management Process

1

INTRODUCTION TO BUSINESS

Learning Objectives

The main objective of this chapter is to make the learners familiar with the nature and scope of business.

1.1 INTRODUCTION

Let us assume that you have decided to buy a particular product. Can you develop a kind of imagination about the number of activities involved in reaching this product to you from the place of its origin? For instance, there is a supplier of raw materials to the producer who then converts these raw materials into usable products, then the producer appoints a dealer who makes the product available at a place which is convenient to you and there are certain banking facilities which impart you the various financial assistance, there is an insurance agent in the market who assumes risk on your behalf and bundles of other activities. Not only a durable item or the non-durable item requires a long chain of activities but even a very small item like pencil or eraser necessitates so many activities to make your purchase possible. The multidimensional activities involved in production, trade, banking, insurance, finance, advertising, packaging, etc. constitute business. Its dictionary meaning conveys the state of being busy. But from this statement, we get the message that every act performed by a person is known as business which is not true. The reason being the element of profit is missing out of this statement. So, any human activity which involves profit is called business. But from this concept, we can say that every activity like sale-purchase, agriculture, industry, profession, and even involvement in theft should be treated as business because all these involve profit motive. Being a more comprehensive term, it requires further clarification through certain definitions.

1.2 MEANING OF BUSINESS

According to Prof. L.H. Hanrey, "Business means any human activity directed towards producing or acquiring wealth through buying and selling of goods". But as per the above definition business is limited up to the exchange activity which is not based upon proper understanding of the things. For that matter if you exchange your old furniture with the new one and in the process you save a little money. Can we call it a business? No, definitely not. Because it should be a continuous feature. According to K. Ashwathappa "Business comprises all profit seeking activities and enterprises that provide goods and services necessary to an economic system. It is the economic pulse of a nation, striving to increase society's standard of living. Profits are a primary mechanism for motivating these activities". This definition which seems to be very clear and more comprehensive also lacks on one issue, i.e., on the front of legality. Whatever activity you do to earn profit that should abide by the country's law. So, from the above definitions and observations, we can come to a conclusion that "Business is an economic activity carried on by human to earn profit in a continuous manner under the purview of rules and regulations of the country".

1.3 NATURE OF BUSINESS

From the above discussion, we can draw certain characteristics of today's business which are as follows:

(i) **It is a Human Activity:** Business is a human activity which makes available goods and services to the society. It is not only dependent on making available the goods and services or the mere production of these but also depends on the exchange of value which is provided in return because if you are engaged in giving gifts to somebody then it will not be treated as business.

(ii) **Continuous Economic Activity:** In business an economic activity must be repeated again and again because if an entrepreneur does not do that it will not be treated as business. For example, if a person sells his own house, this activity does not come under the framework of business.

(iii) **Profit Motive:** Any economic activity which leads to generation of profit is considered as business. Therefore, intension should be to earn profit otherwise if a person is engaged in social service or preaching about the religion cannot be treated as business.

(iv) **Entrepreneurship:** One cannot run any sort of business without the element of entrepreneurship irrespective of the size of the business. Business can only be run by a daring person who has the ability to face risk of loss. Because no business is there where the element of risk is missing. Involvement of element of risk of loss makes the business world more challenging and to face financial challenge is not everybody's cup of tea.

(v) **Creation of Utility:** A man does not produce anything in a way, he only converts the form of resources which are provided by the nature. The business changes the form, place and possession utility of goods and makes them available in usable form. The business creates the utility of the things so that these can be consumed.

1.4 OBJECTIVES OF BUSINESS

After understanding the whole notion of business and its meaning, it seems essential to know the various objectives of the business. But prior to that understanding of three concepts, namely, missions, goals and targets are must. These are discussed as follow:

Mission: It is a statement which defines the overall philosophy and the role that an organization plays in a society. Once the great philosopher of management Peter F. Drucker raised certain questions which are answered by the mission statement of an organization. What is our business? What it will be in the future? What should be its shape in the coming time? It also shows direction to the organization for its continuity and growth. Nowadays, the mission statement appears in the various advertisements of the business organizations. A few examples are:

(a) "Building Trust Worldwide" Maruti
(b) "Connecting People" Nokia
(c) "Leather that Weather" Woodland
(d) "Where growth is a way of life" Reliance
(e) "Serving to grow, growing to serve" Canara Bank
(f) "Let's make things better" Philips

So, from the above mission statements you can very well understand the whole prospective and importance of the mission to survive in the business world. Because with the passage of time and as per the changing requirements of the society, businesses are forced to reshape their organizations and products.

Goals: Where mission indicates the overall philosophy of the business organization, goals refer to the operational side of the business. When the things start appearing into figures indicating yearly budgets, etc., we have the company's goals. A series of such goals converts the statements into reality.

Targets: These have much shorter time span. These can be set for a week, for one month, three or six months or even for a year. By reaching its targets the organization realize its goals and continuous realization will ultimately lead to fulfilment of mission. Having understood the notion of mission, goals and targets, we can proceed to learn the different organizational objectives of the business.

Whenever we implement any sort of planning, there is always a purpose behind it. Therefore, the business is also set to fulfil certain purposes or objectives. Peter F. Drucker says "The object of the business is to create customers for commodities". The following objectives of the business can be understood.

- **Economic Objectives:** The people believe that the main purpose of the business is to earn profit. Profit is the excess of income over expenses. Although profit is the main incentive, motivator, objective indication of growth and development and necessary for survival but people differs on the quantity of the profit and intensions behind generating it. Barnad Shaw writes that "Capitalism has no conscience, its ambition is 'profit' and its 'God' is 'Gold'." But the main essence lies in the economic motive of the business because business confronts with the trade cycles. Hence, to generate profit up to a certain extent is must. Peter Drucker says that the problem of any business is not in the maximization of profit but the achievement of sufficient profit to cover the risks to economic activity and thus to avoid loss. However, it is an absolute necessity for the business enterprises to produce at least the profit required to cover its own future risks, the profit required to stay in business world and to maintain intact the wealth producing capacity of the resources. It means that a business should at least earn the profit up to a certain extent so that it survives in the time of recession otherwise the market forces will wipe it out of the market. It is necessary for both survival and expansion. Because if a business is unable to grow with the passage of time, it leads itself to a disastrous situation.

So, under the economic objectives there should be a perfect blend between maximization of profit and growth so that it can add more products in the market, diversify into new areas, increase market share and also can cut down costs and increase productivity.

- **Social Objectives:** Business and society are the parts of each other, no one can live in isolation. Without society, the imagination of a business is like making castles in the air because society has provided natural, human and financial resources, etc. to the business. Therefore, the optimum utilization of society should be primary consideration of the business. Appropriate use of resources, community development and favourable response towards the government following the rules and regulations and payment of certain taxes at the right time should be the prime considerations of the business. According to Henry Ford "Service first and profit second" means to serve the society should be the primary objective followed by profit. It should be taken care that consumer should not be deceived in any manner and timely and appropriate services should be provided to him. Those businessmen who insisted on and persisted in quality survived competition stayed ahead of others in the market. Persistent quality earns brand loyalty to the product which is a vital ingredient of success like HLL, BPL, Philips, LG and Godrej products. To earn a special niche for oneself in the market, innovation is the key factor in the field of product, advertising and distribution, etc. But all these things cannot be achieved without people who are your employees. Caring for employee satisfaction and taking into consideration their development should be one of social objectives of the business. The businesses which consider the importance of both economic and social objectives are bound to succeed in the market.
- **Human Objectives:** In any business, it is not only the entrepreneur who works but there are three human factors involved in it. One of them is enterprise, other one is employee and the third is customer. Besides entrepreneur, there are thousands of employees who work for the organization and similarly, without customers there is no existence of business. Therefore, to be successful, the satisfaction of all the three is must. Security of investment, and fair return on the investment, good working condition, job security and handsome salary with growth prospects for employees and smooth supply of products and services with reasonable rates are the functions which must be complied with for the success of business. If all sections are satisfied, that business is above board and has succeeded in fulfilling the human objectives of the business.

1.5 SCOPE OF BUSINESS

Business is a vast and interesting subject. If one goes deeper into it, he faces more absorbing and uphill tasks. It encounters with the use of latest scientific and technical know-how, challenges and difficulties it faces from production to the smooth supply of the products to the target audience, problems confronting in raising money and by which method to raise money and the most challenging job of bringing employee together and to spur their motivation level up to a point so that they strive pleasantly to achieve the organizational goals. A business also encounters the most amazing and challenging job of grappling with so many laws and regulations lay down by the government. The consumers, employees and various other interests groups also influence the business.

In keeping with its above mentioned factors it is always difficult to limit the discussion on the subject like scope of business. But with the below factors an endeavour has been made to discuss the nature and scope of business.

- **Vastness:** Earlier there used to be the business in form of sole proprietorship or in partnership forms and that too was within the boundaries of a particular district or state. Then slowly and gradually the bigger form of business organization evolved in the form of joint stock company. Because the earlier forms could not cope up with the ever growing demand of the society and were unable to meet the challenges of mass production. The formation of bigger size companies have gradually started replacing manual labour in manufacturing process and with the advent of automatic machines, production in bulk has become possible. The production philosophy has been replaced by the marketing philosophy where the production is being done by knowing the need of the consumers first and then demand is created. Traditional channels of distribution have been replaced by the new distribution channels, super bazaars, discount houses, trade fairs, different promotional scheme and reshaped world of advertising has become the order of the day in business to meet the present-day challenges. The bigger production level fetches economies of scale and ultimately the benefits pass on to the final buyers. The trend toward growing business into bigger size is quite evident. The companies like IOC, ONGC, SAIL, etc. have shown their presence in the Fortune 500 lists. This scenario has given a kind of dynamism to the business.
- **Globalization:** There used to be a time when business operations were limited up to a particular area. Now the trade barriers are crumbling day by day because the word is shrinking rapidly. Networks of transportation, communication, music, and economics have tied the people of the world together as never before. Political boundaries are no barriers to the business. The fast moving phenomenon of globalization is becoming imperative due to the certain technological explosion, intensity of market competition, and changing lifestyles of the people which has led to the demand for new products. This scenario has occurred due to the multifold exposure of the people to the ever-growing field of information technology which has opened up new vistas for the business. This has added up a new dimension that people have standed learning to be a global manager to meet the challenge of the diversity of the culture to sustain a strong position in the international market.
- **Challenges to the Service Providers:** There was a time when only production and exchange of goods used to come under the scope of business. Service was being considered as the alien part of businesses. But now it is entirely a separate industry which is growing at a very fast pace. These are rapidly growing and increasingly important part of today's global economy. Because services are customer-driven, pleasing the customer

is more important than ever because service-quality strategists emphasis that it is no longer enough simply to satisfy the customer. The strategic service challenge today is to anticipate and exceed the customer's expectations which were a rare phenomenon in yester years' businesses. Because customers are more intimately involved in the service-delivery process than in the manufacturing process, the business needs to go directly to the customer for service-quality criteria. So, the horizons of business have expanded immensely.

- **An interdisciplinary Field:** A principle cause of the expansion of the business is due to the information explosion which has been contributed by the various disciplines. Scholars from various fields—including psychology, sociology, cultural anthropology, mathematics, philosophy, statistics, political science, economics, logistics, computer science and various fields of engineering—have, at one time or another, been interested in business field and its various management theories. In addition, administrators in business, government, church, health care and education all have drawn from and contributed to the study of business which have given immense knowledge of the field to the practitioners. With each new perspective, new questions and assumptions, new research techniques, different technical jargon, and new conceptual frameworks have come up. This has altogether revolutionized the field of businesses.
- **Information Overload:** Since the time immoral, entire civilization have come and gone. In one form or another, business management was practiced in each. Sadly, during those thousands of years of experience, one modern element was missing: a systematically recorded body of knowledge. In early cultures management was something one learned by word of mouth and on trial and error basis not to record about in textbooks, theorized about or experience with in written form. Thanks to the modern print and electronic media, the collective genius of thousands of management theorists and practitioners has been compressed into a veritable mountain of textbooks, journals, research monographs, audio and video tapes and computer disks, etc. Use of Internet has also made it more explosive in nature. Never before have present business had so much relevant information at their fingertips, often as close as the nearest library.
- **Diversification:** Today's business is also characterized by diversification. Earlier people used to stick to the one or two business only. The product portfolio of today's business is expanding like anything. One can understand the concept of diversification by having an overview of Tata's business in India which ranges from salt to steel. Diversification means introducing different lines of products which are not related to each other. Proliferation is another name of the game today. It represents introducing different brands in the same product line. For example, FMCG's giant HLL (Hindustan Lever Ltd.) in India has so many soaps in one time but with different brand names. Nowadays, these measures are used by the companies in the form of certain weapons to face severe competition to sustain in the market as we have never seen before this sort of scenario. The merger and acquisition waves are also sweeping the world. To prevail in the market, we are able to witness some of the biggest mergers in the world which is another feature of today's business. With the repeal of the some of the provisions relating to Monopolies and Restrictive Trade Practices Act, 1969 (MRTP Act), many companies in our country stretched too far in the name of diversification.

- **Foreign Capital and Technology:** There was a time when hardly any country was in the practice of using foreign capital and technology. Because the world is witnessing so many changes and with the implementation of WTO regulations, almost every country has gone international. To pay the international debts, country requires huge amount of foreign capital reservoirs. Most of the countries have been making use of foreign capital and technology to accelerate the pace of their economic growth. There is hardly any country which is not assisted by foreign capital and technology. Foreign capital and technology play a vital role in the shaping of an economy in a big way. India being a developed economy, the importance of foreign capital and technology needs no emphasis as we have to payback lots of international debts as a new and developing economy. Broadly a country can access these types of foreign investment, namely, foreign direct investment (FDI) and portfolio investment (FIIs). While FDIs refers to the direct investment in a foreign country whereas the portfolio investors has only a short-term property interest in investing in equities, banks and other securities.
- **Emphasis on Diversity:** Labour forces and consumers are becoming more diverse in terms of national origin, race, religion, gender, different age categories and personnel preferences around the globe. In today's business, managers are challenged to manage diversity effectively to tap the full potential of every individual's unique combination of abilities and traits. Successful business are the ones which hire the kind of managers who can anticipate and adjust to changing circumstances rather than being passively swept along or caught unprepared. Employers today are hiring managers who can take unfamiliar situations in stride. They are calling for the multilingual and multicultural managers who can manage diversity. Those who are aware of that how to motivate a diverse workforce. Managing across cultures, emphasis on learning foreign languages are other features of today's business. Moving from tolerance to appreciation and managing women and their powers are the other different challenges before the business today. This scenario has led the business to different dimensions.
- **Environmentalism:** Environmental issues such as deforestation, global warming, depletion of the ozone layer, pollution of land, air and water are no longer strictly the issues related to books and conferences. The leading politicians and managers around the world have picked up the environmental banner. The green marketing movement has been gaining momentum around the world. The businesses are challenged today to develop creative ways to make profits without unduly harming the existing environment. Considering the variety of these sources of change in the environment, global managers are challenged to keep themselves abreast and adjust as necessary. Some companies like Daewoo, Hyundai, Maruti, Tata and Hero Honda in India, with their pollution prevention programmes are leading the way. Indeed, cleaning up the environment promises to generate whole new classes of jobs in the future.
- **Competition:** Gone are the days when business was heavily protected and subsidized, licences, quotas and restrictions were the order of the day. Now competition is the name of modern business. Businessmen always stand on the brink of a fear to eliminate from the market. They stand on their feet to cut down costs, to eliminate deficiencies and incessant improvement in the quality is order of the day. But by the competition, consumer is obviously benefitted by the diverse openings of different competitors. According to

Michael Porter "aggressive home based suppliers and demanding local suppliers competing domestic rivals will keep each other honest in obtaining government support". Nowadays, competition is not only from rival firms but also from the ever improving technology. For example, typewriters have been completely wiped out from the market by the computers. Traditional postage telegrams are at the verge of elimination by the increasing use of Internet services. So, today's business is witnessing the manifolds competition which was not prevalent in the past.

- **The Rise of the Rural Market:** The rapid growth of the rural market for a number of products is another important development. The developed economies in the world enjoyed the fruit of sustained growth over a longer period of time but now their markets have been saturated due to the limited population. In the search of growth the Multinational Corporations (MNCs) has started looking for the newer avenues. In the beginning they targeted the underdeveloped and developing nations in their urban areas. In India particularly with the liberalization policy of 1991 of the government of India, so many products were flooded in the Indian markets of genuine prices. This scenario could be witnessed up to 1995-96 but then urban markets of India have also started saturating and the different companies started looking for the newer kinds of market and that was rural market. Earlier rural market due to certain traditional is cultural barriers was not considered by the marketers but now these markets have become the order of the day where around 70 per cent of the population reside in these areas and contributes hefty percentage in the GDP. So, we can say that business have gone to the every nook and corner of the world.

So, from the above discussion, we can conclude that as far as scope of the business is concerned, it is vast and fascinating. It encompasses the use of latest technology and scientific know-how, it has changed its dimension from just producing and exchange of goods as service industry has given a different direction to it. Literature on this subject is ever-growing. Numerous books, journals, monographs and research articles are being written and fulfilment on each functional area of the business which have never seen before. Special courses are being conducted by the various universities and institutions on business as it has taken a thoroughly professional shape over a period of time. It has crossed its boundaries across the borders so the managers have to learn how to cope up with the diversities of race, casts, languages, religion and sex, etc. They have to acquaint different cultures and traditions to be successful in the global market. Therefore, we can say that today's business is entirely different than that of earlier ones and it poses numerous opportunities as well as challenges to the entrepreneurs.

1.6 SUMMARY

Business is an economic activity carried on by human to earn profit in a continuous manner under the purview of rules and regulations of the country. The mission statements reflect the whole perspective and importance of the organizations in a way that they can reshape their organizations and products as per the changing requirements of the society. In a broader manner, business fulfils these objectives namely social, economic and human in one form or the other. There should be a perfect blend between maximization of profit and growth under the economic objectives. It should be taken care by the business that consumer should not be deceived in any manner and timely and appropriate service should be provided to him besides emphasis on quality. Security of investment, fair return on investment, good working conditions for employees and their development are the major considerations in social and human objectives. Latest technology, vast study materials, diversified cultures, globalization and era of information technology have made the scope of the business vast and challenging.

1.7 SELF-ASSESSMENT QUESTIONS

1. What do you understand by the term 'business'? How does business of today differ from that of four to five decades ago?
2. "Profit making is the primary goal of any business enterprise". Discuss.
3. Elaborate the various objectives of the business in detail.
4. Write a detailed essay on the nature and scope of business.

2

UNDERSTANDING INDIAN BUSINESS

Learning Objective

The main objective of this chapter is to make the learners familiar with the various concepts and practices applicable in Indian business system.

2.1 INTRODUCTION

Business is an important institution in society. Be it for the supply of goods or services, creation of employment opportunities, offer of better quality life, or contribution to the economic growth of a country, the role of business is crucial. So the first question arises in anyone's mind is what really a business is? The following definition is an attempt to provide appropriate answer.

> "A business is nothing more than a person or group of persons properly organized to produce or distribute goods or services. The study of business is the study of activities involved in the production or distribution of goods and services–buying, selling, financing, personnel and the like".

Practically the above said definition is true but in theoretical sense it is incorrect. Before any activities can be considered in the business, there must exist both the goal of profit and the risk of loss. Thus, business can be accurately defined by K. Ashwathappa as "Complex field of commerce and industry in which goods and services are created and distributed in the hope of profit within a framework of laws and regulations".

Understanding the Business: To understand any business the critical step is to explore all the factors related to business and properly judging its impact on the business. There are many factors and forces which have considerable impact on any business. All these forces come under one word called environment. Hence, understanding the business means understanding its environment. Environment refers to all external forces which have a bearing on the functioning of business. "Environment factors or constraints", which Barry M. Richman and Melvyn Lopen", are largely if not totally, external and beyond the control of individuals institutional enterprises and their management. These are essentially the 'givers' within which firms and their managements must operate in a specific country and they vary, often greatly, from country to country".

William F. Glueck and L. R. Jauch gave an important characteristic of environment. "The environment includes factors outside the firm which can lead to opportunities for or threats to the firm. Although there are many factors, the most important of the sectors are socio-economic, technological, supplier, competitors and government.

There are two more factors which are not included in definition and which exercise considerable influence on business. They are physical or natural environment and global environment. Therefore, we will study the following environmental factors one by one.

2.2 GLOBAL ENVIRONMENT

Internationalization or globalization of business has become a subject of very serious discussion in the national economic policies and corporate boardroom. International trade is growing faster than world output and international investment is growing much faster than global trade.

Nature of Globalization: Globalization means several things to several people. For some it is a new paradigm–a set of fresh belief, working methods and economic, political and socio-cultural realities in which the previous assumptions are no longer valid. For developing countries, it means integration with world economy. In simple economic terms, globalization refers to the process of integration of world into one huge market. Such unification calls for removal of all trade barriers among countries. Hence, globalization aims at removing isolations of different economies.

Globalization is a new phenomenon to India. We were for long time content in serving internal market which has been vast. Domestic production was insufficient to feed the vast market. We were compelled to import in order to supplement domestic production. We were also exporting to other countries, but our exports were composed of traditional commodities and the direction was mainly erstwhile communist block. Globalization did hardly exist during past five decades. There are other reasons too, which made us within the country's boundaries. For a long time, we did not have industries of the number and magnitude to think of globalization. Vibrant economy filled with robust industries is a prerequisite for internalization. Secondly, for the past five decades, we followed an economic policy which did not encourage competitive spirit among our industrialists. In the name of self-reliance, import substitution, swadeshi and economic sovereignty, we encouraged domestic industries to prosper, however, inefficient they were. We gave them licenses, fixed quotas, imposed tariffs and offered subsidies generously. We put several restrictions on foreign companies desiring to enter Indian soil. This continued till 1990. In 1991, the new industrial policy paved the way for globalization in our economy. The number of global companies entered in India was 164 on 31st December 1991. Major Indian industries also set their subsidiaries abroad. The major Indian players in global arena are Ranbaxy, Essar Gujarat, Arvind Mills, Ballarpur Industries, UB, Reddy's lab and Aditya Birla Group. The process rate increased in late 90s and is now at its youth.

The World Trade Organization was established on 1st Jan. 1995. Governments had concluded the Uruguay Round Negotiations on 15th December 1993 and Ministers had given their political backing to the results by signing the final act at a meeting in Marrakesh, Morocco in April 1994. The 'Marrakesh Declaration' of 15th April 1994, affirmed that the results of the Uruguay Round Would "Strengthen the world economy and income growth throughout the world". The WTO is the embodiment of the Uruguay Round results and the successor to the General Agreement on Tariffs and Trade.

India is a founder member of both GATT (1947) and its successor organization, the WTO. By virtue of its WTO membership, India automatically avails of most favoured nation and national treatment from all WTO members for its exports and its participation in this increasingly rule-based system which is aimed towards ensuring more stability and predictability in the governance of international trade. WTO-related issues of current importance in India relate mainly to rights and obligations emanating from these agreements. The most important issues are:-

(a) Quantitative restrictions (QRs)
(b) Patents
(c) Geographical indications
(d) Agriculture
(e) Services
(f) Market access
(g) Implementation issues
(h) Trade and investment policy

Quantitative Restrictions (QRs): QRs on imports maintained on Balance of Payments (BOP) grounds were notified to WTO in 1997 for 2714 tariff lines at the eight-digit level. In view of the improvement in our BOP, the Committee on BOP Restriction had asked India for a phase out plan for these QRs. Based on presentations before this Committee and subsequent consultations with our main trading partners, an agreement was reached with those countries, except USA to phase out the QRs over a period of six years beginning 1997. The US preferred a dispute under the WTO's Dispute Settlement Mechanism. Pursuant to the report of the Panel and the Appellate body, India and the USA have agreed to a bilateral settlement for determination of a reasonable period of time up to April 1, 2001, within which India has to implement the rulings and recommendations of the Dispute Settlement Body to remove the existing QRs in a phased manner. As on date, the numbers of tariff lines on which QRs exist have come down to 1429 at the eight-digit level.

Trade Related Intellectual Property Rights (TRIPS): The Agreement sets out the minimum standards of protection to be adopted by the Parties, in respect of (a) Copyrights and related rights; (b) Trademarks; (c) Geographical indications; (d) Industrial designs; (e) Patents; (f) Lay out designs of integrated circuits; and (g) Protection of undisclosed information (trade secrets) arid the enforcement of these. A transition period of five years is available to all developing countries to give effect to the provisions of the TRIPS Agreement. Countries that do not provide product patent in certain areas can delay the provisions of product patents for another five years. However, they have to provide exclusive marketing rights for products which obtain patents after 1.1.1995. As per our obligations under the WTO Agreement, the Patents (Amendments) Act, 1999 was passed in March 1999 to provide for exclusive marketing rights.

Patents: The basic obligation in the area of patents is that inventions in all fields of technology, whether products or processes, shall be patentable if they meet the three tests of being novel, involving an inventive step and being capable of industrial application. In addition to the general security exemption which applies to the entire TRIPS Agreement, exclusion from patentability are permissible for inventions whose commercial exploitation is necessary to protect public order or morality, human, animal, plant life or health; or to avoid serious prejudice to the environment. Diagnostic, therapeutic and surgical methods for the treatment of humans or animals and plants and animals other than microorganism may also be excluded from patentability. The patent term provided for in the TRIPS Agreement is 20 years. A Bill to make these and other changes was introduced in Parliament and has been referred to as Joint Select Committee of the Houses.

In respect of plant varieties, there is an obligation to provide for protection by patents or by an effective sui generis or by any combination thereof. The Agreement does not spell out the elements of a sui generis system and it is left to each Government to determine the elements which could be deemed to be providing effective protection. A decision has been taken to put in place a sui generis system as it is perceived to be in our national interest. A legislation to this effect tabled in the Parliament by the Ministry of Agriculture has been referred to as Joint Parliamentary Committee.

Lay-out Designs of Integrated Circuits: India is a signatory to the international agreement (the Washington Treaty) administered by the WIPO. The main obligations of the Washington Treaty are also incorporated in the TRIPS Agreement with some enhancement and cover the protection of intellectual property in respect of lay-out designs that are original in the sense of being the result of their creator's own intellectual efforts. The obligations include national treatment to foreign right holders and a term of protection of 10 years. A legislation giving protection to lay-out designs was introduced in the Rajya Sabha on 20 December, 1999 by the Department of Electronics.

Copyright and Related Rights: In the area of copyright and related rights, i.e., rights of performers, producers of phonograms and broadcasting organizations, the Agreement requires compliance with the provisions of the Berne Convention. Computer programs are to be protected as literary works. The term of protection for copyrights and rights of performers and producers of phonograms is to be no less than 50 years. In case of broadcasting organizations, however, the term of protection is to be at least 20 years.

India is a signatory to the Berne Convention. The Copyright Act, 1957 as amended in 1994 takes care of our own concerns and meets with the requirements of the TRIPS Agreement except in the case of terms of protection of performers' rights. A Bill to increase this term to 50 years was passed by Parliament in December, 1999.

Trademarks: India's trademarks law, The Trade and Merchandise Marks Act (TMMA), 1958 is in its essential features, in accordance with international law. A Bill to amend the TMMA was introduced in Parliament in 1993 so as to provide for protection to service marks also. The Bill could not be passed and subsequently lapsed. A Bill in this regard, however, was passed by Parliament in December, 1999 which, inter alia, provides for protection to service marks.

Geographic Indications: The Agreement contains a general obligation that parties shall provide the legal means for interested parties to prevent the use of any means in the designation or presentation of a good that indicates or suggests that the good in question originates in a geographical area other than the true place of origin of the good. In India, we do not so far have any specific law on geographical indications. Case law, however, enables legal action for protection of geographical indications. It was decided to enact a new law on the subject to take advantage of the provisions of the TRIPS Agreement. A Bill in this regard was passed by the Parliament in December, 1999.

Industrial Designs: Obligations envisaged in respect of industrial designs are that independently created designs that are new or original shall be protected. There in an option to exclude from protection, designs dictated by technical or functional considerations, as against aesthetic consideration which constitutes the coverage of industrial designs. Our law, the Designs Act, 1911 is a very old enactment and needs updating. The Department of Industrial Development prepared a Bill in this regard, which was passed by the Rajya Sabha in December, 1999 and will now have to be passed by the Lok Sabha.

Trade Related Investment Measures (TRIMS): Under the TRIMS Agreement, developing countries have a transition period of 5 years up to 31 December, 1999 during which they can continue to maintain measures inconsistent with the Agreement provided these are duly notified. We notified two Trims, viz., that relating to local content requirements in the production of certain pharmaceutical products and dividend balancing requirement in the case of investment in 22 categories of consumer items. In view of the inconclusiveness of the Seattle Ministerial Conference, where no final decision on the request of developing countries for extension of transition period for elimination of the notified TRIMS was taken, it needs to be seen what final decision is taken by the General Council on this issue.

Tariffs: India's commitments to reduce tariffs to the bound levels by March 1, 2000 exist in respect of non-agricultural and non-textile items and necessary action will be taken to fulfil these obligations.

2.3 TECHNOLOGICAL ENVIRONMENT

Among all the segments of environment, technological environment exerts considerable influence on business. Thus, this section requires more devotion. J.K. Galbraith defines technology as a systematic application of scientific or other organized knowledge to practical tasks. During the last 150 years, technology has developed beyond anybody's comprehensions. Year 1983 was particularly considered by scientists as the year of scientific success. In this year scientists put a billion dollars technology into space, produced the world's first test-tube triplets and obtained evidence of another solar system. A major breakthrough was achieved in the field of genetic technology is to cure dwarfism. Technology, thus, is the most dramatic force shaping the destiny of people and business all over the world.

Status of Technology in India: India, like any other third world country, attended political independence after prolonged colonial rule and exploitation. The country entered the modern world in a state of economic backwardness and poverty of a large section of people. It is obvious that technology must attend to the basic problems of food, clothing, health and housing of people. At the same time, rapid industrial development through latest technology is necessary to catch up with advanced countries.

With these objectives in mind, Government of India set-up series of R & D establishments, space research centre, medical research centres, agricultural research establishments, oil explorations centres, power development projects and the council of scientific and industrial research. Besides, several universities and institutes have been set-up to provide higher education in science, technology and management. As on today there are 4700 intermediate/junior colleges, 144 universities, and 44 deemed universities in the country. Also there are more than 500 science and technological institutions, and 1080 in house research and development laboratories. There is also the Department of Science and Technology, an administrative wing of Government, to coordinate the activities of all research and technical activities in the country.

2.4 ECONOMIC ENVIRONMENT

Economic environment refers to all those economic factors which have a bearing on the functioning of a business unit. Business depends on the economic environment for all the needed inputs. It also depends on the economic environment to sell the finished goods. Naturally, the dependence of business on the economic environment is total and it is not surprising because, as it is rightly said, business is one unit of the total economy.

It is difficult to be precise about the factors which constitute the economic environment of a country. But still there are some factors which have considerable influence. These factors are:-

(a) Growth strategy
(b) Economic system
(c) Economic planning
(d) Industry
(e) Agriculture
(f) Infrastructure
(g) Financial and fiscal sector
(h) Removal of regional imbalances
(i) Price and distribution control
(j) Economic reforms

Out of the above said factors, two are of prime importance:-

1. Economic system
2. Industry

- **Economic System:** The scope of a private business and the extent of government regulation of economic activities depend to a very large extent on the nature of economic system, which is an important part of business environment. Broadly the economic system is divided into three groups.

  (a) Capitalism
  (b) Socialism
  (c) Communism

  (a) Capitalism: The system of capitalism stresses the philosophy of individualism believing in private ownership of all agents of production, in private sharing of distribution processes that determine the functions rewards of each participants, and in individual expression of consumer choice through a free marketplace. In its political manifestation, capitalism may fall in a range between extreme individualisms and anarchism (no government) and the acceptance of some state sanctions.

The capitalist system is also known as free enterprise economy and market economy. Two types of capitalism may be distinguished, viz.,

(i) The old, laissez-faire capitalism, where government intervention in the economy is absent or negligible; and

(ii) The modern, regulated or mixed capitalism, where there is a substantial amount of government intervention.

(b) Socialism: Under socialism, the tools of production are to be organized, managed and owned by the government, with the benefits occurring to the public. A strong public sector, agrarian reforms, controls over private wealth and investment and national self-reliance are the other planks of socialism. Socialism does not involve an equal division of existing wealth among the people, but advocates the egalitarian principle. It believes in providing employment to all and emphasizes suitable rewards to the efforts put in by every worker. Also called Fabian socialism, this philosophy is followed in our country and other social democratic countries in the world.

(c) Communism: Communism goes further to abolish all private property and property rights to income. The state would own and direct all instruments of production. Sharing in the distributive process would have no relationship to private property since this right would not exist. Alternatively called marxism, communism was followed in Russia, China and East European Countries.

- **Industry System:** In the mid-1960s, India had a better industrial base and possessed more prerequisites for industrial growth than South Korea, Malaysia, Taiwan, Thailand and Indonesia. Since then, the country has succeeded in creating a virtually autarkic economy where all outputs and factors were subject to rigid price and quantity controls; where investment was strictly rationed; where there were multiple barriers to entry, investment, foreign trade, and competition, and where the objective of the financial system was to supply subsidized development funds irrespective of returns. Consequently, all the countries, mentioned above, have overtaken India and are far ahead in industrial growth.

  The various administrative controls are industrial licensing, industrial policies and asset classification of monopolies, product reservation for small-scale sector, Foreign Exchange Management Act (FEMA), tariffs and quotas, the miniplant fetish, labour market rigidities, development finance and indulge now availability and essentiality. These are explained as follows:

(a) Industrial Policy: Industrial policy is an important document which lays a wide canvas and sets a tone for implementing promotional and regulatory roles of the government. The term "industrial policy" refers to government's policy towards industries—their establishment, functioning, growth and management.

The policy indicates the respective areas of the large, medium and small-scale sector. It also spells out government's policy towards foreign capital, labour, tariff and other related aspect. Naturally, the industrial development of a country is shaped, guided, fostered, regulated and controlled by its industrial policy.

Industrial policy is probably the most important document which indicates the relationship between the government and the business. But, it has no legal sanction and as such its violation cannot be challenged in a court as is possible in the case of Fundamental Rights guaranteed by the constitution.

This policy was announced on 30th April 1956. The resolution of 1956 made the industrial policy. More socialist oriented and widened the scope of public sector. The resolution classified industries into three categories, having regard to the role which the state would play in each of them.

(i) The first category contained industries "the future development of which will be the exclusive responsibility of the state". Industries in this category were listed in Schedule A of the resolution. Schedule A contained 17 industries. These included railways and air transport, arms and ammunitions, and atomic energy, which were to be developed as Central Government monopolies. In the remaining industries in Schedule A, the expansion of the existing privately-owned units, or the possibility of the state securing the cooperation of private enterprise in the establishment of new units where the national interest so required, was not produced. However, it was made clear that "whenever cooperation with private enterprise is necessary, the state will ensure, either through majority participation in the capital or otherwise, that it has the requisite powers to guide the policy and control the operations of the undertaking.

(ii) In the second category were included industries "which will be progressively state-owned and in which the state will, therefore, generally take the initiative in establishing new undertakings, but in which private enterprise will also be expected to supplement the efforts of state. The industries included in the second category were listed in Schedule B of the resolution. It contained 12 industries like machine tools, fibre-alloys and tools, drugs, fertilizers, synthetic rubber, carbonization of coal, chemical pulp, road transport and sea transport and aluminium and other non-ferrous metals not included in Schedule A.

(iii) The rest of industries were thrown open to the private sector but this did not prevent the state from starting any new undertaking. State will facilitate and encourage the development of these industries in the private sector by providing infrastructural facilities.

Ours is one of the few countries in the world where an entrepreneur is required to obtain an industrial licence from the government before venturing into a new business.

A "licence" is a written permission issued by the Central Government to an industrial undertaking stating such details as the location, the article to be manufactured, production capacity and other relevant particulars. It is also subjected to a validity period within which the licensed capacity should be implemented.

The principal objective of the Foreign Exchange Management Act (FEMA) is to prevent the outflow of Indian currency and to see that the foreign exchange legitimately due to India should be received. In detail, the objectives of the Act are as follows:

(i) To regulate certain payments.
(ii) To regulate dealings in foreign exchange and securities.
(iii) To regulate the transactions indirectly affecting foreign exchange.
(iv) To regulate import and export of currency and bullion.
(v) To conserve the foreign exchange resources of the country and to utilize the same in the interests of the economic development of the country.
(vi) To regulate holding of immovable property outside India.

(vii) To regulate employment of foreign nationals.
(viii) To regulate acquisition, holding, etc. of immovable property in India.
(ix) To regulate foreign companies.

The Act applies to the whole of India and applies to all citizens of India outside India and to branches and agencies outside India of companies or bodies corporate registered in India.

2.5 POLITICAL ENVIRONMENT

The influence of political environment of business is enormous. The political system prevailing in a country decides, promotes, fosters, encourages, shelters, directs and controls the business activities of that countries. A political system which is stable, honest, efficient and dynamic and which ensures political participation of the people, and assures personal security to the citizens, is primary factor for growth of any business.

Two basic political philosophies are in existence all over the world, viz., democracy and totalitarianism. In its pure sense, democracy refers to a political arrangement in which supreme power is vested in the people. Democracy may manifest itself in any of two fundamental manners. If each individual is given the right to rule and vote on every matter, the result is pure democracy which is not, however, workable in a complex society with a large constituency. Hence, the republican forms of organization follow whereby the public, in a democratic manner, elect their representatives who do ruling.

In totalitarianism, also called authoritarianism, individual freedom is completely subordinated to the power of authority of the state and concentrated in the hands of one person or in a small group which is not constitutionally accountable to the people. Societies ruled by a pressure clique–political, economy or military–or by a dictator plus most oligarchies and monarchies belong to this category. The doctrine of fascism and erstwhile Russian Communism Russian Communism are example of totalitarianism.

India is a democratic country. Our political system comprises three vital institutions:-

1. Legislature
2. Executive or government
3. Judiciary

1. **Legislature:** Out of three, legislature is most powerful political institution vested with such powers as policy-making, law-makings, budget approving, executive control and acting as mirror of public opinion. The influence of legislature on business is considerable. It decides such vital aspects as the type of business activities, the country should have, who should own them, what should be their size of operation, what should happen to their earnings and other related factors.
2. **Government as Executive:** Also called the 'state' the term government refers to "the centre of political authority having the power to govern those it serves". For business consideration, we should know what government's responsibilities to business are. Specifically, government's responsibilities towards business are as follows:
   (a) Establishment and enforcement of law
   (b) Maintenance of order

(c) Money and credit
(d) Orderly growth
(e) Infrastructure
(f) Information
(g) Assistance to small industries
(h) Transfer of technology
(i) Tariffs and quotas

3. **Judiciary:** The third political institution is judiciary. Judiciary determines the manner in which the work of executives has been fulfilled. It settles the relationship between private citizens, on one hand, and between citizens and the government upon the other. The power of the judiciary is of dual type:

(i) The authority of the courts to settle legal disputes.
(ii) Judicial review—The authority of the courts to rule on the constitutionality of legislation.

2.6 SOCIO-ECONOMIC ENVIRONMENT

Social and cultural environment refers to the influence exercised by certain social factors which are "beyond the company's gate". All such factors come under one head that is culture.

Culture: In its narrow sense culture is understood to refer to such activities as dance, drama, music and festivals. In its true sense culture is understood as that complex whole which includes knowledge, belief, art, morals, law, customs and other capabilities and habits acquired by individual as a member of a society. The culture has two main characteristics:

(i) Shared value
(ii) Passage of time

Culture of a society is shared by its members. Cultural ethose are passed from one generation to other generation. It is not confined to one particular period of time. The interface between business and culture can be summarized as follows:

(a) Culture creates people.
(b) Culture determines goods and services.
(c) It defines people's attitude to business and to work.
(d) Explains the spirit of collectivism and individualism.
(e) Defines whether people are ambitions or complacent.
(f) Education
(g) Family
(h) Authority
(i) Marriage
(j) Time dimension
(k) Cultural resources.

All the above said factors influence the business in one or other way. Hence, it is important to understand all these factors for a successful business.

2.7 NATURAL ENVIRONMENT

Equally significant, but sadly ignored, are the factors like climate, minerals, soil, landform, rivers and oceans, coastlines, natural resources, flora and fauna, etc. Which have considerable influence on the functioning of a business? It is the natural environment which decides the resources for any business. Manufacturing, which is one of the aspects of business, depends on physical environment for inputs like raw material, labour of various skills, water, fuel, etc. Trade between two regions of a nation or between two nations is the result of geographic factors. Because of natural factors, certain areas are more suitable for production of certain goods and other areas are in need of such goods. Transportation and communication, the main prop of business, depend to a larger extent on geographic factors. Uneven landforms, desserts, oceans, forest, rivers, etc. are barriers to develop this vital infrastructure. Some businesses like mining of coal and ores, drilling of oil and most important agriculture which depends most on nature. Thus, the impact of natural environment cannot be ignored moreover it should be given top priority for any successful business.

2.8 SUMMARY

India is a country of land and people. It has a huge customer base as well as world's most powerful brains. It is rich in its natural resources and is highly adaptive to changing business environment. In some areas like technology and political stability, it requires some wise steps. With all these virtues India has become a favourite destination of other countries to expand their business. India is expanding domestically as well as globally to compete with other powerful business nations so as to get its desired share of world economic growth.

2.9 SELF-ASSESSMENT QUESTIONS

1. Give a brief account of Indian business environment.
2. Discuss the major implications of Industrial Policy on Indian business.
3. Narrate in brief the various Industrial Policy Resolutions.
4. Write short notes on: (i) Economic environment; and (ii) Natural environment.

3

FORMS OF BUSINESS ORGANIZATIONS

Learning Objective

The main objective of this chapter is to make the learners learn about the various forms of business organizations along with their advantages and disadvantages.

3.1 INTRODUCTION

As a matter of common sense, the legal right of any commodity or property is referred to as ownership. Like commodities and properties business units are also owned. This ownership may be in the possession of a single individual or in the hands of few persons or in the hands of government, etc. An owner may possess his property or he may sell his property or he may transfer his property. It also happens in the case of business. This kind of ownership of business by different entities is also known as form of business organization where group of people work together to achieve certain goals with an expectation to earn profit under laws and regulations of the state. The various forms of business organization have evolved through many stages. According to the change of business and industries, we could also witness the manifold changes in the ownership of the business organizations. Certain factors like social, economic and political are responsible for this change.

In the beginning, the area of operation for business was small, the means of transportation were not so developed, the smaller kinds of machines were in practice, the smaller size of population were responsible for production and this is why the size of business was also small. But due to the increase in population, bigger sizes of machines were evolved with a revolutionized transportation and it had led to large-scale production. With the passage of time, the existing form of business organization looked small and it was replaced by another form. For example, the very first form was sole tradership but due to necessities it was replaced by partnership and again due to industrial revolution, bigger sizes of machines, large area of operation and large-scale production had made the size of partnership business a small entity. Then the historical event of 19th century occurred and that was the advent of 'Joint Stock Company' which separated 'management and ownership'. With the background illustrated above, let us discuss the various forms of business organization.

3.2 CLASSIFICATION OF BUSINESS ORGANIZATION

On the basis of ownership, we can classify different business entities into two parts, i.e., private enterprise and public enterprise. Let us discuss them in detail.

3.2.1 Private Enterprise

These organizations are also called non-government enterprises because these are neither established nor controlled by the government. These are managed and controlled by the non-government persons. Under this category, we include sole proprietorship, Hindu-undivided family, partnerships, cooperative society and joint stock companies which are further divided as private company and public company. Let's have brief discussion on these forms of business organizations.

1. Sole Proprietorship

As the name signifies, it is a form of business organization which is managed and controlled by a single person to whom we call 'sole trader'. He is the person who invests the capital, responsible for running the business, enjoys the fruits of profit and also bears the loss and he himself is the owner and manager of the business. Various scholars have defined sole tradership in their own way and a few have been quoted here. According to Louis Henny "The individual proprietorship form of business organization is an organization at the head of which stands an individual as the one who is responsible, who directs its operation and who alone runs the risk of failure". Kimbal and Kimbal define as "The individual proprietor is the supreme judge of all matters pertaining to his business, subject only to general laws of the land and to such special legislation as may affect his particular business". James Stephensen says "A sole trader is a person who carries on business exclusively by and for himself".

On the basis of above definitions, we can conclude that sole tradership is that form of business where a single person invests capital, establishes, directs and manages single-handedly to bear all kinds of profits and losses. So, the business which is run by a single person is known as 'sole trade' and the person who runs it called as 'sole trader'. He is also known as individual entrepreneur, individual owner, individual organizer and sole proprietor.

Special features of sole trade: It is that kind of business which is easy to form and dissolve because it is free from all legal bindings to begin and to wind up. But the liability in this kind of business is unlimited where you are responsible to pay your debts even out of your personal property. There is no distinction between business and businessman and he is free for any occupation. It is suitable in such conditions where area of operation is limited, lesser amount of capital is needed and where somebody wants to attain personal achievement or satisfaction. An entrepreneur, on one hand, enjoys direct relationships with the employees and consumers and on the other hand, enjoys the complete control on the business. But in certain conditions when you are not able to turn up on a particular day, you may bear loss due to absence and if the owner dies then it is difficult for others to continue because there are certain secrets which are only known to the owner. One person may have only limited managerial and investment ability so when it comes to enhance the business there is always a problem with a single person. Therefore, this kind of business has its own advantages and disadvantages.

2. Partnership

As the business progresses, the sole tradership form of business organization becomes small. This is simply because to produce at large scale, invest in a huge manner, to be efficient enough to control larger sort of operation, seems very difficult for a single person. In the growing business the need for more and more capital, limited managerial skill of an entrepreneur, ever increasing risk and limited goodwill are some of the constraints of sole tradership which necessitated the need for partnership. Necessity is the mother of invention seems to be the true saying in case of evolution of partnership, means to remove the maladies of sole tradership, partnership form was evolved. In India, this form of business is directed and controlled through Partnership Act, 1932.

In the simple words, if two or more persons run a business, it together is known as 'partnership'. According to Prof. Henny "The relation existing between persons competent to make contracts who agree to carry on a lawful business in common with a view to private gain". According to Indian Partnership Act, 1932 (Sec. 4) "Partnership is the relation between persons who have agreed to share the profits of a business carried on by all or any one of them acting for all.

On the basis of above definitions, it can be concluded that partnership is an agreement between two or more persons who will share profit and loss on the predetermined basis of a specific business and this business either is carried out by all of them or by any one of them on behalf of others.

It is important to mention here that as per Section 6 of Indian Partnership Act, if 1932 that if two or more persons possess a common property and share profits, they cannot be treated as partners. In that circumstances, these people are called co-owners. In partnership, individual members are called partners and collectively their business is known as 'firm' under whose name they run their partnership business.

Main Features of Partnership

(i) **Number of Partners:** For the partnership, it is essential that there should be at least two members. If at all, due to any circumstances the membership comes down to one, then it would be a compulsory winding up of a partnership. In that situation it would only be a sole tradership. Indian Partnership Act 1932 is silent on the subject of maximum number of partners but this malady has been removed by the Indian Companies Act 1956 where in the Section 11 it is highlighted that in case of ordinary business there can be 20 maximum members whereas in case of banking and insurance business, this number cannot exceed beyond 10.

(ii) **Unlimited Liability:** Like the sole tradership, in partnership also the liability of the partners is unlimited. Therefore, they are not only responsible up to their invested capitals but also from their personal property.

(iii) **Deed:** According to Indian Partnership Act 1932, it is essential that there should be a kind of contract or deed between the partners. It may be in written form or in verbal but if it is written, better it is. All the conditions of the business of partnership are specified in this deed in the beginning of the business so as to avoid any kind of dispute in the future. In the contents of the deed, generally documents relating to followings are included (a) Name and address of the firm where it should be kept in mind that it should not resemble to any other existing name and it should not name like crown, emperor, empress, imperial, king, queen, royal or parliament, etc.; (b) Name and address of the partners; (c) Scope of business; (d) Nature of business; (e) Duration of partnership; (f) Capital invested by partners; (g) Loan to and by partners; (h) Proportion of profit and loss; (i) Inspection of accounts book; (j) Dissolution of partnership.

(iv) **Earning of profit and distribution:** The main purpose of partnership is to earn profit and to distribute it among partners. Any purpose other than that of profit motive cannot be called partnership whose aim may be to serve society in any manner.

(v) **Restriction on transfer of interest:** No partner can transfer his or her share to anybody without the prior consent of other partners. For this purpose, development of consensus is must among the partners.

After knowing certain features of partnership, let us know who can be a partner. Can everybody a partner ? No. According to Indian Partnership Act 1932 (Sec. 30), any person who (1) is not below the age of 18 years (2) should be of sound mind (3) should not have been between declared insolvent and (4) should not have been the person of enemy country. A minor can also be a partner but only to share profit and he cannot access to the books of records.

From the foregoing discussion, we can conclude that partnership is such a form of business organization which is easy to establish. In partnership a huge capital can be invested unlike the sole proprietorship. It increases business efficiency as synergy is developed due to collective efforts of many minds. Due to many partners credit worthiness is increased and you can dare to take more risk. But the position of the partnership falls in between the company and sole tradership. As compared to company, the means and sources are limited with a fear of mutual conflict. Like the sole tradership, your liability remains unlimited and also there is restriction on transfer of share without permission, which does not provide a kind of liberty as in case of company. All these reasons paved the way to give birth to another form of business organization, i.e., joint stock companies.

3. Joint Stock Company

The world could witness two bigger evolutions. One of them was advent of industrial revolution and another was large-scale production. And due to these changes the whole structure of the world changed in terms of trade, industry, politics and at social levels. At earlier times, the structure of markets used to be locals and nationals but now these markets are shaping up into global markets. The people are exposed to diversified media and are able to access any part of the world either physically or in form of products. They have been catered by huge variety of products of different flavour, design and colour. It has enhanced the demand pattern of the consumers and to cater to this kind of demand of the consumers, the marketers realized a different production style which demanded huge amount of capital which was not possible to deliver for the sole tradership and partnership. So, there was a strong feeling of an institution which could meet the growing demand of the people. Therefore, this situation gave birth to a new form of business organization which was named as joint stock company.

These kinds of joint stock companies first evolved in Italy. In 17th and 18th centuries, these kinds of companies were established in England under Imperial Charter Act. But due to excessive speculative activities this form was banned in England in 1720 under Bubbles Act. But with the passage of time, this form was again passed by the parliament of England in 1844. The present form of joint stock companies are the contribution of the Englishmen in India. In 1600 A.D., the first English Company known as the East India Company was established in India by the permission of Royal Charter, then in 1670 Hundson Bay Company was formed and in 1694, Bank of England was incorporated. There used to be unlimited liability of the shareholders in these kinds of companies till 1855. It was after 1855 where the principle of limited liability was accepted and in 1857 Joint Stock Companies Act was passed in India. Then there were so many amendments in Indian Companies Act. In 1913, new companies act was formed in India but it was also amended so many times and finally the Indian Companies Act 1956 came into existence which is still in operation, although it has also been amended for many times but these are known as revolutionary amendments.

Meaning of Company: Section 3 of the Companies Act, 1956 defines the word 'company' as a company formed and registered under the Act or an existing company formed and registered under any of the previous laws. This definition does not bring out the meaning and nature of the company into a clear prospective. The vast majority of companies in India are with limited liability by shares. Therefore, it is desirable to define the term company keeping in mind these types of companies. Various scholars from time to time have contributed to build upon a good definition of the company. The major contributories were Lord Lindley, L.C.B. Gower, Hanney, Justice James and Justice Marshall, etc. As per the combined efforts of these authors, the company is defined as under :

"The company is an artificial person created by law, having separate legal entity, perpetual succession, limited liability and a common seal". This definition is more comprehensive in defining the exact nature of the company.

Features of the Company: On the basis of the above definition, we may spell out the following characteristics of a company:

(i) Artificial Person: A company is created with the sanction of law by the shareholders but is not itself a human being. It is, therefore, called an artificial and since it is clothed with certain rights and obligations, it is called a person. Subsequently a company is accordingly an artificial person. It is independent and distinct from its members. The decision of the House of Lands in Salomon vs Salomon and Co. Ltd. is a well-known authority of this principle where it was argued their company is a separate legal personality and altogether different from its members. A company can sue and be sued in its corporate name.

(ii) Limited Liability: Limited of liability is another major advantage of incorporation. The company, being a separate entity, leading its own business life, the members are not liable for its debts. Each member is bound to pay the nominal value of the shares held by him and his liability ends there if the liability of that member is limited by shares which are a usual phenomenon.

(iii) Perpetual existence/succession: The life of the company is endless. Its shareholders may die or they may transfer their shares or there may be new shareholders but all these things do not disturb the existence of the company, it goes for ever. "An incorporated company never dies". In the words of Professor Gower "Members may come and go but companies remains forever", not even a hydrogen bomb could destroy it. Thus, the death or insolvency of members does not affect the continued existence of the company. The company remains the same entity.

(iv) Transferability of shares: The shares should be capable of being easily transferred was the great object when joint stock companies were established. The share of the member shall be a transferable property in the manner provided by the articles of association. The unique advantage of this is that a member may sell his shares in the open market and get back his money, without affecting the capital structure of the company.

(v) Capital: Every company has authorized share capital which is divided into small shares. The owners of the shares are known as shareholders.

(vi) Common Seal: A company being an artificial person has to work through its directors, officers and officials. But it can be held bound by only those documents which bear its signatures. Common seal is the official signature of a company. When a company has any business or transaction in a place outside India, an exact reproduction of the common seal may be kept there. For such use, there must be power in the articles of association. A person must be properly authorized to use the seal, which shall sign his name, and also put the name of the place and the fact that he has been authorized to do so by the specified resolution.

(vii) Articles of regulations: There are two main documents of the company. One of them is memorandum of association where the main objects of the company are specified and other document is articles of association in which ways and directions are suggested to get those objectives. The directions to managers cannot go beyond these documents.

(viii) Prescribed mode of winding up: It is the another feature of the company that its winding up is also directed by law. "Company is born under rules and dies under rules". Like its inception, its winding up follow a complete and set procedure as prescribed by law.

So, these were some of the major characteristics of the company by which you might have followed the exact nature of this form of business organizations.

Kinds of Joint Stock Companies: Joint stock companies can be classified by different ways especially on the basis of liability and incorporation.

- **On the basis of Incorporation:** The company which is formed or established and it puts the word 'limited' or 'private limited' after its name and which are registered. Following are the different ways of their formation:

  (i) By Royal Character: It is one of the oldest ways of establishing a company. When a company was formed with the prior permission of the King or Queen, it was known as company incorporated under Royal Charter. East India Company is one of the examples of this kind of company.

(ii) By Special Act: When any company is established in the national interest by the special resolution passed by the parliament of the country, it is known as statutory corporation. Reserve Bank of India, State Bank of India and Life Insurance Corporation are some of the live examples of these kinds of companies.

(iii) By Company Act: Apart from statutory companies, all the remaining companies are formed under Company Act 1956 in India. All the companies which we could witness today have either been formed under this act or the existing act of that time.

- **Un-incorporated Companies:** Generally, the bigger sized partnership organizations are known as un-incorporated companies and these organizations do not put limited or private limited after their name. In India, we do not find the example of these types of companies.
- **On the basis of liability:** On the basis of liability the companies can be divided into this parts (i) limited liability company (ii) unlimited liability company.

(i) Limited liability company: Most of the companies in India are of limited liability nature. The liability of the shareholders of these companies is limited up to the nominated value of the shares they possess. The word limited or Ltd. is compulsory to be used with the name clause of the company as per company law. These companies can be of two types: (a) company limited by shares (b) company limited by guarantee.

(a) Company limited by shares: It is a kind of company where the liability of its member remains up to the nominal value of the shares purchased by its members. Beyond the value of the shares nothing can be charged from a shareholder. For example, A has bought 100 shares which value Rs. 1000 and he has already paid Rs. 700 to the company. Now he has to pay only Rs. 300 to the company because he has to pay only up to the value of his shares. Nowadays, this type of companies are most popular around the globe.

(b) Company limited by guarantee: A company limited by guarantee is one having the liability of its members limited by the memorandum to such amount as the members may respectively undertake by the memorandum to contribute to the assets of the company in the event of its being wound up. The liability of the members of a guarantee company is limited by a stipulated sum mentioned in the memorandum. The guaranteed amount can be called up by the company from the members only at the time of winding up if the liabilities of the company exceed its assets. A pure 'guarantee company' does not have a share capital. Generally, these kinds of companies are not established to earn profit but made for social well-being like trade chambers, trusts, sports club, etc.

(ii) Unlimited liability company: A company which is not having any limit on the liability of its members. The members of such a company are liable, in the event of its being wound up, to the full extent of their fortunes to meet the obligations of the company. However, the members are not liable to the company's creditors. The company, being a separate legal entity from the persons who constitute it, is liable to its creditors. Practically these kinds of companies are almost non-existent in India in today's scenario.

- **Private and Public Companies:** Either of the above kinds of companies may be private or public limited company. A private company can be formed by merely two persons by subscribing their names to the memorandum of association. Such a company by its articles must:

(i) Prohibit an invitation to the public to subscribe to its shares and debentures.
(ii) Restrict the rights of its members to transfer shares.
(iii) Limit the number of its members up to fifty, excluding its employee-members provided that where two or more persons hold one or more shares in company jointly, they shall, for this purpose, be treated as a single member.
(iv) A private company cannot issue a prospectus and can start business immediately after receiving the certificate of incorporation.

A public company means a company which is not a private company. Such a company by its articles must follow certain rules :

(i) It may or may not invite money from the public.
(ii) It restricts its minimum number of members to 7 but there is no restriction with regard to the maximum number of members.
(iii) If it decides to invite capital from the public, it has to issue a prospectus containing all information.
(iv) The articles of such a company do not contain provisions restricting the right of members to transfer their shares.

So, with the above background, you can very well distinguish between a private company and a public company and it should not create confusion about the term public company and public enterprise.

Hence, from the above discussion, you can well judge the importance of company form of organization. This kind of organization has permanent existence where death of a member does not have any impact on the life of the organization. The liability of the members remains limited which encourage investments. Whenever you are trapped financially, you can transfer your share. Large-scale production is possible only in this form of organization and being democratic organization you can put forward your grievances. It attracts good and talented people as management is the key to success in this sort of organization. But with these benefits there are certain lacunae also. One confronts with so many difficulties while forming this type of organization as it encourages to speculative activities also. No one is directly responsible for any kind mischievous activities and it leads to irresponsible management. The shareholders are exploited by the promoters. There is no secrecy in such kind of business as thousands of people work in such set-ups. But despite all maladies this form of business organization is the most popular one and suitable in today's environment.

4. Joint Hindu Family Business

It is yet another form of business organization in private sector. Before knowing joint Hindu family business, we must know something about joint Hindu family. Joint Hindu Family means the family which is joint, the family which is undivided and all the members live together. In other words, all the members of a family live and work together. Therefore, we can say that a business is run by a Hindu un-divided family and controlled by the seniormost member of the family.

"When all the members of joint Hindu family carry a business under the control of Karta or Mukhiya of that family, such business is known as Joint Hindu Family Business". This type of business can only be found in India. This type of business is directed under 'Hindu Law'. On the basis of this law, this kind of organization is divided into two parts :

(a) **Dayabhaga:** It is implemented in Bengal, Assam and some parts of South India. Under this pattern, father becomes the full-fledged owner of the property in his life-time and he manages all affairs related to property and business. As per this law, the property can be divided among brothers only, the sons cannot demand property from their father.

(b) **Mitakshara:** In rest of India, mitakshara is in practice. In this case, the senior most member owns the property and manages every function. The son becomes the owner of the property just by his birth. Karta with the help of all family members runs the business. Karta does not possess any right to sell the property of the family.

Management of Joint Hindu Family Business: Joint Hindu Family business is run by the senior most family member. He takes care of all kinds of accounts and he enters into a contract with the other party. In the troublesome hours, he can pledge the prosperity of the family. He cannot be held responsible for the loss but if he does intentionally, he is held responsible. This business is recognized by the Indian Income Tax Act. Two requirements are mandatory as per this law to be recognized as Joint Hindu Family Business (a) There should be a common property. (b) There should be at least two members who can demand the division of the property.

Characteristics of Joint Hindu Family Business

(i) **Control by Hindu Law:** This business is controlled and directed by the Hindu Law. Its rights and duties are specified in this law.

(ii) **Membership:** No endeavour is required to be the member of this business. By birth a family member obtains the membership.

(iii) **Stability:** The death of a member does not have any effect on this business as it continues even after death of a particular member.

(iv) **Liability:** Except 'Karta' the liability of all the members remain limited and up to their share.

(v) **Minor Member:** As one gets membership by birth so even a minor remains the member of this sort of organization.

(vi) **Registration:** As per law, registration of this business is not mandatory. Therefore, it is free from all legal hassles.

(vii) **Restriction on membership of females:** Only male members can obtain the membership of this business, females are barred from being members in this case.

5. Cooperative Organization

In the chain of private sector organization yet another form of business organization exists named as cooperative organization. Although it is one of the oldest kind of organization yet it has gained popularity recently in India. It has evolved through two words Co + operation meaning thereby to work together. It is that kind of organization where men associate themselves voluntarily for a particular task for their financial well-being and development.

Definitions of Cooperative Organization: According to H. Klivert : "Cooperative is a form of organization wherein persons voluntarily associate together as human beings on a basis of equality for the promotion of the economic interest of themselves". According to Prof. Saligman "Cooperation in its technical sense means abandonment of competition in distribution and production and elimination of middleman of all kinds". M.L. Darling defines cooperation that it is something more than a system. It is a spirit which appeals to the heart and mind. It is a religion applied to business. It is a gospel of self-sufficiency and service.

So, on the basis of above discussion, we can conclude that it is a kind of organization where people associate themselves voluntarily on the basis of equal resources to promote their financial and economic interests and to render maximum social service and help to the society.

Main characteristics of cooperative organization

(i) **Voluntary organization:** This organization depends upon the will of the members where there is no place for any deception and ill-will. No undue influence is used, one can be the member at his or her will and also can leave on the same ground.

(ii) **Equal Right:** In this kind of organization the principle of one man one vote applies. Any member can possess number of shares but when it comes to voting he can only use one vote. Therefore, on the basis of number of shares, there is no exploitation.

(iii) **Registration:** Although it is a voluntary organization but for the control of the state on such organization, its registration is compulsory. In India the registration is performed under Cooperative Act, 1912.

(iv) **Democratic Management:** It is run by the elected members whose nominations are done in the annual general meeting on the basis of election. It works on the principle of interest for all by cooperative efforts.

(v) **Cash Transactions:** In this kind of organization generally transactions take place on the basis of cash. Therefore, loss of money or bad debts is not the kinds problems associated with this business.

(vi) **Open Membership:** It is another feature of cooperative organization that anybody could be the member irrespective of his or her religion, caste, creed and sex, etc. Its membership is open for all.

(vii) **Elimination of Middlemen:** The main motto of this sort of organization is to eliminate the middlemen and competition so that the major benefits should reach to common masses.

(viii) **Division of Profit:** The profit earned in a financial year is not divided on the basis of proportion of capital invested by the members but it is distributed in the form of dividend to all the members of the organization.

So, these are the major business organization forms existing in the private sector. Now let us discuss the joint or mixed sector.

3.2.2 Joint or Mixed Sector

The business enterprises which are neither private nor public or the organizations which are established by both government and the private entrepreneurs are called joint sector or mixed organizations. The capital is invested not only by the government but also by the private hands and that may be through inviting money from the public in the form of shares or debentures. The main feature of this kind of organization is that both government sector and private sector work together for the development of the economy. Maruti-Suzuki India Ltd. is the hottest example of the mixed sector where Maruti represents the government of India and Suzuki is a private Japanese company. Haryana Detergents, Dharuhera is the another example of Private-Public enterprise.

3.2.3 Public Enterprises

When the government owns, controls and directs any business entity, it is known as public or government enterprise. Public enterprise should not be confused with public company which falls in the category of private sector. The government enterprises are also known as state enterprises. Prior to independence, the government of India used to look after only few departments like postage and telegram, rail transport and radio, etc. But seeing the scenario of poverty, unequal distribution of wealth and the problem of unemployment led the government to think to adopt socialistic pattern of society. Therefore, the government of India announced its industrial policy in 1956 where it was decided that some industries should be kept by the government so as to provide basic infrastructural facilities to the private sector and to keep the social welfare industry intact in the hands of the government. To attain the socialistic pattern of society, the government thought and planned that for the better development, basic industries and the industries, where huge investment is required, should be kept under the government control.

Meaning of State Enterprise: According to Prof. Roy Chaudhary "State enterprise in business denotes an undertaking which is controlled and operated by the government as its sole owner". According to the Encyclopedia of Britannica, "The term public enterprise usually refers to government ownership and active operation of agencies engaged in supplying the public with goods and services which alternatively might be supplied by private enterprise operations, the same as private, are financed wholly or largely by receipts from sale of goods and services".

So, on the basis of above definitions, it can be concluded that public enterprise is a kind of business organization which is either owned by the government or managed by the government or both the functions are performed by the state.

Forms of State/Public Enterprises

(i) Departmental undertaking
(ii) Public corporation
(iii) Joint stock company
(iv) Public trust

Departmental Undertaking: It is that kind of organization which is fully owned by the government and it is run by any of the departments of the state. Because it is directed by a department that is why it is known as 'Departmental undertaking'. For example, postage or telegram and Indian Railways are such organizations of the central government. These kinds of organizations are privileged in a manner that without the prior permission of the government, nobody can sue to these departments. These are directly controlled by the parliament and their budget is also approved by the parliament only.

Public Corporation: The public corporation is a body with a separate existence which can sue and be sued and is responsible for its own finances. Public corporation is clothed with the power of the government but possesses the flexibility and initiative of private enterprise. These are established with the special act of parliament. General Insurance Corporation (GIC), Life Insurance Corporation (LIC) and Indian Oil Corporation (IOC) are some of the examples of these kinds of establishments. These are run and managed by the board of directors. These organizations are exempted from the budgetary regulations unlike the departmental organizations.

State Enterprises Managed Like a Company: It is one of the important organizations of the government. It is also called 'Government Company'. According to Indian Companies Act 1956, "Government company means any company in which not less than 51% of the paid up capital is held by the central government or by the state government and includes a company which is a subsidiary of a government company". The government has formed separate principles to run these companies. Their accounts, ledgers, audit and budgets are directed through special principles and rules. Steel Authority of India Limited (SAIL), National Fertilizers Limited (NFL), Gas Authority of India Limited (GAIL) are some of the examples of the government companies.

Public Trust: Public trust is also one of the form of government business organizations. Initially, these were meant to control the parts of Kerala and Madras ports but later on they were also applied to develop certain areas. Improvement Trust, Investment Trust and Municipal Improvement Trust are some of the examples.

3.3 SUMMARY

From the above discussion, we can conclude that no form of business organization is perfect in itself. Every form has its advantages and disadvantages and suitability according to the capital available. Scope of business, scale of production, plan of future expansion are also some of other important criteria to go in for a particular form. Before selecting any form of organization, those factors should seriously be taken into account by an entrepreneur and then only the suitable form can be adopted.

3.4 SELF-ASSESSMENT QUESTIONS

1. What do you understand by the term 'Form of Business Organization'? Name the various forms of business organizations.
2. "One man control is the best in the world, if one is able to control everything". Discuss.
3. Define partnership and explain its important characteristics.
4. Why is joint stock company organization known as the best form of business organization? Give reasons.
5. What is a joint stock company ? Explain briefly its important features.
6. Define public corporation. What are its chief features and advantages?

4 COMMERCE, INDUSTRY AND TRADE

Learning Objective

The main objective of this chapter is to make the learners familiar with various types of business activities.

4.1 INTRODUCTION

Business is all around us in the mainspring of modern life. But very few people understand its true nature and role in society. The study of business is essential for training oneself for a career. The study of the principles and practices of business organization helps in understanding events in their right perspective and in tackling the problem of satisfying human wants through the use of available resources. Every human being is busy in one activity or the other to satisfy his unlimited wants and desires. The sum total of human activities may broadly be divided into two categories – economic and non-economic activities. Economic activities are designed to attain the use of the material resources in life. They are concerned with the production, distribution and consumption of goods and services. Human beings undertake economic activities in order to earn their livelihood. For instance, a worker works in the factory, a doctor operates in his clinic, a manager works in his office and lecturer teaches in a class to earn a living for himself/herself and for his/her family. Economic activities may be further classified into three categories, namely, business, profession and employment or service. On the other hand, non-economic activities are carried out not for earning money but on account of the human sentiments of charity, love, sympathy, patriotism, religion, etc. For example, a person goes to temple to offer his prayers.

Concept of Business: Literally the term 'business' implies 'busyness' or the state of being busy. But this is not the proper meaning of business as it covers every human activity. Business is an economic activity which is concerned with earning money and acquiring wealth. It is the human activity directed towards the acquisition of wealth through the production and exchange of goods and services. A business enterprise is an economic institution engaged in the production and/or distribution of goods and services in order to earn profits and acquire wealth.

However, profit is not the sole criterion of business. The early concept of business was based on the goal of profit maximization as reflected in the slogan, 'the business of business is to do business'. This concept later changed to profit with service. The modern concept of business is noticed on the goal of profits through service. Business earns money by supplying the goods and services which can satisfy human wants. Business may be carried on at no profit no loss basis for the welfare of the general public.

The term business should not be confused with commerce and trade. Trade implies simply the buying and selling of goods and services. Commerce includes trade and the activities which facilitate trade. Business is a much wider term embracing not only trade and commerce but industries, or all activities concerned with the production and distribution of goods and services. It means "the whole complex field of commerce and industry, the basic industries, processing and manufacturing industries and the network of ancillary services, distribution, banking, insurance, transport, and so on, which serve and interpenetrate the world of business as a whole". Thus, business may be defined as an economic activity which involves regular production and or exchange of goods and services with the main purpose of earning profits through the satisfaction of human wants.

4.2 SCOPE OF BUSINESS AND TYPES OF BUSINESS ACTIVITIES

Various business activities may be classified into two broad categories– (a) industry and (b) commerce. Industry is concerned with the production of goods while commerce involves their distribution. According to L.H. Haney, "On the one hand, business rests on the technical process of manufacture; on the other hand, it looks to the market. At the junction stands the businessman, either directing the technical process of production or gauging the market, or doing both; but always engaged in buying and selling for the purpose of gain." Industry and commerce may be further subdivided as shown in Fig. 1.

4.2.1 Industry

The term industry is used to refer to the process by which useful things are extracted from the environment, and transformed, processed, fabricated and multiplied into other products. Industry is of the following types:

1. *Extractive Industries:* These industries extract or draw out various products from natural resources such as earth, soil, water, air, etc. The products raised by these industries are provided by nature and collected by human beings. Agriculture, mining, hunting, finishing, lubering, oil exploration, quarrying, etc. are examples of extractive industries. The products of such industries are used by manufacturing and construction industries.
2. *Genetic Industries:* Genetic implies heredity or parentage. Genetic industries involve breeding or reproduction of plants and animals. Plant-breeding nurseries, cattle-breeding farms, poultry farms, fish hatcheries and commercial kernels are examples of genetic industries.
3. *Manufacturing Industries:* These industries are concerned with the conversion or

transformation of raw materials and semi-finished products into finished products. Such industries, therefore, create 'form utility'. Manufacturing industries supply most of the products for daily use. Goods supplied by these industries are known as factory production. Manufacturing industries are of the following types:

(a) *Analytical:* In an analytical manufacturing industry, a basic raw material is analyzed or separated into a number of products. For instance, an old refinery separates crude oil into kerosene, gasoline, diesel oil, lubricating oil and petrol.

(b) *Synthetically:* In these industries, two or more materials are combined or mixed together to manufacture a new product. Soap, plastics, cement, paints, cosmetics, fertilizer, etc. are the products of synthetically industries.

(c) *Processing*: These industries are engaged in the processing of raw material through different stages of production. Examples of processing industry include textiles, sugar, steel, etc.

(d) *Assembling:* In this case, various components or parts are brought together to produce a finished product. Manufacture of bicycles, radios, televisions, watches, automobiles are typical examples of assembly industry.

4. *Construction Industries:* These industries are engaged in the erection or construction of buildings, bridges, roads, dams, canals, etc. Construction industries use the products of extractive industries, e.g., stone, marble, bricks, etc. and also the products of manufacturing industries such as cement, iron and steel, wires, etc. These industries create the basic infrastructure for development. The distinguishing feature of these industries is that their products are made or fabricated at fixed sites. Their products are not carried to the market for sale.

Sometimes, industries are classified into primary and secondary industry. Primary industry consists of extractive and genetic industries which supply basic raw materials for further production. Manufacturing and constructive industries constitute secondary industry. According to scale of operation, industries may be classified as large-scale industry and small-scale industry. Industries requiring huge investment and sophisticated technology, e.g., ship-building, iron and steel, petroleum refining, etc. are known as heavy industry while light industry which requires small investment and simple technology consists of sugar, paper, textiles, etc. But all such classifications are relative rather than absolutely watertight categories.

Industries on the Basis of Economic Activity: Industries may also be classified on the basis of the nature of economic activity carried out in an establishment. The term establishment is defined as an economic unit which is engaged in one or predominantly one economic activity at a single physical location under single ownership control of a firm or enterprise, which may have more than one establishment engaged in different activities at the same location or the same activities in different locations. Each establishment is to be counted separately and classified appropriately.

Like International Standard Industrial Classificaton, 1968, the National Industrial Classification, 1970 groups economic activities which are akin in terms of process type, raw material used and finished goods produced. The classification does not make any distinctions according to the type of ownership or type of economic organization, and except in some cases the classification does not distinguish between large scale and small scale.

National Industrial Classification (NIC)-1970 Divisions of one digit level of classification

0	–	Agriculture, Hunting, Forestry and Fishing
1	–	Mining and quarrying
2, 3	–	Manufacturing
4	–	Electricity, Gas and Water
5	–	Construction
6	–	Wholesale and Retail Trade and Restaurants and Hotels
7	–	Transport, Storage and Communications
8	–	Financing, Insurance, Real Estate and Business Services
9	–	Community, Social and Personal Services
X	–	Activities not adequately defined
Y	–	Repair Services

MAJOR GROUPS Two-digit level of classification

Agriculture, Hunting, Forestry and Fishing

00	–	Agricultural Production
01	–	Plantation
02	–	Livestock Production
03	–	Agricultural Services
04	–	Hunting, Trapping and Game Propagation
05	–	Forestry and Logging
06	–	Fishing

Mining and Quarrying

10	–	Coal Mining
11	–	Crude Petroleum and Natural Gas
12	–	Metal Ore Mining
19	–	Other Mining

Manufacturing

20-21	–	Manufacture of Food Products
22	–	Manufacture of Beverages, Tobacco and Tobacco Products
23	–	Manufacture of Cotton Textiles
24	–	Manufacture of Wool, Silk and Synthetic Fibre Textile
25	–	Manufacture of Jute, Hemp and Mesta Textiles
26	–	Manufacture of Textile Products (including Wearing Apparel other than Footwear).
27	–	Manufacture of Wool and Wool Products, Furniture and Fixtures
28	–	Manufacture of Paper Products and Printing, Publishing and Allied Industries
29	–	Manufacture of Leather and Leather and Fur Products (except repair)
30	–	Manufacture of Rubber, Plastic, Petroleum and Coal Products

31	–	Manufacture of Chemicals and Chemical Products (except Products of Petroleum and Coal)
32	–	Manufacture of Non-Metallic Mineral Products
33	–	Basic Metal and Alloys Industries
34	–	Manufacture of Metal Products and Parts, except Machinery and Transport Equipment
35	–	Manufacture of Machinery, Machine Tools and Parts except Electrical Machinery
36	–	Manufacture of Electrical Machinery, Apparatus, Appliances and Supplies and Parts
37	–	Manufacture of Transport Equipment and Parts
38	–	Other Manufacturing Industries

Electricity, Gas and Water

40	–	Electricity
41	–	Gas and Steam
42	–	Waterworks and Supply

Construction

50	–	Construction
51	–	Activities Allied to Construction

Wholesale and Retail, Trade and Restaurants and Hotels

60	–	Wholesale Trade in Food, Textiles, Live Animals, Beverage and Intoxicants
61	–	Wholesale Trade in Fuel, Light, Chemicals, Perfumery Ceramics and Glass
62	–	Wholesale Trade in Wood, Paper, Other Fabrics, Hides and Skin and Inedible Oils
63	–	Wholesale Trade in all Types of Machinery, Equipment, including Transport and Electrical Equipment
65	–	Retail Trade in Food and Food Articles, Beverages, Tobacco and Intoxicants
66	–	Retail Trade in Textiles
67	–	Retail Trade in Fuel and other Household Utilities and Durables
68	–	Retail Trade in Others
69	–	Restaurants and Hotels

Transport Storage and Communications

70	–	Land Transport
71	–	Water Transport
72	–	Air Transport
73	–	Services Incidental to Transport
74	–	Storage and Warehousing
75	–	Communications

Financing, Insurance, Real Estate and Business Services

80	–	Banking and Similar Type of Financial Institutions
81	–	Provident and Insurance
82	–	Real Estate and Business Services
83	–	Legal Services

Community, Social and Personal Services

90	–	Public Administration and Defence Services
91	–	Sanitary Services
92	–	Education, Scientific and Research Services
93	–	Medical and Health Services
94	–	Community Services
95	–	Recreational and Cultural Services
96	–	Personal Services
97	–	Repair Services
98	–	International and other Extra Territorial Bodies Services
99	–	Services not elsewhere classified.

Activities not adequately defined

XO	–	Persons without any Affiliation to any Particular Industry (including fresh entrants to labour force)
XI	–	Activities not adequately defined (other than that in XO)

Repair Services

YO	–	Repair Services (if not included under 97)

4.2.2 Commerce

Commerce embraces all those activities which ensure a free and smooth flow of goods and services from producers to consumers. It consisted of trade and the activities which facilitate trade. According to James Stephenson, "Commerce is concerned with the exchange of goods; with all that is involved in the buying and selling of goods at any stage in their progress from raw materials to finished goods in the consumers' hands. It covers not only the functions of buying and selling and handling goods but also the many services which must be provided to finance, insure, store and transport goods in the course of these exchanges." Commerce is thus an organized system for the exchange of goods and services between the members of the business world. It serves as a link between producers and consumers.

Role of Commerce: However, the process of exchange is beset with several hindrances. The principal function of commerce is to remove these hindrances so as to ensure a free and interrupted flow of goods and services from producers to consumers. These hindrances have been discussed under:

1. *Hindrance of Person:* The manufacturers and ultimate consumers of goods are often unknown to each other. They are not always situated at the same place. Therefore, certain

persons called traders are required to bridge the gap between them. Various types of traders such as wholesalers, retailers and mercantile agents help to remove the hindrance of persons. Traders play an important role in the field of commerce by establishing a link between sellers and buyers.

2. *Hindrance of Place:* Very often goods are produced at places far away from the points of consumption. Various means of transport remove this barrier of distance and help to establish a link between the two packaging of goods to protect them from damage and pilferage in the course of transit also helps to remove the hindrance of place and thereby creates 'place utility'.
3. *Hindrance of Time:* These days goods are generally produced in anticipation of demand. Therefore, it becomes necessary to store them and make them available as and when the consumers demand them. Warehouses perform this function of storage thereby balancing the time lag between production and consumption. They help to create time utility.
4. *Hindrance of Risk:* During transportation and storage, goods are subject to several types of risk. Goods may be stolen or damaged. Fire, floods, earthquake, storm, riot, etc. and other calamities may result in the destruction of goods. Insurance removes this hindrance by covering the risk of loss or damage of goods. Insurance also helps in the safe transportation and storage of goods.
5. *Hindrance of Exchange:* Large-scale exchange or sale of goods requires safe and economical arrangements for the payment or price. Money serves as the medium of exchange and thereby removes the hindrance of exchange. Banks facilitate exchange by providing credit in various forms. Banking is, therefore, an important part of commerce and banks are useful commercial institutions. Payments for goods and services can be made easily and safely through the banks.
6. *Hindrance of Knowledge:* Exchange of goods can take place only when the seller brings his products to the notice of prospective buyers. Advertising and publicity provide the necessary information to prospective buyers about the utility and features of various products. In this way, they help to remove the hindrance of knowledge.

To sum up, commerce is the sum total of those activities or processes which are engaged in the removal of hindrances of person (through trade), place (through transportation), time (through storage), risk (through insurance), exchange (through banking), and knowledge (through advertising and publicity).

Trade: Trade is that branch of commerce which is concerned with the sale, transfer or exchange of goods and services. It involves the buying and selling of goods and services. Trade is the nucleus of commerce because all commercial services like transportation, storage, insurance, banking, packaging, advertising, etc. revolve around trade. The superstructure of commerce is built upon the foundation of trade. Trade can be classified into the following types:

1. *Internal or Home Trade:* It implies the buying and selling of goods within the boundaries of a country. Payment for the goods sold is made in national currency either in cash or through the banking system. Such trade is also known as domestic trade or inland trade. Internal trade may be further classified into two categories as follows:

(a) *Wholesale Trade:* It refers to the purchase and sale of goods of a specific variety in bulk, a wholesaler buys goods in large quantities directly from manufacturer(s) and sells them in comparatively small quantities to the retailers. Wholesale trade constitutes a link between the producers and the retailers.

(b) *Retail Trade:* It involves the sale of goods to the ultimate consumers. A retailer buys goods from wholesalers or manufacturers and sells them to the final consumers. He serves as the last link in the chain of distribution. Retail trade is carried on in several forms, e.g., department stores, multiple shops, mail-order houses, super bazaars, etc. Small-scale traders like hawkers, peddlers, street stall holders, pavement dealers and neighbourhood stores also carry on retail trade.

2. *International or Foreign Trade:* It consists of the exchange of goods and services between persons or organizations operating in two more countries. International trade involves the use of foreign currency (known as foreign exchange) and international means of transport. A system of international banking has been developed to facilitate payment in the foreign exchange transactions. International means of transport consist generally of shipping and airways. International trade is also carried on between the Governments of different countries. International trade may be further classified into the following categories:

(a) Import Trade: It involves purchase of goods from foreign countries for use in the domestic market.

(b) Export Trade: It is concerned with the sale of domestic goods to foreign buyers or in foreign markets.

(c) Re-export Trade: Re-export trade involves the import of foreign goods with a view to re-export them.

Auxiliaries to Trade: In addition to trade, commerce includes several ancillary services which facilitate exchange of goods and services. These auxiliary services or aids to trade are:

(i) *Transportation:* Transportation carries goods from producers to traders and finally to consumers. It bridges the geographical distances and thereby performs a useful function in commerce. It makes for speed and efficiency in exchange. Transportation provides the wheels of commerce. It is because of transportation that a producer can sell his goods in different parts of the world. It creates 'place utility'.

(ii) *Warehousing or Storage:* It refers to the holding and preservation of goods until they are finally consumed. Goods have to be stored at every stage in the process of exchange. Warehousing performs a useful function by matching supply with the demand. It helps to make available the seasonally produced goods throughout the year. In the absence of warehousing, a producer will have to dispose of the goods as soon as they are produced. Warehousing creates 'time utility'.

(iii) *Insurance:* It facilitates trade by providing a cover against the loss or damage to goods in the process of transit and storage. By getting their goods insured, producers and traders can avoid the risk of loss due to fire, theft, pilferage, etc.

(iv) *Banking:* Banks are traders of money and credit. They help in the buying and selling of goods by providing a convenient and safe mode of payment. Banks also grant credit to businessmen with which they can carry on larger volume of trade.

(v) *Advertising:* Advertising brings goods and services to the knowledge of prospective buyers. It helps to highlight the distinctive features and utility of different products. With the help of such knowledge, consumers can obtain better value for their money. Marketing research helps to know and understand the basic requirements of consumers.

There is a close interrelationship between the different branches of business described above. One cannot function without the support of others. Commerce helps industry before and after production through the purchase of materials and the sale of finished products. Production of goods and services is meaningless unless they are distributed among the consumers. Trade involving buying and selling of goods, maintains a smooth flow of commerce and thereby supports industry. At the same time, industry provides the goods and services for distribution and thereby gives rise to commerce. As industry develops, trade and commerce also grow.

4.3 RELATIONSHIP OF INDUSTRY, COMMERCE AND TRADE

Industry, commerce and trade are interconnected and interdependent. Industry presupposes existence of commerce. Production in a manufacturing industry, for example, is possible when raw material is made available to it through commerce. Similarly, produced goods reach ultimate consumers with the help of commerce. Thus, commerce serves as a link between a producer and a consumer. As production and industry are not possible without commerce, in the same way, no commercial activity is possible in the absence of commerce. Therefore, both industry and commerce are interdependent.

Trade involves transfer of goods from producer to consumers. It is the heart of commerce because all business activities revolve around sale, transfer or exchange. The entire superstructure of commerce is based on the strong and sturdy foundation of trade. Similarly, the specialized commercial activities like banking, insurance, transport, warehousing and advertising, etc. assist in the smooth flow of trade operations. Thus, both are interdependent and interrelated.

To conclude, between the two ends of business activity, i.e., producer and consumer, all the industrial and commercial (i.e., relating to trade and aids to trade) activities are essential for producing and selling goods or providing service to consumers. All of them are interrelated to each other and none can survive in isolation.

4.4 SUMMARY

Industry, commerce and trade are closely related to each other. Industry provides goods and services which are distributed through commerce. No commercial activity is possible in the absence of industry and production. Sound industrial base and infrastructure facilitate trade. At the same time, industry and production cannot survive unless the goods and services are distributed among consumers through commerce. Therefore, industry and commerce are interdependent. Industry provides the base for commerce and commerce serves as the backbone of industry. None of them can exist in isolation as each is essential for other.

4.5 SELF-ASSESSMENT QUESTIONS

1. Differentiate between trade, commerce and industry, explaining the main characteristics of each.
2. "Commerce is the sum total of all those activities which are engaged in the removal of hindrances of person, place, time and exchange." In the light of this statement, discuss the nature and scope of commerce.
3. Define commerce and explain its main components. How does trade constitute the nucleus of commerce?
4. Discuss various obstacles in the exchange of goods and services. How does commerce remove these obstacles?

5 CORPORATE SOCIAL RESPONSIBILITY

Learning Objective

The main objective of this chapter is to give awareness to the students about obligations of a business towards the society.

5.1 INTRODUCTION

Business is an important institution in a civic society. Be it for the supply of goods or services, creation of employment opportunities, better quality life, or contribution to the economic growth of a country, the role of business is crucial.

William F. Glueck and L. R. Jauch gave an important characteristic of environment. "The environment includes factors outside the firm which can lead to opportunities for or threats to the firm. Although there are many factors, the most important of the sectors are socio-economic, technological, supplier, competitors and government.

Managerial environment: It refers to all external and internal forces, which have a bearing on the functioning of the business. According to Barry M. Richman and Melvyn Copen "Environment consists of factors that are largely if not totally, external and beyond the control of individual industrial enterprise and their management. These are essentially the 'givers' within which firms and their management must operate in a specific country and they vary, often greatly, from country to country".

William F. Glucck defines managerial environment "as the process by which strategists monitor the economic, governmental, market, supplier, technological, geographic, and social settings to determine opportunities and threats to their firms.

From the above definitions, we can extract that managerial environment consists of factors that are internal and external, which poses threats to a firm, or these provide opportunities for exploitation.

In a business organization all the activities are being organized and also carried out by the people to satisfy the needs of the consumers. So, it is an activity carried out by the people for the people which means people occupy a central place around which all the activities revolve. It means business is people and a human is always a dynamic entity who believes in change and it may be right to say that the only certainty today is change. It poses a huge challenge for today's and especially tomorrow's businessmen and managers to be aware of specific changes so as to keep themselves abreast with the latest happenings in the field of business to maintain their survival and sustainability in the market. Therefore, the study of business environment is of utmost importance for the managers and practitioners.

5.2 CONCEPT OF SOCIAL RESPONSIBILITY OF BUSINESS

Social responsibility of business refers to what the business does, over and above the statutory requirement, for the benefit of the society. The word responsibility connotes that the business has some moral obligations to the society. The term corporate citizenship is also commonly used to refer to the moral obligations of business to the society. This implies that, just as individuals, corporates are also integral part of the society and that their behaviour shall be guided by certain social norms. The operations of business enterprises affect a wide spectrum. The resources they make use of are not limited to those of the proprietors and the impact of their operations is felt also by many people who are in no way connected with the enterprises. The shareholders, the suppliers of resources, the consumers, the local community and society at large are affected by the way an enterprise functions. Hence, a business enterprise has to be socially very responsive so that a social balance may be struck between the opposing interests of these groups. Goyder argues industry in the twentieth century can no longer be regarded as a private arrangement for enriching shareholders. It has become a joint enterprise in which workers, management, consumers, the locality, government and trade union officials all play a part. If the system, which we know by the name private enterprise, is to continue, some way must be found to embrace many interests, which go to make up industry in a common purpose.

Later, in 1978, while delivering the C.C. Desai Memorial Lecture, he reiterated his plea that if the corporation has to function effectively, it has to be accountable to the public at large; and he sought to equate the suggestion of a responsible company with the trusteeship concept advocated by Gandhiji, the aim of which was to ensure that private property was used for the common good. The declaration issued by the international seminar on the social responsibility of business held in India in 1965 also correlated the Gandhian concept of trusteeship with the social responsibility of business as "responsibility to customers, workers, shareholders and the community." There has been a growing acceptance of the plea that business should be socially responsible in the sense that the business enterprise, which makes use of the resources of society and depends on society for its functioning, should discharge its duties and responsibilities in enhancing the welfare of the society of which it is an integral part. H.S. Singhania classifies the nature of the social responsibility of business into two categories. The first involves the acceptance of the fact that business is not merely a profit-making occupation but a social function, which involves certain duties, and requires that appropriate ethics are followed. For example, a business must obey all the laws, even when they are disagreeable; it should produce the maximum goods of good quality, ensure smooth supplies at competitive prices, pay taxes, shun malpractices, pay a fair wage to employees and a reasonable dividend to shareholders. It is also the duty of a business to undertake new investment and promote the dispersal of economic activity through ancillarisation and the setting up of industries in backward areas so as to spread enterprise and take employment to the doorsteps of labour. In addition to its commercial activity, business also plays a role in promoting social welfare activity, even directly.

5.2.1 Views on Social Responsibility

The contemporary view of social responsibility of business is substantially broader and benevolent than the classical one. According to the classical view, business has only economic objectives and no other responsibility beyond that. Milton Friedman, a Nobel economist and a proponent of this view, argues that there is one and only one social responsibility of business—to use its resources and engage in activities designed to increase its profits so long as it stays within the rules of the game, which is to say, engages in open and free competition, without deception or fraud. Few trends could so thoroughly undermine the very foundations of our free society as the acceptance by corporate officials of a social responsibility other than to make as much money for their stockholders as possible. This is a fundamentally subversive doctrine. The contemporary view of business is an ecological one according to which business is an integral part of the society to serve a social purpose. Proponents like Davis and Blomstorm hold that business is a social institution, performing a social mission and having a broad influence on the way people live and work together. According to Steiner and Steiner, a reasonable approach to social responsibility is as follows:

- Each business must take into account the situation in which it finds itself in meeting stakeholder expectations.
- Business is an economic entity and cannot jeopardize its profitability meeting social needs.
- Business should recognize that in the long run, the general social good benefits everyone.
- The social responsibility expected of a business is directly related to its social power to influence outcomes.
- Social responsibility is related to the size of the company and to the industry it is in.
- A business should fickle only those social problems in which it has competence.
- Business must assume its share of the social burden and be willing to absorb reasonable social costs.

The extent of social orientations of companies varies widely. Further, the social orientation or the extent of social involvement of a company may change over time.

5.2.2 Social Responsibility Models

There are some models which endeavour to describe the evolution and extent of social orientation of companies. Notables ones include Carroll's model, Halal's model and Ackerman's model.

Archie B. Carroll, who defines corporate social responsibility as the entire range of obligations business has to society, has proposed a three-dimensional conceptual model of corporate performance. According to Carroll, a firm has four categories of obligations of corporate performance: economic, legal, ethical, and discretionary.

The firm being an economic entity, its primary responsibility is economic, i.e., efficient operations to satisfy economic needs of the society and generation of surplus for rewarding the investors and further development. Legal responsibilities are also fundamental in nature because a company is bound to obey the law of the land. Ethical responsibilities are certain norms, which the society expects the business to observe though they are not mandated by law. For example, a company shall not resort to bribing or unethical practices, unfair competitive practices, etc. Discretionary responsibilities refer to the voluntary contribution of the business to the social cause, like involvement in community development or other social programmes.nts out that these four categories are not mutually exclusive, and the boundaries between them are difficult, if not impossible, to define. Further, these terms are not value-free and different people may interpret them differently.

Carroll later presented the different categories of responsibilities as a pyramid of corporate social responsibility. Economic responsibilities are at the base of the pyramid, succeeded by legal responsibilities, ethical responsibilities and, finally, philanthropic responsibilities. According to Carroll's pyramid, legal responsibilities come only at the second stage. This is not a right view. A company must inevitably obey the laws, even if it is unable to discharge some of the economic objectives, as long as it exists. Figure 5.1 presents the right perspective.

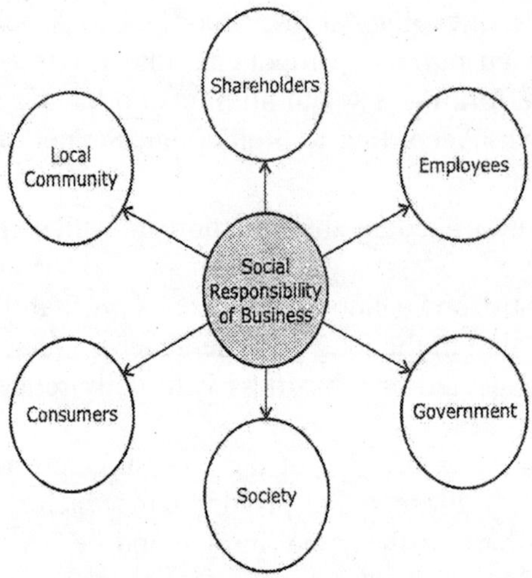

Figure 5.1 Social responsibility of business.

William E Halal's return-on-resources model of corporate performance recognizes the fact that no corporate social posture will be value-free, and this makes corporate social responsiveness a tremendously difficult task. He points out that a firm can only attempt to unite the diverse interests of various social groups to form a workable coalition engaged in creating value for distribution among members of the coalition. Beyond a certain level of economic activity, the social issues at stake may become conflicting. For example, large spending for social cause may affect the profitability of the firm, which could have implications for the stakeholders and the future of the firm. This calls for tradeoffs, which involve both economic and ethical decisions that will not necessarily satisfy the needs of every stakeholder. According to Ackerman's model, there are three phases in the development of the social responsiveness of a company. The first phase is one when the top management recognizes the existence of a social problem, which deserves the company's attention and acknowledges the company's policy towards it by making an oral or written statement. The company appointing staff specialists or external consultants to study the problem and suggest ways of dealing with it characterizes the second phase. The third phase involves the implementation of the social responsibility programmes.

5.2.3 Extent of Social Orientation and Involvement

On the basis of the extent of social orientation and involvement of companies, this can be classified into the following categories:

1. **Anti-social:** Not only that these companies have no social orientation but also they are unfair and unscrupulous in the conduct of the business. Rather than respecting laws and norms in their letter and spirit, attempts may be made to take advantage of the loopholes/ interpretational flexibility or to circumvent the rules and regulations by malpractices. Promoters and top managerial personnel of several organizations have been found to engage in insider trading, price rigging and the like. These businesses may even contribute a part of their ill-gotten money for social purpose to mask their real face or because of some compulsion to which they yield for fear of some reaction or for getting some favours or goodswill.
2. **Indifferent:** These are companies, which have no social orientation beyond discharging the legal as well as the economic responsibilities. The attitude is that going by the rules and regulations is good enough; there is the government and other organizations to work for the social cause and it is not the business of the business.
3. **Peripheral:** These companies are slightly a shade better than the indifferent category. They have little bit of social orientation, often for the namesake.
4. **Socially Oriented:** Companies in this category have a high level of social orientation but their real involvement is constrained by limitations of resource.
5. **Committed and Very Active:** These companies are characterized by high level of social orientation and real involvement in the societal welfare programmes. What distinguishes these companies from those in the preceding category is mostly their ability to commit significant amount of resources to make the social orientation meaningful.

5.3 FACTORS AFFECTING SOCIAL ORIENTATION

Important factors, which influence the social orientation of companies, include the following.

1. **Promoters and Top Management:** The values and vision of promoters and top management is one of the very important factors, which influence the corporate social responsibility.
2. **Board of Directors:** As it is the Board of Directors, which decides the major policies and resource allocation of company, the attitude of the members of the Board is an important influencer of the social orientation.

3. **Stakeholders and Internal Power Relationship:** The attitude of various stakeholders like shareholders, creditors, employees, etc. and the internal power relationship also affect the social orientation of a company. As suggested by the Halal's model described in the previous section of this chapter, a firm can only attempt to unite the diverse interests of various social groups to form a workable coalition engaged in creating value for distribution among members of the coalition. Beyond a certain level of economic activity, the social issues at stake may become conflicting.
4. **Societal Factors:** The social orientation of company is also influenced by certain characteristics of the society and general attitude and expectation of the society regarding the social responsibility of business. For example, a resourceful firm located in a poor community may be expected to contribute to the development of education and health facilities, etc. of the locality whereas such involvement may not be required of a firm in a well-developed community. The orientations or approaches may vary in accordance with the environment. The behaviour or social orientation expected of business may vary between different societies.
5. **Industry and Trade Associations:** Industry and trade associations also influence the behaviour of the firms by establishing professional and ethical codes and norms, education and collective decisions.
6. **Government and Laws:** Laws are society's codification of right and wrong. Business shall play the rules of the game. Anti-trust legislations, legislations to curb corruption, unfair practices, etc. vary between nations. What is right or not anti-law in one country may not be so in some other country. Further, what is legally controlled in some countries have no legal control in some other countries. Besides legislation, there are other methods of government influence like guidelines, persuasion, incentives (like tax exemptions) and pressurizing. The social orientation would also depend on the government's view of social responsibility and the power and earnestness of government agencies (like SEBI, for example) in dealing with defaulting companies.
7. **Political Influences:** Political influences include pressure exerted by special interest groups in society and media to control business practices. These include a variety of non-governmental organizations (NGOs) like consumer interest groups, environmentalists, etc. They use a variety of methods like lobbying to persuade government and public agencies to adopt regulatory measures, conducting public awareness campaigns, and even direct confrontation with the business in some cases.
8. **Competitors:** The competitive forces also influence social orientation of company. Two types of competitive behaviour are often noted. When one or some companies become socially involved, others may be encouraged or provoked to do some thing. Sometimes, there may be competition between companies to out-perform others. The other way by which the society benefits by competitive behaviour is the actions of suing competitors for unfair practices or publicly exposing the misbehaviour of competitors.
9. **Resources:** The financial position and other resources of the company also affect social involvement of companies. It may be noted that the TISCO has been constrained to cap, even though at fairy high level, its social responsibility expenditure.

10. **Ethical Influences:** Another factor influencing the social orientation is the ethical decision-making and self-regulation of business conduct. Some companies have well laid down codes and norms of ethical behaviour. See the previous chapter for more information. Gene Laczniak summarizes five ethical standards that are in vague as follows.
   (i) **The Golden Rule:** Act in the way you would expect others to act towards you.
   (ii) **The Utilitarian Principle:** Act in a way that results in the greatest good for the greatest number.
   (iii) **Kant's Categorical Imperative:** Act in such a way that the action you take could be a universal law or rule of behaviour under the circumstances.
   (iv) **The Professional Ethic:** Take actions that a disinterested panel of professional colleagues would view as proper.
   (v) **The TV Test:** Ask, "Would I feel comfortable explaining to a national TV audience why I took this action?"

5.4 RESPONSIBILITIES OF DIFFERENT SECTIONS

There is no unanimity of opinion as to what constitutes social responsibility of business. The important generally accepted responsibilities of the business to different sections of the society are described below.

1. **Responsibility to Shareholders:** The responsibility of a company to its shareholders, who are the owners, is indeed a primary one. The fact that the shareholders have taken a great risk in making investment in the business should be adequately recognized. To protect the interests of the shareholders and employees, "the primary business of a business is to stay in business". To safeguard the capital of the shareholders and to provide a reasonable dividend, the company has to strengthen and consolidate its position. Hence, it should develop and improve its business and build up its financial independence. Needless to say, to provide dividend, the company should earn sufficient profit. Adequate reserves should be built up so that it will be able to declare a reasonable dividend during a lean period as well. If a company fails to cope with changes in a changing and dynamic world, its position will be shaken, and the shareholders' interests will be affected. By innovation and growth, the company should consolidate and improve its position and help strengthen the share prices. The shareholders are interested not only in the protection of their investment and the return on it but also in the image of the company. It shall, therefore, be the endeavour of the company to ensure that its public image is such that the shareholders can feel proud of their company. It may be mentioned here that the shareholders also have certain responsibilities, which they have to discharge to protect their own interests. They shall not only offer wholehearted support and cooperation in the positive efforts of the company but shall also guide and control properly its policies and activities. At the same time, they shall appreciate the responsibility of the business to other sections of society: to the workers, consumers and the community.
2. **Responsibility to Employees:** The success of an organization depends to a very large extent on the morale of the employees and their wholehearted cooperation. Employee

morale depends to a large extent on the discharge of the company's responsibilities to them and the employer-employee relationship. The responsibility of the organization to the workers include:

(i) The payment of fair wages;
(ii) The provision of the best possible working conditions;
(iii) The establishment of fair work standards and norms;
(iv) The provision of labour welfare facilities to the extent possible and desirable;
(v) Arrangements for proper training and education of the workers;
(vi) Reasonable chances and proper system for accomplishment and promotion;
(vii) Proper recognition, appreciation and encouragement of special skills and capabilities of the workers;
(viii) The installation of an efficient grievance handling system;
(ix) An opportunity for participating in managerial decisions to the extent desirable.

The Committee that conducted the social audit of Tata Iron and Steel Company (TISCO) observes that "not only should the company carry out its various obligations to the employees as well as the larger community as a matter of principle, but this has also led to a higher degree of efficiency in TISCO works and an unparalleled performance in industrial peace and considerable team spirit and discipline which have all resulted in high productivity and utilization of capacity". Thus, by discharging its responsibilities to the employees, the business advances its own interests. It may, however, be pointed out that the expenditure on labour welfare, etc., should have relevance to the financial position of the company and the economic conditions of the nation. This aspect has to be particularly taken note of by public sector enterprises. Such expenditure shall not exceed the socially and economically warranted limits and shall not cause undue burden on the consumers or the general public. It shall not result in the formation of islands of affluence or comfort in the midst of poverty and suffering at the expense of society.

3. **Responsibility to Consumers:** According to Peter Drucker, "there is only one valid definition of business purpose; to create a customer." Drucker observes: "The customer is the foundation of a business and keeps it in existence. He alone gives employment. To supply the wants and needs of a consumer, society entrusts wealth-producing resources to the business enterprise". It has been widely recognized that customer satisfaction shall be the key to satisfying the organizational goals. Important responsibilities of the business to the customers are:

(i) To improve the efficiency of the functioning of the business so as to (a) increase productivity and reduce prices, (b) improve quality, and (c) smoothen the distribution system to make goods easily available.
(ii) To do research and development, to improve quality and introduce better and new products.
(iii) To take appropriate steps to remove the imperfections in the distribution system, including blackmarketing or profiteering by middlemen or anti-social elements.
(iv) To supply goods at reasonable prices even when there is a seller's market.
(v) To provide the required after-sales services.
(vi) To ensure that the product supplied has no adverse effect on the consumer.
(vii) To provide sufficient information about the products, including their adverse effects, risks, and care to be taken while using the products.

(viii) To avoid misleading the customers by improper advertisements or otherwise.
(ix) To provide an opportunity for being heard and to redress genuine grievances.
(x) To understand customer needs and to take necessary measures to satisfy these needs.

Despite the popularity of the Marketing Concept and the growing awareness of consumer rights, consumers all over the world are, by and large, dissatisfied. Consumerism is an organized endeavour of the consumers to protect their rights. In shortage economies like India many businessmen pay scant attention to their responsibilities to consumers. To protect consumer rights and to make the business discharge its responsibilities to them, the consumers should give up their indifferent attitude and build up a strong consumer movement.

4. **Responsibility to the Community:** A business has a lot of responsibility to the community around its location and to the society at large. These responsibilities include:
(i) Taking appropriate steps to prevent environmental pollution and to preserve the ecological balance.
(ii) Rehabilitating the population displaced by the operation of the business, if any.
(iii) Assisting in the overall development of the locality.
(iv) Taking steps to conserve scarce resources and developing alternatives, wherever possible.
(v) Improving the efficiency of the business operation.
(vi) Contributing to research and development.
(vii) Development of backward areas.
(viii) Promotion of ancillarization and small-scale industries.
(ix) Making possible contribution to furthering social causes like the promotion of education and population control.
(x) Contributing to the national effort to build up a better society.

5.5 THE INDIAN SCENARIO

The Indian business sector presents a mixed picture as far as social responsibility is concerned. Shri J.R.D. Tata, who was instrumental in conducting the first social audit in India and perhaps in the world, was of the opinion that while on the side of production, of growth, of efficiency, Indian industry, on the whole, did remarkably well, usually against odds and in spite of crippling infrastructural shortages unknown in advanced countries, on the distributional side, however, its record was often poor and, in some respects, dismal, judged by the size of the blackmarket, the volume of black money and the general corruption that pervaded our economic life. True, many a times the imperfections on the distribution side–mostly hoarding and blackmarketing–mercilessly gouge the unfortunate consumer. "Although it is the trader rather than the manufacturer who is mainly responsible for such diversion of goods and for the resulting heavy burden imposed on the consumer, the fact remains that, to that extent, corporate management of even of large Indian industries has, perhaps unavoidably, failed in the important obligation of ensuring that their goods reach the consumer at fair prices". It is high time the producer realized that his responsibility does not end with producing goods and services; he should ensure that whatever is produced reached the ultimate consumer in time and at reasonable prices. It is gratifying to note that a number of leading companies in India have shown recognition of the social responsibility of the corporate sector. The business community has been instrumental in setting up hundreds of institutions of public service like schools, colleges, management institutes, dispensaries, hospitals, technological institutes, research institutes (medical, scientific and technological), libraries, dharamshalas, cultural institutions, institutes for the dumb, deaf and blind, museums and places of religions worship. Some of the leading enterprises have extended welfare measures like health and medical facilities to people of the surrounding villages. Many businessmen have risen up to the occasion to help the victims of droughts, floods, earthquakes and other natural calamities.

One of the important externalities of industrialization is the serious ecological damage it has inflicted. The problem of environmental pollution caused by industries is very serious in a number of places in our country. Though some enterprises have taken pollution abatement measures, many—both in the private and public sectors—continue to be major offenders against the environment. In fact, some of the public sector enterprises are notorious for their irresponsibility in this matter. As J.R.D. Tata has rightly pointed out, high standards of behaviour and the discharge of social obligations should be expected of or demanded from, not only business and industry but from all economic groups in the country whose actions have an impact on the public weal. This applies in particular to trade unions which, both in India and abroad, have, in recent years, acquired and often misused enormous economic powers, exceeded only by the Government's own. The millions of man-days of production lost in India every year owing to labour unrest and the violent form, which such unrest has taken in many cases, clearly indicate the need for a new approach to trade unionism and recognition of its social obligations.

The participation of labour in management has been suggested as a remedy for many causes of industrial unrest. While it is a welcome suggestion, it should be ensured that the 'collaboration' between labour and capital does not become instrumental in exploiting society.

The social responsibility of business is usually advocated for the private sector, presumably on the assumption that the public sector is socially quite responsible. But the fact remains that the public sector in India is yet to prove that it is more responsive to society than the private sector. In some cases, in fact, the record of the public sector is more dismal than that of the private. As far as the pollution of the environment is concerned, the public sector is as guilty as the private.

Many public sector enterprises in India have undoubtedly failed to discharge their primary responsibilities–increase in the productivity and production, efficiency in the provision of the services, etc. This is reflected in the mounting losses of many public enterprises. Some may argue that the public sector is not, and should not be, profit-motivated. But gone are the days of such philosophy. It has been clearly laid down that the public sector should generate surplus to finance our future development programmes. The huge losses incurred by the Indian public sector are not the result of any charity; they are the inevitable outcomes of inefficiency, irresponsibility and mismanagement at various levels. The failure of the public sector in discharging its primary duties has made the plight of the common man worse than it would have been, for it resulted in shortages, higher prices and more taxes. There is also a very wide gap between the sweet expectations from the public distribution system designed to save the common man from the clutches of the "unscrupulous private sector" and the bitter experiences of the way the public distribution system functions. The least said about the efficiency of the service of the public sector transport undertakings the better. In our country a social audit is indeed, perhaps, more for the public sector than the private sector.

The Sachar Committee suggested that companies in the public sector, which were very much a part of the total corporate sector and accounted for about 70 per cent of the total investment in the corporate sector, must reckon with the social cost and social benefits arising out of any given investment. As a matter of fact, social cost-benefit analysis is accepted as one of the prime considerations for making any investment in the public sector. It is natural, therefore, to expect from the private corporate sector that, in the matter of investment, it will also show a similar consideration of social cost and social benefit. The accountability of the public sector to the people through parliament must find its parallel in the private sector in the form of social accountability, at least to the extent of informing the public about the extent and manner in which it has or has not been able to discharge its social obligations in the cause of its own economic operations. It is in this sense that the social responsibility of business, as far as the private sector is concerned, is another name for social accountability and is, in our view, a mere extension of the principle of public disclosure to which the corporations must be subject. It has also been repeatedly emphasised that the report on social responsibility of the company should not be in a vague or general manner, but should have an element of particularization and certainty.

5.6 ARGUMENTS IN FAVOUR OF AND AGAINST

While there is a lot of appreciation of the idea of social responsibility of the business, there are also people who argue that social involvement of business has certain negative aspects. The important arguments for and against the social involvement of business are given below.

- **Arguments in favour of Social Involvement Business**
  - Business, which survives using the resources of the society, has a responsibility to the society.
  - Business, which is an integral part of the social system, has to care for the varied needs of the society.
  - Business, which is resourceful, has a special responsibility to the society.
  - Social involvement of business would foster a harmonious and healthy relationship between the society and business to the mutual benefit of both.
  - Social responsibilities like recycling of waste may have favourable financial effects.
  - Social involvement may discourage additional government regulation and intervention.
  - Social involvement may create a better public image for the company, which may help it in attracting customers, efficient personnel and investors.
- **Arguments against Social Involvement of Business**
  - Business should confine to its own business. There are government and social organizations to carry out social activities.
  - Involvement in social activities could adversely affect the economic health of a business enterprise. It may be noted that the expenditures on social welfare has been imposing severe burden on TISCO.
  - If the cost of the social involvement of the business is ultimately passed on to the consumers, there is no point in exalting the social involvement of business. Sometimes

there could even be a net loss to the society because of the high cost of the corporate sector undertaking such activities.

- Many companies involve themselves in social activities because of the tax exemptions on the income spent on special social purposes.
- If the social involvement of a business enterprise causes an increase in the price of its products, it could affect its competitiveness both in the domestic and international markets.
- Social involvement of business could lead to an increase in the dominance or influence of business over the society.

5.7 SOCIAL AUDIT AND INDIAN SCENARIO

One important issue related to social responsibility of business is how to evaluate the social performance. In other words, social audit is a tool for evaluating how satisfactorily a company has discharged its social responsibilities. Social audit enables the public as well as the company to evaluate the social performance of the company. Bauer and Fenn Jr. define social audit as "a commitment to systematic assessment of and activities on some meaningful, definable domain of the company's activities that have social impact." According to Ahmed Belkaoui, "social audit, much like the financial audit–is an identification and examination of the activities of the firm in order to assess, evaluate, measure and report their impact on the immediate social environment." In other words, social audit involves:

- Identification of the firm's activities having potential social impact;
- Assessment and evaluation of the social costs and social benefits of such activities;
- Measurement of the social costs and benefits; and
- Reporting, that is presenting in a proper format and manner, the social performance of the firm.

Dr. Clark C. Abet, in his book Audit for Management, suggests that a social Audit should, as far as possible, be approximated to an ordinary commercial audit; that this should be based on a social balance sheet with a "credit" side and "debit" side. He calls them "inputs" and "outputs" or "costs" and "benefits" so far as the social balance sheet is concerned. After suggesting that every "input" and "output" must be measured in monetary terms, he points out that the basic purpose of a business corporation is to maximize the financial return, earned on its financial investment plus the amount of social return on its social investment. To make rational investment decisions in social areas, it is necessary to know the social costs and if we are to assess them by the same measures as of financial investment, this must be expressed in dollar terms. He further asserts that, sooner or later, the social balance sheet must become a mandatory part of the normal commercial balance sheet of the company.

5.7.1 Methods of Social Audit

There is no single universally agreed upon method of social auditing. Some of the important methods of social audit developed by different people or organizations are given below.

(i) Social Process Audit: The aim of the social process audit, also known as programme management audit, is to develop an internal management information system that will allow management to create and administer the social programmes in a better way. This involves the determination of the objectives of the social programmes and a social cost benefit analysis of the programmes with a view to determining whether these objectives have been met.

(ii) Financial Statement Format Audit: Under the financial statement format audit, the social information is presented in the conventional financial statement format, i.e., balance sheet and/or income statement.

(iii) Macro-Micro Social Indicator Audit: The macro-micro social indicator audit attempts to evaluate the micro indicators (i.e., the company's performance) against a set of macro indicators such as national policies.

(iv) Constituency Group Audit: Under this audit, the preference and attitudes of various constituencies (like employees, creditors, suppliers and customers) are identified and measured and the firm's performance is evaluated against the criteria developed for each group.

(v) Partial Social Audit: Partial social audit evaluates any particular aspects of social performance like energy conservation or ecological preservation.

(vi) Comprehensive Audit: Comprehensive audit attempts to evaluate the total performance of the organization including social performance.

(vii) Corporate Rating Approach: In contradistinction to the audits mentioned above, this is an external evaluation of the company's performance by public groups like consumer organizations, social welfare organizations or media.

5.7.2 Obstacles to Social Audit

Social audit encounters a number of problems. The important obstacles are:

- Being a relatively new concept, social audit is yet to gain wide appreciation and acceptance.
- Being a relatively new concept, a clear and generally well-accepted methodology for conducting the social audits is not available.
- There is no agreement as to the items to be included for social audit.
- It is very difficult, and in several cases even impossible, to quantify the social costs and benefits of different activities or items.
- There may be resistance within the company to social audit because of the time, effort, and difficulty involved in the task.
- There may also be resistance because of the fear of a dismal or unsatisfactory picture that may be presented by the social audit.

As the Committee set up by the Tata Iron and Steel Company Limited (TISCO) to conduct the Social Audit of the TISCO points out, though social audits have been undertaken in a number of countries, principally in the USA (to which the practice owes its origin), Japan, the UK and one or two other Western countries, the subject has not yet attained the status of a science. There is no agreement, much less unanimity, among its most ardent proponents, particularly as to its basic principles or its true objectives. It is only a child of the last decade, during which there has been a growing concern about the environment and the problems of pollution, consumer protection, worker's safety and equal employment opportunities. Melvin Anshen, Professor of Public Policy and Business Responsibility at the Graduate School of Business, Columbia University, and an eminent authority on the subject, remarks that "the social audit has been described as an idea whose time has come but which isn't ready to be taken off the drawing board and put to work".

5.7.3 Social Audit in India

Although, the idea of social audit originated in the United States about half a century ago, it is only recently that it received serious attention of corporations even in the advance countries. The first comprehensive social audit in India was conducted by the TISCO in 1980. It was conducted by the Social Audit Committee appointed by the Board of Directors of the company "to examine and report whether, and the extent to which, the company has fulfilled the objectives contained in Clause 3A of its Articles of Association regarding its social and moral responsibilities to the consumers, employees, shareholders, society and the local community." The report of the Committee was a glowing tribute to the endeavours of the company in the discharge of its social and moral obligations to the various segments of the society. Some companies like the Cement Corporation of India have been making some social reporting in their annual reports.

The High Powered Expert Committee on Companies and MRTP Acts (Sachar Committee) observes that the acceptance of the concept of social responsibility must be reflected in the information and disclosures that the company makes available for the benefit of its various constituents – shareholders, creditors, workers and the community and has suggested that a provision may be made in the Companies Act that every company shall give a social report which will indicate and quantify, in as precise and clear terms as possible, the various activities relating to social responsibility which have been carried out by the company in the previous year. The Committee has further suggested that it is possible that a company may be required to alter its Memorandum with respect to the objects of the company so as to carry out its activities as an obligation to the concept of social responsibility. It should be pointed out here that the TISCO had, in 1970, voluntarily incorporated in its Articles of Association its social and moral responsibilities to the consumers, employees, shareholders, society and the local people. The concept of social audit has not yet taken off in India.

5.8 SUMMARY

Viewed in a broad way, the term business typically refers to the development and processing of economic values in society. The scope of business is very wide. It should not be confused with trade. 'Trade' simply denotes purchase and sale of goods, whereas 'business' includes all activities from production to distribution of goods and services. It embraces industry, trade and other activities like banking, transport, insurance, and warehousing, which facilitate production and distribution of goods and services.

India is a country of land and people. It has a huge customer base as well as world's most powerful brains. It is rich in its natural resources and is highly adaptive to changing business environment. In some areas like technology and political stability, it requires some wise steps. With all these virtues India has become a favourite destination of other countries to expand their business. India is expanding domestically as well as globally to compete with other powerful business nations so as to get its desired share of world economic growth.

Business enterprise is a part of society and the business environment has direct relationship with the policy of the enterprise. The environment may impose several constraints on the enterprise. The enterprise, on the other hand, has very little control over its environment. Therefore, the success of an enterprise depends to a very large extent on its adaptability to the environment, i.e., its ability to identify itself with the environment and fit in with the environmental framework. According to Hicks, "The firm can adjust to the environment, or if it has ability, change the environment."

Environment literally means the surrounding external objects, influences of circumstances under which someone or something exist. The environment of any organization is " the aggregate of all conditions, events and influences that surround and affect". Business environment exhibits many characteristics since it is complex, dynamic, multifaceted and it has far reaching impact. For all these reasons dividing environment into external and internal components enables us to understand it better. Every business enterprise thus consists of a set of internal factors and is confronted with a set of external factors.

A conscious identification of the relevant environment enables the organization to focus its attention on those factors, which are initially related to its mission, purpose, objectives and strategies. Depending on its perception of the relevant environment, an organization takes into account those influences in its surroundings, which have an immediate impact on its strategic management process. Having identified its relevant environment, an organization can systematically appraise it and incorporate the results of such an appraisal in strategic planning. The environment of business is an extremely complex and dynamic phenomenon as the environmental factors vary from country to country. In order to cope with the complexity of the environment it is feasible to divide it into different components and sectors. The rationale of the concept of social responsibility is that industry "can no longer be regarded as a private arrangement for enriching shareholders. It has become a joint enterprise in which workers, management, consumers, the locality, government and trade union officials all play a part. If the system which we know by the name private enterprise is to continue, some way must be found to embrace many interests who go to make up industry in a common purpose." It is argued that a company has a number of social responsibilities to the employees, shareholders, consumers and the community. Social responsibility of business is advocated on the ground that the resources it makes use of are not limited to those of the proprietors and the impact of their operations is felt also by many a people who are in no way connected with the enterprises. The shareholders, the suppliers of resources, the consumers, the local community and society at large are affected by the way an enterprise functions. Hence, a business enterprise has to be socially very responsive so that a social balance may be struck between the opposing interests of these groups. Further, companies, which have huge resources at their disposal, have a moral responsibility to care for the society. Besides, discharge of social responsibilities will be in the company's own interest, because it will help build up good rapport with the society and government and improve employee morale and industrial relations. However, there are also arguments against the social involvement of business. It will affect the financial health of companies, it may lead to attempt to dominate the community's affairs, the costs of social involvement may be passed on to the consumers by price increase, for many companies it is a tax saving gimmick, so goes the arguments. A social audit enables the public as well as the company to evaluate the social performance of the company. The "social audit–much like the financial audit–is an identification and examination of the activities of the firm in order to assess, evaluate, measure and report their impact on the immediate social environment." There is no single universally agreed upon method of social auditing. Some of the important methods of social audit developed by different people or organizations include social process audit, financial statement format audit, macro-micro social indicator audit, constituency group audit, partial social audit, comprehensive audit, and corporate rating approach.

5.9 SELF-ASSESSMENT QUESTIONS

1. What do you mean by social responsibility of a business?
2. How can you evaluate the social responsibilities of business in Indian economy?
3. What do you mean by social audit? Why is it compulsory?
4. Explain the benefits and limitations of social responsibilities.

6

INTRODUCTION TO MANAGEMENT

Learning Objective

The main objective of this chapter is to make the learners familiar with the nature and scope of management; to know the difference between management and administration; to understand various levels of management; and to describe the various skills that are essential for the successful managers.

6.1 INTRODUCTION

A business builds up the path of success in due course of time with having brazened out all possible organizational intricacies. With growing complexities managing the business has turned into a thorny mission. It has very much necessitated the need of existence of management theories and practices for solving the organizational intricacies with all effectiveness. Management is essential not only for business concerns but also banks, schools, colleges, hospitals, hotels, religious societies, charitable trusts and other well-thoughtout organizations. Every business unit has some objectives of its own. These objectives can be achieved with the coordinated efforts of several personnel. The work of a number of persons are properly coordinated to achieve the objectives through the process of management is not a matter of pressing a button, pulling a lever, issuing orders, scanning profit and loss statements, promulgating rules and regulations. Rather it is the power to determine what shall happen to the personalities and happiness of entire people, the power to shape the destiny of a nation and of all the nations which make up the world. Peter F. Drucker has stated in his famous book '*The Practice of Management*' that, "the emergence of management as an essential, a distinct and leading social institution is a pivotal event in social history. Hardly ever in human history has a new institution proved indispensable so quickly and even less often as a new institution arrived with so little opposition, so little disturbance and so little controversy?"

Management, in fact, is an imperative aspect of the economic life of mankind that is an organized group activity. It is considered as the indispensable institution in the modern social organization marked by scientific thought and technological innovations. One or the other form of management is essential wherever human efforts are to be undertaken collectively to satisfy wants through some productive activity, occupation or profession. It is management that regulates man's productive activities through coordinated use of material resources. Without the leadership provided by management, the resources of production remain resources and never become production.

Management has achieved an auspicious substance in recent times. We are all intimately associated with many kinds of organizations, the most omnipresent being the government, the school and the hospital. In fact, more and more of major social tasks are being organized on an institution basis. Medical care, education, recreation, irrigation, lighting, sanitation, etc. which typically used to be the concern of the individual or the family, are now the domain of large organizations. Although, organizations other than business do not speak of management, they all need management. It is the specific organ of all kinds of organizations since they all need to utilize their limited resources most efficiently and effectively for the achievement of their goals. It is the most vital forces in the successful performance of all kinds of organized social activities.

Importance of management for the development of underdeveloped economies has been recognized during the last one and a half decade. There is a significant gap between the management effectiveness in developed and underdeveloped countries. It is rightly held that development is the function not only of capital, physical and material resources, but also of their optimum utilization. Effective management can produce not only more outputs of goods and services with given resources, but also expand them through better use of science and technology. A higher rate of economic growth can be attained in our country through more efficient and effective management of our business and other social organizations, even with existing physical and financial resources. That is why, it is now being increasingly recognized that underdeveloped countries are indeed somewhat inadequately managed countries.

The appearance of management concept in modern times may be regarded as a significant development as the advancement of contemporary knowledge. It has made possible organization of economic activity in giant organizations like the Steel Authority of India and the Life Insurance Corporation of India. It is largely through the achievements of modern management that western countries have reached the stage of mass consumption societies, and it is largely through more effective management of our economic and social institutions that we can improve the quality of life of our people. It is the achievements of business management that hold the hope for the huge masses in the third world countries that they can drive out poverty and achieve for themselves well-brought-up standards of living.

6.2 DEFINITION OF MANAGEMENT

Although management as a discipline is about hundred years old, there is no common agreement among the thinkers and practitioners about its specific definition. In fact, this is equally true in case of all social sciences like psychology, sociology, anthropology, economics, political science, etc. As a result of extraordinary and awe-inspiring industrial developments, business organizations have grown in size and complexity, causing far-reaching changes in the practices of management. Changes in management styles and practices have, perhaps, led to changes in management thought. Moreover, management being interdisciplinary in nature has undergone changes because of the developments in behavioural sciences, quantitative techniques, engineering and technology, etc. Since it deals with the production and distribution of goods and services, dynamism of its environments such as social, cultural and religious values, consumers' tastes and preferences, education and information explosion, democratization of governments, etc., have also led to changes in its theory and practice. Yet, a privileged definition of management is required for its teaching and research, and also for improvement in its existing practices.

Various management gurus have tried to define management. But, no definition of management has been unanimously acknowledged by these great thinkers in the field. Let us talk about some of the most important definitions of management:

- Henry Fayol, "To manage is to forecast and plan, to organize, to compound, to coordinate and to control."
- Peter F. Drucker defines, "management is an organ; organs can be described and defined only through their functions".
- According to Terry, "Management is not people; it is an activity like walking, reading, swimming or running. People who perform Management can be designated as members, members of Management or executive leaders."
- Ralph C. Davis has defined Management as, "Management is the function of executive leadership anywhere."
- According to Mc Farland, "Management is defined for conceptual, theoretical and analytical purposes as that process by which managers create, direct, maintain and operate purposive organization through systematic, coordinated cooperative human effort."
- Harold Koontz says, "Management is the art of getting things done through and within formally organized group."
- William Spriegal, "Management is that function of an enterprise which concerns itself with direction and control of the various activities to attain business objectives. Management is essentially an executive function; it deals with the active direction of the human effort."
- Kimball and Kimball, "Management embraces all duties and functions that pertain to the initiation of an enterprise, its financing, the establishment of all major policies, the provision of all necessary equipment, the outlining of the general form of organization under which the enterprise is to operate and the selection of the principal officers."
- Sir Charles Reynold, "Management is the process of getting things done through the agency of a community. The functions of management are the handling of community with a view of fulfilling the purposes for which it exists."
- E.F.L. Brech, "Management is concerned with seeing that the job gets done, its tasks all centre on planning and guiding the operations that are going on in the enterprise."
- Koontz and O'Donnel, "Management is the creation and maintenance of an internal environment in an enterprise where individuals, working in groups, can perform efficiently and effectively toward the attainment of group goals. It is the art of getting the work done through and with people in formally organized groups."
- James Lundy, "Management is principally a task of planning, coordinating, motivating and controlling the efforts of other towards a specific objective. It involves combining of the traditional factors of production land, labour, capital in an optimum manner, paying due attention, of course, to the particular goals of the organization."

- Wheeler, "Management is centred in the administrators or managers of the firm who integrate men, material and money into an effective operating limit."
- Oliver Scheldon, "Management proper is the function in industry concerned in the execution of policy, within the limits set up by the administration and the employment of the organization for the particular objectives set before it."
- Newman, Summer and Warren, "The job of Management is to make cooperative endeavour to function properly. A manager is one who gets things done by working with people and other resources in order to reach an objective."
- Mary Parker Follett defines management as the "art of getting things done through people". This definition calls attention to the fundamental difference between a manager and other personnel of an organization. A manager is one who contributes to the organization's goals indirectly by directing the efforts of others – not by performing the task himself. On the other hand, a person who is not a manager makes his contribution to the organization's goals directly by performing the task himself.

  Sometimes, however, a person in an organization may play both these roles simultaneously. For example, a sales manager is performing a managerial role when he is directing his sales force to meet the organization's goals, but when he himself is contacting a large customer and negotiating a deal, he is performing a non-managerial role. In the former role, he is directing the efforts of others and is contributing to the organization's goals indirectly; in the latter role, he is directly utilizing his skills as a salesman to meet the organization's objectives.
- George R. Terry gives a somewhat more elaborate definition of management. He defines management as a process "consisting of planning, organizing, actuating and controlling, performed to determine and accomplish the objectives by the use of people and other resources". According to this definition, management is a process – a systematic way of doing things. The four management activities included in this process are: planning, organizing, actuating and controlling. Planning means that managers think of their actions in advance. Organizing means that managers coordinate the human and material resources of the organization. Actuating means that managers motivate and direct subordinates. Controlling means that managers attempt to ensure that there is no deviation from the norm or plan. If some part of their organization is on the wrong track, managers take action to remedy the situation.

To wrap up the diverse conventionalization of the concept, it can be observed that various definitions of management do not run opposing to one another. Management is the sum total of all those activities that (i) determine objectives, plans, policies and programmes; (ii) secure men, material, machinery cheaply (iii) put all these resources into operations through sound organization (iv) direct and motivate the men at work, (v) supervises and control their performance and (iv) provide maximum prosperity and happiness for both employer and employees and public at large.

6.3 CHARACTERISTICS OF MANAGEMENT

Management is a distinctive set of activities, which involves the following leading features:

1. **Economic Catalyst:** Management is one of the factors of production that is put together with the land, labour and capital. As industrialization increases, the need for managers also increases. Proficient management is the most critical input in the success of any organized group activity as it is the force, which assembles and integrates other factors of production, namely, labour, capital and materials. Inputs of labour, capital and materials do not by themselves ensure production; they require the catalyst of management to produce goods and services required by the society. Thus, management is an essential ingredient of an organization.
2. **Objective Oriented:** Management is made for a purposeful activity. It coordinates the efforts of workers to achieve the goals of the organization. The success of management is measured by the extent to which the organizational goals are achieved. It is imperative that the organizational goals must be well defined and properly understood by the management at various levels.
3. **Distinctive Process:** Management is a distinct process consisting of such functions as planning, organizing, staffing, directing and controlling. These functions are so interwoven that it is not possible to lay down exactly the sequence of various functions or their relative significance.
4. **Integrative Force:** The essence of management is integration of human and other resources to achieve the desired objectives. All these resources are made available to those who manage. Managers apply knowledge, experience and management principles for getting the results from the workers by the use of non-human resources. Managers also seek to harmonize the individuals' goals with the organizational goals for the smooth working of the organization.
5. **Coordination of Authority:** Management as a team of managers represents a system of authority, a hierarchy of command and control. Managers at different levels possess varying degree of authority. Generally, as we move down in the managerial hierarchy, the degree of authority gets gradually reduced. Authority enables the managers to perform their functions effectively.
6. **Multidisciplinary Subject:** Management has grown as a field of study (i.e., discipline) taking the help of so many other disciplines such as engineering, anthropology, sociology and psychology. Much of the management literature is the result of the association of these disciplines. For instance, productivity orientation drew its inspiration from industrial engineering and human relations orientation from psychology. Similarly, sociology and operations research have also contributed to the development of management science.
7. **Universal Relevance:** Management is universal in character. The principles and techniques of management are equally applicable in the fields of business, education, military, government and hospital. Henry Fayol suggested that principles of management would apply more or less in every situation. The principles are working guidelines, which are flexible and capable of adaptation to every organization where the efforts of human beings are to be coordinated.

6.4 PROCESS OF MANAGEMENT

There is plenty of disagreement among management thinkers on the classification of managerial functional process. Newman and Summer recognize only four steps in management process, namely, organizing, planning, leading and controlling. Henry Fayol identifies five functions of management, viz., planning, organizing, commanding, coordinating and controlling. Luther Gulick states seven such steps in management process under the catch word "POSDCORB' which stands for planning, organizing, staffing, directing, coordinating, reporting and budgeting. Warren Haynes and Joseph Massie classify management process into decision-making, organizing, staffing, planning, controlling, communicating and directing. Koontz and O'Donnell divide the process into planning, organizing, staffing, directing and controlling.

For our purpose, we shall designate the following six as the functions of a manager: planning, organizing, staffing, directing, coordinating and controlling that constitute the management process.

1. **Planning:** Planning is the most elemental and the most all-encompassing step of management process. If people working in groups have to perform effectively, they should know in advance what is to be done, what activities they have to perform in order to do what is to be done, and when it is to be done. Planning is concerned with 'what', 'how', and 'when' of performance. It is deciding in the present about the future objectives and the courses of action for their achievement. It thus involves:
   (a) Determination of long and short-range objectives;
   (b) Development of strategies and courses of actions to be followed for the achievement of these objectives; and
   (c) Formulation of policies, procedures, and rules, etc., for the implementation of strategies, and plans.

   Top management in the context of its basic purpose and mission, environmental factors, business forecasts, and available and potential resources sets the organizational objectives. These objectives are both long-range as well as short-range. They are divided into divisional, departmental, sectional and individual objectives or goals. This is followed by the development of strategies and courses of action to be followed at various levels of management and in various segments of the organization. Policies, procedures and rules provide the framework of decision-making, and the method and order for the making and implementation of these decisions.

   Every manager performs all these planning functions, or contributes to their performance. In some organizations, particularly those, which are traditionally managed, and the small ones, planning are often not done intentionally and scientifically but it is done in modern, bigger and professional organizations. The plans may be in the minds of their managers rather than explicitly and precisely spelt out: they may be nebulous rather than clear but they are always there. Planning is thus the most basic function of management. All managers at all levels of hierarchy perform it in all kinds of organizations.

2. **Organizing:** Organizing involves identification of activities required for the achievement of enterprise objectives and implementation of plans; grouping of activities into jobs; assignment of these jobs and activities to departments and individuals; delegation of responsibility and authority for performance, and provision for vertical and horizontal

coordination of activities. Every manager has to decide what activities have to be undertaken in his department or section for the achievement of the goals entrusted to him. Having identified the activities, he has to group identical or similar activities in order to make jobs, assign these jobs or groups of activities to his subordinates, delegate authority to them so as to enable them to make decisions and initiate action for undertaking these activities, and provide for coordination between himself and his subordinates, and among his subordinates. Organizing thus involves the following sub-functions:

(a) Identification of activities required for the achievement of objectives and implementation of plans.
(b) Grouping the activities so as to create self-contained jobs.
(c) Assignment of jobs to employees.
(d) Delegation of authority so as to enable them to perform their jobs and to command the resources needed for their performance.
(e) Establishment of a network of coordinating relationships.

Organizing process results in a structure of the organization. It comprises organizational positions, accompanying tasks and responsibilities, and a network of roles and authority-responsibility relationships.

Organizing is thus the basic process of combining and integrating human, physical and financial resources in productive interrelationships for the achievement of enterprise objectives. It aims at combining employees and interrelated tasks in an orderly manner so that organizational work is performed in a coordinated manner, and all efforts and activities pull together in the direction of organizational goals.

3. **Staffing:** Staffing is an incessant and fundamental step in management process. After the objectives have been determined, strategies, policies, programmes, procedures and rules formulated for their achievement, activities for the implementation of strategies, policies, programmes, etc. identified and grouped into jobs, the next logical step in the management process is to procure suitable personnel for manning the jobs. Since the efficiency and effectiveness of an organization significantly depends on the quality of its personnel and since it is one of the primary functions of management to achieve qualified and trained people to fill various positions, staffing has been recognized as a distinct function of management. It comprises several sub-functions:

(a) Manpower planning involving determination of the number and the kind of personnel required.
(b) Recruitment for attracting adequate number of potential employees to seek jobs in the enterprise.
(c) Selection of the most suitable persons for the jobs under consideration.
(d) Placement, induction and orientation.
(e) Transfers, promotions, termination and layoff.
(f) Training and development of employees.

As the importance of human factor in organizational effectiveness is being increasingly recognized, staffing is gaining acceptance as a distinct function of management. It need hardly any emphasize that no organization can ever be better than its people, and managers must perform the staffing function with as much concern as any other function.

4. **Directing:** Directing is the function of leading the employees to perform efficiently, and contribute their optimum to the achievement of organizational objectives. Jobs assigned to subordinates have to be explained and clarified, they have to be provided guidance in job performance and they are to be motivated to contribute their optimum performance with zeal and enthusiasm. The function of directing thus involves the following sub-functions:
   (a) Communication
   (b) Motivation
   (c) Leadership
5. **Coordination:** Coordinating is the step of establishing such relationships among various parts of the organization that they all together pull in the direction of organizational objectives. It is thus the process of tying together all the organizational decisions, operations, activities and efforts so as to achieve unity of action for the accomplishment of organizational objectives.

   Mary Parker Follet has aptly highlighted the significance of the coordinating process. The manager, in her view, should ensure that he has an organization "with all its parts coordinated, so moving together in their closely knit and adjusting activities, so linking, interlocking and interrelation, that they make a working unit, which is not a congeries of separate pieces, but what I have called a functional whole or integrative unity". Coordination, as a management function, involves the following sub-functions:
   (a) Clear definition of authority-responsibility relationships
   (b) Unity of direction
   (c) Unity of command
   (d) Effective communication
   (e) Effective leadership
6. **Controlling:** Controlling is the step of ensuring that the divisional, departmental, sectional and individual performances are consistent with the predetermined objectives and goals. Deviations from objectives and plans have to be identified and investigated, and correction action taken. Deviations from plans and objectives provide feedback to managers, and all other management processes including planning, organizing, staffing, directing and coordinating are continuously reviewed and modified, where necessary.

   Thus, controlling itself involves the following process:
   (a) Measurement of performance against predetermined goals.
   (b) Identification of deviations from these goals.
   (c) Corrective action to rectify deviations.

6.5 NATURE OF MANAGEMENT

Management has already been conceptualized as the social process by which managers of an enterprise integrate and coordinate its all available resources for the achievement of common, clear goals. It has developed into a body of knowledge and a separate identifiable discipline during the past six decades. Practice of management as an art is, of course, as old as the organized human effort for the achievement of common goals. Management has also acquired several characteristics of profession during recent times. Large and medium-sized enterprises in India and elsewhere are managed by professional managers – managers who have little or no share in the ownership of the enterprise and look upon management as a career. The nature of management as a science, as art and as a profession is discussed hereunder:

Management as a Science: Development of management as a science is of recent origin, even though its practice is ages old. Frederick W. Taylor was the first manager-theorist who made significant contributions to the development of management as a science. He used the scientific methods of analysis, observation and experimentation in the management of production function. A perceptive manager, as he was, he distilled certain fundamental principles and propounded the theory and principles of scientific management. Many others including Gantt, Emerson, Fayol, Barnard, etc. followed his work. During the last few decades, great strides have been made in the development of management as a systematized body of knowledge, which can be learnt, taught and researched. It has also provided powerful tools of analysis, prediction and control to practising managers. Management scientists who have developed mathematical models of decision-making have particularly strengthened the scientific character of management.

Another characteristic of science in management is that it uses the scientific methods of observation, experimentation and laboratory research. Management principles are firmly based on observed phenomena, and systematic classification and analysis of data. These analyses and study of observed phenomena are used for inferring cause-effect relationships between two or more variables. Generalizations about these relationships result in hypotheses. The hypotheses when tested and found to be true are called principles. These principles when applied to practical situations help the practitioner in describing and analyzing problems, solving problems and predicting the results.

Even though management is a science so far as to possess a systematized body of knowledge and uses scientific methods of research, it is not an exact science like natural sciences. This is simply because management is a social science, and deals with the behaviour of people in organization. Behaviour of people is much more complex and variable than the behaviour of inanimate things such as light or heat. This makes controlled experiments very difficult. As a result, management principles lack the rigour and exactitude, which is found in physics and chemistry. In fact, many natural sciences, which deal with living phenomena such as botany and medicine, are also not exact. Management is a social science like economics or psychology, and has the same limitations, which these and other social sciences have. But this does not in any way diminish the value of management as a knowledge and discipline. It has provided powerful tools of analysis, prediction and control to practising managers and helped them in performing their material tasks more efficiently and effectively.

Management as an art: Just as an engineer uses the science of engineering while building a bridge, a manager uses the knowledge of management theory while performing his managerial functions. Engineering is a science; its application to the solution of practical problems is an art. Similarly, management as a body of knowledge and a discipline is a science; its application to the solution of organizational problems is an art. The practice of management, like the practice of medicine, is firmly grounded in an identifiable body of concepts, theories and principles. A medical practitioner, who does not base his diagnosis and prescription on the science of medicine, endangers the life of his patient. Similarly, a manager who manages without possessing the knowledge of management creates chaos and jeopardizes the well-being of his organization.

The practitioner uses principles of management like the principles of medicine not as rules of thumb but as guides in solving practical problems. It is often said that managerial decision-making involves a large element of judgement. This is true too. The raging controversy whether management is a science or an art is fruitless. It is a science as well as an art. Developments in the field of the knowledge of management help in the improvement of its practice; and improvements in the practice of management spur further research and study resulting in further development of management science.

Management as a Profession: We over and over again pay attention to professionalization of management in our country. By a professional manager, we generally mean a manager who undertakes management as a career and is not interested in acquiring ownership share in the enterprise, which he manages. But, is management a profession in the true sense of the word? Or, is management a profession like the professions of law and medicine? According to McFarland, a profession posseses the following characteristics: (i) a body of principles, techniques, skills, and specialized knowledge; (ii) formalized methods of acquiring training and experience; (iii) the establishment of a representative organization with professionalization as its goal; (iv) the formation of ethical codes for the guidance of conduct; and (v) the charging of fees based on the nature of services.

Management is a profession to the extent it fulfils the above conditions. It is a profession in the sense that there is a systematized body of management, and it is distinct, identifiable discipline. It has also developed a vast number of tools and techniques. But unlike medicine or law, a management degree is not a prerequisite to become a manager. In fact, most managers in India as elsewhere do not have a formal management education. It seems reasonable to assume that at no time in the near future, the possession of a management degree will be a requirement for employment as a career manager.

Management is also a profession in the sense that formalized methods of training is available to those who desire to be managers. We have a number of institutes of management and university departments of management, which provide formal education in this field. Training facilities are provided in most companies by their training divisions. A number of organizations such as the Administrative Staff College of India, the Indian Institute of Management, Management Development Institute, the All India Management Association, and the university departments of management offer a variety of short-term management training programmes.

Management partially fulfils the third characteristic of profession. There are a number of representative organizations of management practitioners almost in all countries such as the All India Management Association in India, the American Management Association in U.S.A., etc. However, none of them have professionalization of management as its goal.

Management does not fulfil the last two requirements of a profession. There is no ethical code of conduct for managers till now as for doctors and lawyers. Some individual business organizations, however, try to develop a code of conduct for their own managers but there is no general and uniform code of conduct for all managers. In fact, bribing public officials to gain favours, sabotaging trade unions, manipulating prices and markets are by no means uncommon management practices. Furthermore, managers in general do not seem to adhere to the principle of "service above self". Switching of jobs by managers evidences, however, little regard is paid to the elevation of service over the desire for monetary compensation. Indeed, such mobile managers are regarded as more progressive and modern than others.

It may be concluded from the above discussion that management is a science, an art as well as a profession. As a social science, management is not as correct as natural sciences, and it is not as fully a profession as medicine and law.

6.6 MANAGEMENT VS ADMINISTRATION

The use of two terms–management and administration has been a controversial issue in the management literature. Some management thinkers do not see any difference between the two terms, while others maintain that administration and management are two different functions. Those who held management and administration distinct include Oliver Sheldon, Florence and Tead, Spriegel and Lansburg, etc. According to them, management is a lower-level function and is concerned primarily with the execution of policies laid down by administration. But some English authors like Brech are of the opinion that management is a wider term including administration. This disagreement is discussed as under:

(i) Administration is concerned with the determination of policies and management with the implementation of policies. Thus, administration is a higher-level function.
(ii) Management is a generic term and includes administration.
(iii) There is no distinction between the terms management and administration and they are used interchangeably.

(i) Administration is a Higher Level Function: Oliver Shelden subscribed to the first viewpoint. According to him, "Administration is concerned with the determination of corporate policy, the coordination of finance, production and distribution, the settlement of the compass of the organization and the ultimate control of the executive. Management proper is concerned with the execution of policy within the limits set up by administration and the employment of the organization in the particular objects before it. Administration determines the organization; management uses it. Administration defines the goals; management strives towards it".

Administration refers to policy-making whereas management refers to execution of policies laid down by administration. Tead, Spriegel and Walter hold this view. Administration is the phase of business enterprise that concerns itself with the overall determination of institutional objectives and the policies unnecessary to be followed in achieving those objectives. Administration is a determinative function; on the other hand, management is an executive function, which is primarily concerned with carrying out of the broad policies laid down by the administration. Thus, administration involves broad policy-making and management involves the execution of policies laid down by the administration as shown in Table 6.1.

Table 6.1 Administration vs. Management

	Basis	*Administration*	*Management*
1.	Meaning	Administration is concerned with the formulation of objectives, plans and policies of the organization.	Management means getting the work done through and with others.

2.	Nature of work	Administration relates to the decision-making. It is a thinking function.	Management refers to of decisions. It is a doing function.
3.	Decision-Making	Administration determines what is to be done and when it is to be done.	Management decides who shall implement the administrative decisions.
4.	Status	Administration refers to higher levels of management.	Management is relevant at lower levels in the organization.

(ii) Management is a Generic Term: The second viewpoint regards management as a generic term including administration. According to Brech, "Management is a social process entailing responsibility for the effective and economical planning and regulation of the operation of an enterprise in fulfilment of a given purpose or task. Administration is that part of management which is concerned with the installation and carrying out of the procedures by which the programme is laid down and communicated and the progress of activities is regulated and checked against plans". Thus, Brech conceives administration as a part of management. Kimball and Kimball also subscribe to this view. According to them administration is a part of management. Administration is concerned with the actual work of executing or carrying out the objectives.

(iii) Management and Administration is Synonymous: The third point of view is that there is no distinction between the terms 'management' and 'administration'. Usage also provides no distinction between these terms. The term management is used for higher executive functions like determination of policies, planning, organizing, directing and controlling in the business circles, while the term administration is used for the same set of functions in the government circles. So there is no difference between these two terms and they are often used interchangeably.

It appears from the above concepts of administration and management that administration is the process of determination of objectives, laying down plans and policies, and ensuring that achievements are in conformity with the objectives. Management is the process of executing the plans and policies for the achievement of the objectives determined by an administration. This distinction seems to be too simplistic and superficial. If we regard chairmen, managing directors and general managers as performing administrative functions, it cannot be said that they perform only planning functions of goal determination, planning and policy formulation, and do not perform other functions such as staffing functions of selection and promotion, or directing functions of leadership, communication and motivation. On the other hand, we cannot say that managers who are responsible for the execution of plans and formulation of plans and policies, etc. do not contribute to the administrative functions of goal determination, and formulation of plans and policies. In fact, all managers, whether the chief executive or the first line supervisor, are in some way or the other involved in the performance of all the managerial functions. It is, of course, true that those who occupy the higher echelons of organizational hierarchy are involved to a greater extent in goal determination, plans and policy formulation and organizing than those who are at the bottom of the ladder.

6.7 LEVELS OF MANAGEMENT

An organization may have different levels of management. Levels of management refer to a line of demarcation between various managerial positions in an organization. The levels of management depend upon its size, technical facilities, and the range of production. We generally come across two broad levels of management, viz., (i) administrative management (i.e., the upper level of management) and (ii) operating management (i.e., the lower level of management). Administrative management is concerned with "thinking" functions such as laying down policy, planning and setting up of standards. Operative management is concerned with the "doing" function such as implementation of policies, and directing the operations to attain the objectives of the organization.

But in practice, it is difficult to draw any clear-cut demarcation between thinking function and doing function. Since the fundamental managerial functions are performed by all managers irrespective of their levels or, ranks. For instance, wage and salary director of a company may assist in fixing wages and salary structure as a member of the board of directors, but as head of wages and salary department, his job is to see that the decisions are implemented.

The real significance of levels is that they explain authority relationships in an organization. Considering the hierarchy of authority and responsibility, one can identify three levels of management, namely:

(i) Top management of a company consists of owners/shareholders, doard of directors, its Chairman, Managing Director, or the Chief Executive, or the General Manager or Executive Committee having key officers.

(ii) Middle management of a company consists of heads of functional departments, viz., Purchase Manager, Production Manager, Marketing Manager, Financial Controller, etc. and Divisional and Sectional Officers working under these Functional Heads.

(iii) Lower level or operative management of a company consists of Superintendents, Foremen, Supervisors, etc.

1. **Top management:** Top management is the ultimate source of authority and it lays down goals, policies and plans for the enterprise. It devotes more time on planning and coordinating functions. It is accountable to the owners of the business of the overall management. It is also described as the policy-making group responsible for the overall direction and success of all company activities. The important functions of top management include:
   (a) To establish the objectives or goals of the organization.
   (b) To make policies and frame plans to attain the objectives laid.
   (c) To exercise effective control of the operations.
   (d) To provide overall leadership to the organization.
   (e) To assemble the resources of money, men, materials, machines and methods to put the plans into action.
   (f) To set up an organizational framework to conduct the operations as per plans.
2. **Middle management:** The job of middle management is to implement the policies and plans framed by the top management. It serves as an essential link between the top management and the lower level or operative management. They are responsible to the top

management for the functioning of their departments. They devote more time on the organization and motivation functions of management. They provide the guidance and the structure for a purposeful enterprise. Without them the top management's plans and ambitious expectations will not be fruitfully realized. The following are the main functions of middle management:

(a) To interpret the policies chalked out by top management.
(b) To prepare the organizational set up in their own departments for fulfilling the objectives implied in various business policies.
(c) To recruit and select suitable operative and supervisory staff.
(d) To collect reports and information on performance in their departments.
(e) To report to top management.
(f) To assign activities, duties and responsibilities for timely implementation of the plans.
(g) To compile all the instructions and issue them to supervisor under their control.
(h) To cooperate with the other departments for ensuring a smooth functioning of the entire organization.
(i) To make suitable recommendations to the top management for the better execution of plans and policies.
(j) To motivate personnel to attain higher productivity and to reward them properly.

3. **Lower or operative management:** It is positioned at the bottom of the hierarchy of management, and actual operations are the responsibility of this level of management. It consists of foreman, supervisors, sales officers, accounts officers, and so on. They are in direct touch with the rank and file or workers. Their authority and responsibility is limited. They pass on the instructions of the middle management to workers.

   They interpret and divide the plans of the management into short-range operating plans. They are also involved in the process of decision-making. They have to get the work done through the workers. They allot various jobs to the workers, evaluate their performance and report to the middle level management. They are more concerned with direction and control functions of management. They devote more time in the supervision of the workers.

6.8 MANAGERIAL SKILLS

A skill is an individual's capability to translate knowledge into action. For this reason, it is manifested in an individual's performance. Skill is not necessarily inborn. It can be developed through practice and through relating learning to one's own personal experience and background. In order to be able to successfully discharge his roles, a manager should possess three major skills. These are conceptual skill, human relations skill and technical skill. Conceptual skill deals with ideas, technical skill with things and human skill with people. While both conceptual and technical skills are needed for good decision-making, human skill in necessary for a good leader.

The *conceptual skill* refers to the ability of a manager to take a broad and farsighted view of the organization and its future, his ability to think in abstract, his ability to analyze the forces working in a situation, his creative and innovative ability and his ability to assess the environment and the changes taking place in it. In short, it is his ability to conceptualize the environment, the organization, and his own job, so that he can set appropriate goals for his organization, for himself and for his team. This skill seems to increase in importance as manager moves up to higher positions of responsibility in the organization.

The *technical skill* is the manager's understanding of the nature of job that people under him have to perform. It refers to a person's knowledge and proficiency in any type of process or technique. In a production department this would mean an understanding of the technicalities of the process of production. Whereas this type of skill and competence seems to be more important at the lower levels of management, its relative importance as a part of the managerial role diminishes as the manager moves to higher positions. In higher functional positions, such as the position of a marketing manager or production manager, the conceptual component, related to these functional areas becomes more important and the technical component becomes less important.

Human skill is the ability to interact effectively with people at all levels. This skill develops in the manager sufficient ability (a) to recognize the feelings and sentiments of others; (b) to judge the possible actions to, and outcomes of various courses of action he may undertake; and (c) to examine his own concepts and values, which may enable him to develop more useful attitudes about himself. This type of skill remains consistently important for managers at all levels.

Table 6.2 gives an idea about the required change in the skill-mix of a manager with the change in his level. At the top level, technical skill becomes least important. That is why, people at the top shift with great ease from one industry to another without an apparent fall in their efficiency. Their human and conceptual skills seem to make up for their unfamiliarity with the new job's technical aspects.

Table 6.2 Skill-Mix of Different Management Levels

Top Management	*Conceptual Skills*
Middle Management	Human Relations Skills
Low Management	Technical Skills

6.9 THE MANAGER AND HIS JOB

Management carries out the functions of planning, organizing, staffing, directing and controlling for the accomplishment of organizational goals. Any person who performs these functions is a manager. The first line manager or supervisor or foreman is also a manager because he performs these functions. The difference between the functions of top, middle and lowest level management is that of degree. For instance, top management concentrates more on long-range planning and organization, middle level management concentrates more on coordination and control and lowest level management concentrates more on direction function to get the things done from the workers.

Each manager is concerned with ideas, things and people. Management is an innovative process for integrating the use of resources to accomplish certain goals. In this process, ideas, things and people are vital inputs, which are to be transformed into output consistent with the goals.

Management of ideas implies use of conceptual skills. It has three connotations. *First*, it refers to the need for practical philosophy of management to regard management as a distinct and scientific process. *Second*, management of ideas refers to the planning phase of management process. *Lastly*, management of ideas refers to distinction and innovation. Creativity refers to generation of new ideas, and innovation refers to transforming ideas into viable relations and utilities. A manager must be imaginative to plan ahead and to create new Ideas.

Management of things (non-human resources) deals with the design of production system, and acquisition, allocation and conversion of physical resources to achieve certain goals. Management of people is concerned with procurement, development, maintenance and integration of human resources in the organization. Every manager has to direct his subordinates to put the organizational plans into practice.

The greater part of every manager's time is spent in communicating and dealing with people. His efforts are directed towards obtaining information and evaluating progress towards objectives set by him and then taking corrective action. Thus, a manager's job primarily consists of management of people. Though it is his duty to handle all the productive resources, but human factor is more important. A manager cannot convert the raw materials into finished products himself; he has to take the help of others to do this. The greatest problem before any manager is how to manage the personnel to get the best possible results. The manager in the present age has to deal efficiently with the people who are to contribute for the achievement of organizational goals.

Peter F. Drucker has advocated that the managerial approach to handle workers and work should be pragmatic and dynamic. Every job should be designed as an integrated set of operations. The workers should be given a sufficient measure of freedom to organize and control their work environment. It is the duty of every manager to educate, train and develop people below him so that they may use their potentialities and abilities to perform the work allotted to them. He has also to help them in satisfying their needs and working under him, he must provide them with proper environment. A manager must create a climate, which brings in and maintains satisfaction and discipline among the people. This will increase organizational effectiveness.

Recently, it has been questioned whether planning, organizing, directing and controlling provides an adequate description of the management process. After an intensive observation of what five top executive actually did during the course of a few days at work, Henry Mintzberg concluded that these labels do not adequately capture the reality of what managers do. He suggested instead that the manager should be regarded as playing some ten different roles, in no particular order.

6.9.1 Role Performed by Managers

1. Interpersonal Roles

Liaison: In this role of liaison, every manager must cultivate contacts outside his vertical chain of command to collect information useful for his organization.

Leader: As a leader, every manager must motivate and encourage his employees. He must also try to reconcile their individual needs with the goals of the organization.

Figurehead: In this role, every manager has to perform some duties of a ceremonial nature, such as greeting the touring dignitaries, attending the wedding of an employee, taking an important customer to lunch, and so on.

2. Informational Roles

Disseminator: In the role of a disseminator, the manager passes some of his privileged information directly to his subordinates who would otherwise have no access to it.

Monitor: As monitor, the manager has to perpetually scan his environment for information, interrogate his liaison contacts and his subordinates, and receive unsolicited information, much of it as result of the network of personal contacts he has developed.

Spokesman: In this role, the manager informs and satisfies various groups and people who influence his organization. Thus, he advises shareholders about financial performance, assures consumer groups that the organization is fulfilling its social responsibilities and satisfies government that the origination is abiding by the law.

3. Decisional Roles

Disturbance Handler: In this role, the manager has to work like a firefighter. He must seek solutions of various unanticipated problems – a strike may loom large a major customer may go bankrupt; a supplier may renege on his contract, and so on.

Entrepreneur: In this role, the manager constantly looks out for new ideas and seeks to improve his unit by adapting it to changing conditions in the environment.

In addition, managers in any organization work with each other to establish the organization's long-range goals and to plan how to achieve them. They also work together to provide one another with the accurate information needed to perform tasks. Thus, managers act as channels of communication with the organization.

Negotiator: The manager has to spend considerable time in negotiations. Thus, the chairman of a company may negotiate with the union leaders a new strike issue, the foreman may negotiate with the workers a grievance problem, and so on.

Resource Allocator: In this role, the manager must divide work and delegate authority among his subordinates. He must decide who will get what.

6.9.2 Characteristics of Professional Managers

1. **Managers think analytically and conceptually:** To be an analytical thinker, a manager must be able to break a problem down into its components, analyze those components and then come up with a feasible solution. But even more important, a manager must be a conceptual thinker, able to view the entire task in the abstract and relate it to other tasks. Thinking about a particular task in relation to its larger implications is no simple matter. But it is essential if the manager is to work towards the goals of the organization as a whole as well as towards the goals of an individual unit.

2. **Managers are mediators:** Organizations are made up of people, and people disagree or quarrel quite often. Disputes within a unit or organization can lower morale and productivity, and they may become so unpleasant or disruptive that competent employees decide to leave the organization. Such occurrences hinder work towards the goals of the unit or organization; therefore, managers must at times take on the role of mediator and iron out disputes before they get out of hand. Setting conflicts requires skill and tact. Managers who are careless in their handling conflicts may later on find that they have only made matters worse.
3. **Managers are responsible and accountable:** Managers are responsible for seeing that specific tasks are done successfully. They are usually evaluated on how well they arrange for these tasks to the accomplished. Managers are responsible for the actions of their subordinates. The success or failure of subordinates is a direct reflection of managers' success or failure. All members of an organization, including those who are not managers, are responsible for their particular tasks. The difference is that managers are held responsible, or accountable, not only for their own work, but also for the work of subordinates.
4. **Managers make difficult decisions:** No organization runs smoothly all the time. There is almost no limit to the number and types of problems that may occur: financial difficulties, problems with employees, or differences of opinion concerning an organization policy, to name just a few. Managers are expected to come up with solutions to difficult problems and to follow through on their decisions even when doing so may be unpopular.
5. **Managers balance competing goals and set priorities:** At any given time, the manager faces a number of organizational goals, problems and needs all of which compete for the manager's time and resources (both human and material). Because such resources are always limited, the manager must strike a balance between the various goals and needs. Many managers, for example, arrange each day's tasks in order of priority the most important things are done right away, while the less important tasks are looked at later. In this way, managerial time is used effectively.

A manager must also decide who is to perform a particular task and must assign work to an appropriate person. Although ideally each person should be given the task he would most like to do, this is not always possible. Sometimes individual ability is the decisive factor, and a task is assigned to the person most able to accomplish it. But sometimes a less capable worker is assigned a task as a learning experience. And, at times, limited human or other resources dictate decisions for making work assignments. Managers are often caught between conflicting human and organizational needs and so they must identify priorities.

This description of these managerial roles and responsibilities shows that managers must 'change hats' frequently and must be alert to the particular role needed at a given time. The ability to recognize the appropriate role to be played and to change roles readily is a mark of an effective manager.

6.10 FUNCTIONS OF MANAGEMENT

Management practices are as old as human civilization, when people started living together in groups, for every human group requires management and the history of human beings is full of organizational activities. Even a smallest human group in our society, i.e., family also needs management. The head of the family acts as top management and the housewife acts as a home manager. She plans about the work to be done, how the work has to be done, who is to do the work and whether the work is done properly or not. She performs all the four functions of management, i.e., planning the budget and day-to-day activities, organizing the things and activities of different people, directing the servants and different members of the family and controlling activities of different members of the family. Family is a very informal type of individuals' cluster. Even if this informal individuals' cluster is not managed properly it will lead to great fuse and confusion.

During the last five decades, management as a discipline has attracted the attention of academicians and practitioners to a very great extent. The basic reason behind this phenomenon is the growing importance of management in day-to-day life of people. Today, the society has large and complex institutions with many people working together. The relationship between managers and managed has changed as compared to the older master-servant relationship making it more complex. People have greater expectations from their jobs. In order to make all these things function properly, people have been trying to evolve some method and techniques. Such attempts have given birth to management as a separate discipline. It has grown over the period of time making itself one of the most respected disciplines. Today, the study of management has become an important fact of human life.

Understanding Management as Concept: The term management can have different meanings, and it is important to understand these different definitions. The term management can be considered as:

> "People who wish to have a career as a manager must study the discipline of management as a means toward practising the process of management".

1. **Management as a process:** Have you ever said "That is a well managed company" or "That organization has been mismanaged"? If you have, you seem to imply that: (i) management is some type of work or set of activities and (ii) sometimes the activities are performed quite well and sometimes not so well.
2. **Management as a discipline:** If you say you are a student of management or majoring in management, you are referring to the discipline of management. Classifying management as a discipline implies that it is an accumulated body of knowledge that can be learned. Thus, management as a subject with principles, concepts and theories. A major purpose of studying the discipline of management is to learn and understand the principles, concepts, and theories of management and how to apply them in the process of managing.
3. **Management as people:** Whether you say, "That company has an entirely new management team" or "She is the best manager I have ever worked for" you are referring to the people who guide, direct and thus, manage organizations. The word management used in this manner refers to the people, manager who engage in the process of management.

4. **Management as a career:** "Mr. Saxena has held several managerial positions since joining the bank upon his graduation from college". This statement implies that management is a career. People who devote their working lives to the process of management progress through a sequence of new activities and, often, new challenges. More than ever before, today's business environment is fast changing and competitive, posing challenges, opportunities, and rewards for individuals pursuing management as a career.

These different meanings of the term management has been related as follows by John M. Ivancevich—

You are referring to management as a process involving set of activities. Since the late nineteenth century, it has been common practice to define management in terms of four specific functions of managers. Planning, organizing, leading and controlling. We can thus say that management is the process of planning, organizing, leading and controlling the efforts of organization members and of using all other organizational resources to achieve stated organizational goals.

All the managers in the organization perform certain functions to get the things done by others. However, what are these functions, which comprise management process, is not quite clear and divergent views have been expressed on this.

Earnest Dale has suggested innovation and representing also as important management functions besides these. Thus, it can be seen that there is no agreement over the various functions of management. These functions have been treated differently over the period of time. Ervin Williams has summarized the various managerial functions developed over the period of time.

All the above functions can be categorized into four fundamental functions of management, i.e., planning, organizing, leading and controlling.

6.10.1 Planning

The planning function is the primary activity of management. Planning is the process of establishing goals and a suitable course of action for achieving those goals. Planning implies that managers think through their goals and actions in advance and that their actions are based on some method, plan, or logic rather than on a....... Plans give the organization its objectives and set up the best procedures for reaching them. The organizing, leading and controlling functions all derived from the planning function.

The first step in the planning is the selection of goals for the organization. Goals are then established for each of the organization's subunits–its division, department, and so on. Once these are determined, programmes are established for achieving goals in a systematic manner.

The organizational objectives are set by top management in the context of its basic purpose and mission, environmental factors, business forecasts, and available and potential resources. These objectives are both long-range as well as short-range. They are divided into divisional, departmental, sectional and individual objectives or goals. This is followed by the development of strategies and courses of action to be followed at various levels of management and in various segments of the organization. Policies, procedures and rules provide the framework of decision-making, and the method and order for the making and implementation of these decisions.

6.10.2 Organizing

After managers develop objectives and plans to achieve the objectives, they must design and develop an organization that will be able to accomplish the objectives. Thus, the purpose of the organizing function is to create a structure of task and authority relationships that serves this purpose.

Organizing is the process of arranging and allocating work, authority, and resources among an organization's members so they can achieve the organization's goals.

Stoner defines "Organizing as the process of engaging two or more people in working together in a structured way to achieve a specific goal or set of goals.

The organizing function takes the tasks identified during planning and assigns them to individuals and groups within the organization so that objectives set by planning can be achieved. Organizing, then, can be thought of turning plans into actions. Organizing function can be viewed as a bridge connecting the conceptual idea developed in creating and planning to the specific means for accomplishing these ideas.

The organizing function also provides on organizational structure that enables the organization to function effectively. Managers must match an organization's structure to its goals and resources, a process called organizational design.

6.10.3 Staffing

Staffing is a continuous and vital function of management. After the objectives have been determined, strategies, policies, programmes, procedures and rules formulated for their achievement, activities for the implementation of strategies, policies, programmes, etc. identified and grouped into jobs, the next logical step in the management process is to procure suitable personnel for manning the jobs. Since the efficiency and effectiveness of an organization significantly depends on the quality of its personnel and since it is one of the primary functions of management to achieve qualified and trained people to fill various positions, staffing has been recognized as a distinct function of management.

As the importance of human factor in organizational effectiveness is being increasingly recognized, staffing is gaining acceptance as a distinct function of management. It need hardly any emphasize that no organization can ever be better than its people, and managers must perform the staffing function with as much concern as any other function.

6.10.4 Directing

Directing is the function of leading the employees to perform efficiently, and contribute their optimum to the achievement of organizational objectives. Jobs assigned to subordinates have to be explained and clarified, they have to be provided guidance in job performance and they are to be motivated to contribute their optimum performance with zeal and enthusiasm.

Once objectives have been developed and the organizational structure has been designed and staffed, the next step is to begin to move the organization toward the objectives. The directing function serves this purpose. It involves directing, influencing and motivating employees to perform essential tasks.

The best human resources employed will be of house if they are not motivated and directed in the right direction to achieve the organizational goals. Managers lead is an attempt to persuade others to join them in pursuit of the future that emerges from the planning, and organizing steps. By establishing the proper atmosphere, managers help their employees to do their best.

Effective leadership is a highly prized ability in organizations and is a skill that some managers have difficulty in developing. The ability requires both task-oriented capabilities and the ability to communicate, understand and motivate people.

6.10.5 Controlling

Finally, the manager must be sure that actions of the organizations members do in fact move the organization towards its stated goals. This is the controlling function of management. The controlling is the process of ensuring that actual activities confirm to plan activities.

Controlling implies that objectives, goals and standards of performance exist and are known to employees and their superiors. It also implies a flexible and dynamic organization which will permit changes in objectives, plans, programmes, strategies, policies, organizational design, staffing policies and practices, leadership style, communication system, etc., for it is not uncommon that employees failure to achieve predetermined standards is due to defects or shortcomings in any one or more of the above dimensions of management.

It may be pointed out that although management functions have been discussed in a particular sequence-planning, organizing, staffing, directing, coordinating and controlling – they are not performed in a sequential order. Management is an integral process and it is difficult to put its functions neatly in separate boxes. Management functions tend to coalesce, and it sometimes becomes difficult to separate one from the other. For example, when a production manager is discussing work problems with one of his subordinates, it is difficult to say whether he is guiding, developing or communicating, or doing all these things simultaneously. Moreover, managers often perform more than one function simultaneously.

Through the controlling function, managers keep the organization on track. Without the controlling functions, other functions loose their relevance. If all the activities are properly planned, organized and directed but there is no control on the activities, then there are full chances that the organization does not achieve its planned goals. Controlling function helps us knowing the deviations but the reasons for such deviations and the corrective actions is to be taken depends on the managers. Hence, the personal ability of the managers makes the controlling function effective or ineffective.

6.11 PRINCIPLES OF MANAGEMENT

Henry Fayol has developed a body of principles of management, the father of modern management. Fayol wrote perceptibly on the basis of his practical experience as a manager. Although, he did not develop an integrated theory of management, his principles are surprisingly in tune with contemporary thinking in management theory.

Fayol held that there is a single "administrative science", whose principles can be used in all management situations no matter what kind of organizations are being managed. This earned him the title of "Universality". He, however, emphasized that his principles were not immutable laws but rules of thumb to be used as occasion demanded.

Fayol held that activities of an industrial enterprise can be grouped in six categories : (i) technical (production), (ii) commercial (buying, selling and exchange), (iii) financial (search for and optimum use of capital), (iv) security (protection of property and persons), (v) accounting (including statistics); and (vi) managerial. However, he devoted most of his attention to managerial activity. He developed the following principles underlying management of all kinds of organizations:

1. **Authority and Responsibility are Related:** Fayol held that authority flows from responsibility. Managers who exercise authority over others should assume responsibility for decisions as well as for results. He regarded authority as a corollary to responsibility. Authority is official as well as personal. Official authority is derived from the manager's position in organizational hierarchy and personal authority is compounded of intelligence, experience, moral worth, past services, etc.

   A corollary of the principle that no manager should be given authority unless he assumes responsibility is that those who have responsibility should also have commensurate authority in order to enable them to initiate action on others and command resources required for the performance of their functions. This aspect of relationship between responsibility and authority is particularly relevant in India where authority tends to be concentrated in higher echelons of management.

2. **Unity of Command:** This principle holds that one employee should have only one boss and receive instructions from him only. Fayol observed that if this principle is violated authority will be undermined, discipline will be jeopardy, order will be disturbed and stability will be threatened. Dual command is a permanent source of conflict. Therefore, in every organization, each subordinate should have one superior whose command he has to obey.

3. **Unity of Direction:** This means that all managerial and operational activities, which relate a distinct group with the same objective, should be directed by one head and one plan. According to Fayol, there should be, "one head and one plan for a group of activities having the same objective". It, however, does not mean that all decisions should be made at the top. It only means that all related one person should direct activities. For example, all marketing activities like product strategy and policy, advertising and sales promotion, distribution channel policy, product pricing policy, marketing research, etc. should be under the control of one manager and directed by an integrated plan. This is essential for the "unity of action, coordination of strength and focusing of effort". Violation of this principle will cause fragmentation of action and effort, and wastage of resources.

4. **Scalar Chain of Command:** According to Fayol scalar chain is the chain of superiors ranging from the ultimate authority to the lowest ranks. The line of authority is the route followed via every link in the chain by all communication, which start from or go to the ultimate authority.

5. **Division of Work:** This is the principle of specialization, which, according to Fayol, applies to all kinds of work, managerial as well as technical. It helps a person to acquire an ability and accuracy with which he can do more and better work with the same effort.

Therefore, the work of every person in the organization should be limited as far as possible to the performance of a single leading function.

6. **Discipline:** Discipline is a *sine qua non* for the proper functioning of an organization. Members of an organization are required to perform their functions and conduct themselves in relation to others according to rules, norms and customs. According to Fayol, discipline can best be maintained by : (i) having good superiors at all levels; (ii) agreements (made either with the individual employees or with a union as the case may be) that are as clear and fair as possible; and (iii) penalties judiciously imposed.
7. **Subordination of Individual Interest to General Interest:** The interest of the organization is above the interests of the individual and the group. It can be achieved only when managers in high positions in the organization set an example of honesty, integrity, fairness and justice. It will involve an attitude and a spirit of sacrificing their own personal interests whenever it becomes apparent that such personal interests are in conflict with organizational interests. It may, however, be emphasized that social and national interests should have precedence over organizational interests whenever the two run counter to each other.
8. **Remuneration:** Employees should be paid fairly and equitably. Differentials in remuneration should be based on job differentials, in terms of qualities of the employee, application, responsibility, working conditions and difficulty of the job. It should also take into account factors like cost of living, general economic conditions, demand for labour and economic state of the business.
9. **Centralization:** Fayol believed in centralization. He, however, did not contemplate concentration of all decision-making authority in the top management. He, however, held that centralization and decentralization is a question of proportion. In a small firm with a limited number of employees, the owner-manager can give orders directly to everyone. In large organizations, however, where the worker is separated from the chief executive through a long scalar chain, the decision-making authority has to be distributed among various managers in varying degrees. Here one generally comes across a situation of decentralization with centralized control. The degree of centralisation and decentralization also depends on the quality of managers.
10. **Order:** Order, in the conception of Fayol, means right person on the right job and everything in its proper place. This kind of order depends on precise knowledge of human requirements and resources of the concern and a constant balance between these requirements and resources.
11. **Equity:** It means that subordinates should be treated with justice and kindliness. This is essential for eliciting their devotion and loyalty to the enterprise. It is, therefore, the duty of the chief executive to instill a sense of equity throughout all levels of scalar chain.
12. **Stability of Tenure of Personnel:** The managerial policies should provide a sense of reasonable job security. The hiring and firing of personnel should depend not on the whims of the superiors but on the well-conceived personnel policies. He points out that it takes time for an employee to learn his job; if they quit or are discharged within a short time, the learning time has been wasted. At the same time those found unsuitable should be removed and those who are found to be competent should be promoted. However, "a

mediorce manager who stays is infinitely preferable to outstanding managers who come and go".

13. **Initiative:** It focuses on the ability, attitude and resourcefulness to act without prompting from others. Managers must create an environment, which encourages their subordinates to take initiative and responsibility. Since it provides a sense of great satisfaction to intelligent employees, managers should sacrifice their personal vanity in order to encourage their subordinates to show initiative. It should, however, be limited, according to Fayol, by respect for authority and discipline.
14. **Esprit de Corps:** Cohesiveness and team spirit should be encouraged among employees. It is one of the chief characteristics of organized activity that a number of people work together in close cooperation for the achievement of common goals. An environment should be created in the organization, which will induce people to contribute to each other's efforts in such a way that the combined effort of all together promotes the achievement of the overall objectives of enterprise. Fayol warns against two enemies of *esprit de corps*, viz., (i) divide and rule, and (ii) abuse of written communication. It may work to the benefit of the enterprise to divide its enemy but it will surely be dangerous to divide one's own workers. They should rather be welded in cohesive and highly interacting work-groups. Over-reliance on written communication also tends to disrupt team spirit. Written communication, where necessary, should always be supplemented by oral communication because face-to-face contacts tend to promote speed, clarity and harmony.

    The other important principles of management as developed by pioneer thinkers on the subject are:

    (a) Separation of planning and execution of business operations.
    (b) Scientific approach to business problems.
    (c) Adoption of technological changes.
    (d) Economizing production costs and avoiding the wastage of resources.
    (e) Fuller utilization of the operational capacity and emphasis on higher productivity.
    (f) Standardization of tools, machines, materials, methods, timings and products.
    (g) Evaluation of results according to criteria of standard levels of performance.
    (h) Understanding and cooperation among the members of the organization set-up.

6.12 SIGNIFICANCE OF MANAGEMENT

Management is concerned with attaining maximum success with a minimum effort. Management is essential wherever group efforts are required to be directed towards achievement of common goals. In this management conscious age, the significance of management can hardly be overemphasized. It is said that, anything minus management amounts to nothing. Koontz and O' Donnel have rightly observed "there is no more important area of human activity than management since its task is that of getting things done through others."

The significance of management in business activities is relatively greater. The inputs of labour, capital and raw material never become productive without the catalyst of management. It is now widely recognized that management is an important factor of growth of any country. The following points further highlight the significance of management:

1. **chievements of group goals:** Management makes group efforts more effective. The group as a whole cannot realize its objectives unless and until there is mutual cooperation and coordination among the members of the group. Management creates teamwork and team spirit in an organization by developing a sound organization structure. It brings the human and material resources together and motivates the people for the achievement of the goals of the organization.
2. **Sound organization structure:** Management establishes proper organization structure and avoids conflict between the superiors and subordinates. This helps in the development of spirit of cooperation and mutual understanding, and a congenial environment is provided in the organization.
3. **Optimum utilization of resources:** Management always concentrates on achieving the objectives of the enterprise. The available resources of production are put to use in such a way that all sort of wastage and inefficiencies are reduced to a minimum. Workers are motivated to put in their best performance by the inspiring leadership. Managers create and maintain an environment conducive to highest efficiency and performance. Through the optimum use of available resources, management accelerates the process of economic growth.
4. **Minimization of cost:** In the modern era of intense competition, every business enterprise must minimize the cost of production and distribution. Only those concerns can survive in the market, which can produce goods of better quality at the minimum cost. A study of the principles of management helps in knowing certain techniques used for reducing costs. These techniques are production control, budgetary control, cost control, financial control, material control, etc.
5. **Change and growth:** A business enterprise operates in a constantly changing environment. Changes in business environment create uncertainties and risk and also produce opportunities for growth. An enterprise has to change and adjust itself in the everchanging environment. Sound management moulds not only the enterprise but also alters the environment itself to ensure the success of the business. Many of the giant business corporations of today had a humble beginning and grew continuously through effective management.
6. **Efficient and smooth running of business:** Management ensures efficient and smooth running of business, through better planning, sound organization and effective control of the various factors of production.
7. **Higher profits:** Profits can be enhanced in any enterprise either by increasing the sales revenue or reducing costs. To increase the sales revenue is beyond the control of an enterprise. Management by decreasing costs increases its profits and thus provides opportunities for future growth and development.
8. **Provide innovation:** Management gives new ideas, imagination and visions to an enterprise.
9. **Social benefits:** Management is useful not only to the business firms but to the society as a whole. It improves the standard of living of the people through higher production and more efficient use of scarce resources. By establishing cordial relations between different social groups, management promotes peace and prosperity in society.

10. **Useful for developing countries:** Management has to play a more important role in developing countries, like India. In such countries, the productivity is low and the resources are limited. It has been rightly observed, "There are no under-developed countries. They are only under-managed ones".

6.13 SCIENTIFIC MANAGEMENT

In the 18th century, the production was affected by industrial revolution, when the management people wanted to increase their production. Their ambitions were fulfilled by the invention of the concept of Scientific Management by F.W. Taylor in the 19th century. F.W. Taylor is the first person to find the concept of Scientific Management and developed it so, he is called as the Father of Scientific Management.

According to F.W. Taylor, Scientific Management consists of a certain philosophy of scientific selection and training of right workers to right job, providing adequate working conditions, providing a system of monetary incentives and supervisors. The workers are selected scientifically and training is provided to both new and existing workers. The workers are placed according to their qualifications and experience. The effective performance of any work depends upon physical working conditions, lighting, ventilation, restrooms, rest periods, drinking water, canteen, recreation, sanitation and the like. The system of monetary incentives should motivate the workers to work well. Management and supervisors should accept responsibility for planning, scheduling, guiding and controlling. It means that planning and execution are different functions.

F.W. Taylor defined Scientific Management as "the substitution of exact scientific investigations and knowledge for the old individual judgement or opinion; either of the workmen or the boss, in all matters relating to the work done in the establishment."

F.W. Taylor firmly believed that the objective of management should be the maximum prosperity for the employer and maximum prosperity to each employee. The prosperity for the employer means lower costs but higher returns. Maximum prosperity to the employee means fair as well as higher wages. These can be achieved through the adoption of Scientific Management.

Basic Principles of Scientific Management: F.W. Taylor has given the principles of Scientific Management which are briefly explained below:

1. **Science not rule of thumb**

   It means the replacement of old method of doing work scientifically. The nature of work performed by each worker should be clearly determined. It includes the allotment of fair work to each worker, standardization of work, adoption of differential piece rate of payment system and the like.

2. **Harmony in-group action**

   F.W. Taylor has emphasized peace and friendship in group action. In other words, dissatisfaction of any worker is to be avoided in the group action. The dissatisfaction is eliminated through scientific selection, training and placing of workers.

3. Cooperation

There should be a cooperation between management and workers. Workers should help the management to get higher profits, better quality products and lower cost of production. Management should give fair wages to workers, recognize the performance of work and acknowledge the indispensability of workers in raising productivity. Then, better cooperation will be achieved. According to Taylor, substitution of war for peace, hearty and brotherly cooperation for discontentment and strife, replacement of suspicious watchfulness with mutual confidence of becoming friends instead of enemies result in cooperation. Mutual understanding and change in thinking are the factors necessary for cooperation.

4. Maximum output

Maximum output is achieved through division of work and assumption of responsibility by management and workers jointly. Maximum output results in the increasing profit to the management and wages and bonus to the workers. Management should provide standard materials, tools and working conditions to perform the work economically and efficiently.

5. Improvement of workers

Under Scientific Management, all the workers should be given opportunity to improve to the fullest, extent possible. It is necessary for the development of company. Workers are scientifically selected and provided with the job training, so, the management should find out the physical, educational and psychological requirements of each job and find suitable person to each job. Systematic training can shape the workers to the job assigned to them.

6.14 SUMMARY

Management is the force that unifies various resources and is the process of bringing them together and coordinating them to help accomplish organization goal. Management is both a science as well as art. It is an inexact science. However, its principles as distinguished from practice are of universal application. Management does not yet completely fulfil all the criteria of a profession. There are three levels of management–top, middle and lower. Managers at different levels of the organization require and use different types of skills. Lower level managers require and use a greater degree of technical skill than high-level managers, while higher level managers require and use a greater degree of conceptual skill. Human skills are important at all managerial levels.

Management is getting the things done through the people with all efficiency and effectiveness. Nowadays, the organizations are surrounded by many complexities and, therefore, managing an organization successfully has become a very difficult task. The managers are required to make an extensive use of the most widely accepted principles of management because without predetermined principles and policies, the organizations cannot be managed efficiently and effectively in this era of global competition.

In every field of study, first there are basic principles, which are practiced later in the forms of certain functions, but management is a field where principles are exclusively based on practical experiences. The above named functions of management, which have been discussed in this lesson, are the backbone of management philosophy. These functions are interrelated as well and we need to perform them in sequenced order for getting the organizational objectives accomplished. But today's environment of business is a perfect blend of all these typical functions. Thus, every function is exercisable according to the situations and perception of managers.

Successful leaders and managers are very energetic. They exert a great deal of effort in order to communicate effectively, solve problems, make decisions, set goals, plan, execute plans, and supervise/evaluate. These are a leader's directional (or thinking) and implementing skills. As a leader, you cannot expect positive results from your subordinates unless you work equally hard at solving problems, making plans, and putting plans and decisions into action. Successful leaders also work hard at accomplishing their missions and objectives while maintaining only the highest possible standards of performance. Therefore, you being student of management should strive to exercise the same degree of effort and excellence.

6.15 SELF-ASSESSMENT QUESTIONS

1. "There is no important area of human activity than management since its task is that of getting things done through people". Discuss.
2. "Management is both a science and an art". Discuss this statement, giving suitable examples.
3. What do you understand by the term "Levels of Management"? Explain with reference to an organization with which you are familiar.
4. What are the functions of a manager? Is mere knowledge of management enough to become successful manager?
5. Discuss basic principles of management along with their significance.
6. Discuss and illustrate the meaning, definition and characteristics of management in modern organizations.
7. What is management? Explain the principles of management with suitable illustrations.
8. "There is no important area of human activity than management since its task is that of getting things done through people". Discuss the statement and explain with examples.
9. "Management starts from planning and ends up with controlling". Discuss this statement, giving suitable examples.
10. Discuss the important functions of management that support the philosophy of modern management thinkers.

7 EVOLUTION OF MANAGEMENT THOUGHTS

Learning Objective

The main objective of this chapter is to make the learners familiar with the various management thoughts and approaches which are essential for blooming managers.

7.1 INTRODUCTION

Organized endeavours, directed by people, responsible for planning, organizing, leading and controlling activities have been in existence for thousands of years. Management has been practiced in some form or the other since the dawn of civilization. Ever since human beings started living together in groups, techniques of organization and management were evolved. The Egyptian pyramids, the Chinese Civil Service, The Roman Catholic Church, the military organizations and the Great Wall of China, for instance, are tangible evidences that projects of tremendous scope, employing tens of thousands of people, were undertaken well before the modern times.

The pyramids are particularly interesting examples. The construction of a single pyramid occupied more than 1,00,000 workers for 20 years. Who told each worker that what did one do? Who ensured that there would be enough stones at the site to keep the workers busy? The answer is managers, regardless of what managers were called at that time. He had to plan what was to be done, organize people and material to do it, lead and direct the workers, and impose some controls to ensure that everything was done as planned. This example from the past demonstrates that organizations have been around for thousands of years and that management has been practices for an equivalent period. However, two pre-twentieth century events played significant roles in promoting the study of management. First is Adam Smith's contribution in the field of management and second is influence of Industrial Revolution in management practice.

Adam Smith's name is typically cited in field of economics for his contribution to classical economic doctrine, but his contribution in Wealth of Nations (1776) outlined the economic advantage that organization and society can gain from the *division of labour*. He used the pin-manufacturing industry for his example. Smith noted that 10 individuals, each doing a specialized task, could produce about 4800 pins a day. However, if each worked separately and had to perform each task, it would be quite an accomplishment to produce even 10 pins a day. Smith concluded that division of labour increased productivity by increasing each worker's skill and dexterity, by saving time lost in changing tasks, and by creating laboursaving inventions and machinery.

Industrial Revolution is another most important aspect that influences management in pre-twentieth century. The major contribution of the industrial revolution was the substitution of machine power for human power, which in turn, made it more economical to manufacture goods in factories. The advent of machine power, mass production, the reduced transportation costs that followed a rapid expansion of the railroads and lack of governmental regulation also fostered the development of big organization.

Now, a formal theory to guide managers in running their organization was needed. However, it was not until the early 1900s that the first major step toward developing such a theory was taken. The periods of evaluation of management thoughts are highlighted in the Table 7.1.

Table 7.1 Evolution of Management Thoughts

Management Thoughts	*Period*
• Early contributions	Upto 19th century
• Scientific management	1900-1930
• Administrative/operational management	1916-1940
• Human relations approach	1930-1950
• Social systems approach	1940-1950
• Decision theory approach	1945-1965
• Management science approach	1950-1960
• Human behaviour approach	1950-1970
• Systems approach	1960s onwards
• Contingency approach	1970s onwards

Thus, management has been recognized and identified as a distinctive branch of academic discipline in the twentieth century.

7.2 FORCES BACKING MANAGEMENT THOUGHTS

Management thoughts have took birth/evolved under the anxiety of political, social and economic forces. These are explained as follows:

1. **Political Forces:** The political forces manifested through the administration of political institutions and government agencies have shaped management thoughts. The important political forces include the political assumptions with respect to property rights,

contractual rights, concepts of justice, judicial processes and attitudes towards governmental control versus laissez-faire. Legal processes, which emanate from political pressures, such as the Union Carbide disaster in Bhopal, have a tremendous impact on management thinking and practice. Political pressures also define the interrelated rights of consumers, suppliers, labour, owners, creditors and different segments of public.

2. **Social Forces:** These evolve from the values and beliefs of a particular culture of people. The needs, education, religion and norms of human behaviour dictate the relations among people, which form social contracts. *Social contracts*, is that unwritten but understood set of rules that govern the behaviour of the people in their day-to-day interrelationships. The same happens between corporations and their constituents—labour, investors, creditors, suppliers and consumers. These social contracts defined relationships, responsibilities and liabilities that influence the development of management thoughts. It gives the society a sense of order and trust in which human affairs can be conducted in relative security and confidence.
3. **Economic Forces:** These forces determine the scarcity, transformation and distribution of goods and services in a society. Every social institution competes for a limited amount of human, financial, physical and information resources. This competition over scarce resources allocates them to their most profitable use and is the motivator of technological innovation by which resource availability can be maximized.

7.3 A FRAMEWORK FOR THE MANAGEMENT THOUGHTS

In the past, the business houses, particularly corporates, did not have a high academic standing and position in the society and it certainly compelled the scholars inculcate the academic interest in the study of business management so that its real fruits could be realized for the stakeholders under reference. There was a widespread belief that management process consisted of hidden tricks, mysterious clues and intuitive knowledge that could be mastered only by a few divinely gifted people. Moreover, the businessmen were very much afraid that through the study of management their tricks and secrets would be exposed.

But the advent of industrial revolution and the introduction of large-scale mechanized production and the resultant growth of trade, industry and commerce necessitated the study of management. The evolution of management thoughts might be better approached through the framework as depicted in Figure 7.1. In the beginning there were two classical schools of management thoughts. These were—the scientific management school and the organizational school. Later on, behavioural school and the quantitative school came into existence. These four schools merged into integration school, which led to the contemporary school of management thoughts.

Among the people who were in search of management principles, techniques and processes, a few emerged as outstanding pioneers. These are—Urwick and Brech, Boulton and Watt, Robert Owen, Charles Babbage, Oliver Sheldon, Lyndall Urwick, Herbert A. Simon, Frederick Winslow Taylor, H.S. Person, Henry L. Gantt, Frank Gilbreth, Harrington Emerson, H.P. Kendall, C.B. Barth, F.A. Halsey, Henri Dennison, Mooney and Reiley, Chester I. Barnard, Elton Mayo, F.J. Roethlisberger and T.N. Whitehead, Mary Parker Follett and Henry Fayol, etc.

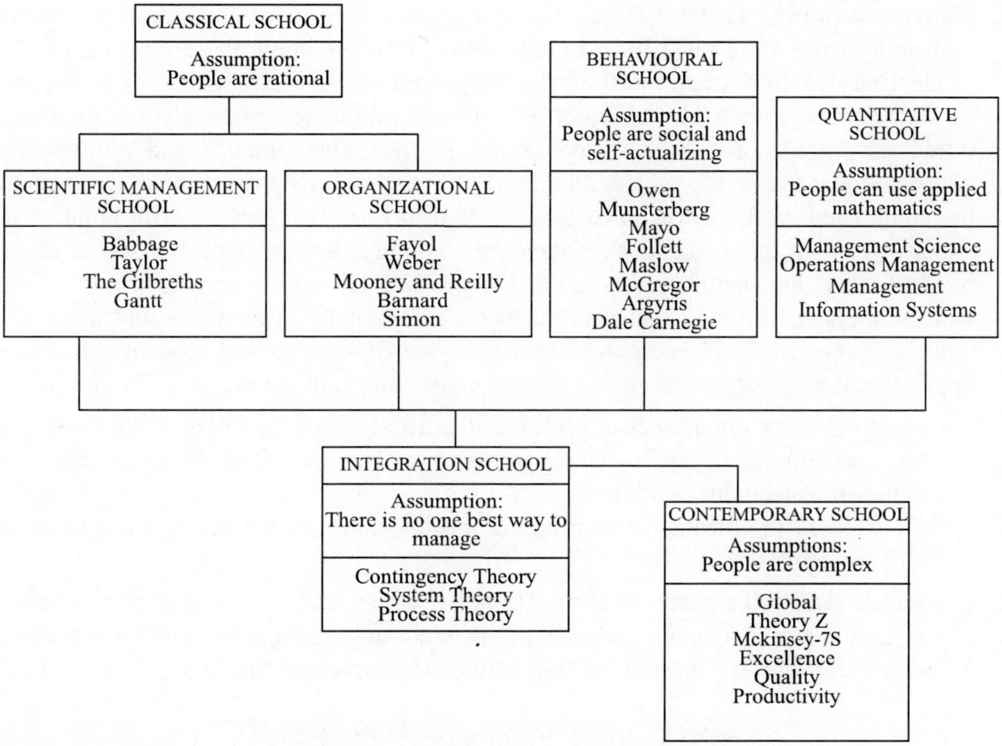

Figure 7.1 Framework for the management thoughts.

7.4 CONTRIBUTION OF LEADING THINKERS

The classical development of management thoughts can be divided into the scientific management, the organizational management, the behavioural management and the quantitative management. The first two (scientific management school and organizational) emerged in the late 1800s and early 1900s were based on the management belief that people were rational, economic creatures choose a course of action that provide the greatest economic gain. These schools of management thoughts are explained as below:

7.4.1 Scientific Management School

Scientific management means application of the scientific methods to the problem of management. It conducts a business or affairs by standards established by facts or truth gained through systematic observation, experiments, or reasoning. The followings individuals contribute in development of scientific management school of management thoughts. They dedicated to the increase in efficiency of labour by the management of the workers in the organization's technical core. They are:

1. **Charles Babbage (1792-1871):** He was a professor of mathematics at Cambridge University from 1828 to 1839. He concentrated on developing the efficiencies of labour production. He, like Adam Smith, was a proponent of the specialization of labour, and he applied mathematics to the efficient use of both production materials and facilities. He wrote nine books and over 70 papers on mathematics, science and philosophy. He advocated that the managers should conduct time studies data to establish work standards for anticipated work performance levels and to reward the workers with bonuses to the extent by which they exceed their standards. His best known book is 'On the Economy of Machinery and Manufacturers' published in 1832. He visited many factories in England and France and he found that manufacturers were totally unscientific and most of their work is guess work. He perceived that methods of science and mathematics could be applied to the operations of factories. His main contributions are as follows:
    - He stressed the importance of division of and assignment to labour on the basis of skill.
    - He recommended profit-sharing programmes in an effort to foster harmonious management-labour relations.
    - He stressed the means of determining the feasibility of replacing manual operations with machines.
2. **Frederick W. Taylor (1856-1915):** He is known as 'father of scientific management'. His ideas about management grew out of his wide-ranging experience in three companies: Midvale Steel Works, Simonds Rolling Mills and Bethlehem Steel Co.

Table 7.2 Taylor's Principles of Scientific Management

	Taylor's Principle	*Related Management Activity*
1.	Develop a science for each job with standardized work implements and efficient methods for all to follow.	Complete time-and-motion study to determine the best way to do each task.
2.	Scientifically select workers with skills and abilities that match each job, and train them in the most efficient ways to accomplish tasks.	Use job descriptions to select employees, set up formal training systems, and establish optimal work standards to follow.
3.	Ensure cooperation through incentives and provide the work environment that reinforces optimal work results in a scientific manner.	Develop incentive pay, such as piece-rate system, to reward productivity, and encourage safe condition by using proper implements.
4.	Divide responsibility for managing and for working, while supporting individuals in work groups for what they do best. Some people are more capable of managing, whereas others are better at performing tasks laid out for them.	Promote leaders who guide, not do, the work; create create a sense of responsibility for group results by panning tasks and helping workers to achieve those results.

Source: *Holt, 1990, p. 38*

As an engineer and consultant, Taylor observed and reported on what he found to be inexcusably inefficient work practices, especially in the steel industry. Taylor believed that workers output was only about one-third of what was possible. Therefore, he set out to correct the situation by applying scientific methods. Taylor's philosophy and ideas are given in his book, 'Principles of Scientific Management' published in 1911. Taylor gave the following principles of scientific management. These are outlined in Table 7.2.

Taylor concluded that scientific management involves a complete mental revolution on the part of both workers and management, without this mental revolution scientific management does not exist.

3. **Henry Gantt (1861-1919):** He was a consulting engineer who specialized in control system for shop scheduling. He sought to increase workers efficiency through scientific investigation. He developed the *Gantt Chart* (Figure 7.2) that provides a graphic representation of the flow of the work required to complete a given task. The chart represents each planned stage of work, showing both scheduled times and actual times. Gantt Charts were used by managers as a scheduling device for planning and controlling work. Gantt devised an incentive system that gave workers a bonus for completing their job in less time than the allowed standards. His bonus systems were similar to the modern *gain sharing* techniques whereby employees are motivated to higher levels of performance by the potential of sharing in the profit generated. In doing so, Gantt expanded the scope of scientific management to encompass the work of managers as well as that of operatives.

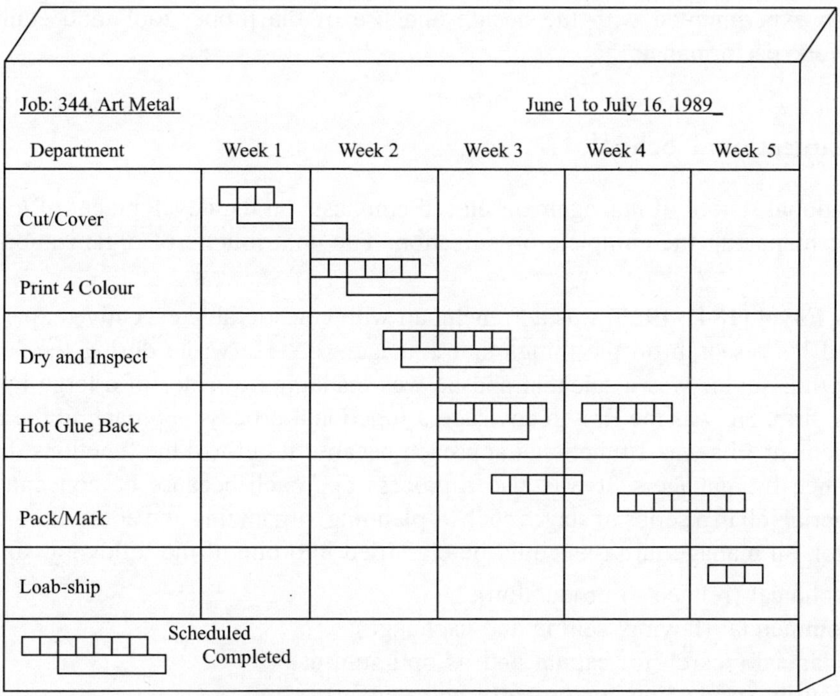

Figure 7.2 Gantt chart for book bindery.

4. **Frank (1868-1924) and Lillian (1878-1972) Gilbreth:** Frank Gilbreth, a construction contractor by back ground, gave up his contracting career in 1912 to study scientific management after hearing Taylor's speak at a professional meeting. Along with his wife Lillian, a psychologist, he studied work arrangements to eliminate wasteful hand-body-motion. Frank specialized in research that had a dramatic impact on medical surgery and, through his time and motion findings, surgeons saved many lives. Lillian is known as 'first

lady of management' and devoted most of her research to the human side of management. Frank Gilbreth is probably best known for his experiments in reducing the number of motions in bricklaying.

The man and wife team developed a classification scheme for the various motions (17 basic hand motions) used to complete a job referring a motion as a *therblig*. Their classification design covered such motions as grasping, moving, and holding. This scheme allowed him to more precisely analyze the exact elements of worker's hand movements. Their scientific motion scheme noted the relationship between types and frequencies of motions and the creation of workers fatigue, identifying that unnecessary or awkward motions were a waste of workers energy. By eliminating inappropriate motions and focusing on appropriate motion, the Gilbreth methodology reduces work fatigue and improves workers' performance.

Gilbreth were among the first to use motion pictures films to study hand-and-body motions. They devised a micro chronometer that recorded time to 1/2,000 of a second, placed it in the field of the study being photographed and thus determined how long a worker spent enacting each motion. Wasted motions missed by the naked eyes could be identified and eliminated. Gilbreths also experimented with the design and use of the proper tools and equipment for optimizing work performance.

7.4.2 Organizational School

The organizational school of management placed emphasis on the development of management principles for managing the complete organization. The contributors of organizational schools are:

1. **Henry Fayol (1841-1925)** was a Frenchman with considerable executive experience who focused his research on the things that managers do. He wrote during the same period Taylor did. Taylor was a scientist and he was managing director of a large French coal-mining firm. He was the first to envisage a functional process approach to the practice of management. His was a functional approach because it defined the functions that must be performed by managers. It was also a process approach because he conceptualized the managerial job in a series of stages such as planning, organizing and controlling. According to Fayol, all managerial tasks could be classified into one of the following six groups:
    - Technical (related to production);
    - Commercial (buying, selling and exchange);
    - Financial (search for capital and its optimum use);
    - Security (protection for property and person);
    - Accounting (recording and taking stock of costs, profits, and liabilities, keeping balance sheets, and compiling statistics);
    - Managerial (planning, organizing, commanding, coordinating and control);

He pointed out that these activities exist in every organization. He focused his work on the administrative or managerial activities and developed the following definition:

- Planning meant developing a course of action that would help the organization achieve its objectives.

- Organizing meant mobilizing the employees and other resources of the organization in accordance with the plan.
- Commanding meant directing the employees and getting the job done.
- Coordinating meant achieving harmony among the various activities.
- Controlling meant monitoring performance to ensure that the plan is properly followed.

2. **Max Weber (1864-1920):** He was a German sociologist. Writing in the early 1900s, Weber developed a theory of authority structures and described organizational activities on the basis of authority relations. He described an ideal type of organization that he called a bureaucracy, a form of organization characterized by division of labour, a clearly defined hierarchy, detailed rules and regulations, and impersonal relationships. Weber recognized that this ideal bureaucracy didn't exist in reality. He used it as a basis for theorizing about work and the way that work could be done in large groups. His theory became the model structural design for many of today's large organizations. The features of Weber's ideal bureaucratic structure are outlined in Figure 7.3.

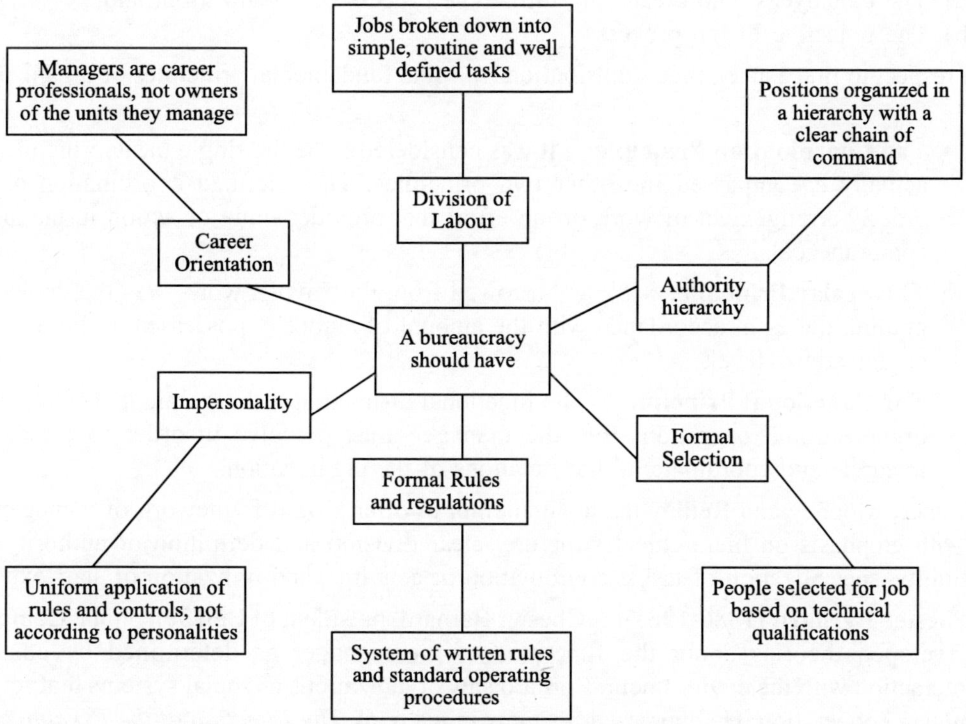

Figure 7.3 Weber's ideal bureaucracy.

The elements of bureaucracy are:

- Labour is divided with clear definition of authority and responsibility that are legitimatized as official duties.
- Positions are organized in a hierarchy of authority, with each position under the authority of a higher one.

- All personnel are selected and promoted based on technical qualifications, which are assessed by examination or according to training and experience.
- Administrative acts and decisions are recorded in writing. Recordkeeping provides organizational memory and continuity over time.
- Management is separate from the ownership of the organization.
- Management is subject to rules and procedures that will insure reliable, predictable behaviour. Rules are impersonal and uniformly applied to all employees.

3. **James D. Mooney and Alan C. Reilly:** James Mooney was a General Motors executive who teamed up with historian Alan Reilly to expose the true principles of an organization in their books. They wrote a book 'Onward Industry' in 1931 and later revised and renamed it as 'Principles of Organization' which had greatly influenced the theory and practice of management in USA at that time. They contended that an efficient organization should be based on certain formal principles and premises. They contended that organizations should be studied from two viewpoints:
   (a) The employees who create and utilize the process of organization; and
   (b) The objective of the process

With respect to first aspect, their contributions to some fundamental principles of organization are:

- **The Coordination Principle:** It was considered to be the single basic principle that actually encompassed the other two principles. They defined coordination as the orderly arrangement of work group effort that provides unity of action in pursuit of common goals.
- **The Scalar Principle:** It was borrowed from the Fayol's work, was the device for grading duties in accordance with the amount of authority possessed at the different organizational levels.
- **The Functional Principle:** The functional distinction is those unique differences in organizational operations that the manager must perceive in order to effectively integrate and coordinate all the functions of the organization.

In essence, Mooney and Reilley made an attempt to offer a rigid framework of management theory with emphasis on hierarchical structure, clear division and definition of authority and responsibility, specialization of tasks, coordination of activities and utilization of staff experts.

4. **Chester Barnard (1886-1961):** Chester Barnard, president of Bell Telephone Company, developed theories about the functions of the manager as determined by constant interaction with the environment. Barnard saw organizations as social systems that require human cooperation. He expressed his view in his book *The Function of the Executive*. He proposed ideas that bridged classical and human resource viewpoints. Barnard believes that organizations were made up of people with interacting social relationships. The manager's major functions were to communicate and stimulate subordinates to high level of efforts.

He saw the effectiveness of an organization as being dependent on its ability to achieve cooperative efforts from a number of employees in a total, integrated system. Barnard also argued that success depended on maintaining good relations with the people and institutions with whom the organization regularly interacted. By recognizing the organization's dependence on investors, suppliers, customers, and other external stakeholders, Barnard introduced the idea that managers had to examine the external environment and then adjust the organization to maintain a state of equilibrium. Barnard also developed set of working principles by which organizational communication systems can maintain final authority for the management team. These principles are:

- Channels of communication should be definitely known.
- Objective authority requires a definite formal channel of communication to every members of an organization.
- The line of communication must be as direct or short as possible.
- The complete line of communication should usually be used.
- Competence of the persons serving at communication centres that is officers, supervisory heads, must be adequate.
- The line of communication should not be interrupted during the time the organization is to function.

5. **Herbert A. Simon:** Simon, the Noble Laureate in Economics (1978), is an American political and social scientist. He started his career in local government. He analyzed the classical principles of management. Due to their ambiguous and contradictory nature, he criticized these principles as 'myths'. He analyzed the problems of management from the socio-psychological viewpoint. But he is best known for his work in the field of decision-making and administrative behaviour. He perceived the modern manager as being limited in his knowledge of a problem and the number of alternative available to him is also limited. Thus, the manager is an administrative man, not an economic man, who makes decision amid bounded rationality and selects not the maximizing alternative. Simon's arguments for the administrative man concept of a manager are highlighted in Table 7.3.

Table 7.3 Economic Man and Administrative Man

Economic Man–Full Rationality	*Administrative Man–Bounded Rationality*
1. Economic man maximizes–selects the best alternative from among all those available to him.	Administrative man satisfies–looks for a course of action that is satisfactory or good enough.
2. Economic man deals with the real world in all its complexity. He is rational. buzzing,	Administrative man recognizes that the world he he perceives is a drastically simplified model of the blooming confusion that constitute the real world.
3. Rationality requires a complete knowledge and anticipation of the consequences that will follow on each choice.	Knowledge of consequences is always fragmentary. Since these consequences lies in the future, imaginations must supply the lack of experienced feeling.
4. Rationality requires a choice among all possible alternative behaviour.	In actual behaviour only a very few of all possible alternatives ever come to mind.

7.4.3 Behavioural School

The school of behavioural management theory involved in recognition on the importance of human behaviour in organization. The major contributors were Figure 7.4.

1. **Robert Owen (1771-1858)** was a British industrialist who was the first to speak out on behalf of the organization's human resources. He carried out experiments and introduced many social reforms. He believed that workers' performance was influenced by the total

environment in which they worked. He criticized industrialists who spent huge sums of money repairing their production machines, but did little to improve the lot of their human machines. Owen worked for the building up of a spirit of cooperation between the workers and managers. He introduced new ideas of human relations, e.g., shorter work hours, housing facilities, education of children, provision of canteen, training of workers in hygiene, etc. He suggested that proper treatment of workers pays dividends and is an essential part of every manager's job.

2. **Hugo Munsterberg (1863-1916)** developed a psychology laboratory at Harvard University where he studied the application of psychology to the organizational settings. Psychology and Industrial Efficiency he argued for the study of scientific study of human behaviour to identify the general patterns and to explain individual differences. Thus, his concern for the human side of business led his peers to consider him to be father of industrial psychology. He successfully documented the psychological conditions associated with varying levels of work productivity, and he instructed managers on ways to match workers with jobs and also how to motivate them. Munsterberg suggested the use of psychological tests to improve employee selection, the value of learning theory in the development of training methods, and the study of human behaviour to determine what techniques are most effective for motivating workers.

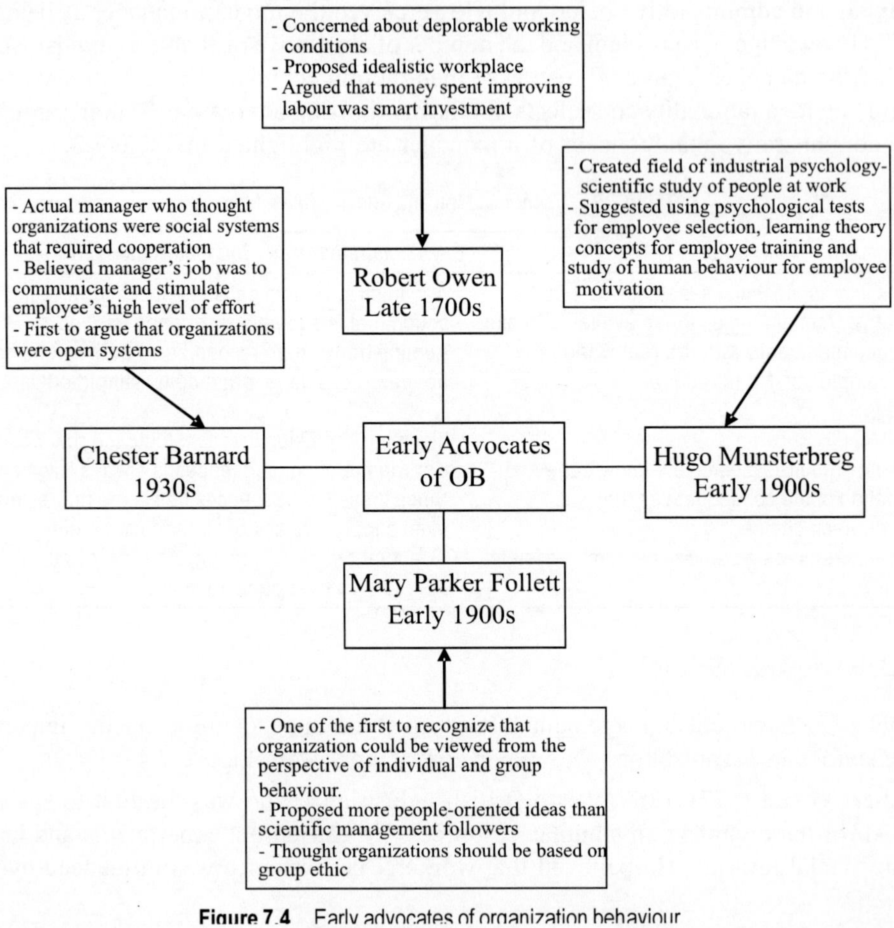

Figure 7.4 Early advocates of organization behaviour

3. **George Elton Mayo (1880-1949):** Mayo was a professor at the Harvard Business School. He served as the leader of the team which carried out the famous Hawthorne Experiments at the Hawthorne plant of the Western Electric Company (USA) during 1927-32. Originally the research was an application of Taylor's management science techniques designed to improve production efficiency.

   Mayo discussed in detail the factors that cause a change in human behaviour. Mayo's first study involved the manipulation of illumination for one group of workers and comparing their output with that of another group whose illumination was held constant. He concluded that the cause of increase in the productivity of workers is not a single factor like changing working hours or rest pauses but a combination of these several other factors. Considerate supervision, giving autonomy to the workers, allowing the formation of small cohesive groups of workers, creating conditions which encourage and support the growth of these groups and the cooperation between workers and management lead to increase in productivity.

   Mayo's contribution to management thoughts lies in the recognition of the fact that worker's performance is related to psychological, sociological and physical factors. Mayo and his associates concluded that a new social setting created by their tests had accounted for the increase in productivity. Their finding is now known as the Hawthorne Effect or the tendency for people, who are singled out for special attention, to improve their performance. Hawthorne study was an important landmark in studying the behaviour of workers and his relationship to the job, his fellow workers and organization. He highlighted that workers were found to restrict their output in order to avoid displeasure of the group, even at the sacrifice of incentive pay. Thus, Hawthorne studies were a milestone in establishing the framework for further studies into the field of organizational behaviour.

4. **Mary Parker Follett (1868-1933):** She was a social philosopher whose ideas had clear implications for management practice. Her contribution towards the understanding of group is of immense value. She believed that groups were the mechanisms through which people could combine their differing talents for the greater good of the organization, which she defined as the community in which managers and subordinates could work in harmony. The mangers and workers should view themselves as partners and as a part of common group. She was convicted that the traditional and artificial distinction between the managers who give the orders and the workers who take the orders obscured their natural relationships. Manager should rely more on their expertise and knowledge to lead subordinates than on the formal authority of their position. Thus, her humanistic ideas influenced the way we look at motivation, leadership, power and authority. The Follett Behavioural Model of control being sponsored by an oriented towards the group, while self-control exercised by both individuals and the group ultimately result in both sharing the power. In the Follett Holistic Model of Control, Follett captured the interactive, integrative nature of self-control groups being influenced by the forces within the work environment.

5. **Abraham Maslow:** He was a humanistic psychologist, proposed a hierarchy of five needs: physiological, safety, social, esteem and self-actualization. He proposed that man was a wanting animal whose behaviour was calculated to serve his most pressing needs. A need can be described as a physiological or psychological deficiency that a person is

motivated to satisfy. Maslow further proposed that man's need could be placed in a hierarchy of needs as shown in Figure 7.5. The study shows that a man has various needs and their order can be determined. The moment the first need of man is satisfied he starts thinking of the second need, and then follows his worry about the third need and the sequence continues till all the needs are satisfied. Maslow's theory is operationalized through two principles.

- The *deficit principle* holds that a relatively well-satisfied need is not a strong motivator of behaviour.
- The *progression principle* holds that, once a need is fairly-well satisfied, behaviour is dominated by the next level in the need hierarchy.

(1) Physiological Needs: This category includes those needs which a man needs to satisfy first of all in order to remain alive. It includes food to eat, house to live in, clothes to wear and sleep for rest.

(2) Safety Needs: After having satisfied the physical needs a man thinks of his safety. Safety needs mean physical, economic and psychological safety. *Physical safety* means saving him from accidents, diseases and other unforeseen situations. *Economic safety* means security of employment and making provision for old age. *Psychological safety* means maintaining his prestige.

(3) Social Needs: Man is a social being and wants to live in society with honour. It is, therefore, necessary that he should have friends and relatives with whom he can share his joys and sorrows.

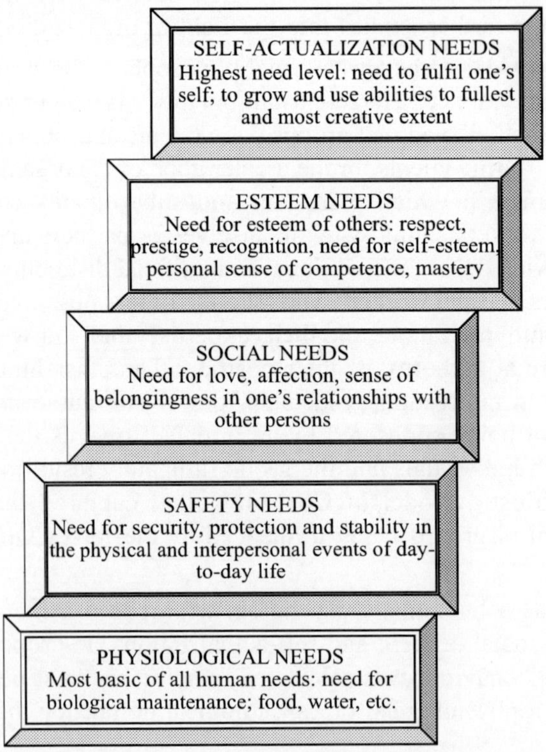

Figure 7.5 Maslow's hierarchy of human needs

(4) **Esteem and Status Needs:** They are called ego needs of man. It means everybody wants to get a high status which may increase his power and authority.

(5) **Self-Actualization Needs:** Last of all man tries to satisfy his self-actualization need. It means that a man should become what he is capable of. For example, a musician wants to be proficient in the art of music, an artist wants to gain proficiency in creating works of art and similarly, a poet wants to be an expert in the art of writing poems.

6. **Douglas McGregor (1906-1964):** He is best known for his formulation of two sets of assumptions–Theory X and Theory Y. McGregor argued that managers should shift their traditional views of man and work (which he termed Theory X) to a new humane views of man and work (which he termed Theory Y).

According to McGregor, Theory X attitudes, that man was lazy and work was bad were both pessimistic and counterproductive. Theory X assumes that people have little ambition, dislike work, want to avoid responsibility, and need to be closely supervised to work effectively.

Theory Y view that man wanted to work and work was good should become the standard for humanizing the workplace. Theory Y offers a positive view, assuming that people can exercise self-direction, accept responsibility and consider work to be as natural as rest of play. McGregor believed that Theory Y assumptions best captured the true nature of workers and should guide management practice. Table 7.4 depicts the assumptions of both these theories:

Table 7.4 Theory X and Y Theory

Traditional Theory 'X'	*Modern Theory 'Y'*
(1) Man by nature is sluggish and shirker.	Man wants to work provided the conditions are favourable.
(2) Mostly people are not ambitious and are afraid to take responsibility.	This theory takes people as enthusiastic, responsible and full of effort.
(3) Under this people want to be directed, meaning thereby that they want somebody to tell them to work and only they will work.	It is thought that the employee has the quality of self-direction and they do not feel the necessity of being directed by somebody else.
(4) Motivation is limited to only physical and security needs.	According to this, physical and security needs motivate for a short time while it is continuous in case of self-actualization and esteem and status needs.
(5) Strict control, threat and punishment are used in order to get work.	If proper environment is provided a person himself performs his work laboriously.

7. **Chris Argyris:** He was an eminent social scientist and a professor of industrial administration at Yale University. He conducts research into personality and organizational life factors and developed the theory that both traditional management practices and organizational structure are inconsistent with the growth and development of the matured personality. Further he argued that the continuing incongruence between one's work environment and one's personality will result in conflict, frustration and failure.

7.4.4 Quantitative School

With the revolutionary change in the application of information technology came the quantitative school of thoughts, which finds its foundation in decision theory, the application of statistics in decision-making and the evolution of mathematical/econometric models that are nurtured by computer technology. This approach is based upon the assumption that mathematical techniques can help the manager in solution of problems. The features of quantitative management school were:

- **Primary Focus on Decision-Making:** The end result of problem analysis will include direct implications for managerial action.
- **Based on Economic Decision Theory:** Final actions are chosen criteria as costs, revenue and rates of return on investment.
- **Use of Formal Mathematical Models:** Possible solutions to problems are specified as mathematical equations and then analyzed according to mathematical rules and formulas.
- **Frequent Use of Computers:** Heavy reliance is placed on computers and their advanced processing capabilities.

The quantitative approach has found favour through the following applications:

1. **Management Science:** Explained later in this chapter.
2. **Operations Management:** It entails the application of quantitative methods to the organizational tasks of production and operations control. The operational management techniques utilizes following basic quantitative techniques:
   - *Forecasting* is the process by which future predictions are formulated through mathematical computations
   - *Inventory control* entails the control of costly inventories through mathematical formulas that determine the proper level of inventory to be maintained as well as the economic quantities to be ordered.
   - *Linear programming* involves the use of computations to allocate scarce resources for their optimal use.
   - *Networks* are complex models, such as Program Evaluation and Review Techniques (PERT) and the Critical Path Methods (CPM) for analyzing, planning and controlling complex operations.
   - *Regression analysis* is used to predict the relationships between two or more variables and to determine how changes in one variable might affect other variables.
3. **Management Information System:** These are integrated programmes for the collection, analysis and dissemination of information to support management decision-making. The total MIS network is more than a machine; it contains human resources, hardware, software and intricate processes. Most MIS networks are computer based due to vast amount of number crunching to be done. That is why the ideal MIS provides accurate, condensed informational analysis to the appropriate manager in a timely manner.

7.4.5 Integration School

In recent years, an attempt has been made to integrate the classical theories with the modern behavioural and quantitative theories into an overall framework that use the best of each approach. These approaches assumed that there is no best way to manage, and all theories have application to the practice of management. Two such integrative developments are explained as follows:

1. **Contingency Theory:** It is based on the notion that the proper management technique in a given situation depends upon the nature and conditions of that situation. The contingency view of management is highlighted in Figure 7.6 contend that an organizational phenomenon exists in logical patterns which managers can come to understand. Along with this organizational understanding comes the development of unique behaviours that have proven successful in particular situations. However, there are no universal solution techniques because every problem situation is unique in itself.

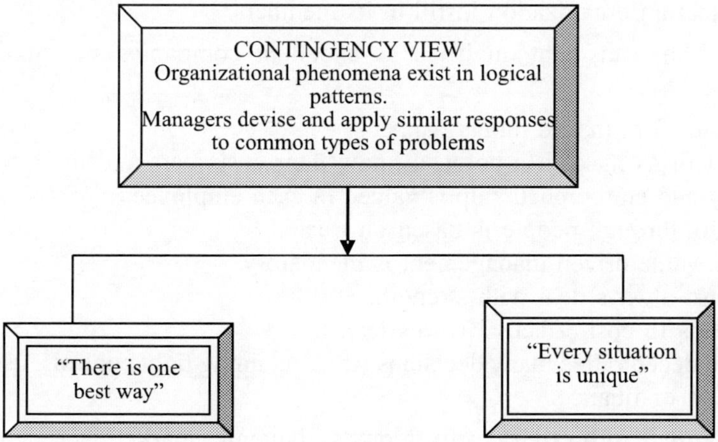

Figure 7.6 The contingency view of management.

2. **Systems Theory:** It has been explained later in this lesson.

7.4.6 Contemporary School

The contemporary school of management thoughts outlines the framework for studying the more recent trends in management practices, such as the impact of global business, Theory Z concepts, McKinsey 7-S approach, the search for excellence, and the concern for quality and productivity. These are explained as follows:

1. **Global:** The recent emergence of a truly global economy is affecting every manager in the world. In today's environment, success in the long-run demands that the manager think globally, even if he can still limit his actions to local market.
2. **Theory Z:** These firms are those which are highly successful American firms that use many of the Japanese management practices. The Type Z firm features long-term employment with a moderately specialized career path and slow evaluation and promotion. Lifetime employment would not be especially attractive to America's mobile workforce and the slow evaluation and promotion processes would not meet the high expectations of American workers.

3. **Mckinsey 7-S:** The 7-S factors are as follows:
    - **Strategy:** The plans that determine the allocation of an organization's scarce resources and commit the organization to a specified course of action.
    - **Structure:** The design of the organization that determines the number of levels in its hierarchy and the location of the organization's authority.
    - **Systems:** The organizational processes and proceduralized reports and routines.
    - **Staff:** The key human resource groups within an organization, described demographically.
    - **Style:** The manner in which manager behave in pursuit of organizational goals.
    - **Skills:** The distinct abilities of the organization's personnel.
    - **Superordinate Goals (shared values):** The significant meanings or guiding concepts that an organization instill in its members.
4. **Excellence:** The firms that qualified as excellent companies shared the following characteristics:
    - A successful firm makes things happen.
    - Successful firms make it a point to know their customers and their needs.
    - Autonomy and entrepreneurship is valued in each employee.
    - Productivity through people is based on trust.
    - Hands on, value driven management is mandatory.
    - A firm must always deal with strength.
    - A firm leads to cost-effective works teams.
    - A firm can decentralize many decisions while retaining tight controls, usually through the function of finance.
5. **Quality and Productivity:** In today's dynamic marketplace, consumers are encouraged to buy a product that demonstrates the highest level of quality at the optimum price. This requires a dedicated and skilled workforce that places utmost importance on quality workmanship.

7.5 APPROACHES TO THE STUDY OF MANAGEMENT

7.5.1 Classical Approach

The classical approach is also known as traditional approach, management process approach or empirical approach. The main features of this approach are as follows:

- It laid emphasis on division of labour and specialization, structure, scalar and functional processes and span of control. Thus, they concentrated on the anatomy of formal organization.
- Management is viewed as a systematic network (process) of interrelated functions. The nature and content of these functions, the mechanics by which each function is performed and the interrelationship between these function is the core of the classical approach.
- It ignored the impact of external environment on the working of the organization. Thus, it treated organization as closed system.

- On the basis of experience of practising managers, principles are developed. These principles are used as guidelines for the practising executive.
- Functions, principles and skills of management are considered universal. They can be applied in different situations.
- The integration of the organization is achieved through the authority and control of the central mechanism. Thus, it is based on centralization of authority.
- Formal education and training is emphasized for developing managerial skills in would be managers. Case study method is often used for this purpose.
- Emphasis is placed on economic efficiency and the formal organization structure.
- People are motivated by economic gains. Therefore, organization controls economic incentives.

The Classical approach was developed through three mainstreams–Taylor's Scientific Management, Fayol's Administrative Management and Weber's Ideal Bureaucracy. All the three concentrated on the structure of organization for greater efficiency.

Merits of Classical Approach

- The classical approach offers a convenient framework for the education and training of managers.
- The observational method of case study is helpful in drawing common principles out of past experience with some relevance for future application.
- It focuses attention on what managers actually do.
- This approach highlights the universal nature of management.
- It provides scientific basis for management practice.
- It provides a starting point for researchers to verify the validity and to improve the applicability of management knowledge. Such knowledge about management is effectively presented.

Shortcomings of Classical Approach

- Weber's ideal bureaucracy suggested strict adherence to rules and regulations, this lead to red tapism in the organization.
- It offers a mechanistic framework that undermines the role of human factor. The classical writers ignored the social, psychological and motivational aspect of human behaviour.
- The environmental dynamics and their effect on management have been discounted. Classical theory viewed organization as closed system, i.e., having no interaction with environment.
- There is positive danger in relying too much on past experiences because a principle or technique found effective in the past may not fit a situation of the future.
- The classical principles are mostly based on the personal experience and limited observations of the practitioners. They are not based on personal experience.
- The totality of real situation can seldom be incorporated in a case study.

7.5.2 Scientific Management Approach

The impetus for the scientific management approach came from the first industrial revolution.

Because it brought about such an extraordinary mechanization of industry, this revolution necessitated the development of new management principles and practices. The concept of scientific management was introduced by Frederick Winslow Taylor in USA in the beginning of 20th century. He defined scientific management as, *"Scientific management is concerned with knowing exactly what you want men to do and then see in that they do it in the best and cheapest way".*

Elements and Tools of Scientific Management: The features of various experiments conducted by Taylor are as follows:

- **Separation of Planning and Doing:** Taylor emphasized the separation of planning aspects from actual doing of the work. The planning should be left to the supervisor and the workers should emphasize on operational work.
- **Functional Foremanship:** Separation of planning from doing resulted into development of supervision system that could take planning work adequately besides keeping supervision on workers. Thus, Taylor evolved the concept of functional foremanship based on specialization of functions. This involve activities of workers as depicted in Figure 7.7.

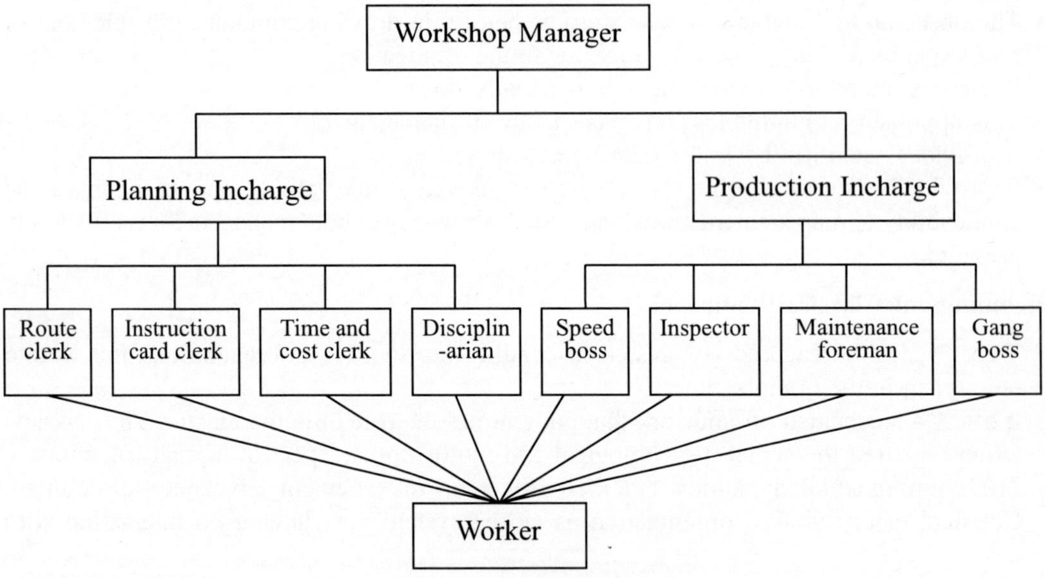

Figure 7.7 Functional foremaship.

- **Job Analysis:** It is undertaken to find out the best way of doing things. The best way of doing a job is one which requires the least movement consequently less time and cost.
- **Standardization:** Standardization should be maintained in respect of instruments and tools, period of work, amount of work, working conditions, cost of production, etc.
- **Scientific Selection and Training of Workers:** Taylor has suggested that the workers should be selected on scientific basis taking into account their education, work experience, aptitudes, physical strength, etc.

- **Financial Incentives:** Financial incentives can motivate workers to put in their maximum efforts. Thus, monetary (bonus, compensation) incentives and non-monetary (promotion, upgradation) incentives should be provided to employees.

Criticism of Scientific Management: The main grounds of criticism are given below:

- Taylor advocated the concept of functional foremanship to bring about specialization in the organization. But this is not feasible in practice as a worker can't carry out instructions from eight foremen.
- Workers were hired on a first-come, first-hired basis without due concern for workers ability or skills.
- Scientific management is production oriented as it concentrates too much on the technical aspects of work and undermines the human factors in industry. It resulted in monotony of job, loss of initiative, over speeding workers, wage reductions, etc.
- Training was haphazard at best, with only minimal use of basic apprentice system.
- Tasks were accomplished by general rule of thumb without standard times, methods or motion.
- Managers worked side-by-side with the workers, often ignoring such basic managerial function of planning and organizing.

7.5.3 Administrative Approach to Management

The advocates of this school perceive management as a process involving certain functions such as planning, organizing, directing and controlling. That's why, it is called as 'functional approach' or 'management process' approach. Fayol's contributions were first published in book form titled 'Administration Industrielle at Generale' in French Language, in 1916. He defined management in terms of certain functions and then laid down fourteen principles of management which according to him have universal applicability. Thus, he was a pioneer in the field of management education. In brief, Fayol's views on management command acceptability even today because they are much in tune with the requirements of management in the present-day world.

Fayol's General Principles of Management

- *Division of Work:* The object of division of work is to produce more and better work with the same effort. It is accomplished through reduction in the number of tasks to which attention and effort must be directed.
- *Authority and Responsibility:* Authority is defined as 'the right to command and the power to make oneself obeyed'. Responsibility coexists with authority and is its other side. Fayol made a distinction between official authority and personal authority, the latter stemming from the manager's own intelligence, integrity, experience, personality, knowledge and skills.
- *Discipline:* It implies respect for agreements designed to secure obedience. It must prevail throughout an organization to ensure its smooth functioning. Discipline requires clear and fair agreements, good supervision and judicious application of penalties.

- *Unity of Command:* Every employee should receive orders and instruction from only one superior and a subordinate should be accountable to only one superior.
- *Unity of Direction:* Each group of activities having one objective should be unified by having one plan and one head.
- *Subordination of Individual to General Interest:* The interest of any one employee or group of employees should not take precedence over the interests of the organization as a whole.
- *Remuneration of Personnel:* The amount of remuneration and the methods of payment should be just and fair and should provide maximum possible satisfaction to both employees and employers.
- *Centralization:* It refers to the degree to which subordinates are involved in decision making. Whether decision-making is centralized (to management) or decentralized (to subordinates) is a question of proper proportion. The task is to find the optimum degree of centralization for each situation.
- *Scalar Chain:* The scalar chain is the chain of superiors ranging from the ultimate authority to the lowest ranks. Communication should follow this chain. However, if following the chain creates delays, cross-communications can be followed if agreed to by all parties and superiors are kept informed.
- *Order:* It is a rational arrangement for things and people. Fayol emphasized both material order and human order. In material order, there should be a place for everything and everything should be in its proper place. In human order, there should be an appointed place for everyone and everyone should be in his and her appointed place.
- *Equity:* Managers should be kind and fair to their subordinates. The application of equity requires good sense, experience and humanistic attitude for soliciting loyalty and devotion from subordinates.
- *Stability of Tenure:* High employee turnover is inefficient. Management should provide orderly personnel planning and ensure that replacements are available to fill vacancies.
- *Initiative*: Subordinates should be provided with an opportunity to show their initiative as a way to increase their skills and to inculcate a sense of participation.
- *Espirit de Corps*: Union is strength, and it comes from the harmony and mutual understanding of the personnel. Management should not follow the policy of 'divide and rule'. Rather it should strive to maintain team spirit and cooperation among employees so that they can work together as a team for the accomplishment of common objectives.

Criticism: Fayol's work has been criticized on the following grounds:

- His theory is said to be too formal. There is no single classification of managerial functions acceptable to all the functional theorists. There is also lack of unanimity about the various terms such as management, administration, etc.
- He did not pay adequate attention to workers.
- The fundamentalists considered their principles to be universal in nature. But many of the principles have failed to deliver the desired results in certain situations.
- There is a vagueness and superficiality about some of his terms and definition.

Table 7.5 Dissimilarity Bvetween Contribution of Taylor and Fayol

Basis of Comparison	*Taylor*	*Fayol*
1. Perspective	Shop-floor level or the job of a supervisor	Top management
2. Focus	Improving productivity through work simplification and standardization	Improving overall administration through general principles
3. Personality	Scientists	Practitioner
4. Results	Scientific observation and measurement	Universal truths developed from personal experiences
5. Major Contribution	Science of industrial management	A systematic theory of management

7.5.4 Human Relations Approach to Management

The criticism of the Scientific and Administrative Management as advocated by Taylor and Fayol, respectively, gave birth to Human Relations Approach. The behavioural scientists criticized the early management approaches for their insensitiveness to the human side of organization. The behavioural scientists did not view the employees mechanically in work situation, but tried to show that the employees not only have economic needs but also social and psychological needs like need for recognition, achievement, social contact, freedom, and respect. Human relations school regards business organization as a psycho-social system.

Elton Mayo of Harvard and his associates conducted a famous study on human behaviour at the Hawthorne plant of the Western Electric Company and this study formed the foundation of this school of management thoughts. The basic hypotheses of this study as well as the basic propositions of the Human Relations Approach are the following:

- The business organization is a social system.
- The employees not only have economic needs but also psychological needs and social needs, which are required to be served properly to motivate them.
- Employees prefer self-control and self-direction.
- Employee oriented democratic participative style of management is more effective than mechanistic task-oriented management style.
- The informal group should be recognized and officially supported.

The human relations approach is concerned with recognition of the importance of human element in organizations. It revealed the importance of social and psychological factors in determining worker's productivity and satisfaction. It is instrumental in creating a new image of man and the workplace. However, this approach also did not go without criticism. It was criticized that the approach laid heavy emphasis on the human side as against the organizational needs. However, the contribution of this approach lies in the fact that it advises managers to attach importance to the human side of an organization.

7.5.5 Social System Approach to Management

It is developed during social science era, is closely related to Human Relation Approach. It includes those researchers who look upon management as a social system. Chester I. Barnard is called as the spiritual father of this approach. According to this approach, an organization is essentially a cultural system composed of people who work in cooperation. The major features of this approach are as follows:

- Organization is a social system, a system of cultural relationships.
- Relationships exist among the external as well as internal environment of the organization.
- Cooperation among group members is necessary for the achievement of organizational objectives.
- For effective management, efforts should be made for establishing harmony between the goals of the organization and the various groups therein.

7.5.6 Decision Theory Approach to Management

Decision theory is the product of management science era. The decision theorists emphasize on rational approach to decisions, i.e., selecting from possible alternatives a course of action or an idea. Major contribution in this approach has come from Simon. Other contributors are March, Cyert, Forrester, etc. The major emphasis of this approach is that decision-making is the job of every manager. The manager is a decision-maker and the organization is a decision-making unit. Therefore, the major problem of managing is to make rational decision. The main features of this approach are:

- Management is essentially decision-making. The members of the organization are decision-makers and problem solvers.
- Organization can be treated as a combination of various decision centres. The level and importance of organizational members are determined on the basis of importance of decisions which they make.
- All factors affecting decision-making are subject matter of the study of management. Thus, it covers the entire range of human activities in organization as well as the macro conditions within which the organization works.

7.5.7 Management Science Approach to Management

Management science is an approach to management that applies mathematical analysis to decision-making. It involves the use of highly sophisticated techniques, statistical tools and complex models. The primary focus of this approach is the mathematical model. Through this device, managerial and other problems can be expressed in basic relationships and where a given goal is sought, the model can be expressed in terms which optimize that goal. The management science approach found its origins during World War II, when highly technical military/production problems become far too complex for traditional management methodology. The major features of this approach are:

- Management is regarded as the problem-solving mechanism with the help of mathematical tools and techniques.
- Management problems can be described in terms of mathematical symbols and data. Thus, every managerial activity can be quantified.

- This approach covers decision-making, system analysis and some aspect of human behaviour.
- Operations research, mathematical tools, simulation, model, etc. are the basic methodologies to solve managerial problems.

7.5.8 Human Behavioural Approach to Management

Human Behavioural approach is a modified version of Human Relations approach. Human Behavioural approach is devoid of any emotional content, which is the core of Human Relations Approach. This approach stresses the individual performing the jobs. Here the attention is directed towards the human aspects of management. The neglect of human factor and the over emphasis on machines and materials led to the development of this approach. The Behavioural approach emphasizes synchronization of group goals within the broader framework of management. It does not consider the goals of the different groups as conflicting with others. Many sociologists, psychologists and social psychologists have shown considerable interest in studying the problems of management. The sociologists who have contributed to management are Blak, Selznick, Homans, Dubin, Dalton, and Katz and Kahn. The social psychologist who have contributed to management are McGregor, Argyris, Leavitt, Blake and Mouton, Sayles, Tannenbaum and his associates, Bennis, Fielder, Stogdill and Herzberg. The behavioural theories have drawn heavily on the work of Maslow. Douglas McGregor built on Maslow's work in explaining his 'Theory X' and 'Theory Y'. Frederick Herzberg develops a two factor theory of motivation. To sum up, many conclusions of the contributions made by behaviouralists can presented as follows:

- People do not dislike work. If they have helped to establish objectives, they want to achieve them. In fact, job itself is a source of motivation and satisfaction to employees.
- Most people can exercise a great deal of self-direction and self-control than are required in their current job. Therefore, there remains untapped potential among them.
- The manager's basic job is to use the untapped human potential in the service organization.
- The managers should create a healthy environment wherein all the subordinates contribute to the best of their capacity. The environment should provide healthy, safe, comfortable and convenient place to work.
- The manager should provide for self-direction by subordinates and they must be encouraged to participate fully in all important matters.
- Operating efficiency can be improved by expanding subordinate influence, direction and self control.
- Work satisfaction may improve as a by-product of subordinates making use of their potential.

Merits of Behavioural Approach

It generated an awareness of the overwhelming role of the human element in organizations. It recognizes the quality of leadership as a critical factor in management success. It recognizes the role of individual psychology and group behaviour in organizational effectiveness.

Shortcomings of Behavioural Approach

Conclusions of behavioural approach discounts theory and stress radical empiricism. This approach neglects the economic dimension of work satisfaction. It is group oriented and anti-individualistic.

Table 7.6 Distinction Between Human Relations and Behavioural Approach

	Human Relations Approach	*Behavioural Sciences Approach*
1.	It laid emphasis on individual, his needs and behaviour.	It stressed upon groups and group behaviour.
2.	It focused on interpersonal relationships	It focused on group relationships.
3.	It was based on the Hawthorne Experiments and so its scope is limited.	It refined the Human Relations approach and has a wide scope. It is much more systematic study of human behaviour in organization.
4.	It was pioneered by Elton Mayo and his associates.	It was pioneered by Feith Davis, Rensis Likert and others.
5.	It laid emphasis on informal groups' motivation, job satisfaction and morale.	The behaviourists studied group dynamics, informal organization leadership, motivation and participative management.

7.5.9 Mathematics or Quantitative Approach to Management

It emphasizes that the organization or decision-making is a logical process and it can be expressed in terms of mathematical symbols and relationships, which can be used to solve corporate problems and conduct corporate affairs. This approach focuses attention on the fundamentals of analysis and decision-making. This brings together the knowledge of various disciplines like Operation Research and Management Science for effective solution of management problems. The Quantitative School quantifies the problem; generate solution, tests the solution for their optimality and then it recommends. The decisions are optimum and perfect as distinguished from the human behavioural approach, in which decisions are 'satisfying'. This approach is devoid of any personal bias, emotions, sentiments, and intuitiveness. The main postulates of the quantitative approach are as follows:

- Management is a series of decision-making. The job of a manager is to secure the best solution out of a series of interrelated variables.
- These variables can be presented in the form of a mathematical model. It consists of a set of functional equation which set out the quantitative interrelationship of the variable.
- If the model is properly formulated and the equations are correctly solved, one can secure the best solution to the model.
- Organizations exist for the achievement of specific and measurable economic goals.
- In order to achieve these goals, optimal decisions must be made through scientific formal reasoning backed by quantification.
- Decision-making models should be evaluated in the light of set criteria like cost reduction, return on investment, meeting time schedules, etc.
- The quality of management is judged by the quality of decisions made in diverse situations.

Table 7.7 Difference Between Quantitative Approach and Scientific Approach

	Quantitative Approach	*Scientific Management*
1.	It makes use of mathematical and statistical techniques in management.	It makes use of scientific approach in management.
2.	It focuses on finding right answers to managerial problems (decision-making).	It focuses on improving efficiency of men and machines (one best way of doing things).
3.	In this operation research is the main techniques.	Time and motion studies are the main techniques.
4.	It is developed by W.C. Churchman.	A movement launched by F.W. Taylor and his associates.
5.	Application of Econometric models.	Application of experiments and research.

7.5.10 System Approach to Management

In the 1960s, a new approach to management appeared which attempted to unify the earlier school of thoughts. This approach is commonly referred to as 'System Approach'. The system approach is based on the generalization that an organization is a system and its components are interrelated and interdependent. "A system is composed of related and dependent elements which, when in interactions, form a unitary whole. On other words, a system may be defined as an organized and purposeful entity of interrelated, interdependent and interacting elements. It is a goal-oriented organism that is composed of parts interrelated in such a way that the total system is greater than the sum of its parts. The elements of each system may themselves be subsystems. These subsystems are functionally related to each other and to the total system. The basic postulates of the system approach are as follows:

- An organization is a system consisting of several subsystems. For example, in a business enterprise production, sales and other departments are the subsystem.
- The position and function of each subsystem can be analyzed only in relation to other subsystem and to the organization as a whole rather than in isolation.
- An organization is a dynamic system because it is responsive or sensitive to its environment. It is vulnerable to changes in its environment.

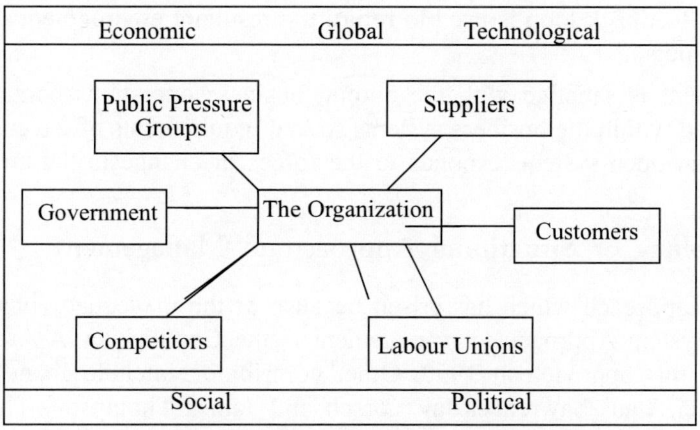

Figure 7.8 Open system view of organization.

Systems are of several types. A *static system*, e.g., a petrol engine operates repetitively completing the same cycle of functions without change or deviation. On the other hand, the *dynamic system* undergoes change, it grows or decays. Biological systems, e.g., plants, animals and human beings are dynamic. A *closed system* is self-dependent and does not have any interaction with the external environment. Physical and mechanical systems are closed systems. A closed system concentrates completely on internal relationships, i.e., interaction between subsystems only. An *open system* approach recognizes the dynamic interaction of the system with its environment in Figure 7.8.

The open system consisting of four basic elements:

- Inputs: These are ingredients required to initiate the transformation process. They include human, financial, material and information resources.

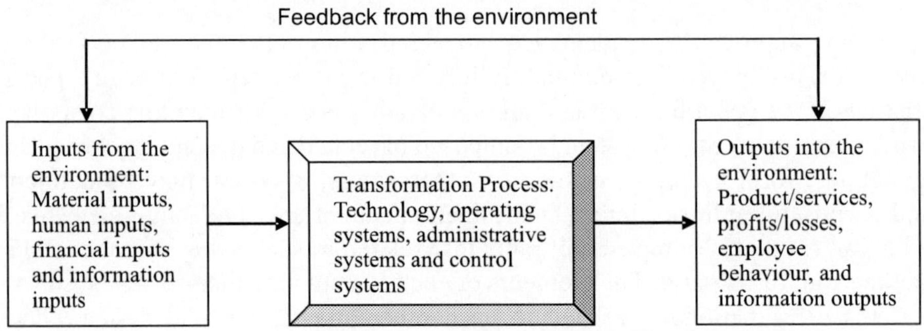

Figure 7.9 Elements of open system.

- Transformation Process: The inputs are put through a transformation process that applies technology, operating methodologies, administrative practices and control techniques in order to produce the output.
- Outputs: The output may be products and/or services, the sale of which creates profits or losses. This process also has by-product outputs such as worker behaviour, information, environmental pollution, community services, and so on.
- Feedback: A feedback loop is used to return the resultant environmental feedback to the system as inputs.

If the environment is satisfied with the output, business operations continue. If it is not, changes are initiated within the business systems so that requirements of the customers are fully met. This is how an open system responds to the forces of change in the environment.

7.5.11 Contingency or Situational Approach to Management

Another important approach which has arisen because of the inadequacy of the Quantitative, Behavioural and System Approach to management is the Contingency Approach. Pigors and Myers propagated this approach in 1950. Other contributors include Joan Woodward, Tom Burns, G.W. Stalker, Paul Lawrence, Jay Lorsch and James Thompson. They analyzed the relationship between organization and environment. They concluded that managers must keep the functioning of an organization in harmony with the needs of its members and the external forces.

Management is situational and lies in identifying the important variables in a situation. The basic theme of contingency approach is that organizations have to cope with different situations in different ways. There cannot be particular management action which will be suitable for all situations. The management must keep the functioning of an organization in harmony with the needs of its members and the external forces.

According to Kast and Rosenzweig, "The contingency view seeks to understand the interrelationships within and among subsystem as well as between the organization and its environment and to define patterns of relationships or configurations of variables. Contingency views are ultimately directed towards suggesting organizational designs and managerial actions most appropriate for specific situations".

The approach has been used in important subsystems of management like organization, design, leadership, behaviour change and operation. The main features of contingency approach are:

- Management is entirely situational. The application and effectiveness of any techniques is contingent on the situation.
- Management action is contingent on certain action outside the system or subsystem as the case may be.
- Management should, therefore, match or fit its approach to the requirements of the particular situation. To be effective management policies and practices must respond to environmental changes.
- Organizational action should be based on the behaviour of action outside the system so that organization should be integrated with the environment.
- Management should understand that there is no one hard way to manage. They must not consider management principles and techniques universal.

Management Variables may depend on the Environmental Variables

Figure 7.10 A conceptual model of contingency approach.

A general framework for contingent management has been shown in the Figure 7.10. However, it is an abstract depiction of the contingency model. In order to operationalize the contingency approach, managers need to know the alternatives for different situations. It may be operationalized as a 'if then' approach to management. The environment (If) is an independent variable where as management (when) is a dependent variable. In this model, a manager has to take four sequential steps:

- Analyze and understand the situation,
- Examine the applicability or validity of different principles and techniques to the situation at hand,
- Make the right choice by matching the techniques to the situations,
- Implement the choice.

Table 7.8 System Approach vs Contingency Approach

	Systems Approach	*Contingency Approach*
1.	It treats all organizations alike irrespective of their size, cultural settings and dynamics	It treats each organization as a unique entity.
2.	It stresses interactions and interdependencies among systems and sub-systems.	It identifies the exact nature of inter-dependencies and their impact on organizational design and managerial style.
3.	It studies organization at an abstract and philosophical level.	It is more down to earth and action oriented.
4.	It is neutral or non-committal on the validity of classical principles of management.	It firmly rejects the blind application of principles regardless of realities of individual situations.
5.	It stresses upon the synergetic effect of organizations and the external input.	It is related to organization structure and design to the environment.
6.	It is vague and complex.	It is pragmatic and action oriented.

7.6 SUMMARY

The study of organization and management is a must to understand the underlying principles of management. The foregoing analysis reveals that management thought is the outcome of diverse contributions of several management thinkers and practitioners. Each of this approach discussed above is an extension of the previous one.

A composite or synthesis of various contributions made over a period of more than a century is the best management theory. The new trends, developments and challenges in the evolution of management thought and movement that will make new demands on managers in India are listed below:

- *Emerging growth of industry and consequent stiff competition from foreign goods, growth of multinational corporations in the context of new liberalized industrial policy.*
- *Greater consciousness and growth of organizations of consumers.*
- *Growing intervention in trade, industry and commerce by the government. Growth of Trade Union Movement, profoundly influenced by political considerations only.*
- *High cost economy and expansion of the services sector including the social sector, public sector and public utility services.*
- *Increasing demand for participation by subordinates in decision-making process. India is heading towards a business management manned by properly trained and educated persons.*
- *Rapid advancement in the field of technology.*

- *Social responsibility and prevention of environmental pollution have aroused much public attention. This is indeed a great challenge to future and government is required to take necessary action in this regard.*
- *Utilization of information as an input and spread of Management Information System.*

7.7 SELF-ASSESSMENT QUESTIONS

1. What are the some early evidences of management practice? Explain why division of labour and the industrial revolution are important to the study of management?
2. "F.W. Taylor is said to be the father of scientific management and Henry Fayol, the father of principles of management". Critically examine the statement.
3. Write a notes on the evolution of management thought. What are the recent trends in management thoughts?
4. Write short notes on the following:
   (a) "Human Behavioural School of thought is a modified version of Human Relations School of thought". Comment.
   (b) What is the System Approach to management? Explain the salient features of this approach.

8 MANAGERIAL PLANNING

Learning Objective

The main objective of this chapter is to make the learners familiar with the nature and process of planning; why it is necessary to do planning; to understand the merits and demerits of planning; to grasp the principles of planning and to understand the various kinds and levels of plans.

8.1 THE CONCEPT OF PLANNING

An organization can be successful in effective utilization of its human financial and material resources only when its management decides in advance its objectives, and methods of achieving them. Without it purposive and coordinated effort is not possible, and what results are chaos, confusion and wastage of resources. Planning involves determination of objectives of the business, formation of programmes and courses of action for their attainment, development of schedules and timings of action and assignment of responsibilities for their implementation. Planning thus precedes all efforts and action, as it is the plans and programmes that determine the kind of decisions and activities required for the attainment of the desired goals. It lies at the basis of all other managerial functions including organizing, staffing, directing and controlling. In the absence of planning, it will be impossible to decide what activities are required, how they should be combined into jobs and departments, who will be responsible for what kind of decisions and actions, and how various decisions and activities are to be coordinated. And, in the absence of organizing involving the above managerial activities, staffing cannot proceed, and directing cannot be exercised. Planning is also an essential prerequisite for the performance of control function, as it provides criteria for evaluating performance. Planning thus precedes all managerial functions.

Definition of Planning: Planning is the process of deciding in advance what is to be done, who is to do it, how it is to be done and when it is to be done. It is the process of determining a course of action, so as to achieve the desired results. It helps to bridge the gap from where we are, to where we want to go. It makes it possible for things to occur which would not otherwise happen. Planning is a higher order mental process requiring the use of intellectual faculties, imagination, foresight and sound judgement.

According to Koontz, O'Donnell and Weihrich, *"Planning is an intellectually demanding process; it requires the conscious determination of courses of action and the basing of decisions on purpose, knowledge and considered estimates."*

Planning is a process, which involves anticipation of future course of events and deciding the best course of action. It is a process of thinking before doing. To plan is to produce a scheme for future action; to bring about specified results, at specified cost, in a specified period of time. It is deliberate attempt to influence, exploit, bring about, and controls the nature, direction, extent, speed and effects of change. It may even attempt deliberately to create change, remembering always that change (like decision) in any one sector will in the same way affect other sectors. Planning is a deliberate and conscious effort done to formulate the design and orderly sequence actions through which it is expected to reach the objectives. Planning is a systematic attempt to decide a particular course of action for the future; it leads to determination of objectives of the group activity and the steps necessary to achieve them. Thus, it can be said that planning is the selecting and relating of facts and the making and using of assumptions regarding the future in the visualization and formulation of proposed activities believed necessary to achieve desired results.

Planning is thus deciding in advance the future state of business of an enterprise, and the means of attaining it. Its elements are:

1. What will be done – What are the objectives of business in the short and in the long run?
2. What resources will be required – This involves estimation of the available and potential resources, estimation of resources required for the achievement of objectives, and filling the gap between the two, if any.
3. How it will be done – This involves two things: (i) determination of tasks, activities, projects, programmes, etc. required for the attainment of objectives, and (ii) formulation of strategies, policies, procedures, methods, standard and budgets for the above purpose.
4. Who will do it – It involves assignment of responsibilities to various managers relating to contributions they are expected to make for the attainment of enterprise objectives. This is preceded by the breaking down of the total enterprise objectives into segmental objectives, resulting into divisional, departmental, sectional and individual objectives.
5. When it will be done – It involves determination of the timing and sequence, if any, for the performance of various activities and execution of various projects and their parts.

8.2 MYTHS ABOUT PLANNING

There are certain commonly prevalent myths and fallacies about planning. An attempt is being made to highlight some of the important concepts of planning by way of its distinguishing features, so as to clarify the misconceptions:

(i) Planning does no attempt to make future decisions: Planning choosing of the more desirable future alternatives open to a company, is the process so that better decisions may be made. Planning provides a frame of reference within which the present decisions are to be made. At the same time, a plan often leads to additional but related decisions. For example, a college plan to introduce a new degree or diploma, necessitates the need for decisions like what should be the duration of the course leading to the degree or diploma, together with detailed curricula in the specific courses to be included, the system of evaluation of examination, and the necessary practical training, if any, etc.

(ii) **Planning is not just forecasting or making projections:** Forecasts are mere estimates of the future, and indicate what may or may not happen. However, corporate planning goes beyond these forecasts and asks questions like:

(a) Are we in right business?
(b) What are our basic goals and objectives?
(c) When shall our present products become obsolete?
(d) Are our markets expanding or shrinking?
(e) Do we want to merge or go for takeover?

(iii) **Planning is not a static process:** Indeed, plans are obsolete as soon as they are executed, because the environment assumed in their preparation may have already changed. Planning is a continuous process. It involves continuous analysis and adjustments of the plans and even objectives in the context of changing circumstances.

8.3 NATURE AND SCOPE OF PLANNING

The nature of planning can be understood by focusing on its following aspects:

1. **Planning is a Continuous Process:** Planning deals with the future, and future, by its very nature, is uncertain. Although the planner bases his plans on an informed and intelligent estimate of the future, the future events may not turnout to be exactly as predicted. This aspect of planning makes it a continuous process. Plans tend to be a statement of future intentions relating to objectives and means of their attainment. They do not acquire finality because revisions are needed to be made in them in response to changes taking place in the internal as well as external environment of enterprise. Planning should, therefore, be a continuous process and hence no plan is final, it is always subject to a revision.
2. **Planning Concerns all Managers:** It is the responsibility of every manager to set his goals and operating plans. In doing so, he formulates his goals and plans within the framework of the goals and plans of his superior. Thus, planning is not the responsibility of the top management or the staff of planning department only; all those who are responsible for the achievement of results, have an obligation to plan into the future. However, managers at higher levels, being responsible for a relatively larger unit of the enterprise, devote a larger part of their time to planning, and the timespan of their plans also tends to be longer than that of managers at lower levels. It shows that planning acquires greater importance and tends to the longer in the future at higher than at lower management levels.
3. **Plans are Arranged in a Hierarchy:** Plans are first set for the entire organization called the corporate plan. The corporate plan provides the framework for the formulation of

divisional departmental and sectional goals. Each of these organizational components sets its plans laying down the programmes, projects, budgets, resource requirements, etc. The plans of each lower component are aggregated into the plans of successively higher component until the corporate plan integrates all component plans into a composite whole. For example, in the production department, each shop superintendent sets his plans, which are successively integrated into the general foremen's, works manager's and production manager's plans. All departmental plans are then integrated in the corporate plan. Thus, there is a hierarchy of plans comprising the corporate plan, divisional/department plans, sectional plans and individual manger's unit plans.

4. **Planning Commits an Organization into the Future:** Planning commits an organization into the future, as past, present and future is tied in a chain. An organization's objectives, strategies, policies and operating plans affect its future effectiveness, as decisions made and activities undertaken in the present continue to have their impact into the future. Some of the plans affect the near future, while others affect it in the long run. For example, plans for product diversification or production capacity affect a company long into the future, and are not easily reversible, whereas plans relating to the layout of its office locations can be changed with relatively less difficulty in the future. This focuses on the need for better and more careful planning.
5. **Planning is Antithesis of Status Quo:** Planning is undertaken with the conscious purpose of attaining a position for the company that would not be accomplished otherwise. Planning, therefore, implies change in organizational objectives, policies, products, marketing strategies, and so forth. However, planning itself is affected by unforeseen environmental changes. It, therefore, needs examination and re-examination, continual reconsideration of the future, constant searching for more effective methods and improved results.

Planning is thus an all-pervasive, continuous and dynamic process. It imposes on all executives a responsibility to estimate and anticipate the future, prepare the organization to cope with its challenges as well as take advantage of the opportunities created by it, while at the same time, influence tomorrow's events by today's pre-emptive decisions and actions.

8.4 IMPORTANCE OF PLANNING

While planning does not guarantee success in organizational objectives, there is evidence that companies that engaged in formal planning consistently performed better than those with none or limited formal planning and improved their own performance over a period of time. It is very rare for an organization to succeed solely by luck or circumstances. Some of the reasons as to why planning is considered a vital managerial function are given below:

1. **Planning is essential in modern business:** The growing complexity of the modern business with rapid technological changes, dynamic changes in the consumer preferences and growing tough competition necessities orderly operations, not only in the current environment but also in the future environment. Since planning takes a future outlook, it takes into account the possible future developments.

2. **Planning affects performance:** A number of empirical studies provide evidence of organizational success being a function of formal planning, the success being measured by such factors as return on investment, sales volume, growth in earnings per share, and so on. An investigation of firms in various industrial products as machinery, steel, oil, chemicals and drugs revealed that companies that engaged in formal planning consistently performed better than those with no formal planning.
3. **Planning puts focus on objectives:** The effectiveness of formal planning is primarily based upon clarity of objectives. Objectives provide a direction and all planning decisions are directed towards achievement of these objectives. Plans continuously reinforce the importance of these objectives by focusing on them. This ensures maximum utility of managerial time and efforts.
4. **Planning anticipates problems and uncertainties:** A significant aspect of any formal planning process in collection of relevant information for the purpose of forecasting the future as accurately as possible. This would minimize the chances of haphazard decisions. Since the future needs of the organization are anticipated in advance, the proper acquisition and allocation of resources can be planned, thus minimizing wastage and ensuring optimal utility of these resources.
5. **Planning is necessary to facilitate control:** Controlling involves the continual analysis and measurement of actual operations against the established standards. These standards are set in the light of objectives to be achieved. Periodic reviews of operations can determine whether the plans are being implemented correctly. Well-developed plans can aid the process of control in two ways.

   First, the planning process establishes a system of advance warning of possible deviations from the expected performance. Second contribution of planning to the control process is that it provides quantitative data which would make it easier to compare the actual performance in quantitative terms, not only with the expectations of the organization but also with the industry statistics or market forecasts.
6. **Planning helps in the process of decision-making:** Since planning specifies the actions and steps to be taken in order to accomplish organizational objectives, it serves as a basis for decision-making about future activities. It also helps managers to make routine decisions about current activities since the objectives, plans, policies, schedules, and so on are clearly laid down.

8.5 ADVANTAGES AND LIMITATIONS OF PLANNING

The importance of formal planning has already been discussed. A vigorous and detailed planning programme helps managers to be future oriented. It gives the mangers some purpose and direction. A sound blueprint for plans with specific objective and action statements has numerous advantages for the organization, which are as follows:

1. **Focuses Attention on Objectives:** Since all planning is directed towards achieving enterprise objectives, the very act of planning focuses attention on these objectives. Laying down the objectives is the first step in planning. If the objectives are clearly laid down, the execution of plans will also be directed towards these objectives.

2. **Ensures Economical Operation:** Planning involves a lot of mental exercise, which is directed towards achieving efficient operation in the enterprise. It substitutes joint directed effort for uncoordinated piecemeal activity, even flow of work for uneven flow, and deliberate decisions for snap judgement costs. This helps in better utilization of resources and thus minimizing costs.
3. **Reduces Uncertainty:** Planning helps in reducing uncertainties of future because it involves anticipation of future events. Effective planning is the result of deliberate thinking based on facts and figures. It involves forecasting also. Planning gives an opportunity to a business manager to foresee various uncertainties, which may be caused by changes in technology, taste and fashion of the people, etc. Sufficient provision is made in the plans to offset these uncertainties.
4. **Facilitates Control:** Planning helps the managers in performing their function of control. Planning and control are inseparable in the sense that unplanned action cannot be controlled because control involves keeping activities on the predetermined course by rectifying deviations from plans. Planning helps control by furnishing standards of control. It lays down objectives and standards of performance, which are essential for the performance of control function.
5. **Encourages Innovation and Creativity:** Planning is basically the deciding function of management. It helps innovative and creative thinking among the managers because many new ideas come to the mind of a manager when he is planning. It creates a forward-looking attitude among the managers.
6. **Improves Motivation:** A good planning system ensures participation of all managers, which improves their motivation. It improves the motivation of workers also because they know clearly what is expected of them. Moreover, planning serves as a good training device for future managers.
7. **Improves Competitive Strength:** Effective planning gives a competitive edge to the enterprise over other enterprises that do not have planning or have ineffective planning. This is because planning may involve expansion of capacity, changes in work methods, changes in quality, anticipation tastes and fashion of people and technological changes, etc.
8. **Achieves Better Coordination:** Planning secures unity of direction towards the organizational objectives. All the activities are directed towards the common goals. There is an integrated effort throughout the enterprise. It will also help in avoiding duplication of efforts. Thus, there will be better coordination in the organization.

8.6 LIMITATIONS OF PLANNING

Sometimes, planning fails to achieve the expected results. There are many causes of failure of planning in practice. These are discussed below:

1. **Lack of reliable data:** There may be lack of reliable facts and figures over which plans may be based. Planning loses its value if reliable information is not available or if the planner fails to utilize the reliable information. In order to make planning successful, the planner must determine the reliability of facts and figures and must base his plans on reliable information only.

2. **Lack of initiative:** Planning is a forward-looking process. If a manager has a tendency to follow rather than lead, he will not be able to make good plans. Therefore, the planner must take the required initiative. He should be an active planner and should take adequate follow up measure to see that plans are understood and implemented properly.
3. **Costly process:** Planning is time-consuming and expensive process. This may delay action in certain cases. But it is also true that if sufficient time is not given to the planning process, the plans so produced may prove to be unrealistic. Similarly, planning involves costs of gathering and analyzing information and evaluation of various alternatives. If the management is not willing to spend on planning, the results may not be good.
4. **Rigidity in organizational working:** Internal inflexibility in the organization may compel the planners to make rigid plans. This may deter the managers from taking initiative and doing innovative thinking. So the planners must have sufficient discretion and flexibility in the enterprise. They should not always be required to follow the procedures rigidly.
5. **Non-acceptability of change:** Resistance to change is another factor, which puts limits on planning. It is a commonly experienced phenomenon in the business world. Sometimes, planners themselves do not like change and on other occasions they do not think it desirable to bring change as it makes the planning process ineffective.
6. **External limitations:** The effectiveness of planning is sometimes limited because of external factors, which are beyond the control of the planners. External strategies are very difficult to predict. Sudden breakout of war, government control, natural havocs and many other factors are beyond the control of management. This makes the execution of plans very difficult.
7. **Psychological barriers:** Psychological factors also limit the scope of planning. Some people consider present more important than future because present is certain. Such persons are psychologically opposed to planning. But it should not be forgotten that dynamic mangers always look ahead. Long-range well-being of the enterprise cannot be achieved unless proper planning is done for future.

8.7 MEASURES TO OVERCOME LIMITATIONS OF PLANNING

Some people say that planning is a mere ritual in the fast changing environment. This is not a correct assessment on managerial planning. Planning may be associated with certain difficulties such as non-availability of data, lethargy on the part of the planners, rigidity of procedures, resistance to change and changes in external environment. But these problems can be overcome by taking the following steps :

1. **Setting Clear-cut Objectives:** The existence of clear-cut objectives is necessary for efficient planning. Objectives should not only be understandable but rational also. The overall objectives of the enterprise must be the guiding pillars for determining the objectives of various departments. This would help in having coordinated planning in the enterprise.
2. **Management Information System:** An efficient system of management information should be installed so that all relevant facts and figures are made available to the mangers

before they perform the planning function. Availability of right type of information will help in overcoming the problems of complete understanding of the objectives and resistance to change on the part of the subordinates.

3. **Carefully Premising:** The planning premises constitute a framework within which planning is done. They are the assumptions of what is likely to happen in future. Planning always requires some assumptions to be made regarding future happenings. In other words, it is a prerequisite to determine future settings such as marketing, pricing, government policy, tax structure, business cycle, etc. before giving the final shape to the overall business plan. Due weightage should be given to the relevant factors at the time of premising. It may be pointed out that the premises, which may be of strategic significance to one enterprise, may not be of equal significance to another because of size, nature of business, nature of market, etc.
4. **Business Forecasting:** Business is greatly influenced by economic, social, political and international environment. The management must have a mechanism of forecasting changes in such environment. Good forecasts will contribute to the effectiveness of planning.
5. **Dynamic Managers:** The persons concerned with the task of planning should be dynamic in outlook. They must take the required initiative to make business forecasts and develop planning premises. A manager should always keep in mind that planning is looking ahead and he is making plans for future, which is highly uncertain.
6. **Flexibility:** Some element of flexibility must be introduced in the planning process because modern business operates in an environment, which keeps on changing. For achieving effective results, there should always be a scope to make necessary addition, deletion, or alternation in the plans as is demanded by the circumstances.
7. **Availability of Resources:** Determination and evaluation of alternatives should be done in the light of resources available to the management. Alternatives are always present in any decision problem. But their relative plus and minus points are to be evaluated in the light of the resources available. The alternative, which is chosen, should not only be concerned with the objectives of the enterprise, but also capable of being accomplished with the help of the given resources.
8. **Cost-Benefit Analysis:** The planners must undertake cost-benefit analysis to ensure that the benefits of planning are more than the cost involved in it. This necessarily calls for establishing measurable goals, clear insight to the alternative courses of action available, reasonable premising and formulation of derivative plans keeping in view the fact that environment is fast changing.

8.8 BASIC PRINCIPLES OF PLANNING

The important principles of planning are as follows:

1. **Principle of contribution to objective:** The purpose of plans and their components is to develop and facilitate the realization of organizational aims and objectives. Long-range plans should be interwoven with medium-range plans, which, in turn, should be meshed

with short-range ones in order to accomplish organizational objectives more effectively and economically.

2. **Principle of limiting factors:** Planning must take the limiting factors (manpower, money, machines, materials, and management) into account by concentrating on them when developing alternative plans, strategies, policies, procedures and standards.
3. **Principle of pervasiveness of planning:** Planning is found at all levels of management. Strategic planning or long-range planning is related to top management, while intermediate and short-range planning is the concern of middle and operative management respectively.
4. **Principle of navigational change:** This principle requires that managers should periodically check on events and redraw plans to maintain a course towards a desired goal. It is the duty of the navigator to check constantly, whether his ship is following the right direction in the vast ocean to reach the distinction as scheduled. In the same way, a manager should check his plans to ensure that these are processing as required. He should change the direction of his plans if he faces unexpected events. It is useful if plans contain an element of flexibility. It is the responsibility of the manager, to adapt and change the direction of plans, to meet the challenge of constantly changing environment that could not be foreseen.
5. **Principle of flexibility:** Flexibility should be built into organizational plans. Possibility of error in forecasting and decision-making and future uncertainties is the two common factors, which call for flexibility in managerial planning. The principal of flexibility states the management should be able to change an existing plan because of changes in environment, without due cost or delay, so that activities keep moving towards established goals. Thus, an unexpected slump in demand for a product will require change in sales plan as well as production plan. Change in these plans can be introduced, only when these possess the characteristics of flexibility. Adapting plans to suit future uncertainties or changing environment is easier if flexibility is an important consideration while planning.

8.9 CATEGORIES AND LEVELS OF PLANNING

8.9.1 Categories of Planning

Planning can be classified on different bases, which are discussed below:

1. **Strategic and Functional Planning:** In strategic or corporate planning, the top management determines the general objectives of the enterprise and the steps necessary to accomplish them in the light of resources currently available and likely to be available in the future. Functional planning, on the other hand, is planning that covers functional areas like production, marketing, finance and purchasing.
2. **Long-range and short-range planning:** Long-range planning sets long-term goals of the enterprise and then proceeds to formulate specific plans for attaining these goals. It involves an attempt to anticipate, analyze and make decisions about basic problems and issues which have significance reaching well beyond the present operating horizon of the enterprise. Short-range planning, on the other hand, is concerned with the determination

of short-term activities to accomplish long-term objectives. Short-range planning relates to a relatively short period and has to be consistent with the long-range plans. Operational plans are generally related to short periods.

3. **Ad Hoc and Standing Planning:** Ad hoc planning committees may be constituted for certain specific matters, as for instance, for project planning. But standing plans are designed to be used over and over again. They include organizational structure, standard procedures, standard methods, etc.
4. **Administrative and Operational Planning:** Administrative planning is done by the middle level management, which provides the foundation for operative plans. The lower level mangers to put the administrative plans into action, on the other hand, do operative planning.
5. **Physical Planning:** It is concerned with the physical location and arrangement of building and equipment.
6. **Formal and Informal Planning:** Various types of planning discussed above are of formal nature. The management carries them on systematically. They specify in black and white the specific goals and the steps to achieve them. They also facilitate the installation of internal control systems. Informal planning, on the other hand, is mere thinking by some individuals, which may become the basis of formal planning in future.

8.9.2 Lelvels of Planning

In management theory it is usual to consider that there are three basic levels of planning, though in practice there may be more than three levels of management and to an extent there will be some overlapping of planning operations. The three levels of planning are:

1. **Top Level Planning:** Also known as overall or strategic planning, top the top management, i.e., board of directors or governing body, does level planning. It encompasses the long-range objectives and policies of organization and is concerned with corporate results rather than sectional objective. Top level planning is entirely long-range and is inextricably linked with long-term objectives. It might be called the 'what' of planning.
2. **Second Level Planning:** Also known as tactical planning, middle level mangers or department heads does it. It is concerned with 'how' of planning. It deals with deployment of resources to the best advantage. It is concerned mainly, but not exclusively, with long-range planning, but its nature is such that the time spans are usually shorter than those of strategic planning. This is because its attentions are usually devoted to the step-by-step attainment of the organization's main objectives. It is, in fact, oriented to functions and departments rather than to the organization as a whole.
3. **Third Level Planning:** Also known as operational or activity planning, it is the concern of department managers and supervisors. It is confined to putting into effect the tactical or departmental plans. It is usually for short-term and may be revised quite often to be in tune with the tactical planning.

8.10 ESSENTIAL STEPS IN PLANNING

Planning is a process, which embraces a number of steps to be taken. It is an intellectual exercise and a conscious determination of courses of action. Therefore, it requires a serious thought on numerous factors necessary to be considered in making plans. Facts are collected and analyzed and the best out of all is chosen and adopted. The planning process, valid for one organization and for one plan, may not be valid for all other organizations or all types of plans, because various factors that go into planning process may differ from organization to organization or plan to plan. For example, planning process for a large organization may not be the same as for a small organization. The steps generally involved in planning are as follows:

1. **Establishing Verifiable Goals or Set of Goals to be Achieved:** The first step in planning is to determine the enterprise objectives. Upper level or top managers most often set these, usually after a number of possible objectives have been carefully considered. There are many types of objectives managers may select: a desired sales volume or growth rate, the development of a new product or service, or even a more abstract goal such as becoming more active in the community. The type of goal selected will depend on number of factors: the basic mission of the organization, the values its managers hold, and the actual and potential ability of the organization.
2. **Establishing Planning Premises:** The second step in planning is to establish planning premises, i.e., certain assumptions about the future on the basis of which the plan will be intimately formulated. Planning premises are vital to the success of planning as they supply economic conditions, production costs and prices, probable competitive behaviour, capital and material availability, governmental control, and so on.
3. **Deciding the Planning Period:** Once upper-level managers have selected the basic long-term goals and the planning premises, the next task is to decide the period of the plan. Business varies considerably in their planning periods. In some instances, plans are made for a year only while in others they span decades. In each case, however, there is always some logic in selecting a particular time range for planning. Companies generally base their period on a future that can reasonably be anticipated. Other factors, which influence the choice of a period, are as follows: : (a) lead time in development and commercialization of a new product; (b) time required to recover capital investments or the payback period; and (c) length of commitments already made.
4. **Findings Alternative Courses of Action:** The fourth step is planning is to search for and examining alternative courses of action. For instance, technical know-how may be secured by engaging a foreign technician or by training staff abroad. Similarly, products may be sold directly to the consumer by the company's salesmen or through exclusive agencies. There is seldom a plan for which reasonable alternatives do not exit, and quite often an alternative that is not obvious proves to be the best.
5. **Evaluating and Selecting a Course of Action:** Having sought alternative courses, the fifth step is to evaluate them in the light of the premises and goals and to select the best course or courses of action. This is done with the help of quantitative techniques and operations research.
6. **Developing Derivative Plans:** Once the plan has been formulated, its broad goals must

be translated into day-to-day operations of the organization. Middle and lower-level managers must draw up the appropriate plans, programmes and budgets for their subunits. These are described as derivative plans. In developing these derivative plans, lower-level managers take steps similar to those taken by upper-level managers – selecting realistic goals, assessing their subunits' particular strength and weaknesses and analyzing those parts of the environment that can affect them.

7. **Measuring and Controlling the Progress:** Obviously, it is foolish to let a plan run its course without monitoring its progress. Hence, the process of controlling is a critical part of any plan. Managers need to check the progress of their plans so that they can (a) take whatever remedial action is necessary to make the plan work, or (b) change the original plan if it is unrealistic.

8.11 SUMMARY

Planning is deciding in advance what is to be done. It is the determination of a course of action to achieve a desired result. A plan is, then, a projected course of action. All planning involves anticipation of the future course of events and, therefore, bears an element of uncertainty in respect of the future course. Fayol pointed out, "The plan of action is, at one and the same time, the result envisaged, the line of action to be followed, the stages to go through, and methods to use. It is a kind of future picture wherein proximate events are outlined with some distinctness, whilst temoteevents appear progressively less distinct." Planning is a mental process requiring the use of intellectual facilities, imagination, foresight, sound judgement, etc.

Planning involves (a) problem-solving (identification of alternatives), and (b) decision-making (selection from alternatives). In planning, manager searches for the alternative courses open to him and then selects from these alternatives to determine general and specific objectives and detailed means for achieving them. Some writers on management starting with F.W. Taylor, the father of Scientific Management Movement, are of the view that planning should be separated from performance but it is recognized by most people that planning and responsibility for planning cannot be completely separated from managerial performance because all managers plan, whether they are at the top, middle, or bottom of the organization structure. The function of planning incorporates forecasting as it is only through anticipation of future that a manager can decide upon the future course of action.

Planning has a primacy over other management functions and is a pervasive element in organizations. It involves the major activities such as setting objectives, determining policies and making decisions. Planning is a higher order mental process requiring the use of intellectual faculties, imagination, foresight and sound judgement. By planning managers minimize uncertainty and help focus the sight of their organization on its goals.

8.12 SELF-ASSESSMENT QUESTIONS

1. "Managerial planning seeks to achieve a coordinated structure of operations". Comment.
2. "Planning involves a choice between alternative courses of action". Comment briefly.
3. "Without planning an enterprise would soon disintegrate, its actions would be as random

as leaves scampering before an autumn wind, and its employes as confused as ants in an upturned ant hill". Comment

4. Describe in detail the steps involved in the planning process.
5. What do you understand by planning? Define its objectives and assess its importance. What should be done to overcome its limitations?

9

DICISION-MAKING

Learning Objective

The main objective of this chapter is to make the learners familiar with the meaning and importance of decision-making; to understand the characteristics and process of decision-making; to understand the various types of decisions and to learn the techniques of decision-making.

9.1 THE CONCEPT OF DECISION-MAKING

More than anything else, the capability to make sound, timely decisions differentiates a successful manager from a non-successful. It is the responsibility of managers to make high quality decisions that are accepted and executed in a timely fashion. On the face of it the decisions should be cohesive, conjectured, contingent, flexible, improved, influencing, intuitional, non-judgemental, objective, operational one. One of the most important functions of a manager is to take decisions. Whatever a manager does, he does through decision-making. Each managerial decision is concerned with the process of decision-making. It is because of this pervasiveness of decision-making that Professor Herbert Simon has said the process of managing as a process of decision-making. According to him, a post or position cannot be said to be managerial level until and unless the right of decision-making is attached to it. As a matter of act, it is the core of executive activities in a business organization.

Decision-making is a mental process. It is a process of selecting one best alternative for doing a work. Thus, it is a particular course of action chosen by a decision-maker as the most effective alternative for achieving his goals. According to D.E. McFarland, "A decision is an act of choice wherein an executive forms a conclusion about what must be done in a given situation. A decision represents a course of behaviour chosen from a number of possible alternatives". In the words of Haynes and Massie, "A decision is a course of action which is consciously chosen for achieving a desired result".

Hence, decision-making is a typical form of planning. It involves choosing the best alternative among various alternatives, in order to realize certain objectives. A decision represents a judgement, a final word, and resolution of conflicts or a commitment to act in certain manner in the given set of circumstances. It is really a mental exercise which decides what to do. Leaders must be able to reason under the most critical conditions and decide quickly what action to take. If they delay or avoid making a decision, this indecisiveness may create hesitancy, loss of confidence, and confusion within the unit, and may cause the task to fail. Since leaders are frequently faced with unexpected circumstances, it is important to be flexible–leaders must be able to react promptly to each situation. Then, when circumstances dictate a change in plans, prompt reaction builds confidence in them.

9.2 CHARACTERISTICS OF DECISION-MAKING

The essential characteristics of decision-making are given below:

1. It is a process of choosing a course of action from among the alternative courses of action.
2. It is a human process involving to a great extent the application of intellectual abilities.
3. It is the end process preceded by deliberation and reasoning.
4. It is always related to the environment. A manager may take one decision in a particular set of circumstances and another in a different set of circumstances.
5. It involves a time dimension and a time lag.
6. It always has a purpose. Keeping this in view, there may just be a decision not to decide.
7. It involves all actions like defining the problem and probing and analyzing the various alternatives which take place before a final choice is made.

9.3 IMPORTANCE OF DECISION-MAKING

As a leader, you will make decisions involving not only yourself, but the morale and welfare of others. Some decisions, such as when to take a break or where to hold a meeting, are simple decisions which have little effect on others. Other decisions are often more complex and may have a significant impact on many people. Therefore, having a decision-making, problem-solving process can be a helpful tool. Such a process can help you to solve these different types of situations. Within business and the military today, leaders at all levels use some form of a decision-making, problem-solving process. There are several different approaches (or models) for decision-making and problem-solving. We would briefly discuss it in this lesson as well.

It is beyond doubt that the decision-making is an essential part of every function of management. According to Peter F. Drucker, "Whatever a manager does, he does through decision-making". Decision-making lies deeply embedded in the process of management, spreads over all the managerial functions and covers all the areas of the organization. Management and decision-making are bound up and go side by side in every activity performed by manager. Whether knowingly or unknowingly, every manager makes decisions constantly.

Right from the day when the size of the organization used to be very small to the present-day huge or mega size of the organization, the importance of decision-making has been there. The significant difference is that in today's complex organization structure, the decision-making is getting more and more complex. Whatever a manager does, he does through making decisions.

Some of the decisions are of routine and repetitive in nature and it might be that the manager does not realize that he is taking decisions whereas, other decisions which are of strategic nature may require a lot of systematic and scientific analysis. The fact remains that management is always a decision-making process.

The most outstanding quality of successful manager is his/her ability to make sound and effective decisions. A manager has to make up his/her mind quickly on certain matters. It is not correct to say that he has to make spur of the moment decisions all the time. For taking many decisions, he gets enough time for careful fact finding, analysis of alternatives and choice of the best alternative. Decision-making is a human process. When one decides, he chooses a course alternative which he thinks is the best.

Decision-making is a proper blend of thinking, deciding and action. An important executive decision is only one event in the process which requires a succession of activities and routine decisions all along the way. Decisions also have a time dimension and a time lag. A manager takes time to collect facts and to weigh various alternatives. Moreover, after decides, it takes still more time to carry out a decision and, often, it takes longer before he can judge whether the decision was good or bad. It is also very difficult to isolate the effects of any single decision.

9.4 DECISION-MAKING PROCESS

The following procedure should be followed in arriving at a correct decision:

1. **Setting Objectives:** Rational decision-making involves concrete objectives. So the first step in decision-making is to know one's objectives. An objective is an expected outcome of future actions. So before deciding upon the future course of efforts, it is necessary to know beforehand what we are trying to achieve. Exact knowledge of goals and objectives bring purpose in planning and harmony in efforts. Moreover, objectives are the criteria by which final outcome is to be measured.
2. **Defining the Problem:** It is true to a large extent that a problem well defined is half solved. A lot of bad decisions are made because the person making the decision does not have a good grasp of the problem. It is essential for the decision-maker to find and define the problem before he takes any decision.

   Sufficient time and energy should be spent-on defining the problem as it is not always easy to define the problem and to-see the fundamental thing that is causing the trouble and that needs correction. Practically, no problem ever presents itself in a manner that an immediate decision may be taken. It is, therefore, essential to define the problem before any action is taken, otherwise the manager will answer the wrong question rather than the core problem. Clear definition of the problem is very important as the right answer can be found only to a right question.
3. **Analyzing the Problem:** After defining the problem, the next step in decision-making is analyzing it. The problem should be thoroughly analyzed to find out adequate background information and data relating to the situation. The problem should be divided into many sub-problems and each element of the problem must be investigated thoroughly and systematically. There can be a number of factors involved with any problem, some of which are pertinent and others are remote. These pertinent factors should be discussed in depth. It will save time as well as money and efforts.

In order to classify any problem, we require lot of information. So long as the required information is not available, any classification would be misleading. This will also have an adverse impact on the quality of the decision. Trying to analyze without facts is like guessing directions at a crossing without reading the highway signboards. Thus, collection of right type of information is very important in decision-making. It would not be an exaggeration to say that a decision is as good as the information on which it is based. Collection of facts and figures also requires certain decisions on the part of the manager. He must decide what type of information he requires and how he can obtain this.

4. **Developing Alternatives:** After defining and analyzing the problem, the next step in the decision-making process is the development of alternative courses of action. Without resorting to the process of developing alternatives, a manager is likely to be guided by his limited imagination. It is rare for alternatives to be lacking for any course of action. But sometimes a manager assumes that there is only one way of doing a thing. In such a case, what the manager has probably not done is to force himself consider other alternatives. Unless he does so, he cannot reach the decision which is the best possible. From this can be derived a key planning principle which may be termed the principle of alternatives. Alternatives exist for every decision problem. Effective planning involves a search for the alternatives towards the desired goal.

   Once the manager starts developing alternatives, various assumptions come to his mind, which he can bring to the conscious level. Nevertheless, development of alternatives cannot provide a person with the imagination, which he lacks. But most of us have definitely more imagination than we generally use. It should also be noted that development of alternatives is no guarantee of finding the best possible decision, but it certainly helps in weighing one alternative against others and, thus, minimizing uncertainties.

   While developing alternatives, the principle of limiting factor has to be taken care of. A limiting factor is one which stands in the way of accomplishing the desired goal. It is a key factor in decision-making. If such factors are properly identified, manager can confine his search for alternative to those which will overcome the limiting factors. In choosing from among alternatives, the more an individual can recognize those factors which are limiting or critical to the attainment of the desired goal the more clearly and accurately he or she can select the most favourable alternatives.

5. **Selecting the Best Alternative:** After developing alternatives one will have to evaluate all the possible alternatives in order to select best alternative. There are various ways to evaluate alternatives. The most common method is through intuition, i.e., choosing a solution that seems to be good at that time. There is an inherent danger in this process because a manager's intuition may be wrong on several occasions.

   The second way to choose the best alternative is to weigh the consequences of one against those of the others. Peter F. Drucker has laid down four criteria in order to weigh the consequences of various alternatives. They are:

   (a) **Risk:** A manager should weigh the risks of each course of action against the expected gains. As a matter of fact, risks are involved in all the solutions. What matters is the intensity of different types of risks in various solutions.

   (b) **Economy of Effort:** The best manager is one who can mobilize the resources for the achievement of results with the minimum of efforts. The decision to be chosen should ensure the maximum possible economy of efforts, money and time.

(c) Situation or Timing: The choice of a course of an action will depend upon the situation prevailing at a particular point of time. If the situation has great urgency, the preferable course of action is one that alarms the organization that something important is happening. If a long and consistent effort is needed, a slow start gathers momentum approach may be preferable.

(d) Limitation of Resources: In choosing among the alternatives, primary attention must be given to those factors that are limiting or strategic to the decision involved. The search for limiting factors in decision-making should be a never ending process. Discovery of the limiting factor lies at the basis of selection from the alternatives and hence of planning and decision-making. There are three bases which should be followed for selection of alternatives and these are experience, experimentation and research and analysis which are discussed below:

In making a choice, a manager is influenced to a great extent by his past experience. He can give more reliance to past experience in case of routine decisions; but in case of strategic decisions, he should not rely fully on his past experience to reach at a rational decision.

Under experimentation, the manager tests the solution under actual or simulated conditions. This approach has proved to be of considerable help in many cases in test marketing of a new product. But it is not always possible to put this technique into practice, because it is very expensive.

Research and analysis is considered to be the most effective technique of selecting among alternatives, where a major decision is involved. It involves a search for relationships among the more critical variables, constraints and premises that bear upon the goal sought.

6. **Implementing the Decision:** The choice of an alternative will not serve any purpose if it is not put into practice. The manager is not only concerned with taking a decision, but also with its implementation. He should try to ensure that systematic steps are taken to implement the decision. The main problem which the manager may face at the implementation stage is the resistance by the subordinates who are affected by the decision. If the manager is unable to overcome this resistance, the energy and efforts consumed in decision-making will go waste. In order to make the decision acceptable, it is necessary for the manager to make the people understand what the decision involves, what is expected to them and what they should expect from the management.

In order to make the subordinates committed to the decision, it is essential that they should be allowed to participate in the decision-making process. The managers who discuss problems with their subordinates and give them opportunities to ask questions and make suggestions find more support for their decisions than the managers who don't let the subordinates participate. The area where the subordinates should participate is the development of alternatives. They should be encouraged to suggest alternatives. This may bring to surface certain alternatives which may not be thought of by the manager. Moreover, they will feel attached to the decision. At the same time, there is also a danger that a group decision may be poorer than the one man decision. Group participation does not necessarily improve the quality of the decision, but sometimes impairs it. Someone has described group decision like a train in which every passenger has a brake. It has also been pointed out that all employees are unable to participate in decision-making. Nevertheless, it is desirable if a manager consults his subordinates while making decision.

7. **Follow-up the Decisions:** Kennetth H. Killer, has emphatically written in his book that it is always better to check the results after putting the decision into practice. He has given reasons for following up of decisions and they are as follows:
   (i) If the decision is a good one, one will know what to do if faced with the same problem again.
   (ii) If the decision is a bad one, one will know what not to do the next time.
   (iii) If the decision is bad and one follows-up soon enough, corrective action may still be possible.

In order to achieve proper follow-up, the management should devise an efficient system of feedback information. This information will be very useful in taking the corrective measures and in taking right decisions in the future.

9.5 TYPES OF DECISIONS

Decisions have been classified by various authorities in various ways. The main types of decisions are as follows:

1. **Programmed and non-programmed decisions:** Professor Herbert Simon has classified all managerial decisions as programmed and non-programmed decisions. He has utilized computer terminology in classifying decisions. The programmed decisions are the routine and repetitive decisions for which the organization has developed specific processes. Thus, they involve no extraordinary judgement, analysis and authority. They are basically devised so that the problem may not be treated as a unique case each time it arises.

   On the other hand, the non-programmed decisions are the one-shot, ill-structured, novel policy decisions that are handled by general problem-solving processes. Thus, they are of extraordinary nature and require a thorough study of the problem, its in-depth analysis and the solving the problem. They are basically non-repetitive in nature and may be called as strategic decisions.
2. **Basic and routine decisions:** Professor George Katona has made a distinction between basic decision and routine decisions. Routine decisions are of repetitive nature and they involve the application of familiar principles to a situation. Basic or genuine decisions are those which require a good deal of deliberation on new principles through conscious thought process, plant location, distribution are some examples of basic decisions.
3. **Policy and operative decisions:** Policy decisions are important decisions and they involve a change in the procedure, planning or strategy of the organization. Thus, they are of a fundamental character affecting the whole business. Such decisions are taken by the top management. On the contrary, operating decisions are those which are taken by lower levels of management for the purpose of executing policy decisions. They are generally concerned with the routine type of work, hence unimportant for the top management.

They mostly relate to the decision-makers own work and behaviour while policy decision influences the work and behaviour of subordinates.

4. **Individual and group decisions:** Individual decisions are those decisions which are made by one individual–whether owner of the business or by a top executive. On the other hand, group decisions are the decisions taken by a group of managers–board, team, committee or a subcommittee. In India, individual decision-making is still very common because a large number of businesses are small and owned by a single individual. But in joint stock Company's group decisions are common. There are both merits and demerits of each type of decision.

9.6 TOOLS OR TECHNIQUES OF DECISION-MAKING

The following are some of the important decision-making techniques:

(a) Qualitative Techniques
(b) Quantitative Techniques

9.6.1 Qualitative-Decision-Making Techniques

There is a great importance of generating a reasonable number of alternatives, so that one can decide upon the better quality items and make better decision.

Generating a reasonable number of alternatives is very useful for solving any complex problem. There are following means of generating the alternatives:

(a) Brainstorming
(b) Synectics, and
(c) Nominal Grouping

(a) Brainstorming: This technique was developed by Alex F. Osborn, and is one of the oldest and best known techniques for stimulating the creative thinking. This is carried out in a group where members are presented with a problem and are asked to develop as many as potential solutions as possible. The member of the group may be experts, may be from other organizations but the members should be around six to eight. The duration of the session may be around 30 minutes to 55 minutes. The premise of brainstorming is that when people interact in a free and exhibited atmosphere, they will generate creative ideas. The idea generated by one person acts as a stimulus for generating idea by others. This generation of ideas is a contagious and creates an atmosphere of free discussion and spontaneous thinking. The major objective of this exercise is to produce as many deals as possible, so that there is greater likelihood of identifying a best solution.

The important rules of brainstorming are as given below:

(i) Criticism is prohibited.
(ii) Freewheeling is always welcome.
(iii) Quantity is desirable.
(iv) Combination and improvements are sought.

One session of brainstorming exercise generates around 50 to 150 ideas. Brainstorming is very useful in research, advertising, management, armed forces, governmental and non-governmental agencies.

Limitations of Brainstorming

The limitations of brainstorming are given below:

(i) It is not very effective when a problem is very complex and vague.
(ii) It is time-consuming.
(iii) It is very costly.
(iv) It produces superficial solutions.

(b) Synectics: This technique was developed by William J.J. Gordon. It is recently formalized tool of creative thinking. The word Synectics is a Greek word, meaning the fitting together of diverse elements. The basic purpose of synectics is to stimulate novel and even bizarre alternatives through the joining together of distinct and apparently irrelevant ideas.

The selection of members to synectics group is based on their background and training. The experienced leader states the problem for the group to consider, group reacts to the problem stated on the basis of their understanding and convictions. When the nature of the problem is thoroughly reviewed and analyzed, group proceeds to offer potential solutions. The leader has to structure the problem and he/she can use various methods to involve the preconscious mind, like role-playing, use of analogies, paradoxes, metaphors and other thought provoking exercises. This helps in generation of alternatives. The technical expert assists the group in evaluating the feasibility of ideas. It also suffers from some limitations of brainstorming. This is more useful and appropriate for solving complex and technical problems.

(c) Nominal Grouping: This was developed by Andre Dellbecq and Andrew Van de Ven. Nominal group is very effective in situations where a high degree of innovation and idea generation is required. It is highly structured and follows following stages:

Stage-1: Around seven to ten participants with different background and training are selected, familiarized with a selected problem like what alternatives are available for achieving a set of objective.

Stage-2: Each member is asked to prepare a list of ideas in response to the identified problem, individually for achieving a set of objective.

Stage-3: After ten minutes, the member shares ideas, one at a time, in a round-robin manner. The group facilitator records the ideas on a blackboard or flip chart for all to see.

Stage-4: Each group member then openly discusses and evaluates each recorded ideas. At this point, it may be rewarded, combined, added or deleted.

Stage-5: Each member votes ranking the ideas privately. Following a brief discussion of the vote, a final secret ballot is conducted. The group's preference is the arithmetical outcome of the individual voter, these are followed by concluding meeting.

9.6.2 Quantitative Techniques

There are a number of quantitative techniques for decision-making that are discussed below:

(a) Stochastic Methods: In many management decisions, the probability of the occurrence of an event can be assumed to be known, even when a particular outcome is unpredictable. Under these conditions of risk, stochastic methods will be useful. Actually, stochastic methods merely systematize the thinking about assumptions, facts and goals that is involved in decisions under conditions of risk.

Three steps are basic to formalizing the factors to be considered in a decision involving probabilities:

(i) The decision-maker should first lay out, in tabular form, all the possible actions that seem reasonable to consider and all the possible outcomes of these actions.

(ii) The decision-maker must then state in quantitative form a probability distribution, projecting chances of each outcome that might result from each act. In this step, it may only be possible to assign probabilities that are reasonable estimates. The key to this step is to state explicitly the various probabilities that might be attached to each act-outcome situation.

(iii) Finally, the decision-maker must use some quantitative yardstick of value (usually rupees) that measures the value of each outcome. It is then possible to calculate an average of the outcome-values weighted by the assigned probabilities; the result is called the expected monetary value.

To illustrate the use of these steps, suppose that a Store Manager of Ramson Limited must decide whether to stock Brand A or Brand B. Either brand can be stocked but not both. If A is stocked and it is a success. The manager can make Rs. 200/-, but if it is a failure, there can be a loss of Rs. 500/-. If Brand B is stocked and it is a success, the manager can make Rs. 400/-, but if it is a failure, there can be a loss of Rs. 300/-. Which brand should be stocked? Without some idea of the probabilities of success and failure of these brands, the manager's thinking cannot be quantified. But assume that the manager's feelings about the probabilities of each outcome are shown in Table 9.1.

Table 9.1 Stochastic Table

Probability of	*Brand A*	*Brand B*
Success	0.80	0.50
Failure	0.20	0.50

(b) Payoff Table: The Store Manager can present the above information in tabular form, showing the conditional values for each strategy (choice of brand) under each state of nature (the combination of uncontrollable factors, such as demand, that determine success or failure). The simplest payoff table as the first step in stating strategies and possible outcomes is shown in Table 9.2.

With the information in Table 9.1 the Store Manager can use subjective estimates of risks assumed above and multiply the conditional values by their probability of occurrence. This calculation will result in expected values. Table 9.2 shows the expected value pay off, using the assumed payoff in Table 9.1 and the above feelings about the probability of success for Brands A and B.

Table 9.2 Payoff Table

	State of Nature (Demand)	
Strategy	*Success*	*Failure*
Stock Brand A	*Rs. 200/-*	*Rs. 500/-*
Stock Brand B	*Rs. 400/-*	*Rs. 300/-*

From the expected value payoff Table 9.3, the store manager can determine the total expected value for each strategy by obtaining the sum of the expected values for each state of nature. If Brand A is stocked, the total expected value is Rs. 60/- (Rs. 160-100); if Brand B is stocked, the total expected value is Rs. 50/- (Rs. 200-150); therefore, under the assumptions in this case, the store manager would decide to stock Brand A, because its total expected value is Rs. 10/- more than if Brand B were stocked. Obviously, if the total expected value for stocking each brand had been negative, the manager would decide not to stock either, because there would probably be a loss under either strategy.

Table 9.3 Expected Value Payoff Table

	State of Nature	
Strategy	*Success*	*Failure*
Stock Brand A	Rs. 160/-	Rs. 100/-
Stock Brand B	Rs. 200/-	Rs. 150/-

(c) Simulation Techniques: Often, when a management problem is too complex to be answered by series of mathematical equations, it is possible to simulate the probable outcomes before taking action. In this way, the manager may rapidly try out on paper (or with a computer) the results of proposed actions before the actions are taken. By trying out several policies, it is possible to determine which one has the best chance of providing the optimum result.

The idea of randomness represented by random numbers is at the heart of simulation. Random numbers are numbers, each of which has the same chance of being selected. Tables of random numbers are now readily available.

One type of simulation is used in queuing problems, one in which the need for personnel or equipment varies over a time period but the determination of the peak demands cannot be estimated because the occurrence is random or due to chance. With simulation, the manager can try out available strategies as they might result in different outcomes, depending upon probabilities from a table of random numbers. For example, the store manager may wish to determine the work schedules for three sales people to serve customers and to decide whether to add a fourth salesperson. The problem arises from not knowing when customers may appear in the store. Experience may indicate the probabilities that at some hours of the day all three sales people will be serving customers, but that at other times the sales people will be idle. In simulating the traffic for a day, the manager may wish to use subjective probabilities for those times in which there are no data from experience, but even if there are no experience data, it is still possible to simulate an activity by using random numbers.

In practice, simulation is carried out by electronic computers. In seconds, a computer can perform thousands of simulation trails and at the same time compile all costs. At the present time, inventory decision rules are commonly tested on computers. The executive specifies such things as reorder points and order quantity and the computer determines the costs of that policy over the same period of time. After many different policies are put through the series of simulation runs, the best policy can be selected.

(d) **Breakeven Analysis:** The simplest approach for showing the relationship of revenue to cost is the breakeven chart. Revenue and cost can be studied by directing attention to : (i) total revenue and total cost, (ii) average revenue and average cost per unit of output, and (iii) changes in revenue and cost. Breakeven analysis directs attention to the first of these. Breakeven analysis implies that at some point in the operations total revenue equals total cost–the breakeven point. This analysis can be handled algebraically or graphically; however, in all cases, the first step is to classify costs into at least two types–fixed and variable.

The distinction between total fixed and total variable costs stresses that only variable costs will increase with an increase in the production rate of output. However, it should be clear that when average cost per unit is considered, fixed cost per unit of output will decline as volume increases–the constant fixed costs are spread over more units of output. Variable costs per unit of output may increase proportionally with an increase in output , or they may decrease per unit of output (for example, if quantity discounts are significant), or they may increase per unit of output (if the quantity of materials is very short and thus price increases as output increases). In most industries, variable costs per unit can reasonably be assumed to be constant, and thus total variable costs will appear as a straight line (linear) when plotted against various quantities of output. The cost-volume-profit relationship can best be visualized by charting the variables. A breakeven chart is graphical representation of the relationship between costs and revenue at a given time.

The simplest breakeven chart makes use of straight lines that represent revenue, variable costs, and total costs. The construction of this chart requires only that the cost and revenue be known at two points (volumes of output), because only two points are required to draw a straight line. The point at the Y intercept (left-hand side of chart) is given by definition: Revenue line will start at zero volume; variable costs also will start at zero volume; fixed costs will be given level on the Y axis because, by definition, they would continue even if there were no production. Cost and revenue data at an actual volume level provide the basis for the necessary second point. All other points on the lines are the results of the assumption of linear relationships for both revenue and costs.

9.7 SUMMARY

Having a logical thought process helps ensure that you will not neglect key factors that could influence the problem, and ultimately your decision. In fact, you should always apply a clear, logical thought process to all leadership situations that you encounter. The seven-step process is an excellent tool that can guide you in solving problems and making those sound and timely decisions. The seven steps are: 1. Identify (recognize/define) the problem. 2. Gather information (facts/assumptions). 3. Develop courses of action (solutions). 4. Analyze and compare courses of action (alternatives/solutions). 5. Make a decision; select the best course of action (solution). 6. Make a plan. 7. Implement the plan (assess the results).

In this chapter, an attempt has been made to make to understand the importance of decision-making in today's context. Decision-making has been defined and various characteristics of decision-making have also been discussed. The unit dimensional types decision, i.e., Organizational vs. Personal, Routine vs. Strategic, Policy vs. Operating, Programmed vs. non-Programmed and Individual vs. Group Decision are discussed. Three phases of decision-making deal with identification, evaluation and selection of alternative to a problem. The decision-making under different conditions has been discussed. Economic man model suggests a logical process of taking decisions, particularly when problem is routine, mechanistic and programmed or when decisions are taken under certainty of conditions.

The decision-making process in a group and its difference from individuals decision making is also discussed. The various qualitative techniques: Brainstorming, Synectics, Nominal Grouping; Quantitative Techniques : Stochastic Method, Payoff Table, Decision Tree, Simulation Technique, Break-even Analysis are discussed.

9.8 SELF-ASSESSMENT QUESTIONS

1. "Decision-making is the essence of management". Comment.
2. "Decision-making is the primary task of the manager". Discuss and explain the scientific process of decision-making.
3. Explain the quantitative techniques of decision-making.
4. Explain the various steps in the process of decision-making. Which one is most important and why?
5. Explain the various types of decisions.
6. What are the principles of decision-making? Design the role of employees' participation in decision-making.
7. What is decision-making? What are its basic characteristics?

10

ORGANIZING

Learning Objective

The main objective of this chapter is to know the meaning, characteristics and nature of organization; to explain steps in designing effective organization; to analyze formal and informal organization; and to understand the nature of different types of organizations.

10.1 INTRODUCTION

Without efficient organization, no management can perform its functions smoothly. Sound organization contributes greatly to the continuity and success of the enterprise. Once Andrew Carnagie, an American industrialist said, "Take away our factories, take away our trade, our avenues of transportation, our money. Leave nothing but our organization, and in four years we shall have re-established ourselves". That shows the significance of managerial skills and organization. However, good organization structure does not by itself produce good performance – just as good constitution does not guarantee great presidents or good laws a moral society. But a poor organization structure makes good performance impossible, no matter how good the individuals may be. The right organizational structure is the necessary foundation; without it the best performance in all other areas of management will be ineffectual and frustrated.

10.2 MEANING AND CHARACTERISTICS OF ORGANIZATION

The term 'organization' connotes different meanings to different people. Many writers have attempted to state the nature, characteristics and principles of organization in their own may. For instance, to the sociologists organization means a study of the interactions of the people, classes, or the hierarchy of an enterprise; to the psychologists organization means an attempt to explain, predict and influence behaviour of individuals in an enterprise; to a top level executive it may mean the weaving together the functional components in the best possible combination so that an enterprise can achieve its goals. The word 'organization' is also used widely to connote a group of people and the structure of relationships.

Some important definitions of organization are given below:

> *"It is grouping of activities necessary to attain enterprise objectives and the assignment of each grouping to a manager with authority necessary to supervise it".*
>
> Koontz and O'Donnel
>
> *"The process of identifying and grouping the work to be performed, defining and delegating responsibility and authority and establishing relationship for the purpose of enabling people to work more effectively together in accomplishing objects".*
>
> Louis A. Allen
>
> *"The structure and process by which a cooperative group of human beings allocates its tasks among its members, identifies relationship, and integrates its activities towards common objectives".*
>
> Joseph L. Massive

From the above definitions, it is clear that organizing is the process of determining the total activities to achieve a given objective, grouping and assigning of activities to individuals, delegating them authority necessary to perform the activities assigned and establishing authority relationship among different positions in the organization.

An analysis of the above definitions reveals the following characteristics of an organization:

1. It is a group of individuals which may be large or small.
2. The group in the organization works under the executive leadership.
3. It is a machine or mechanism of management.
4. It has some directing authority or power which controls the concerted efforts of the group.
5. The division of labour, power and responsibilities are deliberately planned.
6. It implies a structure of duties and responsibilities.
7. It is established for accomplishment of common objectives.
8. It is a functional concept.

Sound organization brings about the following advantages:

1. Facilitates attainment of the objectives of the enterprise.
2. Facilitates optimum use of resources and new technological development.
3. Facilitates growth and diversification.
4. Stimulates creativity and innovation.
5. Facilities effective communication.
6. Encourages better relations between the labour and the management.
7. Increase employee satisfaction and decreases employee turnover.

10.3 NATURE OF ORGANIZATION

The term 'organization' is used in two different senses. In the first sense, it is used to denote the process of organizing. In the second sense, it is used to denote the results of that process, namely, the organizational structure. So, the nature of organization can be viewed in two ways:

(a) Organization as a process; and
(b) Organization as a structure or framework of relationship.

Organization as a process: As a process, organization is an executive function. It becomes a managerial function involving the following activities:

(i) Determining activities necessary for the accomplishment of the business objective.
(ii) Grouping of interrelated activities.
(iii) Assigning duties to persons with requisite competence,
(iv) Delegating authority, and
(v) Coordinating the efforts of different persons and groups.

When we consider organization as a process, it becomes the function of every manager. Organizing is a continuous process and goes on throughout the life time of an enterprise. Whenever there is a change in the circumstances or material change in situation, new type of activities spring up. So, there is a need for constant review and reassignment of duties. Right persons have to be recruited and necessary training has to be imparted to enable them to be competent to handle the jobs.

The process of organization thus, involves dividing the work into rational way and interpreting the activities with work situation and personnel. It also represents humanistic view of the enterprise since it is the people which are uppermost in the process of integration of activities. Continuous review and adjustment makes this dynamic as well.

Organization as a structure or framework of relationships: As structure, organization is a network of internal authority, responsibility relationships. It is the framework of relationship of persons, operating at various levels, to accomplish common objectives. An organization structure is a systematic combination of people, functions and physical facilities. It constitutes a formal structure with definite authority and clear responsibility. It has to be first designed for determining the channel of communication and flow of authority and responsibility. For this, analysis of different types has to be done. Peter F. Drucker suggests following three types of analysis:

(i) Activities analysis,
(ii) Decision analysis, and
(iii) Relations analysis.

A hierarchy has to be built-up, i.e., a hierarchy of positions with clearly defined authority and responsibility. The accountability of each functionary has to be specified. Therefore, it has to be put into practice. In a way, organization can be called a system as well.

The main emphasis here is on relationships or structure rather than on persons. The structure once built is not liable to change so soon. This concept of organization is, thus, a static one. It is also called classical concept. Organization charts are prepared depicting the relationship of different persons.

In an organizational structure, both formal and informal organizations take shape. The former is a pre-planned one and defined by the executive action. The latter is a spontaneous formation, being laid down by the common sentiments, interactions and other interrelated attributes of the people in the organization. Both formal and informal organizations, thus, have structure.

10.4 ORGANIZING PROCESS

The managerial function of organizing may be called as the 'process of organizing'. When the objectives have been set and policies framed, the necessary infrastructure of organization has to be built up. The concentration goes to activities and functions. These form 'the building blocks' of the organizational structure. There are no such rules as to which will lead to the best organizational structure. But the following steps can be of great help in the designing a suitable structure, which will laid in achieving enterprise objectives:

1. **Clear definition of objectives:** The first step in developing an organizational structure is to lay down its objectives in very clear terms. This will help in determining the type, stability and basic characteristics of the organization. In fact, organization activities are detailed in terms of objective to be achieved.
2. **Determining activities:** In order to achieve the objectives of the enterprise, certain activities are necessary. The activities will depend upon the nature and size of the enterprise. For example, a manufacturing concern will have production, marketing and other activities. There is no production activity in retail establishment. Each major activity is divided into smaller parts. For instance, production activity may be further divided into purchasing of materials, plant layout, quality control, repairs and maintenance, production research, etc.
3. **Assigning duties:** The individual groups of activities are then allotted to different individuals according to their ability and aptitude. The responsibility of every individual should be defined clearly to avoid duplication and overlapping of efforts. Each person is given a specific job suited to him and he is made responsible for its execution. Right man is put in the right job.
4. **Delegating authority:** Every individual is given the authority necessary to perform the assigned activity effectively. By authority, we mean power to take decisions, issue instructions, guiding the subordinates, supervise and control them. Authority delegated to a person should commensurate with his responsibility. An individual cannot perform his job without the necessary authority or power. Authority flows from top to bottom and responsibility from bottom to top.
5. **Coordinating activities:** The activities and efforts of different individuals are then synchronized. Such coordination is necessary to ensure effective performance of specialized functions. Interrelationship between different job and individuals are clearly defined so that everybody knows from whom he has to take orders and to whom he is answerable.
6. **Providing physical facilities and right environment:** The success of an organization depends upon the provision of proper physical facilities and right environment. Whereas it is important to have right persons on right jobs, it is equally important to have right working environment. This is necessary for the smooth running and the prosperity of the enterprise.
7. **Establishment of structural relationship for overall control:** It is very essential to establish well-defined clear-cut structural relationships among individuals and groups. This

will ensure overall control over the working of all departments and their coordinated direction towards the achievements of predetermined goals of business.

It is thus clear from the foregoing analysis that organization provides a structural framework of duties and responsibilities. It not only establishes authority relationship but also provides a system of communication. The various processes of organization explained above are technically performed through (a) departmentation, (b) delegation of authority and fixation of responsibilities, and (c) decentralization of authority subject to central control through centralization of decision-making.

10.5 OBJECTIVES OF ORGANIZING

Every economic activity which is deliberately done has some purpose. When a group of people assemble without any pre-planned aim or purpose, it is not an organization but just a mob. But when, for instance they are invited to participate in a conference, an element of purpose has been introduced. A purpose refers to commitment to desired future. Objectives and purposes, generally, are interchangeable terms.

Why should business enterprise organize itself? The answer to this question brings out its objectives. Objectives of a business organization are distinguished from the objectives of other social organizations. To put it more precisely, the nature of an organization (i.e., political, social, religious or economic) can only be known by studying its objectives.

The following may be, generally speaking, the objectives (or purpose) of organizing business:

1. **Effective management of the enterprise:** Effective management largely depends upon effective organization. It is the effective organization which ensures proper balance between authority and responsibility. It achieves a clear line of communication, and defines the areas of work. It is the organization which allows the top management to concentrate on overall planning and supervision, leaving the routine work for the lower levels of administration. It saves the entire enterprise from adhocism, overlappings and inefficiency.
2. **Maximum production at minimum cost:** The activities are allotted according to the principle of division of labour. The efficient system of organization encourages every employee to make his best contribution in raising output. The increase in output and control of wasteful expenditure helps to decrease the cost of production. The profitability of the concern will also go up.
3. **Sustained growth and diversification:** A business enterprise should be a growing organism. With the passage of time, an enterprise must expand its activities. It should also aim at diversification of products and markets.

   A static business soon grows stale and get out of run. It should grow from a small-scale concern to a medium-scale one and from a medium-scale concern to large-scale one. Organization plays an important role in this respect. Execution of policies in organized manner builds the necessary capacity and confidence in undertaking bigger activities.
4. **Cooperation of employees:** The organizational structure will succeed only if employees cooperate in the work. The employees learn working in closer cooperation of others. The management introduces various incentive schemes and gives monetary and other benefits to the employees, so that they work in a team spirit.

5. **Discharging social responsibility:** Maximizing of profits, no doubt, is the motive of every business. Without profit, no business can exist. But business is a part and parcel of society at large. It cannot survive long by exploiting consumers and society. It has to serve the society by providing it with goods of good quality at reasonable prices. It has to ensure smooth supply of goods as per the needs to consumers. The service motto cannot be realized without a well-knit organization structure. So, to discharge social obligation is an important objective of building up sound organization.

The purpose of sound organization is:

(i) to establish an activity-authority environment in which people can perform most effectively.

(ii) to make group action efficient and effective by providing centres for decision-making and a system of communication to effectively coordinate individual efforts towards group-goals.

(iii) to create relationships which minimize friction, focus on the objective, closely define the responsibilities of all parts and facilitate the attainment of the objective.

(iv) to subdivide the management process by which plans are translated into actions so as to make management most effective.

Thus, to sum up we can say that organization is a process by which the manager brings order out of chaos, removes conflicts between people over work or responsibility, and establishes an environment suitable for teamwork.

10.6 PRINCIPLES OF ORGANIZATION

Effective and efficient working of any organization depends on how the managerial function of organization is being performed. The function of organization can be carried effectively with the help of undermentioned principles:

(i) Attention to objectives: An organization is a mechanism to accomplish certain goals or objectives. The objectives of an organization play an important role in determining the type of structure which should be developed. Clearly defined objectives facilitate grouping of activities, delegation of authority and consequently effective coordination.

(ii) Authority and responsibility: Authority should commensurate with responsibility. While assigning the responsibility, authority should also be assigned. If authority is not granted, the subordinates cannot discharge their responsibility properly.

(iii) Continuity: The form of organization structure should be such which is able to serve the enterprise to attain its objectives for a long period of time.

(iv) Coordination: The principal of coordination underlines that there should be proper liaison and cooperation between different departments and units of work. Unity of efforts for the accomplishment of desired objectives is the main aim of organization. This can be achieved through the principle of coordination.

(v) Decentralization: This principle is of great significance to big organizations. Decentralization implies selective dispersal of authority to help departments and units to run effectively and efficiently without frequent interruptions from the top of the enterprise. It requires very careful selection of what decisions to push down into the organization, of what to hold at or near the top specific policy making to guide the decision-making, selection and training of people and adequate control. Decentralization, as such, embraces all areas of management and evidently is of overwhelming significance in organization structure.

(vi) Departmentation: Departmentation is the process of grouping activities into units for purposes of administration. In other words, it denotes grouping of related jobs and activities without violating the principle of homogeneity over which an executive has authority to exercise and assert. The main advantages of departmentation are that it enables individual executive to manage his subordinates effectively since a manageable number of persons are brought under the direct supervision of individual executive.

(vii) Division of work: While structuring organization, division of work, at the very outset, should be considered as the basis of efficiency. It is an established fact that group of individuals can secure better results by having division of work. Therefore, while designing the organization, we should aim at making suitable grouping of activities. This is also called the principle of specialization.

(viii) Efficiency: The organization should be able to attain the predetermined objectives at the minimum cost. It is done so; it will satisfy the test of efficiency. From the point of view of an individual, a good organization should provide the maximum work satisfaction. Similarly, from the social point of view, an organization will be efficient when it contributes the maximum towards the welfare of the society.

(ix) Flexibility: While designing the organization it should be kept in mind that organizational structure should not be regarded as static. Every organization is a living entity in a living environment which is fast changing. As such there must be sufficient room for changing and modifying the structure in the light of environmental changes so that the ultimate objective of the organization is achieved.

(x) Management by exception: It is a fundamental principle that makes any organization effective in its true sense. This principle signifies that problems of unusual nature only should be referred upward and decided by higher level executives in the managerial hierarchy, whereas the routine problems should be passed on to lower levels and resolved there. Application of this principle as such, certainly requires adhering to the principle of delegation of authority. The principle of exception is thus of significant practical utility and applies to all levels in the organization structure.

(xi) Proper balance: It is important to keep various segment or departments of an organization in balance. The problem of balance basically arises when an activity or a department is further divided and subdivided into smaller segments. The problems of balancing also crops up with the growing of any organization in its size and functioning.

(xii) Scalar principle: Scalar chain refers to the vertical placement of superiors starting from the chief executive at the top through the middle level to the supervisory level at the bottom. Proper scalar chain or line of command is prerequisite for effective organization.

(xiii) Span of management: Span of management also refers to span of control signifying the number of subordinates reporting directly to any executive. It is an established fact that larger the number of subordinates reporting directly to the executive, the more difficult it tends to be for him to supervise and coordinate them effectively. This important principle of management should also be kept in mind.

(xiv) Unity of command: Organization structure should also be designed in such a way that there exists unity of command in the sense that a single leader is the ultimate source of authority. This facilitates consistency in directing, coordinating and controlling to achieve the end objectives.

(xv) Unity of direction: This means that each group of activities having the same objectives should have one plan and one head. There should be one plan or programme for each segment of work which is to be carried under the control and supervision of one head or superior. If different plans or policies are followed in one department by the subordinates, confusion is bound to occur.

10.7 ADVANTAGES OF ORGANIZATION

The primary duty of management is to achieve the objectives of the enterprise. The objectives may be social, economic, political or religious. Proper organization of men, materials, money and equipment is necessary. Organization is the mechanism through which management directs, coordinates and controls the business. A sound organization offers the following advantages, which summarizes its importance:

1. **Adoption of new technology:** A properly designed and well-balanced organization permits prompt adoption and optimum use of technological improvements. It has the capacity to absorb changes in the environment of business and to provide a suitable reaction to such changes. A good organization helps in the development of new and improved means of doing things.
2. **Better human relations:** Human beings involved in an organization are only dynamic element of organization. A dedicated and satisfied group of persons proves an asset to any establishment. An organization, built on sound principles, helps harmony in human relations. With properly defined authority, responsibility and accountability, different persons enjoy job-satisfaction. Organization consists of human beings and their satisfaction helps in improving human relations.
3. **Check on corrupt practices:** A weak and unsound organization is source of corruption and inefficiencies. Well organized, well-defined, disciplined and sound organizations boost the morale and motivation of workers. It develops a feeling of involvement, belongingness, devotion, honesty and sincerity among employees. It prevents corruption, inefficiencies and wastage in an enterprise.
4. **Coordination:** Organization facilitates coordination of diverse activities. Different functions are welded together to accomplish the desired objectives. Clear lines of authority and responsibility between various positions; ensure mutual cooperation and harmony in the enterprise. A good organization enables people to work with team spirit.
5. **Creativity, initiative and innovation:** A good organization encourages initiative and creative thinking. Employees are motivated to break new grounds and try unconventional methods. A sound organization offers the scope for recognition of merit followed by financial incentives to the personnel showing creativity.

6. **Enhancement of managerial efficiency:** A sound organization brings a proper coordination among various factors of production and leads to their optimum utilization. It avoids confusion, duplication and delays in work. It motivates the worker by proper division of work and labour. It reduces the work load of executives by delegation of authority.
7. **Growth, expansion and diversification:** Organization provides the framework within which an enterprise can expand and grow. Through organization, management can multiply its strength. In a good organization, the money and effort spent on different activities are in proportion to their contributions. It is through proper organization setup that many firms have grown from humble beginning to a giant size.
8. **Proper weightage to all activities:** A sound organization divides the entire enterprise into different departments, sections and sub-sections according to the functions to be performed by them. Each function of an enterprise has got its own importance. Emphasis is given according to their relative importance. Funds and manpower is allocated to their relative importance.
9. **Specialization:** A sound organization structure provides the benefits of specialization. Various activities are allocated between different individuals according to their qualifications, experience and aptitude. It increases their efficiency. Systematic organization of activities helps to secure economics and to minimize costs.
10. **Training and development:** By delegating authority to lower levels, training and development of future executives is made possible. A good organization puts 'right man at the right job' and provide them right training and managerial development programmes. By appointing employees in different department assigning them different jobs, their training needs can be ascertained.

Thus, organization is the foundation of management. Sound organization is an indispensable mean for efficient management and better business performance. It not only facilitates efficient administration but also encourages growth and diversification. It provides for optimum use of new technology, stimulates innovation and creativity.

10.8 FORMAL AND INFORMATION ORGANIZATION

Formal organization refers to the structure of relationships deliberately built up by the top management to realize the objectives. In this form instructions, responsibility, authority, accountability, lines of command, and positions and authority are clearly defined and declared. Each person is aware of his duties and authority. Every subordinate is expected to obey his supervisor in the formal chain of command. Each individual is fitted in the organization like a cog in the machine. It is designed after careful identification, classification and assignment of business activities. So, it is conscious creation of relationships.

Informal organization refers to the network of personal and social relationships which arise spontaneously when people working together interact on personal whims, likes and prejudices. Such relations are not created by the top management and they are not recognized formally. The informal groups sometimes run parallel to the formal ones. Informal relations are not portrayed on organization charts and manuals. An informal organization provides an opportunity to workers to come close to each other, develop a feeling of cooperation and coordination among themselves.

10.8.1 Difference Between Formal and Informal Organizations

The difference between formal and informal organizations can be enumerated briefly as below:

1. **Authority:** Formal authority is attached to a position and it flows from top to bottom. Informal authority is attached to a person and it flows either downwards or horizontally.
2. **Basis:** A formal organization is based upon rules and procedures, while an informal organization is based upon attitudes and emotions of the people. It depends on informal, social contacts between people working and associating with one another.
3. **Depiction:** Formal organization can be shown in an organization chart or a manual. But an informal organization cannot be depicted in the chart or manual of the enterprise.
4. **Emphasis:** In a formal organization, the main emphasis is placed on authority and functions. In an informal organization the stress is on people and their relationships.
5. **Existence:** A formal organizations exists independently of the informal groups that are formed within it. But an informal organization exists within the framework of a formal structure.
6. **Formation:** Formal organization is deliberately created by management. It is the result of a conscious and deliberate effort involving delegation of authority. On the other hand, informal organization arises spontaneously and no conscious efforts are made to create it. It takes place on the basis of relationships, caste, culture, occupations and on personal interests, etc. No delegation of authority is essential in informal organization.
7. **Nature:** A formal organization is stable and predictable and it cannot be changed according to the whims or fancies of people. But an informal organization is neither stable nor predictable.
8. **Rationality:** A formal organization operates on logic rather than on sentiments or emotions. All activities follow a predetermined course. As an association between like-minded people, an informal organization has little rationality behind it. In an informal organization, activities are influenced by emotions and sentiments of its members.
9. **Set up:** A formal organization is a system of well-defined relationships with a definite authority assigned to every individual. It follows predetermined lines of communication. On the contrary, an informal organization has no definite form and there are no definite rules as to who is to report to whom. Even a low-placed employee may have an informal relationship with an officer far above him in the formal hierarchy.

10.9 FORMS OF ORGANIZATION STRUCTURE

Organization requires the creation of structural relationship among different departments and the individuals working there for the accomplishment of desired goals. The establishment of formal relationships among the individuals working in the organization is very important to make clear the lines of authority in the organization and to coordinate the efforts of different individuals in an efficient manner. In order to organize the efforts of individuals, any of the following types of organization structures may be set up: (i) Line organization, (ii) Line and staff organization, (iii) Functional organization, (iv) Committee organization, (v) Project organization, and (vi) Matrix organization. The nature merits and demerits of line organization, and line and staff organization are discussed as under:

10.9.1 Line Organization

The line organization represents the structure in a direct vertical relationship through which authority flows. It is the simplest from of organization structure and is also known as scalar or military organization. Under this, the line of authority flows vertically downward from top to bottom throughout the organization. The quantum of authority is highest at the top and reduces at each successive level down the hierarchy. Every person in the organization is in the direct chain of command as shown in Figure 10.1.

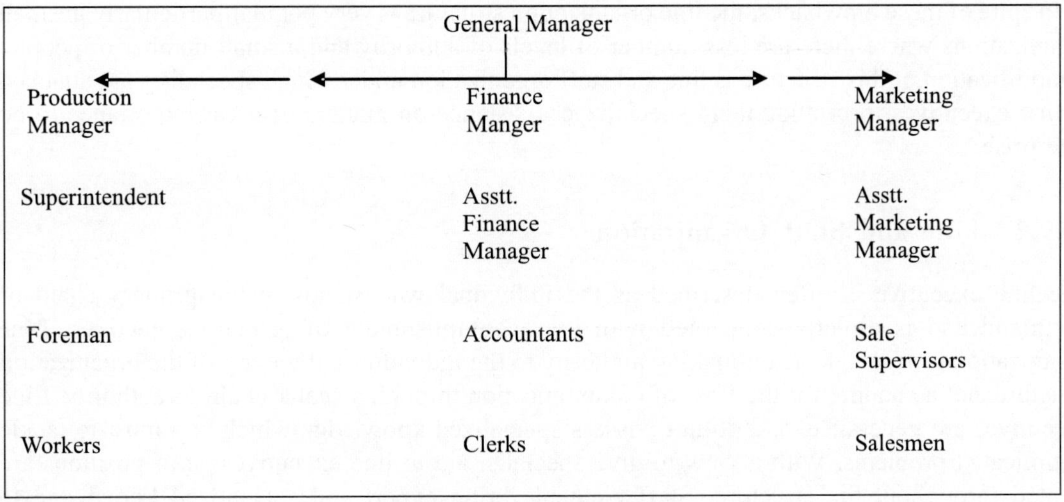

Figure 10.1 Line organization.

In line organization, the line of authority consists of an uninterrupted series of authority steps and forms a hierarchical arrangement. The line authority not only becomes the avenue of command to operating personnel but also provides the channel of communication, coordination and accountability in enterprise.

Advantages of Line Organization

(i) If facilitates unity of command and thus conforms to the scalar principle of organization.
(ii) It ensures excellent discipline in the enterprise because every individual knows to whom he is responsible.
(iii) It facilitates prompt decision-making because there is definite authority at every level. An executive cannot shift his decision-making to others, nor can the blame be shifted.

(iv) It is very easy to establish line organization and it can be easily understood by the employees.
(v) There is clear-cut identification of authority and responsibility relationship. Employees are fully aware of the boundaries of their jobs.

Disadvantages of Line Organization

(i) Line organization is not suitable to big organizations because it does not provide specialists in the structure. Many jobs require specialized knowledge to perform them.
(ii) There is concentration of authority at the top. If the top executives are not capable, the enterprise will not be successful.
(iii) There is partially no communication from bottom upwards because of concentration of authority at the higher levels. If superiors take a wrong decision, it would be carried out without anybody having the courage to point out its deficiencies.
(iv) With growth, the line organization makes the superiors too overloaded with work. If the executive try to keep up with every activity, they are bogged down in myriad details and are unable to pay proper attention to each one. It will hamper their effectiveness.

In spite of these drawbacks, the line organization structure is very popular particularly in small organizations where there are less number of levels of authority and a small number of people. A modification of this structure is line and staff organization under which specialists are attached to line executives to provide them specialized assistance on matters of great importance to be enterprise.

10.9.2 Line and Staff Organization

The line executive is often described as the individual who stands in the primary chain of command and is directly concerned with the accomplishment of primary objectives. Line organization provides decision-making authority to the individuals at the top of the organization structure and a channel for the flow of communication through a scalar chain of authority. Line executives are generalists and do not possess specialized knowledge which is a must to tackle complicated problems. With a view to give specialist aid to line executives, staff positions are created throughout the structure. Staff elements bring expert and specialized knowledge to provide advice to line managers so that they may discharge their responsibilities successfully.

In line and staff organization, the line authority remains the same as it does in the line organization. Authority flows from top to bottom. The main difference is that specialists are attached to line managers to advise them on important matters. These specialists stand ready with their speciality to serve line men as and when their services are called for to collect information and to give help which will enable the line officials to carry out their activities better. The staff officers do not have any power of command in the organization as they are employed to provide expert advice to the line officers. Staff means a supporting function intended to help the line manager. In most organizations, the use of staff can be traced to the need for help in handling details, gathering data for decision-making and offering advice on specific managerial problems. Staff investigates and supplies information and recommendations to managers who make decisions. Specialized staff positions are created to give counsel and assistance in each specialized field of effort as shown in Figure 10.2.

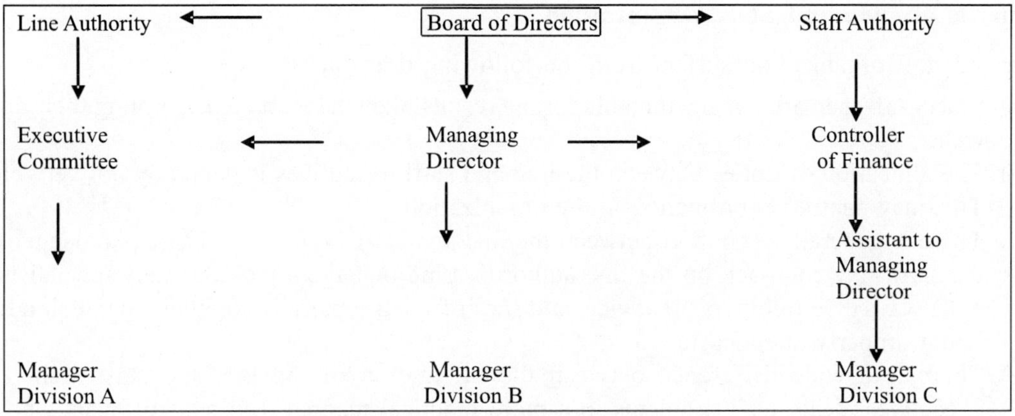

Figure 10.2 Line and staff organization.

Line and staff structure has gained popularity because certain problems of management have become very complex and, in order to deal with them, expert knowledge is necessary which can be provided by the staff officers. For instance, personnel department is established as staff department to advise the line executives on personnel matters. Similarly, finance, law and public relations departments may be set up to advice on problems related to finance and accounting, law and public relations.

The staff officers do not have any power of command in the organization as they are employed to provide advice to the line officers. In most organizations, the use of staff can be traced to the need for help in handing details, gathering data and offering advice on specific managerial problems.

Advantages of Line and Staff Organization

(i) **Better decisions**. Staff specialists help the line executives in taking better decisions by providing them with adequate information of right type at the right moment and expert advice.

(ii) **Flexibility**. Line and staff organization is more flexible as compared to the line organization. General staff can be employed to help line managers at various levels.

(iii) **Proper weightage**. Many problems that are ignored or poorly handled in the line organization can be properly covered in the line and staff organization by the use of staff specialists.

(iv) **Reduction of burden**. Staff specialists relieve the line managers of the botheration of concentrating on specialized functions like accounting, selection and training, public relations, etc.

(v) **Specialized knowledge**. Line managers get the benefit of specialized knowledge of staff specialists at various levels.

(vi) **Unity of command**. Under this system, the experts provide special guidance without giving orders. It is the line manager who only has got the right to give orders. The result is that the enterprises takes advantage of functional organization while maintaining the unity of command, i.e., one subordinate receiving orders from one boss only.

Demerits of Line and Staff Organization

Line and staff organization suffers from the following drawbacks:

(i) Since staff men are not accountable for the results, they may not be performing their duties well.
(ii) The allocation of duties between the line and staff executives is generally not very clear. This may hamper coordination in the organization.
(iii) There is generally a conflict between the line and staff executives. There is a danger that the staff may encroach on the line authority. Line managers feel that staff specialists do not always give right type of advice, and staff officials generally complain that their advice is not properly attended to.
(iv) There is a wide difference between the orientation of the line and staff men. Line executives' deals with problems in a more practical manner. But staff officials who are specialists in their fields tend to be more theoretical.

Superiority of Line and Staff Organization over Line Organization

Line and staff organization is considered better than the line organization because of the following reasons:

(i) Staff makes available expert advice to line executives. This is necessary to deal with complex problems of management. For instance, personnel department is established as a staff department to advise the top executives and other line executives on personnel matters.
(ii) Better decisions are ensured in line and staff organization as compared to a simple line organization.
(iii) Line and staff structure is more suitable for large organizations as expert advice is always available. The line managers can make use of the knowledge of staff specialists to deal with complicated problems. Therefore, line and staff organization is certainly better than line organization.

10.10 SUMMARY

The word organization has two common meanings. The first meaning refers to the process of organizing. The second meaning signifies the institution or group which comes into existence as a result of organizing. The organizing process involves a number of steps, viz., consideration of objectives, grouping of activities into departments, deciding which departments will be treated line and which will be related staff, determining the levels at which various types of decisions are to be made, determining the span of supervision and setting up a coordination mechanism. There are a number of principles of organizing, which should be remembered in the process of organizing.

10.11 SELF-ASSESSMENT QUESTIONS

1. "Organization is an important tool to achieve organizational objectives," Comment.
2. Define organization and discuss its characteristics.

3. Discuss the nature and importance of organization.
4. Explain the meaning of organization and state its principles.
5. What are the important steps in the process of organization?
6. What do you mean by (a) line organization and (b) line and staff organization? Discuss their respective merits and demerits.
7. What do you understand by informal organization? How does it differ from a formal organization?

11 AUTHORITY AND RESPONSIBILITY

Learning Objective

The main objective of this chapter is to understand meaning and sources of authority; to distinguish between delegation and decentralization; to appreciate advantages and disadvantages of decentralization; to understand relationship between Authority and Responsibility; to distinguish between Responsibility and Accountability.

11.1 THE CONCEPT OF AUTHORITY

Authority is the key to managerial functions. Authority is a legal power which is possessed by a person from his superior officers and with the help of which he succeeds in getting the things done by his subordinates. If the managers do not possess required authority, they will not be able to perform their duties properly. A manager is in a position to influence his subordinates only by the use of his authority. It is the authority which enables him to discharge the important functions of planning, coordination, motivation and controlling, etc. in an enterprise. If proper authority is not vested in him, he cannot perform these functions in the required manner and he cannot be held responsible for all these functions in the absence of proper authorities. It is only the authority by virtue of which he dominates his subordinates and gets work done by them.

- "Authority is the right to give order and the power to exact obedience".

  – Henry Fayol

- "Authority is the power to command, to act or not to act in a manner deemed by the possessor of the authority to further enterprise or departmental performance".

  – Koontz and O'Donnell

While concluding the meaning of authority it can be said that authority in ordinary sense of the term is nothing more than a legal right. It empowers an individual to take decisions. He is given a right to command and to exercise control over those who are responsible for the execution of policies and programmes of the enterprise. For decisions taken the authorized person is held responsible and is made answerable to his superiors and the organization as a whole.

11.2 FACTORS FOR SUCCESSFUL USE OF AUTHORITY

For the successful use of authority following factors may be taken into consideration:

1. **Favourable Atmosphere:** For the implementation of authority, favourable atmosphere must be created in the enterprise so that sweet human relations may be established in the enterprise.
2. **Interest in the work:** A very important condition of the successful use of authority is that the employees must have an interest in the work for which they are responsible. If they are not interested in their work, it may be very difficult for the higher officers to implement their authority.
3. **Justified Behaviour:** The second important use for successful implementation of authority is the justified behaviour of the officers towards their subordinates. They must feel and treat all the employees on an equal ground. If they do not do so, the employees may not contribute their efforts towards the attainment of objectives of enterprise.
4. **Mutual Cooperation and Faith:** There must be mutual cooperation and mutual trust between officers and employees of the enterprise for the successful use of authority.
5. **Respect to Superiors:** There must be an atmosphere in the enterprise in which the employees pay their best regards to their bosses. If they do not have a feeling of regard for them, they may not obey their orders.

11.3 SOURCES OF AUTHORITY

There are three different schools of thought about the sources of authority which are discussed below:

11.3.1 Acceptance Theory

This theory states that authority is the power that is accepted by others. Formal authority is reduced to nominal authority if it is not accepted by the subordinates. The subordinates accept the authority if the advantages to be derived by its acceptance exceed the disadvantages resulting from its refusal. The subordinates give obedience to the managers because they visualize the following advantages:

(a) Receipt of financial incentives.
(b) Contribution in attaining the objectives of the enterprise.
(c) Fulfilment of responsibilities.
(d) Appreciation from colleagues.
(e) Setting of an example for others.
(f) Responsibility to leadership of superior
(g) Moral obligation because of regard for old age, experience, competence, etc.

According to acceptance theory, authority flows from bottom to top. A manager has authority if he gets obedience from the subordinates. Subordinates obey the manager because of the fear of losing financial rewards. This theory emphasizes sanctions that a manager can use and overlooks the influence of social institutions like trade unions.

11.3.2 Competence Theory

The supporters of this view assert that an individual derives authority because of his personal qualities and technical competence. Many persons derive informal authority because of their competence. For instance, a person possesses expert knowledge in a particular subject. People will go to him for guidance in that matter even though he has got no formal authority.

11.3.3 Formal Authority Theory

According to this theory, all authority originates in the formal structure of an organization. The ultimate authority in a joint stock company lies with the shareholders. Shareholders entrust the management of the company to the board of directors and delegate to it most of their authority. The board of directors delegates authority to the chief executive and chief executive in turn to the departmental managers, and so on. Every manager or executive possesses authority because of his organizational position and this authority is known as formal authority. Authority conferred by law is also regarded as formal authority. Subordinates accept the formal authority of a manager because of his position in the organization. The subordinates are aware of the fact that if they disregard the formal authority they will be punished according to the rules and regulations of the company. The formal authority theory further states that the superiors have the right to delegate their authority. Thus, formal authority always flows from top to bottom.

11.4 MEANING AND SOURCES OF POWER

Power may be defined as "the ability to exert influence. If a person has power it means that he is able to change the attitude of other individuals".

Power is a method of operating in order to influence the behaviour of others. It is the power politics within the organization that gives rise to power centres in the organization. The power-centres need not necessarily be located at the position of higher authority. Nobody wants to lose power because power can be used in desirable or undesirable ways.

In any organization for sound organizational stability, power and right to do things must be equated, when power and authority for a given person or position are roughly equated, we may call the situations as "Legitimate Power".

11.4.1 Sources of Powers

If we study the origin and sources of power, we cannot forget the name of John French and Berhram Raven. They have written that there are five sources of power which are found at all levels of the organization. They are as follows:

(i) Corrective Power: It is based on the influencer's ability to punish the influence for not carrying out orders or for not meeting requirements.

(ii) Expert Power: This power is based on belief that the influencer has some relevant expertise or special knowledge that the influence does not have. For example, a doctor has expert power on his patients.

(iii) Legitimate Power: The power corresponds to the term authority. It exists when an influencer acknowledge that the influencer is lawfully entitled to exert influence. In this the influence has an obligation to accept this power.

(iv) Referent Power: It is based on the influencer's, desire to identify with or imitate the influence. For example, a manager will have referent power over the subordinates if they are motivated to emulate his work habits.

(v) Reward Power: This power is based on the influencer having the ability to reward the influence for carrying out orders.

In having the study of power the role of the influence in accepting or rejecting the attempted influence is very important. It must be noted that each of the five power bases is potentially inherent in a manager's position and his activities.

11.4.2 Difference between 'Authority' and 'Power'

If we study from close in practice the terms 'Authority' and 'Power' are generally used interchangeably but there is a clear-cut difference between these two words and they are as follows:

1. **Authority a Downward Concept:** Authority is a downward flowing concept; whereas power flows in all directions.
2. **Authority Increases:** It has been observed that authority increases as soon as one goes up in the organizational hierarchy, but it need not necessary be accompanied by more power.
3. **Authority Relationships:** In practice, authority relationships are modified by power politics in the organization. Some individuals may have more power and less authority or more authority and less power. It is the operating mechanism of the organization which is relevant for studying organizational behaviour.
4. **Delegation of Authority:** Authority can be delegated to the lower levels in the organization. The lower we go down the lesser is the authority.
   (i) In actual practice – the power centres may be located at the power levels in the organization. Therefore, one cannot have an idea of power centres in an organization by merely looking at its organization chart.
5. **Positional and Legitimate:** Authority is always positional and legitimate and is conferred on the position. But power is not institutional, rather it is personal. It is acquired by people in various ways and then exercised upon others. It is acquired through political means or by having certain personal attributes.
6. **Right to Command:** Authority is the right to command whereas power is the ability or power to command.

7. **Right to Exercise:** Authority usually resides in the position in the organization, but power is exercised by the person. Authority includes the right to exercise which have been institutionalized.

11.5 DELEGATION OF AUTHORITY AND ITS METHODS

Delegation means devolution of authority on subordinates to make them to perform the assigned duties or tasks. It is that part of the process of organization by which managers make it possible for others to share the work of accomplishing organizational objectives. Delegation consists of granting authority or the right to decision-making in certain defined areas and charging the subordinate with responsibility for carrying through the assigned tasks.

Delegation refers to the assignment of work to others and confer them the requisite authority to accomplish the job assigned.

1. In the words of F.G. Moore – "Delegation means assigning work to others and gives them authority to do it."
2. Louis A. Allen has said – "Delegation is the dynamics of management, it is the process a manager follows in dividing the work assigned to him so that he performs that part which only he, because of his unique organizational placement, can perform effectively and so that he can get others to help him with what remains".
3. E.F.L. Brech has also said – "Delegation is a process of sharing a few or all of the four elements of the management process, i.e., command, planning, coordination and control". He goes on to say that the delegation is not a question of issuing instructions but is a bringing down of the executive's responsibility and transmission of part or all of it to other persons.

Since one person constitutes only one man power, so F.G. Moore has once said that – "Delegation, therefore, is necessary for enlarging his capacity by asking trusted subordinates to share his burden." Without delegation says S.S. Chatterjee, "The very existence of organization is shattered at once. If there are no duties to be divided and no authorities to be shared in the enterprise, the existence of an organization structure is nullified and becomes absurd. Management of that organization becomes impossible without delegation." For this reason activities are to be integrated, coordinated and unity of purpose to be achieved, this necessitates effective delegation.

11.5.1 Methods of Delegation

In a big manufacturing concern the following may be the methods of delegation of authority to ensure better result, unified direction and command and effective delegation:

1. **Administrative Delegation –** When a few of the administrative functions are delegated to subordinate staff it is called administrative delegation. These functions are generally of routine nature, e.g., to maintain discipline, to supervise the work, to recommend for the reward or punishment, etc.

2. **Functional Delegation** – When the enterprise is organized on the basis of functional organization, the delegation of authority is also done on the functional basis. All the heads are given to manage their departments according to their skill, knowledge and experience of course, they are accountable to the chief executives.
3. **Geographical Delegation** – When the work of enterprise is located at different distant places it is not possible for an executive to mange the whole affairs single handly. He then proceeds to delegate his authority to those who are posted at the places where physically he cannot be present round the year. This is known as geographical method of delegating the authority.
4. **Technical Delegation** – This method of delegation of authority is based on technical knowledge and skill. Here the authority is delegated in order to get the advantages of expert and experienced hands and their technical skill.

11.6 ELEMENTS OF DELEGATION AND ITS TYPES

The elements of delegation of authority involve three steps:

1. **Accountability:** The last step in delegation is concerned with creating an obligation to carry out duty or responsibility and render an account of the results achieved through the use of delegated authority. The subordinate must be held accountable for the exercise of authority granted to him. By accepting the duties and authority, a subordinate becomes responsible to his superior.
2. **Authority:** The superior grants authority to the subordinate to carry out the assigned task or duty. This may include right to use resources, spend money, engage people, etc.
3. **Responsibility:** The superior entrusts some responsibility or duty to a subordinate.

- **Authority:** Authority is the sum of the rights entrusted to an individual to make possible the performance of the work delegated. It includes such rights or powers as that spending money, of using certain kinds of quantities of materials, of hiring and firing people. Allen talks of authority of knowledge, authority of position and legal authority. Authority of knowledge according to him is possessed generally by the staff specialists appointed by the company. The consultants more often influence the action of persons in line by virtue of the knowledge possessed by them. Similarly, some persons acquire authority by virtue of their position. For instance, a person close to the person having line authority wields considerable authority. A Private Secretary to Managing Director or even a Staff Assistant may have no formal power and authority. Legal authority is the authority which is entrusted to a person by the law of the land. A company, for instance, is a legal person which enjoys several rights under the Companies Act. The organizations are built on authority relationships between their members. Authority is a building force in an organization and is the key to the executive job. An executive cannot get things done through others without the right to command them.
- **Responsibility:** Responsibility represents the work or duties assigned to a person by virtue of his position in the organization. It refers to the mental and physical activities which must be performed to carry out the task or duty. That means every person who

performs some kind of mental or physical activities as an assigned task has responsibility. In order to enable the subordinates perform his responsibility well, the superior must clearly tell the former as to what is expected of him. In other words, the delegator must determine clearly the task or duty that is assigned to the delegatee. The duty must be expressed either in terms of function or in terms of objectives. If a subordinate is asked to control the operations of a machine, the duty is in terms of function. But if he is asked to produce a certain number of pieces of a product, the duty is in terms of target or objective. Determination of duties in terms of objective will enable the subordinate to know by what standards his performance will be evaluated.

According to Alwin Brown, responsibility is capable of being understood in two senses. In one, it denotes the definition of a part or role to be performed in administration. In the other, it denotes the obligation for the performance of that part. Two meanings are reciprocal. In most circumstances, there is so little difference between the concept of the part and the concept of the obligation that it is more useful to view them as inseparably-related aspects of the same concept, and to refer to them by single term. Taken in this sense, many authors have held that responsibility cannot be delegated. But authority and responsibility are coextensive; and responsibility or duty can be delegated within the framework of authority. In fact, it is the accountability which cannot be delegated. Therefore, it is essential to make a distinction between responsibility and accountability.

Responsibility or duty implies the task assigned to a person to be completed in accordance with the standards laid down. It is his superior who has entrusted this task to him. He should not find any difficulty in expecting it because his superior knows his plus and minus points at work. He would not assign a task which the subordinate is unable to complete. In fact, he has divided and subdivided the task pertaining to this division in such a manner that each one of his subordinates gets the task of his choice. Hence, there is no ground for the subordinate to object the duty assigned to him by his superior unless the superior has acted deliberately in an indicative manner. If he does so, there are other ways to remedy the situation.

Whenever the superior assigns any task to his subordinate, it is implied that he has delegated his responsibility. In this process, though he may hold his subordinate accountable for the task delegated to him, but he continues to be accountable to his own boss on the ground that accountability can never be delegated.

The extent of authority delegated should be commensurate with the responsibilities or duties assigned. In other words, there must be a balance between responsibility and authority. However, in practice, it is very difficult to achieve a balance between responsibility and authority.

According to McGregor, the realities of business place most managers in situations where they cannot effectively control everything that affects the results they are attempting to achieve. Uncontrollable factors include unexpected changes in consumer preferences, action of labour unions, government legislations and the fluctuations of business cycles. The recognition of these problems does not reduce or destroy the utility of this concept. If a manager is abreast of the time, he will make allowance for the unforeseen events outside the control of the subordinate. Many factors prevent a superior to delegate sufficient authority. The risk of losing control is an important factor. Real or presumed non-availability of qualified subordinates, lack of delegating skills and enhancement of one's indispensability are the other factors which cause an imbalance of responsibility and authority. An effective manager is willing to delegate authority as needed to accomplish the desired objectives.

Responsibility cannot be delegated or transferred. The superior can delegate to subordinate the authority to perform and accomplish a specific job. But he cannot delegate responsibility in the sense that once duties are assigned, he is relieved for his responsibility for them. This delegation of tasks does not absolve the superior from his own responsibility for effective performance of his subordinate. In other words, we can say that responsibility is divided into two parts at the time of delegation: (a) operating responsibility; and (b) ultimate responsibility. The subordinate assumes only the operating responsibility for the task. The superior retains ultimate responsibility for getting the job done. If the subordinate fails to perform the job (operating responsibility), the superior is held responsible for this failure (ultimate responsibility). To explain that the ultimate responsibility cannot be shifted or reduced by assigning duties to another. Newman cites the example of a person borrowing money from the bank and then realigning it to his son. This transaction with his son in no way reduces his own obligation and responsibility to repay the money to the bank.

Responsibility may be specific or continuing. It is specific when on being discharged by a subordinate it does not arise again. Thus, a consultant's responsibility is specific. It ceases when the assignment is completed. The responsibility of a foreman is, however, of a continuing nature.

- **Accountability:** Accountability is a logical derivative of authority. When a subordinate is given an assignment and is granted the necessary authority to complete it, the final phase in basic organization relationship is holding the subordinate responsible for results. In other words, the subordinate undertakes an obligation to complete the assignment by the fair use of authority and account for the discharge of responsibility assigned.

Accountability is the obligation to carry out responsibility and exercise authority in terms of performance standards established by the superior. Creation of accountability is the process of justifying the granting of authority to a subordinate for the accomplishment of a particular task. In order to make this process effective, the standards of performance should be determined before assigning a task and should be accepted by the subordinate. An important principle of management governing this basic relationship is that of single accountability. An individual should be answerable to only one immediate superior and no more.

The extent of accountability depends upon the extent of delegation of authority and responsibility. A person cannot be held answerable for the acts not assigned to him by his superior. For instance, if the production manager is given responsibility and authority to produce a specified quantity of certain product and the personnel department is given responsibility and authority for the development of workforce, the production manager cannot be held accountable for the development of workforce. "Accountability is, by the act which creates it, of the same quality and weight as the accompanying responsibility and authority".

- **Accountability cannot be delegated:** Though it is incurred as a result of assignment of duty and conferring of authority, accountability in itself cannot be delegated. The diligent cannot abdicate responsibility. He remains accountable to his superior for that which the latter has delegated to him. Since accountability cannot be delegated, the accountability of persons higher in the hierarchy for the acts of subordinates is unconditional.

11.6.1 Types of Delegation

The important kinds of delegation of authority are as follows:

1. General and Specific Delegation

(i) General Delegation: It is that delegation in which the authority is given to perform general managerial functions, like planning, organizing, directing, etc. The subordinate managers perform these functions and enjoy the authority required to carry out these responsibilities. The Chief Executive exercises over all control and guides the subordinates from time-to-time.

(ii) The Specific Delegation: Specific delegation relates to a particular function or an assigned task. The authority delegated to the production manager for carrying out this function will be a specific delegation. Various departmental managers get specific authority to undertake their department duties.

2. Formal or Informal Delegation

(i) Formal Delegation: Formal delegation has been considered as a part of organizational structure. Whenever a task is assigned to a person, the required authority is also given to him. This delegation is a part of the normal functioning of the organization. Every person is automatically given authority as per his duties. When production manager gets powers to increase production then it is formal delegation of authority.

(ii) Informal Delegation: This delegation does not arise due to position but it arises according to the circumstances of the case. A person may undertake a particular task not because he has been assigned it but because it is necessary to do his normal work.

3. Written or Unwritten Delegation

(i) Written Delegation: Written delegation is normally given through letters, instructions, circulars, etc. Whatever has been delegated it must be in writing.

(ii) Unwritten Delegation: Unwritten delegation is given to the person concerned not in any particular way but through conventions, customs and usages the other party has to do work accordingly.

4. Downward or Upward Delegation

(i) Downwards Delegation: Downwards delegation is a common type of delegation and is used in every type of the working concern. This delegation has been considered as a superior's delegation of authority to his immediate subordinate.

(ii) Upward Delegation: This type of delegation takes place when a subordinate assigns some of his tasks to his superiors. This is an uncommon type of delegation and its instances are very rare.

11.7 PRINCIPLES OF DELEGATION

The following principles may be considered as essential for effective delegation of authority:

1. **Ensure unity of command:** This is one of the common principles of organization advocated by Henry Fayol which stresses that subordinates should have only one boss to whom he should be accountable, to avoid confusion and friction. Of course, in practice, it is not possible to follow this principle.
2. **Establish a climate of confidence:** The subordinate to whom authority is delegated must generally feel free from fear and have a feeling of confidence that delegation will not result in punishment but is an opportunity for his own self-development and growth.
3. **Establish a strong belief in delegation:** For delegation to be successful, the man who delegates must himself be convinced of the need and benefits of delegation. He must also be willing to allow his subordinates to make mistakes although he can be strict if the same mistake is repeated.
4. **Maintain adequate communication:** There should be free and continuous flow of information between the superior and the subordinate with a view to furnish the subordinate with relevant information to help him make decisions and also to interpret properly the authority delegated to him. Plans may change and decisions have to be taken in the light of the changed conditions.
5. **Maintain purity of authority and responsibility:** Authority should be delegated commensurate with responsibility. This is on the assumption that where subordinates are held responsible for performance of certain duties it is fair that they should be vested with the necessary authority to carry out such duties. Although technically it would be inaccurate to stress the questions of equality as the executive does without a certain amount of authority, there must be adequate correlation between duty and authority delegated.
6. **Proper Control Techniques be Developed:** In a good organization proper control techniques be developed and major deviations from standard should be checked. There should be no interference in day-to-day functioning of subordinates.
7. **Proper Selection and Training of Personnel:** Selection of personnel to various jobs should be fair and just. It should not be arbitrary but it must be based on certain principles. Only right persons should be placed on the right job. The person selected must also be given proper training to enable him to handle the post efficiently and to perform the assigned job properly. Proper selection and training helps to develop their self-confidence and morale.
8. **Reward effective delegation:** Effective delegation and successful assumption of authority must be rewarded. This will provide a proper environmental climate for fuller delegation and effective assumption of authority.

9. **Select appropriate subordinate of delegation:** The subordinate should be selected in the light of the work to be achieved. The qualification of the individual concerned may influence the nature of the delegation of authority. This is the purpose of the managerial function of staffing, most carefully considered.
10. **There must be Proper Planning:** An executive must plan as to what is to be achieved, if delegation of authority is made. He should define clearly the objectives to be achieved and the functions to be performed by delegating the authority. The job should be designed and divided in such a way as to achieve the objectives. The subordinates must understand clearly what activities they must undertake and what delegator expects from him.

11.8 VARIOUS STEPS IN THE PROCESS OF DELEGATION

The following steps are essential and they must be kept in mind while delegating:

1. The delegation should define the result expected from his subordinates.
2. Duties should be assigned according to the qualifications, experience and aptitude of the subordinates. They may be described either in terms of activity or set of activities to be performed by a subordinate or in terms of results that are expected from the performance of activities.

   For Example: How much sale is to be achieved by salesman? It is better to assign duties in terms of results expected, because the subordinate knows in advance the terms in which his performance will be judged, while assessing duties and responsibilities.
   The delegator must ensure that subordinates understand and accept the assignment, otherwise delegation would be meaningless or ineffective.
3. Adequate authority must be given to subordinates – The authority to be delegated to each particular subordinate is determined in advance. The delegator confers upon the subordinate the right to act in a specified way within limited boundaries. It decides what actions we may take and what action we cannot take. Proper authority to any subordinate not given in time, will not give or produce expected results.

   For Example: A sales manager, charged with the responsibility of increasing sales of company's product should be given authority to hire competent salesmen, pay wages and incentives, allow concessions, within specified limits.
4. The subordinate must produce expected results from the task assigned to him – It is obligatory on the part of the subordinate that he must give satisfactory performance from the tasks assigned. He becomes answerable for the proper performance of the assigned duties and for the exercise of the delegated authority. Authority without accountability is likely to be misused. Accountability without authority may be frustrating to the subordinates. The extent of accountability depends upon the extent of delegated authority and responsibility. A subordinate cannot be held responsible for acts not assigned to him by his superior. He is accountable only to his immediate superior.
5. Proper evaluation of the performance must be made – In the end, information and control system must be established to check and evaluate the performance of the subordinates to whom authority has been delegated. Duties, authority and responsibility are the three

interdependent essential steps in the process of delegation. In this connection an eminent authority H.W. Newman has said – "These three inevitable attributes of delegation are like a three-legged stool, each depends on the others to support the whole and no two can stand alone." What to delegate and when to delegate are two ticklish questions which a delegator has to answer to himself within the framework of the organization?

An executive according to *Louise A. Allen* can follow the undermentioned rules while delegating:

1. Established goals that are to be attained.
2. Define and enumerate the authority which the delegatee can exercise and the responsibility he has to shoulder.
3. Motivate the subordinate and provide him sufficient guidance. If necessary proper and adequate training should also be given to the delegatee before authority is delegated to him.
4. Ask for the completed work. In between if any help is needed by the delegatee he should be provided with such help either directly through someone who knows the work and is writing of help.
5. Establish an adequate control so as to supervise and provide necessary guidance.

11.9 MERITS OF DELEGATION

1. Delegation helps in avoiding any kind of act at a higher level which may, otherwise undermine the powers vested in the lower level units.
2. *It avoids delay*: Delegation helps in taking timely and accurate decisions. The personnel at lower level, being delegated, act quickly which serves the organization with due economy, efficiency and rapidly.
3. *It avoids overwork*: Delegation shifts some portions of the responsibility and work from the shoulders of the manager. To quote Beach : "The overworked manager who learns the art of delegation, is at one and the same time able to relieve himself of some of his burden, increase the competence of his men, and raise the level of accomplishment of his unit.
4. *It avoids wastage of time:* Present-day management is a complicated process. A manager has to perform various functions as a matter of routine work. It is not possible for him to give proper attention to all matters coming to him. Delegation helps him in transferring the less important subject to his juniors and attends to more important works.
5. *It develops increased sense of responsibility*: Delegation generates an increased sense of responsibility in the subordinate personnel. It also increases their working capacity and helps in enhancing their unspotted calibre which could be helpful for management.
6. *It helps in training the new incumbents:* The lower units that use the delegated power, get a spontaneous feel of their future responsibility. They become aware of the works at the higher level to which they may be promoted. Delegation also helps in developing the managerial personnel within the organization.

11.10 RELATIONSHIP OF AUTHORITY AND RESPONSIBILITY

In every business unit, internal organization is necessary for its efficient and smooth running. Under internal organization, duties are determined and distributed among the employees. All activities are combined and coordinated. The lines of authority are to be determined, a well recognized principle, to be followed for any organization and management.

In the internal organization of any concern, there must be a proper assignment of duties among the various personnel. This means that some people assign and some others have to perform those duties. The former people have an authority. The latter are subordinates to the former. The relationship of authority and subordination among the various personnel and groups should be properly determined. The position of each individual is to be fixed, i.e., whether he is to be in the position of authority or in the subordinate position. This work is very important. In this connection, the following principle is to be followed. The greater the responsibility attached to a post, the higher will be the position of the person holding the post, in the hierarchy. Thus, it is stated that authority should go with responsibility.

When the duties are assigned, there will be two types of employees. Some have authority and others take up responsibility. The former occupy a superior position, while the latter are placed in a subordinate position. Authority refers to the right to make decision and to command subordinate to follow these decisions. It is the supreme coordinating power and is very important for the managerial job. Responsibility refers to the obligation of a subordinate. Every subordinate has to perform the duty assigned to him. The essence of authority is obligation. It arises from the superior-subordinate relationship. It has a meaning, only when it is applied to a person. Authority seems to flow from the superiors to the subordinates. Every manager can see that his orders are executed by persuasion, coercion or economic social sanctions. Persuasion is the best means. Otherwise, the task may not be successfully accomplished, responsibility cannot be delegated. But authority can be delegated.

When these expressions 'Authority' and 'Subordination' are used, they should not create a sense of superiority or inferiority in the minds of the employees. Authority cannot be concentrated in the hands of one or a few individuals. It appears to flow from top to bottom. But it is not really so. There must be de-personalization of orders. This will help in developing good industrial relations among all the employees.

In management literature, responsibility is one of the most misunderstood words, usually, responsibility is referred to as 'Delegation of Responsibility' holding a person responsible or carrying out a responsibility. People use the word responsibility in different senses as referring to a duty, an activity or an authority. Actually responsibility can be defined as the 'obligation' of a subordinate to perform a duty which has been assigned to him.

Thus, obligation is the essence of responsibility. Normally the superior subordinate relationship gives rise to this responsibility as the superior is vested with the authority to require specified services from his subordinates. In case of business, this authority is generally a result of the contractual arrangement under which the subordinate has agreed to perform certain services in return for a monetary reward. In this sense, authority flows from the superior to the subordinate manager to whom certain duties are assigned and responsibility is the obligation of the subordinate to accomplish these duties. Responsibility can be discharged by a single action or it may be a continuous obligation.

11.11 AUTHORITY AND ACCOUNTABILITY

The term 'Accountability' is used by a few writers in the field of management to indicate the managers' liability for the proper discharge of the duties by his subordinates. In the military, the concept of accountability is used to indicate the duty and an officer to maintain accurate records and to safeguard public property and funds.

Thus, the three words confusingly used in varying sense in management literature are authority, responsibility and accountability. A less confusing use would be to use the word 'authority' as referring to the power to get something done, the word 'responsibility' as the liability of the individual for failing to discharge his responsibility. One is thus accountable for failures to his boss. Accountable is similar to tendering of accounts in its case, which refers to discharging of the responsibility. To carry out responsibility, a manager requires adequate authority or power.

11.12 RESPONSIBILITY AND DELEGATION

Whilst a manager can delegate his authority to his subordinates, responsibility cannot be so delegated. A manager is responsible for the performance of his duties even though he may delegate to a subordinate, authority to accomplish a service and the subordinate also in his turn may delegate a part of authority received by him. Therefore, delegation does not absolve a manager of his own responsibilities to perform his duties. In short no manager can shift responsibility to his subordinates. For example, the managing director of a company employed by the board of directors cannot avoid total responsibility for the conduct of the enterprise. Therefore, responsibility cannot be delegated in this sense. A manager cannot relieve himself of his responsibility although he can delegate authority and assign duties to his subordinates.

11.13 DIFFICULTIES IN DELEGATION

There is a fear aspect in delegation which plays a dominant role in a decision as to "what to delegate" and "to whom to delegate". Executive knows for certain that once authority is delegated they will loose the grip over their subordinates and also control over the operations. It is natural that the executives may not like to lose either the grip or control over the operation. But the important psychology is that by their nature executives have no confidence in their subordinates. They feel that the subordinates are not capable of shouldering the responsibility, therefore, the question of delegation of authority does not arise.

Sometimes, executives suffer from inferiority psychosis. They know for certain that though they occupy a position of strength but their knowledge and skill are not up to the mark. Their subordinates are well equipped and thus they may do the assigned job well. No executive would like to delegate when he feels that his subordinate may surpass him.

From the above discussion, we may come to a conclusion that there are three types of fears which discourage delegation and thus create difficulties in delegation. They are:

1. Fear of loosing the grip and control over the operations;
2. Fear of not a better performance by the subordinate to whom the authority may be delegated; and
3. Fear of better performance by the subordinate to whom the authority may be delegated.

The above difficulties arise out of –

1. Existence of element of fear and frustration; and
2. Incapable hands manning the executive positions.
3. Luck of mutual confidence;
4. No favourable management climate;
5. No inter-exchange of ideas and suggestions;
6. No proper and ambiguous definition of common goals to be achieved;
7. Non-independence in thinking and behaviour;
8. Non-existence of atmosphere of teamwork;

Delegation is an important managerial technique. Every effort should be made to encourage delegation. This creates a sense of belonging among subordinates. It develops the personality of the subordinates and helps in evaluating the managerial performance. It also induces a sense of security among both the executives and their subordinates. A favourable management climate should be created for encouraging delegation.

11.14 MEANING OF DECENTRALIZATION

Decentralization is a word that we frequently hear take about by political leaders and business managers. Many of them view decentralization as a panacea or a magical device that will compensate for poor management, encourage participation, increase efficiency, and raise morale. Most people do not have a clear view of what decentralization is and, as often as not when an organization is having "decentralization", it is for the wrong reasons and in the wrong way the term is understood and used.

Earnest Dale mentions four criteria to measure the extent of decentralization in an organization. He states that whenever decentralization is greater.

1. The greater is the number of decisions made at lower levels;
2. The more important are the decisions made lower levels;
3. The more is the number of areas in which decisions can be made at lower levels; and
4. The fewer are the people to be consulted the less is the checking required on the decisions made at the lower levels.

The way many people use the term, decentralization mean about the same thing as delegation– simply pushing authority down to subordinates. But decentralization means much more than simple delegation. Decentralization is a philosophy of the organization and management, one that implies both selectively determining what authority to push down into the organization; developing standing plans (such as policies) to guide subordinates who have this authority delegated to them; and implementing selective but adequate controls for monitoring performance. Thus, decentralization is a philosophy of organization and management which involves both selective delegation of authority as well as concentration of authority through the imposition of policies and selective but adequate controls.

According to McFarland, decentralization is a situation in which ultimate authority to command and ultimate responsibility for results is localized as far down in the organization as efficient management of the organization permits. According to Allen, decentralization refers to the systematic effort to delegate to the lowest levels all authority except that which can only be exercised at central points. Thus, decentralization means reservation of some authority (to plan, organize, direct and control) at the top level and delegation of authority to make routine decisions at points as near as possible to where action takes place.

11.14.1 Essential Characteristics of Decentralization

The essential characteristics of decentralization are:

(i) Decentralization not the same thing as delegation – It is something more than delegation. Delegation means demi-transfer of responsibility and authority from one individual to another. But decentralization means scattering of authority throughout the organization. It is the diffusion of authority within the entire enterprise. Delegation can take place from one person to another and be a complete process. But decentralization is completed only when the fullest possible delegation is made to all or most of the people. Under delegation control rests entirely with the diligent, but under decentralization, the top management may exercise minimum control and delegate the authority of controlling to the departmental managers. It should be noted that complete decentralization may not be possible or desirable, but it certainly involves more than one level in the organization.

(ii) Decentralization is distinct from dispersion – Decentralizing is often confused with the separation of physical facilities which is not correct. Dispersion occurs when plants and offices are located at different places with physical distance between them. Performance of work in dispersed plants and offices does not necessarily lead to decentralization. Decentralization can proceed without separation of facilities and facilities can be separated without decentralization. A company may be highly decentralized even though all physical facilities and employees are located in a single building. Thus, decentralization can take place even without dispersion.

(iii) Decentralization is not a type of organization. Some people believe that a company can decentralize by changing its organizational structure. This is not true. Decentralization may be achieved even without changing the organizational structure as it refers primarily to the systematic delegation authority throughout the organization industries in which markets are less uncertain, production processes technologically less dynamic and competitive relationships more stable, tend to become more centralized.

11.14.2 Gauging the Degree of Decentralization

How decentralized a particular organization is? There are no hard and fast rules, but the following guidelines may be used to test the degree of decentralization in a company:

(i) The narrower the breadth of the control imposed on managers, the greater the decentralization: Thus, a company in which each product-division manager simply has to report once or twice a year on the rate of return his division has earned on its investment is more decentralized. The division in which a variety of day-to-day production, marketing, and personnel decisions are monitored is less decentralized;

(ii) The greater the discretion permitted by the company's policies, procedures and rules, the greater the decentralization;
(iii) The greater the breadth of decision in terms of the number of functions they cover, the more the decentralization. Thus, the company in which division managers are authorized to take production, marketing and personnel decisions is more decentralized than one in which the managers can take only production and personnel decisions;
(iv) The less a subordinate has to check with his superior before taking decisions, the greater is the degree of decentralization – Thus, a company in which a manager does not have to check at all with his superior is more decentralized than one in which the manager must get most of his decisions approved beforehand;
(v) The closer the level to which the decision is made in the relation to the point where the problem arise, the greater the decentralization – Suppose a customer in Maharashtra has a problem, and the western division manager is authorized to make the necessary decisions, then to that extent the company is more decentralized than if the boss in the New Delhi had to make the decisions; and
(vi) The more important are the decisions that can be made at the lower levels, the greater the decentralization – For example, a company in which divisional managers can make equipment purchase decisions of up to Rs. 500,000 is more decentralized than one in which they are authorized to make these decisions up to a limit of Rs. 1,00,000.

11.14.3 Advantages of Decentralization

The merits of decentralization are listed below:

(i) It leads to a competitive climate in the organization.
(ii) It relieves the management of much workload;
(iii) It makes jobs at the lower levels of the organization more attractive and interesting. As a result, the level of motivation of the employee increases;
(iv) It encourages initiative at lower levels where the employees are allowed to participate in the decision-making process;
(v) Decision made closer to the actual situations is likely to be more realistic. Effective decisions are possible because of the speed and first-hand knowledge that decentralization provides.

11.14.4 Disadvantages of Decentralization

(i) It increases the administrative cost due to duplication of specialized services and the appointment of capable executives at lower levels;
(ii) It becomes difficult for top management to exercise control over what people at lower levels are doing or even to know what decisions they are taking;
(iii) Emergency situations cannot be tackled properly in decentralized structure. Adjustment to changing conditions may be difficult; and
(iv) It hampers uniformity in decision-making and consistency of procedures.

11.15 DECENTRALIZATION VS DELEGATION

Though both delegation and decentralization are related concepts, but the distinction between the two terms must be clearly understood. Decentralization could be differentiated from delegation in the following way:

1. Decentralization is simply not an extension of delegation. The purpose of delegation may be confined to relieve the excessive burden of key managerial personnel, but decentralization has a deeper meaning bordering on a new philosophy of organization and management;
2. Delegation could be a routine administrative activity involving only managers and their subordinates while decentralization is a conscious and deliberate organizational action with strategy overtones, to manage growth and expansion under conditions of environmental pressures, challenges and opportunities.
3. Delegation creates authority-responsibility relationship between a superior and his subordinates, whereas decentralization refers to the creation of semi-autonomous decision-making units or even profit centres functionally related to the top management. In other words, decentralization is diffusion of decision-making authority throughout the multiple layers of the organization;
4. Delegation is a process whereby the superior assigns certain tasks and responsibilities within his control to his subordinates, immediately vests part of his decision-making authority in them and precisely it is an obligation from them for proper discharge of authority conferred upon them and for effective performance in the area of delegated activity. But, on the other hand, decentralization refers to structural dispersal of authority for decision-making in various facts of organizational operations throughout the organization in the form of semi-autonomous units, subject to overall control by the top management.
5. Delegation takes place between a superior and a subordinate and is a complete process. It may consist of certain tasks alone. But decentralization involves spreading out the total decision-making power throughout the organization.
6. In case of delegation of authority, the diligent has directive responsibility in relation to his subordinates. But in a decentralized setting, direction is to a large extent substituted by control by the top management. The control mechanism is also elaborate so as to ensure that the dispersal of authority strengthens the entire organization and that the semi-autonomous units have a central focus on viability and vitality of the organization; and
7. Sheer pressure of managerial workload forces managers to delegate a part of their burden to their subordinates, as a matter of necessary with few alternatives. Decentralization, on the other hand, could be only one of the options open to an enterprise out of several alternative ways of organizing expanding operations. This means that delegation of authority could take place without decentralization, whereas there can be no decentralization without delegation of authority.

11.16 CENTRALIZATION OF AUTHORITY

According to Allen, centralization is the systematic and consistent reservation of authority at central points in an organization, while decentralization refers to consistent and systematic dispersal to the lowest levels all authority except that which can only be exercised at central points. Centralization denotes that a majority of the decisions having to do with the work being performed are not made by those doing the work but at a point higher in the organization. Everything that goes to increase the importance of the subordinate's role is decentralization, everything which goes to reduce it is centralization.

Centralization represents certain attitudes and approaches which the management follows. The major implication of centralization is the reservation of decision-making power in regard to planning, organizing, directing and control at the top level. The other implications will depend on the philosophy of management. For instance, in a company where the top management is very particular about the use of authority, it will make all the operations and decisions at lower levels subject to its approval.

Centralization of authority has certain merits also. In case of centralization, most of the decisions are taken not at a point where work is being done, but at a point higher in the organization. They may involve considerable cost and delay in making the decisions. Centralization of authority increases the burden on the top managers and hampers the growth of low-level managers. Because of these disadvantages, absolute centralization is not found in practice. Different organizations follow centralization in different degrees. It should be noted that complete decentralization is also not a feasible proposition of creating an effective organization structure. Some authority must be reserved at the highest level of management. Greater the reservation of authority at the top level, higher is the degree of centralization and lower is the degree of decentralization and vice versa.

11.17 CENTRALIZATION VS DECENTRALIZATION

Centralization and decentralization are the opposite ends of an organization continuum. On the one hand, centralization brings uniformity of policy and action, utilizes the skills of centralized and specialized staff, and enables closer control over operating units. And on the other hand, decentralization tends to effect faster decision-making and action on the spot without consulting higher levels. Decentralization has the effect of motivating the subordinates since they have a greater share in management decision-making.

The question of centralization or decentralization is a matter of degree. It is not possible to conceive of an organization which is exclusively centralized as some decentralization of authority is bound to exist. Likewise, there can be no absolute decentralized structure as the top executive cannot delegate all his authority. The issue of centralization and decentralization has to be decided objectively taking into consideration the size and nature of enterprise, diversity of the company's product, economies of division of labour, location of markets, nature of services to be performed, availability of trained and efficient managers, philosophy of management, etc. Centralization is not a system of management good or bad by itself, capable of being adopted or discarded at the whim of managers or of circumstances; it is always present to a greater or less extent.

11.18 SUMMARY

This chapter has highlighted the concepts of authority, responsibility, accountability, power, delegation, centralization and decentralization. Authority being the sum of the powers and rights entrusted to make possible the performance of the work delegated.

According to Fayol, delegation of work permits reduction in the number of objects to which attention and effort must be directed and has been recognized as the best means of making use of individuals and group of people. Formal delegation is the delegation of authority as per the organizational structure. Whereas, informal delegation of authority is through informal relations. The other type of delegation is bottom up or lateral delegation. It could also be general or specific delegation.

There are three elements of delegation and these are (i) authority, (ii) responsibility, and (iii) accountability.

Authority is the sum of the rights entrusted to an individual to make possible the performance of the work delegated. Responsibility denotes the work or duties assigned to a person by virtue of his position in the organization. Accountability is a logical derivative of authority. It is the obligation to carry out responsibility and exercise authority in terms.

The guidelines for effective delegation are:

(i) Functional definitions;
(ii) Absoluteness of accountability;
(iii) Clarification of limits of authority;
(iv) Proper planning;
(v) Parity of authority and responsibility
(vi) Incentive;
(vii) Selection of right persons;
(viii) Effective communication; and
(ix) Unity of command.

Decentralization is a philosophy of organization which involves both selective delegation and concentration of authority through the imposition of policies and adequate controls. The essential characteristics of decentralization are also discussed in this lesson.

11.19 SELF-ASSESSMENT QUESTIONS

1. "Centralization is not necessarily bad, not is decentralization necessarily good". Elucidate the statement.
2. "Delegation and decentralization are interchangeable terms in management and organization theory". Comment.
3. "Delegation is the key to administrative effectiveness". Elucidate.
4. Distinguish between:
   (a) Authority and accountability
   (b) Authority and power
   (c) Authority and responsibility

5. Explain the term 'Decentralization' and give its principal advantages. What are the factors that govern the degree of decentralization in an organization?
   (a) Responsibility and delegation
   (b) Specific limits of authority
6. State the advantages and limitations of decentralization
7. What are the types of authority? What are the sources of authority?
8. What is meant by decentralization of authority? Distinguish between delegation and decentralization of authority? How would you decide the degree of decentralization?
9. What is the relationship between delegation, control and accountability?

12

RECRUITMENT AND SELECTION

Learning Objective

The main objective of this chapter is to discuss the meaning of recruitment, selection, induction and placement; to explain the various sources of recruitment; to describe the steps involved in the selection process.

12.1 THE CONCEPT OF RECRUITMENT

Selection of a suitable candidate is the most imperative function of personnel department. If a right candidate is not selected, such an error can prove to be very costly for an undertaking. Many organizations, therefore, have developed sophisticated recruiting and selection methods. Manpower planning must precede recruitment and selection. The present and future requirements should also be kept in mind while planning for manpower.

Recruitment is a positive process of searching for prospective employees and stimulating them to apply for the jobs in the organization. In simple words, the term recruitment stands for discovering the sources from where potential employees will be available. The scientific recruitment leads to greater productivity, better wages, high morale, reduction in labour turnover and better reputation. It stimulates people to apply for jobs and hence it is a positive process.

12.2 SOURCES OF RECRUITMENT

Basically there are two sources of recruitment, namely, internal and external

12.2.1 Internal Sources

Best employees can be found within the organization. When a vacancy arises in the organization, it is offered to an employee who is already on the pay roll. Internal sources include promotion and transfer. When a higher post is given to an employee who deserves that post, it stimulates all other employees of the organization to work hard. The employees can be informed of such a vacancy by internal advertisement.

1. **Transfer:** Transfer involves the shifting of an employee from one job to another. At the time of transfer, it is ensured that the employee to be transferred to the new job is capable of performing it. In fact, transfer does not involve any drastic change in the responsibilities and status of the employee. On the other hand, promotion leads to shifting an employee to a higher position carrying higher responsibilities, facilities, status and pay.
2. **Promotion:** Many companies follow the practice of filling higher jobs by promoting employees who are considered fit for such positions. Filling vacancies in higher jobs from within the organization has the following merits:
   (a) **Economy in training costs:** The existing employees are fully aware of the operating procedures and policies of the organization. The existing employees require little training and it results in the economy in training costs.
   (b) **Improves morale:** When an employee from inside the organization is given the higher post, it helps in increasing the morale of all employees. Generally, every employee expects promotion to a higher post (carrying more status and pay) if he fulfils the requirements.
   (c) **No error in selection:** When an employee is selected from inside, there is no possibility of errors in selection since every company maintains complete record of its employees and can judge them in a better manner.
   (d) **No hasty decision:** The chances of hasty decisions are completely eliminated as the existing employees are well tried and can be relied upon.
   (e) **Promotes loyalty:** It promotes loyalty among the employees as they feel secured on account of chances of advancement.
   (f) **Self-development:** It encourages self-development among the employees since they can look forward to occupy higher posts.

Disadvantages: The following are the disadvantages of internal sources:

- For posts requiring innovations and original thinking, this method of recruitment cannot be followed.
- If only seniority is the criterion for promotion then the person filling the vacant post may not be really capable.
- It discourages capable persons from outside to join the concern.
- It is possible that the requisite number of persons possessing qualifications/experiences skills/attitudes required for the vacant posts may not be available in the organization.

In spite of the disadvantages, this is frequently used as a source of recruitment.

12.2.2 External Sources

Every enterprise has to tap external sources for various positions. Running enterprises have also to recruit employees from outside for filling up positions whose specifications cannot be met by internally available employees, and for meeting the additional requirements of manpower. The following external sources of recruitment are commonly used by the enterprises:

1. **Advertisements:** Advertising the job has become a fashion of the day with the large-scale enterprises, particularly when the vacancy is for a higher post or when there are a large number of vacancies. This helps in informing the candidates spread over different parts of the country. This method increases the choice of the management. The necessary information about the company, job descriptions and job specifications may be given in the advertisement itself for the benefit of the candidates. Usually, this method brings in a flood of response from quite unsuitable candidates. This increases the cost of selection of employees. Therefore, advertisement copy should be drafted in such a way that only the suitable candidates are tempted to apply.
2. **Direct Recruitment:** An important source of recruitment is direct recruitment by placing a notice on the notice board of the enterprise specifying the details of the jobs available. It is also known as recruitment at factory gate. The practice of direct recruitment is generally followed for filling casual vacancies requiring unskilled workers. Such workers are known as casual or badly workers and they are paid remuneration on daily wage basis.
3. **Education Institutions:** Jobs in industry have become increasingly varied and complexed to the point where school and college degrees are widely required. That is why, many big organizations maintain a liaison with the colleges, vocational institutes and management institutes for recruitment to various jobs. Recruitment from educational institutions is a well-established practice of thousands of business and other organizations. Organizations which require a large number of clerks or which seek applicants for apprenticeship programmes usually recruit from institutions offering vocational/ professional courses.
4. **Employment Agencies:** Employment exchanges run by the Government are regarded as a good source of recruitment for unskilled, semi-skilled operative jobs. In some cases, compulsory notification of vacancies to employment exchange is required by law. However, in the technical and professional areas, private agencies and professional bodies appear to be doing most of the work. Employment exchanges and selected private agencies provide a nation-wide service in attempting to match personnel demand and supply. They bring the job givers in contact with the job seekers.
5. In a country like India, where there is large-scale unemployment, unemployed persons also contact the employment sections of various organizations to ascertain if they can be casually employed. This source is very useful for recruiting unskilled workers. It does not involve any cost of advertising the vacancies. Whenever regular workers absent themselves in a large number or whenever there is a rush of work, this source of recruitment may be used. This is the cheapest method of getting labour supply on an ad hoc basis.
6. **Labour Contractors:** Labour contractors continue to be a source of recruitment in some industries in India. Workers are recruited through labour contractors who are themselves employees of the organization. The disadvantage of this system is that if the contractor himself decides to leave the organization, all the workers employed through him

may follow suit. This system of recruitment is losing popularity these days. It has been abolished in the public sector enterprises in India.

7. **Recommendations:** Applicants introduced by existing employees, friends and relatives may prove to be a good source of recruitment. Indeed, many employers prefer to take such persons because something about their background is known. When a present employee or a business friend recommends a person, a type of preliminary screening takes place. Some organizations have agreements with the unions of employees to give preference to close relatives of existing or retired employees if their qualifications and experience are suited to the vacant jobs.
8. **Unsolicited Applications:** Many qualified persons apply for employment to reputed companies on their own initiative. Such applications are known as unsolicited applications. They serve as a good source of manpower. A proper record may be kept of such applications and the candidates may be called for interview whenever the need arises.

Filling a vacancy from external sources has the following advantages:

(a) The employees recruited under this system possess varied and broader experience.
(b) Under this system of recruitment, fresh viewpoints are attracted.

Filling a vacancy through external sources suffers from the following disadvantages :

(a) This system is more expensive. The concern has to make huge expenditure on advertisement, holding of written test, interview, training, etc.
(b) This system of recruitment reduces incentive to good work among the lower cadres.
(c) This system of recruitment results in young men being placed over the older and more experienced persons of the lower services. This causes among them more jealousy.

12.3 CONCEPT OF SELECTION

The process of selection leads to employment of persons having the ability and qualifications to perform the jobs which have fallen vacant in an organization. It divides the candidates for employment into two categories, namely, those who will be offered employment and those who will not be. This process is more of 'rejection' since more candidates may be turned away than are hired. That is why, selection is frequently described as a *negative process* in contrast with the positive process of recruitment. The basic purpose of the selection process is choosing right type of candidates to manage various positions in the organization. In order to achieve this purpose, a well-organized selection procedure involves many steps and at each step more and more information is obtained about the candidates.

12.3.1 Difference between Recruitment and Selection

1. Recruitment is a positive process of searching for prospective employees, whereas selection is a negative process because it involves rejection of unsuitable candidates.
2. Recruitment is a relatively simple process as the candidates are required to fill in the prescribed forms and deposit with the employer. But selection is a complex and lengthy

process under which the candidates have to pass through a number of stages before getting the offer for a job.

3. Recruitment is the process of searching for prospective employees and stimulating them to apply for jobs in the organization. On the other hand, selection means employment of workers or establishing a contractual relationship between the employer and the worker.
4. The purpose of recruitment is to create a large pool of applicants for the jobs in the organization. But selection aims at eliminating unsuitable candidates and ensuring most competent people for the jobs.

12.3.2 Significance of Selection

Selection has become a critical process these days because it requires a heavy investment of money to get right types of people. Induction and training costs are also high. If the right types of persons are not chosen, it will lead to a huge loss of the employer in terms of time, effort and money. Therefore, it is essential to devise a suitable selection procedure. Each step in the selection procedure should help in getting more and more information about the applicant to facilitate decision-making in the area of selection.

Absenteeism and employee turnover are the important problems which are being faced by most of the organizations. The intensity of these problems can be reduced if, in the future, all selections are made carefully so that there are 'round pegs in the round holes'. Whenever unsuitable employees are appointed, the efficiency of the organization goes down. Such employees will shirk work and absent themselves from the work quite often. They may also be compelled to leave their jobs. If this happens, all the expenses incurred on the selection and training of such employees will go waste.

Proper selection and placement of personnel goes a long way towards building up a stable workforce. It keeps the rates of absenteeism and labour turnover low and increase the morale of the employees. If the employees are quite suitable according to the requirements of the jobs, they show higher efficiency and productivity. This enables the organization to achieve its objectives effectively.

12.4 STAGES IN SELECTION PROCEDURE

There cannot be a rigid procedure of selection suitable for all types of organizations as shown in Figure. 12.1. The number of steps in the selection procedure and the sequence of steps vary from organization to organization. For instance, some organizations do not hold preliminary interview, test or screening, whereas in other organizations such as commercial banks, preliminary tests are given to eliminate a large number of unsuitable applicants. Similarly, in some cases, medical examination is given before final selection and in others, medical check up follows final selection. Thus, every organization designs a selection procedure which suits its requirements. However, the main steps which could be incorporated in the selection procedure are discussed below:

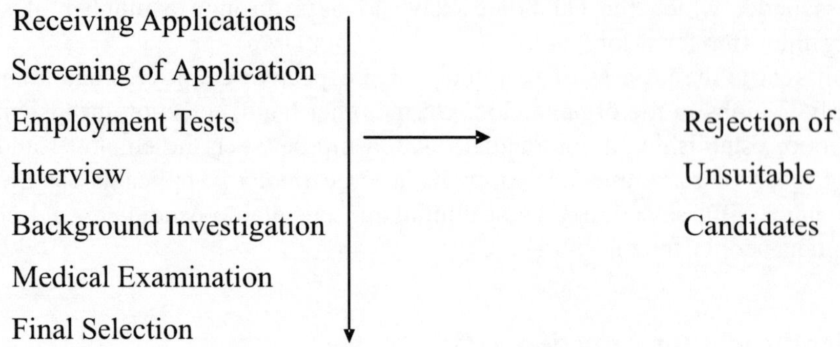

Figure 12.1 Steps in selection procedure.

1. **Preliminary Interview:** In most of the organizations, the selection programme begins with preliminary interview or screening. The preliminary interview is generally brief and does the job of eliminating the totally unsuitable candidates. The preliminary interview offers advantages not only to the organization, but also to the applicants. If an applicant is eliminated at this stage, the organization will be saved from the expenses of processing him through the remaining steps of the selection procedure and the unsuitable candidate will be saved from the trouble of passing through the long procedure. Preliminary interview may take place across the counter in the organization's employment office. It may consist of a short exchange of information with respect to organization's interest in hiring and the candidate's enquiry. It may serve primarily to determine whether it is worthwhile for the applicant to fill in an application blank. Candidates who pass this crude screening are usually asked to fill in the application blank.
2. **Receipt of Applications:** Whenever there is a vacancy, it is advertised or enquiries are made from the suitable sources, and applications are received from the candidates. Standard application forms may be drawn up for all jobs and supplied to the candidates on request. The application form is useful for several reasons. It gives a preliminary idea of the candidate to the interviewer and helps him in formulating the questions to be asked from the candidate. The written information about age, qualifications, experience, etc. may prove to be of great value to the interviewers. Forms make the processing of application very easy since there is uniformity of filling the data in the application form.
3. **Screening of Applications:** After the applications are received, they are screened by the screening committee and a list is prepared of the candidates to be interviewed. Applicants may be called for interview on some specific criteria like gender, desired age group, experience and qualifications. The number of candidates to be called for interview is normally five to seven times the number of posts to the filled up.
4. **Employment Tests:** Employment tests are used to select persons for various jobs. They help in matching the characteristics of individuals with the vacant jobs so as to employ right kinds of personnel. The following types of tests have gained popularity these days:
   (a) **Intelligence Tests:** Intelligence tests are used to judge the mental capacity of the applicant. They evaluate the ability of an individual to understand instructions and

make decisions. They are widely used in all types of organizations for the purpose of proper selection.

(b) Aptitude Tests: Aptitude means the potential which an individual has for learning the skills required to do a job efficiently. Aptitude tests measure an applicant's capacity and his potential of development. Aptitude tests are the most promising indices for predicting a worker's success.

(c) Proficiency Tests: Proficiency tests are designed to measure the skills already acquired by the individuals. They are also known as performance, occupational or trade tests. They are used to test the level of knowledge and proficiency acquired by an applicant. A trade test takes a sample of individual's behaviour which is designed as replica of the actual work situation such as typing. A trade test should be differentiated from the aptitude test. An aptitude test measures the potentials of the applicant to learn skills required on a job.

(d) Interest Tests: Interest tests identify patterns of interest in those areas in which the individual shows special concern, fascination and involvement. These tests suggest what types of jobs may be satisfying to the employees. Interest tests are more often used for vocational guidance. They help the individuals in selecting occupations of their interest.

(e) Personality Tests: Personality tests probe for the qualities of the personality as a whole, the combination of aptitude, interest and usual mood and temperature. It is very difficult to devise and use personality tests because they are concerned with discovering clues to an individual's value system, his emotional reactions, maturity, etc.

(f) Interview: Although application blank and employment tests provide a lot of valuable information about the candidate, yet they do not provide the complete set of information required about the applicant. Hence, interview may be used to secure more information about the candidate. The main purposes of an employment interview are: (i) to find out the suitability of the candidate, (ii) to seek more information about the candidate, and (iii) to give him an accurate picture of the job with details of terms and conditions and some idea of organization's policies. The actual data of the applicant given in the application form may also be checked and more information may be taken from the candidate. This occasion is also utilized for testing the capability and personality of the applicant. Thus, interview affords an opportunity to develop a clear picture of the candidate.

It is customary to have an interview in several stages especially for senior positions. There may be a preliminary interview by the head of the department. The final interview is taken by the interview or selection committee consisting of chairman of the organization, head of department, personnel manager and may be some outside experts. During the interview, the members of the selection committee appraise each candidate according to merits. At the end of interview of each candidate, the chairman consults the members and after a brief discussion finalizes the grading of the candidate. After the completion of interview of all the candidates, a panel is prepared. The number of persons in the panel is generally about two to three times the number of vacancies to be filled up.

Although personal interview is perhaps the most widely used method for selecting the personnel, it has certain limitations too. *Firstly*, it can test only the personality of the candidate and not his skills and ability for the job. *Secondly*, it depends too much on the personal judgement of the interviewer which may not always be accurate. That is why, in most of the organizations, occupational and other tests are given to the candidates before they are called for the final interview.

5. **Medical Examination:** The pre-employment physical examination or medical test of a candidate is an important step in the selection procedure. Though in the suggested selection procedure, medical test is located near the end, but this sequence need not be rigid. The organizations may place the medical examination relatively early in the process so as to avoid time and expenditure to be incurred on the selection of medically unfit persons. Some organizations either place the examination relatively early in the selection procedure or they advise the candidates to get themselves examined by a medical expert so as to avoid disappointment at the end.

   The objectives of physical examination are: (i) to ascertain the applicant's physical capabilities to meet the job requirements; (ii) to protect the organization against the unwarranted claims under the Workmen's Compensation Act or against law suits for damages; and (iii) to prevent communicable diseases entering the organization. The physical examination should disclose the physical characteristics of the individual that are significant from the standpoint of his efficient performance of the job he may be assigned or of those jobs to which he may reasonable be expected to be transferred or promoted. A qualified medical expert appointed by the organization should certify whether the candidate is physically fit to the requirements of a job. A proper medical examination will ensure higher standards of health and physical fitness of the employees and will reduce the rates of accident, labour turnover and absenteeism.

6. **Background Investigation:** A referee is potentially an important source of information about the candidate's ability and personality if he holds a responsible position in some organization or has been the boss or employer of the candidate. Prior to final selection, the prospective employer normally makes an investigation on the references supplied by the applicant and undertakes more or less a thorough search into the candidate's past employment, education, personal reputation, financial condition, police record, etc. However, it is often difficult to persuade a referee to give his opinion frankly. The organization may persuade him to do so by giving an assurance that all information will be treated as strictly confidential.

7. **Final Selection:** After a candidate has cleared all the hurdles in the selection procedure, he is formally appointed by issuing him an appointment letter or by concluding with him a service agreement. The appointment letter contains the terms and conditions of employment and pay scale and other benefits associated with the job.

12.5 INDUCTION AND PLACEMENT

Induction: When an individual successfully clears all the steps involved in selection, he is selected. Induction is concerned with the problem of introducing or orienting a new employee to the organization. It consists of familiarizing new employees with their jobs, introduction with his fellow workers, company policies, etc. It is considered as a part of the selection process. "A good orientation programme will leave the employee firmly established in the new job, comfortable and relaxed in his relations with other members of the department and content with his position in the firm. Though orientation takes a small amount of time from productive activity, it repays the firm many times over in better personnel relations". (Layman and Gubellini).

There are two phases of induction training programme. The first phase is generally conducted by the personnel department. It is concerned with giving the new employee a friendly welcome briefing him in the matters concerned with the company's background, products, health and welfare plans. He may be taken around the factory and introduced to the security officer, time keeper and cashier. The employee may then be asked to report to the department concerned. The second phase of the induction programme is conducted by the head of the department in which he is to work. The employee is given information regarding production process, work rules, working conditions, etc. The employee is then informed about the customs prevalent in the organization such as dress, lunch, refreshments, etc. Good induction is a good business for the firm and a basic desire of most, if not all the new employees. If the new employee is allowed to sink or swim, the adjustment period either is considerably lengthened with consequent losses in productivity, or it is eliminated altogether by resignation, with consequent losses in turnover costs.

Objects of Systematic Induction

(a) To promote a feeling of belongingness and loyalty among the employees.
(b) To provide information to the employee regarding policies of the organization.
(c) To give information to the new employee as to leave rules, location of canteen, etc.
(d) To build confidence in the new employee so that he can become an efficient worker.

The success of induction programme mainly depends on the ability of the persons who conduct it. A comprehensive induction programme usually covers the following:

(a) Accident prevention
(b) Employee's own department and job and how it fits into the general organization.
(c) Organizational culture and ethos
(d) Personnel policy and source of information.
(e) Standing orders including grievance and disciplinary procedures.
(f) Terms and conditions of employment, amenities and welfare facilities available.
(g) The company and its products.
(h) The geography of the plant.
(i) The structure of the organization and the functions of the various departments.
(j) Working routines and production

Placement: The candidates selected for appointment are to be offered specific jobs. There should be a perfect matching of the requirements of the job and the abilities/skills of the employee concerned. Only then effective placement will take place. In practice, right placement is not an easy task. It may take a long time before a candidate is placed on the right job. Generally, the candidate is appointed on probation of one year or so. During this period, he is tried on different jobs. If his performance is satisfactory, he will be offered a permanent post and placed on the job for which he is most suitable. He may need some training to do the job better. Therefore, his training needs must also be identified during the probation period.

If during the probation period, an employee is not found suitable, the management may transfer him to some other job to which he may be expected to do justice. But if the management cannot offer him a job which he can do well, it may sack him or give him time and training to improve himself to do the job better.

12.6 SUMMARY

Once the requirement of manpower is known, the process of recruitment starts. Recruitment is the process of identifying the sources for prospective candidates and to stimulate them to apply for the jobs. Job recruits can be drawn from within or outside the organization. The process of selection leads to employment of persons having the ability and qualifications to perform the jobs which have fallen vacant in an organization. There are several advantages of a proper selection procedure. As the employees are placed in the jobs for which they are best suited, they derive maximum job satisfaction and reap maximum wages. Labour turnover is reduced and the overall efficiency of the concern is increased. Induction and placement help the new employee and the organization to accommodate each other.

12.7 SELF-ASSESSMENT QUESTIONS

1. What is meant by recruitment? How does it differ from selection?
2. Critically discuss the various sources of requirement of employee. What sources of recruitment will you recommend for the appointment of managerial personnel?
3. Discuss in brief the significance of proper selection of personnel. What steps are involved in the selection procedure? Explain.

13 TRAINING AND DEVELOPMENT

Learning Objective

The main objective of this chapter is to elaborate the fundamental concepts relating to training and developments of the employees in modern organizations.

13.1 CONCEPT OF TRAINING

After the selection of people for various jobs, the next function of staffing is to arrange for their training and development. This is because a person, however, carefully selected is not moulded to specifications and rarely meets the demands of his job adequately. Earlier, it was thought that the training of personnel was unnecessary on the ground that the new employees would gradually pick up all the particulars of the job. But as the processes and techniques of production are becoming more and more complicated, it is being increasingly realized that the formal training is important not only for new recruits but also for existing employees. Training function, in fact, has become the corner stone of sound management.

According to Flippo, "Training is the act of increasing the knowledge and skills of an employee for doing a particular job." Training involves the specific job. Its purpose is to achieve a change in the behaviour of those trained and to enable them to do their jobs better. Training makes newly appointed workers fully productive in the minimum of time. Training is equally necessary for the old employees whenever new machines and equipment are introduced and/or there is change in the techniques of doing the things. In fact, training is a continuous process. It does not stop anywhere. The managers are continuously engaged in training their subordinates.

Training is different from education. Training is the act of increasing the knowledge and skill of an employee for doing a particular job. It is concerned with imparting specific skills for particular purposes. On the other hand, education is a broader term concerned with increasing the general knowledge and understanding of the employee's total environment. Thus, when we teach a person how to assemble two objects and tighten a nut, we are training him to do a specific job but when we are giving him a course in engineering, it is education. The distinction between the two is like the distinction between applied and pure sciences.

13.2 PURPOSE OF TRAINING

Training is the act of enhancing the knowledge and skills of an employee for performing a particular job. The main objective of training is to achieve a change in the behaviour of the trainees. In order to achieve this objective, any training programme should try to bring positive changes in:

(i) Knowledge
(ii) Skills; and
(iii) Attitudes.

An attempt to increase the knowledge of a trainee would help him know facts, policies, procedures and rules and regulations pertaining to his job. An attempt to increase his skills would help him learn technical and manual skills necessary to do his job efficiently. The training programme should also mould the attitude of a worker towards other co-workers, supervisor and the organization. It should also create in him a sense of responsibility, interest in his job and appreciation of enterprise's goals and policies.

13.3 BENEFITS OF TRAINING

13.3.1 Benefits of Training to the Organization

The major benefits of training to the organization are discussed below:

1. **Better management:** A manager can make use of training to manage in a better way. To him training the employees can assist in improving his planning, organizing, directing and controlling. For instance, maintaining higher standards of quality, building a satisfactory organization structure, delegating authority and stimulating employees are all assisted by effective training.
2. **Economical operations:** Trained personnel will be able to make better and economical use of materials and equipment. Wastage will also be low. In addition, the rate of accidents and damage to machinery and equipment will be kept to the minimum by the well trained employees. These will lead to less cost of production per unit.
3. **Higher morale:** The morale of employees is increased if they are given proper training. A common objective of training programme will mould employees' attitudes to achieve support for organizational activities and to obtain better cooperation and greater loyalty. With the help of training, dissatisfaction, complaints, absenteeism and turnover can also be reduced among the employees. Thus, training helps in building an efficient and cooperative workforce.
4. **Higher production:** Training increases the skills of the employee in the performance of a particular job. An increase in skills usually helps increase in both quality and quality of output. Training is also of great help to the existing employees. It helps them to increase their level of performance on their present job assignments.
5. **Less Supervision:** If the employees are given adequate training, the need of supervision is lessened. Training does not eliminate the need for supervision, but it reduces the need

for detailed and constant supervision. A well-trained employee is self-reliant in his work because he knows what to do and how to do. Under such situations, close supervision is ordinarily not mandatory.

6. **Preparation of future mangers:** When totally new skills are required by an organization, it has to face great difficulties in the selection process. Training can be used in spotting out promising men and in removing defects in the selection process. It is better to select and train from within the organization rather than seek the skilled employees from the outside sources. Training may be imparted to qualify them for promotion to more responsible jobs.
7. **Quick learning:** Training helps to reduce the learning time to reach the acceptable level of performance. The employees need not learn by observing others and waste a long time if the formal training programme exists in the organization. The qualified instructors will help the new employees to acquire the skills and knowledge to do particular jobs within a short interval of time.
8. **Standardization of procedures:** With the help of training, the best available methods of performing the work can be standardized and taught to all employees. Standardization will make high levels of performance rule rather than the exception. Employees will work intelligently and make fewer mistakes when they possess the required know-how and have an understanding of their jobs and of the interdependence of one job on another.

13.3.2 Benefits of Training to Employees

Training helps the employees or workers in the following ways:

1. **Adaptability:** Training develops adaptability among workers. They don't worry when work procedures and methods are changed.
2. **Confidence:** Training creates a feeling of confidence in the minds of workers. It gives safety and security to them at the workplace.
3. **Higher Earnings:** By imparting skills, training facilitates higher remuneration and other monetary benefits to the workers.
4. **Increased Safety:** Trained workers handle the machine safely. They also know the use of various safety devices in the factory. Thus, they are less prone to industrial accidents.
5. **New Skills:** Training develops skills which serve as a valuable personal asset of the worker. It remains permanently with the worker himself.
6. **Promotion:** Training paves the way for promotion and self-development.

13.3.3 Training Principles and Techniques

According to Pigors and Myres, training principles and techniques include:

1. The material to be learned should be developed in stages.
2. The trainee must want to learn. His motivation to improve his job performance or to learn a new skill must be high.

3. The trainer should tell the trainee as to whether he is learning the job correctly. This is known as feedback.
4. There should be some reward at the conclusion of training, viz., promotion or a better job.
5. This is best accomplished through learning by doing rather than by listening.
6. When the trainee gives correct response, he has learned the job.

13.3.4 Training Procedure

1. First of all, the instructor must be prepared. He should know both his job and how to teach it. On the basis of job analysis and job description, various operations should be planned. In order to avoid delays, everything must be ready before training starts.
2. The next step is the preparation of the trainee. The fact that the employee is learning the job for the first time should be kept in mind. The importance of the job, its relationship with the other jobs and importance of rapid and effective learning, should be explained.
3. The operations should then be presented carefully and patiently. The sequence of the entire job is explained by taking one point at a time.
4. Tthe performance of the trainee should then be tried by asking him to explain each step and do the practical.
5. The employee is then put on the job. In the follow up action, his performance should be frequently checked and questions should be encouraged.

13.4 TYPES OF TRAINING

Various types of training programmes are not mutually exclusive, but invariably overlap and employ many of the same techniques. Some of the more common types of training programmes are examined below:

13.4.1 Induction or Orientation Training

It is a training programme used to induct a new employee into the new social setting of his work. The new employee is introduced to his job situation, and to his co-employees. He is also informed about the rules, working conditions, privileges and activities of the company, what the company does, how it serves the community and other particulars pertaining to the company.

Most of the information is likely to be embodied in an employee handbook which is distributed to all employees, and in the case of a rank and file workers, the orientation may consist only of a brief explanation by a member of the personnel department or the supervisor under whom the employee will work. Induction training can, however, be more elaborate, particularly in the case of supervisory and management employees. Some companies show movies explaining company activities, others arrange for a lecture or a series of lectures on the company and its practices. In some cases, the new employee spends anywhere from a day to several months in each department to gain first-hand experience in the various types of work and an overall view of how the activities of one department affect those of other departments.

In the new employee is an unskilled or a semi-skilled worker, for example, a machine operator, he may be asked to spend some time on the shop-floor in order to familiarize himself with the machines, equipment and working conditions.

In some companies the complete induction programme is divided into two phases. In the *first phase*, induction is done by the personnel department which supplies to the new employee all sorts of information relating to the company. In the *second phase*, induction is done by the supervisor. He has the responsibility of seeing that both the newcomer and the work team accept each other. The supervisor should follow a set induction procedure. A ten step programme provides for:

(a) Greeting the newcomer cordially;
(b) Displaying a personal interest in the newcomer;
(c) Reviewing his terms of employment;
(d) Giving additional information;
(e) Showing the newcomer around;
(f) Explaining the importance of his job in relation to other jobs;
(g) Introducing the newcomer to the rest of the work team;
(h) Telling the newcomer his duties;
(i) Selecting a person who can assist the newcomer on the job; and
(j) Following up frequently.

The induction training not only helps personal adjustment of the new employee to his job and work group but also promotes good morale in the organization. In view of these advantages, many large companies give much importance to induction training.

13.4.2 Refresher Training

As the name implies, the refresher training is meant for the old employees of the enterprise. The basic purpose of refresher training is to acquaint the existing workforce with the latest methods of performing their jobs and improve their efficiency further. Retraining programmes are designed to avoid personnel obsolescence. The skills with the existing employees become obsolete because of technological changes and because of the tendency of human beings to forget. Thus, refresher training is essential because of the following factors:

(a) Rapid technological changes make even the most qualified workers obsolete in course of time because new technology is associated with new work methods and job requirements. Existing workers need to learn new work methods to use new techniques in doing their jobs.
(b) Workers require training to bring them up-to-date with the knowledge and skills and to relearn what they have forgotten.
(c) Refresher training becomes necessary because many new jobs which are created due to changes in the demand for goods and services are to be manned by the existing employees.

The existing talented employees may also be given adequate training to make them eligible for promotion to higher jobs in the organization. It is known as 'training for promotion'. The purpose of training for promotion is to develop the existing employees to make them fit for undertaking higher job responsibilities. This serves as a motivating force to the employees.

13.4.3 Job Training

The object of job training is to increase the knowledge of workers about the jobs with which they are concerned, so that their efficiency and skill of performance are improved. In job training, workers are enabled to learn correct methods of handling machines and equipment, avoiding accidents, removing bottlenecks, minimizing waste, etc.

13.4.4 Promotional Training

Many concerns follow a policy of filling some of the vacancies at higher levels by promoting existing employees. This policy increases the morale of workers. They try to put up maximum efficiency so that they may be considered for promotion. When the existing employees are promoted to superior positions in the organization, they are required to shoulder new responsibilities. For this, training has to be given to them so that they may not experience any difficulty to shoulder the responsibilities of the new position to which they have been promoted.

13.5 METHODS OF TRAINING

There are many methods of training. The method selected should be best suited to a specific organization's needs. The various factors generally considered for selecting a method include skills required, qualifications of candidates, cost, time available, depth of knowledge required, etc. The following methods are usually employed for training:

13.5.1 On the Job Training

Under this method an employee is instructed by some experienced employee, a special instructor or supervisor. The success of this type of training mainly depends on the qualified trainers. Usually training in crafts, trades, technical areas, etc. is given by keeping the unskilled or semi-skilled worker under the guidance of some skilled workers. The increasing labour costs in industry have made it essential that even the simplest job should be carried out in a most economical manner. Therefore, training in improved methods can be given to the new employees. During second world war, millions of workers were trained for different jobs. This method of training proved to be a great success. However, its success largely depends on the trained instructor otherwise the quality of his trainees will be very poor.

Advantages

(a) It is less expensive and consumes less time.
(b) It takes less time as skill can be acquired in a short period.
(c) The production does not suffer under this method.
(d) The trainee learns rules and regulations while learning the job.
(e) The training is under the supervision of supervisors who take keen interest in the training programme.

(f) The workers learn the job in actual conditions rather than the artificial conditions. It motivates employees to learn.

Limitations

(a) The experienced trainers may not be available
(b) The supervisor may not be in a position to devote time and hence faulty training may take place.
(c) The training is highly disorganized and haphazard.
(d) There is a lack of motivation on the part of the trainee to received training.

13.5.2 Apprentice Training

In many industries such as metal, printing and building construction, this system of training is widely in use. The apprentice training may last for four to five years. The worker is usually absorbed by the concerned industry after training period is over. They get practical knowledge on the job and theoretical knowledge in the classroom lecture. The workers get some stipend during their training period. It is the oldest and most common method of training in creates, trades and technical areas.

The standards fixed in apprentice training are slightly rigid. The mechanical apprentice programme in an organization, for example, may take four years. Progress reports are periodically submitted. Like other employees, an apprentice is also entitled to bonus, vacation and other facilities.

Advantages

(a) Trainees receive some stipend during training.
(b) The trainees get valuable skill which carries good demand in the market.
(d) It reduces labour cost and production cost as labour turnover is very low.
(e) The loyalty of the employees is increased.
(c) From employer's point of view, it is cheap source of labour and in addition a skilled workforce is maintained.

Limitations

(b) Rigid standards make this method unsatisfactory.
(d) It is an expensive method.
(c) If a worker fails to learn after long period of training, he may not be absorbed. This may create labour problem in the firm.
(a) The training period is very long and the trainee requires regular supervision which may not be given.

13.5.3 Vestibule Training (Training Centre Training)

Vestibule means a passage or room between the outer door and the interior of a building. In order to reach the inner of a house, one must pass from vestibule. Under vestibule training, workers are trained on special machines in a separate location, i.e., classrooms. The vestibule school is run by the personnel department. Training is given in artificial conditions which are just like the real-life situations.

The supervisor is relieved of training the new employees. He can concentrate on his other important assignments such as quality and quantity of output. This method is followed when the number of persons to be trained is very large.

Advantages

(a) The trainer is a specialist and possesses specialization in teaching.
(b) Since the training is given off the job, trainees can concentrate on learning.
(d) The employee learns the job in a short time.
(c) The instructor can give individual attention as he has no other work assigned to him.

Disadvantages

(a) Training is given under artificial conditions; hence, the worker may not adjust when he is put on actual job.
(b) It is expensive method as duplicate equipment is required.
(c) If demand for workers is uneven, vestibule school may remain unused for a considerable time.
(d) Splitting of responsibilities may lead to organizational problems.

13.5.4 Internship Training

In this method of training students get practical training while they study. A proper liaison is established between the technical institutions and business houses where students are sent during their vacations. Thus, there is a balance between theory and practice and students get practical knowledge while studying.

The chief drawbacks of this method are:

(a) It can be used for training only of skilled and technical workers.
(b) The time taken is usually long.

An example may be given here from M.B.A. (Master of Business Administration) courses being run by various universities of India. A close liaison is kept between the university and industry. The students doing M.B.A. are sent to the different industries during vacations. Thus, they learn practical work also while doing their professional course.

13.5.5 Learner Training

Learners are those persons who are selected for semi-skilled jobs and lack even the basic knowledge of industrial engineering. These learners are first given education in vocational schools where they get knowledge of arithmetic, workshop mathematics and learn the operation of machines. They can be assigned regular jobs after training.

13.6 CONCEPT OF DEVELOPMENT

Executive or management development is a continuous process of learning and growth designed to bring behavioural change among the executives. It implies that there will be a change in knowledge and behaviour of the individuals undergoing development programme. The individual will be able to perform his present assignment better and also increase his potential for future assignments through the acquisition, understanding and use of new knowledge, insights and skills. The learning process involves the implication that there will be changed behaviour on the part of the individuals given the adequate training and education.

Managers develop not only by participating in formal courses of instruction drawn by the organization, but also through actual job experience in the organization. It should be recognized that it is for the organization to establish the developmental opportunities for its managers and potential managers. But an equal, perhaps more important, counterpart to the efforts of the organization are those of the individuals. Self-development is an important concept in the whole programme of management development.

13.6.1 Need and Importance of Development

There is a shortage of trained managers. This shortage is felt particularly during the large-scale expansion of the volume of activities of the organization. It is very difficult to appoint the persons to manage various managerial jobs from the labour markets. The organization has to develop the talented employees and maintain an inventory of executive skills to meet the future demands.

Obsolescence of managerial skills is another factor which calls for continuous executive development. Executive development is not a 'one-shot' affair; it must continue throughout an executive's career. Otherwise, an executive of yesterday will not be acceptable today and an executive of today will not be good enough for the future. Therefore, in order to be dynamic and to change himself according to the needs, a manager must continuously update himself to successfully meet new challenges as they occur.

The performance of a company depends upon the quality of its managers. Companies with similar raw materials, equipment and technical know-how show different results because of the quality of their executives. Quality of management explains the difference in price policy, inventory policy, production policy, marketing policy and labour policy of the organization. Thus, better the management, better are the results of the organization. Executive development, therefore, is of paramount importance to have effective and desired managerial talents to meet the organization's demands.

13.6.2 Objectives of Management Development

The objectives of management development are as follows:

(i) To develop a second line of competent managers for future replacements.
(ii) To ensure adequate managerial talent for the long-term survival and growth of the company.
(iii) To ensure that managerial resources of the organization are properly and fully utilized.

(iv) To prevent managerial obsolescence by exposing the managers to new concepts and techniques in their respective fields of specialization.

(v) To provide opportunities to the managers to reach their maximum capabilities and to fulfil their career expectations.

13.7 METHODS OF MANAGEMENT DEVELOPMENT

A large variety of methods of management development have come into prominence these days. These methods can be classified into two broad categories, namely, (a) on-the-job methods; and (b) off-the-job methods as follows:

13.7.1 On-the-Job Methods

In internal facilities or on-the-job facilities include the practices and facilities given by the enterprise within the organization. Every good concern tries to provide internal development and training facilities to its managers or executives. On-the-job methods include (i) Experience, coaching and understudy, (ii) Position rotation, (iii) Special projects and task forces, and (iv) Committee assignments.

13.7.2 Off-the-Job Methods

Off-the-job methods include the external facilities which are also of two types; firstly for those new entrants who want to tap management as their career, and secondly, junior and middle level managers to equip them with higher skills, and techniques in management. The former type of training is provided by various universities and institutions running M.B.A. programmes. For junior executives various external facilities are provided by the business houses. Off-the-job methods include (i) Special courses or classes (ii) Role playing. (iii) Sensitivity training. (iv) Structured insight. (v) Stimulation. (vi) Conference training (vii) Multiple management. (viii) Special meetings.

(1) On-the-Job Methods

1. **Experience, Coaching and Understudy:** Learning by experience cannot and should not be eliminated as a method of development. The executives may have any title while learning. An understudy may be assistant to someone; or special assistant to someone or any of the regular supervisory or executive positions developing upon his special assignment. He may be assigned as an understudy solely for training, or he may be assigned as a staff man or line assistant to a busy executive who really needs his help. The understudy may have regular duties for which he is solely responsible. Thus, he learns by experience, observation, guidance and coaching. This is a good method for new entrants, promoters and management trainees.
2. **Position Rotation:** The objective of position rotation method is the broadening of the background of trainee in the organizations. If an executive is rotated periodically from one

job to another job, he acquires a general background. The main advantages of position rotating are: provision of general background in all functional areas of the business, training in actual situation and competition among the rotating trainees. Due to rapid specialization, this techniques has become less effective and less useful.

3. **Special Project:** Under special project method, an executive is assigned a project that is closely related to the objectives of his department. For example, a trainee may be asked to develop a system of cost control in the execution of an order. He will study the problem and make recommendations upon it. This project would also help in educating the trainee about the importance of cost and the organizational relationships with the accounting and other departments. Thus, he acquires a knowledge of allied subjects also.

4. **Committee Assignment or Multiple Management:** Under this method an ad hoc committee is constituted. It is to discuss a subject and make recommendations. It is assigned objectives and responsibilities related to work of the organization. It makes a study of the problem and presents its suggestions to the departmental manager. Committee assignment may provide the necessary general background to the trainees because every member of the committee gets a chance to learn from others. It is an important device of educating the executives to acquire general background and to change their behaviour towards the selected problem.

(2) Off-the-Job Training Methods

1. **Special Courses:** The executives are required to attend special courses formally organized by the enterprise with the help of experts from educational institutions. The executives may also be sponsored to attend the courses to be conducted by management institutions. This method is popular these days. However, due to high fee only the big enterprises may send their executives to the management development courses run by management institutions.

2. **Role Playing:** Under role playing method, a conflict situation is artificially created and two or more trainees are assigned different parts to play. The role players are provided with either a written or oral description of a situation and the role they are to play. They are allowed sufficient time to plan their actions. They must act out their parts spontaneously before the class. For instance, a role playing situation may be a supervisor discussing a grievance with an employee or a salesman making a presentation to a purchasing agent. Role playing is used for human relations and leadership training. It aims to give trainees an opportunity to learn human relation skills through practice and to develop insight into one's own behaviour and its effect upon others. Thus, its objective is very narrow. It may be used in human relations training and sales training as both these involve dealing with other people.

   There are various advantages of role playing. *Firstly,* it provides an opportunity for developing human relations, understanding and skills and to put into practice the knowledge they have acquired from text books, lectures, discussions, etc. *Secondly,* the interview may be taped to provide the trainees a chance to listen to their performance and note their strengths and weakness. *Lastly,* knowledge of results is immediate, because the trainees as well as the listeners analyze the behaviour of the role players.

3. **Case Study:** It is a means of simulating experience in the classroom. The trainees may be given a problem to discuss which is more or less related to the principles already taught. He is given an opportunity to apply his knowledge to the solution of realistic problems. Cases may use in following ways:
   (i) They can be used subsequent to the exposition of formal theory under which the trainees apply their knowledge of theory to specific situations.
   (ii) The trainees may be assigned to cases for written analysis and oral class discussion without any prior explanation of pertinent concepts and theory. The case study places heavy demands upon the trainees. It requires that they should have a good deal of maturity and background in the subject matter concerned.

   Case studies are extensively used in teaching law, personnel management, human relations, marketing management and business policy in various educational institutions. Students learn that there is no single answer to a particular problem. The answer of each trainee may differ. Case discussions will help them to appreciate each other's thinking. That is why, case studies are frequently used in supervisory and executive training in business.
4. **Conference Training:** A conference is a group meeting conducted according to an organized plan. The members seek to develop knowledge and understanding by obtaining a considerable amount of oral participation. It is an effective training of both conference members and conference leader. As a member, a participant can learn from others by comparing his opinions with those of the others. He learns the effect of closely controlling and dominating the discussion. Participants can understand how groups actually work and give them a change to discover how they are interpreted by others. Sensitivity training aims at increasing tolerance power of the individuals and their ability to understand others.

13.7.3 Multiple Approach

The different methods outlined above are not mutually exclusive in nature. The typical programme of an executive development includes a number of methods in both categories. Unlike training programmes for operatives, the primary emphasis in executive development should be on self-development. Development which occurs on or near the job has the advantages or providing motivation and of being practicable. As regards the questions of choosing one method against the other, higher the position in the organization, the more important becomes off-the-job methods. The managers are highly educated persons and they can soon learn newer techniques. The important thing is to realize the need and importance of such development programmes and to provide these facilities.

13.8 DISTINCTION BETWEEN TRAINING AND DEVELOPMENT

The terms 'training' and 'development' appear to be synonymous. But there are some differences in the content and techniques of employee training and development. According to Edwin B. Flippo, "Training is the act of increasing the knowledge and skills of an employee for doing a particular job, management development includes the process by which managers and executives acquire not only skills and competence in their present jobs, but also capacities for future managerial tasks of increasing difficulty and scope".

Training is the act of enhancing the knowledge and skills of an employee for doing a particular job. It imparts specific skills for specific purposes. It is mainly job-oriented. Training is given to both new and old employees throughout their stay in the organization. In contrast, management development includes the process by which managers and executives acquire not only skills and competence in their present jobs but also capacities for future managerial positions.

It may be noted here that the term 'training' refers to the programmes that facilitate the learning process which results in development (consequence of training). Hence, the terms 'training' and 'development' are applicable to both managers, executives and non-managerial personnel.

The points of distinction between the two are given below:

1. Training is the act of learning basic skills and knowledge necessary for a particular job or a group of jobs. Development, on the other hand, means growth of the individual in all respects. An organization works for the development of its executives in order to enable them to gain advanced knowledge and competence.
2. The term 'training' is used in the context of imparting skills to operative workers. But the term development is used in the context of management development.
3. Training programmes are directed towards maintaining and improving current job performance, while development programmes seek to develop skills and competence for future jobs.

13.9 SUMMARY

Training is the act of increasing the knowledge and skill of an employee for doing a particular job. Development implies an employee's growth and maturization. A systematic training programme helps in improving the quality and quantity of a worker's output, makes the worker committed and loyal to the organization, facilitates promotion and replacement and reduces spoiled work and accident rate.

13.10 SELF-ASSESSMENT QUESTIONS

1. Define training. Explain the advantages of training to the employees and the organization.
2. Discuss the various methods of training which are used for training the employees.
3. Distinguish between: (a) Training and Education; and (b) Training and Development.
5. Enumerate and explain the methods of Management Development.
4. What do you understand by development? Discuss briefly the systems of Management Development.

14 PERFORMANCE APPRAISAL

Learning Objective

The main objective of this chapter is to make the students learn about the fundamental concepts and methods of performance appraisal.

14.1 INTRODUCTION

Performance appraisal is one of the important sub-functions of staffing in management. Human behaviour is a complex phenomenon because no one can anticipate accurately what exactly a man is going to do. The individual joins an organization to satisfy his objectives. But the organization also has its own goals, which need not to be in conformity with the individual goals. If the goals of the individual and organization are extremely contradictory, a conflict will arise which either result into suppression of human personality or a complete will set back to his work. It is not desirable that individual's personality be suppressed but at the same time organization goals should also be achieved. For monitoring this process of achieving organizational goals, the performance of an individual needs to be assessed after a regular interval so that the desired behaviour could be maintained. This will also help the organization to satisfy the needs and the aspiration of the individual by providing him more facilities, improved working condition and carrier advancement.

According to *Heyel*, "the performance appraisal is the process of evaluating the performance and competencies of an employee in term of the requirements of the job for which he is employed, for the purpose of administration including placement, selection for promotions, providing financial rewards and other actions which require differential treatment among the members of a group as distinguished from action affecting all members equally".

Performance appraisal may also be defined as a process that involves:

(i) Setting work standard;
(ii) Assessing the employees actual performance relative to these standards; and

(iii) Providing feedback to employee with the aim of motivating that person to eliminate performance deficiencies or to continue to perform above par.

How Performance Appraisal differs from Counselling: Counselling follows performance appraisal. It covers two aspects, i.e., 'tell and sell' where the boss tells his subordinates where they stand. He adopts the method of criticism and persuasion. These two are the fundamental tools for counselling. In counselling, the boss discusses the future development by encouraging his subordinates to appraise themselves. Here, the give and take problem-solving approach may be used throughout the counselling meeting. The aim of the counselling is not just to tell the subordinates what they have done wrong. Instead, the boss reveals the root cause of the problem and secures constructive solution. The boss generally avoids criticizing his subordinates and he tries to emphasize the organizational development.

In fact, the performance appraisal process if understood in its comprehension includes the counselling and coaching. Counselling and appraisal differ slightly because the counselling is done on day-to-day basis whereas the appraisal is done after a regular interval. Therefore, it can be said that the performance appraisal would yield dividend only when the proper counselling takes place in an organization.

14.2 SIGNIFICANCE OF PERFORMANCE APPRAISAL

(i) **Career planning and development:** Performance feedback guides career decisions about specific career paths one should investigate.

(ii) **Compensation adjustments:** Performance evaluations help the decision-makers to determine who should receive pay raises. Many firms grant part or all of their pay increases and bonuses on the basis of merit, which is determined mostly through performance appraisal.

(iii) **Equal employment opportunity:** Accurate performance appraisals that actually measure job-related performance ensure that internal placement decisions are not discriminatory.

(iv) **External challenges:** Sometimes performance is influenced by factors outside the work environment, such as family, financial, health, or other personal matters. If these factors are uncovered through appraisals, the human resource department may be able to provide assistance.

(v) **Feedback to human resources:** Good or bad performance throughout the organization indicates how well the human resource are performing.

(vi) **Informational inaccuracies:** Poor performance may indicate errors in job analysis information, human resource plans, or other parts of the personnel management information system. Reliance on inaccurate information may lead to inappropriate hiring, training, or counselling decisions.

(vii) **Job-design errors:** Poor performance may be a symptom of ill-conceived job designs. Appraisal help diagnose these errors.

(viii) **Performance improvement:** Performance feedback allows the employee, the manager and personnel specialists to intervene with appropriate actions to improve performance.

(ix) Placement decisions: Promotions, transfers, and demotions are usually based on past or anticipated performance. Often promotions are a reward for past performance.

(x) Staffing process deficiencies: Good or bad performance implies strengths or weaknesses in the personnel department's staffing procedures.

(xi) Training and development needs: Poor performance may indicate a need for retraining. Likewise, good performance may indicate untapped potential that should be developed.

14.3 APPRAISAL PROCESS

The performance appraisal process generally involves the following steps:

Establish performance standards

↓

Communicate performance expectations to the employees

↓

Measure actual performance

↓

Compare actual performance with standards

↓

Discuss the appraisal with employee

↓

If necessary, initiate corrective action

The appraisal process begins with the establishment of performance standards. At the time of designing a job and formulating a job description, performance standard are usually developed for the positions. These standards should be clear and not vague and objective enough to be understood and measured.

Once performance standards are established, it is necessary to communicate these expectations. It should not be the part of the employees' job to guess that what is expected of them. Unfortunately, too many jobs have vague standards. The problem is compounded when these standards are not communicated to the employees. It is important to note that communication is a two-way street. Mere transfer of information from manager to the subordinate regarding expectations is not communication. Communication only takes place when the transfer of information has taken place and has been received and understood by the subordinate. Therefore, feedback is necessary from the subordinate to the manager. Satisfactory feedback ensures that the information communicated by manager has been received and understood in the way it was desired.

The third step in the appraisal process is the measurement of performance. To determine what actual performance is, it is necessary to acquire information about it. We should be concerned with how we measure and what we measure. To measure actual performance frequently, managers use four common source of information: personal observations, statistical reports, oral reports and written reports. Each has its own strengths and weaknesses. However, a combination of them increases both the number of input sources and possibility of receiving reliable information.

The fourth step in the appraisal process is the comparison of actual performance with standards. The attempt in this step is to note deviations between standard performance and actual performance so that we can proceed to the next phase of the appraisal process—the discussion of the appraisal with the employee.

One of the most challenging tasks facing managers is to present an accurate appraisal to the subordinate and then have the subordinate accept the appraisal in the right spirit. Appraising performance touches on one of the most emotionally charged activities–the assessment of another individual's contribution and ability. The impression that subordinates receive about their assessment has a strong impact on their self-esteem and very important, on their subsequent performance. Of course conveying good news is considerably less difficult for both the manager and the subordinates than conveying the bad news that performance has been below expectations. In this context, the discussion of the appraisal can have negative as well as positive motivational consequences. This is reinforced, for example, when we recognize that statistically speaking, half of all employees are below average.

The final step in the appraisal is the initiation of corrective action when necessary. Corrective action can be of two types. One is immediate and deals predominately with symptoms. The other is basic and deals with causes. Immediate correction action is often described as "putting out fires", whereas basic corrective action gets to the source of deviation and seek to adjust the difference permanently. Coaching and counselling may be done or person may be deputed for formal training courses and decision-making responsibilities and authority may be delegated to the subordinates. Attempt may also be needed to recommend for salary increased or promotions, if these decisions become plausible in light of the appraisal.

14.4 METHODS OF PERFORMANCE APPRAISAL

Here, we will look at how management can actually establish performance standard and devise instruments that can be used to measure and appraise an employee's performance. There are various methods to appraise the employees. No single method is always best. Each has its strengths and weaknesses. Following are the some of the standard methods used by the organizations to measure the performance of their employees:

1. Graphic Rating Scale

The graphic rating scale is the simplest and most popular technique for appraising the performance. It consists of typical rating scale. It lists traits (such as quality and reliability) and arrange of performance values (from unsatisfactory to outstanding) for each trait. The supervisor rates each subordinate by circling or checking the score that best describes his or her performance for each trait. The assigned value for the traits is then aggregated.

The rating method is easy to understand and easy to use. It permits the statistical tabulations of scores in terms of measures of central tendency, skewness and dispersion.

It permits a ready comparison of scores among employees. The scores presumably reveal the merit or value of every individual. However, this method has certain drawbacks also. There is a disadvantage that a high score on one factor can compensate for a low score on another. If a man scores low for quantity of work, this may be counter-balanced by high scores for attendance, attitude, cooperativeness, etc. In practice, rating tends to cluster on the high side with this system.

2. Ranking Method

One of the simplest methods of performance appraisal is ranking method. The supervisor evaluates all the subordinates under him on an overall basis and then rank orders them from exceptional to poor. Each rank indicates the position of an employee in relation to others under the same supervisor. In case these employees have worked under several supervisors each one of these supervisors ranks them according to his own assessment. Finally, all the ranks are grouped to see which one of the employees is rated low. An illustration of this is presented in figure given below, where five subordinates working under three supervisors are ranked.

Subordinates	*Supervisors*			*Mean Rank*
	Subhash	*Usha*	*Bijender*	
Sanjeev	2	4	3	3
Vinod	1	2	1	1.3
Tilak	3	1	2	2
Pradeep	5	3	4	4
Mahesh	4	5	5	4.6

One represents the highest rank. The individual rankings of three supervisors are added and they divided by the number of supervisors. The mean ranks are given in the last column. Since Vinod gets rank of 1.3, he is on an average, the best of all five subordinates.

The difficulty of this system is that the rater is asked to consider rated as a wholeman. It is quite obvious that human personally is very complicated and to ask a human being to pass a judgments on another human being in terms of saying he is 'good' or 'bad' is not only difficult but also undesirable. Asking the appraiser to rank employee on certain desirable traits can reduce the subjectiveness of this method.

3. Paired Comparison Method

Pair comparison force raters to compare each employee with all the employees in the same group who are being rated. For every trait (quantity of work, quality of work, and so on) every subordinate is paired with and compared to every other subordinate.

Suppose there are five employees to be rated. In the paired comparison method one can make chart, as in the following figure, of all possible pairs of employees for each trait. Then for each trait indicate (With a + or –), who is the better employee of the pair. Next the number of items an employee is rated better is added up. In figure, employee B ranked highest (has the most + marks) for quantity of work, while employee A was ranked highest for creativity.

For the trait **'Quantity of Work'**

As compared to	*A*	*B*	*C*	*D*	*E*
A		+	+	–	–
B	–		–	–	–
C	–	+		+	–
D	+	+	–		+ –
E	+	+	+	–	

↓

B ranks highest here

For the trait **'Creativity'**

As compared to	*A*	*B*	*C*	*D*	*E*
A		–	–	–	–
B	+		–	+	+
C	+	+		–	+
D	+	–	+		–
E	+	–	–	+	

↓

A ranks highest here

Note: + means 'better than'– means 'worse than'. For each chart add up the number of +'s in each column to get the highest ranked employee.

4. Forced Distribution Method

Some appraisers suffer from the constant error, i.e., they either rate all workers as excellent, average or poor. They fail to evaluate the poor, average or excellent employees clearly and cluster them closely around a particular point in the rating scale. The forced distribution system is devised to force the appraiser to fit the employees being appraised into predetermined ranges of scale.

The forced distributor system is applicable to a large group of employees. This system is based on the presumption that all employees can be divided into five-point scale of excellent, very good, average, acceptable and poor.

For example, he may be asked to identify and rank employees according to the following percentages:

Percentage of Employees	*Ranking*
10%	Poor
20%	Acceptable
40%	Average
20%	Very good
10%	Excellent

This method obviously eliminates the scope for subjective judgement as the part of the supervisors. Besides this, the system is easy to understand and administer. The objective of this technique is to spread out rating in the form of normal distribution. Many times this categorization is not found in work groups particularly when the group is comparatively small.

5. Checklist Method

In the checklist, the evaluator uses a list of behavioural descriptions and check-off those behaviours that apply to the employees. As figure illustrates on preceding page, the evaluator merely goes down the list and gives 'yes' or 'no' responses.

Once a checklist is complete, the staff of personnel department, not the manager giving the checklist, usually evaluates it. Therefore, the rater does not actually evaluate the employee's performance. He merely records it. An analyst in the personnel department then scores the checklist, often weighting the factors in relationship to their importance. The final evaluation can then be returned to the rating manager for discussion with the subordinate, or someone from the personnel department can provide feedback to the subordinates.

Sample checklist for appraising Sales Clerks

[Answer in Yes/No]

1. Are supervisor's orders usually followed?
2. Does the individual approach customers promptly?
3. Does the individual suggest additional merchandise to customers?
4. Does the individual keep busy when not servicing the customers?
5. Does the individual lose his or her temper in public?
6. Does the individual volunteer to help other employee?

6. Critical Incident Appraisal

With the critical incident method, the supervisor keeps a log of desirable or undesirable examples or incidents of each subordinates work related behaviour. Then every six months or so, the supervisor and subordinates meet and discuss the latter's performance using the specific incidents as examples.

This method can always be used to supplements another appraisal techniques and in that role it has several advantages. It provides you with specific and hard facts for explaining the appraisal. It ensures you to think about the subordinates' appraisal all during the year because the incidents must be accumulated. Keeping a running list of critical incidents should also provide concrete examples of what especially your subordinate can do to eliminate any performance deficiencies. Given below are a few typical incidents from a checklist for the appraisal of an individual in purchase department:

- Displayed unpleasant behaviour to a supplier.
- Consistently absent from work.
- Refused to work overtime when asked for.
- Talked rudely and abruptly on the telephone.
- Created a disturbance with loud speaking.
- Accepted inferior quality goods from a supplier.
- Failed to follow a chain of command.

- Suggested a new method to work.
- Accepted inferior quality goods.
- Developed a new procedure that reduced paper work.
- Rejected a bid that was unreasonably priced.
- Helped fellow employees to solve their problems.

7. Behaviourally Anchored Rating Scales (BARS)

This method assists upon accurate measurement and improvement of job performance through feedback to appraisees. It provides statements of standards against which the performance of an appraisee is evaluated. These standards are put on the scales in BARS. There is one scale for each significant broad performance area or job dimension. While developing BARS, small group discussions are conducted with would-be appraisers and appraisees with a view to identifying the significant dimensions of a job, which need to be evaluated. Different job dimensions identified in this way tend to form varied behaviorally anchored scales. For example, for a managerial position, the significant job dimensions may include: planning, organizing, controlling, leadership, motivation, communication and coordination.

Frequently, the scale is presented vertically with "excellent" performance at the top and "very poor" performance at the bottom. There are a number of scale points ranging between five and nine in between these two extremes. Suppose, five job dimensions have been identified in a particular job. There will be five scales in the appraisal format, each having several anchors illustrating varied amounts of performance along the scales. These scales may also embody statements to facilitate the clarity of the job dimension being evaluated. To cite an example of BARS for the position of an equipment operator, one job dimension in this position is verbal communication. The excellent performance on this scale may contain the following statements: checks verbal instructions against written procedures, checks to ensure he/she heard others correctly, brief replacements quickly and accurately—giving only relevant information. On the other hand, a very poor performance on this scale may contain the following statements: not answers when called, refuses to brief replacements, gives a person relieving him/her inaccurate information deliberately. The appraiser is required to indicate on each scale the level of performance he/she visualizes is revealed by the appraisee's typical job behaviour. While doing so, he/she makes use of the behavioural anchors and dimensions—clarification statements as guidelines and cues to recall the appraisee's job behaviour. Explicitly, it is not possible for the appraisers to place behavioural statements embracing all dimensions of job performance on the scales. Therefore, they merely indicate specific behavioural examples, which can be recalled for each appraisee at appropriate levels on the scale. In this way, these added anchors represent their own examples and rationale for an appraisal at a particular level.

BARS are useful for varied reasons. Their major characteristic relates to behavioural orientation. They are based on job behaviour—what individuals really do on their jobs, which is within their control. Attachment of behavioural anchors to different scales enables the appraisees to understand what they must do to organizing the dimension of a managerial job may include the following: assigns/delegates tasks, identifies alternative approaches to resource applications, coordinates human, financial and material resource applications and divides unit objective into identifiable tasks and sets due dates. This feature of specificity of these scales also enables the appraisers to provide relevant feedback to appraisees why they received a particular level of appraisal, and what they can do to improve their performance. This quality of the scale minimizes subjectivity in appraisal as well as also enables the appraisees to overcome their anxiety related to such appraisals.

BARS also provide participation to both appraisee and appraiser in their development. They become familiar with different aspects of the job as a result of discussions of job dimensions and anchors in small group meetings. This understanding provides guidelines to the appraiser while observing performance and enables the appraisee to judge the expectations of his/her superior. Any conflict between the appraiser and appraisee over the desired performance can be clarified in subsequent discussions. The participation of their ultimate users in the design of BARS also ensures their commitment to this method of appraisal.

As BARS are based on quantity measures, an attempt may be made to relate appraisal scores to current wage and salary structure with a view to ascertaining varying extents of rewards to different behaviours. Thus, the management may link different levels of merit raises to different ranges of scores on BARS. In addition, certain job dimensions can be singled out for bonus administration and allied purposes. Last but not the least, the scales can also be used to identify behavioural criteria to facilitate selection decisions, construct selection tests and specify behavioural training objectives. Explicitly, the job dimensions in BARS can help in formulating training courses, and the behaviour anchors can indicate the specific behaviours to be learned in different content areas. The poor performance areas can be pinpointed to improve performance. Notwithstanding these advantages, BARS form a time-consuming method. Although it is promising, much more research is required to demonstrate its ability to eliminate certain types of rater errors.

8. Management by Objectives (MBO) Method:

This method of appraisal was introduced and made popular by Peter F. Drucker. Management by objectives requires the manager to get specific measurable goals with each employee and then periodically discuss his or her progress towards these goals. You could engage in a modest MBO program with subordinates by jointly setting goals and periodically providing feedback. However, the term MBO almost always refers to a comprehensive, organization wide goal setting and appraisal programme that consists of following steps:

- **(i) Set the organization's goal:** Establish on organization wide plan for next year and set goals.
- **(ii) Set departmental goals:** Here department/heads and their superiors jointly set goals for their departments.
- **(iii) Discuss departmental goals:** Department heads discuss the department's goals with all subordinates in the department and ask them to develop their own individual goals; In other words, how can each employee contribute to the department's attaining its goals.
- **(iv) Define expected results:** Here department heads and their subordinates set short-term performance targets.
- **(v) Performance reviews:** Department heads compare the actual performance of each employee with expected results.
- **(vi) Provide feedback:** Department heads hold periodic performance review meetings with subordinates to discuss and evaluate the latters' progress in achieving expected results.

MBO, thus, is a performance-oriented system. A well thought out MBO system provides the following benefits to the organization.

(i) The setting up of objectives provides a basis for coordinating between and among various units of the organization.
(ii) It establishes a linkage between the performance of the individual and organizations. Hence, both move in the achievement of same objectives.
(iii) It becomes easy to implement because those who carry out the plans also participate in setting up these plans.
(iv) Each employee becomes aware of the exact task that he is supposed to perform leading to better utilization of capacity and talent.
(v) The communication chain between and among employees and units are clearly established facilitating information sharing.
(vi) The performance appraisal is built in the system itself. It provides the guidelines for self as well as evaluation by the supervisor against the set tasks and goals.
(vii) It facilitates the task of employee guidance and counselling.

Notwithstanding the above merits, the result-oriented procedure has several limitations. The procedure is impracticable in situations where the superior is decisive and seldom bothers to involve the subordinates in goal-setting goals. Moreover, the procedure stresses tangible goals (i.e. production) and ignores intangible goals (i.e. morale). This may also cause concealment of poor performance, distortion of data and the fixation of low goals.

MBO is a time-consuming. Taking the time to set objectives, to measure progress and to provide feedback can take several hours per employee per year, over and above the time you spent doing each person's appraisal. Setting objectives with the subordinate sometimes turns into a tug of war with you pushing for higher quotas and the subordinate pushing for lower ones.

14.5 GREY AREAS IN PERFORMANCE APPRAISAL

The ideal approach to performance evaluation is that in which evaluator is free from personal biases, prejudices and idiosyncrasies. This is because when evaluation is objective, it minimizes the potential capricious and dysfunctional behaviour of the evaluator, which may be detrimental to the achievement of the organizational goals. However, a single foolproof evaluation method is not available. Inequities in evaluation often destroy the usefulness of the performance system—resulting in inaccurate, invalid appraisals, which are unfair too. There are many significant factors, which deter or impede objective evaluation. These factors are:

(i) **Halo Error:** It occurs when the rater allows one aspect of a man's character or performance to influence his entire evaluation. It is the tendency of many raters to set their rating is excessively influenced by one characteristic rather than on all subsequent characteristics.

This problem often occurs with employees who are especially friendly or unfriendly toward the supervisor. For example, an unfriendly employee will often be rated unsatisfactory for all traits rather than just for trait "gets along well with others". Being aware of this problem is a major step toward avoiding it. Supervisory training can also alleviate the problem.

(ii) Central Tendency: Many supervisors have a central tendency when filling in rating scales. For example, if the rating scale ranges from 1 to 7, they tend to avoid the highs (6 and 7) and lows (1 and 2) and rate most of their people between 3 and 5. If you use a graphic scale, this central tendency could mean that all employees are simply rated "average". Such a restriction can distort the evaluations, making than less useful for promotion, salary or counselling purposes. Ranking employees instead of using a graphic rating scale can avoid this central tendency problem because all employees must be ranked and this cannot all be rated averages.

(iii) Leniency or Strictness: The leniency bias results when raters tend to be easy in evaluating the performance of employees. Such raters see all employee performance as good and rate it favourably. The strictness bias is the opposite; it results from raters being too harsh in their evaluation. Sometimes, the strictness bias results because the rater wants others to think he or she is a 'tough judge' of people's performance. Both leniency and strictness errors more commonly occur when performance standards are vague.

(iv) Cross cultural biases: Every rater holds expectations about human behaviour that are based on his or her culture. When people are expected to evaluate others from different cultures, they may apply their cultural expectations to someone who has a different set of beliefs or behaviours. In many Asian cultures the elderly are treated with greater respect and are held in higher esteem than they are in many western cultures. If a young worker is asked to rate an older subordinate, this culture value of "respect and esteem" may bias the rating. Similarly, in some Arabic cultures, women are expected to play a very subservient role, especially in public. Assertive women may receive biased rating because of these cross-cultural differences. With greater cultural diversity and the movement of employees across international borders, this potential source of bias becomes more likely.

14.6 SUGGESTIONS FOR IMPROVEMENT

The fact that managers frequently encounter problems with performance appraisal should not lead you to throw up your hands and give up on the concept. There are things that can be done to make performance appraisal more effective. The following are the suggestions in this regard:

(i) Behaviourally based Measures: Many traits often considered to be related to good performance may in fact, have little or no performance relatively. Traits like loyalty, initiative, courage, reliability and self-expression are intuitively appealing as desirable characteristics in employees. But the relevant question is, are individual who are evaluated as high on those traits higher performances than those who rate low? We cannot answer this question. We know that there are employees who rate high on these characteristics and are poor performers. We can find others who are excellent performers but do not score well on traits such as these. Our conclusion is that traits like loyalty and managers may prize initiative, but there is no evidence to support that certain traits will be adequate synonyms for performance in a large cross-section of jobs.

A second weakness in traits is the judgement self. What is loyalty? "When is an employee reliable?" What you consider 'loyalty', I may not. So traits suffer from weak interrater agreement.

Behaviourally derived measures can deal with both of these objectives. Because they deal with specific examples of performance–both good and bad–we avoid the problem of using inappropriate substitute.

(ii) Trained Appraisers: If you cannot find good raters, the alternative is to make good raters. The training of appraisers can make these more accurate raters.

Errors can be minimized through training workers. Training workshops are usually intended to explain to raters the purpose of the procedure, the mechanics of 'how to do it', pitfalls or biases they may encounter and answer to their questions. The training may include trail runs evaluating other classmates to gain some supervised experience. Companies even use videotapes and role playing evaluation sessions to give raters both experience with and insight into the evaluation process. During the training, the timing and scheduling of evaluations are discussed.

(iii) Multiple Raters: As the number of raters increases, the probability of attaining more accurate information increases. If person has had ten supervisors, nine having rated him or her excellent and one poor, we can discount the value of the one poor evaluation. Therefore, by moving employees about within the organizations so as to gain a number of evaluations, we increase the probability of achieving move valid and reliable evaluations.

(iv) Peer Evaluations: Periodically, managers may find it difficult to evaluate their subordinates' performance because they are not working with them every day. Unfortunately, unless they have this information, they may not be making an accurate assessment. And of their goal of the performance evaluation is to identify deficient areas and provide constructive feedback to their subordinates, they may be providing a disservice to these subordinates by not having all the information.

Yet, how do they get this information? One of the easiest means is through peer evaluations. Employees' co-worker, people explicitly familiar with the jobs involved mainly because they too are doing the same thing, conducts peer evaluations. They are the ones most aware of co-workers' day-to-day work behaviour and should be given the opportunity to provide the management with some feedback.

The main advantages to peer evaluation are that (i) there is a tendency for co-workers to offer more constructive insight to each other so that, as a unit, each will improve and (ii) their recommendations tend to be more specific regarding job behaviour-unless specificity exists, constructive measures are hard to gain. But necessary condition for this method is that the environment in the organization must be such that politics and competition for promotion are minimized. This environment can only be found in the most "mature" organizations.

(v) Evaluation Interviews: Evaluation interviews are performance review sessions that give employees essential feedback about their past performance or future potential. Their importance demands preparation. Normally this includes a review of previous appraisals, identification of specific behaviours to be reinforced during the evaluation interview and a plan or approach to be used in providing the feedback.

The evaluator may provide this feedback through several appraisals: tell and sell, tell and listen and problem solving. The tell and sell approach reviews the employee's performance and tries to persuade the employee to perform better. It works best with new employees.

The tell and listen allows the employee to explain reasons, give excuses and describe defensive feelings about performance. It attempts to overcome these reactions by counselling the employee on how to perform better.

The problem solving approach identifies problem that are interfering with employee performance. Then, through training, coaching or counselling goals for future performance are set to remove these deficiencies.

14.7 SUMMARY

Performance appraisal is a critical activity. It includes counselling and coaching as well. Its goal is to provide an accurate picture of past and/or future performance of an employee. To achieve this, performance standards are established. The standards are based on the job-related criteria that best determine successful job performance. Where possible, actual performance is measured directly and objectively. From a wide variety of appraisal techniques, specialists select the methods that most effectively measure employee performance against the previously set standards. Techniques can be selected both to review past performance and to anticipate performance in the future.

The human resources department, often with little input from other parts of the organization usually designs the appraisal process. When it is time to implement a new appraisal approach, those who do the rating may have little idea about the appraisal process or its objectives. To overcome this shortcoming, the human resources department may design and conduct appraisal workshops to train managers.

A necessary requirement of the appraisal process is employee feedback through an evaluation interview. The interviewer tries to balance positive areas of good performance with areas where performance is deficient so that the employee receives a realistic view. Perhaps the most significant challenge raised by performance appraisals is the feedback they provide about the human resources department's performance. Human resources specialists need to be keenly aware that poor performance, especially when it is widespread, may reflect problems with previous human resources management activities.

14.8 SELF-ASSESSMENT QUESTIONS

1. Define performance appraisal. How does it differ from counselling? Describe the process of appraisal.
2. Explain in detail the following:
   (a) Graphic Rating Scale
   (b) Management by Objectives
   (c) Critical Incident Method
   (d) Behaviourally Anchored Rating Scale
3. What are the uses of performance appraisal? Discuss.
4. What are the limitations of performance appraisals? Give suggestions for improvement in performance appraisal.

15

LEADERSHIP

Learning Objective

The main objective of this chapter is to make the students learn about the concept of leadership, leadership styles and theories.

15.1 BACKGROUND

There is a profound difference between manager and leader, and both are essential in a sound management system. To 'manage' means "to bring about, to accomplish, to have charge of or responsibility for, and to conduct". On the other hand, the 'leading' is "influencing, guiding in direction, course, action, opinion". The distinction is critical. Managers are people who do things right and leaders are people who do the right thing. In this lesson, you'll learn that leadership is a very complex art that is essential for the success in mission. In fact, your knowledge of effective leadership principles and concepts coupled with their application at your workplace may prove to be rewarding both professionally and personally.

Let's start with a simple definition of leadership. Leadership is the process of influencing an organized group towards a common goal. This definition sounds easy, but the application can provide a real challenge.

Your goal as a leader in the organization is to do the best job you can at influencing your people towards a common goal. Since you are dealing with a very diverse group of people, it is important to understand the different approaches to motivate them to meet their goals. Leadership style is the pattern of behaviours you use when you are trying to influence the behaviours of those you are trying to lead. Each leadership style can be identified with a different approach to problem solving and decision-making. Possessing a better understanding of the various leadership styles and their respective developmental levels will help you match a given style for a specific situation. The challenge is to master the ability to change your leadership style for a given situation as the person's development level changes.

How can you help your followers increase their development level? Here are some practical ideas:

1. Explain to them what you want to get done.
2. Provide the guidance they might need before they start.
3. Give them the opportunity to complete the task on their own.
4. Give them a lot of positive encouragement.

Your goal should be to help your followers increase their competence and commitment to independently accomplish the tasks assigned to them, so that gradually you can begin to use less time-consuming styles and still get high quality results. Your organization depends on positive, effective leaders at all levels to perform the mission. There is no single leadership style that is appropriate in every situation; therefore, for you to be effective leaders you need to learn to understand your environment, your situation and the circumstances to help you act accordingly. Remember, your success as a leader will depend on your assessment of the situation and your ability to communicate what you want in such a way that others will do as you wish—that is the art of leadership.

15.2 WHAT IS LEADERSHIP

It is difficult to define the term "leadership". However, as a starting point, we may proceed with the workable definition that a leader is one who leads others and is able to carry an individual or a group towards the accomplishment of a common goal. He is able to carry them with him, because he influences their behaviour. He is able to influence their behaviour, because he enjoys some power over them. They are willing to be influenced, because they have certain needs to satisfy in collaboration with him. *French and Raven* have proposed the following bases of power for a person exerting influence:

1. **Legitimate**–That the targets of influence, followers or sub-ordinates understand that the power the leader enjoys is legitimate and they should comply with his orders in order to meet their own goals.
2. **Reward**–That the followers know that the leader has the power to grant promotions, monetary inducements or other rewards if his orders are complied with.
3. **Coercive**–That the followers know that if the leader's orders are not complied with, he has the power to hire, fire, perspire and discharge the followers.
4. **Expert**–That the followers know that the leader possesses specialist's knowledge in the field they lack it.
5. **Referent**–That the followers feel attracted towards him because of his amiable manners, pleasing personality or they feel that he is well connected with high-ups.

It is apparent then that the first three power bases indicate positional power, which one derives from one's position. The other two indicate personal power, which is based on the individual's own characteristics. In any case, the leader exercises his influence because of one or more of these types of power and obtains compliance from the followers. How far he succeeds in his attempts will depend upon several other factors that we will discuss during the course of this lesson.

Leadership is, therefore, regarded as the process of influencing the activities of an individual or a group in efforts towards goal achievement in a given situation. This process, as *Heresy and Blanchard* suggest, can be explained in the form of the following equation:

$$L = f (L, F, S,)$$

That is, the leadership is a function of the leader (L), the follower (F) and other situational variables (S). One who exercises this influence is a leader whether he is a manager in a formal organization, an informal leader in an informal group or the head of a family. It is undoubtedly true that a manager may be a weak leader or a leader may a weak manager, but it is also equally probable that a manager may be a true leader or a leader may be true manager. *A manager who is a true leader as well is always desirable*. Situational variables include the whole environment like the task, the group, organizational policies, etc.

15.3 LEADERSHIP STYLES

Leadership style is the way a managerial leader applies his influence in getting work done through his subordinates in order to achieve the organizational objectives. The main attitude or belief that influences leadership style is the perceived role of the manager versus the role of the subordinates. It depends upon the role of the leader whether he likes to work more of a colleague, facilitator and decision maker and on the other hand the response of the subordinates would determine the particular style to be in application. Broadly speaking, there are three basic leadership styles:

1. **Autocratic or Dictatorial Leadership:** In this leadership style, the leader assumes full responsibility for all actions. Mainly he relies on implicit obedience from the group in following his orders. He determines plans and policies and makes the decision-making a one man show. He maintains very critical and negative relations with his subordinates. He freely uses threats of punishment and penalty for any lack of obedience. This kind of leadership has normally very short life.
2. **Democratic Leadership:** In this case, the leader draws ideas and suggestions from his group by discussion, consultation and participation. He secures consensus or unanimity in decision-making. Subordinates are duly encouraged to make any suggestion as a matter of their contribution in decision-making and to enhance their creativity. This kind of leadership style is liked in most civilized organization and has very long life.
3. **Laissez-faire Free Rein Leadership:** Quite contrary to autocratic leadership style, in this leadership style the leader depends entirely on his subordinates to establish their own goals and to make their own decisions. He lets them plan, organize and proceed. He takes minimum initiative in administration or information. He is there to guide the subordinates if they are in a problem. This kind of leadership is desirable in mainly professional organizations and where the employees are self-motivated. Leader works here just as a member of the team.

We shall now discuss the roots of such leadership styles, i.e., we shall try to understand as to how these different leadership styles have been evolved by the management scholars.

15.4 APPROACHES TO LEADERSHIP STYLES

There are broadly three major approaches to the study of the leadership phenomenon. Attempts have been made to understand this phenomenon by studying (i) traits of the leader, (ii) behaviour of the leader, or (iii) situations in which leadership is exercised. The trait approach was followed during 1930-1960. The behavioural approach attempted to explain leader behaviour in terms of his styles or practices, but altogether neglected the follower and situational characteristics. Therefore, an approach, called the situational approach, which had the potential to incorporate important variables, developed during the 1970s.

15.4.1 Trait Approach

There have always been very few persons in society or organizations who are leaders. The vast majority of people constitute the followers. But what is it that distinguishes leaders from non-leader? Or what make a person the successful leader? It is, perhaps, something that is in-born in him and which the followers lack. This approach stresses the in-born qualities or characteristics of an individual.

One way to identify the traits is to ask the leader himself how he considers himself different from his followers or what distinguishing characteristics he possesses. Another way is to analyze the past and the present of the leader in terms of his family background, education, career events, etc. and build up a list of traits or attributes that the leader possesses. In both cases, a leader's life becomes highly interesting only when he has emerged as a leader. This compilation of a list of traits or attributes does not give any predictive power and therefore, investigators have tended to relate leadership even with handwriting [graphology], skull shape [phrenology] and occult influence of stars [astrology].

A number of studies have been conducted to identify traits or characteristics that can be used to distinguish successful from un-successful leaders or followers. As *Ivancevich et al.* have suggested, the most researched traits include the following:

1. Physical characteristics — Age, appearance and height
2. Social background — Education, social status and mobility
3. Intelligence — Judgement, knowledge, decisiveness and fluency of speech
4. Personality — Alertness, dominance, extroversion, independence, creativity and self-confidence
5. Task-related characteristics — Achievement drive, initiative, persistence, enterprise and task orientation.
6. Social characteristics — Attractiveness, popularity, sociability and interpersonal skills.

Different studies have identified different numbers of traits. With each study, the list of traits studied has become longer and longer. Some traits are, however, common to all the studies. In general, there appears to be a consensus that effective leaders possessed intelligence, social maturity and breadth, inner motivation and achievement drive, and a human relations attitude. However, inability to value the followers' ideas, poor human relations, display of emotional immaturity, and poor communication skills have been regarded as dysfunctional to effective leadership.

Criticism

The trait approach is weak in several respects. But before we list the basic criticisms, we would like to give some examples of leadership that will themselves throw up the main shortcomings of this approach. Mahatma Gandhi, a frail man, not even adequately clothed, but wedded to truth, became the Father of the Indian Nation. Lal Bahadur Shastri, a short stature person, after becoming the Prime Minister, used to be an object of amusement, but not very long thereafter, when the Indian Army marched into Pakistani territory, he became a hero and died at the height of his glory while negotiating a settlement at Tashkent. Indira Gandhi, without much formal education, was in 1971, after the Bangladesh war, acclaimed as 'Chandi' and 'Durga' in Ramlila grounds and presented with a sword, etc. by her staunch critics. But the same "pride of the nation" fell from grace in 1977.

Our purpose is not to comment upon anyone's leadership, but to highlight the fact that the leader remaining the same, his effectiveness has varied in different situations. His or her inborn characteristics are given but whether one succeeds or fails as leader, perhaps, depends upon something else. It seems a person is at his best when he comes across a situation, which needs him. Further, not many things were common among those who succeeded or failed.

In times of crisis, a simpler form of leadership is required. Leaders emerge more easily in unstable situations. Decisions in such situations relate to either/or. Many alternatives are not available. Full cooperation is forthcoming from all corners. But the complexity of decision-making is heightened in the not-so unstable situations when on the spot decisions are not needed and consultation and generation of the search process is possible. Most organizations, no doubt, dynamic but not so unstable as to be crisis-torn, have complex tasks and so, a hierarchy of leaders is required. Therefore, most leadership situations are highly complex and cannot be adequately explained by the trait approach.

We now list criticisms levelled against this approach.

1. There is no finite set of traits to distinguish successful from unsuccessful leaders. Rarely, if ever, do two lists agree on the essential characteristics of the effective leader. A survey by *Bird and Stogdill* shows: (i) Less than 5 per cent of the traits are common in four or more of the studies surveyed, and (ii) leaders are not markedly different from their followers. The same traits are widely distributed among the non-leaders as well.
2. It is difficult to indicate what mix of traits is necessary to make an effective leader. Its measurement is problematic.
3. No consistent relationship is discernible between attributes and leader behaviour.
4. This approach stresses the inborn qualities or characteristics of individuals and therefore, in turn, questions the value of training individuals to assume leadership positions. Training may help improve a person if he possesses the basic traits. Therefore, it was essential first to identify those who possess these traits and then impart training only to such persons. According to this approach, training would be fruitless in the case of others. This view seems to be inappropriate in the light of the aforesaid criticisms and inconsistent with the results of training programmes.

5. Different traits appear necessary for different roles even in the same organization. At lower managerial levels where there is a direct contact between the worker and the supervisor, technical knowledge is of paramount importance. At middle management levels where they interpret and elaborate policies, human relations skills are more important than technical knowledge. At higher managerial levels where ideas are generated, policies are framed, strategic and long-term planning is undertaken, ideational resource possessing conceptual skills gains pre-eminent position. Organizations compete, not with products, with people. So uniformity of traits across all levels is questioned.
6. Leadership in a large organization demands a specialized limited role, but a multiplicity of roles has to be played in a small organization. Therefore, a different combination of traits for the two roles would be required.
7. The approach does not consider what the leader does, ignores followers and their effect on the leader. The effectiveness of leadership is dependent to a large extent on the situation or environment surrounding the leadership or influence process.
8. It requires an initial separation of people into "leaders" and "non-leaders" or "good leaders" and "not so good leaders". But there appears to be no particular correlation between a man's ethics and morals and his power to attract followers.
9. When an individual is faced with a problem, then only the presence or absence of the trait required in that situation becomes known. That is, a trait in order to get expressed needs a situation, without which, the presence or absence of that trait in a particular individual may not be known.

There is, therefore, an increasing recognition of wide variations in the characteristics of individuals who become leaders in similar situations and of even greater divergence in the traits of leaders working in different situations. Despite its shortcomings, no approach is entirely worthless. It is on the basis of its weaknesses that the foundations of new approaches are laid. Thus, the trait approach paved the way for later approaches like the behavioural and the situational.

15.4.2 Behavioural Approach

When it was apparent that the trait basis was not adequate to explain the leadership phenomenon, the theorists directed their attention to the study of leader behaviour. This approach was advocated during the 1950s-1960s. The roots of this approach lie in how the management viewed the workers. Under the spell of the traditional management approach, men were regarded as inert appendages to the machine. It was the function of management to coerce, direct and motivate them through the offer of economic rewards. Management attempted to reduce wastes of time and material to increase efficiency and no consideration was shown to men as assets. In other words, the philosophy was that people were, by nature, lazy uncreative and irresponsible, and so leadership has to be directive. However, during the 1930s, the Hawthorne experiments exploded the myth of management thinking. *Elton Mayo* and his associates discovered the existence of informal groups and informal leaders and laid stress on interpersonal relationships as a significant influence on productivity. Therefore, the scientific management advocates ignored human behaviour and expressed sole concern for output, whereas the human relations movement showed an overriding concern for people.

These two movements gave birth to leaderships studies which characterized leaders as basically adopting a particular leadership style, say, dictatorial/autocratic/authoritarian/ democratic/supportive/consultative/participative or the laissez-faire/free-rein type. These studies were organized to examine the impact of a particular leadership style over individual and group behaviour. The dictatorial leader was one who had absolute authority and used threats and punishments to extract work out of people. An authoritarian leader was one who claimed recourse to authority vested in him to hire, fire and reward people. He issued directions and maintained formal relationship with people. Democratic or participative leaders considered subordinates' views in organizational matters, provided guidance on their work problems and emotionally involved themselves in helping workers achieve organizational as well as individual goals. The laissez-faire or free-rein leader supplied information to the group members, but displayed little emotional involvement and a minimum of participation in the group activities. He lets them decide themselves without laying down any procedures. This amounts to virtual absence of formal leadership or is analogous to abdication of responsibility.

Studies of the type just mentioned were inconclusive and brought out conflicting results. On the whole, it was revealed that authoritarian or autocratic leaders improved production temporarily, but depreciated human assets seriously. In the case of democratic leaders, output was not as high as in the case of the autocratic ones, but quality was better and human problems were minimum. Laissez-faire or free rein leaders evoked an altogether a different response. Here, organization suffered on both the counts-products as well as human relations. In the final analysis, these studies appeared to suggest that leadership style could be either/or, i.e., just of one particular type and the best leadership style was the democratic type involving all workers in decision-making.

In somewhat similar vein, *Tannenbaum and Schmidt* considered a range of leader behaviour [7 points] from the manager able to make decisions which non-managers accept at one extreme of the continuum, and the manager and non-managers jointly making decisions within limits defined by organizational constraints at the other end of the continuum. This continuum suggests that there is scope for a variety of leadership practices, but it is again indicative of the dominant philosophy of a leader. It does not predict that different departments of the same organization could follow different leadership styles. Perhaps, the authoritarian style may be appropriate for the production department, but a democratic style may have to be used in the research and development department. It is also silent in regard to the fact that the same leader could adopt different styles for different matter. *Golembiewski* suggests that different kinds of leadership styles are appropriate for different kinds of problems. There are some roles that are peculiar to the superior, such as setting general goals. The generally appropriate leadership style in such a case is leader centred. For "mixed" roles like relocating machines on which individuals have worked for many years, an appropriate leadership style is group-centred. However, there are some roles that are peculiar to the subordinates such as deciding how to use a tool. In such a case, one may even use the free-rein leadership style.

A number of studies have lent support to the two basic styles of leadership-authoritarian and democratic. Before we discuss some of the important studies, we may point out that various terms like authoritarian, autocratic, leader-centred, task-oriented, job-centred, goal attainment, initiating structure or concern for production leaders have been treated in most studies at par. Terms like democratic, participative, group-centred, employee-centred, relationship-oriented, group maintenance, consideration or concern for people leaders have again been taken to mean more or less the same thing.

1. University of Michigan Studies

The Institute for Social research at the University of Michigan conducted a number of studies to identify styles of leader behaviour that result in increased work-group performance and satisfaction. Their studies resulted in the development of two distinct styles of leadership: (i) the job-centred (task-oriented) leadership style emphasizing the use of rules, procedures, and close supervision of subordinates, and (ii) the employee-centred (relationship-oriented) leadership style emphasizing delegation of authority and responsibility and concern for employee welfare, needs, advancement and personal growth.

The use of both styles led to increase in production, but it was slightly higher in the case of the job-centred leadership style. However, the use of direct pressure and close supervision led to decreased satisfaction and increased turnover and absenteeism. The employee-centred approach led to improved work flow procedures and more cohesion in interaction. This resulted in increased satisfaction and decreased turnover and absenteeism. This fact would obviously suggest the superiority of the employee-centred leadership style.

Criticism

These studies have met with the following criticisms:

1. A serious point of criticism is that these studies fail to point out whether leader behaviour is the cause or effect. A productive group may suggest it to the leader to adopt an employee-centred approach. Whether the employee-centred leadership style makes the group productive or whether the productive group induces the leader to be employee-centred is not clear.
2. It suggests leader behaviour to be of one particular type and static whereas, in practice, it changes from situation to situation. A particular leadership style is appropriate in a normal circumstance and an altogether different one when there is pressure is an extra-ordinary situation.
3. The use of a questionnaire completed by subordinates introduces an element of employee bias in it and may not present the true view of the leadership style. The individuals and groups that are satisfied and attracted towards the leader are more likely to describe the leader as considerate than those who are conflict-ridden and dislike the leader.
4. As in the trait approach, these studies also did not take into consideration the nature of the subordinate's task or the personal characteristics, group characteristics or other situational variables.

2. Ohio State Studies

Initiated in 1945, the Bureau of Business Research studies by *Fleishman and others* at the Ohio State University identified two independent leadership dimensions called Initiating Structure and Consideration which meant more or less the same thing as task behaviour and relationship behaviour of a leader. These concepts were identified as a result of two types of questionnaires: (i) Leader Behaviour Description Questionnaire [LBDQ] completed by the peers, superiors and subordinates; and (ii) Leader Opinion Questionnaire [LOQ] scored by the leaders themselves.

The scores derived from the responses to the questionnaire were used to indicate a manager's style of leadership. These studies revealed that it was just not a question of either/or, rather many shades of styles or combinations of styles are possible. A management may score high on both dimensions, low on both, or high on one and low on the other. A large number of individual research efforts were undertaken to determine the effect of the initiating structure and consideration on group performance and morale. In the beginning, it was widely believed that the most effective leadership style was high on both the initiating structure and consideration. But later the results amply demonstrated that no single style emerged as being the best. In some situations, high initiating structure and high consideration style would prove effective, but in some others, even low initiating structure and low consideration style could prove effective.

Studies show that low consideration and high initiating structure go with grievances and turnover; and so improved consideration and reduced structure would lead to decline in grievances and turnover. However, as *Fleishman and Harris* suggest, there must be certain critical levels beyond which increased consideration or decreased structure have no effect on grievance or turnover rates. But leader behaviour characterized by low consideration is more critical than behaviour characterized by high structure. Apparently, a manager can compensate for high structure by increased consideration, but a low consideration manager cannot compensate by decreasing his structuring behaviour.

Criticism

The Ohio State studies and Michigan studies were being carried out at the same time, but the Ohio State studies marked a break from the rest in the sense that instead of a single continuum, they used two separate dimensions. This was a significant step forward in itself. However these studies suffered from more or less the same weaknesses as the Michigan studies. A few of such weaknesses are listed here:

1. These studies again did not consider the situational factors and the influence of these factors on leader effectiveness. Very little is known about how these styles affect work group performance. An individual's productivity is influenced by many other factors such as his social status within the group, type of technological process employed, his psychological reward from working with a particular type of leader, his expectations of a certain style, etc. Even the formality of the organizational structure was an important influence on the effectiveness of a given leadership style.
2. The use of two questionnaires–one to be completed by the subordinates and the other by the leaders themselves has also come in for severe criticism. The perceptions of the two are not likely to agree. This presents a serious measurement problem: how is leadership style measured–as perceived by the leader or the subordinates?

3. Managerial Grid Study

Blake and Mounton have used "Concern for Production" and "Concern for People" in their Managerial Grid on horizontal and vertical axes respectively. These two terms convey the same meaning as used in the Ohio state studies with the difference that "concern for" shows a predisposition about something and so is an attitudinal dimension, whereas initiating structure and consideration represent behaviours as perceived by others and so, are observed behaviour.

An axis can be divided into 9 points. As the leader advances from 1 to 9 on horizontal scale, his concern for production increases and it becomes maximum when the leader has reached point 9. Similarly, when he travel along the vertical scale, his concern for people becomes maximum when he reaches point 9. This is depicted in the figure given below:

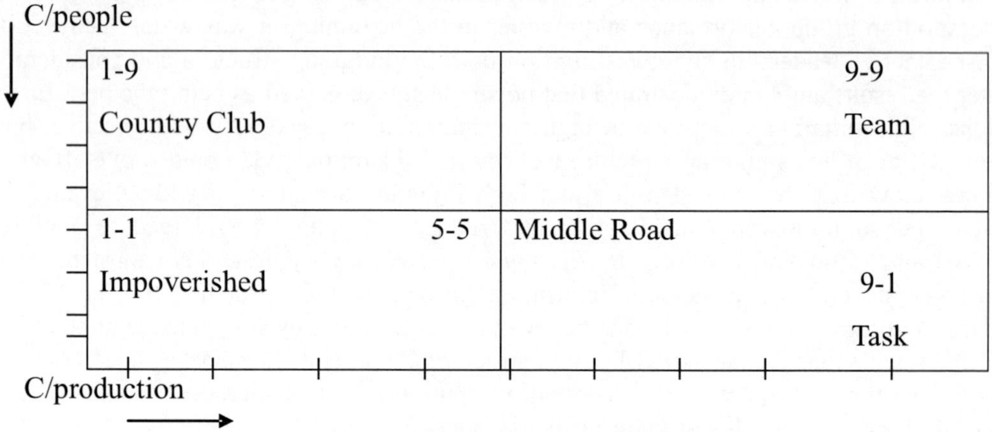

Figure 15.1 The managerial grid leadership style.

The five leadership styles mentioned in the figure above mean the following:

Impoverished (1-1)	Extension of minimum effort to get required work done.
Country Club (1-9)	Thoughtful attention to needs of people for satisfying relationship
Middle of the Road (5-5)	Balancing the necessity to get out work while maintaining the morale of people at a satisfactory level.
Task (9-1)	Interference from human elements permitted to a minimum degree.
Team (9-9)	Committed people having common stake in organizational purpose.

Behavioural Theories: A Final Look

As distinct from the trait approach, behavioural theories endeavoured to explain the leadership phenomenon in terms of the behaviour of the leader. What the leader does was regarded as more important than the leader's personal characteristics. Therefore, the investigators examined the practices or styles that leaders adopted and gave the impression that a leader had a dominant philosophy. A leader was either, say, authoritarian or democratic. For the first time, the Ohio State studies considered two independent leadership dimensions and revealed that leadership style could be any mix of the two dimensions. (They isolated two dimensions of a leader's style, perhaps, only for statistical convenience. In a later work, four to twelve dimensions have been studied.) This research, no doubt, advanced our knowledge, but its stress on effective leader behaviour being characterized by high initiating structure and high consideration or ineffective leader behaviour being marked by low scores on both dimensions, however, seems misplaced. There is a lot of evidence to question this inference. In the military organization during wartime in the field, a high initiating structure and low consideration style would be most appropriate. A similar parallel may be drawn in the case of the firefighting department when a house is on fire.

15.4.3 Situational Approach

Behavioural approach advanced our knowledge in understanding the leadership phenomenon by explaining various combinations of leadership styles. What characteristics an individual possesses did not explain his emergence as a leader nor did it explain what mix of traits one should have to prove effective if one happens to be placed in a leadership position. The trait approach, in effect, explained some of the desirable characteristics that leaders had or a leader should have. But it could not suggest with certainty that one who possesses particular characteristics shall be a leader. The behaviour approach, learning from the weaknesses of the trait approach, went a step further to explain the practices available to a leader in order to discharge his leadership dimensions are available. But this again failed to indicate a "best" style of leadership, which was universally appropriate. As a result, it was recognized that it is not style that matters; in fact, no style is good or bad, it is the situation that makes it so. What makes a style to be effective or ineffective is the situational difference. The behavioural approach failed to consider this situation as an important element. It merely thought of various leadership practices that prove productive or not so productive, but it did not consider its "why".

It is, therefore, clear that it is not a matter of the best style, but of what style is likely to be effective in a particular situation. What is relevant for an industrial setting may not be relevant for an educational institution. What is relevant for an administrative office in an educational institution may not be relevant for the teaching staff. A number of leader behaviour styles may be effective or ineffective depending on the important elements of the situation.

Leader behaviour is affected by several situational factors like managerial characteristics, subordinate characteristics, group factors, organizational factors, etc., which, in fact, constitute the environment of the leader. It is difficult to list all these factors, but it suggests that leadership is a very complex process. The situational theories attempt to provide at least partial examination of how these factors impact on leaderships.

(1) Fiedler's Contingency Theory

Fiedler's Contingency Theory specifies that the performance of a group is contingent upon both the motivational system of the leader and the degree to which the leader has control and influence in a particular situation. That is, a leader's effectiveness is contingent upon the favourableness or unfavourableness of the situation. The favourableness of the situation is dependent upon leader-member relations, the task structure and leader position power. If leader member relations are good, task is structured and leader position power is weak, the situation is regarded as highly favourable. A leader operates in a particular situation and its favourableness or unfavourableness determines the effectiveness of his orientation. It is obviously a question of the kind of leadership style is effective only in a particular situation. Let us now understand these variables.

Leadership style is measured by using an instrument called "esteem for least preferred co-worker" (LPC). Accordingly to this, the respondent has to think of all co-workers he or she has ever had and to describe the one person with whom he or she has been least able to work well, that is, the person he/she least prefers as a co-worker. This need not be someone with whom, he works at the time. The description is made by rating that person on a simple bipolar scale scored from 1 to 8, with 8 representing the most favourable perception of one's least preferred co-worker. The lower the LPC score (an average item value of about 2), the greater is the task-orientation of the least preferred co-worker. Such a person is described in a very negative, rejecting manner with the basic goal of task accomplishment. The higher the LPC score [in the neighbourhood of 5 to 8], the greater is the willingness to perceive even the worst co-worker as having some reasonable positive attributes. Such a person has as his basic goal the desire to be related with others. The person seeks to have strong emotional ties with the co-workers. Over twenty items were used in LPC scales and the score is obtained by summing the item values.

Leader-Member Relations: This variable measures the referent power of the leader, whether the group accepts or rejects him as its leader.

Task Structure: If the task is highly specific, can be done only in one way and the rules and procedures for the task are clearly laid down, leaving no scope for different interpretations, it is said to be highly structured. In this situation, the leader's ability to influence the group is restricted because the task dilutes the leader's potential influence. If the task is completely non-routine, paths to reach the goal are many, the task is regarded as highly unstructured and if the leader possesses more knowledge than the followers do, he has great potential for influence.

Leader Position Power: This indicates the extent to which the leader possesses reward, punishment and legitimate power bases. In most business organizations, leaders have high position power. In most voluntary and social organizations, leaders tend to have low position power.

As Fiedler has considered three additional variables, viz., leader-member relations, task structure and leader position power in addition to leader's employee-orientation, eight combinations of these additional variables are possible ranging from a highly favourable situation to a highly unfavourable situation. The middle position between these two extremes represents a situation intermediate in favourableness for the leader. He plotted his responses indicating the degree of favourableness of the situation on the horizontal scale and employee-orientation [high and low] or LPC score on the vertical scale. Figure 15.2 has emerged as a result.

Above the midline in the figure is positive relationship between LPC score and group performance, i.e., high LPC or employee-oriented leaders performed better. Below that line is negative relationship, i.e., low LPC or task-oriented leaders performed better than high LPC or employee-oriented leaders. Thus, the employee-oriented leader succeeded in situations intermediate in favourableness, whereas the task-oriented leader was successful in highly favourable or unfavourable situations.

These results seem to be quite plausible. The task-oriented leaders performed most effectively in highly favourable situations. Low LPC leaders are basically motivated by task accomplishment. In favourable situations, when tasks are structured but leader member relations are good, even the task-oriented behaviour of the leader seems to be friendly and considerate. The workers perceive it as appropriately fitting the situation and support him. In an un-favourable situation, when the task is unstructured, relations between the two are not good, power position is weak, he becomes more concerned with performance. Employees who wish to perform well are quite anxious and so, they engage themselves in achieving the primary goal of the group. If the leader possesses a more knowledge than the followers, the followers are willing to accept his task-orientation to improve their knowledge for handling unstructured tasks.

Fav. stands for favourable; and Unfav stands for unfavourable;

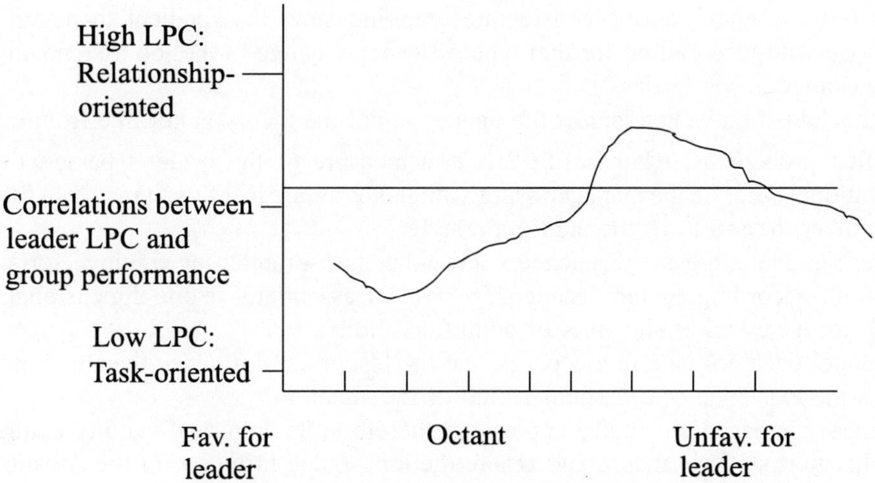

Fav. stands for favourable; and Unfav stands for un-favourable;

Figure 15.2 Correlations between leader's LPC scores and group effectiveness potted for each cell or octant of the situational favourableness dimension.

A high LPC leader obtains better group performance in conditions of moderate or intermediate favourableness in which (i) the task is structured but the leader is disliked and therefore, demonstrates that he cares for the unstructured task and the leader depends upon the willingness and creatively of the group's members to accomplish the goals.

The whole idea can be summarized as follows:

Leadership Style	*Effectiveness is Contingent upon*
Task-oriented	Favourable leadership situation Unfavourable leadership situation
Relationship-oriented	Situation intermediate in favourableness for the leader

Fielder's Contingency Model: An Evaluation—In the past, both consideration and structure have been observed to be effective under different conditions, but Fiedler's contingency theory goes a step ahead and helps resolve confusion about optimum conditions for a considerate, people-oriented leader compared with a more structured, task-oriented leader. It is also one of the first approaches to leadership that included situational factors within its theoretical framework. No doubt, it has not covered subordinate characteristics, group characteristics, etc.– some of the most important elements in the situation, but it has covered some ground in these directions and so, will continue, to inspire researchers in the field. It does not talk in terms of good or bad style, but states that each of the leadership styles can be effective in certain situations. As leadership effectiveness is a function of the leader's motivational base and the interaction of situational factors, the organization may improve the effectiveness of a particular work environment by either modifying the situational factors or attempting to change the manager's leadership style. Here also, Fiedler is of the opinion that it is difficult to train task-oriented leaders to behave as the considerate type and so it is expedient to match existing leadership style with jobs calling for that type of leader. Change in the job assignment may be preferred to change in the leader.

Despite this added understanding of the phenomenon, the theory is not free from criticisms:

(i) The first problem is, what is LPC? It is a measure of the leader's personality or his motivational base. As the manager's motivational bases are in a flux, it may be a futile effort to engineer the job to fit the manager's style.

(ii) Fielder's model suggests that leaders are either task-oriented or employee-oriented and therefore, according to him, leadership style is essentially a one-dimensional concept which we have earlier shown is of doubtful validity.

(iii) His model does not take into account that the leader can influence the situation once he knows the existence of a particular kind of the situation.

(iv) The theory is based on small samples and therefore, its empirical validity is questioned.

(v) The theory is static in nature and ignore the long-range influence of the situation on the leader and the group.

(2) Tri-Dimensional Leader Effectiveness Model and Situational Leadership Theory

Hersey and Blanchard at the Centre for Leadership Studies, Ohio University, have used two concepts—task behaviour and relationship behaviour. Taking a cue from Reddin's 3-D Management Style Theory, they have also added and effectiveness dimension which, in their analysis, represents environment. According to them, what matters is not the actual behaviour as such, but its appropriateness to the environment in which it is used. They regard the leader's basic style as stimulus and it is the response to this stimulus that can be considered effective or ineffective. Unlike those who argue that there is one best style of leadership and make value judgement about the stimulus; the situationalist or environmentalists evaluate the response or results. One may agree that a high concern for both production and people is desirable in organizations, but it may be appropriate even for high-task high-relationship managers to engage in a variety of different behaviours as they face different contingencies or situations in their environment. For example, they suggest that if a manager's subordinates are emotionally mature and can take responsibility for them, the appropriate style of leadership may be low task and low relationship. Thus, any leadership style can be effective or ineffective depending on the environment.

It is, therefore, obvious that it is the interaction of the basic style with the environment that results in a degree of effectiveness or ineffectiveness. Hence, effectiveness may be regarded as a continuum and it is only a question of the degree of effectiveness of a particular style ranging from extremely effective to extremely ineffective.

Situational Leadership Theory: An Evaluation—This seems to be, by so far, the most comprehensive leadership theory and suggests appropriate leadership styles for the varying levels of maturity of the followers. Depending upon the level of maturity of his followers, a leader, in order to be effective, should use a corresponding leadership style from among the four quadrants. The theory is still in a nascent stage and we are not yet aware of any researches based on this theory. However, it appears to us that the leader's judgement of maturity of followers is conditioned by several factors including his personal prejudices. Based on this subjective judgement–for which, in fact, there is no way to be objective, one may adopt an undesired leadership style and prove the theory to be wrong. It is also quite possible, that swayed by other situational variables such as the individual's needs, a leader may adopt a style which, according to theory, is inappropriate for a particular maturity level, but still it may prove to be effective. That is, if the lower order needs of an individual are potent, even the high task and low relationship behaviour may prove effective despite the fact that the individual has high levels of maturity. The theory seems to be sound theoretically, but it may prove to be difficult for application in practice.

(3) Path-Goal Theory

House was baffled by the contradictory findings in the leadership area and so, advanced his own situational theory of leadership. It was, first of all, Evans who talked of the effects of supervisory behaviour on the path-goal relationship and later, *House* developed it into the theory based on Vroom's Expectancy Theory of motivation.

In Vroom's Expectancy Theory of motivation, there are, among others, two key variables: expectancies and valences. Expectancy is the perceived belief concerning the likelihood that a particular behavioural act will be followed by a particular outcome. This degree of belief varies between 0 and 1. Valence is the strength of an employee's preference for a particular outcome. Obviously, for certain things, employee's valences will be positive and for certain others, negative. Expectancy and valence combine multiplicatively to determine one's motivation.

The Path-Goal theory states that an individual's attitude or behaviour can be predicted from (i) the degree to which the job or behaviour is seen as leading to various outcomes (called "expectancy"), and (ii) the evaluation of these outcomes (called "valence"). One is satisfied with the job if one thinks that it leads to things that are highly valued and works hard if one believes that efforts will lead to things that are highly valued. It is the function of the leader to influence the valence (i.e., goal attractiveness) and expectancy (i.e., goal paths) perceptions of subordinates, by increasing personal pay-offs, making the path to these pay-off's easier by clarifying it, reducing road blocks and pitfalls and increasing the opportunities for personal satisfaction in route. This will increase the motivation of the subordinates. In order to enable the leader to help the subordinates reach their highly valued job-related goals, the specific style of leader behaviour is determined by two situational variables—characteristics of the subordinates and the characters of the work environment.

The theory envisages four types of leader behaviour:

(i) Instrumental behaviour is the planning, organizing, controlling and coordinating of subordinate activities by the leader.
(ii) Supportive behaviour shows consideration for employees' needs and their welfare.
(iii) Participative behaviour implies consultation with subordinates and sharing of information with them.
(iv) Achievement-oriented behaviour suggests setting challenging goals for subordinates and also displaying confidence in their ability to do a good job.

The two situational variables mentioned earlier, i.e., characteristics of the subordinate and the characteristics of the work environment moderate the relationship between the leader style and the behaviour of the subordinate. The Path-Goal Theory proposes that leader behaviour will be viewed acceptable to the subordinate to the extent that the subordinate sees such behaviour as either an immediate source of satisfaction, or as needed for future satisfaction. But the subordinate's own characteristics, such as, ability, being internals or externals (whether they believe what happens to them is under their control or because of fate) and needs and motives, influence their perceptions. Accordingly, they view a particular leadership style favourably or unfavourably. For example, a subordinate having the ability to effectively accomplish a task is not likely to view favourably a directive or instrumental behaviour. A subordinate having high safety and security and security needs may accept an instrumental leader style, but those with high social and esteem needs may react more positively to a supportive leader.

The second major variable is the characteristics of the work environment which include three broad aspects: (i) the subordinate's tasks–structured or unstructured; (ii) the primary work group–its characteristics and stage of development; and (iii) the formal authority system or organizational factors such as (a) the degree to which rules, procedures, and policies govern a subordinate's work; (b) high pressures or stressful situations; and (c) situations of high uncertainty. These characteristics of work environment will influence subordinate behaviour in relation to a particular leadership style. For example, the axle assembler in an auto plant-securing front and rear assemblies to chassis springs performs a highly structured and repetitious task. In such a situation, instrumental behaviour would be regarded as unnecessary and inappropriate. A leader who is supportive is likely to have more satisfied subordinates than one who is directive. But a directive leadership style would be welcome where the task is unstructured and there is need for providing clarifications as, for example, if a manager of an industrial relations team gives guidance and direction on how to process a grievance for arbitration.

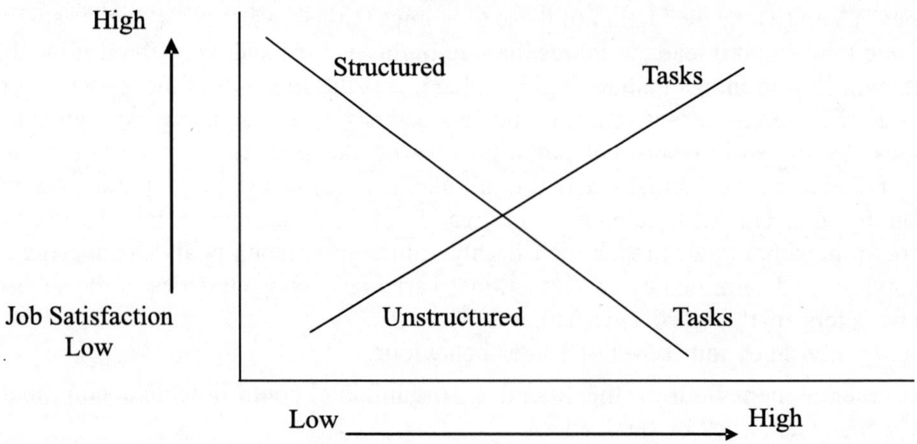

Figure 15.3 Leader directiveness.

Thus, the leader behaviour, modified by the characteristics of the subordinates and the work environment, influences the perceptions of valences and expectancies which can result in higher motivation, satisfaction, and performance. Figure given above shows the effect of the work environment or task structure on leader behaviour and subordinates' job satisfaction.

On the vertical axis, we have shown job satisfaction, ranging from low to high. On the horizontal scale is represented leader directiveness, ranging from low to high. The task structure moderates the relationship between leader behaviour and subordinates' job satisfaction. It may be seen that when the task is structured, the leader who is low in directiveness is more satisfying to the employees, whereas if the task is unstructured, a more directive leader is highly satisfying as he clarifies the ambiguities and therefore, paths to their goals.

Path-Goal Theory: Evaluation–House's Path-Goal Theory of leadership has been formulated and developed only very recently. A few researches that have been undertaken on the basis of the theory have confirmed its basic propositions–that instrumental leader behaviour is more effective than supportive behaviour for subordinates working on unstructured tasks, and supportive leader behaviour results in high employee satisfaction when subordinates are performing structured tasks. The main contribution of this theory lies in the fact that it has identified key leadership styles and situational factors and has shown the relationship between these variables in a complex organizational setting. It highlights that the relationship between the leader and the subordinates does not exist in a vacuum.

A number of situational factors have to be considered before a leader can decide a particular style for a particular group of subordinates. In general, tasks are structured at lower levels and unstructured at higher levels and therefore, it also implies that different leadership style will be required for different occupational groupings and levels of the organization's hierarchy. The chief merit of this theory is in the fact that it not only suggests what type of style may be most effective in a given situation, but also attempts to explain why it is most effective. It gives situation, but also attempts to explain why it is most effective. It gives some indications to the leader of the style he should use in a situation.

Despite this contribution, the theory appears to suffer from the following shortcomings:

(i) The theory is quite complex and its testing poses a serious problem. The measurement of leadership style itself is difficult. Researches have not yet been conducted on participative or achievement-oriented leadership styles to indicate any measurement methodology.

(ii) It looks rather surprising that with subordinates performing routine tasks a leader has to be supportive. This, perhaps, signifies greater emphasis on motivation and satisfaction than performance. Being very recent in formulation, it is still more a tentative tool than a theory.

(4) An Integrative Model of Leadership

We have examined various approaches to study and understand the leadership phenomenon. The Trait approach identified the traits only when a person had emerged, as a leader and therefore, it had no predictive power. Learning from the weaknesses of the trait approach, the foundations of the Behaviour approach were laid, but this approach wholly concentrated on leader behaviour as if it was occurring in a vacuum while other variables were ignored.

Situational theories attempted to fill in these gaps. But no single theory can ever accommodate all the variables and as more and more elaborate theories are advanced, their complexity increases. This fact reduces their applicability in practice. In fact, leadership is such a complex phenomenon that even after integrating the knowledge generated by the formulation and testing of various approaches to the study of leadership, we are not yet nearer to the solution. However, to have a full view of the present state of knowledge in this area, we may talk about an integrative model of leadership as developed by Ivancevich et al.

An Integrative Model of Leadership

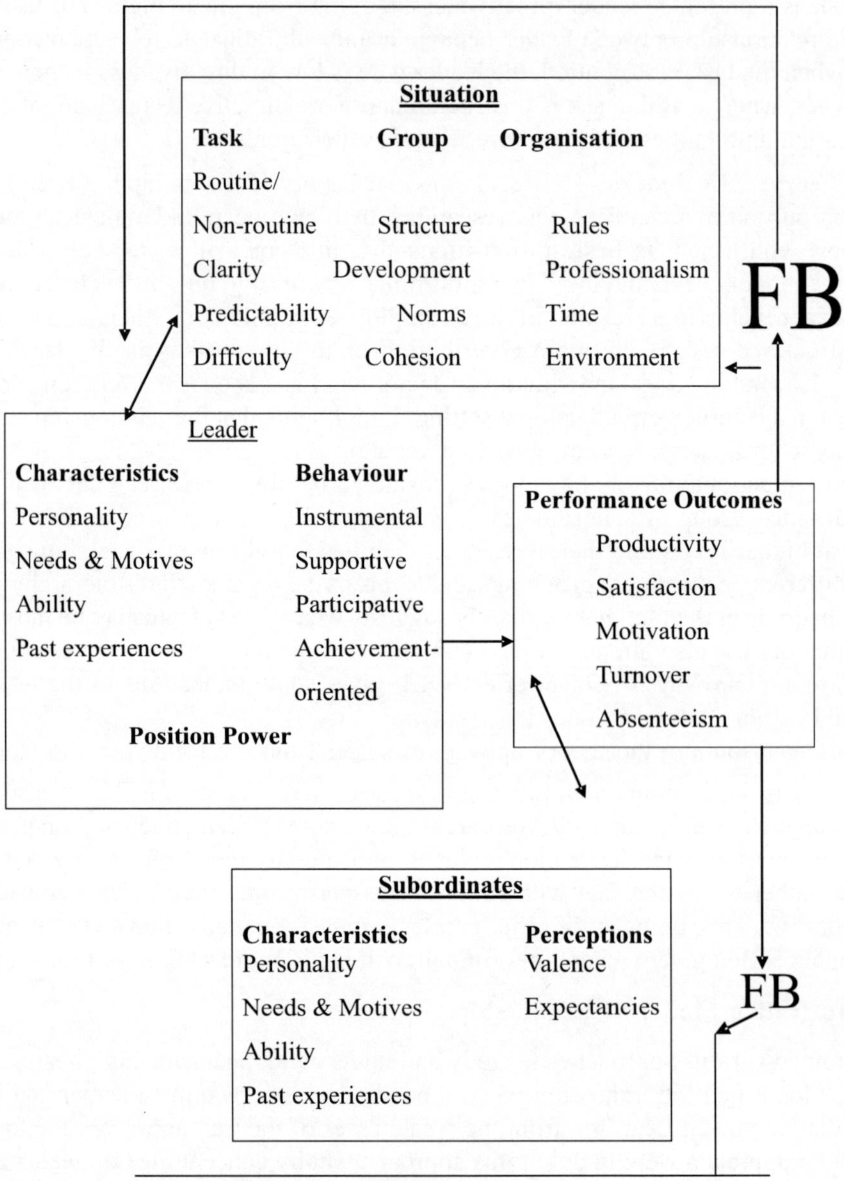

FB stands for feedback.

15.5 SUMMARY

It is beyond doubt that your goal as a leader in the organization is to do the best job you can at influencing your people towards a common goal. Since you are dealing with a very diverse group of people, it is important to understand the different approaches to motivate them to meet their goals. Leadership style is the pattern of behaviours you use when you are trying to influence the behaviours of those you are trying to lead. Each leadership style can be identified with a different approach to problem-solving and decision-making. Possessing a better understanding of the various leadership styles and their respective developmental levels will help you match a given style for a specific situation. The challenge is to master the ability to change your leadership style for a given situation as the person's development level changes.

Some modern management scholars like Ivancevich et al. have identified three major issues in leadership, which have received only scant attention from researchers and theorists. These issues include: (i) leader reward behaviour (ii) the casual relationship between leader behaviour and subordinate behaviour; and (iii) substitutes for leadership.

Management scholars have generally examined the effect of leadership style on subordinate behaviour and have rarely related it to the leader reward behaviour. But whatever little research exists on this issue has shown the strength of the relationship between the positive leader reward behaviour and subordinate satisfaction and performance to be significantly greater than that reported for relationships involving the leader style components. Similarly, the use of negative rewards has been found to have different effects on subordinates, depending on the individual's organizational level. At higher levels, because of ambiguous and vague descriptions of the task, negative rewards are reported to be motivational, whereas at lower levels where tasks are clearly defined, they cause dissatisfaction.

Another interesting issue, though neglected, is whether subordinate behaviour of a particular type is a consequence of leader behaviour or that leader behaviour is a consequence of subordinate behaviour of a particular type. Is it an outcome or a cause? Any efforts that examine these relationships will be of great interest to managers and behavioural scientists.

The third issue concerns our frequent assumption that the subordinates are dependent upon the leader for direction, support, influence, and rewards. In practice, experience and job expertise, professional education and training, help from co-workers and peers, specification of rules, procedures and policies, etc. may reduce the subordinate's dependency on the leader. This does not belittle the importance of leadership. On the other hand, it suggests that individual employees may also be influenced in their work by factors other than leader behaviour.

Towards the conclusion of this lesson it can be summed up that there is no single leadership style that could be most appropriate in every situation; therefore, for you to be effective leaders you need to learn to understand your environment, your situation and the circumstances to help you act accordingly. Remember, your success as a leader will depend on your assessment of the situation and your ability to communicate what you want in such a way that others will do as you wish–that is the art of leadership.

15.6 SELF-ASSESSMENT QUESTIONS

1. "Effective leadership is a function of three factors: the leader, the led, and the situation". Discuss.
2. Explain and illustrate the various approaches accounting for leadership. Which is the best approach?
3. How you will define the leadership? Discuss the main leadership styles with their application.

4. Write short notes on the following:
   (i) Managerial Grid
   (ii) Path-Goal approach.
   (iii) Difference between a leader and manager.

16 COMMUNICATION

Learning Objective

The main objective of this chapter is to make the students learn on the subject matter of the business communication vis-à-vis its nature and importance.

16.1 INTRODUCTION

If you are like the majority of us, you spend more time in communicating than doing anything else. Probably you spend a hefty part of each day in one-to-one speaking, writing and listening. When you are not talking or listening, you are presumably communicating in supplementary ways like–understanding, lettering, gesturing, and drawing. Or perhaps, you are just taking in information by seeing, feeling, or smelling. All of these activities are forms of communication and certainly you do them right through most of your time.

Obviously, such activity, which we are engrossed in so much, has to be significant. Perhaps, it is the most important of all our activities. It is easy to make out that communication is what has enabled us to develop the civilized society. It is one activity that we human beings clearly do better than the other creatures, and it basically explains our dominant role in this universe. Communication has enabled us to organize–to work in groups; and through organization, we have been able to overcome barriers to our existence that we could not have subjugated individually. But we need not discuss further how communication has contributed to our development as human beings. Its role is understandable to all of us. We have to articulate that communication is vital to our success and well-being in enlightened civilization.

16.2 COMMUNICATION EXPLICIT

The word communication has been derived from the Latin word 'communis' that means 'common'. However, communication incorporates, besides commonality, the concepts of transfer, meaning and information. **Communication can be defined as the process through which two or more persons come to exchange ideas and understanding among them.**

The definition involves two aspects in communication:

First, there is something, which is transmitted, such as, facts, feelings, ideas, etc. It implies that there must be a receiver if communication is to occur. The sender of message must consider the receiver while structuring his message from a technical standpoint as well as in delivering it. When the receiver is not considered, there is either no response or there is wrong response.

Second, the definition emphasizes the understanding element in the communication. Sharing of understanding would be possible only when the person, to whom the message is meant, understands it in the same sense in which the sender of the message wants him to understand. Thus, communication involves something more than mere transmission of the message or transmission and physical receipt thereof. The correct interpretation of the message is important from the point of view of organizational efficiency. As such, the greater the degree of understanding presents in the communication, the more the likelihood that human action will precede in the direction of accomplishment of goals.

How do we define communication?

"Communication is something so simple and difficult that we can never put it in simple words," says *T.S. Mathews*.

But we do need a definition to understand the term. In his book Communication in Business, *Peter Little* defines communication as follows:

> "Communication is the process by which information is transmitted between individuals and /or organizations so that an understanding response results."

Another very simple definition of 'communication' has been provided by *W.H. Newman and C.F. Summer Jr*:

> "Communication is an exchange of facts, ideas, opinions, or emotions by two or more persons."

'Information' is the keyword in the first definition communication consists in transmitting 'information'. But this definition does not indicate the objects about which information is to be transmitted. This is precisely what is being done in the second definition. Communication transmits information not only about tangible facts and determinable ideas and opinions but also about emotions. When a communicator passes on or transmits some information, he may also, either deliberately or unconsciously, be communicating his attitude or the frame of his mind. And sometimes the latter may be more relevant to the reality that is being communicated. Often we may have come across words of high praise spoken in a scoffing tone. In such a case, the words signify nothing and the tone is the real thing. Similarly, high-sounding expressions of bravery may be only a mask to conceal a person's timidity and cowardice that may be betrayed by his facial expressions.

The following definition offered by William Scott appears comprehensive and particularly satisfying to the students of 'business communication' since it touches all aspects of the communication process:

> "Managerial communication is a process which involves the transmission and accurate replication of ideas ensured by feedback for the purpose of eliciting actions which will accomplish organizational goals."

This definition highlights four imperative points:

1. The process of communication involves the communication of ideas.
2. The ideas should be accurately replicated (reproduced) in the receiver's mind, i.e., the receiver should get exactly the same ideas as were transmitted. If the process of communication is perfect, there will be no dilution, exaggeration, or distortion of the ideas.
3. The transmitter is assured of the accurate replication of the ideas by feedback, i.e., by the receiver's response, which is communicated, back to the transmitter. Here it is suggested that communication is a two-way process including transmission of feedback.
4. The purpose of all communication is to elicit action.

It is a fairly comprehensive definition and covers almost all aspects of communication. But two comments can be made on it:

1. The concept of ideas should be adequately enlarged to include emotions also.
2. Even in administrative communication, the purpose may not always be to elicit action. Seeking information or persuading others to a certain point of view can be equally important objectives of communication.

16.3 COMMUNICATION PROCESS

It may be clear from the definition of communication discussed earlier that two-way communication takes place when the receiver provides feedback to the sender. For instance, giving an instruction to a subordinate and receiving its acceptance is an example of two-way communication. On other hand, in case of one-way communication, feedback is absent. Here the sender communicates without expecting or getting feedback from the receiver. A policy statement from the chief executive is an example of one-way communication. One-way communication takes less time than two-way communication. In certain situations, one-way communication is more effective to get work from the subordinates.

Two-way communication is superior to one-way communication in the following respects:

(i) Two-way communication is more effective than one-way communication. The feedback allows the sender to refine his communication so that it becomes more precise and accurate.

(ii) Receivers' self-confidence is higher in case of two-way communication as they are permitted to ask questions and seek clarification from the senders.

However, in case of two-way communication, the sender may feel embarrassed when the receiver draws his attention to sender's mistakes and ambiguities. It is therefore, essential to discuss the communication process in comprehensive manner. This lesson discusses the same.

16.3.1 Professional Model to Understand Communication Process

A conventional analysis of communication begins with a definition of the term. Many such definitions exist, so we would have no difficulty finding one suitable for our use. But our approach is not conventional. We do not use words to define words, for, as we will see, such definitions are dangerous. Instead, we use an operational definition. By operational definition, we mean one that demonstrates how something works. The following pages present an operational definition in the form of a model.

In this presentation of the model, we strive to look with scientific diligence into the phenomenon of human communication. We take the event involving one human being communicating with another. We choose a face-to-face oral communication event because this is the communication situation with which we are best acquainted. Later in the chapter, we adapt the model to written communication. Our plan is to take the communication event and place it under the microscope of our minds. Our goal is to show how the process works and how it does not work.

In developing our model, we must incline heavily on the theoretical aspects, as we are not dealing with a subject that has received total factual support. The theoretical material presented, however, represents authoritative thinking on the subject: and research is constantly producing facts that lend support to this thinking. Regardless of its factual bases, this presentation will give us a meaningful understanding of communication and will provide us with principles that we can successfully apply to real-life communication problems.

16.3.2 A Common Misconception

Before beginning our analysis of the model, let us dispense with a common misconception. If you are like most people, you have never thought much about what communication really is.If you have thought about it, probably you have viewed communication as a very normal human activity. This assumption is far from correct.

Human communication at least the verbal part of it is far from being a natural function; that is, it is not the sort of thing we would do if left to nature's devices, as we would many of our other activities. Our hands, for example, would perform their natural functions of picking up and handling things whether we grew up with jungle animals or with civilized people. Likewise, our mouths would take in food and our teeth and jaws would chew it in either event. And most of our other body parts would function naturally without instruction from other human beings. However, we cannot say the same about the major organs used in communication. Our vocal apparatus would not make words if we were not taught to make them. Neither would our brains know them nor do our hands write them without instruction. Clearly, communication is a function that we must learn. It was originated by human beings, and it must be acquired from human beings.

16.3.3 The Communication Environment

Study of the communication process logically is preceded by an analysis of the environment in which communication occurs. This is the sensory environment, in which we find ourselves every moment. It is made up of all the signs existing in the world of reality that surrounds each of us. Your sensory environment is the real world surrounding you as you read these words. It consists of all the signs your senses can detect. More specifically, it is all you can see, taste, smell, hear, or feel in that part of the world that surrounds you.

By 'world of reality' or 'real world' we mean that what actually exists. It contrasts with the world that exists only in people's minds, i.e., world of imagination. Of course, one may argue that what exists in the mind also is real that, right or wrong, the content of a mind exists in that mind. For our purpose, however, we must allow this variation in our definition. It is important to distinguish between what actually is in the world around a communicator and what the communicator says or thinks it is. Often the two are not the same.

By signs we mean everything from the real world that can act as a stimulus to us. In other words, it is everything that our sensory receptors can detect. It is what our eyes can see, our ears can hear, our nostrils can smell, our tongues can taste, and our flesh can touch. It may be a spoken word, the sound of objects crashing together, a printed word, the aroma of a flower, or the movement of a bird. Thus, an individual sign is a portion of the real world that can create a response within us.

From the preceding comment we can deduce the meaning of sensory receptors: those body organs that we use to detect the signs in the real world. Specifically, the term refers to our eyes, noses, ears, mouths, and flesh with its ability to detect surface and temperature differences.

16.3.4 Sign Detection

Our sensory receptors continuously pick up some of the infinite number of signs existing in our communication environment. Stated another way, the signs around us continuously produce responses within us through our receptors. Perhaps this phenomenon can best be explained by an example.

At this very moment, you are looking at this printed page. On it is the words (signs) that your eyes are picking up. We hope that these are the primary signs you are receiving, but there are others. Probably you are picking up some of them from time to time. Perhaps there are various noises around you—voices from another room, the ticking of a clock, a radio playing in the distance, a roommate's movements and sounds. From time to time you may become aware of being hot or cold, or your back may itch, or your sitting position may become uncomfortable. Thus, as you read these pages your sensory receptors are continuously picking up signs from all these parts of the reality that surrounds you.

16.3.5 Sensory Limitations

The number and types of signs, we can detect from the real world, however, are limited by our sensory abilities. In short, the human sensory receptors are restricted. They are not capable of detecting all the signs that we know exist in the real world. For example, our eyes can detect only a small part of the total spectrum of wavelengths; and the ability to detect within these wavelengths varies from person to person. We can see only a fraction of the distance a hawk can see. Our ears can pick up only a narrow band of the vast range of air vibrations, and people's ability to pick up sounds within these ranges varies. As we all know, dogs and birds can hear much that we cannot. Likewise, we can smell only the stronger odours around us, while dogs and most other animals do a much better job of smelling and so. Clearly, our senses are limited and can detect only a small portion of the reality surrounding us.

16.3.6 Selective Perception

Although incapable of detecting all that exists in the real world, our sensory receptors can select some signs and ignore others. Place yourself, for example, in a roomful of talking people, and notice how it is possible to tune in on one conversation and ignore others. Or notice how you are able to focus your vision on one minute object and then expand your view to a much broader picture. All of us have this ability to varying extents, and we can make use of it with all of our senses.

16.3.7 Varying Alertness and Perception

Our detection or non-detection of signs also depends on our receptiveness to signs. There are times when we are keenly alert to our communication environment and times when we are less alert. Certainly you have experienced occasions when you were sleepy, in a daze, or just daydreaming. During such times, you missed many of the signs in your communication environment. When you are asleep, you detect almost none.

16.3.8 The Communication Process

To this point we have seen how each of us lives in an environment of signs and how these signs are with us throughout each day. We have also seen how our ability to detect these signs varies, how we can tune them in or tune them out, and how our alertness to them varies across time. With this knowledge of the communication environment as a foundation, we are now ready to describe the communication process.

Communication is a two-way process in which there is an exchange and progression of ideas towards a mutually accepted direction or goal. For this process to materialize, it is essential that the basic elements of communication be identified. These elements are:

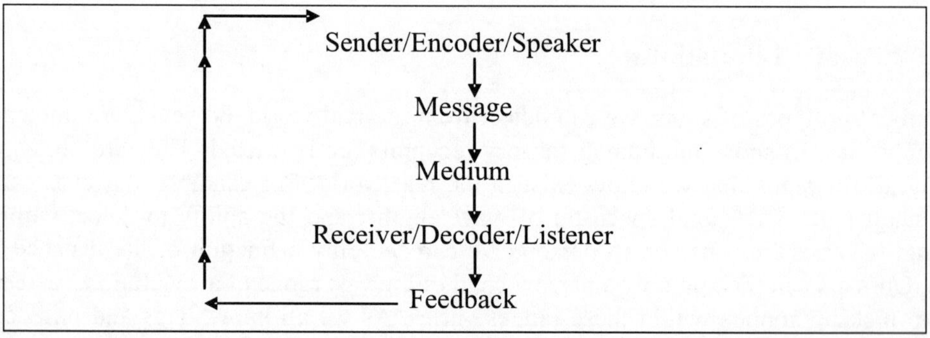

1. **Sender/Encoder/Speaker:** The person who initiates the communication process is normally referred to as the **sender**. From his personal data bank he selects ideas, encodes them and finally transmits them to the receiver in the form of a **message.** The entire burden of communication then rests upon the sender or encoder. His choice of images and words, and the combination of the two is what gets the receiver to listen carefully. In this process

a number of factors come into play, primary among them being an understanding of the recipient and his needs. If the message can be formulated in accordance with the expectations of the receiver, the level of acceptance is going to be higher. For example, a consultant wishes to communicate with the HRD manager of a company. The objective is to secure consultancy projects on training of personnel. If the consultant wishes the HRD manager to communicate with him, he has to ensure that their goals converge. He has a tough task ahead of him. The manager has been interacting with many consultants. Why should he pay heed to the proposal of this consultant? In a situation such as this, a good strategy to be adopted is to expand the purview of the proposal and make it company specific. The result could be highlighted and spelt out in terms of increase in sales. If sufficient preparation has been done, the message too would be formulated in a manner conducive to the interests of the HRD manager.

2. **Receiver/Decoder/listener:** The listener receives an encoded message, which he attempts to decode. This process is carried on in relation to the work environment and the value perceived in terms of the work situation. If the goal of the sender is clear in the mind of receiver the job of **decoding** becomes quite easy and the listener finds the **message** more receptive. The decoding of the message is done in almost entirely the same terms as were intended by the sender. In the example cited above, as soon as the HRD manager realizes that the proposal of the consultant is going to result in tangible benefits, he becomes more receptive and his interest in communication is reinforced.
3. **Message:** Message is the encoded idea transmitted by the sender. The formulation of the message is very important, for an incorrect patterning can turn the receiver hostile or make him lose interest. At this stage the sender has to be extremely cautious. What is the order in which he would like to present his ideas? Suppose he has four points to make. Would he (a) move in the stereotyped manner of presenting them in a sequence or (b) would he like to be innovative and proceed in a creative way? Probability is high that in the first case and he might become monotonous and in the latter case (b) he might touch a wrong spot. How then should the message be formulated and transmitted? The ordering, as stated earlier, should be based on the requirements of the listener so that its significance is immediately grasped. The minute the receiver finds his goals codified in the message, he sits up, listens and responds. The message thus has made an impact.
4. **Medium:** Another important element of communication is the medium or channel. It could be oral, verbal or non-verbal. Prior to the composition of the message, the medium. channel should be decided. Each medium follows its own set of rules and regulations. For example, in oral communication one can afford to be a little informal, but when using the written mode, all rules of communication need to be observed. It must be remembered that anything in writing is a document that would be field for records or circulated to all concerned.
5. **Feedback:** This is the most important component of communication. Effective communication takes place only when there is feedback. The errors and flaws that abound in business situations are a result of lack of feedback. Let us take a look at the typical responses of people involved in miscommunication: “This is not what I meant” or “This is not what I said” or “This was not my intention”. If feedback is solicited on all occasions,

this error can be minimized or even completely done away with. Fallacious statements or erroneous conclusions are made because of lack of confirmation through feedback and discrepancy between the message transmitted and message understood.

Alternative Process of Communication: The sender, according to his ideas, behaviour pattern and intention, selects a message, encodes it, and transmits it to the receiver through a medium–be it oral, verbal or non-verbal. As soon as the message reaches the receiver, he decodes it and gives an internal response to the perceived message. It is noteworthy that the response is not in relation to the actual content but rather to the "perceived content" of the original message. This completes the first phase of the communication process. Interestingly at this point words in themselves have no meaning. It is the perception of a particular word and the intention behind it that assign it meaning. The manner in which the sender and receiver perceive the same word could give rise to difference in encoding and decoding.

In the second phase, the receiver formulates his message, encodes it and transmits it to the original sender-now-turned-receiver. This stage is referred to as providing feedback and is most crucial. Unless and until there is feedback–be it in the verbal or the non-verbal form–we cannot say that effective communication has taken place. If the feedback is in tune with the original intent of the sender, communication proceeds without a hitch. However, there could be moments when the receiver does not agree with the message of the sender. This does not mean that there is breakdown of communication. We can, in such instances, state that effective communication is stalled for the time being. It could resume after subsequent discussions.

For the process of communication to be effective, there should be a well-defined goal in the mind of the sender. Harmony between the goals of the two communicators makes for good and easy progression of ideas and concepts. Whatever be the initial situation, the sender necessarily needs to adhere to the following stages:

1. Create awareness in the mind of the receiver on the topic.
2. Propose his own point of view with clarity and preciseness so as to eliminate possibilities of confusion in the mind of the receiver.
3. Enable smooth flow of discussion through observance of communication strategies.

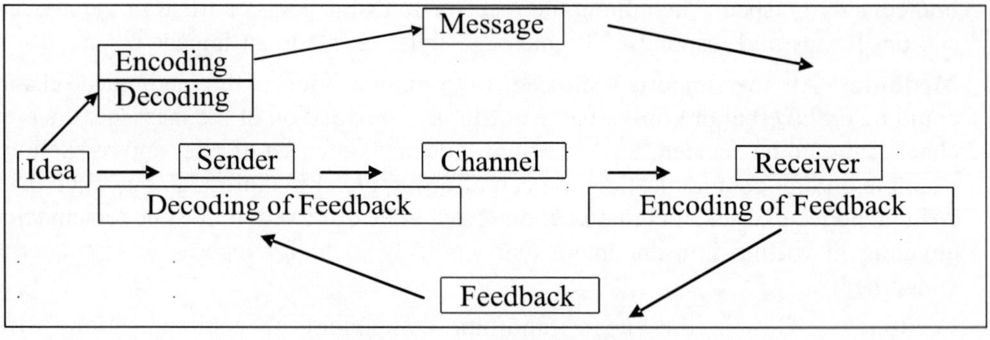

Figure 16.1 Communication process.

4. Reinforce or correct ideas in the mind of the receiver concerning the goal of communication.
5. Achieve the goal of communication.

At the time of transmission and reception of message, all our five senses play an important role in grasping its intent. The sense that is predominantly active at a particular stage, helps in a higher degree of absorption, for example, in the course of the communication, if the visual sense at a particular moment is highly active, we respond only to the visual cues.

16.4 BARRIERS IN COMMUNICATION

The various inadequacies that can be identified through communication evaluation are required to be analyzed in terms of various factors—obstructions and barriers—that impede flow communication. Any managerial action in this regard can be effective only when it strikes at the very root of the factors that lie at the very root of the problem. From this viewpoint, identification of different factors is necessary.

There might be a number of such barriers impeding the flow of communication in the organization. These may be classified as: (i) external (ii) organizational, and (iii) personal factors. However, such a classification does not suggest that these are mutually exclusive. Rather, such a classification is helpful in understanding the nature of communication barriers.

16.4.1 External Barriers

Barriers to communication may be either external to the parties involved or they might be internal to them. External barriers may affect communication in any context, whether organizational or otherwise. Such external barriers may be in the following forms:

1. **Semantic Barriers:** Semantic barriers are obstructions causes in the process of receiving or understanding of the message during the process on encoding and decoding ideas and words. These barriers arise from the linguistic capacity of the parties involved. Words are the principal communication instrument but a common difficulty with the words is that each word has several meanings. For example, in English language, the word 'round' has seventy-five meanings. The Oxford Dictionary records an average of twenty-eight separate meanings for each of the 500 most used words in the English language. Similar is the position in other languages. Thus, words sometimes fail to convey real meanings. Moreover, they work as barriers in communication in the following manner.

   (i) **Badly Expressed Message:** Lack of clarity and precision in a message makes it badly expressed. Poorly chosen and empty words and phrases, careless omission, lack of coherence, bad organization of ideas, awkward sentence structure, inadequate vocabulary, platitudes, numbering repetition jargon, and failure to clarify implications are some common faults found in this case.

   (ii) **Faulty Translations:** Every manager receives various types of communications from superiors, peers, subordinates and he must translate information destined for subordinates, peers and superiors into language suitable to each. Hence, the message has to be put into words appropriate to the framework in which the receiver operates, or it must be accompanied by an interpretation, which will be understood by the receiver. This needs a high level of linguistic capacity. Approximate understanding of words and the consequent faulty translations lead to impaired efficiency and heavy costs.

(iii) **Unqualified Assumptions:** There are certain un-communicated assumptions, which underlie practically all messages. Though a message appears to be specific, it underlying assumptions may not be clear to the receiver.

(iv) **Specialist's Language:** It is often found that technical personal and special groups tend to develop a special, peculiar and technical language of their own. This increases their isolation from others and builds a communication barrier. Whatever be the intention of this special language, it hinders their communication with persons not in their speciality, because of the receiver's ignorance of that type of language.

2. **Emotional or Psychological Barriers:** Emotional or psychological factors are the prime barriers in interpersonnel communication. The meaning ascribed to a message depends upon the emotional or psychological status of both the parties involved. In a communication, apart from the message, there is a meta-message, that is, what one gets out of a message when decoding. Meta-message, the emotions of the receiver play a vital role and he may not be at a wavelength as that of the communicator. Keith Davis opines that these "exist in the people's minds or because of their actions, such as being hard to contact or difficult to understand. These barriers to communication are just at effective as an actual physical wall. Often these human barriers are more like filter paper then a brick wall. They let through some communications, but hold back others, thereby making communication inadequate....This 'half-way' communication gets 'half-way' results". Following are some emotional barriers:

(i) **Premature Evaluation:** Rogers and Roethlisberger in 1952, first pointed out this barrier. Premature evaluation is the tendency of prematurely evaluating communications, rather than to keep an uncompromised position during the interchange. Such evaluation stops the transfer of information and begets in the sender a sense of futility. This barrier can be remedied by 'empathy', non-evaluative listening, where the communication is listened to in a non-committal and unprejudiced way, so that sagacious decision and action can follow.

(ii) **Inattention:** The preoccupied mind of a receiver and the resultant non-listening is one of the major chronic psychological barriers. It is a common phenomenon that people simply fail to react to bulletins, notices, minutes and reports.

(iii) **Loss by Transmission and Poor Retention:** When communication passes through various levels in the organization, successive transmissions of the same message are decreasingly accurate. It is said that in case of oral communications about 30 per cent of the information is lost in each transmission. Even in case of written communication, loss of meaning might occur as far as the appended interpretation, if any, is concerned. Poor retention of the information is again a malady. It is shown that employees retain about 50 per cent of information only, whereas supervisors retain about 60 per cent of it.

(iv) **Undue Reliance on the Written Word:** Written word is no substitute for sound face-to-face relationships and that employees cannot be persuaded to accept companies' viewpoint and policies through 'slick', easy to read, will-illustrated publications, unless there is a fair degree of mutual trust and confidence between the organization and its employees. Further, a written communication might fail to explain the purpose of order, procedure or directive. Chester Barnard has laid down that a communication must appeal to the receiver as consonant with the organization's purpose and with his own personal interest. Written communication often tells what is to be done, but not why it should be done, and it lacks the persuasive quality. Moreover, a written communication can be above the level of readership, and failure to ascertain the response to communication is also there. Hence, written media must be considered as supplementary to productive face-to-face relationships.

(v) **Distrust of Communicator:** It arises out of ill-considered judgements or illogical decisions or frequent countermanding of the original communication by the communicator. Repeated experience of this kind gradually conditions the receiver to delay action or act unenthusiastically, hence making the communication unsuccessful, though apparently it is complete.

(vi) **Failure to Communicate:** It is quite accepted fact that managers often fail to transmit the needed messages. This might be because of laziness on the part of the communicator, or assuming that 'everybody knows', or procrastination or 'hogging' information or deliberately to embarrass.

16.4.2 Organizational Barriers

An organization being a deliberate creation for the attainment of certain specified objectives, day-to-day happenings within it required being regulated in such a manner that they contribute to attain these objectives in the most efficient manner. This is usually attempted through a variety of official measures such as designing the organizational arrangements for performance of various activities, prescribing of various policies, rules, regulations and procedures, laying down of norms of behaviour, instituting a reward-and-punishment system, etc. All the inner processes, including communication in different directions, are markedly affected by these prescriptions. As such major organizational barriers may be as follows:

(i) **Organizational Policy:** The general organizational policy regarding communication acts as an overall guideline to every one in the organization regarding how he is normally expected to behave in this matter. The policy might be in the form of explicit declaration in writing, or as is very commonly the case, it has to be interpreted from the behaviour of organization members, particularly people at the top. If this policy is not supportive to the flow of communication in different directions, communication flow would not be smooth and adequate.

(ii) **Organizational Rules and Regulations:** Organizational rules and regulations affect the flow of communication by prescribing the subject-matter to the communicated and also the channel through which these are to be communicated. The rules may restrict the flow of certain messages and may leave many important ones. On the other hand, communication through proper channel in a specified way prescribed by these rules delays it and works against the willingness of persons to convey the message. This barrier is strongly operative in Indian public sector enterprises where observance of rules and regulations is more rigid.

(iii) **Status Relationships:** The placing of people in superior subordinate capacity in the formal organization structure also blocks the flow of communication and more particularly in upward direction. Greater the difference between hierarchical positions in terms of their status, greater would be the possibility of communication breakdown.

(iv) **Complexity in Organization Structure:** In an organization where there are a number of managerial levels, communication gets delayed, chances of communication getting distorted are more and the number of filtering points is more. This is more true in case of upward communication, because people generally do not like to pass up the adverse criticism either or themselves or of their superiors.

(v) **Organizational Facilities:** Organizational facilities provided for smooth, adequate, clear and timely flow of communication may take a number of forms. Some of these have been mentioned earlier in the communication media such as meetings, conferences, complaint box, suggestion box, open door system, social and cultural gatherings, etc. If these are not properly emphasized generally people fail to make effective communication.

16.4.3 Personal Barriers

While the organizational factors discussed above are, no doubt, important influences operating on communication, a host of factors internal to the two parties-senders and receiver-to this process also exert important influences on its operation, as communication is basically an inter-personal process. Here, for the sake of convenience in the analysis, these barriers have been analyzed separately and these are relevant in the case of downward and upward communication.

Barriers in Superiors

The role of superiors in communication is very vital. Because of their hierarchical relationships with subordinates, they act as barriers in a number of ways discussed below:

(i) **Attitude of Superiors:** The attitudes of superiors towards communication in general or in any particular direction affect the flow of messages in different directions. For example, if this attitude in unfavourable, there is a greater possibility that messages would not flow adequately from and/or to superiors.

(ii) **Fear of Challenge to Authority:** A person in the organization always tries to get a higher position and prestige to satisfy his needs. As such, managers in general try to withhold the information coming down the line or going up as frequent passing of information may disclose their weakness.

(iii) **Insistence on Proper Channel:** One of the basic features of superiors exercising of the authority is that they wish to remain in communication links and they do not like any type of bypassing in communication. Communication through bypassing may, sometimes, be necessary but superiors treat this as the warting of their authority and blocks the flow of communication.

(iv) **Lack of Confidence in Subordinates:** Superiors generally perceive, correct or otherwise, that their subordinates are less competent and capable, they are not able to advise superiors or they may not have some information coming downwards.

(v) **Ignoring Communication:** Sometimes superiors consciously and deliberately ignore the communication from their subordinates to maintain their importance. This works against the willingness of subordinates to communicate.

(vi) **Lack of Time:** Superiors feel, whether correct or otherwise, that they are overburdened with the work and they have time to talk to their subordinates.

(vii) **Lack of Awareness:** Sometimes, superiors may lack the awareness about the significance and usefulness of communication in different directions in general or of particular subject matter. In such a case, communication flow is blocked.

Barriers in Subordinates

Vertical communication in either direction can take place only when subordinates also actively participate in this process. There are various factors in the subordinates that adversely affect such active participation on their part. Some factors, which have been traced in the case of superiors, are also applicable have such as attitude, time availability, awareness about the significance, etc. two factors are more important in the case of subordinates and these are responsible for blocking communication in upward direction.

(i) **Unwillingness to Communicate:** Sometimes, subordinates do not communicate upwards certain information because they are not willing to do so. Thus, if a subordinate feels that he is likely to be adversely affected by a particular piece of information to his superior, he would not be willing to supply it. Information going up is utilized for control purposes and subordinates would not be willing to give any information to their superiors about any unfavourable happening and if its supplication is necessary they would modify the information in such a way so as to protect their own interest.

(ii) **Lack of Proper Incentive:** Lack of motivation to communicate also refrains subordinates to communicate upwards. The reward and punishment system of the organization is more responsible for this. Thus, if a novel suggestion by a subordinate does not evoke any attention from the organization, he would not convey it.

16.5 GATEWAY IN COMMUNICATION

Considering the importance of effective communication in the successful functioning of business organizations, it is essential on the part of the management to overcome these barriers. Though it may not be possible to eliminate these barriers altogether, yet suitable managerial actions in this direction can minimize the effect of these barriers to such an extent that adequate and objective information flow in different directions.

Following measures can be adopted in this regard:

1. It is imperative that organizational policy must be clear and explicit and encouraging the communication flow so that people at all levels realize the full significance of communication. The organizational policy should express in clear and unambiguous terms that organization favours the promotion of communication in the organization.

2. This policy should also specify the subject matter to be communicated. This does not mean that contents of communication are to be prescribed in a completely exclusive manner but that the list should be illustrative and it should emphasize that the subject matter of communication should be determined by the needs of the organization.
3. Though communication through proper channel is essential for orderly flow of information, it should not always be insisted upon. The system of communication through proper channel serves the purpose adequately as far as routine types of information are concerned. However, when and whatever the situation so warrants, this has to be overlooked and persons concerned need being told explicitly that insistence on proper channel is not necessary in all cases.
4. Every person in the organization shares the responsibility of good communication; however, persons at the top have special responsibility in this regard. A successful communication system will only be achieved if top management is determined that it is to be so. It must set good examples itself, clearly expects others to follow them, and check from time to time that there are no bottlenecks.
5. Organization should have adequate facilities for promoting communication. Adequate provision of these facilities is not sufficient, but proper attention must be given towards their proper and effective use. These need being carefully looked into and the responsibility of superior managers in encouraging the use of these facilities through the adoption of supportive attitude and behaviour needs being emphasized.
6. Communication being an interpersonal process, the development of interpersonal relationships based on mutual respect, trust and confidence is essential for its promotion. In large organization, status differentials and class distinctions are overemphasized making interpersonal relationships amongst the executives highly impersonal and official. The organizational climate, therefore, should be radically modified to make it more intimate and personal. A modification in the attitude and behaviour of persons is essential for promotion of communication. Towards this end, an educative programme in communication should be organized for managers at all levels. In this programme, managers should be instructed in the need and significance of communication, need for developing close personal contacts amongst individuals.
7. These should be continuous programme of evaluating the flow of communication in different directions. This would highlight problems in this area identify their causes and thereby enable the adoption of suitable corrective actions.

16.6 COMMUNICATION CHANNELS

Communication channel, formal or informal, requires some subject matter for communication (message, idea, suggestion, complaint, etc.) in the form of words, signs or diagrams, which are called media of communication. In the organization, the managing director wants to issue directions to different departmental heads then he can convene a meeting, summon them to his room, talk to them over the telephone, or send them a memo. All these are the media through which the managing director can communicate. The decision regarding the choice of media is dependent upon the nature and urgency of the message and on the other side on the emotional and intellectual level of the receiver. For communication to be effective the sender has to be very careful and judicious in choice of media. The media of communication can be divided as follows (Figure 16.2):

16.6.1 Verbal Communication

The communication through words, writing speaking and listening constitute verbal communication.

1. **Oral Communication:** Communication with the help of spoken words is known as oral communication. Oral communication may take place in the form of face-to-face conversation and through mechanical devices which include conversation over the telephone, radio broadcasts, interviews, group discussions, meetings, conferences and seminars, announcements over the public address system, speeches, etc. When the communication is oral the sender can ask questions, describe or can make the receiver understand something that is not clear. There are various forms of oral communication depending upon the situation. These are personal instructions, lectures, meetings and conferences, interviews, social and cultural affairs, union channels etc.

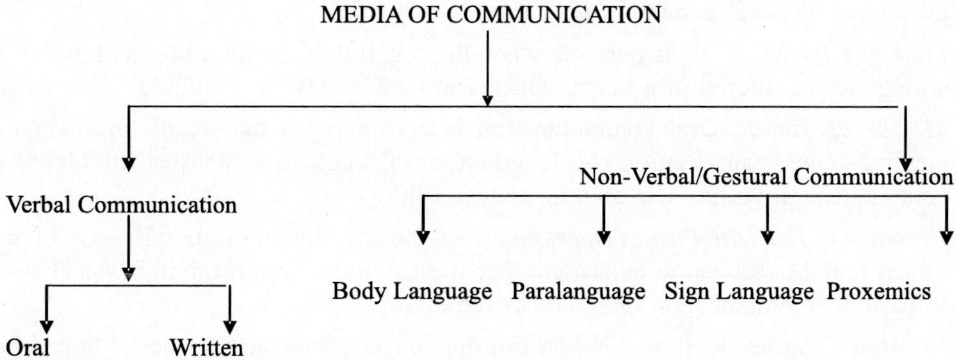

Figure 16.2 Communication channels.

Advantages of Oral Communication

- ***Quickness in Exchange of Ideas:*** The ideas can be conveyed to distant places quickly because this medium does not require message to be written.
- ***Immediate Feedback:*** Oral communication helps in understanding the extent to which the receiver has understood the message through his feelings during the course of conversation.
- ***Flexibility:*** Oral communication has an element of flexibility inherent in it. Flexibility means changing ideas according to the situation or changing ideas according to the interest of the receiver.
- ***Economic Sources:*** It is an economic source of communication because the message is communicated only orally.
- ***Personal Touch:*** Oral communication has a personal touch. Both the sides can

understand each other's feelings, being face to face. The conversation takes place in a clean environment, which increase mutual confidence.

- ***Effective Source:*** Oral Communication leaves much impression on the receiver. It is said that sometimes a thing can be communicated more effectively with the help of some sign. The use of signs or gesticulation can only be made in oral communication.
- ***Saves Time and Increases Efficiency:*** This communication consumes less time and the superiors can utilize the time saved in some other more important works. As a result of this, the efficiency of sender increases.

Disadvantages of Oral Communication

- ***Unfit for Lengthy Message:*** Oral communication is profitable in having a brief exchange of ideas only. It is not possible for receiver to remember long message.
- ***Unfit for Policy Matters:*** Where policies, rules or other important messages is to be communicated, oral communication has no importance.
- ***Lack of Written Proof:*** In the case of oral communication no written proof is left for future reference. Therefore, sometimes difficulty has to be faced.
- ***Expensive Method:*** When less important information is sent to distant places through telephone, etc. oral communication proves costly.
- ***Lack of Clarity:*** This is possible when there is little time for conversation. Sometimes wrong can be uttered in a hurry, which can lead to adverse results.
- ***Misuse of Time:*** Oral communication is considered a misuse of time when during meetings the conversation is lengthened unnecessarily. Parties involved in the communication waste their time in useless talks.
- ***Presence of Both the Parties Necessary:*** In the oral communication it is essential for the sender and the receiver to be present face to face, it does not mean in physical sense. But in written communication one party is required.

2. **Written Communication:** When information is exchanged in the written form, it is called as written communication. It includes personal letters, circulars, memos, telegrams, annual reports, forms and questionnaires, manuals, magazines, newspapers, bulletins, complaint procedures, policy manuals, house journals, trade journals, correspondence, agenda forms, notice board, posters, etc. The limitations of oral communication like the presence of both the parties, lack of proof in the context of future, etc. can be overcome by written communication.

Advantages of Written Communication

- ***Suitable for Lengthy Message:*** The lengthy message can clearly communicate with the help of written communication.
- ***Written Proof:*** Some documents with regard to some special facts have to be kept for future reference. This is possible only through written communication.
- ***Clear Message:*** A message may be long or short, it can be made understandable in a written communication. There is no fear of anything being left out in such a system.
- ***Less Expensive Method:*** Messages are to be sent to distant places, if there is no urgency

involved, it can be sent at a little expense through this method. But if the message is to be sent a distant place quickly, this method is not useful.

- ***Time Saving:*** Under the written communication there is no open conversation with a big human group. Hence, time is not lost in useless talks.
- ***Presence of Both the Parties not Necessary:*** In this system, it is not necessary that the receiver should be present before the sender.
- ***True and Effective:*** The written communication is true and hence effective. A sender sends the information after careful consideration because of written proof it carries with it.
- ***Communication at Different Places:*** When messages have to be sent to different places, written communication proves to be useful.

Disadvantages of Written Communication

- ***Unfit for Uneducated Persons:*** The written communication has no significance for the uneducated people. They can only be made to understand orally.
- ***Lack of Secrecy:*** Because of written proof, nothing can remain secret.
- ***Wastage of Time:*** Because of the organizational constraints it is essential to send less important facts in writing, it shall be the wastage of time, labour and money.
- ***No quick Information about Feedback:*** Some difficulty is felt when the reactions of the receivers are not known immediately. It also becomes difficult to bring an immediate change in the message.

16.6.2 Non-Verbal Communication or Gestural Communication

It uses gestures for exchange of feeling or information. In this messages are conveyed through body movements, facial expression or gesticulation. For example, saying 'yes' or 'no' by the movement of neck. An efficient manager can quickly get the feedback with the help of facial expressions. If there is face-to-face conversation between two persons, they can better understand the feelings, attitude and emotions of each other. The gestures taken by the listener can help the communicator to know their reactions.

Gestural communication is very important to motivate the subordinates, as for instance, handshake with the subordinate or a pat on the back of the subordinate. In this, we are concerned with body movements, space, time, voice tone/pitch, general characteristics of environment, colour, layout/design, and any other kinds of visual and/or audio signals that the communicator may devise. The different forms of gestural communication are gestural news at television, indication by umpire in sports, to accept honour by waving hands.

Advantages of Gestural Communication

- Quick sending of information.
- Less expensive system.
- Quick Feedback.

- Increase in efficiency.
- Time saving.

Disadvantages of Gestural Communication

- Lack of Secrecy.
- Useful for small amount of information.
- Gestures can be misunderstood.
- It is necessary for both the parties to be face to face with each other.
- Lack of written proof.
- Useful only for small messages.

Forms of Non-Verbal/Gestural Communication

1. **Body Language:** It is reflection of our thoughts, feelings and our position in the organization. Body language works through facial expression, eye contact, gestures, head position, body shape, posture and appearance. Like, if an individual slouches or jiggles his feet, he gives the impression of being indifferent, uninterested or distressed. This example shows that body language adds intensity to the process of communication. A resourceful manager should make effective use of it. This results in improving the overall atmosphere and looks of the organization.
2. **Paralanguage:** It means 'Like' language. It is concerned with the manner in which a speaker conveys his meanings through words. It tells a lot about a speaker's educational background, national regional background, his mental state and his place in the organization. Like the word stress makes speech convincing. Proper words stress gives words intended meaning.
3. **Sign Language:** Signs, i.e., visual and audio/sound signals have been in use since time immemorial. Visual signals like pictures, posters, photographs, cartoons, maps, diagrams, drawings and lights, etc. economize on verbal communication. These make communication interesting and motivate the receiver of the message. Drumbeats, alarm signals like sirens/hooters, buzzers, bell ringing are the most commonly used sound signals. These sound signals are important in time management.
4. **Proxemics:** It is study of space language. The distance between the people tells about their relations. Social space is best used for formal/official purposes. For instance, the people who begin conversation and those who are seated at the front are usually considered as the leaders of the group. People seated around a round/oval table will most likely communicate in the form of conference.

16.6.3 Communication Networks

A proper pattern is followed to carry out activities in the business. The board of directors takes the policy decisions, managing directors executes the policy, the departmental managers issue instructions, supervisors give orders and clerks and operatives actually perform the task. All these parties are connected through some channels of communication. The sum total of these channels is known as communication networks. It includes as depicted in Figure 16.3 shown below.

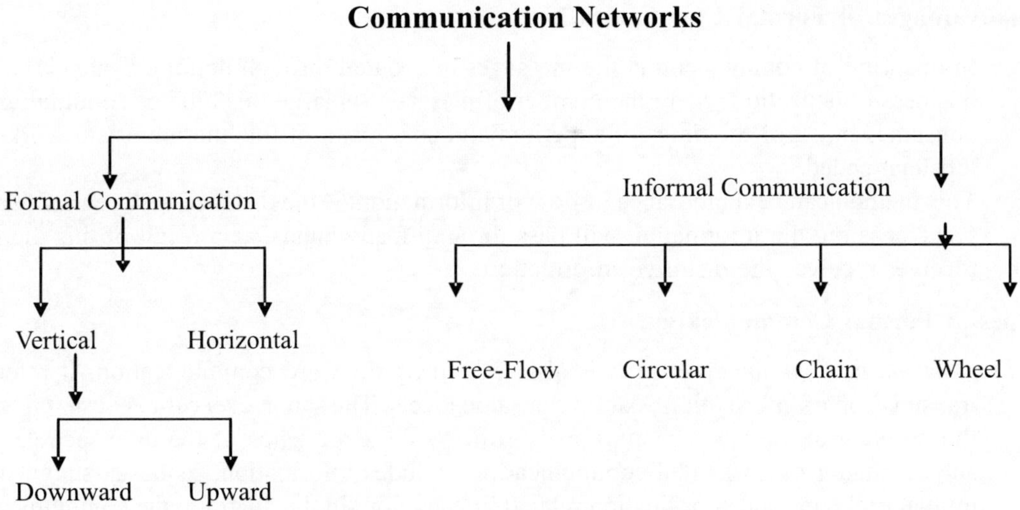

Figure 16.3 Communication networks.

1. **Formal Communication:** It refers to official lines of communication, which follows chain of command. It is the path of communication, which is institutionally determined by the organization. In this exchange of ideas and information is done under the planned organizational structure. It makes it possible for the information to reach the desired place without any hindrance, at a little cost and in a proper way.

Characteristics of Formal Communication

- It can be oral as well as written. Daily works are handled through oral communication, while the policy matters require written communication.
- This communication is adopted where the sender and receiver have some sort of organizational relationship.
- It is related with the authorized organizational messages only, the personal messages are out of its scope.
- Some deliberate efforts are require for the creation of this kind of communication. It is decided in view of the objective of the organization.
- While moving from one person to another, i.e., from worker to foreman, foreman to manager, this kind of communication has to pass through definite channel.

Advantages of Formal Communication

- If helps in maintaining constant relationship between superior and the subordinates as a result of which the dignity of line superiors is maintained. Consequently, it is convenient to control the subordinates and fix their responsibility.
- In formal communication both the superiors and subordinates understand the capability and feeling of each others as they are in direct contact with each other. The manager, thus, makes the information available to the subordinates, as he is well aware of their requirements. Hence, formal communication is clear and effective.

Disadvantages of Formal Communication

- In this kind of communication the messages are routed through definite channels. In big business organization where the number of messages is large this kind of communication consumes much of the times of superiors and as a result of this the important works are left unattended.
- This method can be a hindrance in flow of information. If the distance between sender and receiver is big the information will pass through many hands, as a result of this the final receiver receives the distorted information.

Types of Formal Communication

(a) *Horizontal Communication:* It is also known as sideward communication. It refers to transmission of information positions at same levels. The same level officers use it to solve the problem of the similar nature and profit by the experience of the other people. The subject matter of horizontal communication includes information, requests, suggestions, mutual problems and coordination related information. In the diagram, the communication between a manager and a manager, between a foreman and a foreman and between a worker and a worker is horizontal communication.

(b) *Vertical Communication:* It may move both downward as well as upward.

- Downward Communication: It represents the flow of information from the top level to the lower level of the organization. The basic purpose of downward communication is to communicate policies, procedures, programmes and objectives and to issue orders and instructions to the subordinates. It can be possible through verbal or written orders and instructions, notices, circulars, letters, memos, posters, periodicals, publications, group meetings, etc.
- Upward Communication: It is communication from the lower level to the higher authorities. The subject matter of this communication is suggestions, reactions, reports, complaints, etc. A clean environment in the organization can be maintained by removing the subordinates' problems. It helps the superiors in taking the decision. The upward communication is successful when the relationship between superiors and subordinates is good, otherwise the subordinates never prefer to give right information to superiors and the information, which may harm their interest.

2. **Informal Communication:** It refers to communication among people through informal contacts. In this case, the position and status of parties have no relevance. The communication is entirely based upon the informal relationships like friendship, membership of the same club, same place of birth, etc. In this communication, the superiors will get such information which is not possible to collect through the formal channels. Such communication includes comments, suggestions, etc. It takes place through gesticulation, moving of head, smiling and by remaining quite. It is also called as 'Grapevine Communication' because there is no definite channel of communication.

Characteristics of Informal Communication

- In this kind of communication no superior-subordinate relationship is there. This kind of communication is possible only through social relationships.

- It includes the communication of organizational as well as the individual messages. In other words, the information about the work as well as the individual is collected through this kind of information.
- It is beyond the restriction of the organization, as it follows no definite channels.
- It makes news spread like wild fire. People not only make addition in the existing messages, but also they sometimes change the real meaning of the communication.

Advantages of Informal Communication

- In this type of communication the messages move fast and their effect is great on the people.
- It is done in a free environment. It means that no organizational pressure is there. The opinion of the people about the organization can be easily collected.

Disadvantages of Informal Communication

- This communication is totally unsystematic and the possibility of information to reach the concerned person is very less.
- Most of the information collected through this channel is unreliable and no important decision can be taken on its basis.

Types of Informal Communication

(a) *Free-Flow Communication or All Channel Communication:* Under this no restriction is there on flow of communication. Everyone is free to communicate with each other. This communication is unstructured and flexible.

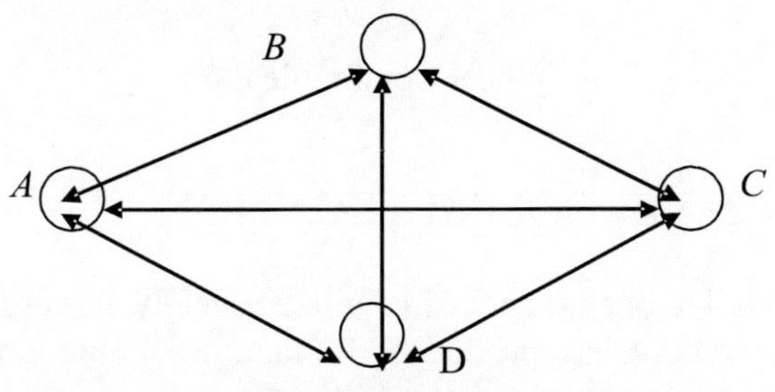

Free-Flow Communication

(b) *Circular Communication:* In this, the message moves in cycle. Each person can communicate with his two neighbourhood colleagues. The basic disadvantage of this communication is that it is very slow.

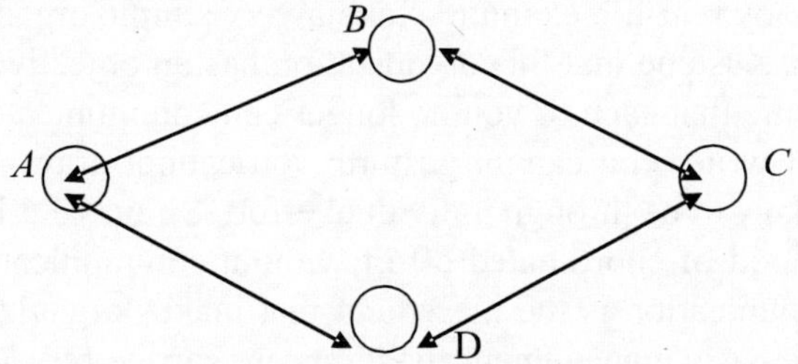

Circular Communication

(c) *Chain Communication:* In this, the message flows in a direct vertical lines along the scalar chain of command. It can flow from top to bottom and bottom top in a line. Thus, the flow of communication takes place through proper channels. No horizontal communication is here.

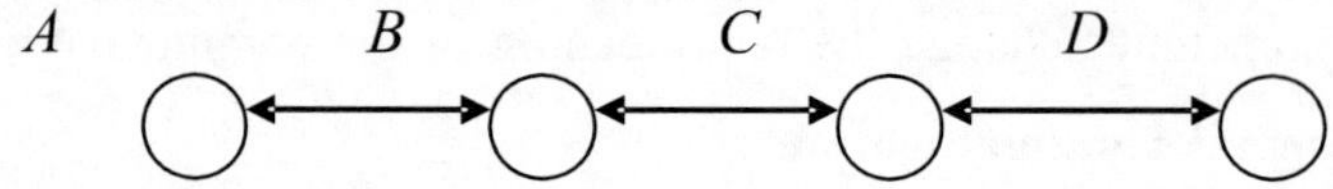

Chain Communication

(d) *Wheel Communication:* In this, all communications pass through the manager who acts as a central authority like the hub of a wheel. The subordinates can communicate with and through one manager. All the instructions and guidance will pass through one person.

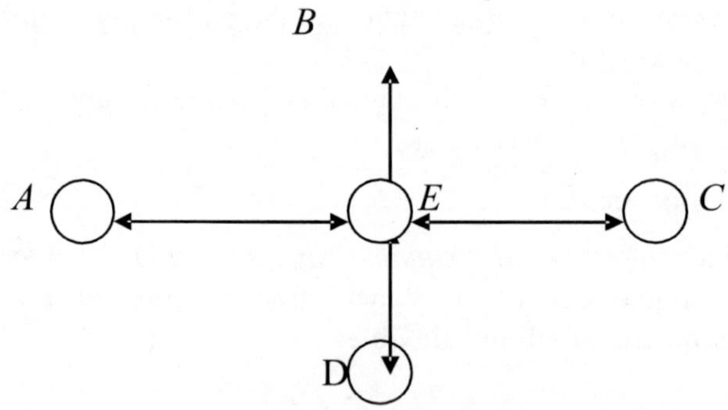

Wheel Communication

16.7 SIGNIFICANCE OF COMMUNICATION

Just as communication is vital to our existence in civilized society, it is essential to the functioning of the organizations our society has produced. In fact, we could go so far as to say that organizations exist through communication; without communication, there would be no organizations. As Herbert Simon expresses it. "Without communication there can be no organization, for there is no possibility then of the group influencing the behaviour of the individual."

If you need proof of the importance of communication to organized activity, you need only apply your good logic to any real-life example. Take a very simple organization made up of just you and one other person. Assume that this organization has an objective–one that is unfamiliar to each of you. Now assume that each of you no longer can communicate. You cannot read; you cannot speak; you cannot write; you cannot gesture; you cannot draw. If the two of you make any progress at all, it is likely to be through individual effort. Strain your imagination as you will, there simply is no likelihood of coordinated effort without communication.

Needless to say, communication is the ingredient that makes organization possible. It is the vehicle through which the basic management functions are carried out. Managers direct through communication; they coordinate through communication; and they staff, plan, and control through communication. Virtually all actions taken in an organization are preceded by communication.

Just how much communicating a business organization needs depends on a number of factors. The nature of the business certainly is one. Some businesses (such as insurance companies) have a much greater need to communicate than do others (such as janitorial services). The company's organization plan also affects the volume of communication, for it generates much of the information flow. Finally, the people who make up the organization affect the extent of communication. As we would point out later, every human being is different. Each one has unique communication needs and abilities. Thus, varying combinations of people produce varying needs for communication.

Although communication needs may be dissimilar in different organizations and different groups of people in such organizations communicate more than we suspect. According to one generally accepted estimate, between 40 and 60 per cent of the work time spent in a typical manufacturing plant involves some form of communication (speaking, writing, listening, and reading). Of course, these percentages are only averages. Some employees spend most of their time communicating. In fact, the higher up the organization structure the employee is, the more communication he or she is likely to do. Typically, top executives spend from 75 to 95 per cent of their time communicating. Unskilled labourers, on the other hand, need to communicate lesser in order to do their work.

Without question, communication is important to business organizations. Therefore, it stands to reason that a business wants its communication to be done well. But all too rarely is a business satisfied with what it gets. Unfortunately, to use the often quoted words of an authority in the field, "Of all the things business executives do, they are worst at communicating".

Communication is the life blood of business. No business can develop in the absence of effective internal and external communication. Besides, communication skills of the employees are given high weightage at the time of their appointment as well as promotion.

16.7.1 Internal Communication

Effective internal communication is considered important for the following reasons:

1. Business has grown in size. Large business houses have a number of branches within the country and even abroad. Some of the multinational corporations are no smaller than huge empires. The central organization of a large business house is its nerve centre. For its healthy and even growth, it is extremely important that the central organization maintains a thorough and up-to-date knowledge of the various activities at the branch offices, and in turn keep the branch offices will acquainted with the activities at the centre, and some kind of link is maintained among the various branches. This calls for an effective and efficient network of communication.
2. Business activity has become extremely complex. This being an age of specialization, planning, production, sales, stores, advertising, financing, accounts, welfare, etc. are handled by different departments. If these departments do not communicate with one another as well as with the management, there will be no coordination among them. This

may give rise to some awkward and embarrassing situations for the management. When production is fully geared up, the stores department may report shortage or non-availability of raw materials. The planners, having spent one full month to work out the details of a new project, may suddenly discover that there are no finances available to execute the project.

3. Effective communication promotes a spirit of understanding and cooperation. If there exists effective communication between the management and the employees, it helps to bring about an atmosphere of mutual trust and confidence. The employees know exactly what is expected of them, the management is aware of the potentialities and limitations of the employees and knows how to exploit the first and make up for the latter. This mutual understanding is extremely beneficial to both the parties. The management gets better returns; the employees get job satisfaction. They also develop a sense of belonging and loyalty to the enterprise.
4. The significance of communication in the context of today's complex organizations is even greater. These organizations being designed on the basis of specialization and division of labour constitute a large number of persons. The larger the size of the organization, the greater generally is the degree of specialization and division of labour and hence, the more urgent is the need for coordination. This coordination requires mutual understanding about the organizational goals, the mode of their achievement and the interrelationship between the work being performed by various individuals; and all this can be achieved through communication only. Effective communication, as such, is essential in any type of human grouping. As Haney has put it, "Communication is imminently essential in business, in government, military organizations. It is difficult, in fact, to imagine any kind of interpersonal activity which does not depend upon communication." Dealing with the problems of communication, then, becomes an important area of activity in management whose objective is the direction of individual efforts in such a way as to secure overall coordination of organizational activities.

16.7.2 External Communication

External communication includes communication with the government agencies and departments on the one hand and distributors, retailers, individual customers and general public on the other.

1. Government agencies and departments. Business organizations are required to deal with licensing authorities, foreign trade offices, customs authorities, banks and other financial institutions, income tax and sales tax offices, post offices, transporters, etc. Quite frequently, they find themselves tricky situations that can be handled only through tactful negotiation are nothing but communication.
2. Distributors, retailers, individual customers, etc. Modern business is a highly competitive phenomenon. Each product of common consumption is available in hundreds of brands, not all of which sell equally well. Marketing research has revealed that the organizations that can communicate better also sell better. Sales are promoted through persuasion and persuasion is a very important aspect of communication.

16.7.3 Communication Skill is Job Requirement

Some areas like personal, public relations, marketing, sales, labour relations call for exceptional communication skills. Professionals like editors, writers, teachers, advocates, researchers, etc., need a highly developed ability to communicate. Executives are also expected to make speeches, prepare pamphlets, brochures, souvenirs, and give interviews to the media in order to project a favourable image of their organization. Thus, the ability to communicate effectively has become a very important job requirement.

16.7.4 Important Factor for Promotion

In an article titled "What Do You Mean I Can't Write?" [Harvard Business Review, May-June 1965], John Fielden lists the ability to communicate as the most essential prerequisite for promotion of the executives. He ranks this ability higher than other essential attributes such as the capacity for hard work, the ability for making sound decisions, academic qualifications and ambition-drive. And this view is endorsed by numerous surveys conducted by a number of American universities and other scholars in the field.

16.8 NATURE OF BUSINESS COMMUNICATION

The role of communication in organized activities is perhaps explained by a real-life illustration. By design, our illustration is both detailed and scant. It is detailed because it consists of examples of the minute and specific communication events that occur in business. It is scant because at best it covers only a sample of an almost infinite number of events.

For this review, we could select any organization, as communication is vital to every conceivable type. Our choice is the Typical Company, manufacturer of a line of quality what sits. The Typical Company is moderately large, with scores of departments and hundreds of workers doing a thousand and one tasks. It employs crews of salespeople who sell the manufactured what sits to wholesalers all over the country. Like most companies in its field, Typical works to move its products from wholesaler to retailer and from retailer to the final consumer. And it works to keep the consumer happy with the purchase. The Typical Company is indeed typical.

Our review begins with the workday of Dan D. Worker, a clerk in Typical's order department. (We could, of course, have selected any of Typical's employees). Dan's daily communication activities begin the moment he awakens. But for our purposes, we shall pick up Dan's activities as he rides to work in a car pool with three co-workers. Of course, Dan and his car-pool companions communicate as they travel. Obviously, communication has a social use, and riding to work is a form of social occasion for Dan and his friends.

Most of their talk is about trivial matters. They talk primarily to entertain themselves and to while away the time. There is a joke or two, some comments about politics, a few words about an upcoming football game, and some talk about plans for a getaway weekend fishing trip. Such talk, of course, is of little direct concern to Typical, except perhaps as it affects the general happiness and welfare of the company's workers.

In time, the conversation drifts to subjects more pertinent to Typical and its operations. Someone mentions a rumour about a proposed change in promotion policy. Then Dan and the others bring up their own collection of rumours, facts, and opinions on the subject. And in the process, they giving, receiving, or handling information. Nothing that he did directly involved making what sits, which, of course, is the Typical Company's main reason for being. Yet the importance of his activities to Typical's operations is unquestionable. Obviously, Dan's work assignment more directly involves communication than do many others at Typical. But there are many other communication-oriented assignments in the company, and every Typical employee's workday is peppered with communication in one form or another. If we were to trace the workday of each Typical employee and combine our findings, we would come up with an infinitely complex picture of the communication that goes on at Typical. We would see that communication indeed plays a major role in Typical's operations.

The importance of communication in business becomes even more apparent when we consider an organization's communication activities from an overall perspective. As we can see from reviewing Dan's half hour at Typical, these activities fall in three broad categories of communication: internal-operational, external-operational, and personal.

16.8.1 Internal-Operational Communication

Internal-operational communication consists of structured communication within the organization that directly relates to achieving the organization's work goals. By 'structured' we mean that such communication is built into the organization's plan of operations. By 'organization's work goals' we mean the organization's primary reason for being—to sell insurance, to manufacture nuts and bolts, to construct buildings, and the like.

The Typical Company, to use a familiar example, has as its major work goals the making and selling of what sits. To achieve these work goals, it has an established plan of operations, in which communication plays a major role. More specifically, each Typical employee has an assignment within the plan. In order for the plan to work, some communicating must be done. Some of the assignments require certain working information. In order for all assignments to be performed as a harmonious and unified effort, certain coordinating information must be communicated. All of this information flow is internal-operational communication.

Specifically, internal-operational communication is carried out through any number of structured activities. In the Typical Company, for example, must of the internal-operational information is entered into the company computer from executive workstations to become part of Typical's database. From the database, programmed reports are developed to give each operations department the information it needs. Then the reports are communicated back to specific workstations; for example, sales reports and inventory records combine to communicate production needs to the production planning department. Finally, the production planning department communicates these needs to the various production departments through a strategically planned work schedule.

Typical's database. From the database, programmed reports are developed to give each operations department the information it needs. Then the reports are communicated back to specific workstations; for example, sales reports and inventory records combine to communicate production needs to the production planning department. Finally, the production planning department communicates these needs to the various production departments through a strategically planned work schedule.

Within each production unit and among production units, of course, additional communicating must go on. Superiors make decisions and transmit them to subordinates. Departments exchange information, and workers communicate working information with one another. Memorandums are written, reports are prepared, and conversations are held—all in the process of coordinating efforts and supplying the information needed for achieving the organization's goals. In every company division and in every activity, similar internal-operational communication occurs.

16.8.2 External-Operational Communication

External-operational communication is that part of an organization's structured communication concerned with achieving the organization's work goals that is conducted with people and groups outside the organization. It is the organization's communication with its publics-suppliers, service companies, customers, and the general public.

In this category fall all of the organization's efforts at direct selling-sales representative's sales spiels, descriptive brochures, telephone call-backs, follow-up service calls, and the like. Also included are all of the organization's advertising efforts-for what is advertising but a deliberate, structured communication with an organization's publics? Radio and television messages, newspaper and magazine space advertising, and point-of-purchase display material obviously play a role in the organization's plan for achieving its work objective. Also in this category is everything the organization does to enhance its public relations. These activities include the organization's planned publicity, and the condition of its physical plant. All these and many more communication efforts combine to make up the organization's external-operational communication.

The extreme importance of an organization's external communications hardly requires supporting comment. Certainly it is obvious that any business organization depends on outside people and groups for its success. It is an elementary principle of business that because a business organization's success depends on its ability to satisfy customers' needs, the organization must communicate effectively with these customers. It is equally elementary that in today's complex business society, organizations depend on one another in manufacturing and distributing and services. This interdependence necessarily creates needs for communication. Like internal communications, these outside communications are vital to an organization's operation.

16.8.3 Personal Communication

Not all the communication that goes on in an organization is operational, however, in fact, much of it is without purpose as far as the organization is concerned. Such communication may be classified as personal.

Personal communication is all the incidental exchange of information and feelings in which human beings engage whenever they come together. Human beings are social animals. They have a need to communicate, and they would communicate even when they have little or nothing to say. In fact, they communicate even when they do not communicate anything.

Much of the time friends spend with one another is devoted to communication, for it is simply the thing to do when people get together. Even total strangers are likely to communicate when they are placed together, such as on a plane trip, in a waiting room, or at a ball game. Such personal communication also takes place in the work situation, and it is part of the communication activity of any business organization. Although not a component of an organization's plan of operations, personal communication can have a significant effect on its success. This effect stems from the influence personal communication can have on the viewpoints (opinions, attitudes, and beliefs) of the organization's members.

Workers' viewpoints towards the organization, their fellow employees, and their assignments directly affect their willingness to do assigned tasks. And the nature of conversation in a work situation affects viewpoints. In a work situation in which heated words and flaring tempers are frequent, the participants are unlikely to make their usual productive effort. A rollicking, jovial work situation is likely to have an equally adverse effect on productivity. No doubt, somewhere between these extremes lie the ideal productive viewpoints.

Organization members' work viewpoint is also affecting the extent of personal communication permitted to them. Outright denial of the communication privilege can lead to emotional upset, for people hold dear their right to communicate. On the other hand, excessive personal communication can interfere directly with their work effort. Probably somewhere in the middle ground lies the optimal policy toward personal communication.

Personal communication can also help form viewpoints (opinions, attitudes, beliefs). As illustrated in the account of Dan's workday at Typical, Dan and his car-pool friends spent some of their conversation time discussing a proposed new promotion policy; and in so doing, each helped crystallize the others' viewpoints. It is a process that determines much of what organization members think about their organization, co-workers and work situation in general. What they think can affect their relationship with the organization and have a direct influence on their productivity.

16.9 SUMMARY

The foregoing discussion merely browses the surface of our mind. It may hopefully help in appreciating the importance of communication to an individual and an organization. It shows how extensive communication is and how it permeates through every segment of the organization in a most complex way. It shows that good communication is vital to the organization's successful operation and equally imperative for a man's personality development. These conclusions, combined with the convincing evidence that most organizational communication is inadequate, leads to yet another conclusion: that communication is an area that deserves further study by those concerned with improving the organizational operations.

Two-way communication is more effective than one-way communication. The feedback allows the sender the refine his communication so that it becomes more precise and accurate. Receivers' self-confidence is higher in case of two-way communication as they are permitted to ask questions and seek clarification from the senders.

Thus, these were the various spices which must be added to make each and every element of the communication process is of its utmost importance and with the absence of any of these elements the communication can't be effective or we can say that the absence of any of the above elements makes the communication process same as a handicap person living his life in the absence of any important part of the body. So, as a business communicator our efforts should be to make communication process as effective as possible and let each element of the process to play its part, suitably well.

16.10 SELF-ASSESSMENT EXERCISE

1. Attempt a suitable definition of the term communication and elaborate your definition through communication process.
2. "The single most significant characteristic of the human race is the ability to communicate." Discuss.
3. "Communication is the sum of all things one person does when he wants to create understanding in the mind of another. It is a bridge of meaning. It involves a systematic and continuous process of telling, listening and understanding." Discuss.
4. Write a note on the need and importance of business communication.
5. What is meant by the communication situation? Do the following constitute communication situations?
   (a) An Englishman speaking in English to an illiterate Indian;
   (b) Two young boys talking to each other in a code language, which they have evolved themselves;
   (c) A man muttering to himself;
   (d) A young lover talking to the moon?
6. What are the various steps in the communication cycle? What is brain drain? Why does brain drain occur?

17 MOTIVATION

Learning Objective

The main objective of this chapter is to understand the meaning of motivation, nature of motivational process and the theories of motivation regarding behaviour and work.

17.1 INTRODUCTION

Generally, people differ by nature, not only in their ability to perform a specific task but also in their will to do so. People with less ability but lots of strength are able to perform better than people with superior ability and lack of will. Hard work is crucial to success and achievement. Albert Einstein underscored this belief when he said, genius is 10% inspiration and 90% perspiration. This 'will' to do is known as motivation. The force of motivation is a dynamic force setting a person into motion or action. The concept of motivation can be traced back to nearly twenty-three centuries ago in the Greek and Indian writings.

The idea that we are motivated to do what brings us the best results for our benefit is found in the early Indian philosophy through writings such as 'Charvak'. The most ancient concept of 'Nirvana', as proposed and propagated by the earliest Aryan thinkers and religious scholars, motivates us to be 'good' people so that we can achieve the final "oneness with God." The Greek view of motivation has been dominated by the concept of hedonism, which is a view that people seek pleasure and comfort, and avoid pain and discomfort. This view was based upon intuition and common sense that an individual does what he does because he believes that it will give him more pleasure than anything else he might do. This philosophy, though still popular, depends excessively upon rational evaluation and does not take into consideration the effect of instincts or even the value system. Hedonism, based on maximizing personal pleasure cannot explain why some people would sometimes risk their own lives to save others in times of crisis or why volunteers would spend so much of their time in collecting money for charitable causes. However, this view prevailed right up to the eighteenth and, nineteenth centuries and is evident in the social and economical philosophies of such famous men as Adam Smith, Jeremy Bentham and John Stuart Mill. The principles of hedonism seems to be too narrow-minded and is empirically insignificant since it does not attempt to evaluate just what the individuals anticipate to be the results of their behaviour and how do they measure pleasure. For example, a person who risked his own life to save another had rationally decided to become a "hero" or did he act on "impulse," believing that it was the right thing to do irrespective of cost or consequences? The principle of hedonism can be more easily explained "after the fact" when the behaviour has already been explained. Thus, even the acts of simple kindness can be explained with the motives of "feeling good" about them or earning the gratefulness of those who have been helped by these acts. Since hedonistic explanations work best in explaining actions after they occur, they cannot be relied upon in predicting behaviour. These limitations of hedonistics viewpoints brought motivation under different light during the late 1800s and early 1900s. William James and Sigmund Freud argue that instinctive behaviour and unconscious motivation are also important elements in human behaviour and these largely determine an individual's interpretation of, and response to, situations.

Instincts, which are inborn or innate predispositions, which are not consciously rational, can explain certain aspects of\human behaviour. These instincts, which influence human behaviour, include the need for autonomy, curiosity, sociability, sympathy, fear, jealousy, love, dominance, harm avoidance, play, and sex. The large number of identified instincts identifies a variety of possible behaviours. The instinct behaviour is like a reflex action, meant for survival and hence caters primarily to physiological needs. It is not learnt and is not dependent upon the consequences of an action. Most instincts are common to all people and would exhibit similar behaviour under similar circumstances. For example, if somebody has a flat tire while driving, the first instinctive reaction is to get mad. The unconscious motivation, of which an individual is unaware, was brought up by Sigmund Freud who suggested that unconscious motives are primarily sexual and aggressive in nature and even though unconscious, they greatly influence everyday behaviour. These unconscious motives are revealed in dreams, symbolism, slips of speech (known as Freudian slip) and hypnotic suggestions. Both the instinctive motivation and unconscious motivation do not stand the scientific analysis and contemporary psychologists explain behaviour by complex cognitive and environmental interactions. The concept of motivation came under scientific scrutiny during 1930s and has led to formulation of many theories and models that try to scientifically explain the concept of motivation.

17.2 DEFINITIONS OF MOTIVATION

The word motivation is derived from motive, which is defined as an active form of a desire, craving or need, which must be satisfied. All motives are directed towards goals and the needs and desires affect or change your behaviour, which becomes goal oriented. For example, if you ordinarily do not want to work overtime, it is quite likely that at a particular time, you may need more money (desire) so you may change your behaviour, work overtime (goal oriented behaviour) and satisfy your needs. Viteles defines motivation as: "Motivation represents an unsatisfied need which creates a state of tension or disequilibria, causing the individual to move in a goal directed pattern–towards restoring a state of equilibrium, by satisfying the need."

17.3 PROCESS OF MOTIVATION

Motivated people are ill constant state of tension. This tension is relieved by drives towards an activity and outcome that is meant to reduce or relieve such tension. The greater the tension, the more activity will, be needed to bring about relief and hence higher the motivation. Thus, the basic motivation process can be depicted as follows:

1. **Effort:** The amount of effort put into the activity identifies the strength of the person's work-related behaviour. Hard work usually reflects high motivation.

   A student who works very hard to get top grades can be referred to as highly motivated. A professor who is engaged in research and publishes many high quality articles is exerting extensive effort relating to his job.
2. **Persistence:** Motivation is a permanent and an integral part of a human being. Its second characteristic is persistence in the efforts. Motivation is continuously goal directed so that once a goal is achieved, a higher goal is selected and efforts are exercised towards this higher goal. For example, a professor who publishes simply to get a promotion and then stops or reduces research efforts would not be considered as highly motivated. Accordingly, high motivation requires persistent efforts.
3. **Direction:** Persistent hard work determines the quantity of effort while direction determines the quality of the anticipated output. All efforts are to be directed towards the organizational goal. This would ensure that the persistent effort is actually resulting into accepted organizational outcomes.

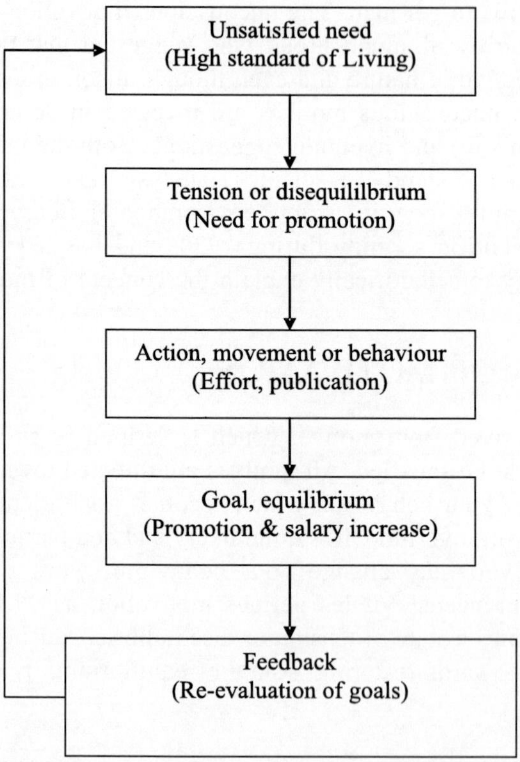

For example, a quality control inspector is consistently expected to direct his efforts in discovering defects in the produced items so that the organizational goal of high quality output is met. As an example, let us assume that a professor has established a goal for him to get a promotion and monetary raise in order to improve upon his standard of living. Thus, the professor will shape his behaviour to achieve that goal. He will thus choose a course of action designed to obtain promotion. This course of action may be five published articles or one published book. He will be highly motivated and will put in persistent efforts in research and publish the desired number of articles or the book. Once the promotion has been obtained the professor will reevaluate his achievement relative to his initially established objective. If the pay raise is not adequate and there are grounds for further promotion and pay raise, the professor will establish a higher goal and strive towards it. This example fits the basic motivational process as follows:

In the above example, if the motivator (publishing) does not serve the required purpose then the professor will look at other alternatives as motivators such as service to the college and community, student guidance and curriculum development, good interactive relations with peers and superiors.

4. **Analysis of situation:** The situation that needs motivational inducement must be sized up so as to ascertain the motivational needs. From organizational behaviour point of view it must be recognized that since the needs of different employees differ both in nature as well as intensity, a composite view of the collective needs of the group is established with appropriate recognition of differences in individual needs.
5. **Selecting and applying appropriate motivators:** A list of all devices of motivation is drawn and a selection made of such motivators that motivate different types of people under different circumstances. Proper timing and the extent of motivation are also to be considered. The individual goals should be given adequate attention within the framework of group goals and the organizational goals.
6. **Follow-up:** It is important to know that the motivators selected are indeed providing the desired motivation. This can be accomplished by getting and evaluating the feedback. If these motivators are not-showing the optimum effect, then alternative motivators should be selected and applied.

17.4 SOURCES OF MOTIVATION

Experts in the organizational behaviour field have a divided opinion as to whether workers are motivated by factors in the external environment such as rewards or fear or whether motivation is self-generated without the application of external factors. It is quite well understood that under the same set of external factors all workers are not equally motivated. Some of these motivational sources are:

17.4.1 Positive Motivation

Positive motivation involves proper recognition of employee, efforts and appreciation of employee contribution towards the organizational goal-achievement. Such motivations improve the standards of performance, lead to good team spirit and pride, a sense of cooperation and a feeling of belonging and happiness. Some of the positive motivators are:

- Praise and credit for work done.
- A sincere interest in the welfare of subordinates.
- Delegation of authority and responsibility to subordinates.
- Participation of subordinates in the decision-making process.

17.4.2 Negative or Fear Motivation

This motivation is based upon the use of force, power, fear and threats. The fear of punishment or unfavourable consequences affects the behavioural changes. Some examples of negative motivation include the fear of failing in the examination, and fear of being fired or demoted. Fear of failure in the examination induces motivation in many students to work harder and pass the course. Similarly, fear of being fired keeps the workers in the line with the organizational rules and regulations as well as do a satisfactory job. While the fear of punishment and actual punishment has resulted in controlling individual misbehaviour and has contributed towards positive performance in many situations and is necessary and useful in many other situations such as disciplining a child or handling a riot. It is not recommended or considered as a viable alternative in the current business and industrial environment. This is based upon the trend and changes in the workforce including higher level of employee education and extensive employee unionization. However, punishment or fear of it is still the most common technique of behaviour modification or control in today's life. When a child misbehaves, he is still spanked. If a worker does not behave according to the way the organization wants him to behave, he is fired. If a person does not behave as the society and law wants him to behave, he is punished by arrest and jail. All religions threaten punishment in the life hereafter if a person does not behave according to God's and religious rules.

Does the punishment system work? Does it change behaviour? Does the prison system reform the criminal? Does spanking make a "good" child? This area has received considerable attention and has become highly controversial. It has been proposed that while punishment has immediate and short-term effect in affecting and changing behaviour, the long-term effects are highly questionable. A driver who gets fined for running a red light where he is supposed to stop may vow never to do it again at that time, but as the time passes, he will do it again.

In the context of organizational behaviour, no worker likes to be criticized, or threatened with employment termination. Specifically, if the worker is punished for an occasional undesired behaviour, it will have a negative effect on his morale, make him bitter with a hostile 'state of mind, affecting negatively his social interaction as well as his sense of loyalty, perhaps resulting in poor performance and productivity and quality.

17.4.3 Extrinsic Motivation

This type of motivation is induced by external factors, which are primarily financial in nature. It is based upon the assumption that the behaviour, which results in positive rewards, tends to be repeated. However, the reward for the desired behaviour should be sufficiently powerful and durable so that it improves the probability of occurrence of desirable behaviour. Money is probably the most important incentive for positive behaviour since money can be used for a number of other resources. These financial incentives and rewards have been a subject of debate whether they really motivate the employees or simply move them to work and perform. These include higher pay, fringe benefits such as retirement plans, stock options, profit-sharing scheme, paid vacation, health and medical insurance, sympathetic supervision and people-oriented company policies.

17.4.4 Intrinsic Motivation

Intrinsic motivation stems from feelings of achievement and accomplishment and is concerned with the state of self-actualization in which the satisfaction of accomplishing something worthwhile motivates the employee further so that this motivation is self-generated and is independent of financial rewards. For example, there are many retired doctors who work free in the hospital because it gives them a sense of accomplishment and satisfaction. Mother Teresa's work in the slums of Kolkata, India, not only motivates the people who work with her but also many others who simply hear about her work and then want to join the team. Similarly, Peace Corps workers work in uncomfortable environments at a minimal pay. Some of the intrinsic motivators are praise, recognition, responsibility, esteem, power, status, challenges and decision-making responsibility.

17.5 THEORIES OF MOTIVATION REGARDING BEHAVIOUR

There are basically two types of theories developed that relate to and define the motivational processes. These are the "content theories" which attempt to determine and specify drives and needs that motivate people to work and "process theories" which attempt to identify the variables that go into motivation and their relationship with each other. These theories are described in greater detail.

17.5.1 The Content Theories of Work Motivation

The content theories have been developed to explain the nature of motivation in terms of types of need that people experience. They attempt to focus on factors within a person that initiate and direct a certain type of behaviour or check certain other type of behaviour. The basic idea

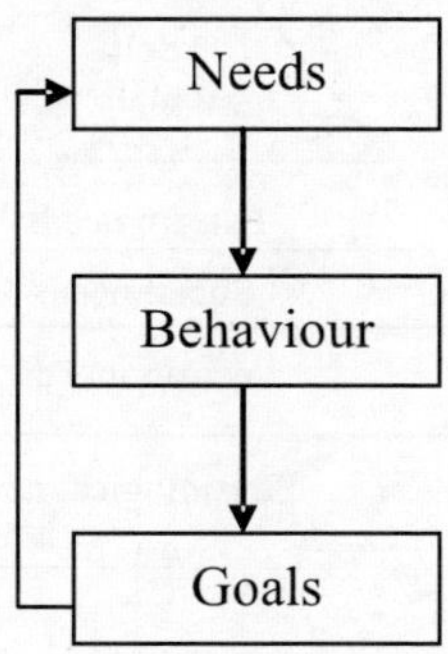

underlying such theories is that people have certain fundamental needs, both physiological and psychological in nature, and that they are motivated to engage in activities that would satisfy these needs. Thus, the nature of needs establishes the nature of motivation that results in a specific behaviour aimed at reaching the goal of satisfying such needs.

Some of the more important content theories are:

1. **Maslow's Model:** Maslow's "needs hierarchy theory" is probably the most widely used theory of motivation in organizations. Abraham Maslow suggested that people have a complex set of exceptionally strong needs and the behaviour of individuals at a particular moment is usually determined by their strongest need. He developed his model of human motivation in 1943, based upon his own clinical experience and formulated his theory of hierarchical needs by asking the same question, what is it that makes people behave the way they do and made a list of answers from which he developed a pattern. His theory is based upon two assumptions. First those human beings have many needs those are different in nature ranging from the biological needs at the lower level, which is the level of survival, to psychological needs at the upper extreme, which is the level of growth. Second that these needs occur in an order of hierarchy so that lower level needs must be satisfied before higher level needs arise or become motivators. Mahatma Gandhi, the Indian leader, once remarked, Even God cannot talk to a hungry man except in terms of food. Similarly, there is a quotation from the Holy Guru Granth Sahib, the holy scripture of Sikhs in India when a holy man says to God, "Take your rosary beads away. I cannot worship and meditate on you when I am hungry." This means that if the people's basic needs which are biological in nature are unsatisfied, then their total attention will be focused upon these needs and it will not be possible to communicate with them about other matter. This model of hierarchical needs explains human behaviour in a more dynamic and realistic manner and is primarily based upon people's inner states as a basis for motivation and the environmental conditions do not play any significant role. Maslow postulates five basic needs arranged in successive layers. These needs continue to change resulting in a change in goals and activities. These five needs are arranged in the form as shown. The first three level needs at the bottom are known as "deficiency" needs, because they must be satisfied in order to ensure the individual's very existence and security and make him fundamentally comfortable. The top two sets of needs are termed "growth" needs because they are concerned with personal growth, development and realization of one's potential.

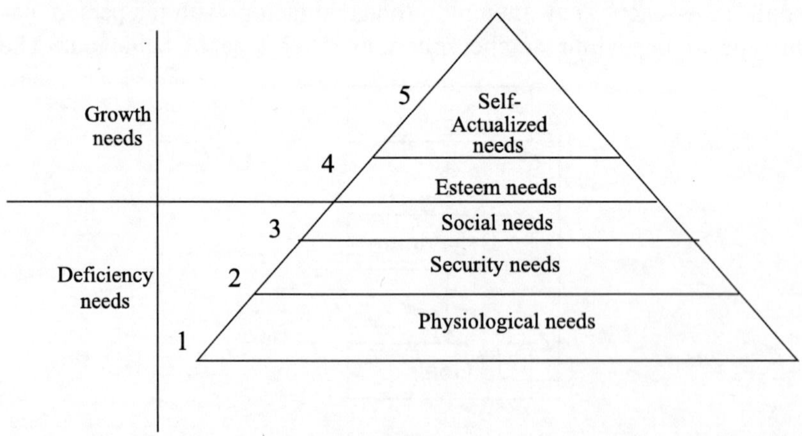

These needs are explained in detail as follows:

(a) Physiological needs: The physiological needs form the foundation of the hierarchy and tend to have the highest strength in terms of motivation. These are primarily the needs arising out of physiological or biological tension and they are there to sustain life itself and include the basic needs for food, water, shelter and sex. Sexual need and desire is not to be confused with love, which is at the third level. Once these basic needs are satisfied to the degree needed for the sufficient and comfortable operation of the body, then the other levels of needs become important and start acting as motivators.

(b) Security and safety needs: Once the physiological needs are gratified, the safety and security needs become predominant. These are the needs for self-preservation as against physiological needs, which are for survival. These needs include those of security, stability, freedom from anxiety and a structured and ordered environment. These safety and security needs are really provisions against deprivation of satisfaction of physiological needs in the future. It also involves a sense of protection against threats and danger of losing the job in the future. In a civilized society such as ours, a person is usually protected from threats of violence or extremes in climate or fear of material safety, so that the safety and security needs dwell upon economic and job security, life and medical insurance and other protective measures to safeguard the satisfaction of physiological needs in the future which may be unpredictable.

(c) Love and social needs: After the needs of the body and security are satisfied, then a sense of belonging and acceptance becomes prominent in motivating behaviour. These needs include the needs for love, friendship, affection, and social interaction. We look for an environment where we are understood, respected and wanted. That is one reason for "polarization" where people of similar background and beliefs tend to group together. "Love thy neighbour" has perhaps a profound meaning.

(d) Esteem needs: This need for esteem is to attain recognition from others, which would induce a feeling of self-worth and self-confidence in the Individual. It is an urge for achievement, prestige, status and power. Self-respect is the internal recognition. The respect from others is the external recognition and an appreciation of one's individuality as well as his contribution. This would result in self-confidence, independence, status, reputation and prestige. People then would begin to feel that they are useful and have some positive effect on their surrounding environment.

(e) Self-actualization needs: This last need is the need to develop fully and to realize one's capacities and potentialities to the fullest extent possible, whatever these capacities and potentialities maybe. This is the highest level of need in Maslow's hierarchy and is activated as a motivator when all other needs have been reasonably fulfilled. At this level, the person seeks challenging work assignments that allow for creativity and opportunities for personal growth and advancement. This need is for soul searching and is inner-oriented. A self-actualized person is creative, independent, content, and spontaneous and has a good perception of reality and he is constantly striving to realize his fun potential. Thus, "what a man 'can' be 'must' be."

Maslow's model is a general model in which an individual's needs interact with each other to some degree. Needs are not necessarily linear, nor is their order so rigid. The relative dominance of many needs is variable and is continuously shifting. For example, a self-actualized person may shift his priority to social needs and love needs, instead of prestige and status, if suddenly there occurs a vacuum due to loss of a loved one. Similarly, a person may not go to the higher need, even when his lower needs are satisfied. It is also likely that a well-prepared elite person may decide to enter a commune, where there is overwhelming emphasis on love and affection, rather than climb the corporate ladder.

Maslow's theory made management aware that people are motivated by a wide variety of needs, and that it must provide an opportunity for the employees to satisfy these needs through creating a physical and conceptual work environment, so that people will be motivated to do their best to achieve organizational goals.

The first level needs in the hierarchy, the physiological needs can be satisfied through such organizational efforts and incentives, as adequate wages and salary, acceptable working conditions in order to improve comfort and avoid fatigue, more leisure time and acceptable work environment in terms of lighting, ventilation, restrooms, working space, heat and noise level. Some bonuses and other fringe benefits will be highly motivational.

The second level needs of safety and security can be satisfied through management's initiative to provide life insurance, medical insurance, job security, cost of living increments, pension plans, freedom to unionize, and employee protection against automation. Law in the form of minimum wages, unemployment benefits, and welfare benefits provides the economic security to some degree. Similarly, unions protect employees against discrimination and indiscriminate firing.

Since first level physiological needs and second level security needs are primarily met by business, industrial, societal and legal environment, the management must take steps to satisfy higher level needs, and must establish as to which of these needs are the stronger sources of motivation. When the third level needs of love and affiliation become motivators, then people find an opportunity in their work environment for establishing friendly interpersonal relationships. The management can satisfy these needs by:

- Providing opportunities for employees to interact society with each other through coffee breaks, lunch facilities and recreational activities such as organized sports programmes, company picnics and other social get-together.
- Creating team spirit by keeping work groups informal wherever possible with friendly and supportive supervision.
- Conducting periodic meetings with all subordinates to discuss matters pertaining to personal achievements and contributions as well as organizational developments.

The fourth level needs of self-esteem involve a feeling of satisfaction and achievement and recognition for such achievement. The management can take the following steps to satisfy these needs:

- Design more challenging tasks and provide positive feedback on performance of employees.
- Give recognition and encouragement for performance and contribution and delegate additional authority to subordinates.
- Involve subordinates in goal setting and decision-making processes.
- Provide adequate training and executive development programmes to help employees successfully accomplish their goals and increase their competency on their jobs.

- Provide some of the symbols for status and respect, such as executive level job title, private secretary, privileged parking, promotion, company car, stock options and write-ups about achievements in the company newspapers.

The fifth and top-level needs of self-actualization long for growth arid creativity and the management can take the following steps to satisfy these needs:

- The employees should be given an opportunity to shape their own jobs.
- Give employees the freedom of expression. This will open the channels of communications further and give the employees an opportunity to get involved. .
- Encourage and develop creativity among employees. Creativity is tied in with freedom of expression and freedom of movement.

Maslow believed that from the point of organizational behaviour the management should strive to create an organizational climate, which motivates employees at all levels of organizational hierarchy. Research has established that top managers generally are more able to satisfy their higher level needs than lower level managers who have more routine jobs. Blue-collar workers who have very little freedom over job operations may not even experience the higher level needs.

2. **ERG Theory:** The ERG need theory, developed by Clayton Alerter is a refinement of Maslow's needs hierarchy. Instead of Maslow's five needs, ERG theory condenses these five needs into three needs. These three needs are those of Existence, Relatedness and Growth. The E, R and G is the initials for these needs.

   (i) **Existence needs:** These needs are roughly comparable to the physiological and safety needs of Maslow's model and are satisfied primarily by material incentives. They include all physiological needs of Maslow's model and such safety needs which financial and physical conditions rather than interpersonal relations satisfy. These include the needs for sustenance, shelter and physical and psychological safety from threats to people's existence and well-being.

   (ii) **Relatedness needs:** Relatedness needs roughly correspond to social and esteem needs in Maslow's hierarchy. These needs are satisfied by personal relationships and social interaction with others. It involves open communication and honest exchange of thoughts and feelings with other organizational members.

   (iii) **Growth needs:** These are the needs to develop and grow and reach the full potential that a person is capable of reaching. They are similar to Maslow's self-actualization needs. These needs are fulfilled by strong personal involvement in the organizational environment and by accepting new opportunities and challenges.

   ERG theory differs from Maslow's theory in proposing that people may be motivated by more than one kind of need at the same time. While Maslow proposes that in hierarchy of needs, a person will satisfy the lower level needs before he moves up to the next level of needs and will stay at that, need until it is satisfied, ERG theory suggests that if a person is frustrated in satisfying his needs at a given level, he will move back to lower level needs. For example, assume that a manager's existence needs are fully satisfied and he looks for more challenging tasks to satisfy his self-esteem needs. If his efforts are frustrated in meeting these challenges, he will move back to existence needs and may ask for more material benefits.

3. **McClelland's Theory of Needs:** Since the lower level needs in Maslow's model are generally satisfied by the business, societal and legal systems, they are no longer strong motivators. Studies conducted by Harvard psychologist David McClelland concluded that from the organizational behaviour point of view the most prominent need is the need for achievement, power and affiliation. The primary motive is the "achievement motive" and is defined as a desire to succeed in competitive situations based upon an established or perceived standard of excellence.

   Individuals with a strong "need for achievement" (known as n Ach), ask for, accept and perform, well in challenging tasks which require creativity, ingenuity and hard work. They are constantly preoccupied with a desire for improvement and look for situations in which successful outcomes are directly correlated with their efforts so that they can claim credit for success. They take moderate and calculated risks and prefer to get quick and precise feedback on their performance. They set more difficult but achievable goals. For themselves, because; success with easily achievable goals hardly provides a sense of achievement. They desire greater pleasure and excitement from solving a complex problem than from financial incentives or simple praise.

   The "need for power" (n Paw) is the desire to affect and control the behaviour of other people and to manipulate the surroundings. Power motivation when applied positively results in successful managers and leaders who prefer democratic style of leadership. Power motivation, applied negatively tends to create arrogant autocratic leadership. The "need for affiliation" (n Aff) is related to social needs and reflects a desire for friendly and warm relationships with others. Individuals tend to seek affiliation with others who have similar beliefs, backgrounds and outlook on life. This results in information of informal groups and informal organizations. It is evident in social circles also that people mix with people of their own kind. Individuals with high "n Aff" tend to get involved in jobs that require a high amount of interpersonal contact; and relations such as jobs in teaching and public relations. From organizational behaviour point of view, these individuals are highly motivated to perform better in situations where personal support and approval are tied to performance. They tend to avoid conflict and exhibit strong conformity to the wishes of their friends.

4. **Herzberg's Two-factor Theory:** Fredrick Herzberg and his associates developed the two-factor theory in the late 1950s and early 1960s. As part of a study of job satisfaction, Herzberg and his colleagues conducted in-depth interviews with over 200 engineers and accountants in the Pittsburgh area. The researchers felt that a person's relation to his work is a basic one and that his attitude towards work would determine his organization related behaviour. The respondents were required to describe in detail the type of environment in which they felt exceptionally good about their jobs and the type of environment in which they felt bad about their jobs. It seems natural to believe that people who are generally satisfied with their job will be more dedicated to their work and perform it well as compared to those people who are dissatisfied with their jobs. If the logic seems justified then it would be useful to isolate those factors and conditions that produce satisfaction with the job and those factors, which produce dissatisfaction.

The basic questions that were asked in the survey were the following two:

- What is it about your job that you like? and
- What is it about your job that you dislike?

Based upon these answers it was concluded that there are certain characteristics or factors that tend to be consistently related to job satisfaction and there are other factors that are consistently related to job dissatisfaction. Herzberg named the factors that are related to job satisfaction as motivational factors, which are intrinsic in nature and factors related to job dissatisfaction as maintenance or hygiene factors which are extrinsic in nature. These factors are described in detail as follows:

(i) Hygiene factors: Hygiene factors do not motivate people. They simply prevent dissatisfaction and maintain status quo. They produce no growth but prevent loss. The absence of these factors leads to job dissatisfaction. The elimination of dissatisfaction does not mean satisfaction and these factors simply maintain a "zero level of motivation." For example, if a person indicated "low pay" as a cause of dissatisfaction, it would not necessarily identify 'high pay' as a cause of satisfaction. Some of the hygiene factors are:

- Wages, salary and other types of employee benefits
- Company policies and administration rules that govern the working environment
- Interpersonal relations with peers, supervisors and subordinates. Cordial relations with all will prevent frustration and dissatisfaction
- Working conditions and job security. The job security may be in the form of tenure or a strong union could support it.
- Supervisor's technical competence as well as the quality of his supervision. If the supervisor is knowledgeable about the work and is patient with his subordinates and explains and guides them well, the subordinates would not be dissatisfied in this respect.

All the hygiene factors are designed to avoid damage to efficiency or morale and these are not expected to stimulate positive growth. Hawthorne experiments were highly conclusive in suggesting that improvements in working conditions or increments in financial benefits do not contribute to motivated performance. A new plant or upgraded facilities at a plant seldom motivate workers if the workers do not enjoy their work and these physical facilities are no substitute for employee feelings of recognition and achievement.

(ii) Motivational factors: These factors are related to the nature of work (job content) and are intrinsic to the job itself. These factors have a positive influence on morale, satisfaction, efficiency and higher productivity. Some of these factors are:

(a) The job itself: To be motivated, people must like and enjoy their jobs. They become highly committed to goal achievement and do not mind working late hours in order to do what is to be done. Their morale is high as evidenced by lack of absenteeism and tardiness.

(b) Recognition: Proper recognition of an employee's contribution by the management is highly morale boosting. It gives the workers a feeling of worth and self-esteem. It is human nature to be happy when appreciated. Thus, such recognition is highly motivational.

(c) Achievement: A goal achievement gives a great feeling of accomplishment. The goal must be challenging, requiring initiative and creativity. An assembly line worker finishing his routine work hardly gets the feeling of achievement. The opportunities must exist for the meaningful achievement; otherwise workers become sensitized to the environment and begin to find faults with it.

(d) Responsibility: It is an obligation on the part of the employee to carry out the assigned duties satisfactorily. The higher the level of these duties, the more responsible the work would feel and more motivated he would be. It is a good feeling to know that you are considered a person of integrity and intelligence to be given a higher responsibility. It is a motivational factor that helps growth.

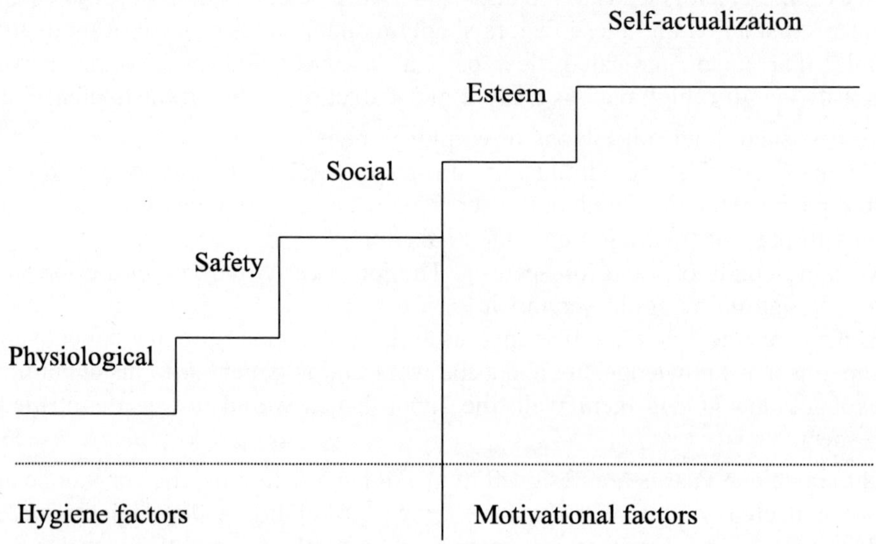

(e) Growth and advancement: These factors are all interrelated and are positively related to motivation. Job promotions, higher responsibility, participation in central decision-making and executive benefits are all signs of growth and advancement and add to dedication and commitment of employees. The Herzberg's two-factor model is tied in with Maslow's basic model in that Maslow is helpful in identifying needs and Herzberg provides us with directions and incentives that tend to satisfy these needs. Also the hygiene factors in Herzberg's model satisfy the first three levels of Maslow's model of physiological needs, security and safety needs and social needs and the motivational factors satisfy the last two higher level needs of esteem and self-actualization.

Some researchers do not agree with Herzberg's model as being conclusive, since the results were based primarily on the responses of white-collar workers (accountants and engineers) and do not necessarily reflect the 'blue collar workers' opinion who may consider hygiene factors as motivational factors. Some studies have found that the effect of hygiene factors and motivational factors are totally reversed on some people. They are highly motivated by financial rewards, organized supervision, well-defined work rules, pleasant working environment and positive employee interaction and do not give much importance to achievement and self-actualization.

Another criticism about Herzberg's two-factor theory dwells upon the method of research and data collection. The theory was developed on the basis of "critical incident" method. According to this method, the respondents were asked to indicate particular incidents, which they felt, were associated with their satisfaction or dissatisfaction with their jobs. This means that the theory is "method bound" and studies that use other methods for measuring satisfaction and dissatisfaction fail to support the validity of Herzberg's theory.

Furthermore, the theory does not take into consideration individual differences in values and outlook as well as the individual's age and organizational level.

However, this theory has contributed to one management programme that has lent itself to the enhancement of motivators. Ii provides valuable guidelines for structuring the jobs in order to include within the job content such factors, which bring about satisfaction.

17.6 THEORIES OF MOTIVATION REGARDING WORK

While "need theories" of motivation concentrate upon "what" motivates persons, "process theories" concentrate upon "how" motivation occurs. These theories identify the variables that go into motivation and their relationship with each other. Some of these theories are explained in more detail as follows:

1. Vroom's Expectancy Model

The expectancy model is based upon the belief that motivation is determined by the nature of the reward people expect to get as a result of their job performance. The underlying assumption is that a man is a rational being and will try to maximize his perceived value of such rewards. He will choose an alternative that would give him the most benefit. People are highly motivated if they believe that a certain type of behaviour will lead to a certain type of outcome and their extent of personal preference for that type of outcome. There are three important elements in the model. These are:

- **Expectancy:** This is a person's perception of the likelihood that a particular outcome will result from a particular behaviour or action. This likelihood is probabilistic in nature and describes the relationship between an act and its outcome. For example, if a student works hard during the semester, he will expect to do well in the final examination. It is not 100% definite that he will indeed do well in the examination. There is some probability attached to this outcome. Similarly, if a person works hard, he may expect to perform better and increase productivity. For example, a worker works hard and is absolutely certain (expectancy = 1.0) that he can produce an average 15 units a day and 60% certain (expectancy = 0.6) that he can produce a high of 20 units per day. This expectation of outcome is known as "first level" outcome.
- **Instrumentality:** This factor relates to a person's belief and expectation that his performance will lead to a particular desired reward. It is the degree of association of first level outcome of a particular effort to the second level outcome which is the ultimate reward. For example, working hard may lead to better performance which is the first level

outcome, and it may result in a reward such as salary increase or promotion or both-which is the second level outcome. If a person believes that his high performance will not be recognized or lead to expected and desired rewards, he will not be motivated to work hard for better output. Similarly, a professor may work hard to improve upon his techniques of teaching and communication (first level outcome) in order to get promotion and tenure (second level outcome). Accordingly, instrumentality is the performance-reward relationship.

- **Valence:** Valence is the value a person assigns to his desired reward. He may not be willing to work hard to improve performance if the reward for such improved performance is not what he desires. It is not the actual value of the reward but the perceptual value of the reward in the mind of the worker that is important. A person may be motivated to work hard not to get pay raise but to get recognition and status. Another person may be more interested in job security than status.

Accordingly, according to this model of motivation, the person's level of effort (motivation) depends upon: *Expectancy:* A worker must be confident that his efforts will result in better productivity and that he has the ability to perform the task well. *Instrumentality:* The worker must be confident that such high performance will be instrumental in getting desired rewards. *Valence:* The worker must value these rewards as desired and satisfactory. Hence, motivation is related to these three factors as:

Motivational Force (M) = Expectancy (E) × Instrumentality (I) × Valence (V).

or $M = (E \times I \times V)$

As the relationship suggests, the motivational force will be the highest when expectancy, instrumentality and valence are all high and the motivational value is greatly reduced when anyone or more of expectancy, instrumentality or valence approaches the value of zero.

The management must recognize and determine the situation as it exists and take steps to improve upon these three factors of expectancy, instrumentality and valence for the purpose of behavioural modification so that these three elements achieve the highest value individually. For example, if a worker exhibits a poorly motivated behaviour, it could be due to:

- Low effort-performance expectancy. The worker may lack the necessary skills and training in order to believe that his extra efforts will lead to better performance. The management could provide opportunities for training to improve skills in order to improve the relationship between effort and performance.
- Low performance-reward instrumentality relationship. The worker may believe that similar performance does not lead to similar rewards. The reward policy may be inconsistent and may depend upon factors other than simply the performance, which the worker may not be aware of or may not consider fair. Low reward-valence. Since the managers may look at the value of a reward differently than the worker, the management must investigate the desirability of the rewards, which are given on the basis of performance. While monetary benefits may be more desirable for some workers, the need to be formally appreciated may be more valuable rewards for others for similar task-oriented activities. The Vroom's model tries to explain as to what factors affect a person's choice of a particular course of action among all available alternatives and why a person would be better motivated towards achievement of certain goals as compared to some other goals. Accordingly, managers must understand and analyze the preferences of particular subordinates in order

to design "individualized motivational packages" to meet their needs, keeping in mind that all such packages should be perceived as generally fair by all concerned parties.

2. Equity Theory

Equity theory is based on the assumption of some researchers that one of the most widely assumed source of job dissatisfaction is the feeling of the employees that they are not being treated fairly by the management or the organizational system. The "Equity theory" has two elements. First, the workers want to get a fair reward for their efforts. This "exchange," meaning reward for efforts, is similar to any other exchange.

If you put in more efforts into your work, you expect to get out of it more rewards. Second, you would compare your rewards with the rewards of others who put in similar efforts. Imagine that you got your MBA from an Ivy League University and are offered a job for $30,000 per year. However, you believe that this offer is not fair and based upon your qualifications and potential contribution to the company; you believe that $35,000 per year would be more equitable. Suppose you do get $35,000 as you hoped for. This would eliminate the inequity and you are happy. A few days into the job you find out that another person with the same degree and background from the same university was hired at the same time at $40,000 per year. You feel that this is unfair by comparison and thus in your mind a state of inequity exists. This inequity can be a source of dissatisfaction.

Equity theory is based upon the recognition that employees are not only concerned with the rewards that they receive for their efforts but also with the relationship of their rewards with the ones received by others. They make judgements of equity or inequity between their inputs and outcomes and the inputs and outcomes of others. For comparison purposes, the inputs can be considered as efforts, skills, education, experience, competence; and outputs can be considered as salary levels, recognition, raises, status and other privileges. When such inequity exists, whether it is perceived or real, employees will feel uneasy about it and will tend to take steps that will reduce or eliminate this inequity. These steps may result in lower or higher productivity, improved or reduced quality of output, increased dedication and loyalty or uncaring attitudes, protests against inequity and voluntary resignation. Equity theory proposes that under-rewarded employees tend to produce less or produce products of inferior equality than equitably rewarded employees, and over-rewarded employees tend to produce more or product of higher quality than equitably rewarded employees. This must be realized that inequity exists when people are either "underpaid" or "overpaid" for similar efforts. However, they are more willing to accept overpayment by justifying such overpayment than by taking steps to reduce this inequity. As formulated by Adams, the equity theory comprises of the following postulates:

- Perceived inequity creates a feeling of resentment and tension within individuals.
- The extent of this tension reflects the magnitude and type of inequity.
- Individuals will be motivated to take steps to reduce this tension.
- The greater the extent of perceived inequity, the greater is the strength of such motivation.

There are a number of steps that a person can take in order to reduce the tension caused by perceived inequity. It must be understood that inequity exists only in the perception of the individual. It may or may not be real. If people are satisfied in spite of any inequity that might exist or if they can justify inequity by one way or another then in their own perceptions, such inequity does not exist. The following are some of the steps people may take to reduce the extent of such inequity.

- They may change their inputs either upwards or downwards to a more equitable level. Overpaid workers may justify overpayment by increased efforts and underpaid workers may reduce their level of efforts and be less interested in work by excessive absenteeism and tardiness.
- They may alter their outcome to restore equity. The workers .may demand better pay and better working conditions for the same input either by staging walkouts and strikes or through organized union negotiations.
- They can change input-outcome ratio to more favourable and equitable levels by distorting the values of the inputs or outcomes. They may artificially increase the importance of the jobs they are doing in their own minds or decrease the value of their own input by believing that they are not really working very hard. For example, if a professor does not get promotion he may justify it by either thinking that "it is not the promotion that counts but helping the students achieves academic excellence" or by believing that "he really did not work very hard in the area of research and publications."
- Employees may resign from their jobs. Employees who feel that they have been inequitably treated at a particular job may find another job where they feel that the input-outcome balance is more favourable and equitable for them.
- People may change the level of comparison with other employees. In the face of equity, the employees may believe either that other people get better outcomes because they do work harder at it or because they belong to different category with which the comparison is not valid or justified. For example, a professor from Business Administration division who did not get promotion may compare it equitably with another professor from Social Sciences division who did get promotion by believing that the requirements for promotion for both divisions are not the same or that the professor from Social Science division did work harder to get his promotion.

3. Goal-Setting Theory

Goal-setting theory is a relatively applied approach to motivation and is based upon the assumption that the type as well as the challenge of the goal induces motivation in the individual to achieve such goal. The theory as proposed by Edwin Locke, studies the processes by which people set goals for themselves and then put in efforts in order to achieve them. The quality of performance is generally shaped by how difficult and how specifically defined the goal is:' General goals such as "do your best," do not lend to accurate performance appraisal and proportionate rewards. Specific goals are clear and tend to give a clear direction to the worker, resulting in improved performance. Similarly, difficult goals, once accepted, lead to higher performance.

- **Goal specificity:** A specific goal identifies the target in quantitative terms. This would enable the worker to evaluate his performance and judge as to how he is doing relative to the goal. For example, if a worker is producing 50 units a day, which is the average output, he may set his goal of 60 units a day to be achieved within seven days. The worker can evaluate this output each day and decide whether he is adequately moving towards that goal. Meeting a goal provides the worker with a sense of achievement, pride and personal satisfaction. General goals, such as "we will produce as much as possible," have little effect on motivation. Specific goals reduce ambiguity and the worker has very clear idea as to what is expected of him.

- **Goal difficulty:** Difficult but feasible goals provide more challenge than easy goals. Reaching an easy target is not competitive and hence hardly exciting. This is particularly true for high need achievers. Goal commitment is independent of whether the goal is set by the worker himself or is assigned by superiors, but depends upon expectations of success and degree of success. Commitment would also depend upon previous rewards for goal achievement.

The most important element of goal setting theory is the acceptance of goal by the workers. Of course, the best way to have the goal accepted by workers is to let them set their own goals within the general organizational guidelines. A goal that one establishes for him becomes an integral part of him. An example is a person's career objective. A person with self-set goals is most likely to strive harder to achieve them. Assigned goals are equally acceptable if these goals are consistent with personal aspirations of workers. Acceptance becomes easier if the workers are encouraged to participate in the goal setting process. Goal acceptance can also be facilitated if the management demonstrates a supportive attitude towards subordinates regarding goal achievement. There is evidence that goal setting, as outlined, improves performance about 90% of the time, and that comparatively high achievers set comparatively more difficult goals and are much more satisfied with intrinsic rewards rather than extrinsic rewards.

4. Management by Objectives (MBO)

A logical extension of goal setting theory is Management by Objectives, which involves systematic and programmatic goal setting throughout an organization. It is a process by which managers and subordinates work together in identifying goals and setting up objectives and make plans together in order to achieve these objectives. These objectives and goals are consistent with the organizational goals.

George Odiorne has explained the concept of MBO as follows:

The system of management by objectives can be described as a process whereby the superior and subordinate managers of an organization jointly identify its common goals, define each individual's major areas of responsibility in terms of results expected of him and use these measures as guides for operating the unit and assessing, the contribution of each of its members. Also known as Goal Management, MBO is based upon the assumption that involvement leads to commitment and when an employee participates in goal setting as well as setting standards for measurements of performance towards that goal, then the employee will be motivated to perform better and in a manner that directly contributes to the achievement of organizational objectives. Some of the elements in the MBO process can be described as follows:

1. **Central goal settings:** The first basic phase in the MBO process is the defining and clarification of organizational objectives. These are set by the central management and usually in consultation with the other managers. These objectives should be specific and realistic. This process gives the group managers and the top mangers an opportunity to be jointly involved. Once these goals are clearly established, they should be made known to all the members of the organization and be clearly understood by them.

2. **Manager-subordinate involvement:** After the organization goals have been set and defined, the subordinates' work with the managers in setting their individual goals relative to organizational goals. Such joint consultation is important because people become highly motivated in achieving objectives that were set by them to start with. The goals of the subordinates are specific and short range and primarily indicate what the subordinate's unit is capable of achieving in a specified period of time. The subordinate must set goals in consultation with the individuals who comprise his unit. In this manner, everyone gets involved in the goal setting.
3. **Matching, goals and resources:** The objectives in themselves do not mean anything unless we have resources and means to achieve those objectives accordingly, management must make sure that the subordinates are provided with necessary tools and materials to effectively achieve these goals. If the goals are precisely set, then the resources requirements can also be precisely measured thus making the resource allocation easier. However, just as in goal setting, the allocation of resources should also be done in consultation with the subordinates.
4. **Freedom of implementation:** The manager-subordinate task force should have adequate freedom in deciding on the utilization of resources and the means of achieving the objectives. As long as these means are within the larger framework of organizational policies, there should be minimum interference by superiors.
5. **Review and appraisal of performance:** There should be periodic review of progress between manager and the subordinates. These reviews would determine if the individual is making satisfactory progress. They will also reveal if any unanticipated problems have developed. They also help the subordinates understand the process of MBO better. They also improve the morale of subordinates since the manager is showing active interest in the subordinate's work and progress. These periodic reviews are necessary since priorities and conditions are constantly changing and these must be periodically monitored.

The concept of MBO is very rich in terms of managerial implications. Managers have a responsibility to assign or set goals in such a manner so as to have the maximum motivational potential. The goals must be tailored to the individual needs and skills, since individuals differ so much in their concept of goals. This would create an optimal performance environment for the employees. When implemented properly MBO has some unique advantages. These are:

1. Since MBO is result-oriented process and focuses on setting and controlling goals, it encourages managers to do detailed planning. As the planning process is improved, it helps in a better overall management system.
2. The managers are required to establish measurable targets and standards of performance and priorities for these targets. Since the goals are set in consultation with subordinates, these are generally more difficult and challenging than if the superiors had imposed them. Additionally, since these targets are tailored to the particular abilities of the subordinates, it obtains maximum contribution from them thus providing optimum utility of human resources.
3. Both the manager and the subordinates know what is expected of them and therefore there is no role ambiguity or confusion.
4. It makes individuals more aware of company goals. Most often the subordinates are concerned with their own objectives and the environment surrounding them. But with

MBO, the subordinates feel proud of being involved with the organizational goals. This improves their morale and commitment.

5. MBO often highlights the area in which the employees need further training. By taking keen interest in the development of skills and abilities of subordinates, the management provides an opportunity for strengthening those areas that need further refinement thus leading to career development.
6. The system of periodic evaluation lets the subordinates know how well they are doing. Since MBO puts strong emphasis on quantifiable objectives, the measurement and appraisal could be more objective, specific and equitable. These appraisal methods are superior to trait evaluation, which is based upon such factors as liability, cooperation, loyalty and self-discipline, since they focus on results and not on some subjective intangible characteristics. This evaluation being more objective can be highly morale boosting.
7. It improves communication between management and subordinates. This continuous feedback helps clarify any ambiguities, refine and modify any processes or any aspects of goals. Also, MBO is a kind of control mechanism so that if there are any deviations discovered between the actual performance and the goals, these can be regularly and systematically identified, evaluated and corrected.

Some of the problems and limitations associated with MBO are as follows:

1. In the classical structure of the organization, the authority flows from top to bottom. This creates rigidity and discipline, which generally lead to better performance. Hence, the top management is usually reluctant to support the process of MBO in which their subordinates would take equal part. Accordingly, MBO can only succeed if it has the complete support of top management.
2. Subordinates may dislike MBO. They may be under pressure to get along with the management when setting goals and objectives and these may be set unrealistically high or far too rigid. This may lower their morale and they may become suspicious about the philosophy behind MBO. They may seriously believe that MBO is just another of the management's trick to make the subordinates work harder and become more dedicated and involved.
3. The emphasis in MBO system is on quantifying the goals and objectives. It does not leave any ground for subjective goals. Some areas are difficult to quantify and more difficult to evaluate. Thus, MBO rewards productivity at the cost of creativity.
4. There is considerable paperwork involved and it takes too much of the manager's time. Too many meetings and too many reports add to the manager's responsibility and burden. Some managers may resist the programme because of this increased paperwork.
5. The emphasis is more on short-term goals. Since goals are mostly quantitative in nature, it is difficult to do long-range planning. This is so because all the variables affecting the process of planning cannot be accurately forecast over the long run due to continuously changing socioeconomic and technical environment. This difficulty affects the stability of goals.
6. Most managers may not be sufficiently skilled in interpersonal interaction such as coaching and counselling which is extensively required.
7. The integration of the MBO system with other systems such as forecasting and budgeting is very poor. This makes the overall functioning of all systems very difficult.

8. Group goal achievement is more difficult. When goals of one department depend upon the goals of another department, cohesion is more difficult to obtain. For example, the production department cannot produce a set quota if it is not sufficiently supplied with raw materials and personnel. Similarly, sales department cannot meet its obligation in sales unless production department keeps pace with sales.
9. It takes a lot of time, perhaps three to five years, to implement the MBO programme properly and fully and some research studies have shown that MBO programmes can lose their impact and potency as a motivating force over time.

17.7 MOTIVATION, PERFORMANCE AND JOB SATISFACTION

Job satisfaction can be defined as the extent of positive feelings or attitudes that individuals have towards their jobs. When a person says that he has high job satisfaction, it means that he really likes his job, feels good about it and values his job highly. It has been established that highly satisfied workers have better physical and mental well-being. It is highly debatable as to which one is the cause and which one is the effect but they are known to be correlation. On the other hand, serious job dissatisfaction results in stress and tension, which is usually the cause of a variety of physiological disorders.

17.7.1 Consequences of Job Dissatisfaction

Job satisfaction or dissatisfaction is of great concern to management since there seems to be a relationship between job satisfaction and job performance. Job dissatisfaction produces low morale among workers and low morale at work is highly undesirable. Accordingly, managers must be constantly watching for any signs of low morale and job dissatisfaction and take corrective action as soon as possible. Some of the indicators of low morale are:

1. **Absenteeism:** Job satisfaction is highly related to absenteeism. Studies have found that less satisfied employees are more likely to be absent from work due to 'avoidable reasons'. This is known as voluntary absenteeism as against involuntary absenteeism due to illness or other emergency reasons, which is unavoidable and is not related to job satisfaction. In an interesting experiment, Frank Smith studied the attendance rate of salaried employees at Sears Roebuck Company on a day of severe blizzard and found that highly satisfied employees were more likely to exert the high level of effort necessary to get to work. In such work units where job satisfaction was low, attendance at work was much lower. Management must be concerned with excessive absenteeism for it disrupts production and business operations.
2. **Early retirement:** Schmitt and McLane to establish relationship between early retirement and job satisfaction have conducted studies. There has been evidence that employees who choose early retirement tend to hold less positive attitudes towards their jobs. Employees with higher-level positions with challenging work opportunities are less likely to seek early retirement than employees with lower-level jobs.
3. **Employee turnover:** High employee turnover disrupts normal operations and continuously replacing the employees who leave is costly and both technically and

economically undesirable. According to Arnold and Feldman, organizational units with the lowest average satisfaction levels tend to have the highest turnover rates. Managerial concern is for such turnover, which is primarily the result of dissatisfactory organizational climate. There are other reasons for voluntary turnover such as alternative places of employment, geographical constraints, family responsibilities, highly marketable employee's special skills, and simply an environment change. Additionally, if such turnover is among poor performers, then the change may be in the best interests of the organization. Turnover may be voluntary which is initiated by the employee and may be due to job dissatisfaction or other personal reasons beyond management control it may be initiated by management and may be due to unsatisfactory conduct exhibited by employees such as incompetence, violation of rules, dishonesty, laziness, insubordination and habitual absenteeism. Turnover could also be due to modernization of plant, lack of orders for the product, materials shortage or generally hard economic times. In any case, the matter of turnover should be seriously investigated and corrective measures taken wherever necessary.

4. **Employee unrest:** Unrest is a general condition of unhappiness with job and may manifest itself in a number of ways. The worker may not attend to his job properly, may be involved in daydreaming, be forgetful or just may not care. He may start complaining about work conditions and find faults with everything that goes on in the work environment. He may enter into formal grievances excessively, and start coming late to work or be absent from work periodically. Sometimes, this unrest becomes so frustrating that it may lead to such undesirable habits as excessive drinking. At its extreme, unrest may affect the mental health and well-being of the worker. If this unrest affects a sufficient number of workers they may take a collective action such as go-slows, work stoppages, strikes and other allied group actions.
5. **Tardiness:** Similar to absenteeism, tardiness is also generally believed to reflect job dissatisfaction. It is assumed that this tardiness is not due to some explainable reason such as getting children ready for school but only due to the fact that employees really do not care much for the job. This is indicated by such employee tardiness as spending excessive time in rest rooms, lingering in the parking lot before coming to work, spending too much time on personal telephone calls, and in general, an attitude of passing time at work rather than spending time for useful productivity.
6. **Union activity:** Studies have shown that satisfied employees are generally not interested in unions and they do not perceive them as necessary. The evidence is strong that job dissatisfaction is a major cause of unionization. Furthermore, the employees feel that individually they are unable to influence changes that would result in the elimination of such factors that cause job dissatisfaction. This job dissatisfaction is primarily caused by lower level needs in Maslow's model of hierarchical needs, such as working conditions and job security rather than higher level needs such as creativity or challenging opportunities. The level of union activities is related to level of job dissatisfaction. Lower levels of job dissatisfaction may result in grievances while higher levels of job dissatisfaction may result in employee strikes.

17.7.2 Job Satisfaction

Job satisfaction results from the employee's perception that the job content and context actually provide what an employee values in the work situation. It can be defined as 'a pleasurable or positive emotional state resulting from the appraisal of one's job or job experience.' This positive emotional state is highly contributory to an employee's physical and mental well-being. Organizationally speaking, high level of job satisfaction reflects a highly favourable organizational climate resulting in attracting and retaining better workers.

17.7.3 Sources of Job Ssatisfaction

Many research studies have been conducted on the subject of job satisfaction and employee morale in order to establish some of the causes that result in job satisfaction. These studies have revealed that certain variables are consistently correlated with job satisfaction. Some of these factors have been grouped into four identifiable, discrete categories. These are:

1. **Organizational factors:** Some of the organizational factors as sources of job satisfaction are:
   - **Salaries and wages:** Salaries and wages play a significant role in determining the level of job satisfaction irrespective of the level of position that an employee holds in the organization. Studies conducted by Locke indicate that pay is a primary determinant of job satisfaction, especially when it is perceived as fair and equitable compared to others and relative to employee's own efforts and contributions. Pay is also the prime mover since it satisfies the first level needs of Maslow's model of motivation. It is also considered a symbol of achievement since higher pay reflects a higher degree of contribution towards organizational operations and welfare.
   - **Promotions:** Promotional opportunities are another source of job satisfaction, especially at higher-level jobs, because a promotion indicates an employee's worth to the organization which is highly morale boosting. A promotion also involves a positive change in higher salary, less supervision, more challenging work assignments, increased responsibility and decision-making freedom.
   - **Company policies:** Organizational structure and organizational policies play an important role in establishing an environment which is conducive to job satisfaction. A highly authoritative and autocratic structure may produce more resentment on the part of employees who may want more open and democratic style of leadership. Organizational policies usually govern employee behaviour, and depending upon how strict or liberal these policies are, can generate positive or negative feelings about the organization. Liberal and fair policies are usually associated with job satisfaction. Employees, who feel unduly constrained because of strict policies or feel that they are not treated fairly, would not be happy with the job.
2. **Work environment:** The work environment factors include the following:
   - **Supervisory style:** It has been established that wherever the supervisors are friendly and supportive to workers, there is job satisfaction. Conversely, it can also be

established that satisfied employees themselves create a social environment at work where supervisors are more considerate of such employees. In any case, a close relationship between the supervisor and the worker and worker's participation in decision-making about such issues that directly concern the worker are highly conducive to job satisfaction.

- **Work group:** The group size and the quality of interpersonal relations within the group play a significant role in worker happiness. Larger group sizes usually lead to lower level of job satisfaction due to the fact that large groups lead to poor interpersonal communication, reduced feeling of togetherness and difficulty in getting to know each other more closely. Smaller groups provide greater opportunity for building mutual trust and understanding. Work group also serves as a social, moral and emotional support system for the employee. If the people in the group exhibit similar societal characteristics, such as attitudes and beliefs, they tend to be drawn closer to each other resulting in a work climate that improves job satisfaction.
- **Working conditions:** Good working conditions are highly desirable because they lead to greater physical comfort. People put a high premium on a clean and orderly work station and factors such as heating, air conditioning, humidity, lighting, noise level, availability of adequate tools and equipment and desirable work schedules all contribute to higher level of satisfaction. While such desirable working conditions are taken for granted, and may not contribute heavily towards job satisfaction, poor working conditions do become a source of job dissatisfaction, simply because they lead to physical discomfort and physical danger.
- **Work itself:** By and large, the work itself plays a major role in determining the level of job satisfaction. The job content has two aspects. One is the "job scope" which involves the amount of responsibility, work pace and the feedback provided. The higher the level of these factors, the higher the job scope and thus higher the level of satisfaction. The second aspect is variety. It has been found that a moderate amount of variety is most effective. Excessive variety produces confusion and stress; and too little variety causes monotony and fatigue, which dissatisfies. Additionally, lack of autonomy and freedom over work methods and work pace creates a sense of helplessness. It is not very motivating for the employees to have their every step and every action determined by their supervisor. It is highly dehumanizing and causes dissatisfaction. Role ambiguity and role conflict are to be avoided because employees feel very unhappy if they do not know exactly what their task is and what is expected of them.

3. **Personal factors:** While the external environment within the organization and the nature of the job are important determinants of job satisfaction, personal attributes of individual employees play a very important role as to whether they are happy at the job or not. People with generally negative attitudes about life and pessimists always complain about everything including the job. Age, seniority and tenure have considerable influence on job satisfaction. It is expected that as people grow older, they usually come up the corporate ladder with the passage of time and move into more challenging and responsible positions. Meeting these challenges and succeeding is a high source of satisfaction. Even if they do

not move up in their position, it is equally natural to assume that with age, people become more mature and realistic and less idealistic so that they are willing to accept available resources and rewards and be satisfied about the situation. Employees who do not move up at all with time are more likely to be dissatisfied with their jobs. Tenure assures job security, and the feeling of job security is highly satisfactory to employees. This means that they can plan for the future without fear of losing the job. Thus, employees with tenure are expected to be highly satisfied with their jobs. Equally important is the intrinsic source of satisfaction, which comes from within the person and is a function of the employee's personality. Some of the personality traits that are directly related to increased job satisfaction are self-assurance, self-esteem, maturity, and decisiveness, sense of autonomy, challenge and responsibility. It can be concluded that the higher the person is on Maslow's model of hierarchical needs, the higher is the job satisfaction.

17.8 SUMMARY

People's work performance depends upon their ability to do their assigned work as well as their "will" to do so. Stronger "will" reflects stronger motivation to achieve a goal. The word motivation is derived from motive which is a need or a desire requiring movement towards the goal of achievement of such need and desire. It is an action, movement or behaviour, which must fulfil the unsatisfied need. The motivation can be positive which requires appreciating employees' efforts resulting in better performance or it could be negative which induces fear and punishment for less efforts. Motivation can also be induced by external factors such as financial rewards for better output or it could be intrinsic in nature, which is inner generated. This means that accomplishing something worthwhile motivates the employee further and this motivation is independent of financial rewards. Historically speaking, the concept of motivation can be traced back twenty-three centuries as reflected in the Greek and Indian writings. These earlier philosophies proposed that we are motivated to do what brings us the best results for our benefit. Similarly, the Greek concept of Hedonism is based upon realizing maximum pleasure while at the same time avoiding pain and discomfort. This brings in the concept of rationality where our actions become utility oriented. These views were held over a long period of time so that the concept of motivation came under scientific study and investigation only in the early 1930s. This study led to a number of theories and models. The content theories of work motivation explain the nature of motivation in terms of types of need that people experience. The concept of motivation is explained by the fact that people have certain fundamental needs; both physiological and psychological in nature and that they are motivated to engage in activities that would satisfy these needs. Abraham Maslow built the needs in order of priority into a hierarchy. The most fundamental needs being physiological needs such as food, clothing, shelter, and so on. Then in order came the needs for safety and security, love and affection, need for respect and self-esteem and finally the self-actualization need which is considered to be the ultimate fulfilment of life. Management can motivate workers by identifying their need level and taking steps to fulfil these needs. ERG theory, developed by Clayton Alderfer, condenses the five needs proposed by Maslow into three and ERG stands for existence, relatedness and growth. The existence needs are roughly comparable to physiological and safety needs of Maslow's model and are satisfied primarily by material incentives. Relatedness needs roughly correspond to social and self-esteem needs and finally, the growth needs are similar to primarily self-actualization needs and partially to esteem needs. McClelland's theory of needs is based upon the premise that lower level needs in Maslow's model are generally taken care of by business, societal and legal systems and hence are no longer motivators. According to this theory, the most prominent need from organizational behaviour point of view is the need for achievement, power and affiliation. The individuals with a high degree of need for achievement, power and affiliation are highly motivated to move towards fulfilling these needs at the highest levels. Herzberg's two-factor theory classifies all the work related factors into two categories. First category contains factors that are known as hygiene factors. These factors prevent dissatisfaction but do not motivate. Some of these factors .are: wages and other benefits, working conditions, organizational rules and policies, cordial relations with peers and superiors, job security, and so on. These factors are designed to avoid damage to efficiency or morale and are not expected to stimulate positive growth. Motivational factors, on the other hand, have a positive influence on morale, satisfaction, efficiency and higher productivity. These are the type of job one enjoys, recognition for employee input and performance, a feeling of accomplishment, increased responsibility and authority and growth and advancement with the organization.

The process theories of motivation put forth hypothesis as to how motivation occurs and identify some of the variables that induce motivation. One such theory is Vroom's expectancy model. This model is based upon the belief that motivation is determined by the nature of reward people expect to get as a result of their job performance. The nature of reward refers to the perceived value that the employee assigns to such a reward. This means that a person will be willing to work hard if he believes that such hard work will lead to better performance and such performance will lead to reward which the employee values. Another process theory of motivation is the equity theory. This theory suggests that employees will be motivated to work hard if they sincerely believe that the management is treating them fairly and equitably. This means that employees are not only concerned with the rewards that they receive for their efforts but also with the relationship of their rewards with the rewards received by others and this would determine the fairness of their rewards in their own minds. Goal-setting theory is a relatively applied approach to motivation and is based upon the assumption that the type of goal as well as the degree of challenge in it would determine the degree of motivation in the individual to achieve such a goal. The goals are generally specific in nature and comparatively more difficult to achieve. A logical extension of goal setting theory is Management by Objectives (MBO), which involves systematic and programmatic goal setting throughout the organization. It is a process by which managers and subordinates work together in identifying goals and setting up objectives and make plans together in order to achieve these objectives. When the subordinates actively participate in the process of goal setting, they are highly motivated to achieve such goals. The primary condition of any motivation at any job is that the employee must like and enjoy his job. If the employees are highly dissatisfied with their jobs, their morale would be very low which would adversely affect their motivation. There are certain indicators that reflect job dissatisfaction. These are: Employee unrest, excessive absenteeism and tardiness, excessive and short-term turnover, destructive union activity, desire of employee to retire early, and so on. Management must continuously monitor the work environment to see signs of any of the above indicators and take necessary corrective action. On the other hand, motivation is closely tied with job satisfaction so that management must take steps and offer privileges, which would make the employees happy with their jobs. Some of these privileges and benefits include equitable wages and salaries, timely promotion, participative style of management, good working conditions, team spirit, and so on. While all these organizational and work related factors are important contributors and catalysts for motivational processes, the most important factor is the person himself. His own attitude towards life in general would determine his attitude towards his job. People with generally negative attitudes about life and pessimists always complain about everything including the job. Accordingly, in addition to providing a healthy work environment, management must ensure that the employee is happy with himself and has a positive outlook on life.

17.9 SELF-ASSESSMENT QUESTIONS

1. What can the management do to satisfy the various level needs of workers as shown in Maslow's model?
2. What are some of the personal factors, unrelated directly to work environment, that affect a person's motivation and his attitude towards his job?
3. Motivation is defined as a drive, which tries to satisfy an existing unsatisfied need. Is this drive within you as an inherited trait or is it the force of environmental factors, which creates this drive? Give examples.
4. Maslow's model of hierarchical needs lists the needs in order of priority so that first level needs must be satisfied before the second level needs become motivators, and so on. How rigid is this order of priority? Explain as to what circumstances would justify a different order of priority.
5. Management by Objectives (MBO) is considered to be the most effective tool of organizational effectiveness. Explain some of the contributions of the concept of MBO towards employee motivation.
6. Job dissatisfaction is highly demoralizing and manifests itself in some of the negative symptoms. Explain in detail some of the indicators of job dissatisfaction and the steps that management can take in eliminating the conditions that cause job dissatisfaction.
7. Explain in detail the Equity theory of motivation. What are some of the standards against which the concept of 'fairness' can be measured?
8. Differentiate between the need theories of motivation and the process theories of motivation. Do these categories complement each other? If so, in what way?
9. Describe in detail Vroom's Expectancy Model of motivation. How are the various factors in the model related to each other? What happens to motivation if one of these factors does not exist? Give examples.
10. According to McClelland's theory of needs, the primary motive is the need to succeed in competitive situations. Do you agree with this concept? Explain your reasons.

18

CONTROLLING

Learning Objective

The main objective of this chapter is to give awareness to the students about the controlling process and its techniques.

18.1 INTRODUCTION

All organizations, business or non-business, face the necessity of coping with, problems of control. Like other managerial functions, the need for control arises to maximize the use of scarce resources and to achieve purposeful behaviour of organization members. In the planning stage, managers decide how, the resources would be utilized to achieve organizational objectives; at the controlling stage; managers try to visualize whether resources are utilized in the same way as planned. Thus, control completes the whole sequence of management process. One reason control is needed is that the best of plans can go awry. But control also helps managers monitor environmental changes and their effects on the organization's progress. Given the pace of change in the organizational environment in recent years, this aspect of control has grown steadily more important. According to Fred Gsteingraber, some of the most pulsing environmental changes are the changing nature of competition the need to speed up the order-to-delivery cycle, the importance of "adding value" to products and services as a way of creating customer demand, changes in workers and organizational cultures, and the increasing need for delegation and teamwork within organization.

18.2 DEFINITION

Control is any process that guides activity towards some predetermined goals. Thus, control can be applied in any field such as price control, distribution control, pollution control, etc. However, control as an element of management process can be defined as the process of analyzing whether actions are being taken as planned and taking corrective actions to make these to conform to planning. Thus, control process tries to find out deviations between planned performance and actual performance and to suggest corrective actions wherever these are needed. For example, Terry has defined control as follows:

"Controlling is determining what is being accomplished, that is evaluating the performance and, if necessary, applying corrected measures so that the performance takes place according to plan."

Based on the definition of control, its following features can be identified:

1. Control is forward looking because one can control future happenings and not the past. However, on control process always the past performance is measured because no one can measure the outcome of a happening which has not occurred. In the light of these measurements, managers suggest corrective actions for future period.
2. Control is both an executive process and, from the point of view of the organizations of the system, a result. As an executive process, each manager has to perform control function in the organization. It is true that according to the level of a manager in the organization, the nature, scope, and limit of his control function may be different as compared to a manager at other level. The word control is also preceded by an adjective to designate a control problem, such as, quality control, inventory control, production control, or even administrative control. In fact, it is administrative control, which constitutes the most comprehensive control concept. All other types of control may be subsumed under it.
3. Control is a continuous process. Though managerial control enables the manager to exercise control at the point of action, it follows a definite pattern and timetable, month after month and year after year on a continuous basis.
4. A control system is a coordinated-integrated system. This emphasises that, although data collected for one purpose may differ from those with another purpose, these data should be reconciled with one another. In a sense, control system is a single system, but it is more accurate to think of it as a set of interlocking subsystems.

18.3 CONTROLLING AND OTHER FUNCTIONS

Control is closely related with other functions of management because control may be affected by other functions and may affect other functions too. Often it is said planning is the basis, action is the essence, delegation is the key, and information is the guide for control. This reflects how control is closely related with other functions of management. In fact, managing process is an integrated system and all managerial functions are interrelated and interdependent. When control exists in the organization, people know what targets they are striving for, how they are doing in relation to the targets, and what changes are needed to keep their performance at a satisfactory level. The relationship of control with major managerial functions can be described as follows:

1. **Planning as the Basis:** Planning is the basis for control in the sense that it provides the entire spectrum on which control function is based. In fact, these two terms are often used interchangeably in the designation of the department, which carries production planning, scheduling, and routing. It emphasizes that there is a plan, which directs the behaviour and

activities in the organization. Control measures these behaviour and activities and suggests measures to remove deviation, if any. Control further implies the existence of certain goals and standards. The planning process provides these goals. Control is the result of particular plans, goals, or policies. Thus, planning offers and affects control. Thus, there is a reciprocal relationship between planning and control, as presented in Figure 18.1.

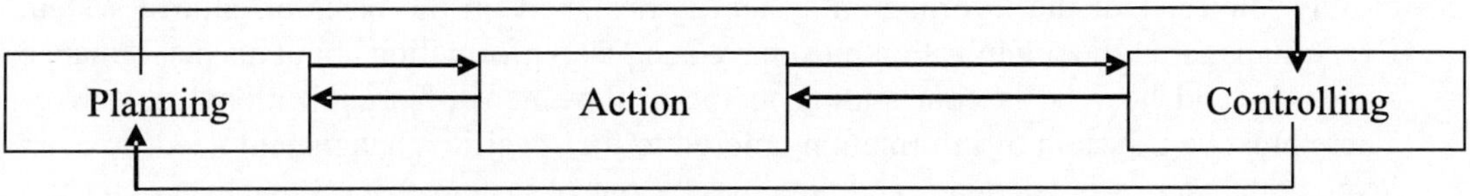

Figure 18.1 Planning and controlling relationships.

Thus, various elements of planning provide what is intended and expected and the means by which the goals are achieved. They provide a means for reporting back the progress made against the goals, and a general framework for new decisions and actions in an integrated pattern. Properly conceived plan become important elements in implementing effective control.

2. **Action as the Essence:** Control basically emphasizes what actions can be taken to correct the deviation that may be found between standards and actual results. The whole exercise of managerial process is taken to arrive at organizational objectives set by the planning process. For this purpose, actions and further actions are necessary; each time there may be correction and change in the actions depending upon the information provided by control procedure. Though it is not necessary that each time a corrective action is taken but control ensures the desirability of a particular action. This is important for organizational effectiveness. Thus, in a real sense, control means action to correct a condition found to be in error or action to prevent such a condition from arising and is never achieved without having action as an essential step.
3. **Delegation as the Key:** Delegation is the key for control to take place because control action can be taken only by the managers who are responsible for performance but who have authority to get the things done. A manager in the organization gets authority through delegation and redelegation. It does not make sense to make someone responsible for achieving results without delegating him adequate authority. In the absence of adequate authority, a manager is unlikely to take effective steps for correcting the various deviations located in the process of analysis. Taking of corrective actions may be seen in the context of controllability of a factor effecting the deviation or non-achievement of organizational objectives. Some of these factors are controllable and some are uncontrollable. A controllable factor is the one which can be controlled by an executive action, while the uncontrollable factors lie outside his jurisdiction. A manager's action is likely to be more effective if more factors are controllable by him. He can have better controllability if he has been authorized to take decisions on various matters concerning him and affecting his action. The best policy of delegation is the matching of responsibility and authority. It suggests that a manager must have corresponding authority as compared to his

responsibility. He has to control the operations, which are exercised by taking action, and action may be taken within the limit of the authority. So the only person who can directly control activities is the one who is directly responsible for them. This is the basic principle for effective organizations.

4. **Information as the Guide:** Control action is guided by adequate information from beginning to the end. Management information and management control systems are closely interrelated; the information system is designed on the basis of control system. Every manager in the organization must have adequate information about his performance, standards, and how he is contributing to the achievement of organizational objectives. There must be a system of information tailored to the specific management needs at every level, both in terms of adequacy and timeliness. Control system ensures that every manager gets adequate information. The criterion for adequacy of information for a manager is his responsibility and authority that is in the context of his responsibility and authority, what type of information a manager needs. This can be determined on the basis of careful analysis of the manager's functions. If the manager is not using any information for taking certain action, the information may be meant for informing him only and not falling within his information requirement. Thus, an effective control system ensures the flow of the information that is required by an executive, nothing more or less. There is another aspect of information for control and other function, that is, the timeliness of information. Ideally speaking, the manager should be supplied the information when he needs it for taking action. For correcting the deviation, timely action is required by the manager concerned. For this purpose, he must have the information at proper time and covering the functioning of a period, which is subject to control. The control system functions effectively on the basis of the information, which is supplied in the organization. However, the information is used as a guide and on this basis, a manager what action can be taken.

18.4 IMPORTANCE OF CONTROL

Organizations try to achieve their objectives through various actions. From this point of view, all the objectives lead to the achievement of organizational objectives. However, the organizations must also monitor whether they are achieving their objectives or not. Thus, control is an integrated action of an organization or manager. It offers help in the following directions:

1. **Organizational Efficiency and Effectiveness:** Proper control ensures organizational efficiency and effectiveness. Various factors of control, namely, making managers responsible, motivating them for higher performance, and achieving coordination in their performance, control ensures that the organization works efficiently. The organization also moves towards effectiveness because of control system. The organization is effective if it is able to achieve its objectives. Since control focuses on the achievement of organizational objectives, it necessarily leads to organizational effectiveness. Looking into the various roles that control system plays in the organization, the management should devise a control system which effectively meets the demands of the organization. The manager can do this if he is aware of the essential features of effective control system.

2. **Policy Verification:** Various policies on the organization generate the need for control. For organizational functioning, managers set certain policies and other planning elements, which later becomes the basis and reason for control. They becomes basis in the sense that organizational performance is reviewed in these lights. They also become the reason for control because through these, an organization tries that its various individuals adhere to such framework. In this process, the organization and its management can verify the quality of various policies.
3. **Managerial Responsibility:** In every organization, managerial responsibility is created through assignment of activities to various individuals. This process starts at the top level and goes to the lower levels. However, when a manager assigns some activities to his subordinates, he remains responsible for that portion of activities for their ultimate performance. It is quite natural that when a person is responsible for the performance of his subordinates, he must exercise some control over them. Thus, the control is required because of the very basic nature of the organization itself. In large organizations, many individuals contribute to the organizational objectives. For efficient performance, they are arranged in hierarchy, forming superior-subordinate relationship throughout the organization. Since each superior is responsible for the activities of his subordinates also, the control flows throughout the organization, beginning at the top level, the only difference being nature and scope of control.
4. **Psychological Pressure:** Control process puts a psychological pressure on the individuals for better performance. The performance of the individuals is evaluated in the light of targets set for them. A person is likely to put better performance if he is aware that his performance will be evaluated. He may feel pressure to achieve the results according to the standards fixed for him. This is further complemented by the reward and punishment based on the performance. Since the performance measurement is one of the basic elements of the control process, it ensures that every person in the organization contributes to his maximum ability.
5. **Coordination Inaction:** Though coordination is the essence of management and is achieved through the proper performance of all managerial functions, control affects this aspect significantly. Control systems are designed in such a way that they focus not only on the operating responsibility of a manager but also on his ultimate responsibility. This forces a manager to coordinate the activities of his subordinates in such a way that each of them contributes positively towards the objectives of the superior. Since this follows throughout the organization, coordination is achieved in the organization as a whole.
6. **Adjustments in Operations:** A control system acts as an adjustment in organizational operations. Every organization has certain objectives to achieve which becomes the basis for control. It is not only sufficient to have objectives but also to ensure that these objectives are being achieved by various functions. Control provides this clue by finding out whether plans are being observed and suitable progress towards the objectives is being made, and acting, if necessary, to correct any deviation. This may result into taking actions more suitable for the achievement of organizational objectives.

18.5 STEPS IN CONTROLLING

The various steps in controlling may broadly be classified into four parts: (i) establishment of control standards; (ii) measurement of performance, (iii) comparison between performance and standards and the communication, and (iv) correction of deviations from standards.

1. **Establishment of Control Standards:** Every function in the organizations begins with plans, which are goals, objectives, or targets to be achieved. In the light of these, standards are established which are criteria against which actual results are measured. For setting standards for control purposes, it is important to identify clearly and precisely the results which are desired. Precision in the statement of these standards is important In many areas, great precision is possible. However, in some areas, standards are less precise. Standards may be precise if they are set in quantities–physical, such as volume of products, man-hours or monetary, such as costs, revenues, and investment. They may also be in other qualitative terms, which measure performance. After setting the standards, it is also important to decide about the level of achievement or performance, which will be regarded as good or satisfactory. There are several characteristics of a particular work that determine good performance. Important characteristics, which should be considered while determining any level of performance as good for some operations are: (i) output, (ii) expense, and (iii) resources. Expense refers to services or functions, which may be expressed in quantity, for achieving a particular level of output. Resources refer to capital expenditure, human resources, etc. After identifying these characteristics, the desired level of each characteristic is determined. It should be reasonable and feasible. The level should have some amount of flexibility also, and should be stated in terms of range–maximum and minimum. Control standards are most effective when they are related to the performance of a specific individual, because a particular individual can be made responsible for specific results. However, sometimes accountability for a desired result is not so simply assigned; for example, the decision regarding investment in inventory is affected by purchase, rate of production and sales. In such a situation, where no one person is accountable for the levels of inventories, standards may be set for each step that is being performed by a man.
2. **Measurement of Performance:** The second major step in control process is the measurement of performance. The step involves measuring the performance in respect of a work in terms of control standards. The presence of standards implies a corresponding ability to observe and comprehend the nature of existing conditions and to ascertain the degree of control being achieved. The measurement of performance against standards should be on a future basis, so that deviations may be detected in advance of their actual occurrence and avoided by appropriate actions. Appraisal of actual or expected performance becomes an easy task, if standards are properly determined and methods of measuring performance which can be expressed in physical and monetary terms, such as production units, sales volume, profits, etc. can be easily and precisely measurable. The performance, which is qualitative and intangible, such as human relations, employee morale, etc. cannot be measured precisely. For such purposes, techniques like psychological tests and opinion surveys may be applied. Such techniques draw heavily upon intuitive judgement and experience, and these tools are far from exact. According to Petor Drucker, it is very much desirable to have clear and common measurements in all

key areas of business. It is not necessary that measurements are rigidly quantitative. In his opinion, for measuring tangible and intangible performance, measurement must be (i) clear, simple, and rational, (ii) relevant, (iii) direct attention and efforts, and (iv) reliable, self-announcing, and understandable without complicated interpretation or philosophical discussions.

3. **Comparing Actual and Standard Performance:** The third major step in control process is the comparison of actual and standard performance. It involves two steps: (i) finding out the extent of deviations, and (ii) identifying the causes of such deviations. When adequate standards are developed and actual performance is measured accurately, any variation will be clearly revealed. Management may have information relating to work performance, data, charts, graphs and written reports, besides personal observation to keep itself informed about performance in different segments of the organization. Such performance is compared with the standard one to find out whether the various segments and individuals of the organization are progressing in the right direction. When the standards are achieved, no further managerial action is necessary and control process is complete. However, standards may not be achieved in all cases and the extent of variations may differ from case to case. Naturally, management is required to determine whether strict compliance with standards is required or there should be a permissible limit of variation. In fact, there cannot be any uniform practice for determining such variations. Such variations depend upon the type of activity. For example, a very minute variation in engineering products may be significant than a wide variation in other activities. When the deviation between standard and actual performance is beyond the prescribed limit, an analysis is made of the causes of such deviations. For controlling and planning purposes, ascertaining the causes of variations along with computation of variations is important because such analysis helps management in taking up proper control action. The analysis will pinpoint the causes, which are controllable by the person responsible. In such a case, person concerned will take necessary corrective action. However, if the variation is caused by uncontrollable factors, the person concerned cannot be held responsible and he cannot take any action. Measurement of performance, analysis of deviations and their causes may be of no use unless these are communicated to the person who can take corrective action. Such communication is presented generally in the form of a report showing performance standard, actual performance, deviations between those two tolerance limits, and causes for deviations. As soon as possible, reports containing control information should be sent to the person whose performance is being measured and controlled. The underlying philosophy is that the person who is responsible for a job can have a better influence on final results by his own action. A summary of the control report should be given to the superior concerned because the person on the job may either need help of his superior in improving the performance or may need warning for his failure. In addition, other people who may be interested in control reports are (i) executives engaged in formulating new plans; and (ii) staff personnel who are expected to be familiar with control information for giving any advice about the activity under control when approached.

4. **Correction of Deviations:** This is the last step in the control process, which requires that actions should be taken to maintain the desired degree of control in the system or operation. An organization is not a self-regulating system such as thermostat which

operates in a state of equilibrium put thereby the engineering design. In a business organization this type of automatic control cannot be established because the state of affairs that exists is the result of so many factors in the total environment. Thus, some additional actions are required to maintain the control. Such control action may be (i) review of plans and goals and change therein on the basis of such review; (ii) change in the assignment of tasks; (iii) change in existing techniques of direction; (iv) change in organization structure; provision for new facilities, etc. In fact, correction of deviation is the step in management control process, which may involve either all or some of the managerial functions. Due to this, many persons hold the view that correcting deviations is not a step in the control process. It is the stage where other managerial functions are performed. Koontz and O'Donnell have emphasized that the overlap of control function with the other merely demonstrates the unity of the manager's job. It shows the managing process to be an integrated system.

18.6 ESSENTIALS OF EFFECTIVE CONTROL SYSTEM

Control is necessary in every organization to ensure that everything is going properly. Every manager, therefore, should have an effective and adequate control system to assist him in making sure that events conform to plans. However, control does not work automatically, but it requires certain design. While the basic principles involved in designing a control system in organizations may be universal the actual system in an organization requires some specific design. In this tailoring of control system, there are certain requirements, which should be kept in mind.

1. **Reflecting Organizational Pattern:** The control should reflect organizational pattern by focusing attention on positions in organization structure through which deviations are corrected. Organization structure, a principal vehicle for coordinating the work of people, is also a major means of maintaining control. Thus, in every area of control, it is not enough to know that things are going wrong unless it is known wherein the organisation structure the deviations are occurring. This enables managers to fix up the responsibility and to take corrective actions.
2. **Promptness in Reporting Deviation:** The success of a thermostat lies in the fact that it points the deviation promptly and takes corrective actions immediately. Similarly, an ideal control system detects deviations promptly and informs the manager concerned to take timely actions. This is done through designing good appraisal and information systems.
3. **Simple:** Control system must be simple and understandable so that all managers can use it effectively. Control techniques which are complicated such as complex mathematical formulae, charts, graphs, advanced statistical methods and other techniques fail to communicate the meaning of their control data to the managers who use them. Effective control requires consistency with the position, operational responsibility, ability to understand, and needs of the individuals concerned.
4. **Objectives:** The control should be objective, definite, and determinable in a clear and positive way. The standards of measurement should be quantified as far as possible. If they are not quantifiable, such as training effectiveness, etc., they must be determinable and

verifiable. If the performance standard and measurement is not easily determinable, many subjective elements enter into the process, which catch the controller and controlled on wrong tooting.

5. **Motivating:** Control system should motivate both controller and controlled. While the planning and control are necessary for economical operations, researches in human relations show that planning and control are, more often than not, antagonistic to good human relations. Sometimes, they may even tend to deprive the people in the organizations one of man's basic needs–a sense of powerful and worthwhile accomplishment The design of control system should be such that aims at motivating people by fulfilling their needs.
6. **Economical:** Control should be economical and must be worth its costs. Economy is relative, since the benefits vary with the importance of the activity the size of the operation, the expense that might be incurred in the absence of control and the contribution the control system can make. The economy of a control system will depend a great deal on the manager's selecting for control only critical factors in areas important to him. If tailored to the job and the size of the enterprise, control will be economical. A large-sized organization can afford highly complicated techniques, sophisticated tools of control and more elaborate system of control, but a small-sized organization cannot afford these because of the cost factor.
7. **Forward Looking:** Control should be forward looking. Though many of the controls are instantaneous, they must focus attention as to how future actions can be confirmed with plans. In fact, the control system should be such that it provides aid in planning process. This is done in two ways: it draws situations where new planning is needed, and it provides some of the data upon which plans can be based.
8. **Pointing out Exceptions at Critical Points:** Control should point exception at critical points and suggest whether action is to be taken for deviations or not. Some deviations in the organizations have any impact while others, though very little in quantity may have great significance. Thus, control system should provide information for critical point control and control on exception. The critical point control stresses that effective control requires attention to those factors critical to appraising performance against an individual plan. The control on exception requires that a manager should take corrective action when there is exceptional deviation. The more a manager concentrates his control efforts on exceptions, the more efficient will be the results of his control.
9. **Flexible:** Control system should be flexible so that it remains workable in the case of changed plans, unforeseen circumstances, or outright failures. As Geotz has remarked, a control system should report such failures and should contain sufficient elements of flexibility to maintain managerial control of operations despite such failures. Having alternative plans for various probable situations can provide much flexibility in control. In fact, flexible control is normally achieved through flexible plans.
10. **Reflecting Organizational Needs:** All control systems and techniques should reflect the jobs they are to perform. There may be several control techniques, which have general applicability, such as, budgeting, costing, etc. However, it should not be assumed that these might be utilized in all situations. The managers should choose an appropriate tool for control, which helps him in controlling actions according to plans.

18.7 BEHAVIOURAL IMPLICATIONS OF CONTROL

Though control should aim at satisfying the needs of the members of the organization, they often take it otherwise. This may be either because of the adverse real impact of control on them or because of misperception of the impact of control. Thus, while designing the control system, it must be kept in mind that almost everybody in the organization not only resents the idea of being controlled but also objects to being evaluated. It means the results of the control may not same as anticipated by those who are exercising control. The major behavioural problems of control can be analyzed by taking the nature of control, perception of those who are being controlled, and action taken by them.

1. **Nature of Control:** Control often puts pressure for engaging in desirable behaviour by those who are subject to control. The basic question is: will they not behave in desirable way if there is no control? Though opinions may differ on this question, often it is recognized that people engage in that behaviour, which provides them satisfaction whether, control or no control. It means if the organizational processes are in tune with the needs of the organizational participants, they can perform well in the absence of control and not in the presence of control. Behavioural scientists have concluded that people try to be self-actualized but the basic problem, which comes in the way, is provided by the organization itself. They are inherently self-motivated. For example, McGregor believes that more people behave according to the assumptions of Theory Y as compared to Theory X. In such a case, if their behaviour is controlled, it may be counterproductive for the organization. The results may be against the organizational interests. Thus, the basic nature of control itself against the very basic nature of the people. However, this is not true in all the cases. Many people may still behave according to the assumptions of Theory X and they need rigid control. In fact, the best control system may be one which focuses attention on the individual needs also, as discussed earlier, otherwise if will provide more behavioural problems and may be detrimental to the organization itself.
2. **Perception of People:** Another behavioural implication of control is the perception of people who are being controlled. Though perception may be that control is against the nature of people, it is further aggravated by the fact that people perceive it to be for benefit of the organization but against them. Thus, perception may be right or otherwise, that control if brings better result, is shared by organization alone whereas it may, be brought by the organizational members. The control in most of the cases is used as a pressure tactic for increasing performance. This is true also because people may produce more if they are aware that their performance is being evaluated. However, increased performance is also determined by several other factors, most important or them being how it is shared between the organization and its members. Thus, if they have positive perception about this aspect also, they will engage in higher performance. In an alternative case, they will take certain actions to thwart the control action. There is another implication of the people's perception about control. The manager may develop some plan for control, but there are many unplanned controls also necessitated by the organizational requirements. Thus, unplanned control is also the part of the organizational control. It is this unplanned control that has more serious repercussion and is more counterproductive. The participants may feel that it is due to improper planning on the part of management. Thus, they are controlled

not because of their own shortcomings but for the shortcomings of others. Naturally this may be more serious for those who are being controlled.

3. **Actions by Participants:** Participants in most of the cases resist control attempt. They will try to escape from the purview of control and may take several actions: (i) they may try to bring behaviour which is satisfying to them but not necessarily satisfying to the organization; (ii) they may engage in a behaviour which may appear to be in conformity with organizational requirements but actually it is not; and (iii) if these are not possible they may try to engage in behaviour as required by the organization. In the first case, people may try to overcome the pressure from control through fanning group. People can stand only to a certain amount of pressure. After this point is passed, it becomes intolerable to them and they will try to find out the alternatives. One of the alternatives is the formation of group if the people cannot reduce the pressure individually. Group helps them to absorb much of the pressure and thus relieves the individual personality. It gets rid of the tension generated by the control and people feel more secure by belonging to a group, which can counteract the pressure. Now the question is: Does the group disappear if the control pressure is off? The answer is generally in negative because by the time, control pressure is off, people have socialized and identified with a particular group and the group has become attractive to them in more than one respect. Thus, they are likely to continue to be the members of the group even after the control pressure is off. Another alternative of overcoming the pressure of control is that an individual solves it at his own level. This happens more so if control pressure affects only a few individuals. In such cases, the individuals may engage in a behaviour, which on the surface seems to satisfy organizational needs but actually it is not so. In such cases, they will try to camouflage the information meant for control like providing wrong information or coming in time at the workplace but not quite engaging in meaningful behaviour or looking busy but without doing anything. This situation is also quite counterproductive. If the individuals are notable to go for any of these alternatives. They will fall in line with organizational control attempt. This situation may, however, cannot be taken as ideal because it may be counterproductive in the long run. People may develop alienation to the work and to the organization which may have adverse affect on their efficiency. Organization in such cases may lose, not only the efficiency of their members but them also.

18.8 CONTROL AND ORGANIZATIONAL FACTORS

The behavioural implications of control, as elaborated above do not mean that control should not be applied in the organization. In fact, control has many positive aspects, as discussed earlier. The basic necessity is that it should suit the participants to make it more effective. From this point of view, it is imperative that various organizational phenomena should be analyzed, which affect the control system. Though there are many such organizational factors and people are engaged in finding out the answer of this basic question, how people can be better controlled for organizational effectiveness, the main factors related directly to control are:

1. **Perception Formation:** The people's perception is affected by a number of factors, as discussed earlier. In organizational situation, it is affected by the action of management,

and the type of relationship between management and employees. The perception of people towards control is a major factor in determining the response to it. Thus, if the perception of people about the control attempt is based on sound organizational climate, mutual trust and belief, there is more likelihood of getting favourable and better response from them. On the other hand, if it is based on general distrust, fear and suspicion, it is always that people resist a possibility that control attempt.

2. **Motivational Dynamics:** The control is affected by the motivational dynamics of people and how the organization is going to satisfy the various needs of the people. The motivational dynamics have twofold role in control. First, how the various attempts at control are in time with the needs of the people. Ideally speaking, a control system should focus adequately on the needs of the participants and must suit them. It means the control system should be tailor-made and no universal because people differ. Thus, all people cannot be satisfied by the same system. Second, the organization itself provides motivation or, demotivation to the people to work. Human beings, being gregarious, seek to remain in the organization. Thus, many of his needs can be satisfied by this phenomenon. However, since organization, as a collectivity of people, has certain norms of behaviour it becomes demotivation for the people if it is not in accordance with the people. Thus, organizational phenomenon of how people are motivated is a crucial factor in control of behaviour of people in the organization. The various factors discussed above suggest that they actually decide the behavioural implications of control rather than the individual factors alone. Thus, real implications may be understood in terms of interaction of individual and organizational factors. While many of the individual factors may be analyzed on the lines suggested earlier in the previous part of the text, the organizational factors may be analyzed throughout the remaining portion of this part.
3. **Organizational Communication:** The organization has to design a communication network for carrying the control, information both downward and upward. Through the downward communication, a superior sends the information about what a subordinate is expected to do; the upward communication is used to get control information from the subordinates, that is, what they have done. Besides, these channels also serve other purposes. Thus, the organization depends to a large extent for exercising control through communication. If the communication system is not quite effective, it will affect the control system also, to that extent, in communicating what is expected from a subordinate and also how he is performing. Often communication blockade is a major source of confusion and frustration in the minds of the people and they resist control.
4. **Organizational Rules and Procedures:** Most of the organizations prescribe some standing measures for providing guidelines for people's actions in the organizations in the form of policies, rules, and procedures. While these elements provide guidelines to them, they, particularly rules and procedures, prescribe rigidity in action. Thus, they leave very little scope for freedom in action. These rules and procedures also take away initiative and generate alienation. Many times, they may not be able to isolate or sense the factors, which have caused a. particular situation. Thus, there may be tendency to put the blame on those who are not really responsible for a situation. Besides, the rules and procedures create more delay in action and consequently the result. Such a phenomenon is more frustrating to the individuals in the organization.

18.9 OVERCOMING BEHAVIOURAL PROBLEMS

Though there are many approaches for overcoming behavioural implications of control because of the various factors involved in this basic issue, here a few important are mentioned in brief. These are as follows:

(i) As far as possible, direct hierarchical pressure should be avoided. This problem can be overcome by structural arrangement.
(ii) Management should build cooperation through participation. This is the problem related with setting right organizational climate.
(iii) Management should build communication network based on open and two-way communication. This is the problem of communication in the organization.
(iv) For obtaining coordination and cooperation in control, group processes must be strengthened. This is the problem of group dynamics.
(v) Management should reinforce both economic and non-economic needs of the people. This is the problem of motivation.
(vi) Management should have long-term perspective in designing control, system, so that frequent and abrupt changes do not take place. This is the problem related with the organizational planning and control.

Many of these issues are being described in this part of the text, while many others have already been discussed in the previous part, and many others will be discussed in other parts of the text. From this point of view, the first basic issue is the means of control.

18.10 CONTROLLING AND MANAGEMENT BY EXCEPTION

One of the most important ways of tailoring controls for efficiency and effectiveness is to make sure that they are designed to point out exception. In other words, by concentrating on exceptions from planned performance, controls based on the time-honoured exception principles allow managers to detect those places: where their attention is required and should be given. This implies the use of management by exception particularly in controlling aspect. Management by exception is a system of identification and communication that signals to the manager when his attention is needed. From this point of view, management by exception can be used in other management processes also though its primary focus revolves round controlling.

Management by exception has six basic ingredients: (i) Measurement assign values to past and present performances. This is necessary because without measurement of some kind, it would be impossible to identify an exception. (ii) Projection analyzes those measurements that are meaningful to organisational, objectives and extends them into future expectations. (iii) Selection involves the criteria which management will use to follow progress towards organizational objectives. (iv) Observation stage of management by exception involves measurement of current performance so that managers are aware of the current state of affairs in the organization. (v) Comparison stage makes comparison of actual and planned performance and identifies the exceptions that require attention and reports the variances to management. (vi) Decision-making prescribes the action that must be taken in order to bring performance back into control or to adjust expectations to reflect changing conditions, or to exploit opportunity. Thus, it can be observed that management by exception is inseparable from other management essentials in many ways. However, the major difference lies in the fact that the superior's attention is drawn only in the case of exceptional differences between planned performance and actual performance. In other cases, subordinate manager takes decisions. However, what is exceptional requires the completion of whole process.

Benefits of Management by Exception: There are various areas where percepts of management by exception are used such as statistical control of product quality, economic order quantities and order points for control of inventories and supplies, break-even points for determining operating, levels, trends in ratios of indirect to direct labour used in apportioning overhead, attitude surveys for gauging employee morale, etc. The use of management by exception is prevalent because of the following factors:

1. Management by exception saves executives' time because they apply themselves on fewer problems, which are important. Other details of the problems are left to subordinates.
2. It concentrates executives' efforts on major problems. Instead of spreading managerial attention across all sorts of problems, it is placed selectively where and when it is needed. Thus, it ensures better utilization' of managerial talents.
3. It facilitates better delegation of authority, increases span of management and consequently provides better opportunities for self-motivated personnel in the organization. It lessens the frequency of decisions at the higher levels of management, which can concentrate on strategic management rather than engaging themselves in operational management.
4. Management by exception makes better use of knowledge of trends, history; and available business data. It forces managers to review past history and to study related business data because these are the foundations upon which standards are derived and from which exceptions are noted.
5. It identifies crises and critical problems and thus avoids uninformed, impulsive pushing of the panic button. It helps in identification of crises because the moment any exceptional deviation occurs, the attention of higher-level managers is drawn. In this way, it also alerts management to opportunities as well as difficulties.
6. Management by exception provides qualitative and quantitative yardsticks for judging situations and people. Thus, it helps in performance appraisal by providing more objective criteria and provides better motivation to people in the organization.
7. It enhances the degree of communication between different segments of an organization. With its focus on results, it seeks to relate causes, regardless of their place in the organization. With overall organizational results. As such it encourages exchange of information between functions and also between a function and cost centre or profit centre to which it reports. Degree of communication determines the organizational cohesiveness and leads it to achievement of objectives.

18.11 SCOPE OF CONTROLLING

For effective control, it is important to know what are the critical areas where control would be exercised. The identification of these areas of control enhances the management to, (i) delegate authority and fixing up of responsibility, (ii) reduce burden of supervising each activity in detail, and (iii) have means of securing satisfactory results. Though controls are needed in every area where performance and results directly and vitally affect the survival and prosperity of the organization, these areas need to be specifically spelled out. The following discussion points out the problems and methods of control in each major area.

1. **Control on Wages and Salaries:** Control over wages and salaries are done by having programme of job evaluation, and wage and salary analysis. The functions are carried on by personnel and industrial engineering departments. Often wage and salary committee is constituted to provide help to these departments.
2. **Control over Capital Expenditure:** Control over capital expenditure is exercised through the system of evaluation of projects, ranking of projects on the basis of their importance, generally on the basis of their earning capacity. A capital budget is prepared for the business as a whole. The budget committee or appropriation committee reviews the budget. For effective control over capital expenditure, there should be a plan to identify the realisation of benefits from capital expenditure and to make comparison with anticipated results. Such comparison is important in the sense that it serves as an important guide for future capital budgeting activities.
3. **Control over Costs:** Control over costs is exercised through making comparison between standard costs and actual costs. Standard costs are set in respect of different elements of costs. Cost control is also supplemented by budgetary control system, which includes different types of budgets. Controller's department provides information for setting standard costs, calculating actual costs, and pointing out differences between these two.
4. **Control over External Relations:** The public relations department regulates external relations. This department may prescribe certain measures to be followed by other departments while dealing with external parties.
5. **Control over Line of Products:** A committee whose members are drawn from production, sales, and research departments exercise control over line of products. The committee controls through studies about market needs. Efforts are made to simplify and rationalize the line of products.
6. **Control over Methods and Manpower:** Control over methods and manpower is keep to ensure that each individual is working properly and timely. For this purpose, periodic analysis of activities of each department is conducted. The functions performed, methods adopted, and time consumed by every individual is studied to eliminate non-essential functions, methods, and time. Many organizations create separate department or section known as organization and methods to keep control over methods and manpower.
7. **Control over Organization:** Organization charts and manuals are used to keep control over organization structure. Organization manuals attempt at solving organizational problems and conflicts, making long-range organizational planning possible, enabling rationalization of the organization structure, helping in proper designing and clarification of each part of the organization, and conducting periodic check of facts about organization practice.
8. **Control over Personnel:** Generally, personnel manager or head of the personnel department, whatever his designation may be, keeps control over personnel in the

organization. Sometimes, a personnel committee is constituted to act as ail instrument of control over key personnel.

9. **Control over Research and Development:** Control over research and development is exercised in two ways: by providing a budget for research and development and by evaluating each project keeping in view savings, sales, or profit potentialities. Research and development being a highly technical activity is also controlled indirectly. Improving the ability and judgement of the research staff through training programmes and other devices does this.
10. **Control over Service Departments:** Control over service departments is effected either (i) through budgetary control within operating departments, or (ii) through putting the limits upon the amount of service an individual department can ask, or (iii) through authorising the head of service department to evaluate the request for service made by other departments and to use his discretion about the quantum of service to be rendered to a particular department: Sometimes, a combination of these methods may be used.
11. **Controls over Policies:** Policies are formulated to govern the behaviour and action of personnel in the organization. These may be written or otherwise, policies are generally controlled through policy manuals, which are generally prepared by top management. Each individual in the organization is expected to function according to policy manuals.
12. **Overall Control:** Control over each segment of the organization contributes to overall organizational control. However, some special measures are devised to exercise overall control. This is done through budgetary control project profit and loss account and balance sheet. Integrating and coordinating budgets prepared by each segment prepare a master budget. The budget committee reviews such budget. This budget acts as an instrument for overall control. Profit and loss account and balance sheet are also used to measure the overall results.

18.12 SUMMARY

Control is any process that guides activity towards some predetermined goals and backward looking approach. Thus, control can be applied in any field such as price control, distribution control, pollution control, etc. It tries to find out deviations between planned performance and actual performance and to suggest corrective actions wherever these are needed.

18.13 SELF-ASSESSMENT QUESTIONS

1. "Control is a fundamental management function that ensures work accomplishment according to plans." Analyze this statement and outline the various steps in control process.
2. Explain the importance of control in a business organization. What are the requirements of an effective control system?
3. In what ways are planning and control related to each other? Explain clearly the essential steps in control process.
4. What are the behavioural implications of control? Discuss some methods of overcoming the behavioural problems of control.

5. "Planning is the basis, delegation is the key, information is the guide, and action is the essence of control." Discuss.
6. Explain the concept of Management by Exception. What are its benefits and limitations?
7. "If you want to control everything, you may end up by controlling nothing." Explain this statement by defining the areas of control.

PART B

Organizational Behaviour

19

INTRODUCTION TO HUMAN BEHAVIOUR

Learning Objective

The main objective of this chapter is to understand the meaning of behaviour; specify the relationship between behaviour and both the individual and his environment; recognize the genetic nature of behaviour and analyze some of the causes of human behaviour in terms of inherited and learned characteristics.

19.1 INTRODUCTION

Human behaviour is most difficult to define in absolute terms as it is the most complex phenomenon to understand. It is primarily a combination of responses to external and internal stimuli. These responses would reflect psychological structure of the person and may be a result of a combination of biological and psychological processes. It is a system by which a human being senses external events and influences, interprets them, responds to them in an appropriate manner and learns from the results of these responses.

Psychologist Kurt Levin has conducted considerable research into the human behaviour and its causes. He believes that people are influenced by a number of diversified factors, both genetic and environmental, and the influence of these factors determines the pattern of behaviour. He called his conception of these influence "the field theory" and suggested that:

$$B = F(P, E)$$

So that behaviour (B) is a function (F) of the person (P) and environment (E) around him. It is important to recognize the effect of the "person" and that of environment individually as well as their interaction and dependence upon each other in order to understand the pattern of behaviour. These two factors are highly linked with each other. Any one of these two factors individually cannot explain fully the behaviour characteristics. An individual's behaviour may change due to a change in the same environment or exposure to a different environment. For example, a person who loses a well-paying job may behave differently when he is unemployed.

Similarly, just the environment in itself cannot be the cause of, or explain, a given behaviour. Different people behave differently in the same or similar environment. However, when the situation demands, the environment may change the behaviour of an individual. For example, certain training programmes or rehabilitation programmes have changed the human attitudes and behaviour. Sometimes, a sudden and unexpected turn of events or a shock can also influence significant and permanent changes in the human behaviour. For example, there are a number of stories in the Indian religious scriptures where a known killer or a dacoit came to a temple and his whole personality and outlook changed. Thus, the environment can change the individual in his or her behaviour. Similarly, the individuals can also change the environment by setting goals and standards and by determination and motivation.

19.2 ORGANIC CHARACTERISTICS

It has been established that certain characteristics of behaviour are genetic in nature and a human being inherits a certain degree of similarity to other individuals, as well as uniqueness in the form of genes and chromosomes. Some of the characteristics such as physical traits including physical height, slimness, dexterity, intellectual capacity and the ability to learn and logicalize are an inherited and have a wide impact on behavioural patterns. According to R.S. Dwivedi, the structure of the nervous system plays a significant part in the emerging pattern of behaviour thus bringing about the integration of human behaviour and personality. Some psychologists believe that some aspects of human behaviour can be explained in terms of neutral activity and neurophysiological processes. Dwivedi further explains: "Integration of human behaviour takes place because of the constant functioning of, effectors and connectors. Here the nervous system is primarily involved in the connecting process. The numerous receptor cells attached to the individual's sense organs tend to convert physical and chemical events from the environment into neural events while the several effect or cells attached to the muscles and glands convert these neural events into responses." These responses result in behavioural activity ranging from simple reflex action to the complex creative activity.

Laymen sometimes easily explain behaviour as a reflection of the state of the nervous system. This causal relationship is referred to continuously during our daily routine impressions and conversations. For example, when somebody loses patience quickly, we tend to brand him as "stupid," and the behaviour is explained by lack of intelligence where intelligence reflects a state of neutral system. Similarly a person whose behaviour is depressive is considered to be having a "nervous breakdown." In other words, it is implied that a man exhibits a certain type of behaviour because he was "born that way," again pointing to genetic structure.

19.3 CAUSES AND PROCESS OF HUMAN BEHAVIOUR

As discussed earlier, both scientific thinkers as well as behaviourists have always been interested in finding out the causes for a given human behaviour. Science has always been involved in explaining a phenomenon by looking at its causes and then establishing a relationship between a cause and its effect. For example, the cause of formation of water is mixing of parts of hydrogen and one part of oxygen in a given manner. Accordingly, the effect of water can be explained by its cause. This relationship is scientific and every time the same cause will produce the same effect. Similarly, the behaviour scientists want to find out the causes for why people behave in a certain way. If these causes can be established, then certain types of behaviour can be predicted, manipulated and controlled.

The assumption that the study of any subject begins in the realm of superstition has some validity. For example, the scientific field of astronomy started as astrology. Similarly, the study and prediction of behaviour has its roots in superstitious beliefs in supernatural phenomenon. Even though such beliefs are not supported by science, they are still socially prevalent. Any conspicuous event, which coincides with some part of general human behaviour, is likely to be seized upon as a cause. Many such beliefs have been extensively discussed of B.F. Skinner. He suggests, for example, the belief of many people that the position of various planets at the exact time of the birth of the individual determines many aspects of this behaviour, such as whether he is temperamental, impulsive, trustworthy, and so on. Millions of people who read the daily horoscope would testify to that belief, even though these horoscopes describe only general characteristics and general predictions which could be interpreted to be applicable to any person, irrespective of when he was born.

The "science" of astrology is taken very seriously in most underdeveloped countries, and even in the technologically and scientifically advanced countries, astrologers are seriously consulted. In India, for example, many business meetings are arranged upon the advice of astrologers. Prime Minister Indira Gandhi of India and President Ronald Reagan of America have been known to arrange important political conferences in consultation with astrologers. The position of planets at birth, as a cause, is not considered as predicting specific actions or unique aspects of behaviour of an individual, but only general characteristics such as whether the person is impulsive or thoughtful, even though some of these general characteristics may be explained as responsible for some specific actions of the individual. For example, a quick but wrong decision can be attributed to "impulsiveness", which is identified by astrology. It is strange that there is lack of serious questioning to its validity, even though the process proposes that all mankind can be divided into 12 monthly categories as far as their behaviour pattern is concerned, even though some astrologers go as far as the particular day and time of birth in order to pinpoint the position of planets at that particular time.

Then there are numerologists who propose another cause of behaviour. This has to do with a person's name. They believe and propose that the choice of a person's name is not a coincidence but a predetermined and predestined phenomenon, which is associated with the person's behaviour. Based upon this philosophy, certain patterns of behaviour are identified and predicted by the number and types of letters in a person's name. Each letter of the alphabet has been assigned a number. Thus, the letters of the name are replaced by their respective numbers. These numbers are then manipulated and an end result of a single number is obtained. This last number can be used to find some behavioural characteristics associated with this number, as explained by numerologists.

Another common practice is to explain behaviour, in terms of certain physical characteristics of a person, the most important of these characteristics being the lines on the palm of the hand. Palmistry or palm reading is many times explained as a science and has been made popular by Cherio and Saint Germain, who practiced the "art" of palmistry and wrote extensively about it. The four major lines on the palm of the hand are the Lifeline, the Heart line, the Brain line or the line of education and intelligence and the Fate line. These major lines are supported by scores of smaller lines, crosses, stars, islands and branches. There are special lines of number of marriages and children and all these lines are supposed to predict not only how long the person will live or whether he will be rich or poor but also such behaviour traits as intelligence, patience, restlessness, trustworthiness, etc.

Another common practice is to explain behaviour in terms of the physical structure of the individual. It is said sometimes that the eyes betray the character of the person. Similarly, certain ideas can be formed about behaviour on the basis of whether the person is fat or tall and slim. Whether there is a correlation between body structure, and behaviour or not has not been scientifically demonstrated. Even if there is such a correlation between the two, it is not always clear which is the independent variable and which is the dependent variable. For example, we cannot be sure whether fat people are jolly because, being at a disadvantage, they develop jolly nature as a competitive edge or whether jolly people are fat because they are free of emotional disturbances and enjoy their life by eating, drinking and not caring too much about their physique.

The theory of "born" leaders suggests that some people behave in a certain manner, because they were born that way. The belief is based upon the assumption that certain behavioural characteristics are genetic in nature and are inherited. If we know that a person has certain inherited qualities and limitations, then we may be able to use our control techniques more intelligently. The causes of human behaviour can be classified into two categories. These are: (1) Inherited characteristics, and (2) Learned characteristics. Let us explain each of these two in more detail.

19.3.1 Inherited Characteristics

Some of the inherited characteristics which may or may not be changed by external forces and may or may not be important determinants of performance are:

1. **Physical characteristics:** Some of these characteristics relate to physical height, slim body, vision, dexterity and stamina, and have some bearing on performance. Manual dexterity, for example, results in quality performance in such jobs that require artistic manoeuvring. Similarly, tall and slim people are expected to dress well and behave in a sophisticated manner, and fat people are assumed to have a jovial nature.
2. **Intelligence:** Intelligence is primarily an inherited trait, even though children of some very intelligent parents have turned out to be less intelligent and vice versa. It is also known that intelligence can be enhanced by proper environment or by proper motivation. Einstein was not considered very intelligent during his earlier years. In any case, intelligence as a trait is related to certain behaviours. Intelligent people are easy to convince if the point is right and they can be expected to be much more stable and predictable.
3. **Sex:** Being a male or female is genetic in nature and can be considered as an inherited characteristic. However, it is highly debatable whether being a male or a female in itself is indicative of any behavioural patterns. Man is expected to be tough while a woman is expected to be gentle. Men "never cry" and women are highly emotional, are some of the stereotyped assumptions that have no basis in genetic influences. These behaviours are developed, if at all, due to differences in treatment that boys and girls receive in the family environment. Even though some work roles are assumed to be the exclusive domain of

woman, such as nurses or airline stewardesses, these roles are being modified to accommodate men in these positions. As far as the administration of the management process is concerned, women in general do not differ from men in their operative behaviours.

4. **Age:** Since age is determined by the date of birth, it is a kind of inherited characteristic. The age may affect the behaviour in physiological as well as psychological ways. Psychologically, young people are expected to be more energetic, innovative, risk taking and adventurous, while old people are supposed to be conservative and set in their ways. Physiologically, with age, older people experience waning of some of their faculties such as memory, stamina, coordination, etc. and hence the related behaviours change as well. According to Lehman, the peak of creative ability is among people between the ages 30 and 40.
5. **Religion:** Religion and religiously based cultures play an important role in determining some aspects of individual behaviour, especially those that concern morals, ethics and a code of conduct. Highly religious people have high moral standards and usually do not tell lies or talk ill of others. They are highly contented and thus strive for the goal of achievement and self-fulfilment. Additionally, the religion and culture also determine attitudes towards work and towards financial incentives.

19.3.2 Learned Characteristics

Some of the behavioural characteristics that account for enormous diversity in human behaviour are a product of our exposure to various situations and stimuli, both within the family and the outside environment. These characteristics are acquired by learning where learning is defined as a "relatively permanent change in behaviour resulting from interactions with the environment." These characteristics involve an individual's attitudes, values and perceptions about the environment around him. They are the result of the parental values and expectations and the values and norms of our cultures and subcultures. The children learn the need and values of being honest and truthful, and the value of love and affections from the family environment. If the parents are always fighting, if the father is always drunk or if the mother resents the child, it is most likely that the child will grow up lacking the closeness of love and respect. Similarly, a loving family instills certain positive values about life in the minds of the children. The physical environment itself has a profound effect on the individual behaviour. Persons who have come through the rigorous routine of the armed forces or students who have been active sportsmen may have learned the spirit of competition as well as cooperation. Similarly, students who have studied in religious schools and convents may have learned different values about truth and human decency. Since inherited behavioural characteristics are more difficult to change or modify, it is the learned characteristics that the managers want to study, predict and control. Hence, these will be discussed in more detail in the following chapters, but a brief familiarity with this factor is necessary here. Some of these learned characteristics are:

1. **Perception:** Perception is the process by which information enters our minds and is interpreted in order to give some sensible meaning to the world around us. It is the result of a complex interaction of various senses such as feeling, seeing, hearing, etc. Sayings

and proverbs like "things are not what they seem" or "all that glitters is not gold," reflect a sense of perception. "One man's meat is another man's poison," is in a psychological sense an indication that different people see and sense the same thing in different ways. Perception plays an important part in human as well as organizational behaviour. For example, if a manager perceives a subordinate's ability as limited, he will give him limited responsibility, even if the subordinate, in fact, is an able person. Similarly, we lose a lot of good friends due to our changed perceptions about them.

Our perception of people differs from our perceptions of inanimate object such as desks, machines because we make inferences about the actions of people that we don't make about objects. Objects don't have beliefs, motives or intentions, people do. The result is that when we observe people, we attempt to develop explanations of why they behave in certain ways. Our perception and judgement of a person's actions, therefore, will be significantly influenced by the assumptions, we make about the person's intend state.

2. **Attitude:** Attitude is a perception with a frame of reference. It is a way of organizing a perception. In other words, it is more or less a stable tendency to feel, think, perceive and act in a certain manner towards an object or a situation. It is a tendency to act in a certain way, either favourably or unfavourably concerning objects, people or events, For example, if I say, "I like my job," I am expressing my attitude about work. Attitude has three elements in it that lead to measurable outcomes. These are feelings, thoughts and behaviours. Feelings and thoughts can be measured by simply asking individuals about their feelings and opinions. Behaviours can be measured either by actual overt actions or simply by asking the person how he would act in a certain situation. Measuring and integrating these three elements can establish a person's attitude towards a given situation. In general, a person may have a positive attitude, which is good outlook of life, or negative attitude, which means continuous complaining about problems in life.

   Organizationally speaking, an employee's negative attitude about work may be reflected by substandard work performance; excessive absenteeism; excessive complaining about work environment or disobedience to rules or authority. These attitudes can be changed either by simple persuasion or by training and coaching. Kelman has identified three processes that act as instruments of change. The first is compliance, which is application of subtle pressure either through reward or punishment in order to change the behaviour, and expecting this change to be lasting. The second process is that of identification with the person who is affecting the change and is acting as a change agent. This change agent could be a close friend who wants you to change and you respect and love him enough to do so to please him. In marriage, for example, both the husband and the wife make a lot of sacrifices and change their behaviours to please each other. The third process is the process of internalization, which is more permanent in nature. This means that the new attitude is integrated with the other attitudes and becomes a part of the person's total personality. This change may occur through internal soul searching and the desire to change that comes from within.

3. **Personality:** When we describe people as quiet and passive or loud and aggressive or ambitious, we are portraying an aspect of their personality. Personality is a set of traits and characteristics, habit patterns and conditioned responses to certain stimuli that formulate the impression an individual makes upon others. This personality may come out as warm

and friendly, or arrogant and aggressive. Many psychologists contend that personality traits develop in the early childhood years and very; few personality changes can be made after the childhood years. Some personality characteristics such as physical build and intelligence are biological in nature, but most traits such as patience, open-mindedness, extrovertness or introvertness, etc. are learned. Some of these personality traits are highly influential in certain organizational operations from organizational behaviour point of view. For example, Tedeschi and Lindskold propose that people who are open-minded seem to work out better in bargaining agreements than people who are narrow-minded. Similarly, people who are extroverts and outgoing are more likely to be successful as managers than those who are introverts.

4. **Values:** Values, according to Milton Rokeach, represent basic convictions that a specific mode of conduct or end-state of existence is personally or socially preferable to an opposite or converse mode of conduct or end-state of existence. They generally identify a person's moral structure on which the concept of good or bad and right or wrong is based. Since values are emotionally charged priorities and are passionately defended, values and behaviour are highly correlated. The values indicate behaviour pattern and while they do not necessarily and accurately predict behaviour, when behaviour occurs, it is likely to be in line with the values one holds. Value system, according to Prof. A Dasgupta, is a framework of personal philosophy which governs and influences the individual's reactions and responses to any situations. These reactions and responses direct individuals in a society to selectively attend to some goals and to subordinate other goals. In other words, value systems represent a prioritizing of individual values in relation to their relative importance. This value system develops from the cultural environment in which the individual is brought up, the concept of nuclear family, religious influences on his code of conduct, respect for traditional concepts of ethics and morality, and degree of faith in the socially inherited religious elements and beliefs.

   These values are highly stable and enduring and once a value is internalized, it becomes, consciously or subconsciously a standard or criterion for defining action, for developing and maintaining attitudes towards relevant objects and situations, for justifying one's own and other's actions and attitudes, for morally defining self and others and for comparing self with others. The value system also determines the form of social organization in terms of family, groups or community and the role and status. Positions of individuals within the community. This will also determine the decision-maker in the family or the opinion leader in the community or the leader in the organizations. Values are important in relation to the study of organizational behaviour because an organization is a composite of attitudes, perceptions, personalities and individual behaviours of managers as well as workers. Values determine what is right and what is wrong where right or wrong is interpreted in terms of perceived values of the decision-maker. Values sometimes overpower even objectivity and rationality. For example, in order to open a profitable manufacturing plant in a developing country, it may be necessary to bribe a government official for granting of the licence. This bribe may be customary and routinely accepted and rationally it could be justified. However, the value system of the management may be such as to consider bribery unethical and hence the value system would overpower rationality. The study of value system of the managerial class becomes significant when one appreciates the areas over which the value system can significantly influence the manager's outlook and behaviour. It is now generally accepted that:

- A manager's value system influences his perception of problems and his understanding of the various situations, which he faces from day-to-day.
- Value system effectively influences a manager's decision-making process as well as his interpersonal behaviour.
- Each manager largely functions within certain ethical and moral parameters and the value systems play an important role in determining the boundaries of such parameters.

Process of Behaviour

If we assume that behaviour is caused, and this assumption is true, behaviour takes place in front of a process. Based on the analysis of behaviour process, three models of behaviour have been developed. These are S-R model, S-O-R model, and S-O-B-C model.

S-R Model: S-R model of human behaviour suggests that the behaviour is caused by certain reasons. The reasons may be internal feeling such as motivation and external environment such as stimulus. A stimulus is an agent, such as, heat, light, piece of information, etc., that directly influences the activity of a person. Stimulus implies that his behaviour is determined by the situation. These are the environmental forces that shape and determine his behaviour at any given moment. The entire situation has been traditionally described as Stimulus-Response (S-R) process.

S-O-R Model: S-O-R model of human behaviour is achieved by inserting O (Organism) in the classical S-R model. The S-O-R model is based upon the stimulus processed by the organism and followed by a behaviour. This O is not passive and immobile as assumed in the S-R model. Rather the O is viewed as a mediating, maintenance and adjustive function between S and R. as a mediating function, the O is constantly active, scanning its surroundings, monitoring its own actions, seeking certain conditions and avoiding others. As a maintenance function, organs of O are responsible for its health and growth. There are three categories of maintenance organs– receptors, i.e., sense organs, connectors, i.e., nervous organs and effectors, i.e., muscles and glands. The adjustment function of the O monitors the person's activities so that he can overcome obstacle and satisfy his needs.

S-O-B-C Model: In this model, S stands for the situation, which is more comprehensive than stimuli of S-O-R model and incorporates all aspects of the environment–immediate stimulus, physical environment and socioculture environment. O is the organism that does not only represent the physiological being as in the S-O-R, model, but also the physiological being which is more complex. B stands for pattern of behaviour, both overt and covert. C stands for contingent consequences, both overt and covert. The interaction among different elements of human behaviour model is complex. The complexity exists because of two reasons.

- There are different variables within each element of the model and different elements interact among themselves with each element affecting others.
- Organism is not only a physiological being but a combination of physiological and socio-physiological being.

Therefore, it has very significant impact on the behavioural process. It is not only O that interacts with the situation and based on his nature, he may perceive the situation in a particular way and behave accordingly.

Overt Behaviour: Behaviour is what a person does. More precisely, it is defined as the observable and measurable activity of human being. This is known as overt behaviour.

Covert Behaviour: Activities that qualify under this category show great variation. These may be in form of mental process like decision-making, or in the form of physical process like machine handling. There is another aspect of behaviour, which is non-observable or measurable, known as covert behaviour like feelings, attitude formation, and perception formation.

19.4 ENVIRONMENTAL IMPACT ON BEHAVIOUR

While behaviour is a reaction to situations and the type of reaction is based upon some inherited and some learned behavioural characteristics, the environment is an important catalyst in determining such type of reactions. If the environment is complementary to established behaviour, then the actions are positively reinforced. However, if the environment is hostile to the values and skills of the worker, then negative reactions take place. For example, some of the coolest people have been known to lose temper under certain situations. Highly skilled people have changed jobs because the environment in the job situations was not conducive to their enhancement. On the other hand, less skilled people have learned skills and forged ahead because of the right environment. The environment surrounding the workplace has two elements. These are physical and social. The physical environment at a workplace is the arrangement of people and things so that this setting has a positive influence on people. Some of the physical factors that influence behaviour are noise level, heat, light, ventilation, cleanliness, accessibility of work tools, space utilization, colour coordination, nature of job, office furnishing and number of people working at a given place. The open communication between the manager and the subordinates has a positive effect on behaviour. The common cafeteria for management and workers in the factories and offices in Japan has been known to be highly motivating to workers. Recent studies in "open wall" office concept showed that some employees were more productive and satisfied with their work place in open space when their jobs did not require private office space.

The social environment relates to interaction among people and respect for numerous social and societal laws, rules and norms created by people to regulate and control behaviour of people. These social influences are affected by family environment, friends, associates, peers at work, and groups to which an individual belongs. Much of the behaviour is an outcome of respect for norms and laws. Norms are unwritten rules and informal expectations about how people behave in certain social situations. For example, standing in the back of a line for a service is expected behaviour from people. Any person cutting in the line will be ridiculed and perhaps not allowed to do so. These norms are useful in standardizing behaviour of all people in a particular environment. "When in Rome, do as the Romans do" is perhaps intended to respect the norms of a certain social group, which you come in contact with.

Rules and laws, on the other hand, are formalized and written standards of behaviour. Both rules and laws are strictly enforced; laws by the legal system and rules by the social system. Laws relate to all members of the society. For example; stealing property of others is illegal and punishable by law and applies to all people within that system. Rules, on the other hand, affect only a particular segment of the society. These may be the rules of a family, a group, a club or an organization. Working from 9 a.m. to 5 p.m. is an organizational rule. Airlines have certain rules about wearing safety belt and smoking. There are rules for visitors visiting a public place or a tourist place. Observing the norms, rules and laws voluntarily makes for an orderly society and allows for predictability of behaviours.

19.5 BEHAVIOUR AS AN INPUT-OUTPUT SYSTEM

We have discussed earlier that human behaviour is a function of the person and his environment where the "person" is primarily shaped by general biological characteristics, and environment, which generates external stimuli. It does not include the possibility of randomness of human behaviour and it assumes that all human behaviour is goal directed so that a measurable correlation exists between the goals and behaviour. The external stimulus is most important since it excites the internal processes to activate and the behaviour takes place, that an external input is necessary to elicit behavioural responses. The basic input-output model can be described as S<->O->B model where S stands for the stimuli generated by the external environment as input, O stands for human organism which is activated by physiological as well as psychological processes, and B stands for behaviour as the output. Before behaviour is exhibited, there is mutual interaction between the stimulus and the organism and except for reflex actions, the organism "decides" as to the type of behaviour outcome. This interaction results in perception and it becomes the cause of human behaviour.

Another input-output model has been proposed by Kolasa, which describes human behaviour in terms of a systems model, which may describe the process in a more objective manner. The input from the external environment is processed and analyzed through a central processing function which is similar to human organism "O" in the previous model except that this central processing region is the crucial region of cognition consisting of perception and such core processes as thinking, reasoning, logic, problem-solving and decision-making.

Here the stimuli forms the input and is transformed into information by various sensory organs. This information is organized by the central information processing function in a manner, which is meaningful to the individual. This organization takes place through the perceptual processes that are formed through experience in the social setting, and is a function of the personality traits as far as the values and the utility of information are concerned. The second step in the behavioural sequence is the analysis of the information, choice of alternatives in dealing with the information, then selecting the most beneficial alternative to the individual and taking action. This step is known as the decision-making and action taking and becomes the output of the system and this output reflects the behaviour of the person.

19.6 BEHAVIOUR AND PERFORMANCE

According to Schermerhorn, Hunt and Osborn performance is a reflection of characteristics. These are:

- Individual's "capacity" to perform
- Individual's "willingness" to perform
- Organizational support

While organizational support basically provides an individual with an "opportunity" to perform which does affect behaviour to some degree, the capacity and the "willingness" are directly associated with the human behaviour. The capacity to perform is an outcome of such competency characteristics as ability and aptitude, which can be considered as, inherited characteristics of behaviour. Ability, which is partly a measure of intelligence, is the basic and important ingredient for effective performance and all the motivation and organizational efforts will not be of any help towards performance if the basic ability does not exist. Accordingly, job performance is facilitated when ability matches the requirements.

Even when the ability fits the task requirements, it does not necessarily result in high performance. To achieve high levels of performance, the individuals must show willingness to perform and put in adequate work effort. The effort or the degree of willingness to perform effectively would depend upon the degree of motivation of the individual. This motivation, which is a behavioural concept, defines the forces within the individual that account for the direction and level of effort relating to a given task. For example, in a classroom setting, all students generally come from a similar background, similar age, and similar abilities and are exposed to the same instructor and similar study requirements, but all students will not get similar grades because some students will be highly motivated to work harder than the others.

Organizational support and resources affect human behaviour in a significant way and the performance is influenced by this behaviour. Physical facilities and technology in the organizational structure, as well as advice and direction from the leaders are highly conducive to positive outlook towards work, resulting in high quality performance. Inadequate support systems such as rush jobs, unavailability of best tools to perform work, unclear guidance and instructions are all influences in a negative way on behaviour and performance. Some of the symptoms of inadequate organizational support are given as follows:

- Lack of time
- Inadequate budgets
- Inadequate tools, equipment, supplies
- Unclear instructions and job related information
- Unfair levels of expected performance
- Lack of job-related authority
- Lack of required services and help from others
- Inflexibility of procedures.

All the above constraints intrude on work performance.

19.7 HUMAN INTERPERSONAL BEHAVIOUR

The basis of our relationships, our loves, hates, commitments and duties make us what we are. These human bonds–complex, universal and so much a part of our daily existence, whether on a personal or sociopolitical level, are largely responsible for the quality of our lives and thoughts, and not the least, our mental health. Schools, colleges and other learning institutions enlighten us on a variety of subjects and equip us to "face life" economically, socially and intellectually. However, there is no school which educates us about ourselves and the ways in which to conduct ourselves in the multitude of relationships that we are called upon to engage in from day to day:

child and parent, brother and sister, student and teacher, employee and boss, servant and master to mention a few. Each one of us learns this independently, through trial and error and sooner or later develops certain typical ways of coping with people and situations.

In the course of our routine interactions, we all have had the experience, some time or the other of facing conflict. Even in our daily interactions with parents, friends, strangers and relatives, we are often faced with the dilemma of either expressing our feelings honestly and directly, thereby running the risk of hurting them and losing their affection and thoughts, and thereby creating uncomfortable undercurrents of hostility and resentment in the relationship. Is it all right to express anger, when one's personal rights are violated, or should one simply keep quiet? How does one express anger without breaking off a relationship? Does one protest when cheated or manipulated, or overlook it? How does one handle an insolent clerk at the Post Office? How does one handle continual nagging at home, or sugar-coated putdown outside, and the endless number of irritant that we encounter in our relationships without completely hassled or fazed?

19.8 DYNAMICS OF HUMAN INTERPERSONAL BEHAVIOUR

One of the causes of stress is the inability to cope with conflict in interpersonal relations. Almost all of us, at some time or the other has experienced the feeling of "being stumped for words", (tongue tied)" not being able to say the right thing at the right time", or "blowing our top" when our emotions overcome us. At these times, we are out of control of ourselves. When this feeling of being out of control persists for a long time, it manifests itself in bodily complaints such as headaches, general fatigue, stomach disturbances, rashes and asthma.

19.8.1 The Fight and Flight Response

How do people generally react, when faced with a conflict? Surprisingly, not very different from animals! Have you ever seen a cat when cornered? Its whole body becomes stiff, eyes dilate, tail stands on edge, hairs stand up, and it starts emitting strange sounds. This is called **fight response**, and may also be termed as 'instinctive', 'survival', or 'protective'. Although slightly modified in present-day civilized person, this response is still very much visible in for example the irate, defensive mother-in-law who wants to vindicate herself before her son, or to take a more common example the bus conductor, who in a loud aggressive voice states that he does not have change. On the other hand, individuals (and so also animals) may opt for the **flight response**, wherein the organism simply 'takes to its heels'. Again its manifestation in modern person is seen in the individual who procrastinates, avoids taking stands, and is constantly eluding or running away from trying or problematic situations, for example, avoiding a friend whom you had promised something, by taking the easy way out: just not being available. The fight and flight responses are built into our systems and are automatically triggered off, in certain situations. They are usually associated with the emotions of fear, anger/frustration, and they were of immense value to our ancestors (e.g., to run as fast as possible, on seeing some danger in the form of a predatory animal) because you didn't have to think. It just happened. The very emotion of fear/rage, by reflex action, aroused the survival instincts, preparing them for fight or flight as the case may be.

However, the main difference between human beings and animals is that while the latter have only two sets of responses–Fight and Flight, humans have a third option, that is, verbal problem-solving ability. But, the Fight and Flight responses when carried to an extreme prevent us from exercising our third option of verbal problem-solving. How does this happen? Manuel J. Smith explains ... Most of our conflicts and problems come from other people and in dealing with other people, our primitive response are insignificant, in comparison with our uniquely human coping ability of verbal assertive problem-solving. Anger-fight and fear-flight actually interferes with this verbal coping ability. When you become angry or afraid, your primitive lower brain centres shut down much to the operation of your new human brain. The blood supply is automatically rerouted away from your brain and gut to your skeletal muscles to prepare them for physical action. Your human problem-solving brain is inhibited from processing information. **When you get angry or afraid,** you just don't think clearly or efficiently.

19.8.2 Non-assertive, Assertive, and Aggressive Behaviour

There are three possible broad approaches to the conduct of interpersonal relations. The first is to consider oneself only and ride roughshod over others ... The second ... is always to put others before one's self .... The third approach is the golden mean. The individual places himself first, but takes others into account.

Joseph Wolpe

Robert Alberti and Michael Emmons distinguish between three types of coping behaviours: Non-assertive, Assertive and Aggressive.

1. Non-assertiveness

An appeaser is one who feeds a crocodile, hoping it will eat him last.

Sir Winston Churchill

Non-assertive behaviour is somewhat similar to the flight response, in that fear stimulating situations; automatically generate inhibited behaviour in the individual concerned. The non-assertive person will not stand up for his own rights, even where it is justified. They are usually at a loss for words, hesitate to express their opinions, thoughts, or needs clearly and allow others to decide for them. They become anxious, and are always giving into requests–even obviously unreasonable ones–are without confidence when criticized though they make half-hearted attempts to defend themselves, and on the whole they are not very happy or satisfied people, because they are always going out of their way to please others, at the cost of self.

The individual who cannot refuse requests, or say 'No' without feeling guilty, hesitates to displease others, to express opinions which differ from others, is easily persuaded by girl salespersons into buying things which they do not need or want; the employee who is afraid to assert herself before her bullying husband, are all examples of non-assertive behaviour. Alberti and Emmons distinguish between general non-assertiveness and situational non-assertiveness. The **generally** non-assertive person is one with very low self-esteem. He has a deep feeling of inadequacy, lack of acknowledgement of self-worth, and usually suffers from actual physical discomforts brought on by extreme anxiety. The **situationally** non-assertive person is on the whole able to cope with people and situations, but certain situations generate mush anxiety in them: the student who can get along well with classmates and people in general, but shivers when they have to face authority figures, like the principal.

2. Aggressiveness

I am the inferior to any man whose rights trample underfoot.

Horace Greeley

There is another class of people, who respond to conflict by becoming aggressive–a fight response. They usually try to subdue other people by shouting in a loud manner, frowning and grimacing, etc. to frighten the other person–they put themselves up by putting others down. We often meet such people. The village 'goonda', or the 'neighbourhood bully' is typical examples of aggressive behaviour. Another common Indian scene, involving aggressive behaviour, is the case= of the woman who refuses to allow anyone near the community tap, till her pots and pans are filled. Aggressive behaviour is easily recognizable. The whole stance of the individual undergoes a transformation. Their body becomes erect and stiff, and slightly bent towards the other individual (they may even take two steps forward and catch hold of the other person's collar), eyes become big, voice is raised ..., and so on.

On the surface, these people usually appear to have level of self-confidence, to be in command of every situation and to be strong and able to cope with life on their terms. But in reality, the aggressive personality covers up an insecure ego. In order to cover up this insecurity, they compensate by becoming overly aggressive, and apparently in command of every situation. Aggressiveness also can be either general or situational. The generally aggressive individual has learned early in life that in order to get what you want, it is okay if you ride roughshod over other people's feelings, rights, etc., whereas the situationally aggressive individual responds with aggression only under certain situations.

Aggressiveness can also be expressed indirectly or passively. On the surface these individuals appear to be very mild and sweet, but in order to get what they want, they will use indirect means–manipulation, trickery, wiles, etc. And if they get angry, they are likely to use sneaky ways to get revenge. They can be so indirect that the person whom they anger was about. Because of the reaction accorded to the aggressive woman and the misery experienced by the passive woman, many women develop the ability to get they want by indirect means, for instance, the woman who will bang the pots and pans in the kitchen to express her anger (when her manipulations do not work out) instead of directly saying what is bothering her. . This brings us to the question, 'Is anger the same as aggression?' No! Anger is not the same as aggression. Anger is a natural emotion, also healthy. But aggression is the destructive or inappropriate expression of anger and is unhealthy. You can reason with an angry person, but not with an aggressive person.

3. Assertiveness

Assertiveness is the golden mean between non-assertiveness and aggression. The assertive individual has a high self-esteem, values self and others, while the non-assertive individual values others but not self, and the aggressive individual values only self but not others.

The assertive individuals, when faced with a conflict are the one who will make use of our third human option of verbal coping ability. Instead of passively giving in to people's demands, on the one extreme, or completely ignoring them on the other extreme, the assertive individual will assess the situation, and take into consideration both points of view.

Assertiveness is a characteristic that is both person and situation specific. For example, if someone makes an unreasonable request–unreasonable for the individual concerned–the assertive person will very simply refuse the request, while acknowledging the other person's feelings. 'I know you will be unhappy, but I don't feel like … (whatever)'. The assertive individual takes responsibility for his responses: **'I** think', **'I** feel', **'and I** like'. **'I** will not'. On the other hand, if the assertive individual is at fault, in that situation, he/she will acknowledge his/her fault or mistake, instead of being defensive and denying it.

19.8.3 Manipulative Coping

In modern society, especially in the upper classes, people are not openly non-assertive, or aggressive. We wear masks and use indirect means to get our way. We are taught, for example, not to be aggressive, it creates bad impressions. So on the surface, we are very sweet, but underneath we are calculating furiously in our minds, the ways in which to "bring the person round ", "get even with so and so", "get rid of those guests" (why did they come today?), "turn down a request (which we have no intention of complying with), etc. It is like a verbal game and the winner is the one who deftly manages to escape, keeping his image intact!

Manipulative coping usually leaves you frustrated, irritated and anxious, and these feelings are eventually expressed by you in verbal fighting or running away. As a result of this unresolved internal conflict between our natural wants and our childhood beliefs, we are left with some really dismal choices:

1. We can do what someone else wants, be frustrated very often, get depressed, withdraw from people and lose our self-respect;
2. We can do what we want angrily, alienate other people and lose our self-respect ;
3. We can avoid conflict by running away from it and the people who cause it, and lose their self-respect.

Role of Anger and the Difference between Anger and Aggression

Anger is a feeling, an emotion just like fear, joy, sorrow, grief, etc. Everyone feels anger, sometime or the other, but the ways in which we show our anger are different. For example, let us say you're walking on the road, and you accidentally brush someone as you pass by. Now, the other person can react in either one of the following ways:

1. Direct put down and verbal aggression: "Damn it, can't you watch where you're going! You fool ..!"
2. Indirect put down: "Can't you see without your glasses on?" or "Oh, have you forgotten to wear your glasses today?"
3. Non-verbal put-down : a dirty look.
4. Saying nothing.

Some people claim that they never get angry. Do not believe them. They do get angry, but they have learned to control it, so as not to openly show it. Such controlled individuals typically suffer from migraine headaches, asthma, ulcer, and skin rashes.

Anger and its expression is a healthy thing, if used constructively. Simple direct verbal expression of your anger is much better than bottling it up or using indirect means–taunting, making snide remarks, or even non-verbal put-downs like, making faces, refusing to talk, sulking, etc., to take revenge on the person who angered you. Even saying simply and forcefully, "I am very angry with you" is preferable to calling names or abusing or physical exertion like banging doors, and throwing things. People often appreciate it when you directly confront them with your anger, rather than do something nasty, or sly to hurt the person concerned. A classic example of this is that of newly weds. After the honeymoon is over, the wife discovers many objectionable habits in her husband. Not wishing to directly confront him, as she is afraid to "spoil their relationship" (or so she thinks), she finds another way out to vent her feelings. When husband goes to work, she rings up her mother and given vent to her hostile feelings. Worse, when all the family gathers together, she berates him in front of everyone–the case of washing your dirty linen in public ... Little does she realize that this mode of expressing anger is much more harmful to their marriage then talking it over with her husband in private. This way only serves to embitter her husband and make him lose his love and respect for her. If on the other hand, she had chosen to courageously assert herself by directly telling him of her feelings; it would have boded much better for their marriage.

Very often people confuse angry feelings with aggressive behaviour. According to Alberti and Emmons ... aggression is not the same thing as anger! Anger is a perfectly natural, healthy human, which may be expressed in a number of ways, including aggressively, non-assertively, assertively or not at all. Anger is a feeling, an emotion we all feel at times. Aggression is a behavioural style of expression.

Dealing with your Anger: A healthy approach to dealing with anger is to:

1. Recognize and allow you to believe that anger is a natural healthy, non-evil human feeling. Everyone feels it, we just don't all express it. You needn't fear your anger.
2. Remember that you are responsible for your own feelings. You got angry at what happened, the other person didn't "make" you angry.
3. Remember that anger and aggression is not the same thing. Anger can be expressed assertively.
4. Learn to relax. If you have developed the skill of relaxing, learn to apply this response, when your anger is triggered.
5. Develop assertive methods for expressing your anger: be spontaneous, don't wait and let it build up resentment; state it directly; avoid sarcasm and innuendo; use honest, expressive language; avoid name-calling; put downs, and physical attacks.
6. Keep your life clear. Deal with issues when they arise, when you feel the feeling–not after hours/days/weeks of "stewing" about it.

Go ahead! Get angry! But develop a positive, assertive style for expressing it . You and those around you will appreciate it.

According to the Vedantic tradition, there are three ways of expressing anger:

1. **Sathvic:** When a person without any attachment to the feeling of anger and without caring for the result for himself, but for the good of the person, to correct him and to offer the whole process to the Divinity in the self or outside and not feeling the responsibility of the doer.

2. **Rajasic:** Where a person wants to correct the evil in the other as well as for the appreciation and does not surrender the process to God. When successful, he claims the success, but when he fails, he blames God.
3. **Tamasic:** Unconscious intervention into the personal problems without being invited to correct them and imposing your own ideas of good and bad and trying to correct them in good faith that you believe you are doing the ultimate good (you are unaware of your own desires).

Dealing with another's anger: When confronted with a direct verbal put-down, the following four steps are valuable-

1. admit it when you are wrong, even in the face of insult.
2. acknowledge the person's feelings.
3. assert yourself about the way he or she is reacting.
4. give a short statement to bring the encounter to an end.

For example, "I apologize for brushing against you. I did not do it intentionally. You're obviously upset, but I do not like you calling me names or yelling at me. I can get your point without that." The best way to handle an indirect put-down is to first ask for more information: "What are you saying?", "What do you mean?" And in case of a non-verbal put-down, it is best to attempt to get the person to use words instead of gestures.

19.9 ASSERTIVE BEHAVIOUR: COMPONENTS AND TECHNIQUES

Have you ever wondered how some people manage to be in perfect control of their lives? Their feelings, relationship, in fact, their whole personality seems to be in perfect concord. They lead a full, interesting, free life, make their own decision, command the respect of others, and reflect an inner glow of contentment and self-worth.

This is not to say that they are the models of perfection, or that they do not undergo any stress whatsoever, but invariably these individuals will have evolved some assertive ways of coping with people and situations without getting unduly anxious. They manage to do this, because they respect themselves, and value their personal judgements, opinions, wishes and needs and more important they recognize these rights in others as well.

- Behaviour which enables a person to act in his or her own best interest, to stand up for herself or himself, without undue anxiety, to express honest feeling comfortably, or to exercise personal rights without denying the rights of others, we call Assertive Behaviour.
- Let us discuss the elements of that complex sentence in greater detail.

➢ *To act in one's own best interest* refers to the capacity to make life decisions (career, relationship, lifestyle, time activities), to take initiative (start conversations, organize activities), to trust one's own judgement, to set goals and work to achieve them, to ask for help from others, to comfortably participate socially.

➢ *To stand up for oneself* includes such behaviours as saying 'No', setting limits on one's time and energy, responding to criticism, or put-downs or anger, expressing or supporting or defending one's opinions.

➢ *To express honest feelings comfortably* means the ability to disagree, show anger, to show affection or friendship, to admit fear or anxiety, to express agreement, or support, to be spontaneous, all without painful anxiety.

- *To exercise personal rights* relates to one's competency (as a citizen, or consumer, as a member of an organization or school or work group, as a participant in public events) to express opinions, to work for change, to respond to violation of one's own rights, or those of others.
- *To not deny the rights of other* is to accomplish the above personal expressions, without unfair criticism of others, without hurtful behaviour towards others, without name-calling, without intimidation, without manipulation, without controlling others.
- Thus, assertive behaviour is a positive self-affirmation, which also values the other persons in your life.

19.9.1 Barriers to Assertiveness

What are some of the barriers to asserting oneself? Alberti and Emmons say, " ... We have found while helping thousands of people to learn to express themselves more effectively, that there are three significant barriers to self-assertiveness:

1. Many people do not believe that they have right to be assertive.
2. Many people are highly anxious/fearful about being assertive.
3. Many people lack the social skills for effective self-expression.

However, research had shown that learning to make assertive responses would inhabit or weaken the anxiety previously experienced in specific interpersonal relations.

19.9.2 Assertive Behaviour at a Glance

Every one is born with unique potential and Free Will—to decide for themselves, to judge for themselves, make mistakes and learn from them, refuse requests, and say 'I don't understand' or change one's mind. As children we had no doubt about these things. Most children are assertive–they know what their rights are and do not hesitate to express them–sometimes from child to adult, we rob ourselves and allow others (due to childhood training and false notions) to rob us of our rights.

As a first step towards becoming assertive, we should become aware of our being assertive individual. The following table illustrates Assertive Behaviour at a Glance. For those who believe that they do not have the right to lead a free, independent life, and still enjoy lasting and good interpersonal relationships, they would be advised to consider the following bill. Most individuals become very disillusioned about people and life in general, or their inability to have close and meaningful relationships and at the same time, retain their identity. The following list will help you to reaffirm your SELF as being of the greatest value!

Assertive Behaviour at a Glance

- You have the right to be treated with respect and dignity.
- You have the right to have and express your own feelings and opinions.

- You have the right to be listened to and taken seriously.
- You have the right to judge your own behaviour, thoughts and emotions, and to undertake the responsibility for their initiation, and consequences upon yourself.
- You have the right to make mistakes and be responsible for them.
- You have the right to say: "I don't know".
- You have the right to say: "I don't understand."
- You have the right to ask for information (including from professionals).
- You have the right to change your mind.
- You have the right to get what you pay for.
- You have the right to choose your profession.
- You have the right to practice your own religion.
- You have the right to ask for what you want (realizing that the other person has the right to say 'no').
- You have the right to acquire knowledge.
- You have the right to say 'No' without feeling guilty.
- Finally, You have the right to do anything so long as it does not violate the rights of others.

19.9.3 Components of Assertive Behaviour

Very often, besides knowing the right words to say, **how we act**, and **how we say something** has an even greater impact.

Your Body: Developing an assertive body image. Your body does communicate. Your style of emotional expression, posture, facial expressions and voice quality are all tremendously important to you in becoming assertive. How does one develop on assertive body image to make your body as well as your words communicate assertively?

Your Inventory of Body Image Components. Methodically check yourself from head to toe, measuring yourself on a scale of assertiveness.

1. ***Eye Contact:*** While addressing another person, where do you look? If you look directly at the person as you speak, it helps to communicate you sincerity and to increase the directness of your message. But if you look down or away much of the time, you present a lack of confidence. Women often have a problem of making eye contact with another person, because many of us have been taught that it is more feminine to look away or look down. In some cultures, like in India, it is considered disrespectful for women to make direct eye contact with men or authority figures. However, making relaxed eye contact is essential when you want to appear assertive and interested and shows respect for the other person. This does not mean staring continuously till the other person becomes uncomfortable. Look at their eyes, then perhaps look away for a few seconds, or drop your gaze slightly so that you are focusing on their mouth, as they speak to you. Practice making good eye contact and be aware of any differences in the quality of your communication. Are you listening better? Are you conveying more interest and receiving more interest in what you are saying?
2. ***Facial Expressions:*** Ever see someone trying to express anger while smiling or laughing? It just doesn't come across. Effective assertion requires an expression that agrees with the

message. Let your face say the same thing your words are saying. With a greater awareness of the feeling in your face, you can begin to more consciously control your facial expression to become more natural

3. ***Body Posture:*** A significant increase in personalizing the conversation, occurs from a slight turn of the torso, say 30 to 45 degrees towards the other person. Relative 'power' may be noticed in an encounter. An obvious example of this is seen in the relationship between a tall adult and a small child; the adult who is thoughtful enough to bend to the child's height will find a considerable difference in the quality of communication.

   In a situation where you are called upon to stand up for yourself, it is useful to do just that–stand up! An active and erect posture lends additional assertiveness to your message, whereas a slumped, passive stance gives the other person an immediate advantage as does any tendency on your part to lean back or move away.
4. ***Gestures:*** A relaxed use of gestures can add depth or power to your message, and can suggest openness, self-confidence and spontaneity on the part of the speaker. However, gesturing must not be erratic or nervous.
5. ***Voice, Tone, Inflection and Volume:*** The way we use our voices is a vital element in our communication. Consider at least three dimensions of your voice:
   - Tone: is it raspy, whiny, soft, angry?
   - Inflection: do you speak in a monotone, or with sing-song effect, or emphasize certain syllables?
   - Volume: do you try to gain attention with a whisper, or overpower others with loudness, or is it very difficult for you to shout, even when you want to?
6. ***Contents:*** What you say is of course important, but honesty and spontaneity of expression is much more important. This means saying, for example, "I am very angry with you" rather than calling names or abusing people. People, who hesitate because they don't know what to say, should make a practice of saying something, to express their honest feelings at the time. It makes a great difference and adds to your assertiveness. Some other components such as fluency, timing, listening, distance/physical contact, even weight and physical appearance, are considered factors in developing assertiveness.

19.9.4 Techniques of Assertiveness

God grant me the confidence to accept the things I cannot change, courage to change those I can, and wisdom to know the difference.

- Anon.

1. ***Broken Record or Persistence:*** One of the most important aspects of being verbally assertive is to be persistent and keep saying what you want over and over again without getting angry, irritated or loud. By practicing to speak as if we were a broken record, we learn to be persistent and stick to the point of the discussion, to keep saying what we want to say, and to ignore all side issues brought up by the person we assert ourselves to. In using broken record, you are not deterred by anything the other person may say but keep saying in a calm, repetitive voice what you want to say until the other person accedes to your request or agrees to a compromise.

2. ***Free Information:*** In order to become an assertive communicator, in social setting, you must master two skills. First you have to practice listening to the clues other people give you about themselves. This free information gives you something to talk about besides the weather, and avoids those awkward silences, when you ask yourself, "What do I say now?" In addition, it makes it easier for people to talk about themselves, when you show an interest in things important to them.

   The second skill is *self-disclosure.* It involves disclosing information about yourself–how you think, feel and react to other person's free information. It allows the social communication to flow both ways. Eye contact is of great value here.
3. ***Fogging:*** This is a skill that teaches acceptance of manipulative criticism by calmly acknowledging to your critic the probability that there may be some truth in what he says, yet allow you to remain your own judge of what you do. It is a very effective skill for desensitizing you to criticism and actually reducing the frequency of criticism from others. It rapidly sets up a psychological distance, boundary lines between you and the person you fog. But fogging should be used with *negative inquiry.* In negative inquiry, you do not respond to your critic's statements with denial, defensiveness, or counter manipulative criticism of your own. Instead, you break the manipulative cycle by actively prompting more information form the critical person in a low-key, unemotional manner.
4. ***Negative Assertion:*** A skill that teaches acceptance of your errors, and faults without having to apologize by agreeing with hostile or constructive criticism of your negative qualities. It allows you to look more comfortably at negatives in your own behaviour or personality without feeling defensive and anxious or resorting to denial of real error, while at the same time reducing your critic's anger or hostility.
5. ***Workable Compromise:*** In using your verbal assertive skills, it is sometimes practical (when you feel that self-respect is not in question) to offer a workable compromise to the other person, or to cooperate when offered one.

19.10 SUMMARY

Human behaviour, being the most complex phenomenon, is most difficult to assess in quantifiable terms. However, since behaviour constitutes a set of responses to external and internal stimuli, some relationship between a given stimuli and its predictable response can be established. There are two factors that have a direct bearing on human behaviour. One is the person himself with regard to some characteristics that he is born with or he acquires because of his family value influences environment to which the person is exposed and the environmental forces that are constantly impacting his personality and behaviour. Both these factors are interlinked so that behaviour cannot be explained in itself by either of the two factors, independent of the other factor. Behavioural characteristics are considered to be both inherited and learned. Inherited behavioural characteristics include physiological aspects, intelligence, sex, age and religion. Learned characteristics include a person's perception about his surrounding environment, his attitude towards life itself and towards other people, his personality and his ethical values. Both the inherited as well as learned characteristics together have an important bearing on the behaviour of a person and knowing the extent of the influences of these factors on the person, his behaviour may be predictable, at least in general terms. The external environment is known to have a considerable effect on a person's behaviour as a response to particular stimuli in the external environment. For example, if a particular situation in the environment is hostile to a person's values and established behavioural pattern, then the behaviour may temporarily change as a response to such a situation. For example, some of the coolest people have been known to lose temper under certain hostile situations. Behaviour can be considered as an input output system. This concept assumes that behaviour is not simply a random phenomenon but is goal directed so that a measurable correlation exists between the goals and behaviour. The external stimulus or input excites the internal processes to activate and the behavioural responses occur. This means that behaviour is related to performance and productivity. Performance is a reflection of three characteristics. These are an individual's "capacity" to perform, his "willingness" to perform and the extent and nature of the organizational support. While organizational support basically provides an "opportunity" to perform which does affect behaviour to some degree, the capacity and the willingness are directly associated with human behaviour.

19.11 SELF-ASSESSMENT QUESTIONS

1. What is interpersonal behaviour? Discuss the important dimensions of interpersonal behaviour with examples.
2. What do we mean by "biological foundations of behaviour?" Is behaviour really founded on "biological" manipulations? Explain your reasoning.
3. Is intelligence an inherited trait or a learned trait? If it is a learned trait, what steps can be taken to improve upon intelligence?
4. Describe some of the learned characteristics of behaviour. Do these characteristics change with changes in the environmental situation? Which of these traits are formed early in years and how difficult it is to change these traits?
5. Describe some of the inherited characteristics of behaviour. Do you believe that these characteristics can be changed or modified? Give reasons.
6. Define the concept of values and ethics. Are these values absolute in nature or differ from person to person and situation to situation? Explain
7. Behaviour is considered to be a function of the person and his environment. Describe the importance of each of these two factors relative to behaviour and explain as to which one of these factors has more impact on behaviour and why?
8. "There are some essentials of an assertive personality". Discuss.
9. Write short note on:
   (a) Defensive behaviour
   (b) Aggressive behaviour
   (c) Non-assertive behaviour
10. Define behaviour. What are the techniques of an assertive behaviour?
11. Discuss the role of anger and the difference between anger and aggression.
12. "Human interaction is the crux of our life and society". Discuss the statement with reference to dynamics of interpersonal behaviour.

20 PERSONALITY AND HUMAN BEHAVIOUR

Learning Objective

The main objective of this chapter is to make the students learn about the word personality and different aspects related to it.

20.1 INTRODUCTION

Personality is a concept that we use in our routine working while dealing with people. We generally talk about people who are close to us or may or may not relate to us. We generally say that a person has good, bad, arrogant or aggressive personality. Thus, the word good, bad, arrogant and aggressive explains that personality is related with the behaviour of an individual. The term personality has been derived from the Latin word 'per sonare' which means to speak through. This Latin word denotes the mask, which the actors used to wear in ancient Greece and Rome. Long ago when plays were performed the numbers of actors used to be less than the number of roles. So the same actor used to change the masks to make people realize that they are performing a different character. Perhaps due to this reason people relate personality to physical and outward appearance. It is also related with social status of the individual, as the person with high social status is having good personality. Thus, in simple sense, personality is sum total of ways in which an individual reacts and interacts with others. Thus,

> *"Personality is the supreme realization of the individuality of a particular living being".*

Personality is a word or characteristics, which is of great importance nowadays in every field of life. Every organization examines the personality of the applicant before he became the employee of the concern. Every entrance test, that may be a professional course, job or future studies have logical, relational and constructive personality assessment questions because they form the personality of an individual. All the interviews are designed with the questions that can bring out the personality of the candidate. According to Gordon Allport,

"Personality is a dynamic organization within the individual of those psychophysical systems that determine his unique adjustments to his environment".

Thus, personality embraces all the unique traits and patterns of adjustments of the individual in his relationship with others and his environment. Personality is a process of change and it is related with psychological growth and development of an individual. According to R.B. Cattel,

"Personality is that which predict of what a person will do in a given situation".

20.2 DETERMINANTS OF PERSONALITY

The factors, which shape, change or develop the personality of an individual, are discussed as under. These determinants of personality can be classified into following categories:

1. **Biological Factors:** The ways an individual sense the external event data, interpret and respond to them are general biological characteristics of human biological system. The study of biological contribution to personality can be divided into:
   (a) Heredity: It is transmission of the qualities from ancestor to descendant through a mechanism lying primarily in the chromosomes of the germ cells. These qualities are present in a person by birth. Heredity refers to those factors like physical stature, facial attractiveness, sex, temperament, muscle composition, energy level and biological rhythms, etc. that were determined at conception. At conception, each parent contributes chromosomes containing thousands of genes, which seems to be transmitter of traits in the child. Saying such as "like father, like son" proves the above discussion. Thus, heredity is generally more important in determining a person's temperament than his values and beliefs.
   (b) Brain: It plays very important role in shaping personality. The structure of brain determines personality. People normally say that a person with more number of lines on his brain is more intelligent. Different people will give value to different things. For some beauty is more valuable than intelligence. However, no conclusive proof is available so far about the nature of relationship between brain and personality.
   (c) Physical Features: Another factor that contributes to personality formation is physical characteristics of an individual. While defining personality some individuals give higher weights to physical features of an individual. The external appearance includes height, weight, colour, facial features, etc. of the individual while determining his personality. The normal belief is that the healthy person is lazy and the thin is angry determines the individual personality. In today's competitive environment for the job of sales executive the physical appearance is an asset of an individual.
2. **Family and Social Factors:** Family plays an important role in early personality development. The infant acquires those behaviour patterns that depend upon the socio-economic level of the family, family size, birth-order, race, religion, parent education level, geographic location, etc. Social factors include the person's interaction with other people throughout his life. The family and social factors are categorize as below:
   (a) Home environment: It is a critical factor in personality development. A child will have soft personality if he will grow in a warm, loving and protective environment. And if everybody in the family is busy in their life and have no concern for each other then

the infant will have rigid personality. The key variable is not the parents per se rather the type of environment that is generated for the child.

(b) Family Members: Parents and other family members have strong influence on personality development of the child. Parents have more impact than other members of the family do in building the child's personality. We generally see that small children behave like their parents. The relationships between the parents and children are higher then between the children and teachers in building child's personality.

(c) Social Group: In addition to home environment and family members, there are other influences from the social placement of the family. Social groups includes the person's interaction with other people which starts with playmates during childhood and continue with peers at work, associates and other work groups. The internal and external work environment continues to influence the people personalities, perception and behaviour throughout his life.

The home environment, family members and social groups influence the socialization and identification process of an individual.

Socialization is a process by which an infant acquires from the wide range of behavioural potentialities that are open to him at birth, those behaviour patterns that are customary and acceptable to family and social groups. It starts with the initial contact between an infant and mother and continues with interaction of infant with other family members and social groups. *Identification process* occurs when a person tries to identify himself with some person whom he feels ideal in the family. Generally, a child in the family tries to behave like his father or mother.

3. **Cultural Factors:** According to Hoebel, Culture is sum total of learned behaviour traits which are manifested and shared by the members of the society. The culture within which a person is brought up is very important determinant of behaviour of a person. Culture is a unique system of perception, beliefs, values, norms, patterns of behaviour and code of conduct that influence the behaviour of the individual. It determines what a person is and what a person will learn. The way of talking and dressing sense of Hindus and Muslims are entirely different, as they are prone to different cultures. Each culture trains its members to behave in the ways that are acceptable to the group. The difference among individual behaviour is also based upon socio-economic classes, ages, education, professions and geographic regions. As skilled have different behaviour pattern than the unskilled workers do.

4. **Situational Factors:** An individual personality is generally stable and consistent; it may change in different situations. An individual life is unique in terms of events and experience, but these experiences sometimes change the structure of the entire personality of an individual. Suppose there is a worker who is very fond of doing work. But sometime due to overload he becomes frustrated from the existing job. Due to this changed situation, his personality composition also changes. Thus, demand of different situation may call for different aspects of one's personality.

5. **Other Factors:**

(a) Temperament: It is the degree to which one responds emotionally. It is distributed according to normal distribution.

(b) Interest: An individual has many interests in various areas. Top executives in any organization do not have common interest. Thus, the organization should provide them job rotation and special training programmes to satisfy their interest.

(c) Character: It means honesty. It is very important requirement for responsible jobs. It is resistance to stealing and cheating others. It is likely that an individual may not steal in normal circumstances, but this can be the demand of undesirable circumstances. For example, if the family of an individual is starving, there is a great probability that one will steal. Thus, before analyzing the undesirable character of an individual, one should study his situation as well.

(d) Schema: It is an individual's belief, frame of reference, perception and attitude which the individual possesses towards the management, job, working condition around him, pay scale, fringe benefits, compensation mechanism, development towards religion, government and satisfaction gained from environment. Thus, the complete behaviour of an individual is dependent upon the external stimuli.

(e) Motives: These are the inner drivers of an individual. They represent goal directed behaviour of individual. Motives help in determining one's behaviour towards a goal.

Thus, the above factors affect the formation and development of personality. At each stage of the life every individual learns from the environment he lives in and the persons he interacts with.

20.3 APPROACHES/THEORIES OF PERSONALITY

1. **Psychoanalytical Theory:** The milestone in the study of personality is Freud's psychoanalytical theory. Freud is of the belief that the personality as a reflection of behaviour has been primarily based on the unconscious nature of personality. The human behaviour and motivation is outcome of following psychoanalytical concepts. Such as:

(a) ID: It is the unconscious part of the human personality. It is most primitive part and is the storehouse of biologically based urges. Example–urges to have food, water, etc. ID is original source of personality present in a newborn or infant. The principal of working for ID is 'Pleasure'. Id tries to satisfy the urge as soon as possible without considering the realities of life.

(b) Ego: Ego manages ID through the realities of the external environment. Ego is conscious in nature and is a mechanism to relate our conscious urge to outside real world. As Ego is conscious and logical part of human personality, ID is guided and governed by Ego. It explains the ways of thinking and behaving. ID demands immediate pleasure at whatever cost, Ego controls it so that the pleasures are granted at appropriate time and in acceptable manner. Ego delays satisfying ID motives and channels the behaviour, which is socially acceptable. It makes people work to live and adjusting to the realities of life. The principle of ego to work is 'Reality Principle'. It takes into account what is possible in this world.

As the function of ID and Ego are contrary there is always ongoing tension between ID and Ego, i.e., between urges and realities of life which keeps Ego to develop more sophisticated thinking skills. Thus, to keep ID under control, Ego is supported by Superego.

(c) Superego: It is higher level restraining force and can be described as the conscience of the person. The conscience creates standards of what is right or wrong. It represents the rules and the norms that check the cultural, moral or ethical behavioural values of the individual in the social environment. However, an individual is not aware of presence and working of superego in oneself. It is developed slowly in a person when he absorbs central values and follows the standards of society. Superego keeps ego to judge what is right or wrong.

Example: A Boy is feeling hungry because of ID. He passes through a shop with food displayed in the window and thus the urge of hunger arises more strongly. But the boy has no penny and the Ego suggest the ways to satisfy hunger that if you don't have money to buy food, steal and run. Then, Superego warns boy that there is something wrong as stealing is considered blundered in society and it is punishable.

2. **Trait Theory:** It visualizes personality as a reflection of certain traits of the individual. This theory was put forward by 'ALLPORT". Trait is a distinctive and personal form of behaviour. There are many traits, which are common to most people, some are unique to a person and other individuals share some. On the basis of trait theory, people can be described as aggressive, loyal, pleasant, flexible, humorous, sentimental, impulsive, cool, and so on. Traits are basic elements of personality and can be used to summarize behaviour. The trait of an individual or 'personal disposition is studied at three levels:

(a) Cardinal Trait Level: ALLPORT defined cardinal traits as those pervasive traits which are so powerful/dominant that rarely all the individual action can be traced back to them. As these are highly influential traits, so they are named after key historical figures like Mother Teresa, Hitler, Romeo, etc. This level describes a trait so broad and so deep in its impact that it overshadows the influence of other traits for the same individual.

(b) Central Trait Level: ALLPORT describes central traits as those that might be referred in careful recommendations or at a rating scale. These are unique and limited in number. The traits at this level means to convey what can be expected from a person most of the time.

(c) Secondary Trait Level: These are least generalized traits of a person. The range of influence of these traits is very narrow. These peripheral traits are specialized to the situation.

Cattell used groups of traits to describe the structure of personality. He put these traits in the following categories:

(a) Surface Traits: Wise-foolish, sociable-seclusive, honest-dishonest, etc.

(b) Source Traits: Trustful-suspicious, relaxed-tense, dominant-submissive, forthright-shrewd, cheerfulness-depressed, etc.

3. **Type Theory:** "Type is simply a class of individuals said to share common collection of characteristics". Type approach discuss the personality in the following ways:

(a) Type on the basis of body build

- Endomorph: They are fat, thick in proportion to their height. They seek comfort, eat too much, jovial, affectionate and liked by all. They are even tempered, show a relaxed posture, easy to get along with others and are tolerant of others. They prefer to be led than to lead.

- Ectomorph: They are thin, long and poorly developed physically. They work well in closed areas and displays restraint, inhibition and desire for concealment. They prefer not to attract attention to him and tend to be distrustful of others. They are anxious, ambitious and dedicated.
- Mesomorph: They are basically strong, athletic and tough. They seek lot of muscular activity, tends to be highly aggressive and self-assertive. They desire action, power and domination and they can run faster and smile brighter.

(b) Type on the basis of nature

- Introvert: The people with following characteristics are introvert such as shyness, social withdrawal, emotional, process the idea within themselves. Introvert can be good scientists and researchers.
- Extrovert: People having following characteristics are extrovert. These are socials, talkative, less emotional, easily makes friends, easily express their ideas and feelings. Extroverts propagate more knowledge and ideas to society. They can be good reporters, actors and marketers.
- Ambiverts/Reserved: These are the people between introverts and extroverts.

(c) Type A and Type B

- Type A: Persons are those who are highly achievement oriented, competitive feel, chronic sense of time urgency and impatient whenever their work slow down. Type A are on fast track of life and are more successful in reaching top slot. They work against opposing forces. Managers in this category are hard drivers, detailed oriented people with high performance standards. These people have difficulty in increasing cordial interpersonal relationships and create a lot of stress for themselves and for the people they deal with. If they have to complete a task within given deadline, they feel pressurized. Researchers have proved that Type A personality profile lead to health problems and specially heart related illness.
- Type B: These kinds of persons are easy going, no competitive drive, feel no emergency. They are relaxed, sociable and have a balanced outlook on life. They are not over ambitious, are more patient and take a broader view of things. In order to meet a deadline they do not feel pressurized. They may be hardworking but feel no pressing conflict with people or time and hence are not prone to stress and coronary problems.

4. **Self-concept Theory:** This theory is organized around the concept that the individual himself largely determines personality and behaviour. It is also termed as organismic or field theories, which emphasize on totality and interrelatedness of all behaviour. There are four factors consider in self-concept theory. These are:

(a) Self-image: Every person has certain beliefs about who or what he is. The beliefs of the individuals are the proof of self-image or self-identity. Thus, self-image is the way one sees himself.

(b) Ideal Self: As discussed earlier self-image indicates the realities of a person as perceived by him, but ideal self indicates the ideal position as perceived by him. It denotes the way one would like to be.

(c) Looking Glass-self: This is the way one thinks people perceive about him and not the way people actually see him. It is the perception of a person about how others perceive his qualities and characteristics. It is a social product, which emerges from face-to-face interaction with others from the very beginning of life. This interaction directs how others see him as an individual.

(d) Real Self: This is what one actually is. An individual self-image is confirmed when other persons response to him, indicate their beliefs about who and what he corresponds with. On the basis of feedback from environment, the person re-evaluates himself and readjusts himself as per the expectation of others. Thus, a balance should be maintained between real self and self-image.

Thus, self-concept plays a very important role in analyzing individual behaviour. It gives a sense of meaningfulness and consistency. On the basis of self-concept a person perceives a situation.

5. **Social Learning Theory:** This theory believes that personality development is a result of social variables. It emphasizes on conscious needs and wants of an individual. This theory uses "reinforcement and punishment approach" in understanding personality. It looks at personality as some total of all that a person has learned from outside stimuli. There is mutual interaction between external environment and behaviour. For example, if an individual receives bad behaviour from society, the frustration causes and reinforces aggression as a personality trait. And if he receives good behaviour from people in terms of praise, this reinforces good behaviour. Learning can also occur from observation; we watch the behaviour of other people, draw observation about them and express our own behaviour.

20.4 PERSONALITY AND HUMAN BEHAVIOUR

Personality is a set of relatively stable characteristics or dimensions of people that account for consistency in their behaviour in various situations. Personality is a major determinant of what will be done and how it will be done in the job where most of the working day is spent in interacting with other people. In any organization every individual's personality reveals how he work with superiors, subordinates and other people, how an individual adjust himself to a particular situation and how he reacts to the changes occurring in the existing jobs or on the new job. Some of the important personality factors or dimensions that determine what kind of performance will be achieved or what kind of behaviour is exhibited at work are:

1. **Self-concept and Self-esteem:** *Self-concept* is the way individuals define themselves as so who they are and what is their identity. *Self-esteem* is the degree of respect; liking or disliking an individual has for him. It is a measure of self-confidence and respect for one's abilities and motivation. It denotes the extent to which an individual regards himself as capable, successful, important and worthy. People with high self-esteem are very friendly, affectionate, find it easy to form interpersonal attachment and find good in other people. They tend to take on more challenging assignment and contribute significantly to their organization if the organization rewards them suitably for their efforts. They are high performers. Low self-esteem people are usually critical of others, are generally depressed

and blame others for their own failure. They contribute to poor performance, which in turn leads to low self-esteem.

2. **Authoritarianism:** A closely related term to authoritarian is "dogmatism" which refers to the rigidity of a person's beliefs. Authoritarianism refers to blind acceptance of authority. Authoritarian people believe in obedience and respect for authority. They believe that there should be status and power differences among people in organization. The individual with high authoritarian personality is intellectually rigid, judgemental of others, deferential to those above and exploitative of those below, distrustful and resistant to change. They rightly adhere to conventional values, are conservative, endorse parental control for keeping the family together, are concerned with toughness and power, are close minded and are generally less educated. Where the job demands sensitivity to feelings of others, tact and ability to adapt the complex and changing situations, the persons with high-authoritarian personality would be negatively related to performance.
3. **Need Patterns:** Every individual have needs for achievement, affiliation, autonomy and dominance at work. People with:
   (a) *High need for achievement* engage themselves totally in work in order to feel proud about their achievements and success.
   (b) *High need for affiliation* work with great cooperation with others.
   (c) *High need for autonomy* prefers to work in the environment where the supervision is less.
   (d) *High need for dominance* is effective in an environment where they can enforce their legitimate authority.
4. **Bureaucratic Personality:** This kind of persons has respect for rules and regulations. Thus, on this account it differentiates from authoritarian person whose respect for authority is blind. Bureaucratic persons are not innovative; even not ready to take risk and they keep themselves at ease while following other directions. They value subordination, rules, conformity, impersonal and formal relationship. In the routine and repetitive work they are better supervisors.
5. **Machiavellianism:** It refers to manipulation of others as a primary way of achieving one's goals and gaining and keeping control of others. The extent to which an individual is Machiavellian is measured by Mach Scale. People with high score on Mach Scale have high self-confidence and self-esteem. They are cool and calculating, logical in assessing the system around them. They have no hesitation in using others or taking advantage of others in order to serve their own goals, willing to twist and turn facts to influence others and try to gain control of people, event and situation by manipulating the system to their advantage. As they thoughtfully and logically approach their situation, they are skilled in influencing others. They are successful in exploiting structured situations and vulnerable people.
6. **Tolerance for Ambiguity:** Because of rapid changes an individual have to work in an environment which is full of uncertainty. They should develop high level of tolerance for ambiguity. People or managers with high tolerance level of ambiguity can work effectively without much stress. But the people with low tolerance for ambiguity can work effectively in structured work setting but it is difficult for them to work in changed conditions.

7. **Locus of Control:** It is the extent to which individual believe that they control their own lives or external forces control their lives. In other words, the degree to which people believe that they are masters of their own fate

   The individual with '*internal locus of control*' believes that he is master of his own destiny. He believes that his internal traits determine what happens in a given situation and he controls events concerning his own life. The person with this kind of personality seeks opportunities for advancement and relies more on their ability and judgement at work. The study proves that the persons with internal locus of control are highly confident. They use their own wisdom and energy while working on any projects.

   The individual with '*external locus of control*' tends to believe that events occur purely by chance and because of the factors beyond their control. They feel that the outside forces are affecting the events in his life and the individual is at the mercy of destiny, chance or other people. The person with this kind of personality are generally inactive and they allow events occur own their own.

8. **Risk Taking:** This shows the willingness of individual to take or avoid risk. It shows how long a manager take to make a decision and how much information he requires before taking a decision. High-risk taker takes rapid decision with less available information. The propensity to assume risk is dependent upon the nature of job. An accountant performing auditing activities should be risk averse; on the other hand, in the expectation of higher return a high risk-taking propensity results high performance for a stock trader's brokerage firm. As a general saying is higher the risk, higher the return.

20.5 PERSONALITY ASSESSMENT TESTS

1. **Subjective Test:** This includes interviews, observations, case studies, etc. A person is interviewed and observed carefully to judge his capabilities and capacities. Sometimes a person is also judged with the help of case studies and autobiographies. The judgement and critical remarks about the case studies and autobiographies help in judging the personality of a person.
2. **Objective Tests:** It includes questionnaire, K.G. Aggregation, etc. These kinds of tests give stress on the mental ability, capabilities rather than on personal appearance of a person.
3. **Projective Test:** In this, the test like WAT (Words Association Test) and TAT (Thematic Aptitude Test) are conducted. These tests play a major role in analyzing the personality of a person. These tests comprise of words and pictures. And the person is judged by his/her reaction to the picture and words.

All these tests have been devised to assist the personality of the person in the most effective manner.

20.6 SUMMARY

Every individual possesses a unique set of traits and characteristics, which remain stable overtime. This uniqueness and consistency form the aspects of personality. It is the stability of these characteristics that sometimes assist in predicting behaviour of a given person. There are many factors like biological characteristics, family and social groups, cultural and social factor, which contributes towards formation of personality. An individual can be manifested in various forms like authoritarian personality, bureaucratic personality, Machiavellian personality, and so on. There are many theories that are developed in predicting the behaviour of an individual on the basis of various attributes. Some tests are also designed for assessing the personality of an individual.

20.7 SELF-ASSESSMENT EXERCISE

1. What are the various dimensions of personality that are related with interpersonal and organizational behaviour?
2. Give a brief account of the factors contributing personality. What are the various tests for assessing personality?
3. Define personality. How personality does relate to organizational behaviour?
4. Briefly describe the various theories of personality.

21 PERCEPTION AND HUMAN BEHAVIOUR

Learning Objective

The main objective of this chapter is to highlight the meaning, components and factors influencing the perception.

21.1 INTRODUCTION

The psychological processes that allow an individual to adjust his behaviour are called perception. The behaviour of an individual is inclined by his personality, motives and efforts. The behaviour and performance provides satisfaction to the employees who get stimulated to work more and develop his personality and work quality.

21.2 DEFINITION OF PERCEPTION

Perception may be defined as "a cognitive process by which people attend to incoming stimuli, organize and interpret such stimuli into behaviour". Perception can also be defined as "a process by which individuals organize and interpret their sensory impressions in order to give meaning to their environment". The environment is a stimulus to influence behaviour, because the stimuli are attended, organized and interpreted to arrive at certain forms of behaviour. The sensory organs, i.e., eyes, nose, ears, skin and tongue, are used to change the stimuli into behaviour through their attention, recognition and interpretation processes. Individuals do not accept the information or stimuli unless they are evaluated and interpreted by the mental processing system. Individuals attend to the stimuli, recognize and translate them into meaningful information, which inspire them to act and perform the job. These processes are known as perpetual process. When employees get satisfaction through their performance, either by meeting their physical or mental needs, they perceive the organization in the right perspective. It helps them understand the functions and achieve satisfaction.

21.3 COMPONENTS OF PERCEPTION

Perception is a process of sensory organs. The mind gets information through the five sense organs, viz., the eyes, ears, nose, tongue and skin. The stimulation coming to these organs may be through action, written messages, oral communication, odour, taste, touch of the product and people. The perception starts with the awareness of these stimuli. Recognizing these stimuli takes place only after paying attention to them. These messages are then translated into action and behaviour.

1. **Stimuli:** The receipt of information is the stimulus, which results in sensation. Knowledge and behaviour depend on senses and their stimulation. The physical senses used by people are vision, hearing, touch, smell and taste. Intuitions and hunches are known as the sixth sense. These senses are influenced by a larger number of stimuli, which may be action, information, consideration and feelings, etc. The stimuli may be in the form of objects or physical commodities. The human body itself is developed through the acceptance of the stimuli. The mind and soul are the victims of these stimuli occurring in the surroundings of the people. The family, social and the economic environment are important stimuli for the people. The physiological and psychological functions are the result of these stimuli. The intensive and extensive forms of stimuli have a greater impact on the sensory organs. The physical work environment, sociocultural environment and other factors have certain stimuli to influence the employee's perception. In all, the perception begins only when people deal with stimuli; that is, stimulating factors give information about the situation.
2. **Attention:** People selectively attend to stimuli. Some of the stimuli are reacted to while others are ignored without being paid any attention. The stimuli that are paid attention depend purely on the people's selection capacity and the intensity of stimuli. Educated employees pay more attention to any stimuli, viz., announcement of bonus, appeal for increasing productivity, training and motivation. The management has to find out suitable stimuli, which can appeal to the employees at the maximum level. If the attention of the employees is not drawn, the organization cannot expect proper behaviour from the employees. An organization should be aware of all those factors, which affect the attention of the employees. During the attention process, sensory and neural mechanisms are affected and the message receiver becomes involved in understanding the stimuli. Taking employees to the attention stage is essential in an organization for making them behave in a systematic and required order.
3. **Recognition:** After paying attention to the stimuli, the employees try to recognize whether the stimuli are worth realizing. The messages or incoming stimuli are recognized before they are transmitted into behaviour. Perception is a two-phase activity, i.e., receiving stimuli and translating the stimuli into action. However, before the stage of translation, the stimuli must be recognized by the individual. The recognition process is dependent on mental acceptability. For example, if a car driver suddenly sees a child in front of his running car, he stops the car. He recognizes the stimuli, i.e., the life of the child is in danger. His mental process recognizes the danger after paying attention to the stimuli. If he does not pay attention to the stimuli, he cannot recognize the danger. After recognizing the stimuli, he translates the message into behaviour.

4. **Translation:** The stimuli are evaluated before being converted into action or behaviour. The evaluation process is translation. In the above example, the car driver after recognizing the stimuli uses the clutch and brake to stop the car. He has immediately translated the stimulus into an appropriate action. The perception process is purely mental before it is converted into action. The conversion is translation. The management in an organisation has to consider the various processes of translating the message into action. The employees should be assisted to translate the stimuli into action. For example, the announcement of bonus should be recognized as a stimulus for increasing production. The employee should translate it into appropriate behaviour. In other words, they should be motivated by the management to increase productivity. During the translation period, psychological mechanism commonly known as sensory and mental organs is affected. They influence perception. The incoming stimuli are interpreted and perception is developed.
5. **Behaviour:** Behaviour is the outcome of the cognitive process. It is a response to change in sensory inputs, i.e., stimuli. It is an overt and covert response. Perceptual behaviour is not influenced by reality, but is a result of the perception process of the individual, his learning and personality, environmental factors and other internal and external factors at the workplace. The psychological feedback that may influence the perception of an employee may be superior behaviour, his eye movement, raising of an eyebrow, the tone of voice, etc. The behaviour of employees depends on perception, which is visible in the form of action, reaction or other behaviour. The behavioural termination of perception may be overt or covert. The overt behaviour of perception is witnessed in the form of physical activities of the employees and covert behaviour is observed in the form of mental evaluation and self-esteem. The perception behaviour is the result of the cognitive process of the stimulus, which may be a message, or an action situation of management function. Perception is reflected in behaviour, which is visible in different forms of employees' action and motivation.
6. **Performance:** Proper behaviour leads to higher performance. High performers become a source of stimuli and motivation to other employees. A performance-reward relationship is established to motivate people.
7. **Satisfaction:** High performance gives more satisfaction. The level of satisfaction is calculated with the difference in performance and expectation. If the performance is more than the expectation, people are delighted, but when performance is equal to expectation, it results in satisfaction. On the other hand, if performance is less than the expectation, people become frustrated and this requires a more appealing form of stimulus for developing proper employee work behaviour and high performance. It is essential to understand the factors that influence the perception process and mould employees' behaviour towards the corporate objectives and self-satisfaction. Individuals observe several stimuli everyday. They confront these stimuli, notice and register them in their minds, interpret them and behave according to their background and understanding. Employees confronted with stimuli select only a few stimuli of their choice and leave other stimuli unattended and unrecognized. Factors influencing the selective process may be external as well as internal, organizational structures, social systems and characteristics of the perceiver.

21.4 FACTORS INFLUENCING THE PERCEPTION PROCESS

There is no doubt that stimuli play a significant role in the perception process as various factors relating to the perception process have been noticed by behavioural experts. The factors influencing perceptions are the perceiver's characteristics, object and situations. However, they can be analyzed under specific heads such as the perceiver's characteristics, personal factors, internal factors, organizational structures and social conditions.

21.4.1 Perceiver's Characteristics

Perception depends on how an individual views the objects and situations. Some employees may perceive the workplace as incorporating favourable working conditions, while others may perceive it as a place of good pay. The perception is not actual reality, but it is the viewing of the reality, which differs from person to person according to their respective characteristics. Perceptions of the object are influenced not only by individual's characteristics but also by the characteristics of other employees, the manager's personality and employee's views from their perception of the workplace. The characteristics of employees, viz., attitude, motives, interests, habits, experience, expectations, learning and personality have a greater influence on perception formation.

1. **Personality:** Personality has different levels of perception. The personality of a perceiving person considerably affects the stimuli transformation behaviour process. Young people perceive objects and situations in the original form. Experienced persons perceive the objects as per their personality levels. Perception influences learning, which is a developing factor of personality. The personality has a wider impact on the perception process too. Persons can view objects and situations as per their personality levels. The age, sex, motivation, learning levels, etc. influence perception.
2. **Motives:** The motives and desires of employees cause them to view stimuli differently as per their level and angle. Helpful motives of the employees will always assist the management. If they desire to develop themselves and the organization, they will perceive objects and situations positively. Employees having low motives will not work sincerely. The perception will differ depending on different types of motives. An indecisive manager perceives his supervisors differently. Personal insecurity of a manager results in doubtful perception about his supervisors, irrespective of their intentions. People who are dubious are prone to see others as dubious persons. Motives are reflected in actions based on perception.
3. **Learning:** Learning levels of employees have a great impact on their perceptions. It is an important factor influencing perception formation. Educated persons have higher perceptions than the less educated persons. Attitudes are developed according to the learning levels.
4. **Interest:** The interest of individuals draws more attention and recognition to stimuli. Less attention and recognition lowers the impact of stimuli or objects on behaviour. If employees lack interest, behaviour pattern will be less effective, and the perception will be weak. Managers cannot influence the employees in their work culture. Since individual

interests vary from person to person, the perception is also different. However, the management tries to create interest among the employees to have higher perception of the organization.

5. **Habits:** Habits die-hard and therefore individuals perceive objects, situations and conditions differently according to their habits. Many employees learn quickly. Others are slow in perceiving a stimulus. Some employees are not bothered about the management. They do not perceive the object correctly. Some people work by smoking or chewing pan. Thus, the habits of people have different perception levels.
6. **Experiences:** The experience of employees' result in different levels of perception. A young employee takes time to understand the object and situation. Experienced employees generally understand objects quickly and correctly. However, in contradictory situations, it is difficult to correct aged persons, whereas the young are easily moulded towards achieving the objectives of the organization.
7. **Expectation:** Expectations distort the perceptions. People see what they expect to see. If they see the object and the situation differently from their expectations, they get frustrated. They are unable to modify their behaviour. The employees may expect more inclination towards them positively in terms of payments and fringe benefits; therefore, they perceive the management from that angle. The real stimuli are not properly perceived if expectations exist there on. The management has to evolve expectations for proper perception.
8. **Attitude:** The attitude and aptitude of employees influence perception formation. If they have positive attitudes towards the management, they directly perceive the stimuli given by management. In case of negative attitudes, the employees suspect the management's approach. Employees of high aptitude have a desire and attitude for growth. They behave positively towards the management of an organization.

21.4.2 External Factors

The perception process is influenced by external factors, which may be objects and situations. The external points related to objects and situations have great influence on the perception process. The external factors may be the size, interest, contrast, repetition, motion, familiarity, novelty and others.

1. **Size:** The size of the object or stimulus has a greater impact on the perception process because the size influences attention and recognition in a more effective manner. Employees are greatly influenced by tall and well-built managers as compared to the normal-sized individuals. The engineering department pays more attention to big and, attractive machines; big-sized objects have a natural attraction and get more attention.
2. **Situations:** Situations have a great influence on people's perceptions. A favourable work environment develops a positive attitude and work culture because the perception process is easily channelised and rightly directed. The management style and functioning of the organization influences the employee's mental state through attention and recognition. Work relations also have some impact on perception forces.

3. **Repetition:** Repeated stimuli have more impact on performances than a single statement. Repetition has the advantage of being attention-catching. When stimuli are waning, repetition generates fresh attention and recognition. Supervisors repeat orders several times to have them followed by employees.
4. **Objects:** Objects are external factors influencing the perceiver because he has no control over them. The physical and internal attributes of objects are influencing factors of perception. The physical and time proximity, complex nature of objects, presentation of messages and the territorial approach of the management have great impact on the perception.
5. **Novelty:** Novel actions get more attention. New ideas and model preaching will draw the attention of the perceiver. Changing jobs reduce monotony. Novel objects and situations are recognized clearly by the perceivers.
6. **Motion:** People pay more attention to the moving objects than to stationary objects. This is just the impact of eyes on the mind. Workers are more attentive towards working machines than stationary machines. The video films of some training programmes create more of an impact on employees than others.
7. **Intensity:** Scholars on human behaviour have revealed that the more intense the stimuli, the higher the attention and recognition in the perception process. A strong voiced manager has more impact on supervisors and employees. It is observed that managers use voice modulation to get the attention of employees. Bright letters and strong appeal have more impact on people than normal letters and low appeal. More attention results in a higher recognition and behaviour pattern. The intensity varies as per the needs of the organisation. The same type of intensity may not be useful for all the situations and objects.
8. **Familiarity:** Employees would like to hear and see those programmes with which they are familiar. Training programmes demonstrated in the language of the employees are highly attended and recognized. Examples, which are known and easily understood, are used for motivating employees.
9. **Contrast:** Contrasting objects have more impact on behaviour. Employees pay more attention and recognition to contrasting objects and situations. Machines making noises are hardly noticed, but a machine coming to a halt is immediately noticed, because of contrast stimuli. Normal communication and performance have less impact than abnormal and contrast communication. The purpose of contrast stimuli is to attract more attention and recognition. However, if the contrast is not helpful in drawing more attention, it should be avoided and more attention-drawing stimuli should be exercised for gaining a real perception of work behaviour.

21.4.3 Internal Factors

Internal factors are within the personal control of the perceivers. They use these factors when they so desire. They are based on the individual's psychological setup, economic and social background, learning, personality and motivation.

1. **Psychological setup:** Factors such as attitude, interest, preferences, likings and other psychological bent of mind distort the perception process. People perceive what they like to perceive because of their attitudinal and mental approaches. These factors are the outcome of not only the self-factors of the individuals but their actions and interaction with other people. People working with employees do help in the foundation of the psychological setup. One person's problem may be another person's satisfaction. For example, giving a higher bonus is a state of satisfaction to employees, but becomes a problem for managers.
2. **Personality:** The personality of the perceiver as well as the stimulator has an impact on the perception process. The age, sex, race, dress, facial expressions and body postures of both the persons have a direct influence on the perception process. If the perceiver is female and the stimulator is male, the perceiver gets some influences only if she prefers males. Otherwise, the perception process will be disturbed. The ethnic personalities have some influence on perception. Physical and mental characteristics, work pattern and age similarities affect the perception process.
3. **Motivation:** The pattern of motivation in an organization helps to develop perception building. Motivated people have the right perceptions about the stimuli, whereas the loco-profiled workers are doubtful about the message given by the management for the development. The approach of the female managers to problems is given more attention and recognition. Motivational theories have revealed the perception processes of particular categories of employees. Attention is drawn towards their needs, satisfaction and achievement desires. The mental state of motivational desire influences the perception process. Stimuli based on external factors receive varied degrees of attention and recognition. Internal factors, i.e., factors related to employees and managers, have different degrees of impact on the attention and recognition process while being translated into behaviour, which results in performance.
4. **Learning:** The state of learning influences the perception process. Highly educated persons can easily and rightly perceive the management's problem. They cooperate in problem solution. On the contrary, less educated employees are less concerned about the management. They perceive the management as a separate and superior part of the organization, who tend to exploit the labour, irrespective of the reality. People perceive as per their levels of learning. It is therefore essential for the organization to make its employees knowledgeable and educated for their effective performance and behaviour. The learning of managers and workers is a twin requirement.
5. **Economic and Social background:** The employee perceptions are based on economic and social backgrounds. The employee's level of understanding depends upon their economic and social backgrounds. Socially and economically developed employees have a more positive attitude towards development rather than less developed employees. However, developed employees are prone to decision-oriented functions. Conflicts between managers and employees will increase in this case. The problems can be resolved only through proper perception processes.

21.4.4 Organizational Structure

The perceptual process is influenced by the organizational structure and process. The perceptual structure, perceptual grouping, constancy, context, defence, workplace and process have been recognized as important factors influencing the perceptual process.

1. **Perceptual constancy:** Perceptual constancy plays an important role in the perception process. The stability and unchangeability of objects help in the constant perception process of people. The constancy of stimuli helps in easy perception because people become accustomed to the stimuli. The size, shape, place and colour of objects and situation are easily observed if they are constant. Constant stimuli make the perception process easy and effective.
2. **Perceptual context:** The context of the stimuli with reference to objects and situations has a meaningful impact on the perceiver. If the perceiver has the confidence that the stimuli are relevant to their work and awards, they may pay more attention to the perception process, policies and objectives relevant to employees. Welfare is paid more attention. Verbal communication in the relevant context is given more perceptual consideration.
3. **Perceptual defence:** The defensive role of the management is well recognized by the employees. There are many areas where employees develop conflicts, which are resolved by the management. Such functions, which provide defence to conflicting views, are given more importance by employees. People like to defend their professions, work and work relations, if they are satisfied. On the contrary, dissatisfied workers criticize their own work and workplace. Many workers perceive conflicts as not being very serious. They only perceive conflicts as casual and to be expected, without any significant features. Some employees, however, find conflicts alarming. They react to warning signs and perceive the situation differently. Managers can find different perceptions for their actions because they view the situation from the angle of defence.
4. **Perceptual grouping:** The manager generally groups all the stimuli together to influence the employees. The grouping is done based on closure, continuity, similarity and proximity. The closure doctrine of grouping is based on the Gestalt Principle of Psychology wherein the individuals perceive the whole object although the whole unit does not exist. For example, the manager perceives that all the members cooperate with him in achieving computerization, whereas some members really oppose mechanization. The manager tries to close the disagreement and maintains uniformity in agreement for mechanization. On the other hand, if the members do not withdraw their disagreement, they observe their individual perceptions. The continuity principle emphasises that the stimuli should continue to make an impact on the perceiver. Discreet stimuli may, however, distort the perception process. The continuity principle is different from the closure principle as missing stimuli are applied in the latter case, whereas a continuous link is maintained in the former case. It is observed that only continuous and related stimuli are easily attended and recognized. The obvious and continuous flow of stimuli may produce the desired behaviour. The similarity principle assumes that similar stimuli are easily attended, recognized and perceived. The similarity has its own impact on the employees. For example, employees wearing special clothes at the workplace automatically carry the message of the

organization. Similarity in age, sex, education and other characteristics have a direct impact on the employee's perception. The proximity principle refers to the grouping of the segments into one unit. Nearness of stimuli will be perceived as wholesome for the group. All the stimuli are considered one because of physical proximity. For example, all the employees in one-cadre will be considered as one group which is stimulated by the proximity of stimuli. Departmental employees are considered single group employees because of proximity. They are motivated on the basis of proximity stimuli.

5. **Perceptual process:** The relationship between employees and managers is crucial in the perceptual process. Employees may perceive a low output with pleasure to influence their supervisor. The management has a different perception of performance and evaluation. Some may perceive a self-fulfilling prophecy by the management, when they have too high or too low expectation from employees. High expectation inspires managers to motivate their employees positively. Managers develop subjective attitudes many times about the performance and process. Besides, the employees' efforts are also considered for performance and process valuation. During the work process, some employees are troublemakers and some are loyal. The perceptual process is an important factor for the perception process of management and employees.
6. **Perceptual structure:** The organizational structure influences the perception of employees and other people related to the organization. The departmentalization, decentralization, delegation of authority and other structural frameworks have important bearings in the mind of employees. An adequate amount of decentralization makes employees feel that the organization is welfare-oriented. Similarly, too much centralization gives rise to the feeling of suspicion in the minds of employees. Structure itself becomes a flow chart of perception. Work relations and the decision-making authority provide an important understanding of organizational perception. If the employees view the structure positively, they willingly contribute to the development of the organization.
7. **Perceptual workplace:** The perceptual process is affected by the workplace too. The climate temperature, noise, smoke and other factors have a direct bearing on the perception and psychological traits of employees. Consequently, the perceptual process is different for different employees. Some employees develop a positive perception while others develop a negative perception of the workplace. All employees perceive the same situation and object differently because of the varied nature of their workplace.

21.4.5 Social Factors

Social conditions have much influence on the perception process. Perceivers and the perceived objects have complex characteristics. They are perceived differently in different situations. The attributes of objects are important considerations influencing the selectivity process of perception. Attributes of objects, the subject, the situations and the perceiver have become so important that a separate theory known as attribution theory has been developed under the perception theory. Social factors consider how one person behaves towards the other person and how other people behave towards him. The interaction between the manager and his subordinates is considered under social factors, which include the stereotyping effect, the halo effect, contrast effect and projection. These are:

1. **Contrast effect:** Like stereotyping and halo effect, the contrast effect is another factor of social perception, i.e., perception in a group. People perceive differently in many cases. Whatever the manager emphasises, the employees may take different views of the stimulus. For example, manager asks employees to increase productivity for getting a bonus. Employees may view this stimulus or message as the manager being bothered about his promotion. If employees develop this perception and translate it into practice, the stimulus will work against the purpose. The contrast effect is an error of social perception. Politicians generally produce a contrast effect amongst their audience. The contrast effect occurs because of doubtful relations, swift conclusions, unfavourable attitudes, and so on.
2. **Halo effect:** The halo effect occurs only when a single factor is taken for performance evaluation or perception, with the process ignoring other important considerations. For example, if an employee is considered good on one account, he is treated as good on all accounts. But, in the real field, he may not be good on every account. The halo effect is related to the personality assessment based only on a single trait. If a manager is found to be intelligent, he is considered good for cooperation, dependability and for other purposes. The halo effect arises on account of the nuclear expression of traits, which are not frequently encountered and have moral implications. The perception process becomes deceptive if only one factor is given more importance. If an employee possesses all desirable qualities except that of loyalty to the manager, he is not put in the same perceptual setup as the personally loyal employees, having no profession attributes and work devotion. The halo effect is an attribution. Error or perceptual error should be avoided in the perception process. The communicating authority should be well aware of the halo effect for proper motivation.
3. **Projection:** Generalization leads to projection. People have the habit of projection although it may not be correct. People may project future events differently from the reality in many cases. Personal attributes, objects and situations are to be considered before projection. However, projection may not be always incorrect. If it is properly evaluated and placed, the projection may give the correct perception. For example, if a manager is trustworthy, he may also treat his employees trustworthy. Contrary to this, many employees may not be trustworthy. Similarly, a manager who is good may not necessarily consider his employees good too. Thus, the projection process differs from person to person, place to place and object to object, and this has an ultimate impact on the perception process.
4. **Stereotyping effect:** The perception process takes the shortest method in some cases and considers only routine effects. Stereotype judgement is based on an ideal situation or the type of impression formed about the group. It is the consideration of individual's characteristics as being representative of the whole group. If an employee is found well behaved, the whole group of employees is considered to be good. If, in an organization, a manager is helpful, it is generalized that the organization is very helpful and sympathetic towards employees. It is an inductive method wherein conclusions are aggregated from individual performance; that is, it accumulates particular cases to arrive at general conclusions. Stereotyping is generalization, which has the advantages of being time saving, accurate and common. For example, assume that the management has previously found that sportsmen and athletes have been very successful workers in the factory. They were

ambitious; hardworking and can easily overcome adverse situations. In future selection process, the management may appoint such sportsmen and athletes without undergoing many selection procedures. Similarly, many decisions are taken on the basis of the stereotyping effect. The generalization may prove disastrous if it is relied on heavily without proper scrutiny and examination of individual characteristics. The most important stereotyping effects are observed in the form of age, sex, nationality and social status. The stereotyping effects under social perception consider the attributes, traits and other qualities of a member of a social organization. These qualities are generalised as the qualities of the social organization or group. However, there may be perceptual errors, because the generalized attributes and qualities may not be found in all the cases. Therefore, the perception process takes into consideration the amount of perceptual errors when deriving conclusions based on stereotyping effects. Favourable and unfavourable traits are always calculated and evaluated to find their impact on the behaviour or decision taken. Stereotyping has become an important factor of social perception, which is based on ethnic groups–socio-economic groups, demographic groups, and so on. The individual difference in the group is recorded to evaluate the perceptual errors in arriving at stereotyping effects. The belief factor in stereotyping effects has become an important tool to arrive at certain decisions. One can conclude that an organization has a democratic manager. The common characteristics are the basis of belief. If a manager belongs to the said democratic organization, one can believe that he will also have the same characteristics. The errors may be there in belief because of ignoring variations in characteristics and holding mistaken beliefs. The beliefs or stereotyping effects are modified from time to time to arrive at correct perception behaviour and decisions.

21.5 PERCEPTION MODELS

Perception models are related to the perception objectives and perceptual setup to achieve objectives. Broadly speaking, perception model may be selected from among the decision-making model, the satisfying model, implicit favourite model and the intuitive model. Each has its respective advantages.

21.5.1 Decision-making Models

There are different types of decision-making models. Of these, the optimizing model, the individual decision-making model and the ethical decision-making model are some of the important perception models based on the decision-making process. These are:

1. **Ethical decision-making model:** The decision-making process involves ethical considerations, which are utilitarian, consistent and just. Utilitarianism refers to the greatest good for the greatest number of people. Goals like productivity, profitability, economy and efficiency are considered under the ethical decision-making process. Consistency with the existing rules and regulations are important for making ethical decisions. Right decisions are preferred, as they do not antagonize any person. Equitable distributions of benefits and

costs are the basic point of justice. Ethics are based on cultures and social setup. Ethical decisions have a moral support and long lasting features. Ethics and culture influence the decision-making process at every stage, i.e., ascertaining the needs for decisions, identification of the decision criteria, allocation of weight to the criteria, development of the alternatives, evaluation of the alternative; and selection of the best alternatives. The needs and attitudes are developed as per the ethics and culture of society.

2. **Individual decision-making model:** Individuals think before they act in their own manner and method. They follow the simple process of decision-making. They consider their decision the best because the decision is taken as per their individual outlook. Some individuals prefer satisfying decisions while others take maximisation of uses as the best decision. However, there are people who do not bother about the decision process, but take a swift decision based on their personal whims and discretion. The majority of the people use a simple decision-making process. Neatness, promptness, enthusiasm, attitudes, preferences and education have a great influence on the individual's decision-making process.
3. **Optimizing model:** The optimising decision-making model assumes the rationality, goals and preferences for arriving at the final choice of maximising the outcome. Rationality assumes that people prefer consistency and value maximising. People are logical and objective-oriented. They are goal-oriented and use the steps of optimizing to select the best alternative. People are clear about their preferences and choice methods. They are knowledgeable about the need for a decision, can identify the decision criteria, assign proper weights and values, develop alternatives, evaluate the alternatives and select the best alternative. The decision-makers list the needs, which are more thrusting and less thrusting. The criteria dividing the steps are weighed and evaluated to find various alternative solutions to a problem. First, alternatives are developed in different forms. Secondly, the alternatives are evaluated as per the weighted criteria. Different alternatives are related and ranked. The alternative having the maximum weights is rated as the best and given the first rank. The decision thus arrived gives maximum value or optimises the use of resources.

21.5.2 Satisfying Model

The satisfying or bounded rationality model is used to arrive at suitable decisions. When people face complex problems, they require at least those solutions, which may satisfy them to a minimum level. A simple and satisfying model is constructed within the limits of rationality. All the problems are analyzed, their complexities are understood and solutions are put forward for conspicuous choices. The difference between the optimizing and satisfying model is that all alternatives are not evaluated under satisfying model as is done in the former case. Instead, only those alternatives are evaluated which are satisfactory and sufficient. Only those alternatives, which are good enough, are selected for getting satisfaction. If satisfying attributes exist in alternatives, the further search of good enough attributes continues till the best alternative is arrived at. The satisfying model considers only simple and limited models. Only those alternatives are considered which are commonly known and are within the limits of the decision-makers.

Remote, non-feasible alternatives are not considered, and only useful and approachable decisions are used for solving problems.

1. **Implicit Favourite Model:** Like the satisfying model, the implicit favourite model solves complex problems by simplifying the process. An alternative will be considered and evaluated only when it is identified as a favourite, which is implicitly known to the decision-maker. In this case, the decision-maker is neither rational nor objective. He implicitly selects a preferred alternative. The implicit favourite is the right choice. It has been revealed by research that people prefer an implicit favourite decision which may or may not be the optimizing alternative. In the implicit favourite model, the problem is first identified. Thereafter, implicit favourite alternatives are developed to find the required solutions. Evaluation criteria to judge each and every alternative as the favourite are developed. Using the criteria, the alternatives are reduced to a lower number, viz., one or two. If these alternatives do not fulfil the requirements of the decisions, new implicit favourite alternatives are developed, evaluated and selected as discussed already.
2. **Intuitive Model:** The implicit favourite model gives birth to the intuitive model, which believes in one's own decision as favourable. The implicit favourite model requires even evaluation of the alternatives. Intuition is considered the best criterion to select an alternative as the best alternative solution to the problem. Intuition is one's own inner feeling or sixth sense. It depends on one's own experience and knowledge. Many decisions taken at the unconscious level of the mind are very useful. Intuitive and rational decisions are not opposite to each other, but are complementary to each other. Intuitive decisions result from quick decision-making processes, although they are not always dependable. The management should rationally evaluate intuitive decisions.

21.6 SUMMARY

Behaviour is a fatality of the environment, which is observed in the form of stimuli. The sensory organs perceive the stimuli as per their learning and personality. The reverse functions are also correct. The perceptions, if modified through adequate and qualitative stimuli, help to develop learning and personality. Improved behaviour has better performance and rewards, which provide more satisfaction to the employees. A satisfied employee tries to learn and work effectively. An organization grows with the developed employees. Perception is therefore an important and initial step for developing an organizational behaviour. It is a cognitive process, which selects, organizes and interprets the stimuli. It overlay the base for behaviour. Although, perception may not be a real-world presentation, it is an imaginary understanding of the situation. The behaviour of an individual is guided by perception. People perceive differently as per their learning and personality. The perceptual world of a manager is different from the perceptual world of employees. Social factors also influence the perception process. Employees coming from a poor family have different perceptions of an organization from those coming from rich families. The levels of education, family background and political situation have a direct impact on the perception level.

21.7 SELF-ASSESSMENT QUESTIONS

1. "Behaviour is the perceptional problem". Comment.
2. "Employees of different organizations have different perceptions". Explain.
3. Define the components and models of perception.
4. Do you think the behaviour is natural and should be ignored?
5. What do you mean by perception in the context of organization?

22
ATTITUDES AND HUMAN BEHAVIOUR

Learning Objective

The main objective of this chapter is to understand how attitudes affect human behaviour and to identify how attitudes are developed so that mangers can affect attitudes by controlling various factors.

22.1 INTRODUCTION

Attitude is the major factor, which affect the behaviour of a person or an organization. It manipulates the perception of objects and people, exposure to and comprehension of information, choice of friends, co-workers, and so on. The importance of attitudes in understanding psychological phenomenon was given formal recognition early in the history of social psychology. From the time of the concept's entry into the language of psychology until now, interest in attitudes has been strong and growing. However, over the years attitudes have been studied with differing emphases and methods. For example, between the period of 1920s and up to World War II the attention of attitude researchers was directed principally towards definitional issues and attitude measurement.

In addition, there were studies concerned with relationship of attitudes to some social variables. World War II brought with it a growing concern about the place of the attitude concept in understanding prejudice, particularly anti-Semitism. This period also brought the measurement of attitudes and opinions concerning various facts of soldiering and war. After the war, the subject of attitudes was taken up by academicians, particularly in the context of attitude change. Till now, the researchers have developed a loosely structured theoretical framework formulating the psychological processes underlying attitude change and the direct application of the study of attitudes to contemporary social problems.

22.2 MEANING AND CONCEPT OF ATTITUDES

Attitudes may be defined in two ways conceptual and operational. Even there is a quite difference in the conceptual definition of the term attitude. The term attitude first entered in the field of social phenomenon, it was natural to conceive of attitude as a tendency, set, or readiness to respond to some social objects. Some authors define attitude as a mental and neural state of readiness, organized through experience, exerting directive or dynamic influence upon the individual's response to all objects and situations with which it is related. From this point of view, attitude implies a heightened responsiveness to certain stimuli. Many researchers have defined attitude in terms of effect and evaluation.

For example, Krech and Crutchfield define attitude as an enduring organization of motivational, emotional, perceptual, and cognitive processes with respect to some aspect of the individual's world. Thus, attitudes are beliefs imbued with emotional and motivational properties and are expressed in a person's favourability towards an object. The evaluative nature of attitude is also emphasized by Katz and Scotland when they define attitude as a tendency or predisposition to evaluate an object or symbol of that object in a certain way. Evaluation consists of attributing goodness-badness or desirable-undesirable qualities to an object.

In addition to conceptual approach, there is operational approach in defining the term attitude. The concept of attitude is operationalized in a number of ways; but in most cases, studies rely on some kind of questionnaire to measure attitudes. Taking attitudes from this point of view, only evaluative aspect of attitudes has been taken into account. For example, Fishbein has noted that most measures of attitudes tap an underlying dimension of favourability-unfavourability and, therefore, attitudes should be regarded as synonymous with evaluating meaning. Thus, in practice, the term attitude often is used in a generic sense to any reports of what people think or feel or the ways in which they intend to acts.

22.2.1 Attitude, Opinion and Belief

An opinion is generally the expression of one's judgement of a particular set of facts or an evaluation of the circumstances presented to him. Thurstone defines opinions as expressions of attitudes. However, Kolasa observes that an opinion is response to a specifically limited stimulus, but the response is certainly influenced by the predisposition with which the individual is operating that is the attitude structure. Undoubtedly, attitudes are basic to opinions as well as to many other aspects of behaviour. Although attitudes tend to be generalized predisposition to react in some way towards objects or concepts, opinions tend to be focused on more specific aspects of the object or the concept. McCormick and Tiffin observe that the measurement of attitudes is generally based on the expressions of opinions. But we should distinguish between attitude scale like a thermometer or barometer, which reflects the generalized level of individuals' attitudes towards some object or concept, and opinion survey which typically are used to elicit the opinions of people toward specific aspects of, for example, their work situation.

A difference can also be made between attitude and belief. A belief is an enduring organization of perceptions and cognitions about some aspects of individual's world. Thus, belief is a hypothesis concerning the nature of objects, more particularly, concerning one's judgement of the probability regarding their nature. In this sense, belief is the cognitive component of attitude, which, reflects the manner in which an object is perceived. Kolasa observes that beliefs are stronger than opinions; we hold them more firmly than we do the more changeable evaluations of minor or transitory events represented by opinions.

22.2.2 Attitude and Behaviour

Individual's behaviour is not a simple and direct stimulus-response relationship; rather it is affected by the individual concerned, as is explained by S-O-B model. The work situation is interpreted by individual, and attitudes play an important part in which the situation is interpreted. Only after individual's interpretation and comparison does the response occur. This means that response expected of a purely objective and rational consideration of the work situation and its characteristics may not be the actual response of the individual. His response depends completely on how he interprets the situation and on his own personal attitudes towards the situation. Obviously, attitudes are an important consideration because of their central position in the process transforming work requirements into effort. Attitudes have been thought as serving four functions and thereby affecting the behaviour, as discussed below:

1. **Ego-defensive:** The ego-defensive function of attitudes acknowledges the importance of psychological thought. Attitude may be required and maintained to protect the person from facing threats in the external world or from becoming aware of his own unacceptable impulses. Ego-defensive attitudes may be aroused by internal or external threat, frustrating events, appeals or to the build-up or repressed impulses, and suggestions by authoritarian sources. The attitude influences his/her behaviour by affecting his perception of the situation accordingly.
2. **Instrumental:** Attitude serves as a means to reach at a desired goal or to avoid an undesired one. Instrumental attitudes are aroused by the activation of a need or cues that are associated with the attitude object and arouse favourable or unfavourable feelings.
3. **Knowledge:** The knowledge function of attitudes is based on a person's need to maintain a stable, organized and meaningful structure of the world. Attitudes that provide a standard against which a person evaluates aspects of his world serve the knowledge function too.
4. **Value Orientation:** The value-orientation function takes into account attitudes that are held because they express a person's values or enhance his self-identity. These attitudes arise by conditions that threaten the self-concept, appeals to reassert the person's self-image, or by cues that engage the person's values and make them salient to him.

These functions of attitudes affect the individual's way of interpreting the information coming to him. Since attitudes intervene between work requirements and work responses, information about how people feel about their jobs can be quite useful in prediction about work response. Thus, these types of attitudes can portray areas of investigation for making the individual and the organization more compatible.

22.3 THEORIES OF ATTITUDE FORMATION

There are so many theories that have been projected to explain the attitude formation and change. Although, these theories have many limitations, they provide useful thinking about the processes underlying attitude formation. These theories are organized into major groupings according to the nature of the psychological processes postulated to underlying formation and change of attitudes. These theories may broadly be classified into three categories: cognitive-consistency theories, functional theories and social judgement theories. However, there is frequent discontinuity between various groupings because related approaches have focused on different sets of phenomena. Nevertheless, such classification is valid from practical point of view.

22.3.1 Cognitive Consistency Theories

Attitudes do not exist in isolation; indeed, a complex structure results which, appears to have at its heart a consistent tendency to maintain balance and resist change from influences of various types. In general, these theories are concerned with inconsistencies that arise between related beliefs, bits of knowledge, and/or evaluations about an object or an issue. Through various consistency theories differ in several respects, including the form of inconsistency about which they are concerned, all of them have in common the idea that the psychological tension created by this unpleasant state leads to attempt for reducing the inconsistency. There are four important theories under this group.

1. **Balance Theory:** The basic model of balance theory has been provided by Heider. The theory is concerned with consistency in the judgement of people and/or issues that are linked by some form of relationship. There are three elements in the attitude formation; the person, other person, and impersonal entity. Two generic types of relationships are considered to exist between the elements; linking or sentiment relations and unit relations. The linking relations encompass all forms of sentiment or effect, while unit relationships express the fact that two elements are perceived as belonging together. Both linking and unit relations can be positive and negative. In a three element system, balance exists if all three relations are positive or if two relations are negative and one is positive. Imbalance exists if all three relations are negative or if two relations are positive and one is negative. People tend to perceive other and objects linked to them so that the system is balanced. Thus, if a perceiver likes a source who favours a certain position on an issue, the balancing process induces the perceiver to favour that position too. The balanced states are stable and imbalanced states are unstable. When imbalanced states occur, the psychological tension created motivates the person to restore balance cognitively by changing the relations. Thus, a person's attitudes towards an object depend on his attitudes towards a source that is linked with the object.

   The basic model of Heider has been criticized on some grounds. For example, the theory does not consider the degree of linking or unit relationship nor the relevance to the perceiver of the elements and relations. Consequently, there are no degrees of balance or imbalance, and it is not possible to make quantitative predictions about the degree of attitude change.

   In the extension of balance model, Abelson has suggested four methods in which a person can resolve imbalance in cognitive structures: denial, bolstering, differentiation, and transcendence. Denial involves denying a relationship when imbalance occurs. Bolstering involves adding element in the structure that is adding another issue in the main issue.

Differentiation involves splitting one of the elements into two elements that are related in opposite ways to other elements in the system and negatively related to each other. Transcendence involves combining elements into larger, more superordinate units from a balanced structure. These processes occur in hierarchy so that a person's attempts to resolve imbalance in the ordering are discussed. The ordering is based on the assumption that the person will attempt the least effortful resolution first. This theory helps in understanding the role of persuasive communication and interpersonal attractiveness in changing the attitudes.

2. **Congruity Theory:** Osgood and Tannenbaum have proposed the congruity theory of attitudes which is similar to the balance theory. The focus of the theory is on changes in the evaluation of a source and a concept, which are linked by an associate or dissociate assertion. Congruity exists when a source and concept that are positively associated have exactly the same evaluations and when a source and concept those are negatively associated have exactly the opposite evaluations attached to them. Congruity is a stable state and incongruity is unstable one. As such, incongruity leads to attitude change, and the theory states how much attitudes towards the source and towards the concept change in order to resolve the incongruity.
3. **Affective Cognitive Consistency Theory:** This theory, propounded by Rosenberg, is concerned with the consistency between a person's overall attitude and effect towards an object or issue and his beliefs about its relationship to his more general values. Rosenberg has related attitudes to one aspect of cognitive structure-means-end relationship between the object or issue and the achievement of desired and undesired values or goals. The theory is also called structural because it is concerned mainly with what happens within the individual when an attitude changes. It proposes that the relationship between the affective and the cognitive components of the attitude change when an attitude is altered.

   The theory postulates that a person's effect towards or evaluation of the attitude object tends to be consistent with this cognitive structural component. When there is inconsistency beyond a certain level of tolerance, the individual is motivated to reduce the inconsistency and thereby to change one or both components to make them more consistent. The theory, thus, suggests that changes in the affective component produce changes in the cognitive component in order to bring about consistency between the two. The theory also suggests that persuasive communication can be used to change the attitudes. The persuasive communication conveys information about how the attitude object or issue furthers the attainment of certain desirable ends or conveys persuasive material that results in a re-evaluation of the goals themselves.
4. **Cognitive Dissonance Theory:** The cognitive dissonance theory, proposed by Festinger, has had by far the greatest impact on the study of attitudes. At first sight, this theory may appear similar to the affective cognitive theory. The difference between the two is that this theory (dissonance) tends to tie in the third component of the attitudes (behavioural tendency) with cognitions about the attitude object. Rather than dealing with only one belief, this theory deals with relationship a person's ideas have with one other, it states that there are three types of relationships between all cognitions: dissonance, consonance, and irrelevance. Cognitions are dissonant whenever they are incompatible; or if they are opposed to one's experience about the relationship of events. Cognitions are

consonant when one follows from the other on the basis of logic or experience. Cognitions are totally irrelevant when two events are not interrelated. The presence of dissonance gives rise to pressures to reduce or eliminate the dissonance and avoid the further increase of dissonance. Dissonance varies in magnitude. The total amount of dissonance is a function of the proportion of relevant elements that are dissonant with one another relative to the total number of consonant and dissonant elements, each weighted by the importance of the elements for the person. Higher the degree of dissonance, higher would be the attempt to reduce it. Dissonance is reduced through three methods: changing a behavioural cognitive element, changing an environmental element, and adding a new cognitive element. The basic model of Festinger applies to several situations affecting behaviour of persons. In each behaviour, the person experiences dissonance when he engages in behaviour contrary to his attitudes. Since magnitude of dissonance is a function of the relative number and important elements, the amount of justification a person has for engaging in the attitude-discrepant behaviour is an important determinant of the amount of dissonance he experiences. Justification adds consonant element to the otherwise dissonant situation. For example, when a person has to choose among a number of alternatives, he experiences conflict before the decision. After the decision, he experiences dissonance because the positive features of rejected alternatives and negative features of selected alternative dissonant with the choice. To overcome this dissonance, the justification process starts. Dissonance reducing changes have the net effect of increasing the valuation of the chosen alternative and decreasing the valuation of rejected alternatives.

22.3.2 Functional Theory

Functional theory considers how attitudes and efforts are related to the motivational structure of the individual. The theory focuses on the meaning of the influence situation in terms of both the kinds of motives that is arouses and the individual's method of coping and achieving his goals. An understanding of the functions served by attitudes is important for attitude change procedure since a particular method may produce change in individuals whose attitudes serve one particular function, but may produce no change in an opposite direction in individuals for whom the attitudes serve a different function.

The most prominent person who visualized functional theory is Katz and he suggests four functions of attitudes: utilitarian or instrumental function, ego-defensive, value orientation, and knowledge, as discussed earlier. It can be seen that there is some similarity in parts of this theory to cognitive dissonance theory. What Katz points out is that when an attitude serves an adjustive function one of the two conditions must prevail before it can be changed; (i) the attitude and the activities related to it no longer provide the satisfaction they once did; or (ii) the individual's level of aspiration has been raised shifts in the satisfaction which come from behaviours bring with them changes in the attitudes. When new behaviours inconsistent with attitudes bring satisfaction these attitudes then must be adjusted. However, Katz functional theory has not stimulated much research except for the work on changing ego-defensive attitudes.

Kelman has given another approach about the functional approach of attitudes. His theory is directed towards the types of social relationships that occur in social influence situations. Kelman has distinguished three processes of attitude formation and change compliance, identification, and internalization.

These processes derive functional meaning primarily from their emphasis on the motivational significance of the individual's relationship to the influencing agent, or from the differing types of social integration that they represent. Compliance occurs when an attitude is formed or changed in order to gain a favourable reaction from other person or group. Identification occurs when a person forms or changes his attitude because his adoption helps him establish or maintain a positive self-defining relationship with the influencing agent. Internalization involves adopting an attitude because it is congruent with one's overall value system. The individual perceives the content of the induced attitude as enhancing his own values. This approach makes an important contribution towards an understanding of the conditions that influence the maintenance and stability of attitude change.

22.3.3 Social Judgement Theory

The social judgement theory, formulated originally by Sherif and Hoveland, attempts to explain how existing attitudes produce distortions of attitudinally related objects and how these judgements mediate attitude change. Accordingly, a person's own stand on an issue, that is, initial attitude, serves as an anchor for the judgement of attitudinally related stimuli. The person's initial attitude on an issue provides a point of reference against which he evaluates other opinions. These views can be considered in terms of attitudinal continuum and can be considered comprising latitudes. The latitude of acceptance, which is the range of opinions the individual finds acceptable, encompasses the opinion that best characterizes his own stand. The attitude of rejection, which is the range of opinions the individual finds objectionable, encompasses the opinion he finds most objectionable. The attitude of non-commitment is the range of opinions that the person finds neither acceptable nor unacceptable.

22.4 FACTORS AFFECTING ATTITUDE FORMATION

The attitudes are learned. Though there are different approaches as how learning works and is acquired by individuals, generally it is held that individuals learn things from the environment in which they interact. Thus, for attitude formation, all those factors must be taken into account from which people learn. Such factors may be analyzed in term of group, then to larger Starting from the family as a group, an individual moves in a close group, then to larger groups, and finally to the society as a whole. Apart from these groups the individual's psychological make-up, particularly his personality, is also responsible for shaping his behaviour and attitudes; thus in order to understand the various factors and how they affect the attitudes, both these category of factors should be analyzed.

22.4.1 Group Factors

The influence of groups on the attitudes of individuals is inversely proportional to the distance of the group from the individual. From this point of view, three types of groups have different types of effect on the attitudes of a person.

1. **Family:** The term family may be used in a variety of ways: it may include a nuclear family which means the immediate group of father, mother, and children; an extended family which includes nuclear family and other relatives. Both these types of family have influence on the attitudes of individuals. In fact, when a person starts learning anything about the world, he learns it through his mother which is known as the process of socialization. In this socialization process, he learns and forms attitudes also. Gradually, when the child grows up he comes in contact with others in the family but does not make significant contact with persons outside his family. Family has two important roles. First, other family members have certain personality characteristics, evaluative criteria, and attitudes, and the family as a whole has certain attitudes and values, which are shared by all other persons. Second, family mediates the influence of larger social systems on the individual's attitudes, values, and personality characteristics. As an individual interacts with other family members, he simultaneously both influences the personality characteristics and attitudes of others and in turn is influenced by others. Since a family is a primary group, the attitudes of family members tend to converge and are typically more homogeneous than would be the case if they were not in the family.
2. **Reference Groups:** The awareness and learning of behaviour alternatives is accomplished efficiently through the influence of reference groups. A reference group is any interacting aggregation of people that influences an individual's attitudes of behaviour. This group may include family or other types of groupings, either primary or secondary groups. Reference groups serve important inputs to an individual's learning of his attitudes and awareness of alternative behaviours and lifestyle. This happens through the process of socialization. Socialization, as discussed earlier, is a process by which a new member learns the value system, the norms, and the required behaviour patterns of the society, organizations, or groups in which he is entering. Though all groups with which an individual makes contact have influence on his attitudes, the values and norms of the primary groups play a very important role in influencing attitudes, opinions, and beliefs of the members of the group.
3. **Social Factors:** The social classes have important influence on individual's attitudes. They have the important task of transmitting cultural behaviour patterns to specific groups and families. They define the expectations of society for groups of people and for families within the groups. The family then transits these cultural expectations to the individual. Thus, social classes restrict behaviour between individuals of differing social classes, especially in intimate relationships. People have their close relationships with people of similar classes, which tend to restrict attitude formation in similar patterns of other members. This is so because attitudes and values provide goals, which aid alternative evaluation and provide motivation for research and evaluation. These are transmitted differently among social classes.

22.4.2 Personality Factors

Personality factors are important in attitude formation. However, many personality characteristics themselves are determined by group and social factors, as discussed earlier.

Personality differences between individuals are very important Concomitant of the discussion of attitudes. This area has been the subject of great interest of research and study, particularly with respect to broader area of prejudice and social functioning. Various studies show that there is positive relationship between different personality factors and attitudes. Adrono *et al.* show that there was a coherent pattern of ethnocentric attitudes including anti-semitism among persons having authoritarian personality. The ethnocentric stuck to the straight and narrow, holding conventional values, not being able to accept certain socially unacceptable impulses and, therefore, in the main, projecting these on others.

McClosky has found a relationship between personality correlates of conservatism and liberalism. He found that the conservative attitudes characterized these at the lower end of the intelligence scale with less education and with less awareness of current events. Various other research studies also show positive relationship between personality variables and particular attitudes. Since personality itself is influenced by various group and in understanding attitude formation, these factors, particularly former ones, must be analyzed.

22.5 ATTITUDE MEASUREMENT

The subjective attributes of people are attitude. They can be regarded as constructs in the sense that they are conceptualizations of human qualities that are formed on the basis of either rational consideration of statistical evidence. Thus, people may vary along each of a number of attitudinal dimensions. Keeping this measurement aspect into consideration, the attitude might be defined operationally by describing the measurement systems that psychologists use to measure attitudes. Attitude measurement, developed largely by social psychologists, is concerned with efforts to tap these attitudes as they are characteristics of individual. There are many methods of attitude measurement. In pulling together numerous methods dealing with attitude measurement, Summers uses the following organization which, in effect, is classification of methods of attitude measurement : (i) self-report (usually elicited with, questionnaires dealing with beliefs, feelings, and behaviours) ; (ii) indirect tests (such as projective techniques and disguised approaches); (iii) direct observation techniques; and (iv) psychological reaction techniques.

However, attitude measurement of employees in organizations is most commonly carried out with self-respect questionnaires. Measurement of attitudes based on questionnaires uses several scaling methods. There are three types of attitude scaling which are commonly used in attitude measurement: Thurstone type of scale, Likert scale, and semantic differential. The Thurstone type of scaling goes back to the early work of Thurstone and Chave, who collected a large number of statements relating to the area in which attitudes were to be measured. These statements may be relating to any object about which attitudes are to be measured. The statements are both favourable and unfavourable, and are placed in piles: most favourable statement being placed in pile 1 and the most unfavourable one being placed in pile 11. Other statements are placed in between, their position depending on the degree of favourability or unfavourability. The scale is then presented to the respondents. Each respondent checks the statement with which he agrees. His attitude score is then based either on the average or the median scale of the statements that he has checked.

Soon after Thurstone scale, Likert experimented with certain other varieties of attitude scales. Liker's attitude scale uses five points. The statement relating to the measurement of attitudes is given to the person concerned and he is asked to check one of the five points given for every statement. These points show degree of agreement or disagreement with the given statements. The Likert scale is considered better as compared to Thurstone because of several positive facts. For example, in this scaling, there is not much problem in making numerous statements because for every aspect, only one statement is required which will show both positive and negative degrees.

Seiler and Hough refer to Likert scaling as equally or more reliable than the Thurstone, and faster and equally or more valid. The semantic differential, an attitude scaling technique that lends itself to various applications, was developed by Osgood, Suci, and Tannenbaum. Semantic differential means the successive all vocation of a concept to the point in the multidimensional space by selection from among a set of given scaled semantic alternatives. For any given purpose it consists of several or many pairs of opposite adjectives or phrases, with scale values in between. In using this scale, the respondent marks the position along each scale that reflects his attitude to the attitude object. Scale values (often ranging from 1 to 7) are associated with the different responses and individual's attitude score usually is the sum of these. Apart from these measures of attitudes, certain other scales have also been developed. These include the Guttman technique, the error-choice method, and the sentence completion method.

22.6 ATTITUDE CHANGE IN BEHAVIOUR

There is often a paradox of attitudes in that people need them to provide stability to social world yet world is a changing one and people must change their attitudes appropriate to the situation. The attitude change appropriate to organizational requirement is more important because attitudes affect behaviour and only certain behaviour is desirable from organization point of view.

Organizations adopt a number of techniques for changing attitudes of their members so that their behaviour corresponds with the organizational requirement. However, whatever the techniques for attitudes change are adopted, they can be effective only if basic characteristics of attitudes and their nature are kept inconsideration. Though various theories of attitude formation and change have been presented earlier which help in understanding attitudes and the techniques through which they can be changed, the change techniques can be more effective, if three basic factors (as discussed below) are considered adequately:

1. **Characteristics of Attitudes:** In understanding attitude change, the analysis of attitude characteristics is an important element. Theories attitudes suggest numerous types of their characteristics. Such characteristics may be (i) extremeness of the attitude (ii) multiplexity, (iii) consistency, (iv) interconnectedness, (v) consonance of the attitude cluster .of which the focal attitude is a part, (vi) the number and strength of the needs which are served by the attitude, and (vii) centrality of related values.
2. **Personality of Attitude Holder:** The personality factors of attitude holder are also important in attitude change in the sense that some persons are more pursuable as compared to others. This is so because of personality differences. Such differences change the natural of attitudes because attitudes are subjective qualities. Persuability is the tendency of a person to accept a persuasive communication. It commonly refers to a response to a direct influence attempt.

3. **Group Affiliation:** Individuals often express their attitudes in terms of group. This is more so in the case of less extreme attitudes. This is so because membership in the group prevents existing attitudes from being disturbed by filtering the information. As will be discussed later, one of the powerful bonds which, hold the group together is the fact that members think alike. Information likely to cause dissonance or inconsistency is either omitted or perceived according to group norms with some modification or is rejected or considered irrelevant. Though people are not always exposed to information in the concept or groups and information, which may change their attitudes impinges upon them from many sources, even outside the group, their membership still influences the way the new information is perceived. This is particularly true of primary groups, such as family, friendship group, etc.
4. **Methods of Attitude Change:** Various methods have been adopted for attitude change. Cohen has classified them into four categories: Communication of additional information approval and disapproval of a particular attitude, group influence, and inducing engagement in discrepant behaviour. However, in some way or the other, all these methods involve introducing discrepancies among the elements making up the individual's attitude in the hope that elements win be rebalanced through changing the affective component of the attitude. Thus, in practice, the central variable in attitude change is the feeling comment associated with the attitude object. Thus, from organization's point of view, a manager may take the following actions in bringing out change the attitudes of organizational members. Such a course of action may be in the form of group action, persuasion through leadership, persuasion through communication, and the influence of total situation.

   Several personality factors suggest different types of persuability. First is level of self-esteem of the person. The more inadequate a person feels and the more social inhibitions he has, the more likely is he to be persuable. People with a great deal of confidence in their own intellectual ability are not only more resistant to change but more willing to expose themselves to discrepant information. Related to the personality factors, there is a style of thinking referred to as close minded or dogmatism. Dogmatism is a farm of authoritarianism where there is admiration of those in authority and hatred far those opposed to authority.

   Taking these characteristics of attitudes, there may be two types of attitude change: congruent and incongruent. The congruent change involves an increase in the strength of an existing attitude, either to make a positive attitude even more favourable or to make a negative attitude more strongly negative. An incongruent change is .one in which the direction of change is opposite to the originally held attitude. Congruent change is easier to produce than incongruent one-specially when the attitude held is extreme, central in the attitude system, and interconnected with supporting attitudes. Another characteristic involved in changeability of attitudes is their simplicity. The number of acts involved in the cognition and the number of facts to which it is related makes the attitude simple or complex. It is more likely to produce change in simple attitude than the complex one. The degree of interconnectedness determines the changeability of attitudes.

   There is a strong belief in the cause and a decreasing tendency to admit that other causes might be valid. Dogmatism is a relatively closed system in which the beliefs and disbeliefs are isolated from one another. It tends to be organized around some central authority theme, which must be protected at all costs. In dogmatism, there is high degree of rejection of opposing beliefs, a relatively low level of interconnection among belief systems, and complex cognitions about positively valued objects as against cognitions about negatively valued objects. In such cases attitude change is often resisted. However, personality factors should not be overemphasised in attitude change because the change makes much more sense in the context of total change attempt situation.

Usually, attitudes which are strongly supported by other attitudes are more resistant to change. Similarly, depending on how many social wants support them and the strength of these wants, the attitudes may be more or less changeable. Attitudes which reflect the core or principal component of an individual's personality would most likely be very resistant to change.

22.7 SUMMARY

Attitude is the bent of one's mind toward an object or subject. It involves liking or disliking people, work and objects. Desire is an attitude, which directs people to adopt certain behaviour. Attitude is developed through learning, although the family, society and nation exert great influence in the attitude formation of people. Attitude is a combination of popular belief and interest. For example, the attitude of male workers is that female workers cannot perform hard work. Attitude is learned and expressed, apart from being primarily acquired by people through interaction with members of family and society. Attitude formation is related to the cognitive aspects of behaviour.

22.8 SELF-ASSESSMENT QUESTIONS

1. What is the concept of attitudes? How do attitudes differ from opinions and beliefs? How do attitudes affect behaviour?
2. What are the various theories of attitude formation and change?
3. What are the various factors responsible for attitude formation? How can these factors be controlled?
4. What are the various methods of attitude measurement? How does attitude measurement help the management?
5. What are the various factors, which must be taken into account in attitude change? Discuss some methods for attitude change.

23 LEARNING AND VALUES

Learning Objective

The main objective of this chapter is to understand learning as a factor affecting learning behaviour and to know the reinforcement for inducing positive leanings and values in human behaviour.

23.1 INTRODUCTION

An important tool of individual behaviour in an organization is learning. The learning depends upon one's personality, perception and situation. Its process and outcome are motivating factors in an organization. The learning process is the process by which individuals acquire the knowledge and experience to be applied in future behaviour. It may be intentional and incidental. It encompasses the total learning process from the beginning of life to its end, going through reflexive responses to knowing abstract concepts and complex problem-solving. It involves motivation, cues, response and reinforcement. Motivation acts as a spur to learning. Motivation decides the degree of involvement for the search of knowledge. The learning starts with motivation, which is given direction by cues. Motives are stimuli, while cues are attention and recognition of the stimuli for learning. Cues guide employees to behave in the right way. If behaviour is shaped through the learning process, the response is visible. Response accepted for behaviour becomes reinforcement, which moulds the behaviour of employees. If an employee is motivated to learn about computers, he tries to find out the cues of its uses in employment. Getting favourable cues, he responds to learning. With constant reinforcement of computer operation, he acquires the changed behaviour of computer handling.

23.2 DEFINITION OF LEARNING

Several authors have defined learning in different ways. All of them have accepted that learning shapes human behaviour. Employees may learn knowingly or unknowingly in the organization.

Tim R. V. Davis and Fred Luthans have defined learning as a cognitive and modelling process for acquiring knowledge and experience. They have analyzed different theories of learning for explaining the learning process. Robbins has stressed upon learning as a "relatively permanent change in behaviour that occurs as a result of experience". He has opined on experience only, although an employee might change his behaviour as a result of a social process. Learning is a process of observation, action, reaction and response to some stimuli.

Learning is a process of change in behaviour. The outcome of learning is a permanent change in behaviour. Therefore, learning is a permanent change in behaviour as a result of a cognitive process. A temporary change in behaviour is not learning because it is purely reflexive. Change in behaviour is the necessary outcome of learning. If it were purely theoretical, it would not be learning. A cognitive change process in the mind of an employee resulting in behaviour is learning. "Learning is the process by which an activity originates or is changed by reacting to an encountered situation, provided that the characteristics of the change in activity cannot be explained on the basis of native response tendencies, maturation or temporary states of the organism".

This definition includes almost all the attributes of learning. It reveals that learning is the inferred process, which influences behaviour. The learning is an original activity for the employee. He gets new things or may change his process as a result of observation and cognitive processes. The learning can take place only when the employee reacts to the stimuli, evaluates and accepts the stimuli for changing his behaviour. Learning must be deliberately accepted. It does not include maturity, temporary changes in behaviour and the natural process of behaviour. Behaviour is learned through a cognitive process. It is not a spontaneous and natural process. A child knowing the language of her mother is not learning, because it is a natural process. Children learn good habits and sports on account of their environment, which is a stimulus of learning. The learning process starts with motives and continues with cues, responses and reinforcements until the learner acquires the required changes in behaviour permanently. Learning to drive a car is a good example of a learning process.

The learning process is a mental and habit formation process. Attention is paid to certain stimuli used for learning, which are recognized and translated into reinforcement and behaviour. If the learner gets a reward for his improved behaviour, he forms it into behaviour. Proper habits motivate the employee who makes efforts in the right direction. The efforts result in satisfaction and become a stimulus for further learning. The employee pays further attention, recognizes and translates stimuli to strengthen habits. This process continues and the employee learns and effects permanent changes in his behaviour, which become a part of his habits. The habit helps in recognition of good behaviour. A habit motivates an employee to perform better. It helps him pay proper attention. He learns constantly and effects a permanent change in behaviour. Learning improves behaviour. This process continues and the employee learns in the process.

23.3 PROCESS OF LEARNING

1. **Stimuli:** Stimuli are any objects and language, which draw the attention of people. Employees get stimuli from the actions of their superiors. Superiors tell and advice employees who pay attention to these stimuli. All the stimuli may not be fully attended to. Literary works are also stimuli, which are given attention by educated employees. Stimuli

are provided at jobs by perks and scores. Universities and colleges also impart stimuli for learning. Stimuli provide quality performances. Practical training and vocational teaching are forceful stimuli. The stimuli available at work are numerous. Social, political, cultural and geographical factors provide varieties of stimuli for learning.

2. **Attention:** The degree of attention depends upon the nature of stimuli. Technical and interesting stimuli are highly attended. Employees generally accept career-oriented stimuli. The personality levels of employees influence their desires to learn, motives for need fulfilment and tension reduction. Employees having more values of life pay more attention to the stimuli for acquiring more knowledge and experience. People's creative attitudes are favourable factors for learning and paying more attention to available stimuli.
3. **Recognition:** Attention-paid stimuli are recognized as acceptable factors of improvement and new lifestyles. Employees paying attention to stimuli are recognizing the stimuli for learning purposes. The levels of recognition depend upon the levels of values, preferences, needs and desires of the employees. When objectives are unclear, employees do not pay attention and do not recognize the training as a fruitful process of improvement. In the learning process, employees as useful factors for their well-being and satisfaction must observe unambiguous activities for recognition.
4. **Translation:** Recognized stimuli are evaluated at the mental level to eliminate the irrelevant points for accepting a part of the stimulus for changing behaviour. The evaluation and appraisal of the recognized stimuli helps in reinforcement. An activity will not take place unless it is found useful by employees. The translation and evaluation process is a crucial point for implementing the stimuli in behaviour through reinforcement. Employees behave properly through attitude changes, objectivity, mental and physical development. It is observed in better performances.
5. **Reinforcement:** Reinforced perception is learning. The perception process includes stimuli, attention, recognition, translation and behaviour. Perception leads to learning, but perception itself is not learning unless it is reinforced. Repeated action is reinforcement. Reinforcement may be positive, negative, punishment and extinction. Learners learn as per their perception levels. Generally, positive reinforcement is more effective for making permanent changes in behaviour.
6. **Behaviour:** Learning changes behaviour through reinforcement of perceived knowledge. It makes permanent changes in behaviour. A temporary change in behaviour is not learning. Positive behaviour gives rewards to employees.
7. **Reward:** Employees expect rewards for learning. If the translated behaviour provides a reward, it is accepted, otherwise it is not accepted. Employees develop their behaviour into habits. Rewards may be monetary or non-monetary. A non-monetary reward includes job satisfaction, status recognition and task achievement. Professional satisfaction is attached to the behaviour, which influences the form of reward. The behaviour of employees decides the level and form of reward. The reward reinforcement makes employees learn more than positive reinforcement behaviour.
8. **Habits:** A permanent change in behaviour becomes a habit, which helps continuous improvement in behaviour and performance. Employees develop the habit of self-appraisal and development. It helps to inspire creativity and confidence in employees who are

encouraged to behave properly again and again. Right behaviour is reinforced repeatedly. Habits help the development of capability and capacity of employees. Habits translate theoretical knowledge into practice. Skill development requires habitual performance.

9. **Motives:** Motives depend on the level of satisfaction. Employees getting more satisfaction through learning develop high motives. Less satisfied learners have low motives. Learning is complete only when motives are fully realized and translated into efforts.
10. **Efforts:** Habits help achieve good efforts and performance. This is a continuous process. Efforts are the automatic outcome of good habits, which are acquired through the learning process. Self-development is possible through self-effort. Employees willing to develop themselves are self-motivated and effort-oriented. Efforts become the stimuli for learning after development of the standard of employees. Self-learning has been observed when employees have developed good habits and right motives. The learning process itself provides all these opportunities.

The learning process is totally associated with the mental process, inspiration and action. Stimuli reach only the unconscious mind. If it pays attention to stimuli it goes to the inner-level of the mind at subconscious level. Attention is paid by the subconscious mind, which analyses the stimuli and filters out irrelevant stimuli from the employees' angle. The relevant stimuli are attended to, but a smaller portion of the stimuli attended is recognized by the clear mind.

Recognition of stimuli is done only by the clear mind. The stimuli recognized further go to the inner part of the mind only when the clear mind has received them and the feeling cell of the mind evaluates their utilities. A felt mind has the capacity to evaluate and appraise the recognized stimuli. The evaluated stimuli if found correct are stored at the level of the feeling cell of the mind. The stored stimuli or retention works for mobilizing the function through reinforcement. Repeat and recall are mobilizing factors for action. Similarly, a tense mind gets reinforcement; it compels and forces the heart to activate the body for action and behaviour. Intensity at the mental level activates the heart to function. The level, quality and direction of intensity give the behavioural function a real shape.

Behaviour is the outcome of intensified stimuli. Behaviour producing reward helps the mental process to think and rethink again and again at all the five levels of the mind. The reward itself becomes a stimulus, which is attended, recognized, translated and reinforced respectively by the unconscious, subconscious, clear, felt and intense mind. It reaches to the heart level, and consequently this process develops into a habit. Permanent changes in behaviour converge in the form of a habit.

23.4 MODELS OF LEARNING

Theories of learning have been developed as models of learning which explain the learning process by which employees acquire a pattern of behaviour. Inborn ability and aptitude to learn new skills and the degree to which the learner participates in the process are considered under models of learning. Some models believe that individuals cannot learn independently. They require the help of experts and personal involvement in the learning process. Other theories believe that employees can learn by observation. Their drive and motives are helpful for the learning process.

No one can learn unless they are willing to learn. Employers have to provide adequate opportunities and incentives to employees so that they can get drives for the learning purpose. It is also believed by some theorists that learning is a stimulus–response process.

Stimuli are essential for the learning purpose. The stimuli provide understanding and insights to the employees. The learning process helps further learning. Previous learning helps further learning. For example, learning of language and mathematics helps in the learning of higher education. Learning is a constant process, which provides reinforcement to employees to avoid forgetfulness and take up learned behaviour. The basic purpose of any theory is to explain a phenomenon in a better manner so that a learner can acquire it easily and permanently. A perfect theory explains how, when, why and other aspects of learning. Although, there is no perfect and universal model of learning, theorists have devised models of learning under classical, operant and social.

23.4.1 Classical Model of Learning

The classical model of learning developed with experience of the material process accompanied with learning stimuli. Pavlov propounded this model. In Indian mythology, some examples have been observed where the learner took the assistance of natural phenomena to make a pupil learn a new process of functions. Ivan Pavlov, a Russian physiologist, observed that a dog started secreting saliva with the ringing of a bell, as the ringing of the bell was accompanied by the showing a piece of meat to the dog. It is a natural phenomenon that a dog secretes saliva when meat is put before the mouth of dog. If the natural phenomenon known as unconditioned stimulus is accompanied by an artificial phenomenon known as conditioned stimulus, the dog generated a conditioned response ultimately, as the process was repeated constantly. The unconditioned response, i.e., the secreting response, becomes a conditioned response after sometime as the dog learnt that the ringing of a bell meant the availability of meat.

The classical model of learning believes that the unconditioned and conditioned stimuli would be repeated several times to get the net result of a conditioned stimulus which would be a conditioned response. In the Pavlov theory, the dog learnt to secrete saliva (conditioned response) at the ringing of a bell (conditioned stimulus), after repeatedly performing the functions of unconditioned stimulus (showing meat) and conditioned stimulus (ringing bell) simultaneously. Later on, the unconditioned stimulus was separated from the conditioned stimulus to get a conditioned response. Employees can be conditioned accordingly. The conditioned stimulus may be changed to get the result of second or third conditioned stimulus. Employees can learn the new conditioned stimuli if they are repeatedly given new stimuli along with the old unconditioned stimulus. The monetary incentives are generally accepted as the unconditioned stimuli for motivating employees. If these stimuli are accompanied with non-monetary incentives for some period, employees learn to work hard with non-monetary incentives. People have a natural liking for dance, drama, exhibitions, etc., which can be used for getting conditioned response from them. Learning while you work in the factory provides conditioned response to the employees. Reinforcement of the unconditioned stimulus and conditioned stimulus is needed to get a conditioned response. Conditioned stimuli with reinforcement help in learning. Reinforcement makes the conditioned stimulus behave as an unconditioned stimulus to get its natural response.

Classical conditioning is passive and creates reflexive behaviour. It is elicited. It is a natural process, which may be useful in the primitive stage of an employee's knowledge. An advanced employee may not get the benefit of classical conditioning, which is purely a formation of a Stimulus - Response link habit. Repeated pairing of a conditioned stimulus with an unconditioned stimulus would result in a conditioned response. Learning car driving is based on stimuli-response (S-R) behaviour where the driver is immediately alerted to a response as he confronts a boy in front of his running car, i.e., conditioned stimulus. Initially, he starts with unconditioned (natural) stimuli and later on he develops conditioned (artificial) stimuli. In Indian industries, classical conditioning is an important method of learning when employees start with certain natural phenomena along with an artificial work style to arrive at new methods of working.

23.4.2 Operant Model of Learning

The operant or instrumental model of learning is a developed form of classical learning, i.e., the S-R link habit. Employees behave in a particular manner because they would like to get a reward (Response). Reward or the desired results acquire certain behaviour traits. Reward creates drives and motives to acquire certain behaviour amongst employees. B.F. Skinner, a Harvard psychologist, propagated operant learning. He argues that behaviour increases and develops to acquire certain benefits. The desired behaviour is the outcome of acquired benefit or reward. Employees do not accept behaviour, which is not rewarded. The reinforcement of behaviour is contingent upon the reward.

Employees work hard to get additional benefits. The learning process starts with the reward or response. Learned employees for the sake of customer satisfaction, employee productivity and shareholder wealth improve corporate functions. The learning takes place for the said responses. The classical conditioning has the stimulus as the beginning of learning, whereas operant learning starts with the response, which becomes a stimulus for the learning process. The reward develops habits, motives and efforts for providing them with stimuli for learning. The employees pay more attention, recognize properly and translate their recognition into behaviour. It is a clear fact that learning starts with reward and performance satisfaction. People do not like to learn a process, which is not rewarded. Behaviour is improved through learning for rewards and benefits. In the absence of a reward and response, behaviour is not shaped, and the learning process does not take place or continue in the future. The environment of the factory becomes a stimulus for leaning. It is the reverse of classical learning where the stimulus provides the response. The reward or response itself becomes a source of drive and motivating factors. The drive can be developed by a variety of responses or events. The drive helps to develop the habit of learning for achievement. The habit is developed or learned through motives, which improve the efforts of the employees. Efforts provide satisfaction because they feel happy while performing a job. Effort encourages and becomes a stimulus for learning. More attention is paid to job content and context, because it has been recognized as a source of reward.

Translation and reinforcement help behaviour, which assures reward. A particular behaviour is learnt to get a given reward. Reinforcement strengthens behaviour, which in turn is aimed at acquiring the reward, which drives habit and motivates efforts for a proper performance. Motives lead to behaviour, which is satisfying. It is a known law of effect that reward strengthens habits because of lessening drive. It is R-S link behaviour, which becomes a habit if rewarded. Reinforcement has become an important factor to shape stimuli into behaviour. Reinforcement may be positive or negative. Positive reinforcement assures reward, whereas, negative reinforcement avoids unpleasant conditions. Employees are alerted to avoid unpleasant happenings through learning.

For example, proper operation of machines is needed to avoid accidents or casualties. Negative reinforcement, i.e., avoidance of unpleasant events is useful for learning the proper handling of electric appliances and machines. The positive and negative reinforcement change behaviour, which if rewarded becomes a habit. Punishment and extinction are not part of the process of learning. They are used to avoid unpleasant behaviour. Modem theorists do not believe in punishment and extinction because they may be averse to the learning process. On the contrary, reward and response are taken for learning. The larger the reward, the larger will be the reinforcement and stimulus to learn. To change the desired behaviour into habit, reward is an inevitable point and conversion factor.

The classical learning process lays emphasis on changing unconditioned stimuli to conditioned stimuli. If the conditioned stimulus has been acquired through the process of pairing with unconditioned stimulus, learning is acquired, as it will give a conditioned response. Operant learning emphasizes response, which stimulates learning by changing the present behaviour into the required behaviour. The S-R connection in classical learning is changed to the R-S connection in operant learning. The reward or response need not be financial. It may be non-financial and psychologically satisfying to the employees. The classical theory believes that employees will fulfill their basic and other needs if they work hard or in a learned manner. On contrary, the operant learning theory emphasises that the required learning and behaviour is adopted for getting basic and other needs. A manager works for getting social recognition. He learns to manage efficiently to gain recognition. He learns to manage efficiently to gain recognition and fame. Scientific research and technological development is related to operant learning.

23.4.3 Social Learning Model

Employees learn from their surroundings, peers, parents, teachers and other people. They learn socially by observation, and the importance of the perception process has been recognized under the social learning model. Stimuli, attention, retention, reproduction and reinforcement have been accepted as basic components of social learning. Employees pay attention to several social stimuli, which occur in their surroundings. They do not pay attention to all stimuli, but pay attention to only those stimuli, which are attractive, easy to recognize, important and useful. The attended stimuli are recognised and translated by employees. The learning level depends upon how much the recognized stimuli are retained in the mind of employees. The retention process is helpful for storing information. Stimuli, which are translated as useful and satisfactory, must be retained for reproduction and recall purposes. The recall provides reinforcement and behaviour. If rewards are provided, the behaviour will become a habit. The learning process is completed when employees show changes in behaviour, which becomes a habit, i.e., permanent change in behaviour. Social learning has become a more useful process of learning because it goes beyond the process of classical operant learning by recognizing the fact that there are more points and subjects of learning than the antecedent stimuli of classical and contingent consequences of operant learning. Social learning refers to the learning process through vicarious process, modelling and self-control.

Social learning includes the vicarious process, which is useful for learning, which involves observational learning. Millar and Bollard propounded the vicarious process wherein they believe that learning can take place through imitation process. Social learning includes the socialization process. It refers to learning through social action, reaction and interaction. The language, customs, functions and performances are the outcome of social, cultural and political phenomena. Culture and religion are accepted for teaching the new generation about life style and behavioural patterns in society. People observe others and acquire a mental picture of the act and its consequences, which may be reward and punishment. If the consequences are positive and satisfactory as per social norms, people like to imitate and perform with repetition. If people find that the consequences are negative and full of problems, the imitated acts will be rejected. It is not a discrete performance with discrete response consequences. Operant learning is discrete response stimuli whereas social learning is a continuous response stimuli connection.

Modelling is effectively applied for shaping behaviour. It is used for the improvement of human behaviour. The behaviour leads to performance improvement. It is capable of meeting the technical skill requirements. A favourable environment increases the probability of attention and retention. Role-playing and demonstration is modelled on the target behaviour. The behaviour is acquired as a result of the modelled process of existing behaviour. Continuous intermittent factors help develop behaviour. Modelling procedures have a favourable impact on behaviour and habits.

23.5 REINFORCEMENT

Reinforcement is the crucial factor in the learning process. This is also known as the method of shaping employees' behaviour. Perception becomes learning only through reinforcement.

Perception = Stimuli → Attention → Recognition → Translation

Behaviour Learning = Stimuli → Attention → Recognition → Translation Reinforcement Behaviour → Habit

Reinforcement is the repeated use of the translated stimuli to induce new behaviour. It increases the strength of response and induces repetitions of the response, which is the outcome of the translated and evaluated stimuli. When reward is attached to behaviour, it becomes a habit. Reinforcement increases the possibility of specific responses occurring in future as a result of evaluated stimuli or uses.

Learning = Input → Process → Output
= Stimuli → Reinforcement → Behaviour

Reinforcement is (he instrument or process of learning in all the models discussed already. No stimuli can take the shape of behaviour unless reinforcement or repetition takes place during the learning process. A learner of car driving learns until such time it becomes a part of the total habits of the learner. The behaviour, i.e., learning car driving becomes a habit because the learner gets rewarded for his behaviour in the form of the satisfaction of car driving. Reinforcement is the repeated exposure of knowledge for translation into practice and habit. New behaviour or change in behaviour is the output of learning, which is the outcome of stimuli input through reinforcement. Classical, operant and social learning models lay emphasis on reinforcement. Reinforcement is another term for conditioning. The stimuli, response and social activities are conditioned to arrive at a new behaviour or change in behaviour. Behaviourists have proposed conditioning of employees for proper behaviour. Repetition, adherence, stimulus, generalization or discrimination, converting theory into practice is various forms of reinforcement.

A habit is formed through repeated rewards attached to behaviour. While conditioning explains how employees learn from cues or stimuli, operant (instrumental) conditioning refers to response or goal directed activities. Social conditioning is concerned with social recognition and acceptability. Employees learn in this case through modelling various observation or self-understanding. Reinforcement is a cognitive process. The stimuli are translated into habit through an effective, cognitive and behaviour process. Reinforcement, being cognitive in nature, is environmentally based. The law of effect is used in reinforcement for getting the reward. Goal-oriented reinforcement is long lasting and increases the strength of response.

23.6 TYPES OF REINFORCEMENT

Reinforcement may either be positive and negative, extrinsic and intrinsic, primary and secondary, and in the form of punishment and extinction. It is used to shape the behaviour of employees. Systematical reinforcement of successive steps will move employees closer to the desired response. They reinforce improvement in their behaviour.

1. **Positive and Negative Reinforcement:** Positive reinforcement consists of events that assure achievement of a specific response or the desired behaviour. Getting technical skills assures the desired result of reward, and the changing of behaviour into a permanent habit of technical performance, when response is pleasant as a result of the repetitive efforts of employees, is called as positive reinforcement. It means that positive reinforcement assures desired consequences and pleasant achievements through strengthening of the present behaviour or presenting new behaviour. Positive reinforcement strengthens behaviour for pleasant performance and reward. It is the presentation of attractive results. Negative reinforcement does not give an unpleasant response, but avoids an unpleasant response. Negative reinforcement is the termination or withdrawal of an unpleasant and undesirable result. It helps employees escape from aversive or disagreeable conditions.

   Negative reinforcement is the termination of unattractive results. It is not punishment because punishment discourages behaviour, and negative reinforcement avoids unpleasant or disagreeable behaviour. Appreciation of an employee, who is successful in performing a task if constantly repeated, will be positive reinforcement. Repeatedly warning employees against the careless handling of electrical machines would be negative reinforcement as it attempts to avoid accidents. Negative reinforcement strengthens and increases a particular type of behaviour, as the employees learn how to avoid and prevent accidents while operating electric machines. The withdrawal or avoidance will result in a specific kind of behaviour. Negative reinforcement is not punishment because the latter decreases and discourages behaviour, while the former increases and strengthens behaviour to avoid something undesirable. If an employee does not bother about undesirable results and handles the electric machine carelessly, he will face punishment by his supervisor or meet with an accident. In both the cases, behaviour decreases. If the employees do not follow negative reinforcement, they are punished. Employees learn to escape and avoid unpleasant jobs. They may avoid punishment by being alert enough to avoid undesirable events. For example, employees are not very active and good performers when the supervisor is not present in the factory. If a supervisor comes at a particular time, the employees become active before his entry into the factory. It is a negative reinforcement that employees avoid unpleasant rewards in the presence of the supervisor by non-working and being non-active. If employees do not bother about the supervisor and do not exercise negative reinforcement, i.e., avoiding inaction, they will be punished by the supervisor for non-working and for their laxness. Negative reinforcement simply avoids unpleasant tasks, but it does not assure a pleasant performance for which positive reinforcement is essential in the organization.

2. **Extrinsic and Intrinsic Enforcement:** The employees to learn a particular type of behaviour externally use extrinsic reinforcement. The environment in the factory helps exercise extrinsic reinforcement. The employee is influenced by external cues and stimuli. The relationship between the supervisor and employees, monetary incentives and favourable work conditions are several examples of external reinforcement. The behaviour of and instructions by peers and seers are used for moulding the behaviour of the employees. Extrinsic reinforcement is external and has other activities influencing the learning process as reinforcement. Intrinsic reinforcement is internal and uses self-reinforcement. When the employee develops his own understanding of the problem, it is self-reinforcement. Intrinsic reinforcement is self-realization and improvement of behaviour. Feelings and motives become intrinsic reinforcement. Intrinsic reinforcement is considered a more forceful process of learning. Extrinsic reinforcement will not be effective unless intrinsic reinforcement is applied for learning. It is self-appraisal and development. Extrinsic reinforcement is evaluated by employees and, if accepted as useful, will be converted into intrinsic reinforcement. Extrinsic and intrinsic reinforcement are used for learning purposes. Intrinsic reinforcement is personal and relates to satisfaction, recognition, challenges, growth and responsibilities.

   Extrinsic reinforcement is ultimately evaluated at the level of intrinsic reinforcement. The success of reinforcement depends on how much it influences the internal drive of the employees. In extrinsic reinforcement, for example, monetary incentives would be ineffective if it is not internally accepted as the drive for learning and improvement in behaviour.

3. **Primary and Secondary Reinforcement:** Primary reinforcement directly influences primary motivational drives. It is related to the primary needs of people. The employees are reinforced to learn by adopting primary functions or basic needs. Children learnt languages and mathematics through primary reinforcement. For example, they are told that A is Apple, B is Banana because they are used to the words apple and banana. Therefore, the first letter of these fruits will help them understand the letters. The example of fruits is the primary reinforcement. Primary reinforcement is mainly observed in classical learning wherein the artificial reinforcement is accompanied with the natural or primary reinforcement to make a long-lasting impact of artificial reinforcement.

   The secondary reinforcement is closely related to the operant learning, wherein the rewards are taken as the drives and motives for learning. Secondary reinforcements are artificial and new in their characters. They are first introduced to the learner for adoption in their learning process. Technical education first introduces the machine and its components before detailing its operation. Secondary reinforcements have become significant for understanding complex human behaviour. This reinforcement is used for motivation and modifying behaviour.

4. **Punishment and Extinction:** Punishment is also a method of learning, although it is very crude and undesirable. It is generally used to make the employees learn a particular type of behaviour. However, it is the least accepted aspect of learning. Supervisors use punishment to modify the behaviour of employees. Punishment is not a well-thought reinforcement. It is the reverse of reinforcement for altering behaviour. Punishment is used in an illiterate society to learn behaviour. Indian workplaces generally use punishment for mending the behaviour of employees, although it is the reverse of reinforcement and learning. There is no shortage of examples where employees learn to attend work in time and perform correctly because of fear of punishment. Fear psychosis is helpful to the learning process. It is a complex and cumbersome method of learning, and cannot be used as an effective reinforcement. On the contrary, punishment decreases reinforcement and consequently the learning process and results. It weakens behaviour and ultimately decreases productivity. Punishment is the appreciation of an undesirable process or the facing of noxious consequences. It is designed to discourage a particular type of behaviour. It creates unpleasant conditions to eliminate undesirable behaviour. Negative reinforcement presents pleasant conditions to avoid unpleasant consequences. Punishment is an unpleasant condition to prevent undesirable behaviour. Punishment focuses on unpleasant reinforcement and undesirable behaviour. Punishment does not contribute to learning the desired response. On the other hand, it creates an undesirable atmosphere and discourages learning for favourable results. Only positive and negative reinforcements help in learning and getting a favourable outcome. Extinction is the withdrawal of desirable consequences and is contingent upon employee's behaviour. The withdrawal of desirable consequences occurs after behaviour has taken place. In this process, neither reward nor punishment follows undesirable behaviour. Ignoring undesirable behaviour is extinction.

   For example, if an employee misbehaves with his colleagues, the supervisor ignores his behaviour. Ignoring this behaviour will extinguish undesirable behaviour. When learned response is not reinforced, it is extinction. The behaviour fades with the neglect of response. Eliminating any reinforcement for maintaining behaviour is called extinction. Punishment and extinction are not true learning processes as there is no effective reinforcement for the learning process. Learning is expected through undesirable stimuli and reinforcement, or avoiding both stimuli and reinforcement to check undesirable behaviour. Positive and negative reinforcement help learning because they provide favourable behaviour and avoid non-favourable behaviour.

23.7 TECHNIQUES OF REINFORCEMENT

Reinforcement plays a crucial role in human resources management such as learning, training, improvement, development and modification. It increases the strength of desired behaviour. Employees are psychologically treatment through reinforcement for delivering good results. If rewards are attached to behaviour, employees develop reinforcement into habits. The pattern and timing of reinforcement are important factors to determine the results of reinforcement. Some type of reinforcement is essential to produce change in behaviour and result in the effective performance of the organization. However, the speed, place and timing of reinforcement have much bearing on behaviour change.

23.7.1 Schedules of Reinforcement

The schedule of reinforcement should be properly decided for getting the full result of learning. The schedule of reinforcement may be continuous or intermittent. Intermittent is further classified on interval and ratio basis into fixed and variable.

1. **Continuous schedule:** A continuous schedule incorporates each and every item of learning in a systematic order. It reinforces the accepted stimuli to get the desired behaviour. Learners get stimuli and cues repeatedly till they learn the desired behaviour. Continuous reinforcement assures a specific habit. The machine operators are continuously told to operate the machine. They are first given a theoretical perception before putting this into practical usage. They operate the machine in the presence of the supervisor who constantly describes the use of each and every part of the machine till they learn how to operate the machine effectively.
2. **Intermittent schedule:** An intermittent schedule does not include demonstration of each and every item of learning as in the case of the continuous schedule. Reinforcement is given after a gap to make the learner repeat himself during the learning process. Intermittent reinforcement provides more opportunities to learn because the learner applies his mind during the interval of not getting instruction. It promotes more resistance to extinction. Desired behaviour is observed easily through reinforcement repeated after a gap and not every time. It is clarified with a simple example of a machine operator in the factory. When the foreman continuously attends the learning of operation process to make the learners conversant with each and every point of his demonstration, the learners are dependent on the trainer and may not apply their minds during performance. However, in the case of intermittent reinforcement, the foreman comes after a certain time and explains whatever is not clear to the employees. He is not present continuously. In this case, the learner applies his mind and tries to think clearly when the trainer is absent, because the trainer will not be present always to solve all his problems. The trainer comes after a gap of time. The time interval depends on the number of employees engaged in learning and the nature of learning. Within the time interval, employees repeat the reinforcement given by the trainer when he has left after instruction. The gap between the first instruction and the second instruction makes the employees learn the behaviour demonstrated in the first instruction. The intermittent schedule helps in the modification of behaviour and the extinction of unfavourable behaviour. The discontinued and discrete schedule helps understand the work profoundly. Reinforcement after a gap recalls previous good behaviour and avoids non-desirable behaviour. Behaviour becomes resistant to extinction. Intermittent reinforcement may be based on an internal ratio.
3. **Interval schedule:** Reinforcement is done with a uniform time interval. The critical variable is time, which may be fixed or variable.

4. **Fixed interval schedule:** A fixed interval schedule has a constant variable. The learner attends to the learning process at fixed intervals of a week, fortnight, month or year. Reinforcement is given after a specified period of time. The time interval is fixed for a particular learning process. Since there are different learning processes, the fixed interval varies from one job to another. At the beginning of learning, a short interval is desirable which may extend further at a later stage of learning. Monetary reinforcement is generally at fixed intervals. The time interval is fixed after research to make the interval an effective and useful learning process. Too long or too short an interval may hamper the learning process and consequently the results or response of reinforcement.
5. **Variable interval:** The time schedule is not fixed. The learner is unaware as to when he will get the reinforcement. The supervisor has told the employees to work seriously. If anyone is found inactive at any time, he may be punished. The supervisor reinforces his decision at random or at any time not known to the employees. Reinforcement is given in an irregular or unsystematic manner. Unlike fixed interval intermittent reinforcement, the time of reinforcement is not known or certain in case of the variable interval. It makes employees aware of their functions and disciplines all the time, to avoid any punishment during a random visit by the supervisor. In the case of the fixed interval, the employees are aware of the time of the supervisor's visit, and so try to be alert only at that time. At any other time, they are inactive and careless. A variable interval having uncertainty of reinforcement becomes more effective and useful.
6. **Fixed ratio schedule:** The difference between interval and ratio is that the critical value is time in the former case and the number of responses in the latter. The reinforcement is initiated after getting a fixed number of responses. For example, reinforcement is fixed after twenty responses. Rewards attached to the output also follow a case fixed ratio schedule. The response of wage is linked to the reinforcement of output. Reinforcement is given after a certain number of responses. If the reward is paid with the response, employees try to have a larger number of responses to get the reward. Bonus linked with productivity is a very good example of fixed ratio reinforcement.
7. **Variable ratio schedule:** Reinforcement varies with the response and is not in a fixed ratio. Reward varies from individual to individual in case of the variable ratio schedule. Reinforcement is not fixed to the number of stimuli. It varies from individual to individual, depending upon their levels of personality. Fixed ratio reinforcement may produce different responses because of different levels of understanding of employees. Variable reinforcements based on different levels of personality are expected to produce almost similar responses. The fixed and variable interval as well as fixed and variable ratio provides opportunities for modification and development of behaviour. Any schedule of reinforcement is not foolproof. Every reinforcement has its advantages and disadvantages. Therefore, considering the environment and level of employees, reinforcement schedule will be selected. Continuous reinforcement is useful for newly appointed employees with unstable and low frequency responses. It provides early satisfaction, but fades with the withdrawal of reinforcement. Intermittent reinforcement is effective with stable and high frequency responses. A variable schedule gives better results and high performances than the fixed schedule. A variable interval schedule provides opportunities for high responses

and more stable and consistent behaviour because of the uncertainty involved. Employees tend to behave sincerely because an element of surprise is involved in variable schedule.

23.8 VALUES

Employees have certain values in life. They view life from different angles which are reflected in their work performance. Learning helps them to develop high values towards their jobs and the organization. Values refer to the basic convictions, which lead to formation of conduct or social preferences. Values are a combination of different attitudes and attributes of individuals. They help employees decide what is right, good, desirable, and favourable, and so on. One value may be useful for a person, but may not be effective for others. The intensity attributes or value system has relative importance. Values are a code of conduct developed by an individual and the social system. Honesty, self-respect, equality, sincerity, obedience, truthfulness, etc. are various examples of values. Values are significant in organizational behaviour. Employees behave properly if they give importance to values. Learning may help provide opportunities for development of values. Employees would be aware of what ought to be done or what ought not to be done by giving importance to values.

Behaviour is modified only if people are aware of right or wrong things, which are the deciding components of values. Learning aims to develop values so that employees can perform and behave properly. Values influence objectives too, because values shape the attitude and behaviour of employees. For example, obedient employees perform efficiently without creating any problems for the management. Disciplined employees feel directed towards objectives, and learning helps employees develop high values and favourable behaviour.

23.8.1 Sources of Values

People develop values from different sources, e.g., parents, friends, teachers, society, religion, workplace and national characteristics. Parents are the initiators of values. Mother and father always tell us what is right or what is wrong. They ask their children to do right things and avoid wrong things. Every family has certain values, which are inculcated in the children. Brothers and sisters play significant roles in developing values. Parental guidance paves the value systems on which children develop their attitude and behaviour. That is why, it is said that children of a good family will be good and hard workers. Children in their attitudes and behaviour incorporate parent's talk about society, friends, nations and work values, and these values. Friends influence each other to resort to particular behaviour. Good company helps develop good values. Teachers teach several good values to be adopted by students. Teachers are real instructors of value to learners. Society has a great impact on shaping the inter-behaviour of people, which provides value formation. Club members encourage (Different values depending upon their respective characters. Values are learnt and developed through religious factors. God, universe, fortune and suffering are attached to value application in behaviour. For example, righteous behaviour pleases god and vice versa. A pleased god showers fortune and a displeased god give suffering, as per several examples of religious and cultural beliefs. Indian society believes that good values are related to godly pleasure, which give satisfaction to people. Workplaces teach honesty, responsibility, diligence, endurance, and so on. People should be honest and responsible while performing a job. Good values have become strong forces for good behaviour whereas bad values destroy social and economic ties. Misery, suffering and dissatisfaction are associated with bad values. Good values give satisfaction as they help one to perform better. National characters have a great impact on the values exercised by the people. Warring nations have been developing warring and fighting values as real factors for satisfaction. Peace-loving nations develop peace values in people. Based on different sources of value formation, values are different. Learning strengthens good values and avoids bad values through positive and negative reinforcements respectively. The social learning process helps in developing various types of values.

23.8.2 Types of Values

Values may be of different types, depending upon their sources of formation, namely, family values, economic values, social values, religious values and national values. Family values preach methods of living in a family. The behaviour of family members with each other depends on the values developed. For example, the relationship between parents and children, brother and sister, and so on have certain behavioural values. A father will treat his children affectionately. Similarly, children are expected to honour and respect their parents. There are different family values, which are bases of satisfaction and happiness in the family. Economic values give importance to money, financial resources and property formation. If an employee is unable to develop himself and his family, he has not given due importance to economic values. In the modern age, people recognise economic values more than other values. Economic well being is considered a symbol of status and satisfaction. Social values refer to the methods of behaviour in society. Social recognition and social satisfaction are related to social values. If a friend helps other friends, he values friendship and selflessness. Religious values are often observed in India where large sections of the people are governed by religious values and acceptances. Religious leaders shape lives of people through the preaching of religious values such as having faith in god, non-interference in others' lives, job fulfilment, being active, non-attachment, etc. The aim of life is told to them and this incorporates several relevant values to shape the behaviour of people. It is also referred to as a terminal value. People practice instrumental values for the development of family and society. Values at the workplace are covered under economic values, whereas values of behaviour accepted in the organization are known as instrumental values. For achieving satisfaction, national values are preached by national leaders. Mahatma Gandhi preached some significant values to the people of the nation. Truth and non-violence were the two important values preached by him. Different values are attached to particular generations. The modern generation below the age of 30 is freer, leisure-minded, and flexible, and so on. Learning programmes should be designed in such a way that the employees can develop high values for corporate development and their satisfaction as well. Instrumental values of honesty, responsibility, ambition, courage and independence may achieve the terminal values of self-respect, security, accomplishment, happiness and self-satisfaction. Older people are conservative, loyal and quality-oriented whereas the younger generation is flexible, leisure liking and believes in building up relations. Good values are to be explored, initiated and developed for the modification of performance behaviour in an organization. Learning has a great role to play in achieving this objective.

23.9 SUMMARY

Learning is a self-development process. People are interested in self-development. Self-analysis, appraisal and improvement help to learn and acquire the required behaviour. Reinforcement has a major role in the learning process. Further, the human species, unlike animal possess an extremely high proportion of unused mental capacity at birth. Human being has very few instincts or innate response tendencies relative to lower animals. While this may be detrimental to man in the sense that he is helpless for a long period in his early years, it is favourable in the sense that he has greater capacity for adaptation in response to changed survival conditions. This is because of his learning capacity. As such, learning becomes an important concept in the study of human behaviour.

23.10 SELF-ASSESSMENT QUESTIONS

1. What is reinforcement? Discuss its use in organization.
2. Explain the importance of values and reinforcement for learning process.
3. Discuss the nature of classical conditioning and operant conditioning. What are the differences between these?
4. Discuss the learning process in an organization.
5. Analyze the role of learning theory for understanding human behaviour.

24

EMOTIONAL INTELLIGENCE AND BEHAVIOUR

Learning Objective

The main objective of this chapter is to give awareness to the students about emotions, their types and emotional intelligence.

24.1 INTRODUCTION

The world is changing rapidly but the changes of the recent past have been unprecedented in the history of human civilization. The advent of information technology and satellite television has revolutionized the entire world leaving the business world no exception. Due to the globalization process more firms have started moving out from their domestic to international markets. This phenomenon of internationalization has not only led to the products being flown out the national boundaries but also the workforce got intermingled in the world business map. These cross-cultural interactions have changed the mindset of people in general and the younger ones in particular. This phenomenal revolution has led to multifarious changes in the business making the task of business managers more complicated in attaining the managerial effectiveness, Managerial effectiveness which is the ability of a manager in making his best contribution towards the organizational goals and objectives seem to be possible through emotional intelligence.

24.2 EMOTIONS

There are so many terms, which are interrelated. Therefore, we need to clarify these terms: affect, emotions, and moods.

Affect is a generic term that covers a broad range of feelings that people experience. It's an umbrella concept that encompasses both emotions and moods.

Emotions are intense feelings that are directed at someone or something.

Finally, **moods** are feelings that tend to be less intense than emotions and that lack a contextual stimulus. Emotions are reactions to an object, not a trait.

They are object specific. You show your emotions when you are happy about something, angry with someone, afraid of something. Moods, on the other hand, aren't directed at an object. Emotions can turn into moods when you lose focus on the contextual object. So when a work colleague criticizes you for the way you spoke to a client, you might become angry with him. That is, you show emotion (anger) toward a specific object (your colleague). But later in the day, you might find yourself just generally dispirited. You can't attribute this feeling to any single event; you're just not your normal, upbeat self. This affective state describes a mood.

A related term that is gaining increasing importance in organizational behavior is emotional labour. Every employee expends physical and mental labour when they put their bodies and cognitive capabilities, respectively, into their job. But most jobs also require **emotional labour**. This is when an employee expresses organizationally desired emotions during interpersonal transactions. The concept of emotional labour originally developed in relation to service jobs. Airline flight attendants, for instance, are expected to be cheerful, funeral counsellors sad, and doctors emotionally neutral. But today the concept of emotional labour seems relevant to almost every job. You're expected, for example, to be courteous and not hostile in interactions with co-workers. And leaders are expected to draw on emotional labour to II charge the troops. Almost every great speech, for instance, contains a strong emotional component that stirs feelings in others. As we proceed in the ensuing paragraph, you'll see that it's because of the increasing importance of emotional labour as a key component of effective job performance that an understanding of emotion has gained heightened relevance within the field of organisational behaviour.

24.3 FELT VERSUS DISPLAYED EMOTIONS

Emotional labour creates dilemmas for employees when their job requires them to exhibit emotions that are incongruous with their actual feelings. Not surprisingly, this is a frequent occurrence. There are people at work with whom you find it very difficult to be friendly. Maybe you consider their personality abrasive. Maybe you know they've said negative things about you behind your back. Regardless, your job requires you to interact with these people on a regular basis. So you're forced to feign friendliness. It can help you to better understand emotions if you separate them into felt versus displayed.

Felt emotions are an individual's actual emotions. In contrast, **displayed emotions** are those that are organizationally required and considered appropriate in a given job. They're not innate; they're learned. "The ritual look of delight on the face of the first runner-up as the new Miss Universe is announced is a product of the display rule that losers should mask their sadness with an expression of joy for the winner. Similarly, most of us know that we're expected to act sad at funerals regardless of whether we consider the person's death to be a loss, and to pretend to be happy at weddings even if we don't feel like celebrating. Effective managers have learned to be serious when giving an employee a negative performance evaluation and to cover up their anger when they've been passed over for promotion. And the salesperson that hasn't learned to smile and appear friendly, regardless of his or her true feelings at the moment, isn't typically going to last long on most sales jobs. The key point here is that felt and displayed emotions are often different. In fact, many people have problems working with others simply because they naively assume that the emotions they see others display is what those others actually feel this is particularly true in organizations, where role demands and situations often require people to exhibit emotional behaviours that mask their true feelings.

24.4 EMOTION DIMENSIONS

There are many emotions. These may be reflected in different ways. These are discussed as follows:

Variety: There have been numerous efforts to limit and define the fundamental or basic set of emotions. Research has identified six universal emotions: anger, fear, sadness, happiness, disgust, and surprise. One factor that has strongly shaped what is and isn't listed in this basic set is the manner in which emotions were identified. Researchers tended to look for universally identified facial expressions and then convert them into categories (see Exhibit 24.1). Emotions that couldn't be readily identified by others through facial expressions, or which were considered a subset of one of the basic six, were not selected.

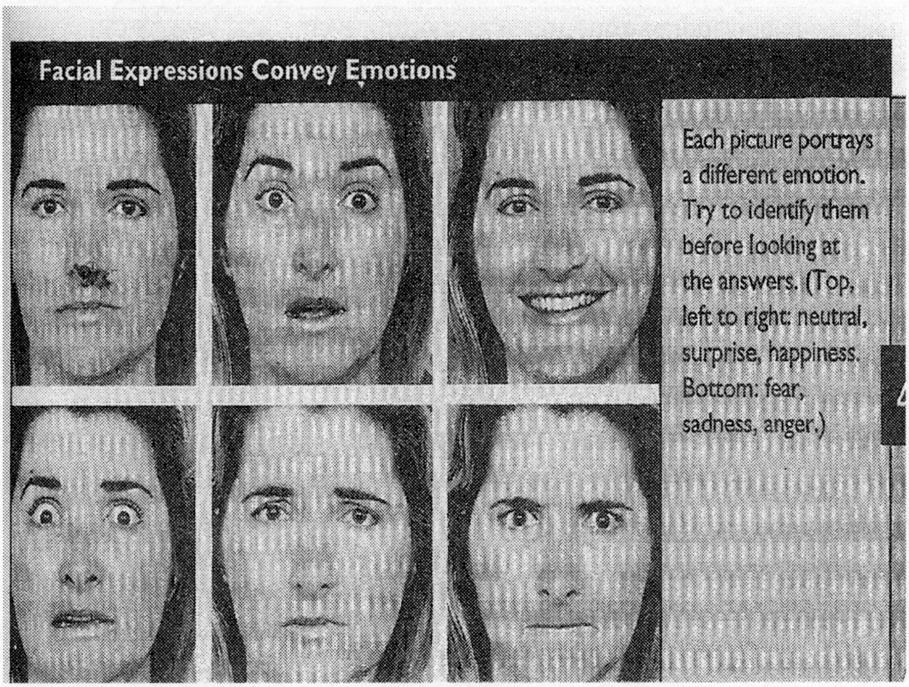

Exhibit 24.1

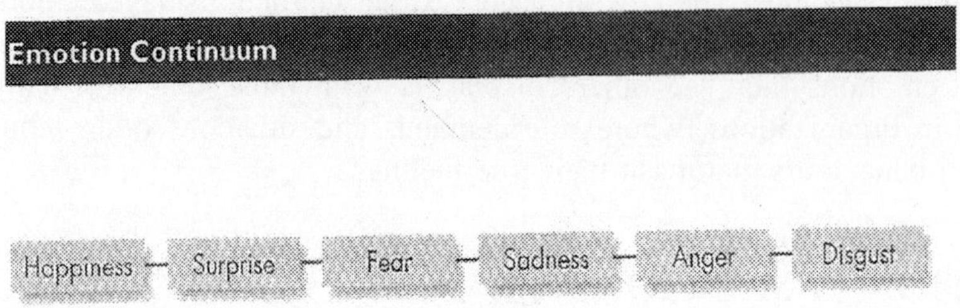

Exhibit 24.2

Exhibit 24.2 illustrates that the six emotions can be conceptualized as existing along a continuum. The closer any two emotions are to each other on this continuum, the more people are likely to confuse them. For instance, happiness and surprise are frequently mistaken for each other, while happiness and disgust are rarely confused. e.g., I get angry after receiving a poor performance appraisal. I fear that I could be laid off as a result of a company cutback. I'm sad about one of my co-workers leaving to take a new job in another city. I'm happy after being selected as employee-of-the month. I'm disgusted with the way my supervisor treats the women on our team. And I'm surprised to find out that management plans a complete restructuring of the company's retirement program.

Intensity: People give different responses to identical emotion-provoking stimuli. In some cases this can be attributed to the individual's personality. Other times it is a result of the job requirements. People vary in their inherent ability to express intensity. You undoubtedly know individuals who almost never show their feelings. They rarely get angry. They never show rage. In contrast, you probably also know people who seem to be on an emotional roller coaster. When they are happy, they are ecstatic. When they're sad, they're deeply depressed. And two people can be in the exact same situation with one showing excitement and joy, while the other is calm and collected. Jobs make different intensity demands in terms of emotional labour. For instance, air traffic controllers and trial judges are expected to be calm and controlled, even in stressful situations. Conversely, the effectiveness of television evangelists, public-address announcers at sporting events, and lawyers can depend on their ability to alter their displayed emotional intensity as the need arises.

Frequency and Duration: Emotional labour that requires high frequency or long durations is more demanding and requires more exertion by employees. So whether an employee can successfully meet the emotional demands of a given job depends not only on which emotions need to be displayed and their intensity, but also how frequently and for how long the effort has to be made.

24.5 CAN PEOPLE BE EMOTIONLESS?

Some people have severe difficulty in expressing their emotions and understanding the emotions of others. Psychologists call this alexithymia (which is Greek for "lack of emotion"). People who suffer from alexithymia rarely cry and are often seen by others as bland and cold. Their own feelings make them uncomfortable, and they're not able to discriminate among their different emotions. Additionally, they're often at a complete loss to understand what others around them feeling. Does this inability to express emotions and read others mean that people who suffer from alexithymia are poor work performers? Not necessarily. Consistent with our discussion on matching personality types with appropriate jobs, people who lack emotion need to be in jobs that require little or no emotional labour. These people are not well suited to sales and managerial positions. But they might very well be effective performers, for instance, in a job writing program code or in any work that is confined exclusively to computer interaction.

24.6 GENDER AND EMOTIONS

The evidence does confirm differences between men and women when it comes to emotional reactions and ability to read others. In contrasting the genders, women show greater emotional expression than men; they experience emotions more intensely; and they display more frequent expressions of both positive and negative emotions, except anger. In contrast to men, women also report more comfort in expressing emotions. Finally, women are better at reading nonverbal and paralinguistic cues than are men.

Why do they differ? Three possible answers have been suggested. One explanation is the different ways men and women have been socialized. Men are taught to be tough and brave; and showing emotion is inconsistent with this image. Women, on the other hand, are socialized to be nurturing. This may account for the perception that women are generally warmer and friendlier than men. For instance, women are expected to express more positive emotions on the job (shown by smiling) than men, and they do. A second explanation is that women may have more innate ability to read others and present their emotions than do men. Third, women may have a greater need for social approval and, thus, a higher propensity to show positive emotions such as happiness.

24.7 EXTERNAL CONSTRAINTS ON EMOTIONS

An emotion that is acceptable on the athletic playing field may be totally unacceptable when exhibited at the workplace. Similarly, what's appropriate in one country is often inappropriate in another. These facts illustrate the role that external constraints play in shaping displayed emotions. Every organization defines boundaries that identify what emotions are acceptable and the degree to which they can be expressed. The same applies in different cultures. These can be expressed as follows:

1. **Organizational Influences:** If you can't smile and appear happy, you're unlikely to have much of a career working at a Disney amusement park. And a manual produced by McDonald's states that its counter personnel "must display traits such as sincerity, enthusiasm, confidence, and a sense of humour." There is no single emotional "set" sought by all organizations. Expressions of negative emotions such as fear, anxiety, and anger tend to be unacceptable except under fairly specific conditions. For instance, one such condition might be a high-status member of a group conveying impatience with a low-status member. Moreover, expressions of intense emotion, whether negative or positive,

tend to be typically unacceptable because they're seen as undermining routine task performance. Again, there are exceptional conditions in which this isn't true–for example, a brief grieving over the sudden death of a company's CEO or the celebration of a record year of profits. But for the most part, consistent with the myth of rationality, well-managed organizations are expected to be essentially emotion free.

2. **Cultural Influences:** Cultural norms in the United States dictate that employees in service organizations should smile and act friendly when interacting with customers. But this norm doesn't apply worldwide. In Israel, smiling by supermarket cashiers is seen as a sign of inexperience, so cashiers are encouraged to look somber. In Moslem cultures, smiling is frequently taken as a sign of sexual attraction, so women are socialized not to smile at men. The foregoing examples illustrate the need to consider cultural factors as influencing what is or aren't considered as emotionally appropriate. What's acceptable in one culture may seem extremely unusual or even dysfunctional in another. And cultures differ in terms of the interpretation they give to emotions.

24.8 THE CONCEPT OF EMOTIONAL INTELLIGENCE

For decades, a lot of emphasis has been put on certain aspects of intelligence such as logical reasoning, math skills, spatial skills, understanding analogies, verbal skills, etc. Cumulatively known as Intelligence Quotient (IQ), was the thrust area of judgement as far as a person's suitability to a particular was concerned. But the researchers were puzzled by the fact that while IQ could predict the academic performance and to some degree, the professional and personal potential; yet there was something missing in the equation. Some people with fabulous IQ scores were doing poorly in the professional life; one could say that they were wasting their potential by thinking, behaving and communicating in a way that hindered their chances to succeed, and the major missing part in the success equation was identified as cognitive skills. The discovery of cognitive skills and abilities though appears to be outside the scope of IQ yet is unquestionably important for.

If there are some critical ingredients of human intelligence independent of those measured by IQ, their discovery and elucidation will contribute a better, more complete theory of human success with proper blend of Emotional Quotient (EQ). It states that high levels of emotionally intelligent leaders create a climate in which information sharing, trust, health, risk-taking, and learning flourish. The basic message, that effectiveness in organizations is at least as much about EQ as IQ, resonated deeply; it was something that people knew in their guts but that had never before been so well articulated.

Scales fell from the eyes of managers when they heard of emotional intelligence concept as coined by two American psychologists, Peter Salovey of Yale and John Mayer of the University of New Hampshire. Managers were not ready to accept as to how the human qualities such as empathy, self-awareness and emotional control could be of any use in organizational setting. But the entire storm of controversy on the subject came to an end with the Daniel Goleman's bestseller 'Emotional Intelligence: Why It can Matter More than IQ. In fact, he gave the world a new dimension of emotional intelligence while stating that EQ accounts for about 80 per cent of a person's success in life. Though emotional intelligence might have marked its presence as an academic catch phrase, yet it is fast developing the main psychological mantra of organizational development in the recent times. The concept emotional intelligence came out of the term emotion, which refers to a feeling with its distinctive thoughts, psychological and biological states, and ranges of propensities to act. So it may be an agitation or disturbance of mind, passion, any vehement but definitely related to the person's mental state. There can be a number of emotions like anger, sadness, fear, enjoyment, surprise, love disgust, and shame, etc.

A manager's ability to balance the emotions with the reason to maximize long-term happiness, i.e., capacity of effectively recognizing and managing one's own emotions and those of others may be termed as emotional awareness or emotional management skills. In the words of Daniel Goleman emotional intelligence, "The ability to motivate oneself and persist in the face of frustration; to control impulse and delay gratification; to regulate one's moods and keep distress from swamping the ability to think; to empathize and to hope". In fine the concept of emotional intelligence is an umbrella term that captures a broad collection of individual skills and dispositions, usually referred as soft skills or inter or intrapersonal skills that are outside' the traditional areas of general intelligence and technical or professional skills. In the most general way, the development of emotional intelligence (EO) is the building of skills and understandings related to the ways we feel, manage and act on our emotions. These shape the way we interact with ourselves and with others. EO includes components such as self-control, delaying of gratification, prioritizing, recognizing and communicating emotions and perhaps one of the most critical elements is empathy. Emotional intelligence is the combination of skills, understandings and habits that shape the ways we think, feel and act. The latest researches in neurobiology have brought out that human beings operate from two minds, i.e., the rational mind and the primitive mind, which is purely the emotional mind. The rational mind is centered in the neo-cortex, the outer part of the brain and allows human beings to plan, learn, remember, love, care and also to make moral and ethical distinctions.

On the contrary the emotional mind is the source of basics emotions like anger, sadness, fear, lust, surprise, disgust, etc. and help the individuals in attaining emotional competence. Emotional competency is the learned capability that leads to outstanding performance in life. This means that emotional intelligence actually contributes to rational thought. It is now believed that your feelings take precedence over your thoughts in making decision, because a rational mind take littler longer to register and respond than the emotional mind. In this kind of emotional reaction, there is an extended appraisal of the situation, both thoughts and cognition plays a key roulette determining what the emotion be aroused. The ability of an individual to monitor one's own and other's feeling and emotions, to discriminate among them and to use the available information in steering one's own as well as other's behaviour has attained much significance–even in the information age. A growing body of research on the human brain proves that, for better or worse, leader's mood affects the emotions of the people around them. The reason for that lies in what scientists calls the open loop nature of the brain limbic system, our emotional centre. A closed loop system is self-regulating, whereas an open-loop system depends on external source to manage itself. Our limbic system's open-loop design lets other people change our very physiology and hence, our emotions. In organizations mood start at the top tends to move the fastest because everyone watches the boss/leader, and the subordinates take their emotional cues from him. Thus, the entire phenomenon creates a strong link between emotional intelligence and managerial effectiveness irrespective of the managerial style.

Emotional Intelligence (EI) refers to an assortment of noncognitive skills, capabilities, and competencies that influence a person's ability to succeed in coping with environmental demands and pressures. It's composed of five dimensions:

Empathy: The ability to sense how others are feeling.
Self-awareness: The ability to be aware of what you're feeling.
Self-management: The ability to manage one's own emotions and impulses.
Self-motivation: The ability to persist in the face of setbacks and failures.
Social skills: The ability to handle the emotions of others.

Some of the EQ fundamentals are:

- Socializing effectively
- Motivating yourself
- Managing feelings
- Controlling yourself and delaying gratification
- Committing to noble goals
- Building empathy and hope

Some EQ applications/outcomes are:

- Team-building
- Problem-solving
- Inclusion/tolerance
- Conflict resolution.
- Community
- Communication

"Emotional intelligence involves the ability to monitor one's own and others' feelings and emotions, to discriminate among them and to use this information to guide one's thinking and actions."

The specific competencies involved in emotional intelligence include

- Using emotions in adaptive ways to facilitate cognitive activities and motivate behaviour (Mayer & Salovey, 1997)
- Understanding emotions and emotional knowledge
- Regulating emotion in the self and others
- Appraising and expressing emotions in the self and others

The Four-Branch model of Emotional Intelligence: (Peter Salovey)

- Ability to identify emotion in other people
- Ability to identify emotion in one's physical and psychological states
- Ability to express emotions accurately and to express needs related to them
- Ability to discriminate between accurate/honest and inaccurate/dishonest feeling

Emotional Facilitation of Thought (Using Emotional Intelligence)

- Ability to use emotional states to facilitate problem-solving and creativity
- Ability to redirect and priorities thinking on the basis of associated feelings

- Ability to generate emotions to facilitate judgment and memory
- Ability to capitalize on mood changes to appreciate multiple points of view

Emotional Understanding

- Ability to understand transitions among emotions
- Ability to understand relationship among various emotions
- Ability to understand complex feelings, emotional blends and contradictory states
- Ability to perceive the causes and consequences of emotions

Emotional Management

- Ability to monitor and reflect on emotions
- Ability to manage emotions in others
- Ability to manage emotions in oneself
- Ability to engage, prolong or detach from an emotional state
- Ability to be open to feelings, both pleasant and unpleasant

EQ competencies are learnable and profitable. Learn how to turn daily conflicts into opportunities to practice valuable lifelong skills such as anger management, listening, oral communication and critical thinking.

Principles Of Emotional Intelligence:

- Use positive social skills in handling relationships
- Show empathy and understand others' points of view
- Regulate and copy positively with emotional and behavioural impulses.
- Be positive goal and plan oriented
- Be aware of one's own feelings and those of others

24.9 IMPORTANCE OF EMOTIONAL INTELLIGENCE

Knowledge of emotions can help a manager to better understand the selection process in organizations, decision-making, motivation, leadership, interpersonal conflict, and deviant workplace behaviours in the following ways:

1. **Motivation:** Motivation theories basically propose that individuals are motivated to the extent that their behaviour is expected to lead to desired outcomes. The image is that of rational exchange: the employee essentially trades effort for pay, security, promotions, and so forth. But people aren't cold, unfeeling machines. Their perceptions and calculations of situations are filled with emotional content that significantly influences how much effort they exert. Moreover, when you seem people who are highly motivated in their jobs, they're emotionally committed. People who are engaged in their work "become physically, cognitively, and emotionally immersed in the experience of activity, in the pursuit of a goal". So, are all people emotionally engaged in their work? No, But many are. And if we focus only on rational calculations of inducements and contributions, we fail to be able to explain behaviours such as the individual who forgets to have dinner and works late into the night, lost in the thrill of her work.

2. **Leadership:** Effective leaders almost all rely on the expression of feelings to help convey their messages. In fact, the expression of emotions in speeches is often the critical element that results in individuals accepting or rejecting a leader's message. "When leaders feel exited, enthusiastic, and active, they may be more likely to energize their subordinates and convey a sense of efficacy, competence, optimism, and enjoyment". Politicians, as a case in point, have learned to show enthusiasm when talking about their chances for winning an election, even when polls suggest otherwise. Corporate executives know that emotional content is critical if employees are to buy into their vision of their company's future and accept change. When new visions are offered, especially when they contain distant or vague goals, change is often difficult to accept. So when effective leaders want to implement significant changes, they rely on the evocation, framing, and mobilization of emotions, by arousing emotions and linking them to an appealing vision, leaders increase the likelihood that managers and employees alike will accept change.
3. **Interpersonal Conflict:** Few issues are more intertwined with emotions than the topic of interpersonal conflict. Whenever conflicts arise, you can be fairly certain that emotions are also surfacing. A manager's success in trying to resolve conflicts, in fact, is often largely due to his or her ability to identify the emotional elements in the conflict and to get the conflicting parties to work through their emotions. And the manager, who ignores the emotional elements in conflicts, focusing singularly on rational and task concerns, is unlikely to be very effective in resolving those conflicts.
4. **Deviant Workplace Behaviours:** Negative emotions can lead to a number of deviant workplace behaviours. Anyone who has spent much time in an organization realizes that people often engage in voluntary actions that violate established norms and that threaten the organization, its members, or both. These actions are called employee deviances. They fall into categories such as production (e.g., leaving early, intentionally working slowly); property (e.g., stealing, sabotage); political (e.g., gossiping, blaming co-workers); and personal aggression (e.g., sexual harassment, verbal abuse). Many of these deviant behaviours can be traced to negative emotions. For instance, envy is an emotion that occurs when you resent someone for having something that you don't, which you strongly desires. It can lead to hateful deviant behaviours. Envy, for example, has been found to be associated with hostility, backstabbing and other forms of political behaviour, negatively distorting others' successes; and positively distorting one's own accomplishments.
5. **Decision-making:** Negative emotions can result in a limited search for new alternatives and a less vigilant use of information. On the other hand, positive emotions can increase problem-solving and facilitate the integration of information. You can improve your understanding of decision-making by considering 'the heart' as well as 'the head.' People use emotions as well as rational and intuitive processes in making decisions. Failure to incorporate emotions into the study of decision processes will result in an incomplete (and often inaccurate) view of the process.
6. **Ability and Selection:** People who know their own emotions and are good at reading others' emotions may be more effective in their jobs. That, in essence, is the theme underlying recent research on emotional intelligence. Further, the employer should know the EI and consider it as a factor in selection, especially in jobs that demand a high degree of social interaction.

24.10 SUMMARY

As one consultant aptly put it, "You can't divorce emotions from the workplace because you can't divorce emotions from people. Managers who understand the role of emotions will significantly improve their ability to explain and predict individual behaviour. Emotions can hinder performance, especially negative emotions. That's probably why organizations, for the most part, try to extract emotions out of the workplace. But emotions can also enhance performance in two ways. First, emotions can increase arousal levels, thus acting as motivators to higher performance. Second, emotional labour recognizes that feelings can be part of a job's required behaviour. So, for instance, the ability to effectively manage emotions in leadership and sales positions may be critical to success in those positions. The critical moderating variable is the complexity of the individual's task. The more complex a task, the lower the level of arousal that can be tolerated without interfering with performance. While a certain minimal level of arousal is probably necessary for good performance, very high levels interfere with the ability to function, especially if the job requires calculative and detailed cognitive processes. Given that the trend is toward jobs becoming more complex, you can see why organizations are likely to go to considerable efforts to discourage the overt display of emotions–especially intense ones–in the workplace.

24.11 SELF-ASSESSMENT QUESTIONS

1. Describe some of the inherited characteristics of behaviour. Do you believe that these characteristics can be reflected by emotions? Comment.
2. Describe the fundamentals and principles of EI.
3. Explain the types of emotions and their role in organizations.
4. Is Emotional Intelligence an inherited trait or a learned trait? If it is a learned trait, what steps can be taken to improve upon EI?
5. What do you mean by emotions? How they can be changed by external environment?

25

STRESS MANAGEMENT AND BEHAVIOUR

Learning Objective

The main objective of this chapter is to make the students learn about the concept of stress and its sources and effects and ways to manage stress.

25.1 INTRODUCTION TO THE CONCEPT

The concept of stress denotes physical and mental revelation to prevailing within the mental environment of a human being. Stress is a neutral phenomenon whereas distress has a negative connotation. Stress may be classified in three ways as shown below:

Low stress	*Optimum stress*	*High stress*
Performance is traditional lesser uncertainty known environment narrow span of control	High motivation high morale high and satisf-actory performance high supervision and moral support	Area of task is novel uncertainty of operation and result unknown environment wide span of control

Stress is inevitable for every individual. A pioneer researcher *Hans Selye* opined that 'stress is the spice of life, the absence of stress is death'. Stress and strain are the two sides of the same coin. Life is a dynamic organism so is the concept of stress.

A close nexus may be established among the variables time, stress and productivity. Time may be considered as a linkage between stress and productivity. Increase in stress warrants entailing more time and reduction in productivity. The multidimension of stress that infects an individual has been projected in the following way:

Workplace, job related stress	*Interpersonal stress*	*Intrapersonal stress*	*Inter-organizational stress*
Conflict in the workplace, time management, sexual harassment noise, overcrowding, overload of work, work ethos and values, nature of job transfer, punishment, reward travelling.	Interpersonal conflict, relationship with peers, relationship with superiors, relationship with subordinates, insubordination relation with customers, dealers, interpersonal communication.	Confliction situation, conflict management, personal difference, difference in decision-making, perceptional difference.	Noise, heat, lighting, limited space, limited resource, career constraints, competition from new recruits, void from retirement/leave of existing staff.

Under current of ego battles between bosses can cause stress for subordinates and peers. The employee faces embarrassing stress in this situation as he or she cannot take side with either of the boss, and has to pretend to support, individually and severally, both of them. This is a case of interpersonal and intrapersonal conflict and organizational behaviour leading to stress.

25.2 SOURCES OF STRESS

Stress and strain exert serious pressure, both mental and physical, upon the business executives. The pressure for stress and strain is emerging owing to various factors, which have been elaborated in this section.

1. **Role Analysis Technique (RAT):** Stress evaluation entails role analysis, role classification, role identification and role to be performed by an employee is a process of stress management. It would also highlight the expectation from the employees ahead of doing the work and thus helps in reducing work stress.
2. **Effectiveness vs. Efficiency:** While measuring the degree of stress, we may have to weight as to how effectively the work has been accomplished. Effectiveness denotes accomplishment of goals and objectives while efficiency hints at cost reduction. A work may be accomplished with hundred per cent efficiency but even the objective or target could not be achieved, then such efficiency becomes meaningless. Tension and stress would definitely mount on the face of the employees. It is a biggest challenge before organization behaviour.
3. **Uncertainties and Changes in Future:** The business enterprises under WTO regime have been exposed to a hung in balance (HIB) situation where nobody can predict accurately as to what is stored in future. Planning process is no longer recognized as sufficient equipment to meet this managerial stress. To enable the business executives to bear the burden of stress arising from uncertainties and changes, we require a mix of prescriptions. The rapidity of decision-making ability for an executive matters in controlling the stress and strain. Besides formulating strategies and plans, the corporate entities are supposed to translate plans into strategic business decisions.
4. **Sexual Harassment at Workplace:** One of the usual allegations leading to mental stress is arising out of gender variation in work place. There are certain jobs dominated by male

folk such as management and the female occupation such as secretarial work. However, it is theoretically difficult to give a comprehensive definition of stress and strain. But we generally conceive it as a mental state of affairs but under extra caution and alertness emerging from workplace environment, psychological preparedness to perform a given business task from a given table, amongst a group of fellow workers, with simultaneous accountability to higher authority or boss and the responsibility of extracting desired work output from the subordinates. This manifests the all-round stress that is put on the corporate executives from within the workplace itself. Here the stress has emerged from gender diversity in the workplace often resulting in sexual harassment. We find it cumbersome to give a concrete definition of harassment. Harassment (T. Chakrabarty (1997) is generally taken to cover staring and bearing sexual, derogatory or demeaning remarks or jokes. The Supreme Court in a landmark judgment on 13 August, 1997 held that sexual harassment is a cognizable offence and punishable under law.

We may recognize that stress is not always bad either for the individual or for the organization. Often stress helps to bring out the best in the individual. Stress, on the other, may have different effects on the employee, namely, physical problems, (heart disease, pressure, exhaustion); psychological problems (change of mood, defying attitude, non-compliance with office order, disrespect to the superior, dissatisfaction on the job); behavioural problems (tardiness,m absenteeism, inability to work in a group with harmony, individualistic outlook, turnover, unmindfulness, accident). The task of the management in an organization is to acknowledge the constraints emerging from strain and draw up suitable action plan to overcome the stress. Although whole problem may not be easy to overcome but the management can bring out some strategy to counter the stress. Management ought to create an environment to reduce or prevent job stress on an individual or an entity, such as prioritization of activities, including better time management. Time management technique may be applied at the workplace, such as urgent telephone calls, E-mail and similar message screened by the subordinates may be attended by the executives while the routine matters may be left for the office assistants. Other techniques include role analysis, role identification, career counselling services, leisure and recreational facilities, motivating with monetary incentives, employee assistance programme (EAP), workshop on stress and strain, display of video cassette and film show. All these measures will go a long way in reducing stress in workplace.

25.3 THE NATURE OF STRESS

Many people think of stress as a simple problem. In reality, however, stress is complex and often misunderstood. To learn how job stress truly works, we must first define it and then describe the process through which it develops.

Stress has been defined in many ways, but most definitions say that stress is caused by a stimulus, that the stimulus can be either physical or psychological, and that the individual responds to the stimulus in some way. Here, then, we define stress as a person's adaptive response to a stimulus that places excessive psychological or physical demands on him or her.

Given the underlying complexities of this definition, we need to examine its components carefully. First is the notion of adaptation. As we discuss presently, people may adapt to stressful circumstances in any of several ways. Second is the role of the stimulus. This stimulus, generally called a stressor, is anything that induces stress. Third, stressors can be either psychological or physical. Finally, the demands the stressor places on the individual must be excessive for stress to result. Of course, what is excessive for one person may be perfectly tolerable for another. The point is simply that a person must perceive the demands as excessive or stress will not result.

25.3.1 The Stress Process

Much of what we know about stress today can be traced to the pioneering work of Dr. Hans Selye. Among Selye's most important contributions were his identification of the general adaptation syndrome (GAS) and the concepts of stress and distress.

The GAS begins when a person first encounters a stressor. The first stage is called 'alarm.' At this point, the person may feel some degree of panic and begin to wonder how to cope. The individual may also have to resolve a 'fight-or-flight' question: Can I deal with this, or should I run away? For example, suppose a manager is assigned to write a lengthy report overnight. Her first reaction may be 'How will I ever get this done by tomorrow?'

If the stressor is too extreme, the person may simply be unable to cope with it. In most cases, however, the individual gathers his or her strength (physical or emotional) and begins to resist the negative effects of the stressor. The manager with the long report to write may calm down, call home to tell her kids that say she's working late, roll up her sleeves, order out for dinner, and get to work. Thus, at stage 2 of the GAS, the person is resisting the effects of the stressor.

Often, the resistance phase ends the GAS. If the manager completes the report earlier than she expected, she may drop it in her briefcase, smile to herself, and head home tired but happy. On the other hand, prolonged exposure to a stressor without resolution may bring on phase 3 of the GAS: exhaustion. At this stage, the person literally gives up and can no longer fight the stressor. For example, the manager may fall asleep fail to finish the report.

Distress and Eustress. Selye also pointed out that the sources of stress need not be bad always. For example, receiving a bonus and then having to decide what to do with the money can be stressful. So can getting a promotion, gaining recognition, getting married and similar 'good' things. Selye called this type of stress **eustress**. As we will see later, eustress can lead to a number of positive outcomes for the individual.

Of course, there is also negative stress. Called **distress**, this is what most people think of when they hear the word stress. Excessive pressure, unreasonable demands on our time, and bad news all fall into this category. As the term suggests, this form of stress generally results in negative consequences for the individual.

For purposes of simplicity, we will continue to use the simple term stress throughout this chapter. But as you read and study the chapter, remember that stress can be either good or bad. It can motivate and stimulate us, or it can lead to any number of dangerous side effects.

25.3.2 Individual Differences and Stress

We have already alluded to the fact that stress can affect different people in different ways. Given our earlier discussion of individual differences back in lesson of Interpersonal Behaviour, of course, this should come as no surprise. The most fully developed individual difference relating specifically to stress is the distinction between Type A and Type B personality profiles.

Type A and B Personality Profiles

Type A and Type B profiles were first observed by two cardiologists, Meyer Friedman and Ray Rosenman. They first got the idea when a worker repairing the upholstery on their waiting room chairs noted that many of the chairs were worn only on the front. This suggested to the two cardiologists that many heart patients were anxious and had a hard time sitting still—they were literally sitting on the edges of their seats!

Using this observation as a starting point, Friedman and Rosenman began to study the phenomenon more closely. They eventually concluded that their patients were exhibiting one of two very different types of behaviour patterns. Their research also led them to conclude that the differences were personality based. They labelled these two behaviour patterns Type A and Type B.

The extreme **Type A** individual is extremely competitive, very devoted to work, and has a strong sense of time urgency. Moreover, this person is likely to be aggressive, impatient, and highly work oriented. He or she has a lot of drive and motivation and wants to accomplish as much as possible in as short a time as possible.

The extreme **Type B** person, in contrast, is less competitive, is less devoted to work and has a weaker sense of time urgency. This person feels less conflict with either people or time and has a more balanced, relaxed approach to life. She or he has more confidence and is able to work at a constant pace.

A common-sense expectation might be that Type A people are more successful than Type B people. In reality, however, this is not necessarily true—the Type B person is not necessarily any more or less successful than the Type A. There are several possible explanations for this. For example, Type A people may alienate others because of their drive and may miss out on important learning opportunities in their quest to get ahead. Type B, on the other hand, may have better interpersonal reputations and may learn a wider array of skills.

Friedman and Rosenman pointed out that people are not purely Type A or Type B; instead, people tend toward one or the other type. For example, an individual might exhibit marked Type A characteristics much of the time but still be able to relax once in a while and even occasionally forget about time.

Friedman and Rosenman's initial research on the Type A and Type B profile differences yielded some alarming findings. In particular, they suggested that Type A's were much more likely to get coronary heart disease than were Type B's. In recent years, however, follow-up research by other scientists has suggested that the relationship between Type A behaviour and the risk of coronary heart disease is not all that straightforward?

Although the reasons are unclear, recent findings suggest that Type A's are much more complex than originally believed. For example, in addition to the characteristics already noted, they are likely to be depressed and hostile. Any one of these characteristics or a combination of them can lead to heart problems. Moreover, different approaches to measuring Type A tendencies have yielded different results.

Finally, in one study that found Type A's to actually be less susceptible to heart problems than Type B's, the researchers offered and explanation consistent with earlier thinking: Because Type A's are compulsive, they seek treatment earlier and are more likely to follow their doctors' orders!

25.3.3 Hardiness and Optimism

Two other important individual differences related to stress are hardiness and optimism. Research suggests that some people have what are termed hardier personalities than others. **Hardiness** is person's ability to cope with stress. People with hardy personalities have an internal locus of control, are strongly committed to the activities in their lives, and view change as an opportunity for advancement and growth. Such people are seen relatively unlikely to suffer illness if they experience high levels of pressure and stress. On the other hand, people with low hardiness may have more difficulties in coping with pressure and stress.

Another potentially important individual difference is optimism. **Optimism** is the extent to which a person sees life in positive or negative terms. A popular expression used to convey this idea concerns the glass half filled with water. A person with a lot of optimism will tend to see it as half full, whereas a person with less optimism (a pessimist) will often see it as half empty. Optimism is also related to positive and negative affectivity. In general, optimistic people tend to handle stress better. They will be able to see the positive characteristics of the situation and recognize that things may eventually improve. In contrast, less optimistic people may focus more on the negative characteristics of the situation and expect things to get worse, not better.

Cultural differences also are important in determining how stress affects people. For example, research by Cary Cooper suggests that American executives may experience less stress than executives in may other countries, including Japan and Brazil. The major causes of stress also differ across countries. In Germany, for example, major causes of stress are time pressure and deadlines. In South Africa, long work hours more frequently lead to stress. And in Sweden, the major cause of stress is the encroachment of work on people's private lives.

Other research suggests that women are perhaps more prone to experience the psychological effects of stress, whereas men may report more physical effects. We should add, however, that the study of individual differences in stress is still in its infancy. It would therefore be premature to draw rigid conclusions about how different types of people handle stress.

25.4 CAUSES OF STRESS

Many things can cause stress. It has mainly two broad categories: organizational stressors and life stressors. It also shows three categories of stress consequences: individual consequences, organizational consequences, and burnout.

25.4.1 Organizational Stressors

Organizational stressors are various factors in the workplace that can cause stress. Four general sets of organizational stressors are task demands, physical demands, role demands, and interpersonal demands.

1. **Task Demands.** Task demands are stressors associated with the specific job a person performs. Some occupations are by nature more stressful than others. The jobs of surgeons, air traffic controllers, and professional football coaches are more stressful than those of general practitioners, airplane baggage loaders, and football team equipment

managers. In a study of representative sample of stressful jobs from among a total set of 250 jobs, it was found that the job of the US president was found to be the most stressful, followed by the jobs of firefighter and senior executive. Towards the middle of the distribution are jobs such as mechanical engineer, chiropractor, technical writer, and bank officer. The jobs of broadcast technician, bookkeeper, and actuary were among the least stressful jobs in this study.

Beyond specific task-related pressures, other aspects of a job may pose physical threats to a person's health. Unhealthy conditions exist in occupations such as coal mining and toxic waste handling. Security is another task demand that can cause stress. Someone in a relatively secure job is not likely to worry unduly about losing that position. threats to job security can increase stress dramatically. For example, stress generally increases throughout an organization during a period of layoffs or immediately after a merger with another firm. This has been observed at a number of organizations, including AT & T, Safeway, and Digital Equipment.

A final task demand stressor is overload. Overload occurs when a person simply had more work than he or she can handle. The overload can be either quantitative (the person has too many tasks to perform or too little time to perform them) or qualitative (the person may believe he or she lacks the ability to do the job). We should note that the opposite of overload may also be undesirable. Thus, a moderate degree of workload related stress is optimal, because it leads to high levels of energy and motivation.

2. **Physical Demands.** The physical demands of a job are its physical requirements on the worker; these demands are a function of the physical characteristics of the setting and the physical tasks the job involves. One important element is temperature. Working outdoors in extreme temperatures can result in stress, as can working in an improperly heated or cooled office. Strenuous labour such as loading heavy cargo or lifting packages can lead to similar results. Office design also can be a problem. A poorly designed office can make it difficult for people to have privacy or promote too much or too little social interaction. Too much interaction may distract a person from his or her task, whereas too little may lead to boredom or loneliness. Likewise, poor lighting, inadequate work surfaces, and similar deficiencies can create stress.
3. **Role Demands.** Role demands also can be stressful to people in organizations. A role is a set of expected behaviours associated with a particular position in a group or organization. As such, it has both formal (i.e., social and implicit) requirements. People in an organization or work group expect a person in a particular role to act in certain ways. They transmit these expectations both formally and informally. Individuals perceive role expectations with varying degrees of accuracy, and then attempt to enact that role. However, "errors" can creep into this process, resulting in stress-inducing problems called role ambiguity, role conflict, and role overload.
4. **Role ambiguity.** arises when a role is unclear. If your instructor tells you to write a term paper but refuses to provide more information, you will probably experience ambiguity. You do not know what the topic is, how long the paper should be, what format to use, or when the paper is due. In work settings, role ambiguity can stem from poor job descriptions, vague instructions from a supervisor, or unclear cues from coworkers. The

result is likely to be a subordinate who does not know what to do. Role ambiguity can thus be a significant source of stress.

5. **Role conflict.** occurs when the message and cues from others about the role are clear but contradictory or mutually exclusive. One common form is interrole conflict–conflict between roles. For example, if a person's boss says that to get ahead one must work overtime and on weekends, and the same person's spouse says that more time is needed at home with the family, conflict may result. Intra-role conflict may occur when the person gets conflicting demands from different sources within the context of the same role. A manager's boss may tell her that she needs to put more pressure on subordinates to follow new work rules. At the same time, her subordinates may indicate that they expect her to get the rules changes. Thus, the cues are in conflict, and the manager may be unsure about which course to follow.

   Intra-sender conflict occurs when a single source sends clear but contradictory message. This might occur if the boss says one morning that there can be no more overtime for the next month but after lunch tells someone to work late that same evening. Person-role conflict results from a discrepancy between the role requirements and the individual's personal values, attitudes, and needs. If a person is told to do something unethical or illegal, or if the work is distasteful (for example, firing a close friend), person-role conflict is likely. Role conflict of all varieties is of particular concern to managers.

   A final consequence of a weak role structure is **role overload**, which occurs when expectations for the role exceed the individual's capabilities. When a manager gives an employee several major assignments at once while increasing the person's regular workload, the employee will probably experience role overload. Role overload may also result when an individual takes on too many roles at one time. For example, a person trying to work extra hard at his job, run for election to the school board, serve on a committee in church, coach Little League baseball, maintain an active exercise program, and be a contributing member to his family will probably encounter role overload.

6. **Interpersonal Demands.** A final set of organizational stressors consists of three interpersonal demands: Group pressures, leadership, and interpersonal conflict. Group pressures may include pressure to restrict output, pressure to conform to the group's norms, and so forth. For instance, as we have noted before, it is quite common for a work group to arrive at an informal agreement about how much each member will produce. Individuals who produce much more or much less than this level may be pressured by the group to get back in line. In individual who feels a strong need to vary from the group's expectations (perhaps to get a pay raise or promotion) will experience a great deal of stress, especially if acceptance by the group is also important to him or her.

   Leadership style also may cause stress. Suppose an employee needs a great deal of social support from his leader. The leader, however, is quite brusque and shows no concern or compassion for him. This employee will probably feel stressed. Similarly, assume an employee feels a strong need to participate in decision-making and to be active in all aspects of management. Her boss is very autocratic and refuses to consult subordinates about anything. Once again stress is likely to result.

   Finally, conflicting personalities and behaviours may cause stress. Conflict can occur when two or more people must work together even though their personalities, attitudes, and behaviours differ. For example, a person with an internal locus of control—that is, who always wants to control how things turn out—might get frustrated working with an external person who likes to wait and just let things happen. Likewise, a smoker and a non-smoker who are assigned adjacent offices obviously will experience stress. The working with Diversity box describes another example of how interpersonal demands–in the form of harassment–can result in stress.

25.4.2 Life Stressors

Stress in organizational settings also can be influenced by events that take place outside the organization. Life stressors generally are categorized in terms of life change and life trauma.

1. **Life Change.** Thomas Holmes and Richard Rahe first developed and popularized the notion of life change as a source of stress. A **life change** is any meaningful change in a person's personal or work situation. Holmes and Rahe reasoned that major changes in a person's life can lead to stress and eventually to disease. The study summarizes their findings on major life change events. Note that several of these events relate directly (fired from work, retirement) or indirectly (change in residence) to work.
2. **Life Trauma.** Life trauma is similar to life change, but it has a narrower, more direct, and shorter-term focus. A life **trauma** is any upheaval in an individual's life that alters his or her attitudes, emotions, or behaviour. To illustrate, according to the life change view, a divorce adds to a person's potential for health problems in the following year. At the same time, the person will obviously also experience emotional turmoil during the actual divorce process. This turmoil is a form of life trauma and will clearly cause stress, much of which may spill over into the workplace.

   Major life traumas that may cause stress include marital problems, family difficulties, and health problems initially unrelated to stress. For example, suppose a person learns she had developed arthritis that will limit her favourite activity, skiing. Her dismay over the news may translate into stress at work. Similarly, a worker going through a family breakup will almost certainly go through difficult periods, some of which will affect his or her job performance.

25.5 EFFECTS OF STRESS

Stress can have a number of consequences. As we already noted, if the stress is positive, the result may be more energy, enthusiasm, and motivation. Of more concern, of course, are the negative consequences of stress. Referring back to our discussion in this lesson, we see that stress can produce individual effects, organizational effects, and burnout.

We should first note that many of the factors listed are obviously interrelated. For example, alcohol abuse is shown as individual effects, but it also affects the organization the person works for an employee who drinks on the job may perform poorly and create a hazard for others. If the category for a consequence seems somewhat arbitrary, be aware that each effect is categorized according to the area of its primary influence.

1. **Individual Effects:** The individual effects of stress, then, are the outcomes that mainly affect the individual. The organization also may suffer, either directly or indirectly, but it is the individual who pays the real price. Stress may produce behavioural, psychological, and medical effects.
2. **Behavioural Effects:** The behavioural effects of stress may harm the person under stress or others. One such behaviour is smoking. Research has clearly documented that people who smoke tend to smoke more when they experience stress. There is also evidence that alcohol and drug abuse are linked to stress, although this relationship is less well documented. Other possible behavioural consequences are accident proneness, violence, and appetite difficulties.
3. **Psychological Effects:** The psychological effects of stress relate to a person's mental health and well-being. When people experience too much stress at work, they may become depressed or find themselves sleeping too much or not enough. Stress may also lead to family problems and sexual difficulties.
4. **Medical Effects:** The medical effects of stress affect a person's physical well-being. Heart disease and stroke, among other illnesses, have been linked to stress. Other common medical problems resulting from too much stress include headaches, backaches, ulcers and related stomach and intestinal disorders, and skin conditions such as acne and hives.
5. **Organizational Effects:** Clearly, any of the individual effects just discussed can also affect the organization. Other results of stress have even more direct consequences for organizations. These include decline in performance, withdrawal, and negative changes in attitudes.
6. **Performance:** One clear organizational effects of too much stress is a decline in performance. For operating workers, such a decline can translate into poor-quality work or a drop in productivity. For managers, it can mean faulty decision making or disruptions in working relationships as people become irritable and hard to get along with.
7. **Withdrawal:** Withdrawal behaviours also can result from stress. For the organization, the two most significant forms of withdrawal behaviour are absenteeism and quitting. People who are having a hard time coping with stress in their jobs are more likely to call in sick or consider leaving the organization for good. Stress can also produce other, more subtle forms of withdrawal. A manager may start missing deadlines or taking longer lunch breaks. An employee may withdraw psychologically by ceasing to care about the organization and the job. As noted above, employee violence is a potential individual consequence of stress. This also has obvious organizational implications as well, especially if the violence is directed an employee or at the organization in general.
8. **Attitudes:** Another direct organizational effect of employee stress relates to attitudes. As we just noted, job satisfaction, morale, and organizational commitment can all suffer, along with motivation to perform at high levels. As a result, people may be more prone to complain about unimportant things, do only enough work to get by, and so forth.
9. **Burnout:** Burnout, another effect of stress, has clear implications for both people and organizations. Burnout is a general feeling of exhaustion that develops when a person simultaneously experiences too much pressure and has too few sources of satisfaction.

Burnout generally develops in the following way. First, people with high aspirations and strong motivation to get things done are prime candidates for burnout under certain conditions. They are especially vulnerable when the organization suppresses or limits their initiative while constantly demanding that they serve the organization's own ends.

In such a situation, the individual is likely to put too much him or her into the job. In other words, the person may well keep trying to meet his or her own agenda while simultaneously trying to fulfil the organization's expectations. The most likely effects of this situation are prolonged stress, fatigue, frustration, and helplessness under the burden of overwhelming demands. The person literally exhausts his or her aspirations and motivation, much as a candle burns itself out. Loss of self-confidence and psychological withdrawal follow ultimately.

25.6 MANAGING STRESS IN THE WORKPLACE

Given that stress is widespread and so potentially disruptive in organizations, it follows that people and organizations should be concerned about how to manage it more effectively. And in fact they are. Many strategies have been developed to help manage stress in the workplace. Some are for individuals and others are geared toward organizations.

1. **Time Management:** Time management is often recommended for managing stress. The idea is that many daily pressures can be eased or eliminated if a person does a better job of managing time. One popular approach to time management is to make a list every morning of the things to be done that day. Then you group the items on the list into three categories: critical activities that must be performed, important activities that should be performed, and optional or trivial things that can be delegated or postponed. Then, of course, you do the things on the list in their order of importance. This strategy helps people get more of the important things done everyday. It also encourages delegation of less important activities to others. The Talking Technology box illustrates how managers can better manage their time by using their cellular telephones more selectively.

   The organization's culture also can be used to help manager stress. In some organizations, for example, there is a strong norm against taking time off or going on vacation. In the long run, such norms can cause major stress. Thus, the organization should strive to foster a culture that reinforces a healthy mix of work and nonwork activities.
2. **Support Groups:** A final method for managing stress is to develop and maintain support groups. A support group is simply a group of family members or friends with whom a person can spend time. Going out after work with a couple of co-workers to a basketball game, for example, can help relieve the stress that builds up during the day. Supportive family and friends can help people deal with normal stress on an ongoing basis. Support groups can be particularly useful during times of crisis. For example, suppose an employee has just learned that she did not get the promotion she has been working toward for months. It may help her tremendously if she had good friends to lean on, be it to talk to or to yell at.

3. **Role Management:** Somewhat related to time management is the idea of role management, in which the individual actively works to avoid overload, ambiguity, and conflict. For example, if you do not know what is expected of you, you should not sit and worry about it. Instead, ask for clarification from your boss. Another role management strategy is to learn to say 'no'. As simple as saying 'no' might sound, a lot of people create problems for themselves by always saying 'yes'. Besides working in their regular jobs, they agree to serve on committees, volunteer for extra duties, and accept extra assignments. Sometimes, of course, we have no choice but to accept an extra obligation (if our boss tells us to complete a new project, we will probably have to do it). In many cases, however, saying 'no' is an option.
4. **Relaxation:** A related method of managing stress is relaxation. We noted at the beginning of the chapter that coping with stress requires adaptation. Proper relaxation is an effective way to adapt. Relaxation can take many forms. One way to relax is to take regular vacations. A recent study found that people's attitudes towards a variety of workplace characteristics improved significantly following a vacation. People can also relax while on the job. For example, it has been recommended that people take regular rest breaks during their normal workday. A popular way of resting is to sit quietly with closed eyes for ten minutes every afternoon. (Of course, it might be necessary to have an alarm clock handy!).
5. **Organizational Coping Strategies:** Organizations are also increasingly realizing that they should be involved in managing their employees' stress. There are two different rationales for this view. One is that because the organization is at least partly responsible for creating the stress, it should help relieve it. The other is that workers experiencing lower levels of harmful stress will function more effectively. Two basic organizational strategies for helping employees manage stress are institutional programmes and collateral programmes.

   Many firms today also have employee fitness programmes. These programmes attack stress indirectly by encouraging employees to exercise, which is presumed to reduce stress. On the negative side, this kind of effort costs considerably more than stress management programmes, because the firm must invest in physical facilities. Still, more and more companies are exploring this option. Both Tenneco and L.L. Bean, for example, have state-of-the-art fitness centres for their employees.
6. **Institutional Programmes:** Institutional programmes for managing stress are under taken through established organizational mechanisms. For example, properly designed jobs and work schedules can help ease stress. Shift work, in particular, can cause major problems for employees, because they constantly have to adjust their sleep and relaxation patterns. Thus, the design of work and work schedules should be a focus of organizational efforts to reduce stress.

   Finally, supervision can play an important institutional role in managing stress. A supervisor can be a major source of overload. If made aware of their potential for assigning stressful amounts of work, supervisors can do a better job of keeping workloads reasonable.
7. **Exercise:** Exercise is one method of managing stress. People who exercise regularly are less likely to have heart attacks than inactive people. More directly, research has suggested

that people who exercise regularly feel less tension and stress, are more self-confident, and show greater optimism. People who do not exercise regularly feel more stress, are more likely to be depressed, and experience other negative consequences.

8. **Collateral Programmes:** In addition to institutional efforts aimed at reducing stress, many organizations are turning to collateral programmes. A collateral stress programme is an organizational programme specifically created to help employees deal with stress. Organizations have adopted stress management programmes, health promotion programmes, and other kinds of programmes for this purpose. More and more companies are developing their own programmes or adopting existing programmes of this type. For example, Lockheed Martin offers screening programmes for its employees to detect signs of hypertension. The Mastering Change box provides other examples.

   Finally, organizations try to help employees cope with stress through other kinds of programmes. For example, existing career development programmes, like the one at General Electric, are used for this purpose. Other companies use programmes promoting everything from humour to massage as antidotes for stress. Of course, little or no research supports some of the claims made by advocates of these programmes. Thus, managers must take steps to ensure that any organizational effort to help employees cope with stress is at least reasonably effective.

25.7 SUMMARY

Stress is a person's adaptive response to a stimulus that places excessive psychological or physical demands on that person. According to the general adaptation syndrome perspective, the three stages of response to stress are alarm, resistance, and exhaustion. Two important forms of stress are eustress and distress.

Type A personalities are more competitive and time-driven than Type B personalities. Initial evidence suggested that Type A's are more susceptible to coronary heart disease, but recent findings provide less support for this idea. Hardiness, optimism, cultural context, and gender may also affect stress.

Stress can be caused by many factors. Major organizational stressors are task demands, physical demands, role demands, and interpersonal demands. Life stressors include life change and life trauma.

Stress has many effects. Individual effects can include behavioral, psychological, and medical problems. On the organizational level, stress can affect performance and attitudes or cause withdrawal. Burnout is another possibility.

Primary individual mechanisms for managing stress are exercise, relaxation, time management, role management, and support groups. Organizations use both institutional and collateral programmes to control stress.

People have numerous dimensions to their work and personal lives. When these dimensions are interrelated, individuals must decide for themselves which are more important and how to balance them.

25.8 SELF-ASSESSMENT QUESTIONS

1. What can be done to prevent burnout? If someone you know is suffering burnout, how would you advise that person to recover form it?
2. What are the major stressors for a student?
3. Is an organizational stressor or a life stressor likely to be more powerful?
4. Do you practice any of the stress reduction methods discussed in the text? Which ones? Do you use others not mentioned in the text?
5. Do you consider yourself a Type A or a Type B person? Why?
6. Do you agree that a certain degree of stress is necessary to induce high energy and motivation?
7. Describe one or two recent times when stress had both good and bad consequences for you.
8. Describe a time when you successfully avoided stage 3 of the GAS and another time when you got to stage 3.
9. Can a person who is a Type A change? If so, how?

26

CONFLICT MANAGEMENT

Learning Objective

The main objective of this chapter is to make the students learn about the concept of conflict management, objectives, factors responsible for conflict, conflict process, and types of conflict.

26.1 CONCEPT OF CONFLICT

The Webster's Dictionary defines conflict as "a battle, contest of opposing forces, discord, antagonism existing between primitive desires, instincts and moral, religious, or ethical ideals." Conflict occurs when two or more people or organizations disagree because their needs, wants, goals, or values are different. Hurt feelings, anger, bruised egos, and poor communication are all the precursors to conflict. However, conflict is not the end of the world, or your team or group.

Some tools have been developed that will help us all recognize conflict and deal with it so that our group or team can move on, stronger than before. Most of us have been in a conflict at some point in our lives. But did we know that conflict was coming? Could we have seen it, and "headed it off at the pass"? The visible quarters of conflict may include: body language, disagreements, regardless of issue, withholding bad news, surprises, strong public statements, airing disagreements through media, conflicts in value systems, desire for power, increasing lack of support, open disagreement, lack of candor on budget problems or other sensitive issues, lack of clear goals, no discussion of progress, failed goals, and inability to evaluate leaders fairly, thoroughly, or at all. Many people think of conflict as negative. But conflict can be both negative and positive. Conflict is negative when it…

- Damages the spirit of the team or an individual
- Divides people and groups, and makes cooperation difficult
- Leads to harmful behaviour, like fighting or name-calling

- Makes people or group focus on their differences
- Takes attention away from other activities

But it can be positive or constructive when it…

- Brings about solutions to problems
- Causes real communication
- Clears up important problems or issues
- Develops understanding and skills
- Gets everyone involved in solving issues
- Helps people learn more about each other and cooperate
- Release emotion, anxiety, and stress in a positive way

While the definition of conflict and our feelings about it tend to be negative, conflict itself does not need to be negative! How we manage our conflict can sway the outcome, our feelings about the way it was handled, and the people involved conflict.

26.2 CONFLICT MANAGEMENT

Conflict management is what we're doing when we identify and deal with conflict in a reasonable manner. To manage conflict the management Gurus say that we must develop and use skills like effective communication, problem solving, and negotiating. When we resolve issues, we need to focus on the things we need or desire as a group, and not things needed or wanted by individuals. This promotes working with each other instead of against each other. There are some proven strategies that you can use to help resolve conflicts within your groups. The Ohio Commission on Dispute Resolution and Conflict Management in USA describes five popular styles.

26.2.1 Style 1: Collaborating

- **Why should I collaborate?** Cooperation will help everyone achieve their goals and keep relationships healthy.
- **A collaborator's attitude:** Talking through the conflict will help us find creative ways to solve our problems where everyone is satisfied in the end.
- **When should I collaborate?**
  - Everyone trust each other.
  - No one wants total decision or resolution power.
  - Everyone needs to have a part in the decision.
  - Everyone involved will change their thinking as more information is available.
  - People need to work through personal hurts and disappointments.
- **When should I choose another method?**
  - When you need a resolution that won't take a lot of time and money.
  - When some may take advantage of others' trust.

26.2.2 Style 2: Compromising

- **Why should I compromise?** Winning something while losing a little is sometimes okay.
- **A compromiser's attitude:** We should all meet halfway to do what is best for the group and each of us can still get part of what we want.
- **When should I compromise?**
    - No one at the table has more position or power than anyone else and everyone is equally committed to the group's goals.
    - Time can be saved by agreeing on a situation that works for everyone "for now".
    - Achieving all of your goals are only somewhat important.
- **When should I choose another method?**
    - Things that are important to you may be lost in the fray.
    - Someone's demands are too great for the rest of the table.

26.2.3 Style 3: Accomodating

- **Why should I accommodate?** Our commonalities are more important than other issues and facing differences may hurt relationships.
- **An accommodator's attitude:** I will please others by playing down how important the issue or conflict is in order to protect relationships.
- **When should I accommodate?**
    - Issues not as important to you as it is to others.
    - You know you can't win.
    - Everyone agreeing is the most important thing.
    - The things people have in common are more important than their differences.
- **When should I choose another method?**
    - Some ideas don't get attention.
    - Credibility and influence can be lost.

26.2.4 Style 4: Competing

- **Why should I compete?** Resolving a conflict is associated with competition and winning.
- **A competitor's attitude:** I must use all of my power to win the conflict.
- **When should I compete?**
    - You know you're right.
    - A quick decision is necessary.
    - Strong personalities are overshadowing other people.
    - Defending your rights or position.
- **When should I choose another method?**
    - Can make conflict worse.
    - Those on the losing end may attempt to get back at the winners.

26.2.5 Style 5: Avoiding

- **Why should I avoid?** Not the right time or place to address this issue.
- **An avoider's attitude:** I avoid conflict by leaving, avoid, or putting off discussions.
- **When should I avoid?**
    - Conflict is small and the future of a relationships is at stake.
    - There is no time to devote to conflict resolution.
    - Other issues are more important than the conflict.
    - There is no chance of getting your concerns heard.
    - One party is too emotionally involved and others can better resolve the conflict.
    - More information is needed.
- **When should I choose another method?**
    - Decisions may be made by default.
    - Putting off or avoiding issues may make matters worse.

Conflict occurs when the message and cues from others about the role are clear but contradictory or mutually exclusive. One common form is interrole conflict–conflict between roles. For example, if a person's boss says that to get ahead one must work overtime and on weekends, and the same person's spouse says that more time is needed at home with the family, conflict may result. Intrarole conflict may occur when the person gets conflicting demands from different sources within the context of the same role. A manager's boss may tell her that she needs to put more pressure on subordinates to follow new work rules. At the same time, her subordinates may indicate that they expect her to get the rules changes. Thus, the cues are in conflict, and the manager may be unsure about which course to follow.

Intrasender conflict occurs when a single source sends clear but contradictory message. This might occur if the boss says one morning that there can be no more overtime for the next month but after lunch tells someone to work late that same evening. Person-role conflict results from a discrepancy between the role requirements and the individual's personal values, attitudes, and needs. If a person is told to do something unethical or illegal, or if the work is distasteful (for example, firing a close friend), person-role conflict is likely. Role conflict of all varieties is of particular concern to managers. Research has shown that conflict may occur in a variety of situations and lead to a variety of adverse consequences, including stress, poor performance, and rapid turnover.

26.3 MANAGING CONFLICT

Some people aren't willing to admit that they may not be the best at conflict management, but that doesn't mean that they aren't sometimes involved in the management process. You can't change the way that people behave or approach conflict, but you can arm yourself with some tools to help you successfully navigate conflict when not everyone is on the same page.

- **Sherman Tanks**—These intimidators get "in your face" to argue and state opinions as facts.
    1. Get their attention by using their first name to begin a sentence.

2. Maintain eye contact; give them time to wind down.
3. Stand up to them without fighting; don't worry about being polite.
4. Suggest you sit down to continue discussions.

- **Snipers**—These individuals take potshots in meetings but avoid one-on-one confrontations.
  1. Expose the attack; draw them out in public and don't let social convention stop you.
  2. Get other opinions—don't give in to the sniper's views.
  3. Provide the sniper with alternatives to a direct contest.
- **Chronic Complainers**—These people find faults with everyone, except themselves.
  1. Politely interrupt and get control of the situation.
  2. Quickly sum up the facts.
  3. Ask for their complaints in writing.
- **Negativists**—These individuals know that nothing new will work; they'll disrupt group brainstorming sessions.
  1. Acknowledge their valid points.
  2. Describe past successes.
  3. Avoid "you're wrong, I'm right" arguments.
- **Exploders**—These individuals throw tantrums that quickly escalate.
  1. Give them time to regain self control.
  2. If they don't, shout a neutral phrase such as "STOP!"
  3. Take a time-out or have a private meeting with them.

26.4 STEPS FOR ANALYZING CONFLICT

How can you manage conflict and disagreements in ways that strengthen instead of damage personal and professional relationships? These five steps which could help you out…

- **STEP 1: ANALYZE THE CONFLICT**

  Don't be afraid to ask questions of everyone involved. Take in answers from a variety of sources, and gain as much information as you can.
- **STEP 2: DETERMINE YOUR MANAGEMENT STRATEGY**

  When you understand the basis of the conflict and everyone involved, you will need to develop a plan to manage the conflict. There are many plans to choose from, so you can pick the one that is most appropriate for your situation.
- **STEP 3: PRE-NEGOTIATION**

  Steps must be taken for discussion to begin. This to think about includes:

  (i) Someone has to start the conversation! If neither party is willing to do so, bring in an outsider who will remain neutral to begin discussions.

  (ii) Everyone must be ready to come to the table, to work together, and resolve the issues.

  (iii) The group must agree on rules for the discussion. Some ideas of things to include are: ways we'll communicate and how we'll make the final decision.

(iv) BE ORGANIZED! Location, time, place and materials must all be in order for conflict management to work.

(v) Everyone at the table must agree on what information is put on the table, relevant to the conflict, and how the group will get answers to questions.

- **STEP 4: NEGOTIATION**

  Negotiations should be discussions that include:

  (i) Reasons, needs, concerns and motivations for differing positions

  (ii) Current options

  (iii) Evaluation of all the current options

  (iv) Written agreement that documents what everyone understands

  (v) Everyone must be confident that all parties will follow through with their parts of the agreement. Make sure everyone is on the same page and understands the expectations.

- **STEP 5: POST-NEGOTIATION**

  Once negotiation is complete, the group should take the actions they decided upon.

  (i) Individuals should get support from outside parties who may have been involved in some way. Outsiders must be on board with the terms of the agreements reached during Step 4.

  (ii) Communication and working together should continue throughout this process.

Reflection: Identify a time when you've been in a conflict. How did you behave? Did you escalate or de-escalate the situation? If you could replay the situation, what would you do differently? Identify times when you have behaved like one of the "conflict problem people" listed in the brochure. How can we keep ourselves in check so that we don't repeat past mistakes? How can you implement the strategies contained in this lesson in your club or group?

26.5 STRATEGIES FOR MANAGING CONFLICT

Methods for Managing Conflict: Given the right opportunity and motivation all conflict can be resolved but not always to the satisfaction of all parties. The effect of disagreement and the methods for resolution depend on how conflict is managed by the participants.

The following are some common methods that can help to effectively manage conflict.

- **Third Party Intervention.** Using this strategy requires a third party that is unbiased and is not taking sides to support either party in conflict. The third party may be known or unknown to the parties involved or may even be from a different location. Some assumptions in using a third party are:

  (1) The third party is trusted or respected by participants.

  (2) Te third party is an expert, has knowledge or is competent to give a decision about the issue(s) in dispute.

  (3) The third party has the power or authority to rule over the decision.

- **Suppression.** "We all get along here", "we run a happy ship", "don't rock the boat", and "nice people don't fight", are the voices of suppression. People who use suppression play down their differences in a belief it is better to "go along to get along."

- **Power or Dominance.** Power is often used to settle differences. The source of power may be physical, or vested by authority or position. Power strategies, however, result in a win-lose situation. In other words, in order for somebody to gain something, somebody else has to lose something. Normally the loser will not support the final decision in the same way as the winner, and may even attempt to sabotage the decision.
- **Integration or Collaboration.** This approach requires all parties in a conflict situation to recognize the legitimate abilities and expertise of each other in the process of resolution. This method attempts to find an acceptable solution that does not necessarily require giving and getting as in a compromised solution. The group problem solving concept is considered the optimum form of managing conflict because it encourages a common search for creative alternatives to resolve the conflict that is rewarding to all parties.
- **Denial or Avoidance.** With this approach, individuals attempt to reduce or get rid of the conflict by denying it exists, both parties shun each other or dodge the issue of disagreement.
- **Compromise or Negotiation.** Compromise and negotiation are often regarded as virtues in our culture. Compromise is an agreement between parties about what each should give or get in a particular situation. "You give a little, and I'll give a little so we can meet each other halfway", is a way we have been taught to get along with others. It is believed all parties will profit from the compromise or at least have a feeling of being treated fairly. Negotiation reaches an impasse when one or all participants become set in what they are willing to give and limits have been reached. The compromise, therefore, would allow all parties to reach an agreement with which all would be somewhat satisfied or rewarded.

(4) All parties involved will accept the decision of the third party.
(5) All parties believe a just and fair decision will be rendered.

26.6 SUMMARY

The term conflict was originally defined as "striking at another", "to fight with an enemy or do battle with opposing forces." Later meanings included "being antagonistic", or "a clash between contradictory impulses within an individual."

Conflict is inevitable because people will always have different viewpoints, ideas, and opinions. The issue is how will you deal with or relate to these differences. It is unfortunate that negative connotations are often associated with conflict, because, if properly managed, conflict is highly constructive and essential to cross-cultural interactions.

There are three levels of conflict. If we are to have a clear understanding of conflict, it is important to know the three levels and their relationship to each other. Level one: intrapersonal conflict is an experience that takes place within the individual. *Ask the group for an example. (An example would be a soldier who feels guilty about telling sexual or ethnic jokes but vigorously participates when friends are around.).* Level Two: Interpersonal conflict is experienced between individuals in the same location, *e.g., coworkers, roommates, team members. It exists whenever people interact or come together to accomplish a common goal or objective.* Level Three: Intragroup conflict is defined as conflict between groups in the same organization or command.

Sources of intragroup conflict are often caused by issues of group cohesion, such as "sticking together, leadership and status, power or influence and lack of or limited resources."

Trying to identify or determine the cause of conflict is sometimes difficult. Heightened emotions or bad feelings may cloud the real cause of any conflict and detract soldiers from examining the facts. The cause of conflict can also have multiple factors which makes it difficult to isolate just one cause. The following is a list of common causes in conflict situations:

- *Different values and beliefs.*
- *Perception differences.*
- *Diverse goals or objectives.*
- *Group status or identity.*
- *Race, ethnicity, or gender differences.*
- *Personality clash or conflict.*
- *Disagreement on how things should be done.*
- *Tension and stress.*

Many believe that the negative characteristics of conflict occur because group members become closed minded to any compromises. It often occurs when someone wants his or her own way. Hostility among group members is normally followed by an assumption of competition that someone will win and someone will lose. These negative forces have destructive consequences.

Earlier we stated conflict was neither good nor bad. If viewed as a natural process, conflict is the opportunity to explore and resolve differences in a constructive manner. Conflict is constructive when individuals or group members have a new understanding of the functions of healthy conflict and avoid the destructive negative forces.

During our discussion here, we defined conflict, explored various levels of conflict, and identified sources of conflict, and strategies to manage interpersonal conflict. Additionally we discussed the positive aspects, components of conflict and how it can contribute to individual and group problem solving. We examined six strategies for effectively managing interpersonal conflict and the negative and positive attributes of each. Are there any questions about the methods for resolving conflict?

26.7 SELF-ASSESSMENT QUESTIONS

1. Describe in detail characteristics and role of conflict management and its agents.
2. What are the reasons for not managing the conflict? What can management do to overcome such reasons?
3. Describe in detail the various steps that are essential to be taken in the conflict process. Give examples where necessary.
4. Define conflict. What are the factors responsible for conflict? State and explain different strategies for conflict management.

27 ORGANIZATIONAL CHANGE

Learning Objective

The main objective of this chapter is to make the students learn about the concept of management of change, objectives, factors responsible for change, change process, types of changes, steps in managed change and change agents, etc.

27.1 CONCEPT OF ORGANIZATIONAL CHANGE

In the present time, every organization faces dynamic and changing environments, which in turn requires them to adapt to theses changes. Changes simply mean the alteration of status quo. Changes are necessary in every organization to keep the level of given stability. Organizational changes include changes in attitudes, nature and interest of the employees, technological and environmental changes related to organization and changes in rules and regulation affecting the organization. The management of every organization should continuously monitor the outside environment and be innovative and creative to find new and better utilization of organizational resources so that customers' needs are competitively met and their problems can be properly solved. The environment includes the social environment, cultural and religious environment, biological and physical environment, natural calamities and opportunities, regional environment, educational and philosophical environment and other external as well as internal environments of the organization.

In order to bring success in any organization, changing pattern of production, finance, human resources and communication should be analyzed and managed. The management of the organization has to be alert to the changes, which generally affect the working of the organization. An organization faces its own change in structure, authority, responsibility and job restructuring by introducing various absorption, mergers, liquidation and other reorganizational activities. Often, changes can be managed by introducing other changes. According to Barney and Griffin, "the primary reason cited for organizational problems is the failure by managers to properly anticipate or respond to forces for change".

Change refers to something which occurs to an organization, a group or an individual. A managed change relates to the active involvement of the organization, group or individual in making things occur with a view to accomplish the best interests of both the individual and the organization. Change means managed change which can be used to solve problems more readily, learn from experiences, adapt to new conditions and become more competent. Organizational change refers to a relatively enduring alteration of the present state of an organization or its components or interrelationships amongst the components, and their differential and integrated functions, in totality or partially, in order to attain greater viability in the context of the present and anticipated future environment.

It may embrace activities such as amalgamation and bifurcation, diversification, reorganization, restructuring, change in design or the introduction of new systems involving the total organization or its sections. It may also include change of people, task and technology as well as change in processes, customs, norms and culture of the organization. The change may be aimed at one or more of such aspects and tends to be correlated. A change in tasks may cause changes not only in people, structure and techniques but also in the relationships between these components of the organization, and may lead to reallocation of resources. Management of organizational change may encompass anticipation of needs for changes, decision about the required changes and initiation and implementation of changes, ensuring that they are stable and lasting in nature.

27.2 GOALS AND TYPES OF ORGANIZATIONAL CHANGE

27.2.1 Goals of Organizational Change

The organizational change has a number of goals, explicit and implied. Invariably, the most obvious common goals are: higher performance, acceptance of new techniques, increased motivation, greater innovation, enhanced cooperation, decreased turnover, etc. Underlying these goals are two basic objectives: changes in an organization's level of adaptation to its changing environment, and changes in the internal behavioural patterns of employees.

There is the goal of modification in adaptation level. Organizations are constantly striving to adapt themselves in a better way to their external environmental conditions. As the management is not able to control completely the environmental conditions, it frequently induces internal organizational changes with a view to cope more effectively with new challenges stemming from outside in the form of enhanced competition, technological advancements, government legislation and compelling social requirements. Organizational changes are induced in response to these environmental conditions. Sometimes changes are introduced in anticipation of future requirements by proactive organizations which tend to change their environmental conditions as well as themselves.

There is the objective of achieving modification in behavioural patterns of employees which arises when an organization's level of adaptation does not improve unless its employees behave in a different way in relationship to each other and their jobs. Organizations do not function through computers, but involve people to make decisions in their unique patterns arising from a set of formal and informal behavioural patterns and procedures. Accordingly, any organizational change, irrespective of whether it is induced through a new structural design or a training programme, aims to get employees to adopt new behavioural patterns and procedures relating to each other and their jobs. To succeed in achieving organization-wide impacts, it is necessary that these new patterns embrace not only superior-subordinate relations but also different work groups and larger subsystems of the entire organization.

27.2.2 Types of Change

For operational enhancement of the organization there are various organizational domains where changes can be made. The various types of changes that have considerable impact on organizational culture are:

1. Task Approach: Job performed by individuals, motivational process, job structure and job design are restructured as per changes.
2. Structural Change: It involves change in the structural designs such as chart, authority, responsibility, procedures and policies. Decentralized operations and participative management is major area of concern for management in organizational structure. The structural changes have major impact on the organization's social climate and members are required to develop team spirit to make on the spot decision at the point of operations.
3. Strategic Change: This change is related to change in the mission of the organization. A single mission has to be changed to the multiple missions with the changing need of the environment. The strategy, programmes, procedures, budgeting, rules and regulation are designed, redesigned and restructured according to changes.
4. Process-oriented/Technological Change: These changes are related to technological development, information processing, automation and use of robotics in the manufacturing operations. The techniques are changed as per the needs of the work flow, physical layouts, work methods, procedures and work standards. The tools and techniques are modified under the organizational changes. This would affect the organizational culture and hence changes in the behaviour patterns of members.
5. People-oriented Change: People give more importance to the motivation and reward system. They are particular about their skills, selection and training and performance appraisal. These changes are directed towards performance improvement as well as developing a sense of self actualizations among the members. These can be developed by closer interactions with employees and by special behavioural training and modification sessions.

27.3 FORCES FOR CHANGE

More and more organizations today face a dynamic and changing environment. This, in turn, makes these organizations either to change or parish.

There are five specific forces that are acting as stimulants for change.

(i) World Politics: We have called for seeing OB in a global context while business schools have been preaching a global perspective since the early 1980s, no one–not even the strongest proponents of globalization–could have imagined how world politics would change in recent years. A few examples make the point: the fall of the Berlin Wall, the reunification of Germany, Iraq's invasion of Kuwait, and the breakup of the Soviet Union. Almost every major U.S. defence contractor, for instance, has had to rethink its business and make serious changes in response to the demise of the Soviet Union. Companies like Hughes Electronics, Lock-heed Martin, Raytheon, and Northrop Grumman have each cut tens of thousands of jobs since the early 1990s.

(ii) **Competition:** has changed the entire spectrum of business. The global economy means that competitors are as likely to come from across the ocean as from across the town. Heightened competition also means that established organizations need to defend themselves against both traditional competitors who develop new products and services, and small, entrepreneurial firms with innovative offerings. Successful organizations will be the ones that can change in response to the competition. They will be fast on their feet, capable of developing new products rapidly and getting them to market quickly. They will rely on short production runs, short product cycles, and an ongoing stream of new products. In other words, they will be flexible. They will require an equally flexible and responsive workforce that can adapt to rapidly and even radically changing conditions.

(iii) **Economic Shocks:** have continued to impose changes on organizations. In recent years, for instance, interest rates have become more volatile and the economies of individual countries have become more interdependent. When interest rates rise, for example, the market for new home loans and refinancing declines. For many mortgage brokerage firms, revenue declines and layoffs ensue. Similarly, the profitability of US security firms such as Merrill Lynch and Dean Witter is increasingly linked to the health of foreign economies and markets.

(iv) **Technology:** is changing jobs and organizations. The substitution of computer control for direct supervision, for instance, is resulting in wider spans of control for managers and flatter organizations. Sophisticated information technology is also making organizations more responsive. Companies like AT& T, Motorola, General Electric, and Chyrsler can now develop, make, and distribute their products in a fraction of the time it took them a decade ago. And, as organizations have had to become more adaptable, so too have their employees. Many jobs are being reshaped. Individuals earlier doing narrow, specialized, and routine jobs are being replaced by work teams whose members can perform multiple tasks and actively participate in team decisions.

(v) **Changing Nature of the Workforce:** For instance, almost every organization has to adjust to a multicultural environment. Human resource policies and practices have to change in order to attract and keep this diverse workforce. And many companies are spending large amounts of money on training to upgrade the skills of employees.

Lewin in his three steps model introduced "force-field analysis" to induce, implement and manage change. This analysis is based upon the assumption that we are in state of equilibrium when there is balance between forces that induce change and forces that resist change. Kurt Lewin argued that successful change should follow following steps:

- ***Unfreezing:*** Lewin believes that the change should not come as a surprise to members of the organization. Sudden, unannounced change would be socially destructive. The management must pave the way by "unfreezing the situation", so that members would be willingly and ready to accept the change. Unfreezing means the status quo and this is considered to be an equilibrium state. It makes the individuals or organizations aware and prepare for the change. Unfreezing can be possible in one of the three ways as depicted in figure. These are— Driving Forces, which direct behaviour away from the status quo, can be increased.

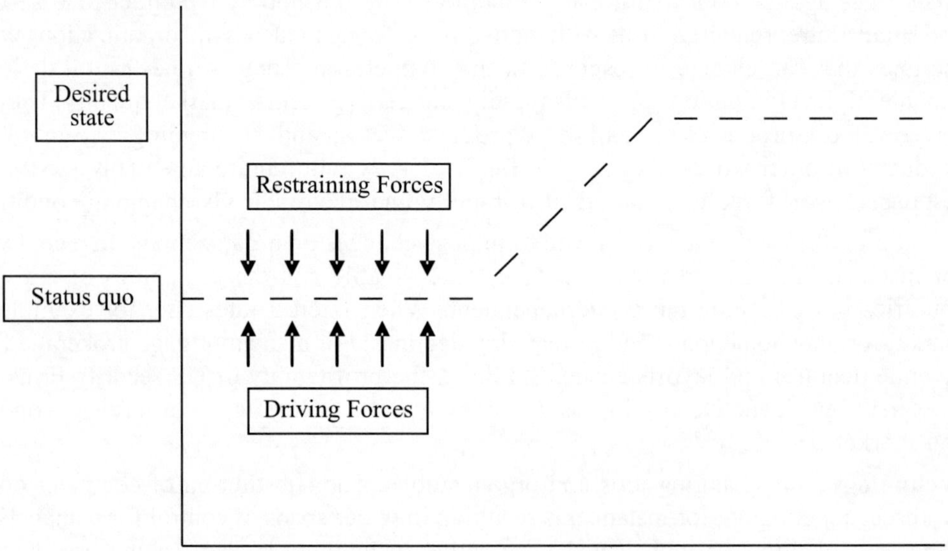

Restraining Forces, which hinder movement from the existing equilibrium or it forces hinder movement away from the status quo, can be decreased. The third alternative is to combine the first two approaches.

- ***Movement or Changing:*** This a stage at which the individual being changed learn new behaviour, methods of working, new thinking, perception of new roles, etc.
- ***Refreezing:*** It is stabilization of change intervention by balancing driving and restraining forces. It means that what has been learned is integrated into actual practice. At this stage, the individuals learned new beliefs, feelings and behaviour. The new behaviour must replace the former behaviour completely for successful change to take place.

The change process is not a one time application but a continuous process due to dynamism and ever changing environment. Lewin concluded that to achieve change, we must overcome the status quo. The change forces are known as driving forces and the forces that resist change are known as restraining forces as shown below:

Driving Forces → Equilibrium → Restraining Forces

Managers who are trying to implement change must analyze this balance of driving and restraining forces. For effective change the driving forces should be strengthen and the restraining forces should be weaken successfully.

27.4 THE CHANGE PROCESS

Once, the need for change and the goals of such a change are recognized and accepted, the management must introduce the change process in such a manner that such change is more or less permanent and the management does not shift back to the original and more familiar ways of doing things. To make the change more lasting, Kurt Lewin proposed 3 phases of the change process for moving the organization from the present to the future. These stages are: (1) Unfreezing, (2) Changing, and (3) Refreezing.

(i) Unfreezing: According to Schein, unfreezing is the process of breaking down the old attitudes and behaviours, customs and traditions so that they start with a clean slate. This can be achieved by making announcements, holding meetings and promoting the ideas throughout the organization via bulletin boards, personal contacts and group conferences.

The unfreezing process basically cleans the slate so that it can accept new writings on it which can then become the operational style.

(ii) Changing or Moving to the New Condition: Once the unfreezing process has been completed and the members of the organization recognize the need for change and have been fully prepared to accept such change, their behaviour patterns have to be redefined. H.C. Kellman has proposed three methods of reassigning new patterns of behaviour. These are:

(a) Compliance: Compliance is achieved by strictly enforcing the reward and punishment strategy for good or bad behaviour. Fear of punishment, actual punishment or actual reward seems to change behaviour for the better. For example, many people have stopped smoking because of warning given by the Surgeon General of United States that smoking causes cancer of the lungs.

(b) Identification: Identification occurs when members are psychologically impressed upon to identify themselves with some given role models whose behaviour they would like to adopt and try to become like them. Many public organizations use celebrities as role models in advising young people not to try drugs.

(c) Internalization: Internalization involves changing the individual's thought processes in order to adjust to a new environment. Members are left alone to look themselves and they are given freedom to learn and adopt new behaviour in order to succeed in the new set of circumstances. Sometimes, soul searching brings about a new dimension to the philosophy of existence and thus brings about changes in such behavioural patterns that are not considered socially or professionally redeeming.

(iii) Refreezing: Refreezing occurs when the new behaviour becomes a normal way of life. The new behaviour must replace the former behaviour completely for successful change to take place. Also, it should be permanent in nature. Accordingly, it must be continuously reinforced so that this new acquired behaviour does not diminish or extinguish.

This must be clearly understood that the change process is not a one time application but a continuous process due to dynamism and ever changing environment. Accordingly, the phenomena of 'unfreezing, changing and refreezing' are a cyclical one and remain continuously in process.

The implementation of this three steps change model can be seen in the case of kidnapping victims or prisoners of war or in deprogramming of some religious cultists. The prisoners of war, for example, may be brainwashed into believing that they are fighting a losing and immoral war and that their enemy is really their friend, by certain shock treatments which involve three steps of unfreezing, changing and refreezing process as explained before. If these prisoners return back to their own country, the process can be repeated to bring them back to their original behaviour.

Another methodology to induce, implement and manage change was also introduced by Kurt Lewin, who called it "force-field analysis". This analysis is based upon the assumption that we are in a state of equilibrium when there is balance between forces that induce change and forces that resist change. To achieve change, we must overcome this status quo. The change forces are known as driving forces and the forces that resist change are known as restraining forces as shown below:

Driving forces → Equilibrium ← Restraining forces

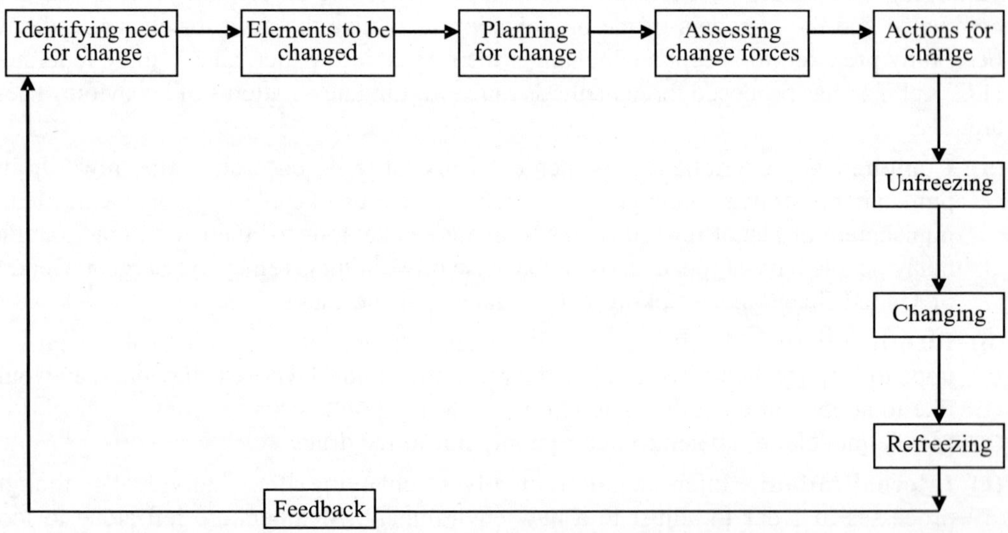

Managers who try to implement change must analyze this balance of driving and restraining forces and then strengthen the driving forces or weaken the restringing forces sufficiently so that change can take place.

27.5 ACTION RESEARCH AND CHANGE

Action research refers to a change process based on the systematic collection of data and then selection of a change action based on what the analyzed data indicate. Their importance lies in providing a scientific methodology for managing planned change.

The process of action research consists of five steps: diagnosis, analysis, feedback, action, and evaluation. You'll note that these steps closely parallel the scientific method.

(i) **Diagnosis:** The change agent, often an outside consultant in action research, begins with gathering information about problems, concerns, and needed changes from members of the organization. This diagnosis is analogous to a physician's search to find what specifically ails a patient. In action research, the change agent asks questions, interviews employees, reviews records, and listens to the concerns of employees.

(ii) **Analysis:** The information gathered during the diagnostic stage is then analyzed. What problems do people key in on? What patterns do these problems seem to take? The change agent synthesizes this information into primary concerns, problem areas, and possible actions.

(iii) **Feedback:** Action research includes extensive involvement of the change targets. That is, the people who will be involved in any change program must be actively involved in determining what the problem is and participating in creating the solution. So the third step is sharing with employees what has been found from steps one and two. The employees, with the help of the change agent, develop action plans for bringing about any needed change.

(iv) **Action:** Now the action part of action research is set in motion. The employees and the change agent carry out the specific actions to correct the problems that have been identified.

(v) **Evaluation:** Finally, consistent with the scientific underpinnings of action research, the change agent evaluates the effectiveness of the action plans. Using the initial data gathered as a benchmark, any subsequent changes can be compared and evaluated.

Action research provides at least two specific benefits for an organization. First, its problem focused. The change agent objectively looks for problems and the type of problems and determines the type of change action. While this may seem intuitively obvious, a lot of change activities are not done this way. Rather, they're solution centred. The change agent has a favourite solution–for example, implementing flexitime, teams or a management by objectives programme–and then seeks out problems that his or her solution fits. Second, because action research so heavily involves employees in the process, resistance to change gets reduced, if not vanished.

27.6 STEPS IN MANAGED CHANGE

The first step in the change process is to identify the need for change and the area of change as to whether it is a strategic change, process-oriented change or employee-oriented change. This need for change can be identified either through internal factors or through external forces that may be in place. Once the need for change is identified, the following general steps can be taken to implement such change.

(i) **Develop new goals and objectives:** The managers must identify as to what new outcomes they wish to achieve. This may be a modification of previous goals due to changed internal and external environment or it may be a new set of goals and objectives.

(ii) **Select an agent for change:** The management must decide as to who will initiate and oversee this change. A manager may be assigned this duty or even outside specialists and consultants can be brought in to suggest the various methods to bring in the change and monitor the change process.

(iii) Diagnose the problem: It is important to gather all pertinent data regarding the area or the problem where the change is needed. This data should be critically analyzed to pinpoint the key issues. Then the solutions can be focused on those key issues.

(iv) Select methodology: Because of natural resistance to change, it is very important to chart out a methodology for change which would be correct and acceptable to all. Members' emotions must be taken into consideration while devising such methodology.

(v) Develop a plan: This step involves putting together a plan as to what is to be done. For example, if the company wants to develop and implement a flexitime policy, it must decide as to what type of workers will be affected by it or whether flexitime should be given to all members or only to some designated workers.

(vi) Strategy for implementation of the plan: In this stage, the management must decide on the "when", "where" and "how" of the plan. This includes the right timing of putting the plan to work, how the plan will be communicated to workers in order to have the lesser resistance and how the implementation will be monitored.

(vii) Implementation of the plan: Once the right timing and right channels of communication have been established, the plan is put into action. It may be in the form of simple announcement or it may require briefing sessions or in-house seminars so as to gain acceptance of all the members and specially those who are going to be directly affected by the change.

(viii) Receive and evaluate feedback: Evaluation consists of comparing actual results to the set goals. Feedback will confirm if these goals are being met so that if there is any deviation between the goals and the actual performance outcomes, then corrective measures can be taken.

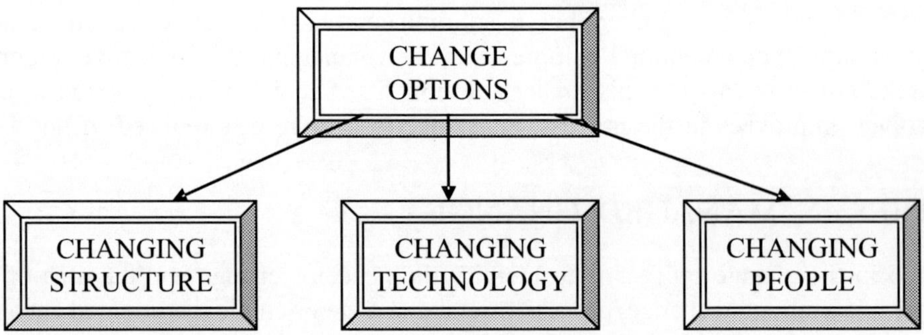

27.7 THE CHANGE AGENTS AND THEIR CHARACTERISTICS

The change agents are those factors that are responsible for bringing about the change in the individual behaviour patterns. This is the most important type of change since other types of changes such as in strategy, structure or process can always be introduced simply by the management and most often these changes are accepted by the workers and also because behaviour is a highly complex phenomenon and it may require a number of strategies to make desirable changes in human behaviour. These change agents may either be the initiators of change or serve as catalysts for such change. Four types of change agents have been identified.

(i) **Outside pressures:** These are pressures from the external environment and are directed towards change in the entire organization. These may be in the form of government intervention if there are serious quality or safety defects. The government may also get involved if there are labour strikes for a long period of time or mass demonstrations against the organization.

(ii) **Internal organizational development:** This can come slowly and through and within the organization itself. This may include redefinement of goals as well as participative goal setting such as MBO (Management by Objectives), work redesign, team development, and so on.

(iii) **Individual change:** This change is the modification of behaviour within the individual where personal goals may be better served in the changed environment of the organization. For example, in a government job, if a person who is habitually coming late to work without any obvious repercussions or reprimands, might change his behaviour if the organization starts taking notice of such tardiness in a negative way.

(iv) **Changes from central management:** The organizational change may come from the top management who may be convinced about its necessity and may direct the structural, strategic or technological changes that would be beneficial to the organization and its members.

There have been a number of change agents that have been at work in changing the organizational processes and structures. In America, for example, Ralph Nader, a consumer advocate has been responsible for many changes in the area of quality and safety of many products and especially in the automobiles. In addition, forces such as women's liberation movement and strong labour unions have brought about changes that have affected the work ethics of the organizations and work roles of its members.

Similarly, in India where the bureaucratic structure is deeply embedded in the organizational system, changes are being brought about by government regulations and by social pressures to give more freedom to the workers, to bring about equal opportunity for employment, irrespective of religion or gender and to keep pace with the changing world in technological processes.

The change agent may be in the form of a consultant who helps the client find solutions to the organizational problems. It could also be in the form a trainer who trains the client to achieve a set of skills that could be used in bringing about the change for desired outcomes. This change agent must have certain characteristics which would identify it to be more effective than others.

The way a change agent manages the process of change is indicated by certain factors and characteristics which have been identified by Havelock and Shaskin. The first letters of these factors together spell "HELP SCORES". These are:

(i) **Homophily:** It is the degree of closeness and similarity between the change agent and the client. The closer the relationship, the easier and more successful the change is likely to be. It is similar to listening to our close friend whom we trust and whose advice we seriously take.

(ii) **Empathy:** It involves understanding of feelings and emotions and thoughts of others by putting ourselves in others' shoes. This sincere understanding leads to improved communications between the client and the change agent which is very helpful in bringing about the desired change.

(iii) Linkage: It refers to the degree of collaboration between the change agent and the client. The tighter the linkage, the more likely is the success.

(iv) Promixity: The change agent and the client should have easy access to each other. The closer the proximity the better the relationship between the two and easier to develop the collaborative linkage.

(v) Structuring: This factor involves proper and clear planning of all activities that are related to change. If these activities are planed in step-by-step sequential factors, then the implementation would be easier.

(vi) Capacity: This factor refers to the organization's capacity to provide the resources that are needed for successful organizational development effort and implementation. These resources must be adequate and available when needed.

(vii) Openness: Openness refers to the conceptual environment which is conducive to the development of respect and understanding for each other's ideas, needs and feelings. The degree of openness between the change agent and the client would considerably affect the outcome of the programme.

(viii) Reward: All members expect that the change will bring potential benefits. These rewards should be both in the short run as well as in the long run. The greater the potential for rewards, the more determined the effort would be in making the required change.

(ix) Energy: Energy refers to the amount of effort put into the change process. This effort involves both the physical and psychological energy. The client's energy must be well spent and channelled precisely into the change programme itself. The energy of the change agent should not be spread over too many clients, for in that case, each of the clients individually may not receive the needed energy.

(x) Synergy: Synergy simply means that the whole is more than the sum of its parts. This means that the previous nine factors involving a variety of people, resources, energies and activities together result in synergy, if they support success mutually as well as individually, they are as favourable to the programme as possible.

These ten factors whose initials spell "HELP SCORES", describe the personal characteristics of successful change agents who have profound influence on the organizational development programmmes and processes of change.

27.8 RESISTANCE TO CHANGE

One of the well-documented findings from studies of individual and organizational behaviour is that organizations and their members resist change. In a sense, this is positive. It provides a degree of stability and predictability to behaviour. If there weren't some resistance, organizational behaviour would take on characteristics of chaotic randomness. Resistance to change can also be a source of functional conflict. For example, resistance to a reorganization plan or a change in a product line can stimulate a healthy debate over the merits of the idea and result in better decision-making. But there is a definite downside to resistance to change. It hinders adaptation and progress.

Resistance to change doesn't necessarily surface in standardized ways. Resistance can be overt, implicit, immediate, or deferred. It is easiest for management to deal with resistance when it is overt and immediate. For instance, a change is proposed and employees quickly respond by voicing complaints, engaging in work slowdown, threatening to go on strike, or the like. The greater challenge is managing resistance that is implicit and/or deferred. Implicit resistance efforts seem to be subtle but has serious ramifications—loss of loyalty to the organization, loss of motivation to work, increased errors or mistakes, increased absenteeism due to "sickness"—and hence more difficult to recognize. Similarly, deferred actions cloud the link between the source of the resistance and the reaction to it. A change may produce what appears to be only a minimal reaction at the time it is initiated, but then resistance surfaces weeks, months, or even years later. Let's look at the sources of resistance. For analytical purposes, we have categorized them by individual and organizational sources. In the real world, the sources often overlap.

27.8.1 Individual Resistance

Individual sources of resistance to change reside in basic human characteristics such as perceptions, personalities, and needs. The following summarizes five reasons why individuals resist change.

(i) Habit: Every time you go out to eat, do you try a different restaurant? Probably not. If you're like most people, you find a couple of places you like and return to them on a somewhat regular basis.

As human beings, we're subservient to our habit. Life is complex enough; we don't need to consider the full range of options for the hundreds of decisions we have to make everyday. To cope with this complexity, we all rely on habits or programmed responses. But when confronted with change, this tendency to respond in accustomed ways becomes a source of resistance. So when your department is moved to a new office building across town, it means you're likely to have to change many habits : waking up ten minutes earlier, taking a new set of streets to travel, finding a new parking place, adjusting to the new office layout, developing a new lunchtime routine, and so on.

(ii) Security: People with a high need for security are likely to resist change because it threatens their feelings of safety. When Sears announces it's laying off 50,000 people or Ford introduces new robotic equipment, or Indian banks thought of computerization in early 80's many employees at these firms feared that their jobs are in jeopardy.

(iii) Economic factors: Another source of individual resistance is the concern that change will lower one's income. Changes in job tasks or established work routines also can arouse economic fears if people are concerned that they won't be able to perform the new tasks or routines to their previous standards, especially when pay is closely tied to productivity.

(iv) Fear of the unknown: Changes substitute ambiguity and uncertainty for the known. The transition from high school to college is typically such an experience. By the time we're seniors in high school, we understand how things work. You might not have liked high school, but at least you understood the system. Then you move on to college and face a whole new and uncertain system. You have traded the known for the unknown and the fear or insecurity that goes with it.

Employees in organizations hold the same dislike for uncertainty. If, for example, the introduction of TQM means production workers will have to learn statistical process control techniques, some may fear they'll be unable to do so. They may, therefore, develop a negative attitude toward TQM or behave dysfunctionally if required to use statistical techniques.

(v) **Selective information processing:** Individuals shape their world through their perceptions. Once they have created this world, it resists change. So individuals are guilty of selectively processing information in order to keep their perceptions intact. They hear what they want to hear. They ignore information that challenges the world they've created. To return to the production workers who are faced with the introduction of TQM, they may ignore the arguments their bosses make in explaining why knowledge of statistics is necessary or the potential benefits the change will provide them.

27.8.2 Organizational Resistance

Organizations, by their very nature, are conservative. They actively resist change. You don't have to look far to see evidence of this phenomenon. Government agencies want to continue doing what they have been doing for years, whether the need for their service changes or remains the same. Organized religions are deeply entrenched in their history. Attempts to change church doctrine require great persistence and patience. Educational institutions, which exist to open minds and challenge established doctrine, are themselves extremely resistant to change. Most school systems are using essentially the same teaching technologies today as they were 50 years ago. The majority of business firms, too, appear highly resistant to change.
Six major sources of organizational resistance have been identified.

(i) **Structural Inertia:** Organizations have built-in mechanisms to produce stability. For example, the selection process systematically selects certain people in and certain people out. Training and other socialization techniques reinforce specific role requirements and skills. Formalization provides job descriptions, rules, and procedures for employees to follow.

The people who are hired into an organization are chosen for fit; they are then shaped and directed to behave in certain ways. When an organization is confronted with change, this structural inertia acts as a counterbalance to sustain stability.

(ii) **Limited focus of change:** Organizations are made up of a number of interdependent subsystems. You can't change one without affecting the others. For example, if management changes the technological processes without simultaneously modifying the organization's structure to match, the change in technology is not likely to be accepted. So limited changes in subsystems tend to get nullified by the larger system.

(iii) **Group Inertia:** Even if individuals want to change their behaviour, group norms may act as a constraint. An individual union member, for instance, may be willing to accept changes in his job suggested by management. But if union norms dictate resisting any unilateral change made by management, he's likely to resist.

(iv) **Threat to expertise:** Changes in organizational patterns may threaten the expertise of specialized groups. The introduction of decentralized personal computers, which allow managers to gain access to information directly from a company's main frame, is an example of a change that was strongly resisted by many information systems departments in the early 1980s. Why? Because decentralized end-user computing was perceived as a threat to the specialized skills held by those in the centralized information systems departments.

(v) **Threat to established power relationship:** Any redistribution of decision-making authority can threaten long-established power relationships within the organization. The introduction of participative decision-making or self-managed work teams is the kind of change that is often seen as threatening by supervisors and middle level managers.

(vi) **Threat to established resource allocations:** Those groups in the organization that control sizable resources often see change as a threat. They tend to be content with the way things are. Will the change, for instance, mean a reduction in their budgets or a cut in their staff size? Those that most benefit from the current allocation of resources often feel threatened by changes that may affect future allocations.

27.9 OVERCOMING RESISTANCE TO CHANGE

Six tactics have been suggested for use by change agents in dealing with resistance to change. Let's review them briefly.

(i) **Education and communication:** Resistance can be reduced through communicating with employees to help them see the logic of a change. This tactic basically assumes that the source of resistance lies in misinformation or poor communication. If employees receive the full facts and get any misunderstandings cleared up, resistance will subside. Communication can be achieved through one-on-one discussions, memos, group presentations, or reports. Does it work? It does, provided that the source of resistance is inadequate communication and that management-employee relations are characterized by mutual trust and credibility. If these conditions don't exist, the change is unlikely to succeed.

(ii) **Participation:** It's difficult for individuals to resist a change decision in which they have already participated. Prior to making a change, those opposed can be brought into the decision-making process. Assuming that the participants have the expertise to make a meaningful contribution, their involvement can reduce resistance, obtain commitment, and increase the quality of the change decision. However, against these advantages are the negatives: potential for a poor solution and great time consumption.

(iii) **Facilitation and support:** Change agents can offer a range of supportive efforts to reduce resistance. When employee fear and anxiety are high, employee counselling and therapy, new-skills training, or a short paid leave of absence may facilitate adjustment. The drawback of this tactic is that, as with the others, it is time-consuming. Additionally, it's expensive, and its implementation offers no assurance of success.

(iv) **Negotiation:** Another way for the change agent to deal with potential resistance to change is to exchange something of value for a lessening of the resistance. For instance, if the resistance comes from a group of few powerful individuals, a specific reward package can be negotiated that will meet their individual needs. Negotiation as a tactic may be necessary when resistance comes from a powerful source. Yet one cannot ignore its potentially high costs. Additionally, there is the risk that, once a change agent negotiates with one party to avoid resistance, he or she is open to the possibility of being black mailed by other individuals in positions of power.

(v) Manipulation and cooptation: Manipulation refers to covert influence attempts, twisting and distorting facts to make them appear more attractive, withholding undesirable information, and creating false rumors to get employees to accept a change are all examples of manipulation. If corporate management threatens to close down a particular manufacturing plant if that plant's employees fail to accept an across-the-board pay cut, and if the threat is actually untrue, management is using manipulation. Cooptation, on the other hand, is a form of both manipulation and participation. It seeks to "buy off" the leaders of a resistance group by giving them a key role in the change decision. The leaders' advice is sought, not to seek a better decision, but to get their endorsement. Both manipulation and cooptation are relatively inexpensive and easy ways to gain the support of adversaries, but the tactics can backfire if the 'targets' become aware that they are being tricked into or used. Once discovered, the change agent's credibility may drop to zero.

(vi) Coercion: Last on the list of tactics is coercion, that is, the application of direct threats of force upon the resisters. If the corporate management mentioned in the previous discussion really is determined to close a manufacturing plant if employees don't acquiesce to a pay cut, then coercion would be the label attached to its change tactic. Other examples of coercion are threats of transfer loss of promotions, negative performance evaluations, and a poor letter of recommendation. The advantages and drawbacks of coercion are approximately the same as those mentioned for manipulation and cooptation.

27.10 SUMMARY

Today the major forces which are exerting pressure for change on organizations are the globalization of markets, instantaneous communications travel at the speed of sound, political realignments, changing demographics, technological transformations, shortening product life cycles, corporate alliances, flattening organizations, and the like. Though change is the only constant factor in organizations, yet the pace of change has been considerably accelerated by these forces.

Lewin's three phases of the change process include: unfreezing, changing and refreezing. Unfreezing means unlearning of old things in order to learn a new thing. Changing refers to accepting a new behaviour. Refreezing means providing opportunities for new behaviour to get integrated into actual practice.

The reasons for individual resistance to change may lie in economic, psychological, and sociological factors. Organizational resistance to change may emanate from its reward system, resource limitations, organizational politics, structural rigidities, faulty introduction of change, poor record of change implementation, and so on.

Depending upon its situation, organization can broadly draw upon six strategies for managing resistance to change: education and communication, participation and involvement, support, incentives, manipulation and cooptation, and coercion.

27.11 SELF-ASSESSMENT QUESTIONS

1. What are the various types of changes? Under what circumstances would each be desirable?
2. What are the reasons for resistance to change? What can management do to overcome such resistance?
3. Describe in detail the three steps in the change process. Give examples where necessary.
4. Describe in detail characteristics and role of change agents.
5. Define change. What are the factors responsible for change? State and explain action research.
6. Are all managers change agents? Discuss. Identify the role of change agents in an organization.
7. "Resistance to change is an irrational response". Do you agree or disagree? Discuss. How does Lewin's three-step model of change deal with resistance to change?
8. What do you mean by planned change? What are its objectives?
9. "Organizational change has to be managed on technological, social and economic dimensions". Elaborate. What precautions must be taken in a democratic set-up to make a change acceptable to the personnel?

28 ORGANIZATIONAL DEVELOPMENT

Learning Objective

The main objective of this chapter is to make the students learn about the concept of organizational development and various OD interventions.

28.1 INTRODUCTION

Organization Development (OD) offers an approach to bringing about a positive change in organization efficiency and effectiveness. OD is a process of planned change organization-wide to increase organization effectiveness through changing the methods or process by which work is done. Planned changes are instrumental for development. Many changes with traditional and modern techniques are taken place for organization development. Organization development is an intervention strategy to bring out changes in beliefs, attitudes, structures, processes and interaction. It requires proper environment study, support, training and reward system. OD takes organization to higher levels of performance by excelling. It aims at building internal competencies and teams in the organization. It focuses on behaviour and uses various behavioural tools.

The basic concept behind organizational development is to improve organizational efficiency by modifying human behaviour rather than technological innovations, because without the committed involvement of human element, all the technology has a limited meaning. It started with the emergence of applied behavioural science, social psychology, training and feedback. OD has been defined in different ways:

In general terms, it is an effort to improve an organization's effectiveness by dealing with individual, group, and overall organizational problems from both a technical standpoint and a human standpoint. At the heart of OD is a concern for improving the relationships among the organization's personnel.

- OD is the art of learning to solve problems and take advantage of opportunities to keep improving through the process of carrying out changes in the internal environment to conform to the fast changing external environment.

- OD is the planned process of change in the organization's culture through the utilization of behaviour science technology, research and theory. Emphasis is on management of people in the change process (Burke). OD is a planned approach to respond effectively to change in its environment.
- OD is a powerful change strategy. It uses process consultation where the consultation works with the leader and group to diagnose and enables them to solve their own problems. It is participative, collaborative and problem focused approach. OD taps the experience and expertise of members as they work on their problems to generate solutions.

According to Harold Rush, "Organization development is a planned, managed and systematic process to change the culture, systems and behaviour of an organization in order to improve the organization's effectiveness in solving its problems and achieving its objective".

28.2 FEATURES OF ORGANIZATION DEVELOPMENT

Organization development attempts to develop the whole organization through an open communication by increasing the adequacy and accuracy of information. "Organization development is collection of planned change interventions, built on humanistic-democratic values, that seek to improve organizational effectiveness and employees well-being". The main features of organization development are:

1. **System Orientation:** The organizations are complex systems comprising of many subsystems which must work together in harmony and synchronization. The systems are divided into subsystems and there are number of variables that affect these subsystems. These subsystems themselves interact with each others. The interaction of all the subsystems is channelised for better performance of the organization. Thus, system management is the basic tenet of corporate development. All the system of the organization like marketing, finance, personnel, production and communication and their subsystems are properly interlinked for making better utilization of resources. For example, advertising, personal selling, publicity and public relation are linked together to make marketing system effective. The working relationships and personal interactions are formalized to make organization development easy and smooth.
2. **Humanistic Approach:** Organization development includes human values. Organization development can be possible with employees' development. The employees' development is possible through open communication, interpersonal relationship, empowerment and constructive discussion. It is possible through change agents who actually introduce and manage change in organization. They stimulate, facilitate and coordinate the development function. They analyze the existing systems and evolve suitable methodology for development. Thus, organization development is basic objective of change agents.
3. **Action Research:** It is very important for organization development. It reveals the problems, identifies them and finds their possible solution. Action research is a data based system. It improves the problem solving skills of the individuals. Management coordinates all the activities of the system, subsystems, groups and teams. Feedback from them is necessary for self correcting actions. Their relationships and work experience are used for improvement. All this contribute in organization development.

4. **Intervention:** The organization development interventions are the building blocks which are planned activities designed to improve the organization's functioning through participation of organizational members. It is an effective change in the organization structure and process. It includes career planning, team building, job designing and redesigning. It involves application of behavioural science in different fields of the organization. The planned, continued and organized efforts of individual, interpersonal, group, intergroup are needed for organization development. People, structure, technology and environment are intervened for a better performance. For effective interventions, proper feedback from each employee is important.

According to French and Bell, 1990 and Backhard, 1969, OD has following characteristics:

- with the use of external consultants.
- using behaviour science knowledge and action research, and
- to increase organization effectiveness and health,
- through planned interventions,
- systematic, long-range, planned, change effort,
- organization-wide,
- managed from the top.

28.3 OBJECTIVES OF ORGANIZATIONAL DEVELOPMENT

OD programmes vary because they are tailored to unique situations. In general, OD programmes develop social processes such as trust, problem-solving, communication and cooperation to facilitate organizational change and enhance personal and organizational effectiveness. The objectives of organization development are highlighted in the following lines:

1. To increase personal responsibility for planning, implementing the plans and be aware and responsible for the consequences. This will build enthusiasm individually and group wise and will involve communication, feelings, open competition as well as compromise, conflict resolution, etc. This will increase a sense of self-direction for all people within the organization. It improves organizational performance and innovativeness.
2. To encourage an analytical approach to problem-solving in a team spirit and open manner, where the problems and differences are confronted and resolved instead of problem-avoiding or decision-postponing approach.
3. To build and enhance interpersonal trust, communication, cooperation and support among all individuals and groups throughout the organization at all levels. It increases a sense of belonging in employees and towards the organization. Thus, the organizational goals become the goals of the members of the organization.
4. To assign decision-making and problem-solving responsibilities to skilled and knowledgeable persons who are closer to the scene of operations and sources of information, rather than to a person with a particular role or at a particular hierarchical level.
5. The management should be goal-oriented rather than process oriented. Organization development helps managers to manage according to the relevant objectives. All efforts should be directed and channelled towards related objective in the area of responsibility.

6. OD represents a viable strategy for improving organization effectiveness and enhancing the quality of work life of members.
7. Develop a satisfying work experience capable of building enthusiasm and encourage personal willingness to change.
8. Deepen the sense of organizational purpose (or vision) and align individuals with that purpose. OD keeps work organization productive as well as hospitable for members.

These objectives help the organization in examining its current methods of operations, its norms and values and in generating and evaluating alternative ways of operating and utilizing the full potential of human resources. It focuses on developing total organization.

28.4 HISTORY OF ORGANIZATION DEVELOPMENT

Bell and French have stated that organization development emerged largely from applied behavioural sciences. It has four major sources:

1. The invention of the T-group and innovations in the application of laboratory training insights to complex organization.
2. The invention of survey feedback technology.
3. The emergence of action research.
4. The evolution of the Tavistock socio-technical approaches.

They further add that the importance for applying OD approaches has changed to an increasingly turbulent environment. OD are organizational transformation, organizational culture, the learning organization, high-performance teams, total quality management, business process re engineering. OD was first introduces in India in Larsen and Toubro and Bharat Heavy Electricals Ltd., Bhopal plant in the mid-1970s as a formal and structural part. It had a slow growth for over 25 years in spite of introduction of laboratory training by Udai Pareek, Roltlynton and other professionals. Laboratory training was considered as an important instrument for development. It has following advantages: it helps the management to meet the challenges of change, it makes the people happier and more satisfied and corporate policies are made more flexible. In the post-liberalization period, every company has been forced to seek change.

Peculiarities of Indian's Way of Managing and Need for OD (S. Ramanarayan, 1998)

1. Indian culture is strongly hierarchy-based and OD facilitator must explain the need for change, what is to be changed and how it is going to benefit the target group.
2. Indian mindset is tradition-bound, fatalistic and more resistance to change.
3. The Indian mind that governs organizations is much less system driven and more people and relationship driven.
4. When faced with uncertainties, Indian organizations are forced to work for short-term goals rather than long-term ones.

28.5 ORGANIZATIONAL DEVELOPMENT: SOME VALUES

Organizational development is dependent upon organizational values. These values are incorporated for employees and corporate growth, for improved participative process and collaboration of different functional features. The corporate values include:

1. **Respect for People:** Individuals are perceived as being responsible, conscientious, and caring. They should be treated with dignity and respect.
2. **Trust and Support:** The effectiveness and healthy organization is characterized by trust, authenticity, openness and a supportive climate. Thus, management and employees must develop trust and support for the organization development.
3. **Power Equalization:** The equitable power vested with the hierarchy is a welcome step. Effective organization de-emphasizes hierarchical authority and control.
4. **Open Discussion or Confrontation:** Openness of problems and solutions removes misunderstanding. Thus, problems shouldn't be swept under the rug. They should be openly confronted.
5. **Participation:** It brings changes in the working process for the betterment of the corporate philosophy. The more that people who will be affected by a change are involved in the decisions surrounding that change, the more they will be committed to implementing those decisions. In this way, people get an opportunity to demonstrate their qualifications.

Thus, Organizational Development can be defined as, "An effort planned, organization wide, managed from the top, in order to increase organizational effectiveness and health, through planned intervention in the organization's processes using behavioural science knowledge.

28.6 ORGANIZATION DEVELOPMENT PROCESS

Organization development is a slow and continuous process. The process is designed, reviewed and implemented. The problems, diagnosis and suggestions are designed under organization development. The outcomes are evaluated and the momentums of functioning are accelerated. Kurt Lewin argued that successful change should follow—unfreezing, movement or change and refreezing. The following Figure 28.1 describes how the unfreezing-change-freezing analogy

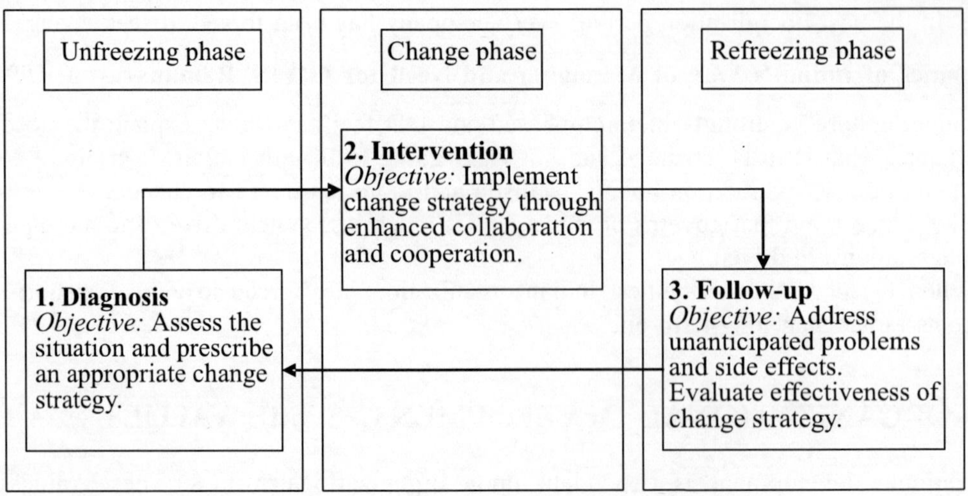

Figure 28.1 Organizational development process.

applies to Organization Development (OD). The process of organization development involves following steps:

Unfreezing prepares the members of a social system for change and then helps neutralize initial resistance. Lewin believes that the change should not come as a surprise to members of the organization. Sudden, unannounced change would be socially destructive. The management must pave the way by "unfreezing the situation", so that members would be willingly and ready to accept the change.

Unfreezing means the status quo and this is considered to be an equilibrium state. It makes the individuals or organizations aware and prepare for the change. Unfreezing can be possible in one of the three ways. These are:

- Driving Forces, which direct behaviour away from the status quo, can be increased.
- Restraining Forces, which hinder movement from the existing equilibrium or it forces hinder movement away from the status quo, can be decreased.
- The third alternative is to combine the first two approaches.

Driving Forces → Equilibrium → Restraining Forces

Managers who are trying to implement change mustm analyze this balance of driving and restraining forces. For effective change the driving forces should be strengthen and the restraining forces should be weaken successfully.

Movement or Changing: This a stage at which the individual being changed learn new behaviour, methods of working, new thinking, perception of new roles, etc.

Refreezing: It is stabilization of change intervention by balancing driving and restraining forces. It means that what has been learned is integrated into actual practice. At this stage, the individuals learned new beliefs, feelings and behaviour. The new behaviour must replace the former behaviour completely for successful change to take place. It is necessary to follow up on problems, complaints, unanticipated side effects.

OD model introduced here is based on Lewin's approach to handling change. Diagnose is carried out during the unfreezing phase. Change is then carefully introduced through tailor made intervention. Finally, a systematic follow-up refreezes the situation. Each phase is critical to organizational change and development. Thus, the following three-phase sequence makes OD an ongoing system of planned change. The catchall term used to describe this process is organizational development. These are explained as below:

28.6.1 OD Diagnosis

Because of the expenses of conducting a diagnosis, management teams need to identify at the outset the specific problems areas or subunits that deserves close examination. Diagnosis that is over comprehensive is a waste of time. Therefore, the management must select the relevant domain and can turn to three important aspects of the diagnostic phase:

(a) ***Unfreezing the situation:*** An OD programme should not come as a surprise. Some unfreezing–making announcements, holding meetings and launching promotional campaign in the organization's newsletter and on bulletin boards–can help start things. All these activities help deliver clear message: "We can improve the effectiveness of our organization while increasing our personal satisfaction if we all cooperate in a comprehensive programme of finding out where we are, where we want to go and how we can get there". This message prepares people for interviews, questionnaires, unfamiliar consultants and group activities that could be threatening if they came as surprises. One word of caution: during the unfreezing phase, care needs to be taken to avoid creating unrealistic expectations.

(b) ***Designing the diagnostic strategy and* interpreting *the diagnostic data:*** Those about to tackle an OD diagnosis will find it helpful to view the typical organization as an iceberg. For getting some feedback in the organization at large it is important to examine the organization climate. Organization climate is determined by knowing the attitudes and perceptions the employees have about the organization's leadership, products, pay, employee benefits, discipline, policies and goals. In measuring organizational climate, we are interested in learning about the *informal organization*, which is analogous to the part of an iceberg that rests under the water. Following Figure 28.2 depicts the organizational iceberg:

The **Formal aspects** are readily observable and oriented to structural considerations. The formal aspects are visible, if there is something wrong with the formal aspects, we can adjust them. If some one is inefficient, we can find out why and try to deal with the problem.

Visible Features (Formal Aspects)–The Formal Organization
Objectives, Structure, Policies and plans, Formal Authority, Rules, Task Design, Technology, Formal channel of communication, Performance, Jon Definition, Job Descriptions, Forms of Departmentalization, Span of Control, Operating policies, Efficiency measures.

Hidden Features (Informal Aspects)–The Informal Organization
Opinions, Attitudes, Feelings, Values, Power and Politics, Interpersonal conflicts, Interpersonal conflict (e.g., role conflict and role ambiguity), Blocked communication channels, Technical and behavioural problems, Group norms and sentiments, Perception of trust and openness, Value orientation, Employee Satisfaction.

Figure 28.2 Organizational iceberg.

The **Informal aspects** are hidden from view and oriented to social-psychological process and behavioural consideration. Usually, we do not know what is going on in the informal organization until problems begins.

However, there are ways of measuring organizational climate and dealing with a trouble situation before it becomes too serious. A complete diagnosis of every feature listed in figure would be prohibitively expensive and time-consuming and so it is important to select the right diagnostic strategy for the information sought. Four approaches are widely used. These are:

(i) Review of records: Nowadays organizations possess a wealth of recorded information and data in response to the government's increased demand. When change agents have the time and patience to carry out a thorough records search, they are often rewarded with valuable information about the relative health or sickness of the organization. Much can be learned by review of human records for signs of excessive absenteeism and turnover or for patterns of grievances. Similarly, studies of financial records can yields telling signs of cost overruns and other financial problems.

(ii) Interviews: By using a carefully compiled list of specific questions and general, open-ended questions, a skilled interviewer can discover a great deal about both individuals and the organization at large.

(iii) Survey questionnaires: These are most widely used diagnostic strategy today. Questionnaires may be administered to people assembled in groups, or they may be mailed individually. They may be constructed in-house or purchased. Some of the more sophisticated published survey questionnaires include in the purchase price scoring and statistical analysis.

(iv) Direct observation: It is well known that people tend to say one thing and do another. When this kind of discrepancy is likely to be a problem, management may choose to have a neutral third party observe organizational members at work.

Each of these strategies has its appropriate place in OD diagnosis. By balancing the respective strengths and weaknesses of the various approaches, it is possible to develop a diagnostic strategy based on two or more approaches.

The Six-Box Model of MARVIN R

This diagnostic model can help in identifying processes and activities as to which box give signs of troubles/problems. Weisbord identifies six critical areas–purpose, structure, rewards, helpful mechanisms, relationships and leaderships, where things must go right if the organization is to be successful. These areas are affected by environment Model as given in Figure 28.3.

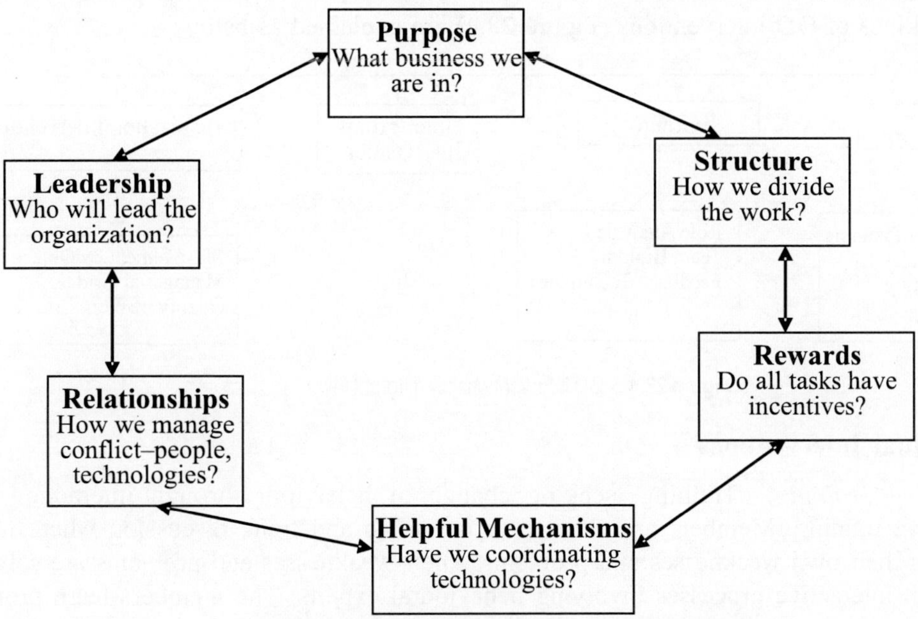

Figure 28.3 Marvin R. Weisbord organizational model.

According to Weisbord, one should look to both the formal and informal aspects of each box. Commonly one finds that formal arrangements are inappropriate, but informal system works around the deficiencies by developing methods to correct them. He suggests, before choosing interventions, a thorough diagnosis should be done based on multiple boxes.

28.6.2 OD Intervention

An OD intervention is defined as the set of structured activities in which selected organizational units (target groups or individuals) engage with a task(s) where task goals are related to organizational improvement. All the activities which are planned and carried in order to bring about improvements are called as interventions. These cover the action planning and implementations. An intervention, in OD terms, is a systematic attempt to correct an organizational deficiency uncovered through diagnosis. Management teams, working either alone or in collaboration with an outside consultant are responsible for selecting OD interventions.

OD strategy, on the other hand, can be defined as an overall plan for relating and integrating different organizational improvement activities over a period of time to accomplish objectives.

Characteristics of OD interventions:

- An OD intervention focuses on organizational process apart from substantive content of an activity.
- An OD intervention focuses on work team as the unit of analysis and change towards effective behaviour.
- OD would view change as an ongoing process and would rely on a collaborative management of work culture.

Different kinds of OD interventions (Figure 28.4) are explained as below:

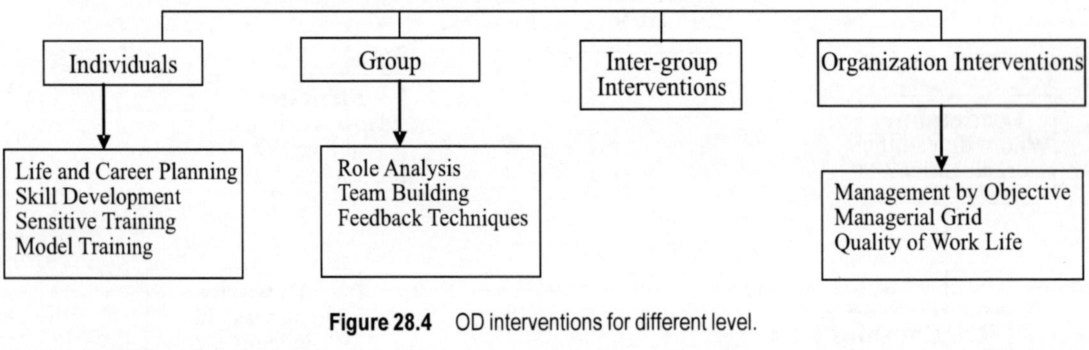

Figure 28.4 OD interventions for different level.

(1) Individual Interventions

(a) *Sensitive Training*: Training, seeking change of behaviour through interaction, is sensitive training. Members are allowed to have free and frank discussion where they discuss their own weaknesses and problems. Their weaknesses and problems are solved through interactive processes involving behavioural experts. The members learn proper behaviour through participation, under the guidance of some expert behaviorists. They express their beliefs, ideas and attitudes with the experts who try to modify them through practical orientation. Practical training is imparted to them by these unbiased experts. Employees are taught self-awareness based on their own behaviour and perception. Greater sensitivity is made use of to understand their attitudes. Employees are put under training to understand better about themselves and about others. They develop observation and listening skills, greater openness, increased tolerance and conflict resolution style. The employee understands what others think about him. The self-perception is developed through understanding himself and perceiving how other perceives him. It is more realistic and leads to self-perception and group cohesiveness. Sensitive training provides the wisdom to understand about himself, others and the organization.

(b) *Life and Career Planning:* Many employees today have no clear plans for their lives on their careers, things just happen. But individuals can be challenged to take grater responsibility for the direction of their lives. One company that helps its people rise to the challenge of actively managing their own careers is prudential, the well-known insurance giant.

(c) *Laboratory Training:* Individual intervention requires laboratory training wherein the employees' attitudes, values and lifestyles are changed to make organization more effective. It is expected that the employees learn skills which are applied and reinforced on the job. Laboratory training provides situations in which the trainees themselves experience the methods of development and behaviour in the organization through their own interactions. The employees experiment on themselves on how to improve and fit themselves for growth and development of the organization. The laboratory method of training includes role playing, game playing, modeling, encountering and simulation.

Role Playing is a spontaneous acting of a realistic situation. Real-life situations are used to teach the trainees, while other trainees stand by and watch. Other trainees are considered as observers and critics.

Game Playing is a group exercise of sequential decision-making. Workers perform the job in groups. There may be two or more groups who exercise their decision-making process with a competitive start. The decision of each group is processed and again put up for discussion.

Modelling is based on the social learning process of observation and imitation. It develops the skills of handling the encountered behaviour. Modelling relies upon demonstration, explanation, practice and feedback.

Encountering involves dividing the group into small participating groups. They are unstructured and are sensitive to others feelings. Encountering develops reasonable group activity. These sub-groups are training groups known as T-groups. These groups have variations on account of their sensitivity and human potentials. All the training groups performs during the decision-making process under their respective environment.

Simulation is the experiments of different dimension of work life. It includes physical setting, organizing, hierarchy, modelling roles and design production tasks. It is recreating reality, communication patterns, decision-making styles and conflict resolution.

(d) *Skill Development:* When carried out alone, this intervention is considered part of management training and development. Unlike most OD interventions, skill development deals with content rather than process. For example, when an OD diagnosis uncovers the inability of a group of engineers in the research and development department to write objectives and formulate plans, the deficiency can be corrected through appropriate training. Similarly, managers at all levels can be trained to polish their skills in areas such as delegation, problem-solving, conflict resolution and leading. Emphasis in skill development clearly in on learning "how to do it".

(2) Group Intervention

(a) *Role Analysis:* A role, once again, is a prescribed way of behaving. In an unhealthy organization, many people do not know what their roles are or should be, and if they do know, their roles typically are in direct conflict with those of coworkers. In a healthy organization, everyone knows his or her role, and those roles mesh in a way that encourages cooperation and reduces dysfunctional conflict. For this reason, many OD programmes call for some sort of role analysis, which is the systematic clarification of independent tasks and job behaviour.

(b) *Team Building:* It is essential for task performance. It is a family concept helping all the members of the corporation for improving the performance. Special task force (for task accomplishment), field force (identifies role and goal setting) and financial teams (relationship between resources and manpower allocation) are examples of teams associated with corporate development. The structure, task, relationship, process, role analysis and role identification are analyzed under team building process. The basic ingredients of team building are supportive environment, skills and role clarity, super-ordinate goals and team rewards. The potential team problems are overcome for its successful building. The benefits of team building are greater motivation, increased productivity, better quality of work, higher job satisfaction, better resolution of conflict and increased willingness to change.

(c) *Survey Feedback:* In survey feedback, data gathered through personal interviews and/or survey questionnaires are analyzed, tabulated into understandable form, and shared with those who first supplied the information. The main purpose of survey feedback is to let people know where they stand in relation to others on important organizational issues so that constructive problem solving can take place. Effective feedback should be:

(i) Relevant: Only information that is meaningful to the recipients should be fed back.
(ii) Understandable: To ensure clear communication, language and symbols should be familiar to the recipients.
(iii) Descriptive: Data should be in the form of real-life examples with which the recipients can identify.
(iv) Verifiable: The form of presentation should allow recipients to test the validity and accuracy of the data fed back to them.
(v) Limited: Too much feedback causes an information overload, and so only significant highlights should be presented.
(vi) Controllable: Recipients should be given information on situations that they can directly control.
(vii) Comparative: Comparative data let recipients know where they stand in relation to others.
(viii) Inspiring: Recipients must see feedback information as a beginning and a stimulus for action rather than as a final statement.

Target Group	Interventions Designed to Improve Effectiveness
Individuals	– Life and career-planning activities – Coaching and counselling – T-group (sensitivity training) – Education and training to increase skills, knowledge in the area of technical task needs, relationship skills, process skills, decision-making, problem-solving, planning goal-setting skills – Grid OD phase 1 – Work redesign – Gestalt OD – Behaviour modelling
Dyads/Triads	– Process consultation – Third-party peace-making – Role negotiation technique – Gestalt OD
Teams and Groups	– Team Building–Task directed and process directed – Gestalt OD – Grid OD phase 2 – Interdependency exercise – Process consultation – Role negotiation – Role analysis techniques – Startup team-building activities – Education in decision-making, problem-solving, planning, goal-setting in group setting – Team MBO – Appreciation and concerns exercise – Socio-technical system (STS) – Visioning – Quality of Work Life (QWL) programmes – Quality circles – Force-field analysis – Self-managed teams
Inter-group Relations	– Inter-group activities–Process directed and task directed – Organizational mirroring – Partnering – Process consultation – Third-party peace-making at group level – Grid OD phase 3 – Survey feedback
Total Organization	– Socio-technical systems (STS) – Parallel learning structures – MBO (participation forms) – Cultural analysis – Confrontation meetings – Visioning – Strategic planning/strategic management activities – Grid OD phases 4,5,6 – Interdependency exercise – Survey feedback – Appreciative inquiry – Search conferences – Quality of work life (QWL) programmes – Total Quality Management (TQM) – Physical Settings – Large-scale systems changes

Figure 28.5 Typology of OD interventions based on target groups .

Feedback that meets these criteria should be fed back to organizational subgroups, as the situation allows, until all employees have had a chance to see where and how they fit. At that point, interventions such as life and career planning, skill development, team building, and role analysis can be introduced.

(3) Inter-group Interventions

Organizational development seeks an inter-group development. Conflict situations between groups are identified and analyzed. Confrontation meeting (mirroring) may be used for inter-department cooperation. Inter-group development seeks to change the attitudes and perceptions that groups have of each other. A popular method for improving inter-group relations is problem-solving. In this method each group meets independently to develop lists of perceptions of itself, the other group, and how it believes the other group perceives it. The groups then share their lists, after which similarities and differences are discussed. Differences are clearly articulated and the groups look for the causes of the disparities. The groups can now move to the integration phase, i.e., working to develop solutions that will improve relations between the groups. Basically organization mirroring is meant to give feedback to work groups regarding how other groups view each other. The aim of this intervention is to improve inter-group relations and increase organizational effectiveness.

(4) Organizational Interventions

The important intervention of total organization is Grid OD intervention which is used to bring about change in the entire organization and improve organization effectiveness. It is based on managerial grid of Blake and Mouton (1964) Various six phases of OD grid training are summarized in Figure 28.6.

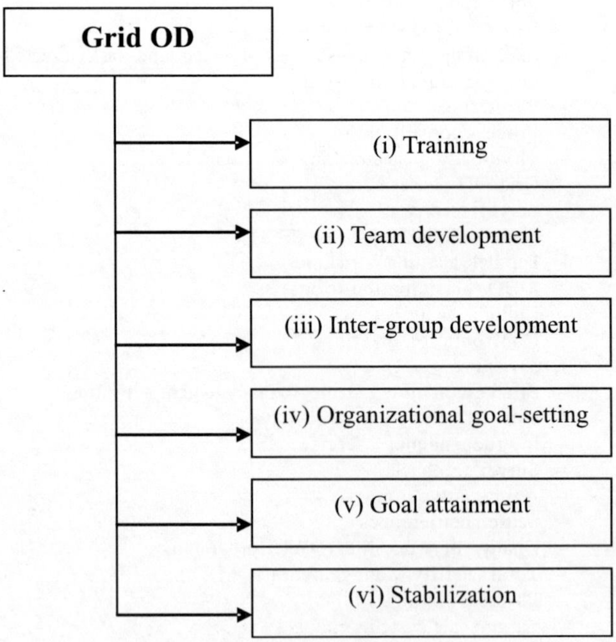

Figure 28.6 OD grid training.

(i) Laboratory–Seminar Training: The purpose of this is to introduce the participants to the overall concepts and materials used in grid training. In this first focus on training, e.g., manager's styles–training to managers is imparted so that high score on both, i.e., concern for production and concern for people is achieved which is desirable.

(ii) Team Development: Members of the same department are brought together to chart how they are going to attain 9, 9 position on the grid. In this emphasis is on improving both boss-subordinate relationships and team effectiveness. Here focus is laid on diagnosis meetings, task achievement, building relationships, role clarification and mutual expectations.

(iii) Inter-group development: Here trust is on improving coordination, cooperation, relieve tensions and solve problems jointly. Here focus is on group-to-group. Conflict situations between groups and identified and analyzed. Another intervention is third party peace making. It is designed as an inter-group intervention where OD consultant acts as a mediator in a conflict situation.

(iv) Organizational goal-setting: Members agree upon the important goals for the organization, in the manner of management by objectives.

(v) Goal attainment: In this participants attempt another strategy used is to accomplish the goals which they set.

(vi) Stabilization: Stabilize positive changes and identify new areas of opportunity for the organization after evaluation of overall programme is conducted.

The other OD intervention strategy is *Transactional Analysis,* it makes the employees understand themselves. People understand their own ego states and those of others to understand the principles behind the transaction. It suggests more meaningful ways to interact with one another. It is used for developing the managerial personnel and employees. It helps to understand and analyze the transactions with others. The transaction may be complementary, crossed, ulterior or others. It also helps process consultation, third part peace-making and team-building.

28.6.3 Follow-up

Effective OD programmes do not end abruptly when the intervention phase is completed but, rather, require a carefully monitored refreezing period to ensure lasting change. This follow-up phase has two objectives: the effectiveness of OD interventions needs to be evaluated, and steps need to be taken to maintain the changes that have been introduced. These two objectives are explained below:

(a) *Evaluating the OD programme:* Evaluating changes in any complex social system is never easy. A statistical analysis of 126 studies involving OD intervention yields following insights:

   (i) *combined interventions* were more effective at improving employee attitudes and satisfaction than were single technique interventions;

   (ii) *team building* was the most effective OD intervention for improving attitudes and satisfaction; and

   (iii) OD intervention tends to have a stronger influence on *attitudes* than on satisfaction.

From a research perspective, objective evaluation should be a part of every OD programme, even though they are difficult, time-consuming, expensive and hence largely unappealing from an administrative standpoint. Claims of improvement because of an OD programme are virtually impossible without an objective evaluation of results.

(b) *Maintaining positive change:* The purpose of any OD programme is to induce organizational members to behave differently. Although the various OD interventions are designed to persuade individual to experiments with new modes of behaviour, permanent behaviour change is a different matter. Only skilful unfreezing and exciting, relevant, and innovative OD interventions will generate individual commitment. But after enthusiasm among organization members is achieved and the culture shifts in a positive direction, no barrier to change is too great to be overcome.

28.7 SUMMARY

In general, OD efforts are designed to bring changes in the conceptual environment of an organization as well as in the outlook of the organizational members. Each member begins to see himself as a resource to others and is willing to lend his support to his colleagues when it is needed. The conceptual environment brings about open and free expression of feelings, emotions and perceptions. The change must be for the better so that it develops the organization and such organizational development should be directed towards improvement in organizational health and welfare of the members. The basic purpose of such development is to improve the operational as well as interpersonal skills of employees and it also helps members to develop interpersonal competence including communication skills and an insight into themselves and others. It improves communication channels at all levels of the hierarchy and build team spirit among workers as that their inter-group relationships are highly cordial.

28.8 SELF-ASSESSMENT QUESTIONS

1. What do you mean by organizational development? Explain why OD is necessary even in a stable environment.
2. What do you mean by OD interventions? Describe the various OD interventions and explain as to how they improve the functioning of the organizations.
3. Describe in detail the objectives of OD programme.
4. 'Organization Development process is useful'. Comment. How is it carried out?

29 LEADING MANAGEMENT THINKERS: AN OVERVIEW

Learning Objective

The main objective of this chapter is to let the students be familiar with very concise biographical sketches of great management thinkers and practitioners in the world so that necessary inspirations may be drawn in this regard.

29.1 INTRODUCTION

They articulate that the pen is mightier than the sword and the authority of words is so passionate; it can cut through systems, strategies, operations and observation of masses. That is the strength of verbal phrasing when words are expressed with clarity, vision and profound perceptions; they evolve into management thoughts and principles. People with this gift then become what we have phrased 'Management Gurus'. Worldwide, there are renowned personalities known for their management concepts, principles and practices. The likes of such 'management celebrities' are F.W. Taylor, Henry Fayol, P.F. Drucker, Elton Mayo, Tom Peters, Edward De Bono, Philip Kotler, Peter Senge, Bob Watermann, Stephen Covey and many more.

Who are the leading and influential management thinkers? That was the simple question that inspired the author to think and breifly outline the biographical sketches of the leading and original thinkers of management. A lot of hardwork was required to answer this basic question and finally it became possible to provide a very brief account of these business gurus.

29.2 MANAGEMENT THINKERS: INTERNATIONAL

1. Frederick Winslow Taylor

Frederick Winslow Taylor, the father of scientific management, was born on March 20, 1865, into an upper class liberal Philadelphia family. His father, a Princeton graduate and lawyer, made enough money from mortgages and did not have to keep a regular job. His mother was a spirited abolitionist and feminist who was said to have run an Underground Railroad station for runaway slaves. Both parents were Quakers and believed in high thinking and plain living. Parental authority was not questioned and children were seen and not heard in the Taylor family. Family members referred to each other as "thee" and "thou". At an early age Taylor learned self-control and his Quaker upbringing helped him to avoid conflicts with his peers and to resolve disagreements among them.

Taylor was a compulsive adolescent and was always counting and measuring things to figure a better way of doing something. At age twelve, he invented a harness for him to keep from sleeping on his back, hoping to avoid the nightmares he was having.

At age twenty-five, Taylor earned an engineering degree at the Stevens Institute of Technology in New Jersey while holding a full time job. To date, no one has broken that record.

Another of his achievements was his winning of the US Lawn Tennis Association doubles championship where he used a patented spoon-shaped racket that he himself designed.

Even though he excelled in math and sports and had a degree from an exclusive college, Frederick chose to work as a machinist and pattern maker in Philadelphia at the Enterprise Hydraulic Works.

After his apprenticeship at the hydraulic works plant, he became a common labourer at the Midvale Steel Company. He started as shop clerk and quickly progressed to machinist, foreman, maintenance foreman, and chief draftsman. Within six years he advanced to research director, then chief engineer. While working there he introduced piecework in the factory. His goal was to find the most efficient way to perform specific tasks. He closely watched how work was done and would then measure the quantity produced.

Taylor's work was taking place in a time period when there was much industrial change happening after the Civil War. National industries grew out of local trades–steel, glass, textiles, and shoes and what were small factories became large plants. Owners of capital became wealthier with mass production, and workers received little for their efforts. Problems included carelessness, safety, inefficiencies, and soldiering (worker foot dragging) on the job. Taylor sought to get past the futile incentive bonuses that management thought would remedy the problems. He believed that incentive wages were no solution unless they were combined with efficient tasks that were carefully planned and easily learned. He proposed that management should work cooperatively in a supportive role "Not only did Taylor have some definite ideas about work and how it should be studied, organized, and rewarded, but it appears he also knew something about organizational change".

Taylor believed that the secret of productivity was finding the right challenge for each person, and then paying him well for increased output. At Midvale, he used time studies to set daily production quotas. Incentives would be paid to those reaching their daily goal. Those who didn't reach their goal would get the differential rate, a much lower pay. Taylor doubled productivity using time study, systematic controls and tools, functional foremanship, and his new wage scheme. He paid the person not the job.

At age thirty-seven, Frederick became a consulting engineer. Unfortunately, he did not understand the resistance of the people most threatened by his system supervisors and middle managers. He focused on cost cutting methods when a problem called for new customers and products. At the Simonds Roller Bearing Company he increased productivity while improving speed and accuracy. Taylor's critics said he was too harsh because his innovative plan caused people to lose their jobs, referring to his replacing of 120 workers with only 35 at Simonds.

In practice, Taylor "took a harsh, often ruthless approach" to chopping heads rather than saving jobs. He believed that unions wouldn't be necessary if workers were paid their individual worth.

As a consultant, Frederick's most important client was Bethlehem Iron Company, later known as Bethlehem Steel Company. In 1901, he and another Stevens graduate made Bethlehem "the world's most modern factory and potentially a prototype for manufacturers and engineers in other industries" by installing production planning, differential piece rates, and functional foremanship. Among Taylor's other contributions to Bethlehem in 1901 were a real time analysis of daily output and costs, a modern cost accounting system, reduced yard worker's ranks from 500 to 140, doubled stamping mill production, and lowered cost per ton of materials handled from eight cents to four cents. He successfully implemented cost saving techniques even though he added clerks, teachers, time-study engineers, supervision and staffing support positions. While at Bethlehem, Taylor and Manusel White co developed the Taylor-White system for heat-treating chrome-tungsten tool steel, which won Frederick international recognition.

Despite his many impressive achievements, Taylor made enemies. Some managers were also landlords and when Taylor reduced the yard force population, they thought he would depopulate South Bethlehem. Ironically, that is exactly what they had hired Taylor to do, but they never expected that he would actually do it. In fact, displaced workers were moved to other jobs and did not lose employment. After disputes with new management at Bethlehem, Taylor was eventually fired in May 1901.

Taylor did not suffer financially from losing his job, but the event did hurt his self-esteem. He began to concentrate on his home and hobbies and with his wife, Louise Spooner, adopted three orphaned children. After Bethlehem, Frederick never worked for money again.

Much of his famous book, "The Principles of Scientific Management", was written from transcripts of talks Taylor gave at his estate years after he stopped working for money. The system he describes in his book is an actual composite of everything he had learned from trying different things at many companies. Taylor did what he could to fit as much of his thinking to his client's problems and motives for each particular situation. Consultants use this type of process today." He was the first person in history to make a systematic attempt to improve both output and work life in factories".

In his last years Frederick felt misunderstood by quick-fix managers and zealous unionists, and wronged by consultant imitators. His energy was sapped by the constant attention he paid to his wife's severe illnesses.

While on a speaking tour in the Midwest, in 1915, he contracted influenza. He was admitted to a hospital in Philadelphia and celebrated his fifty-ninth birthday there. He died the next day.

Taylor's core values: The rule of reason, improved quality, lower costs, higher wages, higher output, labour-management cooperation, experimentation, clear tasks and goals, feedback, training, mutual help and support, stress reduction, and the careful selection and development of people. He was the first to present a systematic study of interactions among job requirements, tools, methods, and human skill, to fit people to jobs both psychologically and physically, and to let data and facts do the talking rather than prejudice, opinions, or egomania.

2. Henry Fayol

Henry Fayol (1841-1925) was a French engineer. His key work was Administration Industrielle et Generale, 1916. He belongs to the Classical School of Management Theory and was writing and exploring administration and work about same time as F.W. Taylor in USA.

While both have a task focus, their approaches are quite different. Fayol was particularly interested in authority and its implementation while Taylor concentrated on work organization (e.g., efficiency). In many ways their views were illustrating some of the differences between the USA and Europe. American theorists do not always lead the views and attitudes towards organizations and management. He advocated a consistent set of principles that all organizations need to run properly.

Fayol was a key figure in the turn-of-the-century Classical School of Management Theory. He saw a manager's job as: Planning, organizing, commanding, coordinating activities, and controlling performance. He noticed that most of these activities are very task-oriented, rather than people-oriented. This is very like Taylor and Scientific Management.

Fayol laid down the following principles of organization (he called them principles of management): Specialization of labour; Authority; Discipline; Unity of command; Unity of direction; Subordination of Individual Interests; Remuneration; Centralization; Scalar chain; Order; Equity. Equality of treatment (but not necessarily identical treatment); Personnel tenure; Initiative. Thinking out a plan and do what it takes to make it happen; and Esprit de corps; Harmony, cohesion among personnel.

Out of 14, the most important elements are specialization, unity of command, scalar chain, and, coordination by managers (an amalgam of authority and unity of direction).

3. Elton Mayo

Elton Mayo was one of the key figures involved in Hawthorne Studies and his work laid the foundation for the many later management and organizational thinking. He worked in areas of motivation and commitment and worker-management relations. "The relation of working groups to management was one of the fundamental problems of... industry."

He highlighted the importance of communication between management and the workers and identified the now accepted notion, which work satisfaction lay in recognition, security, and sense of belonging, rather than monetary rewards. Communication between managers and workers was the key because of the problems caused when they didn't communicate well–they were on different tracks–workers 'logic of sentiment', managers motivated by 'logic of cost and efficiency'. Conflict was bound to arise in such circumstances. Touched on new area of human emotions, he raised the awareness of individual's reactions and need for managers to show respect towards their staff and workers.

Other associated ideas included work as a group activity, that it is social, the peer group (informal groups) is highly significant in work relationships, workers are influenced by social demands inside and outside work, alongside formal structures and groups were the informal ones, which should be harnessed and used for greater productivity.

4. Douglas Mcgregor

Douglas McGregor was born in 1906 in Detroit, where his grandfather Thomas McGregor in about 1895 founded McGregor Institute to aid Great Lakes sailors and other transient labour. The

Institute, housing and feeding 1000 men each year, was continued by the son, Murray McGregor. It had a strong religious emphasis. Here Douglas McGregor grew up. During high school and much of college, he worked as night clerk and played the piano and organ at the chapel services. In this way, he became acquainted with working men and their problems. In 1936, the Institute was discontinued and the $100,000 plant was given to the Goodwill Industries.

Douglas McGregor attended Oberlin College and Wayne Universities, graduating from the latter in 1932. He received a Ph.D. degree from Harvard in 1935 in Experimental Psychology, carrying an A grade in every course.

On his way through college he was married and discontinued college work for five years to save enough money to start a family. Starting as a gasoline station attendant in Buffalo he became district manager of stations in the Detroit area.

On his graduation from Harvard he taught there for two years and then went to the Massachusetts Institute of Technology, where he has been since 1937. He was the first full time teacher of psychology in that institution. His position on resigning to come to Antioch was Professor of Psychology and Executive Director of the Industrial Relations Section of MIT.

At MIT about two thirds of his time was spent at teaching and as Director of the Industrial Relations Section, and about one third as consultant in industry. From 1943-1945, he was on leave from MIT and was Director of Industrial Relations for the Dewey Almay Company of Cambridge, manufacturer of rubber goods. He has been consultant in human relations for that company since 1940.

The general manger of Dewey Almay Company stated that McGregor liked to explore and experiment in industrial relations with the Dewey Almay Company. Sometimes the boldness of his experiments were disconcerting, but because he always turned out to be right, the company came to give him an entirely free hand in determining its industrial relations policy. Not only does the company have full confidence in him, but also "the workmen worship him."

Since 1939 Douglas McGregor has served as consultant for a dozen industries and labour undone in the East and Middle West. This work has covered wage and salary administration, contract negotiation, foremen training, grievance handling, executive development programmes, union and management cooperation programmes, and problems of organizational structure and function. He is a member of the panel of arbitrators of the American Arbitration Association and tree arbitrated labour disputes for many companies and unions. He has been a frequent speaker before many management and labour groups in the United States and Canada and has led conferences on human relations for small groups of top executives in a number of nationally known companies.

The combination of teaching, educational administration and practical experience provides an exceptionally good background for a president of Antioch. The understanding with the college is that he will continue to give part of his time to industrial relations consultation, thus sharing the co-op plan with the students.

5. Abraham Maslow

Abraham Harold Maslow was born on April 1, 1908 in Brooklyn, New York. He was the first of seven children born to his parents, who themselves were uneducated Jewish immigrants from Russia. His parents, hoping for the best for their children in the new world, pushed him hard for academic success. Not surprisingly, he became very lonely as a boy, and found his refuge in books.

To satisfy his parents, he first studied law at the City College of New York (CCNY). After three semesters, he transferred to Cornell, and then backs to CCNY. He married Bertha Goodman, his first cousin, against his parents' wishes. Abe and Bertha went on to have two daughters.

He and Bertha moved to Wisconsin so that he could attend the University of Wisconsin. Here, he became interested in psychology, and his schoolwork began to improve dramatically. He spent time there working with Harry Harlow, who is famous for his experiments with baby rhesus monkeys and attachment behaviour.

He received his BA in 1930, his MA in 1931, and his Ph.D. in 1934, all in psychology, all from the University of Wisconsin. A year after graduation, he returned to New York to work with E. L. Thorndike at Columbia, where Maslow became interested in research on human sexuality.

He began teaching full time at Brooklyn College. During this period of his life, he came into contact with the many European intellectuals that were immigrating to the US, and Brooklyn in particular, at that time–people like Adler, From, Horney, as well as several Gestalt and Freudian psychologists.

Maslow served as the chair of the psychology department at Brandeis from 1951 to 1969. While there he met Kurt Goldstein, who had originated the idea of self-actualization in his famous book, *The Organism* (1934). It was also here that he began his crusade for a humanistic psychology–something ultimately much more important to him than his own theorizing.

One of the many interesting things Maslow noticed while he worked with monkeys early in his career was that some needs take precedence over others. For example, if you are hungry and thirsty, you will tend to try to take care of the thirst first. After all, you can do without food for weeks, but you can only do without water for a couple of days! Thirst is a "stronger" need than hunger. Likewise, if you are very thirsty, but someone has put a chokehold on you and you can't breath, which is more important? The need to breathe, of course. On the other hand, sex is less powerful than any of these. Let's face it; you won't die if you don't get it!

He spend his final years in semi-retirement in California, until, on June 8 1970, he died of a heart attack after years of ill health.

6. Peter F. Drucker

Peter F. Drucker–writer, management consultant and university professor–was born in Vienna, Austria in November 1909. After receiving his doctorate in Public and International Law from Frankfurt University in Frankfurt, Germany, he worked as an economist and journalist in London before moving to the United States in 1937.

Peter Drucker published his first book, *The End of Economic Man*, in 1939. He then joined the faculty of New York University's Graduate Business School as Professor of Management in 1950. Since 1971, he has been Clarke Professor of Social Science and Management at the Claremont Graduate University in Claremont, California. The university named its management school after him in 1987. Peter Drucker has written 35 books in all: 15 books deal with management, including the landmark books *The Practice of Management* and *The Effective Executive*; 16 cover society, economics, and politics; 2 are novels; and 1 is a collection of autobiographical essays. His most recent book, *Managing in the Next Society*, was published in the year 2002.

Peter Drucker also served as a regular columnist for The Wall Street Journal from 1975 to

1995 and has contributed essays and articles to numerous publications, including the Harvard Business Review, The Atlantic Monthly, and The Economist. Throughout his career, he has consulted with dozens of organizations ranging from the world's largest corporations to entrepreneurial startups and various government and non-profit agencies. Experts in the worlds of business and academia regard Peter Drucker as the founding father of the study of management.

For his accomplishments, Peter Drucker was awarded the Presidential Medal of Freedom by President George W. Bush on July 9, 2002. A documentary series about his life and work appeared on CNBC 10 times from December 24, 2002 to January 3, 2003.

7. Henry Mintzberg

Henry Mintzberg, (born September 2, 1939) is an internationally renowned academic and author on business and management. He is currently the Cleghorn Professor of Management Studies at the Desautels Faculty of Management of McGill University in Montreal, Quebec, Canada, where he has been teaching since 1968, after earning his Master's degree in Management (MBA) and Ph.D. from the MIT Sloan School of Management.

Professor Mintzberg writes prolifically on the topics of management and business strategy, with more than 140 articles and thirteen books to his name. His seminal book, *The Rise and Fall of Strategic Planning*, criticizes some of the practices of strategic planning today and is considered required reading for anyone who seriously wants to consider taking on a strategy-making role within their organization.

Professor Mintzberg has recently published a book entitled *Managers Not MBAs* which outlines what he believes to be wrong with management education today and, rather controversially, singles out prestigious graduate management schools like Harvard Business School and the Wharton Business School at the University of Pennsylvania as examples of how obsession with numbers and an overzealous attempt at making management into a science actually can damage the discipline of management. He also suggests that a new masters programme, targeted at practising managers (as opposed to younger students with little real-world experience), and emphasizing practical issues, may be more suitable.

Ironically, although Professor Mintzberg is quite critical about the strategy consulting business, he has twice won the McKinsey Award for publishing the best article in the Harvard Business Review.

In 1997 he was made an Officer of the Order of Canada. In 1998, he was made an Officer of the National Order of Quebec.

8. Blake, Robert

Actor Born Michael Gubitosi (professionally known as Robert Blake), on September 18, 1933 in Nutley, New Jersey. Introduced to the entertainment industry at an early age, Blake spent his childhood performing with his family's vaudeville act. After moving to California, he had a five-year stint with MGM Studios, where he appeared in a string of *Our Gang* shorts, including *Dad for a Day* (1939) and *Alfalfa's Double* (1940). Later that year, Blake had a bit part in the romantic comedy *I Love You Again* starring Myrna Loy and William Powell.

During the 1940s, after landing the lead part in the drama *Mokey* (1942), Blake appeared in over 70 films, including *The Horn Blows at Midnight* (1945) and *Humoresque* (1946), as well as an unaccredited but pivotal role in *The Treasure of the Sierra Madre* (1948). Throughout the 1950s, he moved into adult roles with parts in mediocre action films like *Apache War Smoke* (1952), *Screaming Eagles* (1956), *The Tijuana Story* (1957), and *Battle Flame* (1959).

During the 1960s, Blake landed more noticeable roles in the World War II adventure *PT 109* (1963) and the mammoth religious epic *The Greatest Story Ever Told* (1965). In 1967, Blake offered a chilling portrayal of homicidal drifter Perry Smith in the film adaptation of Truman Capote's *In Cold Blood.*

In 1975, Blake was cast in the role for which he is best remembered—that of the title character in the cop series *Baretta*. The gritty drama enjoyed three years on the air, during which Blake earned an Emmy Award for Outstanding Lead Actor in a Drama Series. Following the show's cancellation in 1978, Blake worked sporadically in a slew of TV movies, most notably *Of Mice and Men* (1981) and *Blood Feud* (1983).

For the next 10 years, Blake virtually withdrew from the spotlight. In 1993, he staged an unlikely comeback, receiving an Emmy nomination for his performance as a New Jersey accountant-turned-mass murderer in the TV drama *Judgement Day: The John List Story*. His most recent film credits include the crime capers *Money Train* (1995) with Jennifer Lopez and Wesley Snipes and *Lost Highway* (1997) with Patricia Arquette and Bill Pullman.

In 1964, Blake married actress Sondra Kerry; they had two children before divorcing in 1983. In 2000, he wed Bonny Lee Bakley, with whom he had a daughter.

In May 2001, Blake made headlines when Bakley was murdered while waiting in a car outside a restaurant where the couple had just dined. Blake maintained his innocence throughout the ensuing investigation, but after almost a year, the police arrested him and his bodyguard in connection with the murder. In March 2005, he was acquitted of the murder charge, as well as one count of soliciting murder. But eight months later, a jury in a civil suit found the actor liable for the murder and ordered him to pay $30 million in damages to Bakley's children.

9. Victor H. Vroom

Victor H. Vroom, the John G. Searle Professor of Organization and Management, is an international expert on leadership and decision-making. He came to Yale in 1972 as Chairman of the Department of Administrative Sciences and Associate Director of the Institution for Social and Policy Studies. When the School of Management was founded in 1976, Professor Vroom was named to its original board of permanent officers.

A native of Canada, Professor Vroom received his B.Sc. and M.Sc. degrees in psychology from McGill University in 1953 and 1955. After receiving his Ph.D. in psychology from the University of Michigan in 1958, he was named Study Director at the university's Institute for Social Research. He served as Assistant Professor of Psychology at the University of Pennsylvania and later as Professor of Psychology and Industrial Administration at Carnegie-Mellon's Graduate School of Administration. He continued in that role until his move to Yale.

Professor Vroom's research has focused on issues of motivation and of leadership in organizations. He is the author of nine books and over fifty articles. His 1964 book, Work and Motivation, is regarded as a landmark in that field and continues to be widely cited by scholars. In 1971, he collaborated with Professor Edward Deci in writing Motivation in Management, which sold over 100,000 copies and was totally revised in 1992.

In 1973, he began his famous work on leadership with the publication of Leadership and

Decision-making, written with Phillip Yetton. The ideas in that book have stimulated more than a hundred research studies by scholars and may be found in virtually every textbook on management and leadership published in the last two decades. His latest book on leadership, The New Leadership: Managing Participation in Organizations was coauthored with Professor Arthur G. Jago and published by Prentice Hall in 1988. It has since been translated into German, Spanish and Korean.

Professor Vroom has received awards for his research by the American Psychological Association, the McKinsey Foundation, and the Ford Foundation, and is one of a select number of behavioural scientists whose autobiographies are contained in Management Laureates. His work was also profiled in Life and Works of Management Thinkers, a book dealing with the fourteen foremost contributors to management theory during the twentieth century. In 1998, the Society of Industrial and Organizational Psychology honoured him with its Distinguished Scientific Contribution Award. In addition, he has served as a consultant to many government agencies and to over 100 major corporations in the United States and abroad. He has been elected to Fellowships in the American Psychological Association, the American Psychology Society, the Society for the Psychological Study of Social Issues, and the Academy of Management. Professor Vroom has also been elected President of the Society of Industrial and Organizational Psychology.

10. Weber Max

Weber Max (b. April 21, 1864, Erfurt, Prussia [Germany] – d. June 14, 1920, Munich, Ger.), German sociologist and political economist best known for his thesis of the "Protestant Ethic," relating Protestantism to capitalism, and for his ideas on bureaucracy. Through his insistence on the need for objectivity in scholarship and his analysis of human action in terms of motivation, Weber profoundly influenced sociological theory.

Weber was born in Erfurt, the eldest son of an aspiring liberal politician whose family had become wealthy in the German linen industry. The father soon joined the more compliant, pro-Bismarckian "National-Liberals" and moved to Berlin, where he became a member of the Prussian House of Deputies (1868-97) and the Reichstag (1872-84). As such he became part of the Berlin social milieu and entertained in his housemen prominent in scholarship and politics.

Helene Weber, the sociologist's mother, was raised in Calvinist orthodoxy. Though she gradually accepted a more tolerant theology, the Puritan morality of her mother remained intact within her. As a result of the social activities of her husband she came to feel increasingly estranged from him, and, after the deaths of two of her children and the serious illness of young Max, she was aghast at his inability to share her prolonged grief. He, in turn, tended to adopt a traditionally authoritarian manner at home and to demand absolute obedience from wife and children.

Weber left home to enroll at the University of Heidelberg in 1882, interrupting his studies after two years to fulfil his year of military service at Strassburg (Strasbourg). During this time, he became very close to the family of his mother's sister, Ida Baumgarten, and her husband, the historian Hermann Baumgarten, whose influence on Weber's intellectual development was profound.

After his release from the military, Weber was asked by his father to finish his studies at the University of Berlin, where he could live at home. This was perhaps because his father considered the influence of the Baumgartens subversive of his son's character. From 1884 until his marriage in 1893, Weber left his father's house only for a semester of study at Göttingen in 1885, and for some brief periods of military manoeuvres with his reserve unit.

During most of his formative years as a scholar in legal and economic history, Weber was thus continually subject to his parents' conflicting and unanswerable claims on his loyalty. Since he spent his mid- and late-20s working simultaneously in two totally unremunerative apprenticeships–as a lawyer's assistant and as a university assistant–he was financially unable to leave home until the autumn of 1893. At that time he received a temporary position in jurisprudence at the University of Berlin and married Marianne Schnitger, a second cousin.

After his marriage, Weber paid unwitting homage to his Calvinist forebears by continuing a compulsive work regimen that he had begun after his return to Berlin in 1884. Only through such bondage to his labour, believed Weber, could he stave off a natural tendency to self-indulgence and laziness, which, if tolerated, would lead to an emotional and spiritual crisis.

Weber's great capacity for disciplined intellectual effort, together with his unquestionable brilliance, brought the reward of meteoric professional advance. Only a year after his appointment at Berlin, he became a full professor in political economy at Freiburg, and then, in the following year (1896), at Heidelberg. Following his doctoral and postdoctoral theses on the agrarian history of ancient Rome and the evolution of medieval trading societies, Weber wrote a comprehensive analysis of the agrarian problems of the German east for one of Germany's most important academic societies, the Union for Social Policy (1890), and important essays on the German stock exchange and the social basis of the decline of Latin antiquity. He was also politically active in these years, working with the left-liberal Protestant Social Union (Evangelisch-Soziale Verein).

The high point of his early scholarly career was his inaugural address at Freiburg in 1895, in which he pulled together some five years of study on the agrarian problems of Germany east of the Elbe into a devastating indictment of the ruling Junker aristocracy as historically obsolete. In Weber's view, the existing liberal parties were in no position to challenge and replace the Junkers. Nor was the working class ready to accept the responsibilities of power. Only the nation as a whole, educated to political maturity by a conscious policy of overseas imperial expansion, could bring Germany to the level of political maturity attained by the French in the revolutionary and Napoleonic eras and by the English in the course of their imperial expansion in the 19th century. Weber's Freiburg address thus advanced an ideology of "liberal imperialism," attracting to its support such important liberal publicists as Friedrich Naumann and Hans Delbrück.

In the months following his father's death in August 1897, an increasing nervousness plagued the young scholar. His return to teaching in the autumn brought a brief respite, which ended in the first months of 1898 with the first signs of the nervous collapse that was to prostrate him between mid-1898 and 1903. For five years, he was intermittently institutionalized, suffering sudden relapses after slow recoveries and vain efforts to break such cycles by travelling.

In 1903, Weber was able to resume scholarly work, though he did not teach again until after World War I. Although he had resigned his professorship at Heidelberg at the height of his illness, he came into an inheritance in 1907 that made him financially independent. The nature of his most important work after his partial recovery suggests that his prolonged agony had led him to develop brilliant insights into the relationship of Calvinist morality and compulsive labour, into the relationship between various religious ethics and social and economic processes, and into many other questions of lasting importance. Indeed, all of Weber's most important work appeared in the 17 years between the worst part of his illness and his death.

A brief glance at *The Protestant Ethic and the Spirit of Capitalism,* Weber's best known and most controversial work, illustrates the general trend of his thinking. Weber noted the statistical correlation in Germany between interest and success in capitalist ventures on the one hand, and Protestant background on the other. He then went on to attribute the relationship to certain accidental psychological consequences of the notions of predestination and the calling in Puritan theology, notions that were deduced with the greatest logical severity by Calvin and his followers.

In Calvin's formulation, the doctrine of predestination invested God with such omnipotence and omniscience that sinful humanity could know neither why nor to whom God had extended the grace of salvation. The psychological insecurity that this doctrine imposed on Calvin's followers, stern believers in hellfire, was too great, and they began to look for loopholes that would indicate the direction of divine will. The consequence was an ethic of unceasing commitment to one's worldly calling (any lapse would indicate that one's state of grace was in doubt) and ascetic abstinence from any enjoyment of the profit reaped from such labours. The practical result of such beliefs and practices was, in Weber's estimation, the most rapid possible accumulation of capital.

Weber never denied the claim of his critics that highly developed capitalist enterprises existed centuries before Calvin, and he was well aware that there were other preconditions, material and psychological, for the development of capitalism. In response to these criticisms, Weber argued that, before Calvinism, capitalist enterprise was always fettered by the passive or active hostility of the prevalent religious order. If some capitalists were, by virtue of their skepticism, able to escape the guilt feelings that conventional morality dictated, it was nevertheless a fact that never before had religious convictions enabled people to conceive of their success in the accumulation of capital as a sign of God's everlasting grace. The Puritans, Weber argued, had accepted the cloak of worldly asceticism voluntarily, as a means of alleviating otherwise unbearable spiritual burdens. In so doing, however, they helped to create the enormous structure of modern economic life, which came irresistibly to determine the life and values of everyone born into it. Thus, 'fate decreed that the cloak should become an iron cage.'

Weber published *Die protestantische Ethik und der Geist des Kapitalismus* (1904-05; *The Protestant Ethic and the Spirit of Capitalism,* 1930) in the journal he had just begun to edit, *Archiv für Sozialwissenschaft und Sozialpolitik.* In 1905–10, he published a number of exchanges in his *Archiv* between himself and critics of his thesis. During these years, however, which he spent in Heidelberg when he was not on one of his numerous journeys through Europe, the middle-class German culture in which he had been nurtured experienced its first spasms of disintegration. The Protestant morality that he had come to accept as inescapable destiny came under attack from the youth movement, from avant-garde literary circles such as the one centred on the poet Stefan George, from Neoromantics influenced by Nietzsche and Freud, and from Slavic cultural ideals, exemplified in Tolstoy and Dostoyevsky.

Weber's political sociology is concerned with the distinction between charismatic, traditional, and legal forms of authority. Charisma refers to the gift of spiritual inspiration underlying the power of religious prophecy and political leadership. In many of these later concerns, Weber touched, sometimes explicitly, on themes that had first been broached by Nietzsche.

His acute interest in social phenomena such as mysticism, which are antithetical to the modern world and its underlying process of rationalization, paralleled a late awakening of Weber's aesthetic and erotic faculties. In 1910, amid the crumbling social order of European middle-class society, Weber began a series of important discussions with Stefan George and his close disciple, the poet Friedrich Gundolf. At roughly the same time, he embarked on an extramarital affair, probably his first experience of sexual intimacy; one of his most brilliant later essays contains a penetrating analysis of the conflicting relationships between eroticism, ascetic and mystical modes of religiosity, and the general process of rationalization ("*Theorie der Stufen und Richtungen religioser Weltablehnung,*" 1916; "Religious Rejections of the World and Their Directions").

During this same period Weber was engaged in efforts to gain respect for sociology as a discipline by defining a value-free methodology for it, and in his analysis of the religious cultures of India and China for purposes of comparison with the Western religious tradition. Also of critical importance in his last decade were his stoical examination of the conditions and consequences of the rationalization of political and economic life in *Wirtschaft und Gesellschaft* (1922; *Economy and Society,* 1968) and journal articles.

Indeed, Weber's most powerful impact on his contemporaries came in the last years of his life, when, from 1916 to 1918, he argued powerfully against Germany's annexationist war goals and in favour of a strengthened parliament. He stood bravely for sobriety in politics and scholarship against the apocalyptic mood of right-wing students in the months following Germany's defeat. After assisting in the drafting of the new constitution and in the founding of the German Democratic Party, Weber died of a lung infection in June 1920.

Weber's significance during his lifetime was considerable among German social scientists, many of whom were his personal friends in Heidelberg or Berlin; but because of the fact that little of his work was published in book form during his lifetime and because most of the journals in which he published had restricted audiences of scholarly specialists, his major impact was felt after his death. The only exceptions were his formulation of "liberal imperialism" in 1895, his widely discussed thesis on Protestantism and capitalism, and his extensive attack on German foreign and domestic policies during World War I in the pages of the *Frankfurter Zeitung,* which stimulated liberal sentiment against the government's war aims and led Gen. Erich Ludendorff to view him as a traitor.

In general, it may be said that Weber's greatest merit as a thinker was that he brought the social sciences in Germany, hitherto preoccupied largely with national problems, into direct critical confrontation with the international giants of 19th century European thought – Marx and Nietzsche – and that through this confrontation he helped create a methodology and a body of literature dealing with the sociology of religion, the sociology of political parties, small group behaviour, and the philosophy of history. His work continues to stimulate scholarship.

11. Kenneth Blanchard

Few people have impacted the day-to-day management of people and companies more than Ken Blanchard. A prominent, gregarious, sought-after author, speaker, and business consultant, Dr. Blanchard is universally characterized by his friends, colleagues, and clients as one of the most insightful, powerful, and compassionate people in business today.

When Ken speaks, he speaks from the heart with warmth and humour. His unique gift is to speak to an audience and communicate with each individual as if they were alone and talking one on one. He is a polished storyteller with a knack for making the seemingly complex easy to understand.

From his phenomenal best-selling book, The One Minute Managers, coauthored with Spencer Johnson, which has sold more than ten million copies and remains on best-seller lists, to the library of books coauthored with Sheldon Bowles, Raving Fans, Gung Ho!, Big Bucks!, and High Five!, Ken's impact as a writer is far-reaching. His book on spirituality in the workplace, Leadership by the Book, coauthored with Phil Hodges and Bill Hybels, is giving new meaning to Servant Leadership.

Ken is chief spiritual officer of The Ken Blanchard Companies, an international management training and consulting firm that he and his wife, Dr. Marjorie Blanchard, founded in 1979 in San Diego, California. He is also a visiting lecturer at his alma mater, Cornell University, where he is a trustee emeritus of the Board of Trustees. Ken is cofounder of The Center for Faith Walk Leadership, which is dedicated to helping leaders walk their talk in the marketplace.

Ken has received several awards and honours for his contributions in the fields of management leadership and speaking. The National Speakers Association awarded him its highest honour, the "Council of Peers Award of Excellence." He was inducted into the HRD Hall of Fame by Training magazine and Lakewood Conferences. He received the Golden Gavel Award from Toastmasters International.

12. Tom Peters

Tom Peters (b. 1942) is a native of Baltimore. He studied engineering at Cornell, before heading to the west coast to get his MBA and Ph.D. at Stanford. He saw active service in the Vietnam War with the US Navy. In the mid-1970s he joined McKinsey as a consultant, leaving in 1981 to set up his own firm, now part of the Tom Peters Group.

In 1982 appeared *In Search of Excellence* (written with Robert Waterman, a fellow McKinsey partner). This became the best-selling management book of the twentieth century–the first to reach the best-seller charts. This was soon followed by the nearly as successful *A Passion for Excellence* (1985).

The book has achieved a cult following. It tied in with the need in the United States in the early 1980s to feel good about being American again. It showed that significant parts of American industry and business *were* excellent; others could be too. Its simplistic rhetoric earned Peters a wrap over the knuckles from the venerable Peter Drucker. He chided Peters for making "managing sound so incredibly easy. All you have to do is put that book under your pillow and it will get done."

'In Search of Excellence' was an American classic. It contained really great stories of do-and-dare about 43 excellent American companies. It was not long on theorizing. It is liberally spruced with nuggets of home-spun wisdom: "If a window of opportunity appears, don't pull down the shade."

Excellence in business depends on eight ingredients.

(1) activism, with people who "do it, fix it [and] try it"
(2) excellent companies "learn from the people they serve".
(3) they promote entrepreneurship and autonomy
(4) management learns from a "hands-on" approach
(5) workers are valued as the key to achieve productivity

(6) excellent companies stick to their knitting, exploiting their core competencies and not pursuing wild goose chases
(7) they keep their form simple and their staff lean;
(8) they know how to be simultaneously tight-fitting and expansive.

Peters has always been in favour of delegation in a company. The manager can't know everything. If he tries he'll get snowed under in useless detail.

A Darwinian approach to the achievement of excellence had to be adopted to achieve excellence. It is better to do something wrong than do nothing: people should not be terrified of making mistakes. The next time they try they'll learn from it and do it right, or hopefully better. So excellence could be gained incrementally, through a series of small steps bonded by a central message.

He is not a captive to consistency. A lot of the excellent companies praised by him in *Excellence* have not stood the test of corporate time. Some have disappeared. In today's world of shifting industry boundaries, the notion of telling a company to stick to its knitting seems akin to an order for corporate suicide. But Peters doesn't mind changing his tune.

He believes now that there are no excellent companies. He modified the message. It was no longer enough to be excellent: companies have to stand out from the crowd. Companies have to shrink, even deconstruct. They have to innovate. They must make the workplace more interesting.

Old structures are redundant. They were obstructing progress. In *Liberation Management* (1992) pronounced the death of middle management in with the sentence: "... middle managers as we have known them are cooked geese." The individual employee increasingly has to brand himself or herself. He prophesies an increasing number of women workers. He welcomes this, women are better than men at working in teams.

He believes that "90 per cent of white-collar jobs will be totally reinvented/reconceived in the next decade". His interest in crafting the new corporate citizen led to the production of a series of books including *The Brand You 50* (1999) and *Project 50* (1999).

Peters is a consummate performer, injecting the same messiahnism into his public appearances as is found in his books. A lecture by Tom Peters is a performance, a spectacle even. He is never static. Someone (at an obvious loose end) once calculated that he walks seven miles on stage while giving a lecture. He gives about a hundred talks a year throughout the world. He jokes that that's why he called his first horse "Frequent Flyer".

Tom Peters and Robert Waterman were also instrumental in the development of the 7Ss method of isolating management strengths and weaknesses, developed with their former colleague at McKinsey, Richard Pascale.

13. Michael Porter

Michael E. Porter is the Bishop William Laurence University Professor at the Harvard Business School. He has an almost "living legend" status in the world of management thinking. He has written eighteen books and countless articles. In addition to his teaching he consults widely with the Monitor Group which he helped establish. Above and before everything he is an educator, either by the spoken or by the written word. But he is not a performer or management superstar. *The Economist* once commented that he was as likely to write a best-selling management blockbuster like ... (the reader can no doubt supply an example) as to give a lecture wearing a bra and stockings (what an awful image!). Few of his books are available in paperback. He has advised both the public and private sectors throughout the world. Not only has he been showered with academic and business awards, he has even received civic medals usually reserved for military heroes or extraordinary sports people. Porter was for many years active in the US military's reserve and was a celebrated college footballer, baseballer and golfer in his youth.

Porter was born in a university town – Ann Arbor, Michigan. His father was an army officer. He studied mechanical and aerospace engineering at Princeton and then switched to business, earning an MBA and a Ph.D. in economics from Harvard. He later joined the faculty there.

Porter has always been obsessed by competition. His first widely-read book *Competitive Strategy* (1980) is now in its 63rd imprint. In it he analyses competition. There is natural competition and tension between existing players in an industry; threats of new entrants to the market; the prospect of substitute products or services; the bargaining power of suppliers; and the bargaining power of consumers.

There are three ways to compete effectively: produce a product or service either more cheaply; produce something that is better and different from the competition; and dominate a niche market and close out the competitors. He defined the latter as differentiation.

He did not believe many companies could do all three or even two at a time. The particular strategy chosen depended on what type of company you had. He noted five: global; fragmented; emerging; mature; and declining.

The company also had to look at the series of links that went into its provision or production. He called this The Value Chain (and the name has stuck). He isolated five primary activities in any value chain. These are: internal logistics–getting the necessary materials; production or provision ; external logistics and distribution; marketing; and after-sales services.

These were each accompanied by a range of secondary activities. Each company's value chain in turn fitted into a wider value system.

Porter subsequently moved from competition between firms to competition between nations. In *The Competitive Advantage of Nations* (1990) he examined how some states were wealthy and why others were not. The important element here were National Value Systems. He visualized these as akin to a four-sided diamond. The four components were: domestic rivalry – the tougher it was the better; traditional economic resources; infrastructure, including the education level of its citizens; and the cluster phenomenon.

The latter was very important, thought frequently overlooked. These were concentrations of particular types of industry in defined geographical areas. They embraced the low-tech Portuguese cork-makers and Silicon Valley. These areas can use economies of scale to attract workers and increase efficiency, as well as cross-subsidization and skills pools.

His study of national economies has been extensive, though not always welcome. In *Can Japan Compete?* (2000) he showed that the long and protracted recession suffered by Japan was the inevitable result of successive post-war Japanese governments' policies.

His most recent research on competition has involved a look at America's inner cities. He argues wealth creation is a sounder panacea for poverty and inequality reduction than redistributing wealth from elsewhere.

He has academically colonised much of the east coast of the United States with various centres supplied with full-time research staff working on a plethora of projects dear to his academic heart, from competition to inner-city development.

14. Paul Hersey

Paul Hersey's Situational Leadership has been used to train well over 10,000,000 managers and sales people from more than 1,000 businesses and other organizations. He is an internationally known behavioural scientist and highly successful entrepreneur.

Hersey is recognized as one of the world's outstanding authorities on training and development in leadership, management, and selling. In addition to his teaching, he is a consultant, on a continuing basis, to industrial, government, and military organizations.

He is former faculty member of Northern Illinois University, California State College a Chico, University of Arkansas, and Ohio University. Dr. Hersey also served in the roles of Chairman of the Department of Management and Dean of the School of Business. Dr. Hersey has also served as Project Director for the Industrial Relations Center of the University of Chicago, Training Director at Kaiser Aluminum and Chemical Company, and Department Head at Sandia Corporation.

Dr. Hersey has authored or co-authored numerous papers, articles, and books including Management of Organizational Behaviour: Utilizing Human Resources, Organizational Change Through Effective Leadership and Selling: A Behavioural Science Approach. His most recent books include The Situational Leader, Situation Selling, and Situational Service: Customer Care for the Practitioner, and Situational Parenting.

15. Jack Welch

Jack Welch is the former CEO of General Electric. Born in Salem, Massachusetts, the son of a bus conductor, he studied chemical engineering at the university of Massachusetts, gaining a Ph.D. in the same subject from the university of Illinois. He joined General Electric's plastics division in 1960. He devoted the rest of his working life to the company.

His rise was meteoric. At age 33, he became one of the company's youngest general managers. He subsequently served as vice president and sector executive for the consumer products and services sector and finally he was vice chairman and executive officer. In December 1980, after a little over twenty years in the company, he was named GE's eighth CEO, the youngest in the company's history.

Welch had an immense impact on corporate America, setting standards of best practice for its senior executives. He always led by example. He had shown during his rise to greatness the potential of GE's plastics divisions. He also laid the foundations for the success of GE Capital. As CEO he took a number of innovative steps to promote the disparate elements of what had become an unmanageable conglomerate. He announced to the various sectors that unless they could become either the number 1 or the number 2 in their respective industries they would be spun off. He commented: 'My main job was developing talent. I was a gardener providing water and other nourishment to our top 750 people. Of course, I had to pull out some weeds, too.' His talent-nurturing sometimes took unusual forms. He also introduced the practice of establishing 'anti-groups' within certain divisions whose role was to put forward the opposite to official policy in a deliberate attempt to encourage debate and discourage group-thinking.

He earned a reputation for being endlessly creative, never being hide-bound by convention when it came to solving a problem.

He introduced Six Sigma Quality Management at GE, after its usefulness had been shown in Motorola. St Augustine asked God to make him perfect "but not yet". He was an early advocate of Six Sigma, a means of achieving near-perfection in manufacturing by gradual, incremental steps, monitored by specially-trained experts called Black Belts and Master Black Belts.

Welch also became known for his desire to communicate. He is reputed to have written three to four thousand notes to members of his staff every year. GE's financial success came at the expense of extensive layoffs. During the process of streamlining the company, over 100,000 workers lost their job. His perceived ruthlessness earned him the moniker "Neutron Jack". He hated bureaucracy of any form, and always sought people who were dedicated to change. He was also an active teacher at the GE Leadership Centre in Crottonville.

After nearly two decades at the helm Jack Welch prepared for departure followed by a smooth succession. The person who was to take up his mantle was chosen from within the GE organization, through a long and rigorous process. This resulted in the anointing of Jeffrey Immelt as the prospective CEO from April 2001 when Welch promised to "walk away and keep walking". Things didn't just go to script. GE had acquired the Honeywell Company in 1990, and Welch announced he wanted to stay in charge to oversee the integration of this prized plant into his garden. However, the takeover was scuttled when the European Commission raised objections that the resultant company would have a dominant and potentially distorting role in the aviation financing sector in Europe. Welch was thus denied a last charge towards the setting sun. Most observers felt this did not do him any harm. At GE he was a larger-than-life figure.

Since retiring Jack Welch has continued to consult a number of Fortune 500 firms. He also found the time to write his memoirs: Jack: Straight from the Gut *(2001). Outside the US the book had the less macho subtitle of* Jack: What I've Learned Leading a Great Company and Great People *It went to number one in the best-sellers' chart in America. He has since added* Winning: The Ultimate Business How-To Book *(2005). This "...is a book for the people in business who sweat, get their nails dirty, hire, fire, make hard decisions, and pay the price when those decisions are wrong."*

16. Henry Mintzberg

Henry Mintzberg who witnessed his latest book: *Why I Hate Flying*, a brilliantly sardonic look at management in the airline industry. Next in line is a book exploring management education, one of Mintzberg's longest held bugbears. Indeed, as befits an iconoclast, a common theme throughout Mintzberg's career has been a willingness to bite the hand that feeds him. For a man employed by two business schools–Montreal's McGill and France's INSEAD–he has proved a relentless thorn in the side of conventional b-school education. The fruit of his dissatisfaction was the International Masters Programme in Management, a thoroughly global programme which encourages managers to break free of the limitations of functional, and other, perspectives.

His career began with his Ph.D. research which saw him examining what managers actually did. Hardly rocket science, but a strangely unusual strategy. The result was *The Nature of Managerial Work* (1973) was the result–one of the few (very few) books which actually examines what managers do rather than discussing what they should do.

Since then, Mintzberg has set the agenda in the sphere of strategic management with a combination of academic rigour and a devotion to seeking out new perspectives which has generally set him apart from his contemporaries. This reached a climax with the publication of *The Rise and Fall of Strategic Planning*, a coherent tour-de-force which sounded the death knell for the strategic orthodoxy which had long dominated management thinking and education. His most recent strategy book is *Strategy Safari*.

Mintzberg is working on his next book Developing Managers, Not MBAs. No doubt the book will include more of Mintzberg's forthright opinions on the subject as expressed in a recent interview: I think every MBA should have a skull and crossbones stamped on their forehead and underneath should be written: 'Warning: not prepared to manage.'

29.3 MANAGEMENT THINKERS: INDIANS

29.3.1 Management Gurus: Indian Scene

Micro-scooping on India for the purpose, we too have prominent 'Management Gurus', from legends to contemporary trendsetters. But before we investigate into their works, a noticeable fact is that these management thinkers have studied, travelled, worked, operated, managed and made their presence felt in many parts of the globe. The following are leading names for Indian Management Thinkers.

1. C.K. Prahalad

If you wish to refer to one of the greatest Indian business thinkers, C.K. Prahalad should be on the top of your list. He needs no introduction; every management student in India and internationally knows the name C.K. Prahalad. He is known not only for his prolific works also for his management perceptions and strategies.

C.K. Prahalad was a professor, researcher, speaker, author and prominent consultant. Business Week has called him "a brilliant teacher at the University of Michigan" and also described him as "maybe the most influential thinker on business strategy today."

In addition to serving as the Harvey C. Freuhauf Professor of Business Administration at the University of Michigan Business School, Prahalad specializes in corporate strategy and the role of top management in large, diversified, multinational corporations.

In 1994, he co-authored the best-seller, Competing for the Future, with Gary Hamel. Translated into 14 languages, it was named the Best-Selling Business Book of the Year in 1994. Prahalad is particularly well known for the work he has conducted with fellow strategy expert Gary Hamel. This includes the articles The Core Competence of the Corporation (Harvard Business Review, May-June, 1990), Competing in the New Economy: Managing Out of Bounds (Strategic Management Journal, Vol. 17, No. 3, March, 1996) as well as the best-selling book *Competing for the Future: Breakthrough Strategies for Seizing Control of Your Industry and Creating the Markets of Tomorrow* (1994).

He won numerous awards. The most recent include the McKinsey Prize three times, the SMR-PWC award, and the ANBAR Electronic Citation of Excellence.

A prominent world-class guru, Professor Prahalad has consulted with the world's foremost companies, such as Ahlstrom, AT&T, Cargill, Citicorp, Eastman Chemical, Kodak, Oracle, Philips, Quantum, Revlon, Steelcase, and Unilever. In addition, he serves on the Board of Directors of NCR Corporation, Hindustan Lever Limited and the World Resources Institute.

His latest book, 'The Fortune at the Bottom of the Pyramid: Eradicating Poverty Through Profits', proves that the future will develop from serving the poor, because the innovations that are developed are superior—top quality, low price, high volume and world-scale. Only the best innovations will work for both sides of the equation, those in poverty and those in the "developed" countries.

2. Gita Piramal

More often than not, a journalist's viewpoint is considered to be critical, biased and dynamic. But a journalist with a Ph.D. in business history is a potentially intense combination. This profile describes, Gita Piramal an author who has written for many years on the corporate sector for leading Indian and international publications such as the Financial Times and the Economic Times, and is a consulting editor of the World Executive's Digest. She also has been involved in the making of television programmes on Indian business for the BBC and Plus Channel. In 1986, she co-authored India's Industrialists, and in 1991 contributed to Business and Politics in India—A historical perspective, published by the Indian Institute of Management, Ahmedabad. She divides her time between London and Mumbai.

Through her works, she describes the Indian corporate sector with Indian historical and political references as the foundation. How earlier systems have an influence on contemporary operations and radical changes or 'Business Mantras' required to keep abreast in this dynamic environment.

Gita Piramal is one of India's foremost business writers. She is now the managing editor of The Smart Manager, India's first world-class management magazine.

3. Sumantra Ghoushal

If you attempt to visualize a mentor, an author and a consultant in one being you are sure to find one personality, Sumantra Ghoushal. Born in India, educated in the US and currently living in Europe, he is a teacher, author and consultant in the field of international management. He is also founding dean of the Indian School of Business in Hyderabad, a new venture jointly sponsored by Northwestern University and the London Business School.

He has published eight books, over forty-five articles and several award-winning case studies. The book "Managing across Borders: The Transnational Solution", co-authored with Christopher A. Bartlett, has been listed as one of the fifty most influential management books and they have become one of the world's most respected business thinkers.

His most recent work focuses on the need to develop strategy, which encompasses people. He has been critical of the current fad for knowledge management.

4. Ram Charan

If you want to know how to strip down a concept to its core meaning and then put it into action, you should consider the works of Ram Charan. He is a highly acclaimed business advisor, speaker, and author. Ram has coached some of the world's most successful CEOs. For 35 years, he has worked behind the scenes at companies like GE, KLM, Bank of America, DuPont, Novartis, EMC, Home Depot and Verizon.

Ram is a favourite among executive educators. He won the Bell Ringer (best teacher) award at GE's famous Crotonville Institute. He won similar awards at Wharton and Northwestern. He was among Business Week's top ten resources for in-house executive development programmes.

Apart from authoring fine books, he also tailors his books for specific client companies such as Gateway, Ford, and EDS. His articles have been published in Harvard Business Review, Fortune, Time, Information Week, Leader to Leader, Director's Monthly, Directorship, The Corporate Board and USA Today. Ram is a director of Austin Industries and The Six Sigma Academy. He was elected a Fellow of the National Academy of Human Resources. He serves as a co-host for the Fortune Forum on Corporate Governance and also serves on the National Association of Corporate Directors' Blue Ribbon Commission on Corporate Governance.

He is known for his practical, real-world perspective. His expertise entails areas of business like: Profitable Growth, Business Acumen, Leadership, Execution: Discipline of Getting Things Done, Tools for Changing a Social System, Global Matrix Organization, Innovation, Corporate Governance, Succession & Leadership Pipeline, Building Top Management Teams.

5. Arindham Chaudhuri

Speaking of contemporary business thinkers, another fine entrepreneur, educator, author and enterprising personality are Arindham Chaudhuri.

Professor Chaudhuri is the Dean, Centre for Economic Research & Advanced Studies at IIPM (The Indian Institute of Planning & Management, New Delhi). In the year 1996, he founded Planman Consulting, which is now one of the fastest growing Indian Management Consulting Firms. After being associated with the production and marketing of two Bengali movies, in the year 2001 he formally launched Planman Life: A fully dedicated production and communications venture.

His latest book 'Count Your Chickens Before They Hatch' for which he got an unprecedented seven figure record advance has created a new benchmark in India by selling more than 80,000 copies in just 8 months! It has been in all national bestseller lists from the first week of inception, till date.

As a management consultant he specializes in the areas of Strategic Vision, Leadership, Social Sector Consulting, Comparative Management Techniques and Global Opportunities & Threat Analysis.

His contribution to the field of management studies in India can be found in the iconoclastic "**Theory ' i ' Management**" which he has developed for India Inc. "Theory 'i' Management" is about India centric management ideas. For the last few years, he has been conducting workshops on Leadership and Strategic Vision exclusively for CEOs, MDs, Directors and Presidents from the corporate sector. From the Managing Director of Hero Motors to the President of Tata Chemicals, from the Executive President of A.V. Birla Group to the CEO of Ernst & Young... have all taken leadership training workshops from him. As a celebrated speaker he is regularly invited to speak at various annual conferences and national conventions. He also happens to be highest paid speaker in the country.

An economist by passion and education, during Bill Clinton's historic visit to India he launched his Great Indian Dream—India can beat America, a series of seminars for every Indian. Held in all the metros of India, these seminars had thousands of people pouring in from all walks of life. In these seminars he not only highlights the inherent strengths of the Indian culture but also talks about an alternative resource mobilization and allocation package for an Indian turnaround. To facilitate social activities based on this he has started the Great Indian Dream Foundation in memory of his brother Aurobindo Chaudhuri.

He was recently rated as one of the 50 leading thinkers in South Asia by Wilton Park (an organization supported by the European Commission and British foreign office).

Further, he was awarded the Academic Gold Medal while completing the Postgraduate Diploma in Planning and Management from IIPM. Prof. Chaudhuri was awarded "Management Guru 2000 Award" by Chennai based Om Venkatesa Society which annually honours management experts.

6. Shiv Khera

In this dog-eat-dog business world, if you are not self-motivated, self-confident and unique, you will be trampled over. At such times look into the works of the distinguished management guru and motivator, Shiv Khera. His gospel:- "Winners don't do different things, they do things differently".

Shiv Khera is the founder of Qualified Learning Systems Inc. An educator, business consultant, a much sought after speaker and a successful entrepreneur. He has taken his dynamic personal message around the world. Shiv has been recognized as a 'Louis Marchesi Fellow' by the Round Table Foundation. His client list includes the who's who of the corporate world. He has authored three best-sellers, amongst other books. His first book "You Can Win", which came out in 1998, has sold over a million copies worldwide. His second book "Living With Honour" hit the stands in August 2003, becoming an instant best-seller. Then within a span of six months in February 2004, his third book "Freedom is Not Free" was released, also to become a best-seller.

His first two books are on an individualistic level, where he defines the winning edge as achieving excellence rather than perfection, as excellence paves the way for progress. He also conveys that it is better to be honourable than to be honoured. His work offers direction for living with pride in a cluttered environment. His latest book concentrates on society. Here he firmly believes that a progressive society is the basis for individual progress of its people.

Transforming his years of experience as a motivator into a practical tool, he has developed a core programme/workshop known as the Blueprint for Success (BPS). This programme motivates people to recognize their true potential and gain success–personally and professionally.

Apart from the prominent business thinkers mentioned above, India also presents other management thinkers who have a substantial influence on business minds and operations. To name a few as an illustration are: Venkatram Ramaswamy; Vijay Vishwanath; Partha Bose; Rita Bhimani; Jeetendra Jain; Ashwath Damodaran and J.S. Chandan.

29.4 SUMMARY

The idiom 'Management Guru' describes a person who is thinker, experienced, inventive and who develops business management perspectives that provide beneficial outlooks and practices. With reference to the slogan 'An idea is only a thought until it is materialized', the most successful Business Thinkers are those who have ensured the successful implementation of their thoughts.

In the past, the benefit of such resourceful business practices was limited to only those people who were privileged to have communication links with knowledgeable business tycoons. But presently, in a global order, the exposure has broadened. Perspectives and practices of international and Indian management personalities are now available to almost anyone in the form of workshops and seminars and other similar modes. So with an open mind, thinks 'WOW', act now and pay attention and participate with our Management Gurus who have been/are willing to impart their knowledge to the business world in particular and the whole society in general.

29.5 SELF-ASSESSMENT QUESTIONS

1. Discuss the biographical sketches of classical and modern management thinkers at international level.
2. “The personal lives of great management thinkers has not been quit satisfactory”. Comment.
3. “Indian management thinkers are equally good in their contribution in terms of literature”. Discuss and elaborate.

GLOSSORY

Abnormal Loss: An abnormal loss is where total revenue does not cover total cost. It is a situation where a firm is making below normal profits. If abnormal losses persist in an industry, firms will tend to leave, prices will rise and normal profits will be restored.

Abnormal Profit: Profits exceed the amount a firm must receive to carry on production. Also known as supernormal profit. If abnormal profits persist in an industry this will tend to attract new firms in, supply will increase, prices will fall and normal profits will be restored. If there are barriers to entry then abnormal profits may persist in the long run.

Acceleration: A contract clause that requires payment of the full amount of the debt owed if a payment is missed or another triggering event (such as bankruptcy of the debtor) occurs. This type of clause often appears in promissory notes or loan agreements.

Accounting: The recording, classifying, summarizing, and interpreting of events of a financial character. These events can include income, expenses, and cash flow.

Accounts Payable: Trade accounts of businesses representing amounts owed for goods or services received.

Accounts Receivable. Trade accounts of businesses representing amounts due for goods sold or services rendered.

Accrual-Basis Accounting: An accounting system in which income is recorded when it is earned rather than when it is paid, and expenses are recorded when an obligation is established rather than when the money is paid.

Agent: A person granted the authority to act on behalf of another person or entity, known as the "principal". The actions and decisions of the agent can be binding on the principal.

Amortization: The periodic expense of an amount paid for an intangible asset over a period of time. New businesses are able to amortize their start-up expenses over at least a 5-year period.

Annual Growth Factor: A percentage by which sales and cost of sales (COS) will increase over a one-year period.

Appreciation: The increase in the value of an asset.

Arbitration: A form of alternative dispute resolution in which a neutral third party (an arbitrator) considers the competing parties, arguments and evidence and renders a decision or award. Arbitration can be binding or non-binding.

Asset Category: The indication of whether an asset is either land, a building, equipment or a start-up cost.

Asset Life: The number of year's service expected from an asset.

Asset: Anything that an individual or an entity owns that has value. Cash, equipment and stocks are all considered assets.

Assign: To give or sell a right or an interest. The person who receives the right or interest is the "assignee" and the person making the transfer is the "assignor."

At-will Employment: The policy allowing employers or employees to end an employment relationship at any time for any reason–or for no reason at all. In some states, the law may place practical limits on this policy.

Audit: An examination of a company's financial records and the accounting systems, controls, and records that produced them.

Audit Legal: A review or examination of an individual's or organization's records to determine legal compliance or proper record keeping.

Award: A decision rendered by a court or arbitrator that one party in a dispute is owed money and that the other party or parties are liable.

Balance sheet: A report listing the balances of the assets, liabilities, and equity as of a specific date. Also a financial statement that includes a company's assets and liabilities. A company's net worth is equal to its assets minus its liabilities.

Bankruptcy: A condition in which a business cannot meet its debt obligations and petitions a federal district court for either reorganization of its debts (Chapter 11) or liquidation of its assets (Chapter 7). In the action the property of a debtor is taken over by a receiver or trustee in bankruptcy for the benefit of the creditors. The action may be voluntary or involuntary.

Banner Ad: A common form of online advertising, banner ads come in a variety of sizes and typically appear on a Web page as a box or rectangle containing text, images, animation or other effects. Users who click on a banner typically follow a hyperlink to the advertiser's website.

Barriers: This generally refers to factors inhibiting the free movement of resources, e.g., restrictive laws relating to the movement of goods, capital and labour.

Boston matrix: A grid containing four types of product, used as a means of analyzing the product range of a business. The four types of product are cash cows, dogs, problem children or wild cards and stars.

Black economy: Unrecorded production. The Black economy results from activity that has not been recorded through the tax system or other conventional means of recording.

Bonds: Securities issued by the US government, corporations, federal agencies, or state or local municipalities.

Bonus: A cash award granted to employees by the employer, usually based on personal and/or company performance. Bonuses can also come in the form of extra vacation time, gifts and other non-monetary awards.

Bookmark: A marker or address that identifies a website or web page. Most Web browsers, such as Microsoft Internet Explorer (which calls bookmarks "Favorites"), allow users to save and organize bookmarks as a convenient way to mark Websites for future reference.

Boutique: A small company or firm that specializes in a particular industry or provides a limited service, such as investment banking firms that concentrate solely on technology companies.

Breach of contract: A violation of or failure to perform according to the terms and conditions of an agreement.

Broadband: A high-speed transmission medium. T-1, ISDN, DSL and cable modems are broadband media. Besides downloading Web pages more quickly, broadband can also transmit high-quality streaming video.

Broken Link: A hyperlink that does not work, usually because the URL is incorrect or the Web page to which the link refers has been moved or deleted.

Browser: Software that lets you view websites. Most browsers display text, images, graphics, animation and other online content. Popular browsers include Netscape Navigator and Microsoft Internet Explorer.

Business organization: A business organization aims to meet needs by providing goods or services to customers. All organizations have a formal structure; aim to achieve objectives; use resources; require direction; are legally regulated.

Business Plan: A planning document that describes a company, its market, its management team, its potential, its competitors, and all other relevant information about its business and its prospects.

Business type: The legal structure of the business. Types include Sole Proprietorship, Partnership, S Corporation, C Corporation, or Limited Liability Company.

Cash cows: Products that produce a large amount of revenue because they have a large share of an existing market which is only expanding slowly.

Corporation: A corporation where the entity is taxed separately from its owners under subchapter C of the Internal Revenue Code.

Cafeteria Plan: An employee benefit plan where employees use pretax salary or wages to create their own customized benefits package. Employees may be able to take cash (which becomes taxable) for unused credits or convert more pretax dollars to pay for more benefits. Also known as a flexible benefits plan.

Cancellation Fee: A fee for breaking a contract. Many cellular phone service contracts impose a cancellation fee for ending the contract before the end of its term.

Capital Expenditures: Business spending on additional plant equipment and inventory.

Capital: (1) assets less liabilities, representing the ownership interest in a business, (2) a stock of accumulated goods, especially at a specified time and in contrast to income received during a specified time period, (3) accumulated goods devoted to the production of goods, and (4) accumulated possessions calculated to bring income.

Caption: The text accompanying an illustration or photograph.

Cash: Coins and currency, cheques, money orders, credit card slips, and deposits in bank accounts.

Cash Discount: An incentive offered by the seller to encourage a buyer to pay within a stipulated time. For example, if the terms are 1%/10/net 30, the buyer may deduct 1 per cent from the amount of the invoice (if paid within 10 days); otherwise the full amount is due within 30 days.

Cash Equivalents: Investments of high liquidity and safety with a known market value and a very short-term maturity. Examples include Treasury bills and money market funds.

Cash Flow. An accounting presentation showing how much of the cash generated by a business remains after both expenses (including interest) and principal repayment on loans are paid. A projected cash flow statement indicates whether the business will have cash to pay its expenses, loans, and make a profit. Cash flows can be calculated for any given period of time, normally done on a monthly basis or yearly basis.

Cash plan: A report listing the cash the business will generate from sales and use for expenses. It also shows how much cash is left over or how much additional cash the business needs.

Cash sales: The portion of sales paid for with cash.

Circulation: The number of copies that a publication distributes or sells. Also refers to the number of people who have an opportunity to observe a piece of outdoor advertising, such as a billboard or poster.

Close: The point during the sales process when the customer agrees to buy a product or service.

Closing: Actions and procedures required to effect the successful conclusion of a business transaction, such as a real estate purchase or loan consummation.

Cold Call: An unscheduled contact, either on the phone or in person, between a seller and a prospective customer.

Collateral Document: A legal document covering the item(s) pledged as collateral on a loan.

Collateral: Something of value pledged to support the repayment of an obligation or loan. Examples include real estate and certificates of deposit.

Common Law: Law made by judges in individual cases, rather than by the legislature.

Common stock: Ownership in a corporation resulting from investment. Common stockholder rights usually include a right to vote, share in dividends, purchases additional shares, and share in cash if the corporation is liquidated.

Compensation: Direct and indirect monetary and non-monetary rewards given to employees based on the value of the job, their personal contributions and their performance.

Competitive advantage: A distinct characteristic that makes your product or service more appealing than your competitor's.

Compromise: The settlement of a dispute or claim.

Consideration: The inducement to a contract. Some right, interest, profit, or benefit accruing to one party, or some forbearance, detriment, loss, or responsibility given, suffered, or undertaken by the other.

Consultants: Paid professionals that perform a certain job function for your business. Consultants can include attorneys, accountants, and advertising/marketing agencies.

Contingency Fee: A common legal fee arrangement that relies on the collection of monetary damages for the plaintiff before any legal fees are owed. Most common in litigation (such as in personal injury lawsuits), it allows the client to receive legal services while paying the attorney little or no money up front.

Contingent Liability: A potential obligation that may be incurred dependent upon the occurrence of a future event. Two examples are: (1) the liability of a guarantor of a promissory note if the primary borrower fails to pay as agreed and (2) the liability that would be incurred if a pending lawsuit are resolved in the other party's favour.

Controlled Circulation: Publications, generally business oriented, delivered only to readers who have some special qualifications. Generally, these publications are free to the qualified recipients, who must complete registration questionnaires in order to receive them. Also called 'qualified circulation.'

Corporate Bonds: Debt instruments issued by corporations, as distinct from ones issued by a government agency, typically interest-bearing with a fixed maturity.

Corporation: A form of organization that provides its owners and shareholders with certain rights and privileges, including protection from personal liability, if proper steps are followed. Corporations may take a number of forms, depending on the goals and objectives of the founders. Types include C, S and non-profit corporations. Corporations are regarded as "persons" in the eyes of the law and may thus sue and be sued, own property, borrow money and hire employees.

Cost of Goods Sold: This term represents the cost of buying raw materials and producing the goods that a company sells. It also includes the cost of the company's labour force and overhead costs.

Cost of Sales (COS): The cost of a product or service sold to customers.

Credit Rating: A formal evaluation of an individual or a company's credit history and capability of repaying debt.

Credit sales: The portion of sales sold on credit terms.

Credit terms: The arrangements agreed upon by the buyer and seller as to when payments for products and services are to be made.

Current assets: Assets which are either cash, will turn into cash, or will be used up within one year.

Current liabilities: Debts the business must pay within one year.

Current market value: What someone is willing to pay you for an item should you choose to sell it today.

Current Ratio: The ratio of the company's current assets to its current liabilities. A current ratio of less than 1-to-1 typically indicates a poor credit risk. A current ratio of greater than 2-to-1 typically indicates a good credit risk.

Customer profile: A written description of your customers. Usual methods for developing customer profiles include demographics, geographic, and psychographics.

Customer: Someone who has bought or made the decision to buy a product or service.

Cyclical Industry: An industry that has natural high and low sales periods based on the time of year, season or other factors.

Damages: A cash compensation ordered by a court or arbitrator to offset losses or suffering caused by another's fault or negligence. Damages are a typical request made of a court or arbitrator when persons sue for breach of contract or tort.

Database: A computer program that helps users organizes information. Databases range from simple collections of rows and columns (similar to a spreadsheet) to complex systems that process and manipulate millions of records in a variety of ways.

Debenture: Debt instrument evidencing the holder's right to receive interest and principal installments from the debtor.

Debt Financing: The provision of long-term loans to small business concerns in exchange for debt securities or a note.

Debt service: The total payment of principal and interest on loans.

Decision-Maker: The person within a company who ultimately decides which products or services to buy.

Deed of Trust: A document that, when properly delivered, transfers a security interest in real property.

Defaults: The nonpayment of principal and/or interest on the due date as provided by the terms and conditions of a promissory note or loan agreement.

Demand Letter: A letter from a lawyer on behalf of a client that demands payment or some other action. Demand letters often threaten litigation if the other party does not perform.

Demographic: A descriptive classification for consumers, such as age, sex, income, education, household size, home ownership or other defining characteristics.

Demographics: A means of separating customers into groups by factors such as age, gender, income, or education.

Depreciation: The reduction in value of an asset over its useful life. An accounting procedure that spreads the cost of purchasing an asset over the useful lifetime of the asset.

Direct Mail: Marketing or advertising materials sent directly to a prospective customer via the US Postal Service or a private delivery company.

Direct Marketing: The process of sending promotional messages directly to individual consumers, rather than via a mass medium. Includes methods such as direct mail and telemarketing.

Disability Benefits: Benefits paid to an employee who cannot work because of disability, usually limited to what is not covered by workers compensation. Disability benefits are usually a percentage of the employee's prior income and generally run for a limited time.

Distributions: Amounts paid to, or withdrawn by, the owners of a Sole Proprietorship, Partnership, S Corporation, or Limited Liability Company.

Dividends: Distributions of money by a corporation to its stockholders.

EBITDA: Earnings before interest, taxes, depreciation, and amortization.

E-Check: A method of automatically paying for goods or services that works much like direct deposit in reverse. Companies keep a customer's voided check on file, which allows them to debit the customer's bank account for the amount owed.

EDI (Electronic Data Interchange): The exchange of standardized document forms between computers for business use. EDI has traditionally been a very complex and expensive undertaking. As more companies build inexpensive, standards-based networks around the Internet, however, EDI systems are becoming cheaper and easier to use.

Embossing: To raise a design or letters already printed on a card.

Employee benefits: Expenses for employees in addition to salaries and wages. Employee benefits include retirement plans, health plans, dental or vision plans, life insurance plans, paid vacations, holidays, or sick leave.

Employee Manual: A handbook that describes a company's personnel procedures, policies and benefits.

Employee Retirement Income Security Act (ERISA): A broad-reaching law that establishes the rights of pension plan participants, standards for the investment of pension plan assets, and requirements for the disclosure of plan provisions and funding.

Employer ID Number (EIN): An identification number assigned to businesses for taxpaying purposes by the IRS or state taxing authorities. An Employer ID Number is required for partnerships, corporations, and trusts, and it may be required for sole proprietorships that have employees. Also called a Federal ID Number or Taxpayer ID Number.

Employment Agreement: An agreement that sets forth the rights and obligations of employees and employers. Typical employment agreements oblige employees to keep trade secrets confidential and to not solicit other employees after their departure.

Entrepreneur: One who assumes the financial risk of the initiation, operation, and management of a given business undertaking.

Equal Employment Opportunity (EEO): Federal legislation prohibiting employment discrimination based on age, race, sex, religion or ethnic background.

Equity: The investment in the business by the owner(s).

Equity Financing: The provision of funds for capital or operating expenses in exchange for capital stock, stock purchase warrants, and/or options in the business financed, without any guaranteed return, but with the opportunity to share in the company's profits.

ESOP (Employee Stock Ownership Plan): A retirement-type plan in which a trust holds stock in the employees' names. Employees receive cash from the stock only when they leave the company or perhaps when the company is sold.

Exempt Employee: Employees who are not bound to overtime regulations and minimum wage laws. Who is exempt depends on level of responsibility or professional status.

Exit Interview: An interview conducted at the end of an employee's term of employment to obtain employment feedback and to remind the employee of his or her confidentiality obligations.

Expense forecast: An estimate of the business's future costs.

Expenses: Costs incurred by the business.

Extranet: An intranet that is open to certain external users, such as suppliers and clients. These external users may log onto an extranet in a one-way relationship or they may connect their own intranet with the host intranet, creating a two-way relationship.

Fair Use: A legal doctrine that authorizes use of copyrighted materials for certain purposes without the copyright owner's permission.

Financial Reports: Reports concerning the financial aspects of a business, such as: balance sheet and P & L a/c are two financial reports.

Financing: New funds provided to a business, either by way of equity infusion, or loans.

Fixed Annuities: Investment contract sold by an insurance company that guarantees fixed payments, either for life or for a specified period, to the annuitant. The insurer takes both the investment risk and the mortality risk.

Fixed Costs: Costs of doing business, such as rent and utilities that remain generally the same regardless of the amount of sales of goods or services.

Fixed inventory: A system where the inventory level remains constant.

Flow Chart: A graphical representation for the definition, analysis, or solution of a problem, in which symbols are used to represent operations, data, flow, equipment, etc.

Foot Traffic: Consumer activity produced by visitors at stores, trade show exhibits or by popular retail locations.

Foreclosure: The act by the mortgagee or trustee upon default, in the payment of interest or principal of a mortgage of enforcing payment of the debt by selling the underlying secured property.

Franchise: An agreement under which the franchiser (owner of the rights) licences the franchisee (the business owner) the right to sell a given product/service or to use certain trademarks or trade names, usually within a designated area.

Franchise fees: Cash paid to a franchiser for the use of a franchise.

Franchising: A relationship in which the franchiser provides a licensed privilege to the franchise to do business and offers assistance in organizing, training, merchandising, marketing, and managing in return for a consideration. Examples of franchises include Burger King and Taco Bell.

Freeware: Software that is available for anyone to use, free of charge. Most freeware is still copyrighted, however, which means that it can't be further distributed or licensed.

Full-Service Agency: A firm that handles all aspects of the advertising or public relations process, including planning, design, production and placement. Many full-service agencies also handle marketing communication, public relations, sales promotion and direct marketing.

General partner: A partnership investor who manages the business and assumes responsibility for the partnership's debts and other obligations.

Giveaway: A gift given to potential customers at trade shows and other marketing events to remind them of a product or service. Also known as a 'freebie' or a 'gimme.'

Gross profit: Sales minus the cost of sales.

Guarantee: A promise to step in and perform another's obligation if that person should fail or default.

Guarantor: A person who makes a legally binding promise either to pay another person's obligation or to perform another person's duty if that person defaults or fails to perform.

Hard Sell: Aggressive, high-pressure sales techniques.

Health Maintenance Organization (HMO): A system of managed health care in which patients must see approved health care providers. HMOs typically offer coverage with no deductibles and low per-visit fees.

High-Yield Bonds: A bond that has a rating of BB or lower and pays a higher yield to compensate for the greater credit risk.

Income Statement: A record of the financial performance of a company over a period of time. It records all the income generated by the business during the period and deducts all its expenses for the same period to arrive at net income, or the profit for the period.

Independent Contractor: A worker who works on a specific project for a specified period of time. Independent contractors are not subject to tax withholdings and usually don't receive benefits granted to full-time employees.

Infringement (of copyright): Any unauthorized use of a copyrighted work other than fair use.

Infringement (of patent): Violation of a patent through production, use or sale of a patented invention or its functional equivalent without the patentholder's permission.

Infringement (of trademark): Unauthorized use of a protected trademark or service mark or use of a confusingly similar mark.

Inquiries: Consumer response to a company's advertising, or to other promotional activities such as coupons. Used to measure the effectiveness of promotions.

Insolvency: The inability of a borrower to meet financial obligations as they mature, or having insufficient assets to pay legal debts.

Interest expense: The cost of borrowing money.

Interest Rate: Percentage of a sum of money charged for the use of the money. Borrowing $100 for one year at a 10 per cent simple interest rate would cost $10.

Interest: (1) An amount paid a lender for the use of funds, or (2) cost of using credit or another person's or company's money. Interest is usually calculated as a rate per a period of time, typically a year.

Internet: A network of networks, built upon a set of widely used software protocols that links millions of computers around the world. Services such as email and the Web use the Internet to transfer data.

Intranet: A private corporate network built with Internet-based protocols and software applications.

Inventory: Items the business owns and intends to sell to customers.

Invoice: A bill prepared by the seller of goods or services. Invoices tell purchasers how much they owe.

Joint Venture: An agreement between two or more partners ('joint ventures') to pursue collaboratively a particular project or business, with a sharing of profits or losses.

Judgement by Confession: The act of debtors permitting judgement to be entered against them for a given sum with a statement to that effect, without the institution of legal proceedings.

Judgement: Judicial determination of the existence of indebtedness or other legal liability.

Jurisdiction: The authority of a court to hear and decide a case. For a decision to be valid, a court must have both "subject matter jurisdiction" (the ability to hear the type of case at issue) and "personal jurisdiction" (authority over the parties).

Labour: Costs paid to employees directly involved with bringing goods or services to the customer.

Lease: A contract by which a tenant (the 'lessee') takes possession of office space, furniture, equipment or other property for a specified rent and specified amount of time. At the end of a lease, the property reverts back to its owner (the 'lessor').

Letter of Credit: A document issued by a bank guaranteeing payment of a customer's debt up to a set amount over a set period of time. Letters of credit are used extensively in international trade.

Letter of Intent (LOI): An agreement, usually non-binding, documenting the general terms of a proposed business relationship. Often used as a prelude to a binding, definitive agreement.

Liability: Any debt or obligation due now or potentially in the future. Liability is synonymous with legal responsibility.

Lien: A charge upon or security interest in real or personal property maintained to ensure the satisfaction of a debt or duty ordinarily arising by operation of law.

Limited Liability Company (LLC): A flexible business structure, popular with small businesses, offering owners the advantage of limited personal liability and the choice of being taxed like a partnership or a corporation.

Limited Liability Partnership (LLP): A type of partnership recognized in many states that protects individual partners from personal liability for negligent acts committed by other partners and employees not under their direct control. Some states restrict this type of partnership to professionals, such as lawyers, accountants and architects.

Limited partner: A partnership investor who has no control over the business and is not subject to the same liabilities as the general partners.

Line-of-credit loan: A current liability that extends the cash available in the business's checking account by the upper limit for the loan agreement.

List Broker: A person or company, who prepares, rents and maintains mailing lists.

Litigation: Lawsuits instituted through the judicial process.

Loan Agreement: An agreement for the borrowing of money, typically containing pertinent terms, conditions, covenants and restrictions.

Logo: A symbol that a company uses to represent itself or its brand.

Long-Term Debt: Obligations or liabilities that a company owes in one year or more.

Long-Term Government Bonds: Securities issued by the US government and debt issues of federal agencies having a maturity of 10 years or more.

Long-term liabilities: A formal loan where the term of the loan is greater than one year.

Mailing List: Names, addresses and sometimes phone numbers of consumers or businesses aggregated by buying characteristics such as age, income, education, size of household or business and ownership of property. Mailing lists are used for direct mail and to generate sales leads.

Market Share: The percentage of a product category's sales, in dollars or units, that a particular brand, product line or company controls.

Marketing Communications: The process and techniques involved in marketing, promoting or selling products or services through creative, visual or written communications. Also known as "marcom."

Marketing plan: A written explanation of how you plan on reaching customers, making sales, and reaching your financial goals.

Marketing Plan: A company plan for marketing products and services and increasing sales.

Maturity Extension: Extension of payment beyond the original date established for repayment of a loan.

Maturity: In general, the period and date when payment of a loan is due. As applied to securities and commercial paper, the period and date when payment of principal is due.

Mediation: A form of alternative dispute resolution in which a neutral party (a mediator) seeks to promote and negotiate a settlement between opposing parties in a dispute. There is no mechanism to compel the parties to settle; they must voluntarily agree to any settlement.

Medium: A type of publication or communications method that conveys news, entertainment and advertising to an audience. Examples include newspapers, television, magazines, radio, billboards and the Internet.

Merger: Typically, a combination of two or more corporations into one corporation.

Minimum cash balance: The minimum amount of cash the business needs to keep on-hand at all times.

Mission statement: A series of brief sentences or paragraphs that describe the purpose of your business, its products or services, customers, markets, and philosophy.

Mortgage: An instrument giving legal title to secure the repayment of a loan made by the mortgagee (lender).

Mortgage-Backed Bonds: Securities backed by mortgages issued by FMLMC and FNMA or guaranteed by GNMA. Investors receive payments out of the interest and principal on the underlying mortgages.

Multimedia: Information that combines different types of content, such as text, images, animation, video and audio.

Municipal Bonds: Debt obligation of a state or local government entity. The funds may support general government needs or fund special projects. The interest on these bonds is typically exempt from federal income taxes, and most state and local taxes.

Negligence: An action or omission falling below the standard of care that a reasonable person would exercise in the same situation.

Net income: The amount the business makes when sales exceeds all expenses.

Net loss: The amount the business loses when all expenses exceed sales.

Net Sales: Sales after discounts and returns.

Net worth: The owner's equity in the business.

Netiquette: A code of conduct that governs behaviour on the Internet. Netiquette, for example, requires Internet users not to send unsolicited commercial email, or "spam," to large numbers of other users. Many Internet Service Providers and discussion groups will ban users who consistently violate these rules.

Non-disclosure Agreement (NDA): A contract in which a person or business agrees to maintain the confidentiality of proprietary information or trade secrets and not disclose such information without authorization. Employees, consultants, business partners and investors are often asked to sign nondisclosure agreements.

Non-exempt Employee: Employees who are protected by wage laws that mandate payment for every hour of overtime worked.

Non-profit Corporation: A form of corporation in which no stockholder or trustee shares in profits or losses and which usually exists to accomplish some charitable or educational function. These organizations are exempt from corporate income taxes, and donations to these groups may be tax deductible.

Non-qualified Stock Options (NSOs): Non-qualified stock options may be granted to employees, consultants, contractors and others. When non-qualified stock options are exercised the holder must pay ordinary income tax on them, even if the shares have not yet been sold.

Notes payable: Formal loans due in less than one year.

Notes Receivable: A secured or unsecured receivable evidenced by a note.

Organization: An organization is a body which is set up to meet a set of needs.

Operating expenses: Selling, general, and administrative expenses that are necessary to run the business. Examples include salaries, insurance, advertising, and rent. Any expenses other than cost of sales.

Operating income: The amount of profit earned during the normal course of operation.

Operating plan: A written explanation of how you plan on running your business. An operating plan should include a description of your business facility, required operating equipment, supplier and vendor relationships, and needed personnel.

Organizational chart: A diagram of the relationships and responsibilities of individuals or functional departments within your business.

Overnight Delivery: A service promising delivery of packages by a designated time of the next business day.

Overrun: A quantity of printed material or other manufactured product that exceeds the amount ordered.

Ownership: The person, people or institution who legally possesses an item.

Parent Company: A company that owns a majority stake (51 per cent or more) of another company's shares. It may have its own operations, or it may have been set up solely for the purpose of owning the operating company.

Partnership: A business that is unincorporated and organized by two or more individuals. A legal relationship existing between two or more persons or entities contractually associated as joint principals in a business.

Patent: A patent secures to an inventor the exclusive right to make, use and sell an invention for a designated period of time. See information at www.uspto.gov.

Pay Period: The frequency with which payroll is processed and paychecks are issued.

Payroll Taxes: The cost of employing someone. Payroll taxes include FICA, federal and state unemployment taxes, worker's compensation, and state short-term disability programmes.

Peak Period: In wireless telephones, the high-use period of the business day when wireless service providers charge their highest rates, typically 7 a.m. to 7 p.m.

Performance Review: A mechanism for regular discussion and evaluation of an employee's job performance.

Peripheral: Any hardware device, such as a modem, printer or mouse that operates separately from a computer's CPU.

Personnel Plan: A written description of your business's staffing requirements. It should include a breakdown of your needs by position and the number required.

Power of Attorney: A written authorization that lets one person act as an agent for another and to make binding decisions for the principal. A power of attorney can be limited to specific types of decisions or it can be general.

Preferred stock: Ownership in a corporation resulting from investment. Preferred stock carries certain preferences over common stock, such as a prior claim of dividends. Often preferred stock has no or limited voting rights. A class of stock with a liquidation preference before payment is made to the common stockholders. Preferred stock is the security most used by venture capital investors.

Press Kit: A collection of publicity materials, including press releases and general company information that is packaged and sent to media organizations.

Press Release. A document that communicates information to the press. Press releases can publicize good news such as positive earnings and new product or service launches.

Prime Rate: Interest rate which is charged business borrowers having the highest credit ratings, for short-term borrowing.

Product life cycle: A phenomenon where a product experiences rapid growth until it matures and growth slows. Eventually, sales will decline and the product will disappear from the marketplace entirely.

Profit & Loss (P&L): A report listing sales, expenses, and net income.

Profit Sharing: Employee incentives in which a company distributes or receives a portion of the business's profits to employees.

Promotion: Forms of communication that calls attention to products and services, typically by adding extra value to the purchase. Includes temporary discounts, allowances, premium offers, coupons, contests and rebates.

Promotional plan: A written description of the activities you plan on using to promote your products or services. Promotional activities can include advertising, personal selling, public relations, and sale promotion.

Property, plant, and equipment: Assets that are used in the business, which exist physically, and are not for sale to customers.

Proprietorship: The most common legal form of business ownership; about 85 per cent of all small businesses are proprietorships. The liability of the owner is unlimited in this form of ownership.

Prospect: A prospective customer who has the capacity to buy a product or service, but who has not yet decided to do so.

Prospecting: The process by which salespeople determine whether or not a business or an individual could qualify as a potential customer.

Proxy: A right given to an agent, most often in the context of shareholder voting in corporations.

Public Domain: A copyright term that means a particular work is free for all to use without permission. Works in the public domain include those that were never copyrighted, those for which the copyright has expired and public documents.

Public Relations: Communication with various sectors of the public to influence their attitudes and opinions in the interest of promoting a person, product or idea.

Publicity: Information with news value used to promote a product, service or idea in the media.

Purchase Order: A form that contains pricing, quantity and other purchasing information.

Rentable Square Feet: The total square feet available for lease. Typically, when landlords quote a price per square foot, they are talking about rentable square feet.

Resale Carrier: A company that buys telephony services in bulk and sells them to others at a markup.

Retainer: A contract between a lawyer and a client in which the lawyer agrees to provide certain legal services for money. The agreement formalizes the lawyer-client relationship and explains the relative duties of lawyer and client toward one another.

Return on Investment: The amount of profit (return) based on the amount of resources (funds) used to produce it. Also, the ability of a given investment to earn a return for its use.

Right of First Offer: The right to be the first person offered a particular item (such as stock or real estate).

Right of First Refusal: The right to be the first person allowed to purchase a certain item (such as stock or real estate) if it is ever offered for sale.

Roaming: Using a wireless phone outside the home service area defined by the service provider. Roaming often incurs higher per-minute rates as well as daily access fees and long distance charges.

State Corporation: A form of corporate organization where the profits of the entity pass through to shareholders and are taxed on their personal returns under subchapter State of the Internal Revenue Code.

Salary: Regular compensation paid to an employee as a condition of employment. Salary is generally computed on an annual or a monthly basis.

Sales: Revenue generated from the sale of products and services.

Sales mix: The portion of sales forecasted between the various products and services being offered.

Sales Tax: A tax on retail products based on a set percentage of retail cost.

Search Engine: Software that indexes Web pages and allows users to search for particular keywords. Public search engines such as Lycos, AltaVista and Google constantly index Websites and add information about these sites to their databases. Many individual Websites also use their own built-in search engines.

Second-Day Delivery: A service that promises to deliver packages by the end of the second day after the package was sent.

Security Deposit: Money that a lessee must give a lessor as a guarantee that the lessee will make payments.

Server: A computer on a network that offers shared hardware or software resources to multiple users. The term may apply in a general sense to a computer that "serves" shared files or applications over a LAN, or it may apply to a computer running a specific application, such as a Web server or mail server.

Sexual Harassment: Uninvited sexual advances or related conduct that creates an intimidating, hostile or offensive work environment. Sexual harassment is prohibited by the federal Civil Rights Act of 1991 as well as by various state laws.

Shareholder Agreement: A written agreement between a corporation and its shareholders governing the nature of the relationship and the conduct of certain corporate activities (such as distribution of profits and resolution of shareholder disputes).

Shareware: Software that anyone may download for free and pass along to others. The creators of shareware programs usually ask users to pay a small fee if they use the product after a specified period of time.

Silent Ringer: A phone or battery pack that signals incoming calls by vibrating or flashing a light.

Sister Company: Sister companies share the same parent company or individual owner. Like a subsidiary, a sister company is typically a separately incorporated business.

Social Security Tax: Provides benefits for retired workers and their dependents as well as for the disabled and their dependents.

Soft Sell: The technique of using low-pressure appeals in sales.

Sole Proprietorship: A business entity that involves just one individual who owns and operates the enterprise.

Spam: Slang term for unsolicited commercial email. "Spamming" people with unwanted commercial email solicitations is considered unethical and it is now illegal in several US states. Most ISPs will terminate a user's account if they use it to send spam.

Stock Option: A right to buy a given amount of company stock at a given price for a given period of time.

Stockholders: Those persons holding some share of the business's equity through stock ownership. Also known as shareholders or equityholders.

Strategic alliance: An agreement between two or more companies for the purpose of doing business.

Streaming Media: Streaming technology lets users play audio or video files as they download, rather than waiting for the whole file. Popular streaming media platforms include QuickTime, RealPlayer and Windows Media Player.

Sublease: The act of a tenant leasing the property it is leasing to yet another tenant, called a sublessee.

Subsidiary: A company owned by a parent company, a subsidiary is a separate legal entity listed as a corporation or LLC that is required to file its own taxes.

Supplies: Items that a business needs to provide products or services, but are not sold to customers.

Target Market: A specified audience or demographic group that an ad, product or service is intended to reach.

Tax Credit: A dollar-for-dollar reduction in the tax. Can be deducted directly from taxes owed.

Tax Deduction: A part of a person's or business' expenses that reduces income subject to tax.

Teleconferencing: A meeting conducted by telephone among people in different locations.

Telemarketing: Using the telephone to sell, promote or solicit products and services.

Telephony: A catchall word describing the world of communications — from wireless phones to digital computer communications to voicemail systems.

Telnet: An Internet-based protocol for connecting to a remote host or server. Telnet was once the main way to access other computers over the Internet, and it supported a variety of text-based email, file transfer, chat and information retrieval programs.

Temporary Employee: An employee, often hired and paid by a third party, who fills in staffing shortages caused by special projects, seasonal coverage, leaves of absence or other reasons.

Tenant Improvements: Refurbishing a rental space for a new tenant. Improvements may include repainting, remarketing and moving walls. In high-vacancy markets, landlords often entice tenants with money for tenant improvements. In tight rental markets, tenants may be on their own.

T-Notes: T-Notes are negotiable debt obligations of the Government with maturities of 1 to 10 years.

Tracking: Overnight shipping companies typically enable their customers to find out when a package was picked up, when it passed through certain regional shipping centres and airports, and when it was delivered. Tracking information is available either through toll-free phone numbers or Websites.

Trademark: A name, phrase, logo, image or combination of images used to identify and distinguish a business from others in the marketplace. The term is often used to include service marks, which apply to businesses providing services as opposed to selling products. Trademarks can be either registered or unregistered, with different levels of protection.

Trustee: A person or legal entity that holds money or property for the benefit of another. The owner of the money or property is known as the beneficiary. In most cases, the trustee and the beneficiary can be the same person.

Two-Way Paging: A feature of some pagers that lets users transmits confirmation that a message has been received.

Unemployment Compensation: Money paid to eligible people who have lost a job and are actively looking for work. Unemployment compensation is partially paid by the employer's unemployment insurance contributions.

Unfair Competition: A broad term describing illegal commercial activity ranging from trademark infringement to false advertising. Federal and state laws regulate unfair competition, and the remedies available range from money damages to court injunctions.

Unit cost: The cost of a single product or service.

Unit price: The selling price of a single product or service.

Unsecured Debt: A debt that is not guaranteed by a specific piece of real or personal property. If the debtor defaults, the creditor does not have the right to seize specific property to satisfy the debt.

Up sell: A technique to increase the value or quantity of a sale by suggesting additional options or upgrades. For example, a fast-food restaurant may up sell by suggesting that a customer buy a larger drink or an order of French fries.

Usable Square Feet: The amount of space renters can actually use. Usable square footage is usually less than rentable square footage because it deducts common areas such as public corridors, elevators, lobbies and bathrooms.

Usenet: An Internet service that provides thousands of discussion lists, or newsgroups, on a variety of topics. Users can read newsgroup postings or they can add their own. Most newsgroups are completely open, although some are moderated. You can view Usenet newsgroups with special software built into browsers and email programs or via one of several Web-based services.

VAR (Value Added Reseller): A company that modifies or improves a system in some way and then resells it. A VAR might, for example, integrate a software application with its clients' other systems or it might buy hardware components and build complete systems.

Variable cost or expense: A cost or expense that increases or decreases with the level of sales.

Variable inventory: A system where the inventory level fluctuates with sales.

Vendor financing: Buying from vendors on credit terms.

Venture Capital Limited Partnership: Investment vehicles organized to raise capital for start-up companies or those in the early process of developing products or services. The limited partners invest in the limited partnership to provide investment capital.

Venture Capital: Money used to support new or unusual commercial undertakings; equity, risk or speculative capital. This funding is provided to new or existing firms that exhibit above-average growth rates, a significant potential for market expansion and the need for additional financing for business maintenance or expansion.

Vicarious Liability: When a person is held legally responsible for the actions of another even though that person did not directly cause the harm. For example, employers are sometimes held vicariously liable for the damages caused by their employees.

Vision statement: A series of brief sentences of paragraphs that describes the 'big goals' that your business hopes to achieve over time. It can also present the ultimate heights you believe your business can reach and what you want your business to be after a certain period of time.

Voicemail: An automated service that answers phone calls and records incoming messages. Enhanced voicemail services add features such as personalized greetings, longer recording times and more saved messages.

Warranty: A guarantee about the performance of a product, or a promise to perform a specific act, such as repairing or replacing a defective or broken product.

Web page: A page in a Web document. Unlike printed pages, a Web page may be just a few words long or it may include thousands of words, images and other content.

Wi-Fi: Shorthand for "wireless fidelity," this is a high-frequency wireless local area network. Wi-Fi can be used to connect to the internet wirelessly.

Workers' Compensation Insurance: Government-mandated insurance that covers business′ financial obligations for its employees' work-related injuries.

Workgroup: Two or more networked computers that share files or other resources. A large network may consist of several smaller workgroups, each having different levels of access to various types of data.

Working Capital: The difference between current assets and current liabilities. Working capital finances the cash conversion cycle of a business — the time it takes to convert raw materials to finished products to sell and receive cash.

World Wide Web (WWW): An Internet service that links collections of documents, or Websites, both internally and to other sites. In addition to formatted text, Web pages may include graphics, audio, video and other multimedia content.

BIBLOGRAPHY

Aitken, J. (1997) 'Managing the New Organization: Some Problems of Institutional Transition–The New Zealand Perspective'. Public Administration and Development 17 (1): 41-48.

Alvesson, M. and Willmott, H. (1992) Critical Management Studies. Sage Publications, London.

Anthony, P.P. (1986) The Foundation of Management, London, Tavistock.

Appelbaum, S.H. and Santiago, V. "Career Development in the Plateaued Organization". Career Development International 2(1): 11-20 (1997).

Argyris, C. (1997) "Justice and Effectiveness". Organization Development Journal 15(2): 21-28.

Arnold, J. and Johnson, K. (1997) "Mentoring in Early Career". Human Resource Management Journal 7(4):61-70.

Arrington, J. and others. (1997) "A Question of Color: a Debate on Race in the US Workplace". Harvard Business Review 75(5): 118-132.

Ashwathapa, K., Organisational Behaviour, Himalaya Publishing House, New Delhi, 1996.

Aswathappa, K., Business Environment for Strategic Management, Himalaya Publication House, Mumbai.

Barker, R.A. (1997) "How Can We Train Leaders if We Do Not Know What Leadership is?". Human Relations 50(4): 343-362.

Barnes, P. (1997) "Lessons of Reform in the Ontario Civil Service". Public Administration and Development 17(1): 27-32.

Bartlett, C.A. and Ghoshal, S. (1989) Managing across borders: The transnational solution. Hutchison Business Books.

Bartlett, C.A. and Ghoshal, S. (1992) What is a global manager? Harvard Business Review, September-October.

Baruch, Y. and Peiperl, M. (1997) "High Fliers: Glorious Past, Gloomy Present, Any Future?". Career Development International 2(7), 355-359.

Basu C. R., Business Organization and Management, 2nd edition, Tata McGraw-Hill Ltd.

Bhavani, K. and Phoenix, A. (1994) Shifting Identities, Shifting Racisms. Sage

Bhote, K.R. (1997) "What do Customers Want, Anyway?" Management Review 86(3): 36-40.

Blake, R.R. (1997) "Promise and Performance in the Emergence of Grid Organization Development" Organization Development Journal 15(2): 69-78.

Blunt, P. and Jones, M.L. (1997) "Exploring the Limits of Western Leadership Theory in East Asia and Africa". Personnel Review 26(1/2): 6-23.

Boucher, C. (1997) "How Women Socially Construct Leadership in Organizations: a Study Using Memory Work". Gender, Work and Organization 4(3): 149-158.

Brech, E. F. L., Organization: The Framework of Management, 2nd edition, Longman.

Briggs, R.O. and de Vreede, G.-J. (1997) "Meetings of the Future: Enhancing Group Collaboration with Group Support Systems". Creativity and Innovation Management 6(2): 106-116.

Brocklehurst, M. (1997) "A Sense of Identity: the Difference Between Being at Work and Working at Home". Flexible Working 2(5): 22-23.

Brown, M. (1997) "The Survival of the Flattest". Human Resources (31): 99-101.

Brown, R.B. (1997) "You Can't Expect Rationality From Pregnant Men: Reflections on Multi-Disciplinarity in Management Research". British Journal of Management 8(1): 23-30.

Browne, J. and Prokesch, S.E. (1997) "Unleashing the Power of Learning". Harvard Business Review 75(5): 147-161.

Bryman, A. (1992) Quantity and Quality in Social Research. Routledge

Burke, R.J. and Black, S. (1997) "Save the Males: Backlash in Organizations". Journal of Business Ethics, 16(9): 933-942.

Burke, W.W. (1997) "The New Agenda for Organization Development". Organizational Dynamics 26(1): 7-20.

Burrell, G. and Morgan, G. (1992) Sociological Paradigms and Organisational Analysis. Ashgate

Callendar, G. and Johnston, J. (1997) "The Australian Way of Government and Public Sector Commercial Reform: From a Lucky to a Clever Country?" Public Administration and Development 17(1): 55-70.

Camillus, J. (1997) "Shifting the Strategic Management Paradigm". European Management Journal 15(1): 1-7.

Cetron, M. and Davies, O. (1997) "Get Ready for a Digitized Future: Smart Toasters, Media Butlers, and More". The Futurist 31(4): 18-23.

Cherrunilam, Francis (2003), Business Environment, New Delhi: Vikas Publishing House Private Limited.

Cherrunilam, Francis, Business Environment, Himalaya Publication House, New Delhi.

Chhabra, T.N. and Suri, R.K.(2000), Management Process and Perspectives, 1st edition, Kitab Mahal.

Coff, R.W. (1997) "Human Assets and Management Dilemmas: Coping with Hazards on the Road to Resource-Based Theory". Academy of Management Review 22(2): 374-402.

Cornish, E. (1997) " The Futurist Forecasts 30 Years Later". The Futurist 31(1): 45-48.

Coviello, N.E., Brodie, E. and Munro, H.J. (1997) "Understanding Contemporary Marketing: Development of a Classification Scheme". Journal of Marketing Management 13(6): 501-522.

Covin, T.J. and Stivers, B.P. (1997) "Knowledge Management Focus in US and Canadian Firms". Creativity and Innovation Management 6(3): 140-150.

Coyne, K.P., Hall, S.J.D. and Clifford, P.G. (1997) "Is Your Core Competence a Mirage?" The McKinsey Quarterly (1): 40-54.

D. J. Levinson, "A Conception of Adult Development", American Psychologist, vol. 41.
Dearlove, D. (1997) "Letting Go is Hard to Do". Human Resources (30): 87-90.
Deligonul, S. (1997) "An Epistemological Cross-perspective for Positioning Team Research". Quality Management Journal 4(2): 127-158.
Demarest, M. (1997) "Understanding Knowledge Management". Long Range Planning 30(3): 374-384.
Denton, K.D. "Down with Diversity (at Least Some of it): a Case for Cultural Identity". Empowerment in Organizations 5(4): 170-175.
Dodoo, R. (1997) "Performance Standards and Measuring Performance in Ghana". Public Administration and Development 17(1): 115-121.
Dorothy Marcic, "Organizational Behavior: Experience and Cases" Fifth edition
Douglas S. Basil, (1971) Leadership Skills for Executive Action, American Management Association, New York, p. 79.
Drucker, P.F., Dyson, E., Handy, C., Saffo, P. and Senge, P.M. (1997) "Looking Ahead: Implications of the Present". Harvard Business Review 75(5): 18-26.
Duke, C. (1997) "Equal Opportunity Versus Elitism? Culture Change for a New 'Old' University". Gender, Work and Organization 4(1): 47-57.
Duncan, J. 1973, Decision Making and Social Issues, Hindale, III : Richard D Irwin. Inc.
Earnest R. Hilgard and Gordon Power, Theories of Learning, Prentice Hall.
Easterby-Smith, M. (1994) Evaluating Management Development Training and Education. Gower
Easterby-Smith, M., Thorpe, R. and Lowe, A (1991) Management Research: An Introduction. Sage
Eder, P. (1997) "The Emerging Interactive Society". The Futurist 31(3): 43-46.
Eisenhardt, K.M. Kahwajy, J.L. and Bourgeois, L.J. (1997) "How Management Teams Can Have a Good Fight". Harvard Business Review 75(4): 77-85.
Elton Mayo, the Human Problems of an Industrial Civilization, Macmillan Publishing Company, New York.
Emery, F.E. (1997) "The Next Thirty Years: Concepts, Methods and Anticipations". Human Relations 50 (8): 885-935.
Frank, R. and Porter, J. (1997) "The Inspiration of Experience". Management Review 86(1): 33-36.
Fred Luthans, Organisational Behaviour (8th ed.), Irvin/Tata McGraw-Hill.
French, Wendell L., (1997) Human Resource Management, All India Publishers and Distributors Registered, Chennai.
Garnett, H., Koenen-Grant, J. and Rielly, C. (1997) "Managing Policy Formulation and Implementation in Zambia's Democratic Transition". Public Administration and Development 17(1): 77-91.
Garratt, R. (1987) The Learning Organisation, A.M.E.D./Fontana
Gini, A. (1997) "Moral Leadership: an Overview". Journal of Business Ethics 16(3): 323-330.
Giroux, H.A. (1983) Theory in Resistance in Education. Heinemann Education Books
Glueck, William (1980), Business Policy and Strategic Management, Auckland: McGraw-Hill International Book Company.
Gore, J.M. (1993) The Struggle for Pedagogies. Routledge, London

Griffin, C. (1987) Adult Education as Social Policy. Croom Helm

Guan, L.S. (1997) "Sustaining Excellence in Government: the Singapore Experience". Public Administration and Development 17(1): 167-174.

Hambleton, B. "Why do People Work?". Modern Management 11(5): 26-27.

Handy, C. & Gordon, C. (1988) Making Managers, Pitman

Handy, C. (1989) The Age of Unreason, London: Hutchinson

Harold Koontz and Cyril O'Donnell (1976). Management A Systems and Contingency Analysis of Management Functions, McGraw-Hill Kogakusha Ltd. Tokyo, p. 198.

Hauschildt, J. (1997) "Innovation, Creativity and Information Behaviour". Creativity and Innovation Management 5(3): 169-178.

Hawkins, P. (1997) "Organizational Culture: Sailing Between Evangelism and Complexity". Human Relations 50(4): 417-440.

Haynese and Massie, (1990) Management Analysis, Concepts and Cases, Prentice-Hall of India, New Delhi, p. 147.

Heifetz, R.A. and Laurie, D.L. (1997) "The Work of Leadership". Harvard Business Review 75(1): 124-134.

Henry Fayol, 1996 General and Industrial Managements, McGraw-Hill, New York.

Herrera, L.A. and Pereyra, R.R. (1997) "Review of the Management Literature 1996". IFLA Journal 23(5/6): 371-380.

Hill, H. (1997) "Distance No Object–Collaborative Software Comes of Age". Flexible Working 2(6): 6-7.

Hofstede, G., (1980) Culture's Consequences, Sage

Holloway, W. (1992) Work Psychology and Organisational Behaviour. Sage

Hussey, D. (1997) "Strategic Management: Past Experiences and Future Directions. Part I & II". Strategic Change 6(5): 261-271.

Hussey, D.E. (1997) "Glossary of Techniques for Strategic Analysis". Strategic Change 6(2): 97-115.

J.R. Bigg, G.N. Plants and L.F. Miller, (1950) Dynamics of Participative Groups, M.O. : Swift and Co..

Jit S. Chandan, Organizational Behaviour, Vikas Publishing House.

Jordan, J. and Jones, P. (1997) "Assessing Your Company's Knowledge Management Style". Long Range Planning 30(3): 392-398.

Kaul, M. (1997) "The New Public Administration: Management Innovations in Government". Public Administration and Development 17(1): 13-26.

Kazagozoglu, N. (1997) "Managerial Perspectives on Organizational Learning". Creativity and Innovation Management 5(2): 123-133.

Keith Davis, Human Behaviour at Work, Tata McGraw-Hill, New Delhi.

Kets de Vries, M.F.R. and Balazs, K. (1997) "The Downside of Downsizing". Human Relations 50(1): 11-50.

Kim, W.C. and Mauborgne, R. (1997) "Fair Process: Managing in the Knowledge Economy". Harvard Business Review 75(4): 65-75.

Kleiner, A. and Roth, G. (1997) "How to Make Experience Your Company's Best Teacher". Harvard Business Review 75(5): 172-177.

Kootnz & O'Donnell, Principles of Management.

Kuhn, T.S. (1962) The Structure of Scientific Revolutions Chicago, Chicago University Press

Lam, S.S.K. and Woo, K.S. "Measuring Service Quality: a Test-Retest Reliability Investigation of SERVQUAL". Journal of the Market Research Society 39(2): 381-396.

Laurie J. Mullins, Management and Organisational Behaviour (2nd ed.), Pitman.

Leavy, B. (1997) "Strategic Renewal - is Disruptive Revolution Unavoidable?" Strategic Change 6(5): 283-298.

Legge, Karen, (1995) Human Resource Management, Rhetorics and Realities, Macmillan Press Limited, London.

Leonard, D. and Straus, S. (1997) "Putting Your Company's Whole Brain to Work". Harvard Business Review 75(4): 111-121.

Lewis, S. (1997) "Family Friendly Employment Policies: a Route to Changing Organizational Culture or Playing About at the Margins?". Gender, Work and Organization 4(1): 13-23.

Liff, S. and Cameron, I. (1997) "Changing Equality Cultures to Move Beyond 'Women's Problems'". Gender, Work and Organization 4(1): 35-46.

Lincoln, Y.S. and Guba, E.G. (1985) Naturalistic Enquiry. Sage

Linstead, S. (1997) "The Social Anthropology of Management". British Journal of Management 8(1): 85-98.

Longenecker, C.O. (1997) "Why Managerial Performance Appraisals are Ineffective: Causes and Lessons". Career Development International 2(5): 212-218.

Louis A. Allen, Management and Organization, McGraw-Hill Kogakusha, Ltd.

Lovelock, R. and Ashworth, R. (1997) "Steering Ideas Through the Corporate Maze - a Guide for Managers". Modern Management 3(11): 9-11.

Lyotard, J.F. (1984) The Post Modern Condition: A Report of Knowledge. Manchester, Manchester University Press

Maier, N.R.F. (1967). Assets and Liability in group production Solving : The Need for an integrative function. Psychological Review; 4, 239-249.

Mangham, I. (1995) Special Issue of Oganisation. Vol. 2., No 2

Marsick, V.J. & Watkins, K.E. (1990) Informal and Incidental Learning in the Workplace, International Adult Education Series, Routledge

Mazen, A.M. (1997) "Team Defensiveness: a Neglected Root Cause". Quality Management Journal 4(2): 24-50.

McCune, J.C. (1997) "Management's Brave New World". Management Review 86(90): 11-14.

McDonald, F. and Potton, M. (1997) "The Nascent European Policy Towards Older Workers: Can the European Union Help the Older Worker? Personnel Review 26(4): 293-306.

McIntosh, N. (1997) "Aspects of Change in the Canadian Federal Public Service". Public Administration and Development 17(1): 123-129.

Milburn, T. (1997) "Bridging Cultural Gaps". Management Review USA 86(1): 26-29.

Mintzberg, H. (1973) The Nature of Managerial Work, Harper and Row

Moon, C. and Stanworth, C. (1997) "Ethical Issues of Teleworking", Business Ethics: A European Review 6(1): 35-45.

Morris, B. and Nocera, J. (1997) " Is Your Family Wrecking Your Career?". Fortune 135(5): 40-50.

Morrison, L.J. Colman, A.M., and Preston, C.C. (1997) "Mystery Customer Research: Cognitive Processes Affecting Accuracy". Journal of the Market Research Society 39(2): 349-361.

Murray, C. (1997) "How to Write a Telework Agreement". Flexible Working 2(2): 6-8.

Narayan, B., (1998) Human Resource Management, A.P.H. Publishing Corporation, New Delhi.

Nelson, T. and Coxhead, H. (1997) "Increasing the Probability of Re-engineering/Culture Change Success Through Effective Internal Communication". Strategic Change 6(1): 29-48.

Orpen, C. (1997) "The Downside of Downsizing: Managing an Organization to its Right Size". Strategic Change 6(4): 195-209.

Paper, D.J. and Johnson, J.J. (1997) "A Theoretical Framework Linking Creativity, Empowerment and Organizational Memory". Creativity and Innovation Management 6(1): 32-44.

Paul, Srivastava, Strategic Management, Cinicinnati: South-Western Publishing Conmpany.

Pearson, C.A.L. (1997) "Achieving Customer Service Quality Through teamwork: the Murdoch University Case". Empowerment in Organizations 5(2): 96-112.

Pedler, M., Burgoyne, J.G. and Boydell, T. (1991) The Learning Company. McGraw-Hill

Pickard, J. and Argyris, C. (1997) "A Yearning for Learning". People Management 3(5): 34-35.

Prasad Manmohan, Management Concepts and Practices, 1st edition 1998; Himalaya Publishing House.

Quintas, P., Lefrere, P. and Jones, G. (1997) "Knowledge Management: a Strategic Agenda". Long Range Planning 30(3): 385-391.

Raelin, J.A. (1997) "Action Learning and Action Science: Are They Different?". Organizational Dynamics 26(1): 21-34.

Reason, P. and Rowan, J. (Eds) (1991) Human Inquiry. Wiley

Reed, M. & Hughes, M. (Eds.) (1992) Rethinking Organisation: New Directions in Organisation Theory and Analysis, Sage, London

Richard L. Daft, "Organizational Theory and Design" Sixth edition.

Richardson, A.M., Mikkelsen, A. and Burke, R.J. (1997) "Work Experiences and Career and Job Satisfaction Among Professional and Managerial Women in Norway". Scandinavian Journal of Management 13(2): 209-218.

Rieple, A. (1997) "The Paradoxes of New Managers as Levers of Organizational Change". Strategic Change 6(4): 211-225.

Robbins Stephen P. and Decenzo David A., Fundamentals of Management, 3rd Edition, Pearson Education Asia.

Robbins Stephen P. and Mary Coulter (2000), Management, Prentice-Hall of India.

Rowbotham, D. and Jubb, R. (1997) "Competencies: Measuring the Unmeasurable". Management Development Review 9(5), 25-29.

Rubin, J. (1997) "Gender, Equality and the Culture of Organizational Assessment". Gender, Work and Organization, 4(1): 24-34.

Saiyadain, Mirza S., (1994) Human Resource Management, Tata McGraw-Hill Publishing Company Ltd., New Delhi.

Salaman, G. (Ed) (1992) Human Resource Strategies. London, Sage.

Sawayama, A. (1997) "Back to Basics: the New Success Factors in Japanese Companies". Strategic Change 6(3): 125-132.

Schein, E.H. (1997) "Organizational Development and the Organization of the Future". Organization Development Journal 15(2): 11-20.

Sekhran, Uma, (1989) Organisational Behaviour : Test and Cases, Tata McGraw Hill Publishing Company Limited, New Delhi.

Senior, B. (1997) "Team Roles and Team Performance: is There Really a Link?". Journal of Occupational and Organizational Psychology 70(3): 241-258.

Sharma, R.A., (2000) Organisational Theory and Behaviour, Tata McGraw Hill Publishing Company Limited, New Delhi.

Silverman, D. (1994) Interpreting Qualitative Data. Sage

Simpson, R. (1997) "Have Times Changed? Career Barriers and the Token Woman Manager". British Journal of Management (8):S121-S130.

Smith, C. (1997) "Career Transitions of Dual-Career Couples: an Empirical Study". Career Development International 2(5): 229-237.

Smith, J. (1997) "Government Reform in Canada". Public Administration and Development 17(1): 33-39.

Smith, K. and Berg, D. (1997) "Cross-Cultural Groups at Work". European Management Journal 15(1): 8-15.

Snell, R.S. (1990) Managers' Development of Ethical Awareness and Personal Morality Personnel Review, 19 (1), pp.13-20

Sparrow, P. (1997) "Job-based Flexibility–Challenging Times for HRM". Flexible Working 2(5): 26-28.

Stainer, A. and Stainer, L. (1997) "Ethical Dimensions of Re-Engineering". Strategic Change 6(6): 357-365.

Stephen P. Robbins, Organisational Behaviour (9th ed.), Prentice-Hall, India.

Stewart, T.A. (1997) "Get With the New Power Game". Fortune 135(1): 34-38.

Stewart,R. (1986) The Reality of Management, Cox-Wyman

Storey, J. (1992) Developments in the Management of Human Resources: An Analytical Review, Blackwell, Oxford

Storey, J. (Ed) (1989) New Perspectives on Human Resource Management, Routledge, London

Storey, J., Mabey, C. and Thomson, A. (1997) "What a Difference a Decade Makes". People Management 3(12), 28-30.

Tanton, M. and Fox, S. (1987) The Evaluation of Management Education and Development: Participant Satisfaction and Ethnographic Methodology. Personnel Review, 16, 4: 33-40

Taylor, B. (1997) "The Return of Strategic Planning–Once More With Feeling". Long Range Planning 30(3): 334-344.

Taylor, P. and Walker, A. (1997) "Age Discrimination and Public Policy". Personnel Review 26(4): 307-318.

Tersine, R., Harvey, M. and Buckley, M. (1997) " Shifting Organizational Paradigms: Transitional Management". European Management Journal 15(1): 45-57.

Thomas Cummings, "Organization Development and Change" Sixth edition

Thornberry, N. (1997) "A View About 'Vision' ". European Management Journal 15(1): 28-34.

Von Krogh, G., Nonaka, I. and Ichijo, K. (1997) "Develop Knowledge Activists!". European Management Journal 15(5): 475-483.

Wageman, R. (1997) "Critical Success Factors for Creating Superb Self-Managing Teams". Organizational Dynamics 26(1): 49-61.

Williamson, O.E. (Ed) (1995) Organisation Theory: From Chester Bernard to the Present and Beyond. New York, Oxford University Press

Winterton, J. and Winterton, R. (1997) "Does Management Development Add Value?". British Journal of Management, (8): S65-S76.

Wolfe Morrison, E. and Robinson, S.L. (1997) "When Employees Feel Betrayed: a Model of How Psychological Contract Violation Develops". Academy of Management Review 22(1): 226-256.

www.123india.com
www.afocus.indiainfo.com
www.analytictech.com/mb021/fayol.htm
www.arnoldporter.com
www.bharatbook.com
www.bizcarta.com/knowledge.../BizCarta_KC_Glossary_001.pdf
www.bombaybiz.com
www.books.google.com/books/YVcreativity22&f/.htm
www.business-standard.com
www.businesswireindia.com
www.cmie.com/kommon/bin
www.crisil.com
www.datamationindia.com
www.deccanherald.com
www.economicexpert.com/a/Henry:Mintzberg.htm
www.explorehr.org/.../Individual_and_Organizational_Resistance.html
www.financialexpress.com
www.findarticles.com
www.globaltel.com/Glossary.asp
www.google.com/downloads.cas.psu.edu/leadership/pdf/conflictmanagement.pdf
www.google.com/search downloads.cas.psu.edu/leadership/pdf/conflictmanagement.pdf
www.hdfcbank.com
www.hinduonline.com
www.hindustantimes.com
www.ibid.informindia.co.in
www.indiainfoline.com
www.jaxworks.com/glossary.htm
www.members.shaw.ca/pdg/dynamics-of-interpersonal-behaviour.html
www.omictimes.indiatimes.com
www.probizbrokers.com/terminology.htm
www.probizbrokers.com/terminology.htm
www.riseofthewest.com/thinkers/weber03.htm
www.riseofthewest.com/thinkers/weber03.htm
www.samachar.com
www.schandgroup.com
www.scribd.com/doc/.../MGT502-Organizational-Behavior
www.scribd.com/doc/21393300/Conflict-Management
www.scribd.com/doc/9177627/Organisational-Change
www.searchindia.com
www.sify.com
www.situational.com/WhoWeAre/CLS/PaulHersey.aspx

www.sofindia.indiatimes.com
www.som.yale.edu/Faculty/vhv1/BIO1.htm
www.statemaster.com/encyclopedia/Strategy-dynamics
www.synergos.org
www.tribuneindia.com
www.universalteacherpublications.com/mba/ebooks/ob/ch2/page2.htm

Yammarino, F.J. and Atwater, L.E. (1997) "Do Managers see Themselves as Others See Them? Implications of Self-Other Rating Agreement for Human Resources Management". Organizational Dynamics 25(4): 35-44.

I

ANNEXURE

LEADING INDIAN COMPANIES AT A GLANCE

1. Acer India Private Limited
2. Activa Softech Limited
3. Aditya Birla Group
4. Ador Fontech Limited
5. Ador Powertron Limited
6. Ador Welding Limited
7. Air Deccan
8. Air India
9. Air Sahara
10. Air-India Express
11. AirTel Bharti
12. Alang Ship Recycling Yard
13. Amdocs
14. Amol Group
15. AmSoft Systems
16. Anand Software and Training
17. Apollo Hospitals
18. Archies Limited
19. ARJ Allana Group
20. Arvind Mills
21. Ashok Leyland
22. Bajaj Auto
23. Balaji Telefilms
24. Bank of India
25. BEL
26. Bharat Petroleum
27. Bharat Sanchar Nigam Limited
28. Bharti Telecom
29. Bharti Televentures
30. BHEL
31. Birla Corporation Limited
32. Blue Lotus Communications Consultancy
33. Bombay Dyeing
34. Bondit Construction Chemicals
35. BPL Group
36. Canara Bank
37. Canarys Automations Pvt Ltd.
38. Caritor Inc
39. CavinKare
40. Chitransh Electronics Equipment India
41. Cipla
42. Coal India Limited
43. Comtek Services Pvt. Ltd.
44. Covansys India Limited
45. D.K. Agencies Pvt. Ltd.
46. Dabur India Limited
47. Deccan Aviation
48. Deepak Mittal & Co.
49. Dena Bank
50. Development Credit Bank
51. DishnetDSL
52. Dr. Reddy's Labs
53. DSP Merrill Lynch
54. East-West Group

55. Eicher Motors
56. Ek Tar Ltd.
57. Energy Machine Tools Pvt. Ltd.
58. Engineers India Limited
59. Envision Labs Private Limited
60. Essar Construction Ltd.
61. Essar Oil Limited
62. Essar Power Limited
63. Essar Shipping Limited
64. Essar Steel Limited
65. Evalueserve
66. Fertilizers and Chemicals Travancore Limited
67. Frost and Sulivan
68. GAIL
69. Go Air
70. Godrej Group
71. HDFC Bank
72. Hero Cycles Ltd.
73. Hero Honda Motors Limited
74. Hindalco Industries
75. Hindustan Aeronautics Ltd.
76. Hindustan Book Agency
77. Hindustan Cables Ltd.
78. Hindustan Computers Ltd. (HCL)
79. Hindustan Copper
80. Hindustan Lever Limited (HLL)
81. Hindustan Machine Tools (HMT)
82. Hindustan Motors
83. Hindustan Paper Co. Ltd.
84. Hindustan Pencils Ltd.
85. Hindustan Petroleum
86. Hindustan Platinum
87. Hindustan Radiators
88. Hindustan Times
89. Hindustan Zinc
90. Hitachi Metglas
91. IBP
92. ICICI Bank
93. i-flex Solutions
94. i-Gate Global Solutions
95. IL&FS
96. Inbpo.net
97. India InfoMedia
98. India Today Group
99. Indian Airlines
100. Indian Oil Corporation
101. Indian Overseas Bank
102. Indian Potash Limited
103. India Times Group media
104. IndiGo Airlines
105. Indo Gulf Fertilisers
106. Infolink Technologies
107. Infosys
108. Infotech Enterprises Limited
109. Ispat India
110. ITC Limited
111. Jet Airways
112. Jindal Steel
113. Jiwanjot Industries, Amritsar
114. Keltron
115. Khatau Mills
116. Kingfisher Airlines
117. Konkan Railway Corporation
118. Kotak Mahindra Bank
119. Kotak Mahindra Finance
120. Larsen and Toubro (L&T)
121. Loreal India Private Limited
122. Maarga Systems
123. Madras Rubber Factory (MRF)
124. Mahanagar Telephone Nigam Limited
125. Mahindra & Mahindra
126. Mahindra British Telecom
127. Malwa Industries, VSO Group ludhiana
128. Manaksia Limited
129. MarileSoft
130. Maruti Udyog Limited
131. MindTree Consulting
132. Modi Group
133. MTNL
134. National Aluminium Company (NALCO)
135. National Small Industries Corporation
136. National Thermal Power Corporation
137. NDTV India
138. Neilsoft Ltd
139. NeST Group of Companies
140. Neyveli Lignite Corporation

141. Nicholas Piramal
142. NIIT
143. Nirma Limited
144. Oberoi Group of Hotels
145. Oil India Limited
146. ONGC
147. Paramount Airways
148. Pamolive Colgate
149. Patni Computer Systems
150. Peepal Technology and Management Consulting Pvt. Ltd.
151. Perot Systems
152. Polaris Software
153. Power Finance Corporation
154. Power Trading Corporation of India
155. Proactive Lab
156. Progeon
157. Punjab National Bank
158. Ramco Systems
159. Ranbaxy Laboratories Limited
160. Raymond Textiles
161. Reachwell Software Services Private Limited
162. Real Soft Solutions & Consultancy
163. Rediff.com
164. Reliance Capital
165. Reliance Industries Limited
166. Reliance Infocomm
167. Renaissance Seers Consultants Pvt.Ltd
168. Saksoft
169. Sasken Communication Technologies Limited
170. Satyam Computer Services
171. Shapoorji Pallonji Group
172. Sharekhan
173. Shipping Corporation of India Ltd.
174. Siemens Ltd.
175. Simple Solutions
176. Spice Jet
177. Star India Network
178. State Bank of India
179. Steel Authority of India Limited
180. Swaraj Mazda Ltd.
181. Syndicate Bank
182. TAFE Tractors
183. Tamil Nadu Mercantile Bank Ltd.
184. Tata Chemicals
185. Tata Consultancy Services Limited (TCSL)
186. Tata Infotech
187. Tata Motors (TTM)
188. Tata Steel (TISCO)
189. Tata Tea Ltd.
190. Techno Developers' Group
191. The Rozaleenda Group, Inc.
192. Titan Watches
193. Torrent (Group)
194. Toyo Engineering India Limited
195. TVS Motors
196. Union Bank of India
197. United Beverages Group (UB Group)
198. Videocon Electronics
199. Vijaya Bank
200. VSNL
201. Wipro

INDEX